SUPPLEMENT X
Madison Smartt Bell to John Edgar Wideman

American Writers
A Collection of Literary Biographies

JAY PARINI
Editor in Chief

SUPPLEMENT X
Madison Smartt Bell to John Edgar Wideman

Charles Scribner's Sons
an imprint of the Gale Group
New York • Detroit • San Francisco • London • Boston • Woodbridge, CT

Charles Scribner's Sons
1633 Broadway
New York, New York 10019

1 3 5 7 9 11 13 15 17 19 20 18 16 14 12 10 8 6 4 2

Library of Congress Cataloging-in-Publication Data

American writers; a collection of literary biographies.

Leonard Unger, editor in chief. p. cm.

The 4-vol. main set consists of 97 of the pamphlets originally published
as the University of Minnesota pamphlets on American writers; some have been
rev. and updated. The supplements cover writers not included in the original series.
Supplement 2, has editor in chief, A. Walton Litz; Retrospective suppl. 1, c1998, was edited by A. Walton Litz & Molly Weigel; Suppl. 5
has editor-in-chief, Jay Parini. Includes bibliographies and index.
Contents: v. 1. Henry Adams to T. S. Eliot - v. 2. Ralph Waldo Emerson to Carson McCullers - v. 3. Archibald MacLeish to George Santayana - v. 4. Isaac Bashevis Singer to Richard Wright - Supplement: 1, pt. 1. Jane Addams to Sidney Lanier. 1, pt. 2. Vachel Lindsay to Elinor Wylie. 2, pt.1. W.H. Auden to O. Henry. 2, pt. 2. Robison Jeffers to Yvor Winters. - 4, pt. 1. Maya Angelou to Linda Hogan. 4, pt. 2. Susan Howe to Gore Vidal. 5. Russell Banks to Charles Wright.
ISBN 0-684-19785-5 (set) - ISBN 0-684-13662-7 1.
American literature-History and criticism. 2. American literature-Bio-bibliography. 3. Authors, American-Biography. I. Unger, Leonard. II. Litz, A. Walton. III Weigel, Molly. IV. University of Minnesota pamphlets on American writers.

PS129 .A55 810'.9 73-001759

ISBN 0-684-80649-5

Acknowledgment is gratefully made to those publishers and individuals who have permitted the use of the following material in copyright.

Madison Smartt Bell
Excerpts from "One Art," in *My Poor Elephant Elephant: 27 Male Writers at Work,* by Madison Smartt Bell. Edited by Eve Shelnutt. Longstreet Press, 1992. Reproduced by permission. Excerpts from *My Silk Purse and Yours: The Publishing Scene and American Literary Art,* by George Garrett. University of Missouri Press, 1992. Copyright © 1992 by The Curators of the University of Missouri. Excerpts from *For the Love of Books: 115 Celebrated Writers on the Books They Love Most,* by Ronald B. Shwartz. Compilation by Ronald B. Shwartz. Grosset/Putnam, 1999. © 1999. All rights reserved. Reproduced by permission. Excepts from *The Atlanta Journal-Constitution,* June 12, 1989. Reproduced by permission. Excerpts from *BOMB Magazine,* fall, 2000. Reproduced by permission. Excerpts from *Booklist,* vol. 89, April 1, 1993. Copyright © 1993 by the American Library Association. Reproduced by permission. Excerpts from *Four Quarters,* vol. 9, spring 1995. © 1995 by La Salle College. Reproduced by permission. Excerpts from "An Interview with Madison Smartt Bell," by Mary Louise Weaks. *The Southern Review,* vol. 30, January 1994. Copyright 1994 by Louisiana State University. Reproduced by permission of the author.

Wendell Berry
Excerpts from "A Native Hill," "Long-Legged House," in *The Long-Legged House,* by Wendell Berry. Harcourt, Brace & World, Inc., 1969. Copyright © 1965, 1966, 1968, 1969 by Wendell Berry. All rights reserved. Reproduced by permission. Excerpts from *The Hidden Wound,* by Wendell Berry. Houghton Mifflin, 1970. Reprinted by permission of Houghton Mifflin Company. All rights reserved. Excerpts from "To the Unseeable Animal," in *Farming: A Hand Book,* by Wendell Berry. Harcourt Brace Jovanovich, Inc., 1970. Copyright © 1967, 1968, 1969, 1970 by Wendell Berry. All rights reserved. Reproduced by permission. Excerpts from "Reverdure," in *Clearing,* by Wendell Berry. Harcourt Brace Jovanovich, 1977. Copyright © 1974, 1975, 1977 by Wendell Berry. All rights reserved. Reproduced by permission. Excerpts from *The Unsettling of America: Culture & Agriculture,* by Wendell Berry. Sierra Club Books, 1977. Copyright © 1977 by Wendell Berry. All rights reserved. Reproduced by permission. Excerpts from "The Country of Marriage," in *The Country of Marriage,* by Wendell Berry. Harcourt Brace Jovanovich, 1977. Copyright © 1971, 1972, 1973 by Wendell Berry. All rights reserved. Reproduced by permission. Excerpts from "The Making of a Marginal Farm," in *Recollected Essays: 1965–1980,* by Wendell Berry. North

Editorial and Production Staff

List of Subjects

Introduction

This supplement to our series brings together a wide range of articles on American writers, most of them contemporary, although a couple of them reach back to neglected, but important, writers from the literary past. An effort has been made to demonstrate the variety and high quality of writing on this continent, and the subjects have all been chosen with those aspects in mind. Readers will find these eighteen essays both lively and intelligent, designed to interest readers unfamiliar with the work and to assist those who know the work quite well by providing a sense of context—biographical and critical.

American Writers had its origin in a series of monographs that appeared between 1959 and 1972. The Minnesota Pamphlets on American Writers were incisively written and informative, treating ninety-seven American writers in a format and style that attracted a devoted following of readers. The series proved invaluable to a generation of students and teachers, who could depend on these reliable and interesting critiques of major figures. The idea of reprinting these essays occurred to Charles Scribner, Jr. (1921–1995). The series appeared in four volumes entitled *American Writers: A Collection of Literary Biographies* (1974).

Since then, nine supplements have appeared, treating well over two hundred American writers: poets, novelists, playwrights, essayists, and autobiographers. The idea has been consistent with the original series: to provide clear, informative essays aimed at the general reader. These essays often rise to a high level of craft and critical vision, but they are meant to introduce a writer of some importance in the history of American literature, and to provide a sense of the scope and nature of the career under review. A certain amount of biographical and historical context is also offered, giving a context for the work itself.

The authors of these critical articles are mostly teachers, scholars, and writers. Most have published books and articles in their field, and several are well-known writers of poetry or fiction as well as critics. As anyone glancing through this volume will see, they are held to the highest standards of good writing and sound scholarship. Each essay concludes with a select bibliography intended to direct the reading of those who want to pursue the subject further.

Supplement X focuses on contemporary writers, many of whom have received little sustained attention from critics. For example, Madison Smartt Bell, Kaye Gibbons, Alice Hoffman, Lorrie Moore, Tom Robbins, and David Foster Wallace have been written about in the review pages of newspapers and magazines, and their fiction has acquired a substantial following, but their work has yet to attract significant scholarship. That will certainly follow, but the essays included here constitute a beginning.

Some of important writers from the past—such as Claude McKay, Marjorie Kinnan Rawlings, and Anaïs Nin—have already attracted a good deal of sustained attention, and their work is often taught in college courses, but for various reasons their careers have not yet been discussed in *American Writers*. It is time they were added to the series.

The poets included here—from Wendell Berry (also a novelist and essayist) and Anthony Hecht to Thomas McGrath and Sharon Olds—are well known in the poetry world, and their work has in each case been honored with major literary prizes. These poets have been widely anthologized as well. Nevertheless, the real work of assimilation, of discovering the true place of each poet in the larger traditions of American poetry, has only begun. In each case, these poets are written about by critics who are themselves poets, and the depth and eloquence of their essays should be obvious even to casual readers.

Writers from various ethnic and cultural backgrounds have contributed a great deal to contemporary literature, and several of the strongest among writers of fiction—Ishmael Reed, John Edgar Wideman, and Amy Tan—are considered in this volume. There is also a lively essay here on the gay poet-memoirist, Paul Monette, who died of AIDS only a few years ago. These writers, once thought of as writing from the margins, have become central to the American literary tradition.

The critics who contributed to this collection represent a catholic range of backgrounds and critical approaches, although the baseline for inclusion was that each essay should be accessible to the nonspecialist reader or beginning student. The creation of culture involves the continuous reassessment of major texts produced by its writers, and my belief is that this supplement performs a useful service here, providing substantial introductions to American writers who matter, and it will assist readers in the difficult but rewarding work of close reading.

—*JAY PARINI*

Contributors

Susan Balée. Author of *Flannery O'Connor: Literary Prophet of the South,* as well as numerous article on British and American literature. She holds a Ph.D. in English from Columbia University. MARJORIE KINNAN RAWLINGS

Kim Bridgford. Director of the writing program at Fairfield University, where she is an associate professor of English and poetry editor of *Dogwood.* Her poetry has appeared, or is forthcoming, in *North American Review, The Christian Science Monitor,* and *The Georgia Review,* and her fiction in *Redbook, The Massachusetts Review,* and *Witness.* She is the recipient of a 1999–2000 NEA Fellowship. SHARON OLDS

Gerry Cambridge. Editor of the Scottish-American poetry magazine, *The Dark Horse,* whose books include *The Shell House; "Nothing But Heather!": Scottish Nature Poems, Photographs, and Prose;* and *Madame Fi Fi's Farewell and Other Poems.* He is the recipient of the 1997–1999 Brownsbank Fellowship, a writing residency at Hugh MacDiarmid's cottage in South Lanarkshire, Scotland. ANTHONY HECHT

John Cooley. Professor of English at Western Michigan University. ANNE LABASTILLE

Patricia Ferreira. Assistant professor of English at Norwich University. JOHN EDGAR WIDEMAN

Dean Flower. Professor of English at Smith College and advisory editor of *The Hudson Review.* He has written essays and reviews for such journals as *The New England Quarterly, The Massachusetts Review, Essays in Criticism,* and *The Hudson Review.* He has edited works by Henry James and Henry David Thoreau. WENDELL BERRY

Denise Gess. Visiting assistant professor of creative writing at the University of North Carolina, Wilmington. Author of two novels, *Good Deeds* and *Red Whiskey Blues,* and a forthcoming book of nonfiction *The Night of Two Sunsets.* ALICE HOFFMAN, LORRIE MOORE

Tracie Church Guzzio. Assistant professor of English, State University of New York at Plattsburgh. Author of essays on Charles Chesnutt, Clarence Major, and John Edgar Wideman, and a forthcoming book on John Edgar Wideman's work. ISHMAEL REED

Brian Henry. Assistant professor of English at the University of Georgia and editor of *Verse.* Author of *Astronaut,* a collection of poetry, and numerous reviews and essays that have appeared in such journals as the *Times Literary Supplement, The Kenyon Review, Boston Review, The Yale Review,* and *The Antioch Review.* DAVID FOSTER WALLACE

Brian Kent. Lecturer at the University of Vermont, where he teaches writing and American literature. He has published articles about Stephen King and is completing a book about Gore Vidal. TOM ROBBINS

Melissa Knox. Author of *Oscar Wilde: A Long and Lovely Suicide,* and *Oscar Wilde in the 1990s: The Critic as Creator.* She has published articles about Henry James, Thomas De Quincey, William Butler Yeats, and Anaïs Nin. PAUL MONETTE, ANAÏS NIN

Veronica Makowsky. Professor of English and Women's Studies and Associate Dean of the College of Liberal Arts and Sciences at the University of Connecticut. She is the editor of *MELUS* and author of *Caroline Gordon: A*

Biography and *Susan Glaspell's Century of American Women.* She has published numerous articles on such Southern authors as William Faulkner and Walker Percy. KAYE GIBBONS

David Mason. Professor of English at Colorado College. Author of *The Poetry of Life and the Life of Poetry.* THOMAS MCGRATH

Donna Seaman. An editor for *Booklist* and author of articles and reviews in such publica-

tions as the *Chicago Tribune, Newsday,* the *Los Angeles Times,* and the *Ruminator Review.* Editor of the anthology *In Our Nature: Stories of Wildness.* MADISON SMARTT BELL

Stephen Soitos. Author of *The Blues Detective: A Study of African American Detective Fiction* and works centering on German Expressionist painting, Brazilian art, and African American art and literature. CLAUDE MCKAY, AMY TAN

SUPPLEMENT X
Madison Smartt Bell to John Edgar Wideman

Madison Smartt Bell

1957–

MADISON SMARTT BELL was called a wunderkind after he set out a straight flush of five critically acclaimed works of fiction in four years. He began in 1983 with his first novel, *The Washington Square Ensemble,* published when he was twenty-five years old, and concluded with the nearly simultaneous release of *The Year of Silence* and his first short story collection, *Zero db and Other Stories,* in 1987. And this was not merely beginner's luck. Designated as one of *Granta*'s Best Young American Novelists in 1996 by such illustrious judges as Robert Stone, Anne Tyler, and Tobias Wolff, Bell has sustained this remarkably high level of creative fervor and productivity. He has become not only a superb literary craftsman but also a profoundly spiritual and moral writer, and he has emerged as one of the most brilliant and daring historical novelists of his time.

Tennessee-born and raised, Bell chose in his earliest works to portray not his home turf but New York City, which he adopted as his domicile circa 1980. New to the metropolis, hence acutely sensitive to its barely controlled chaos, he vividly and purposefully conveys the edgy energy of the streets and the endemic friction between various races and cultures, the well-off and the destitute, the ruthless and the barely functional. In his first three novels Bell comes across as a quintessential savvy and hip New Yorker, yet he declared himself a southern writer right from the start, pointing not only to his Tennessee roots but to the enormous impact southern literature had on his sensibility and imagination.

In his contribution to *For the Love of Books: 115 Celebrated Writers on the Books They Love the Most* (1999), Bell cites Robert Penn Warren's *All the King's Men* (1946), which he read for the first time at age fifteen, as a tremendous influence:

> I must have read this book once a year for the following ten years. I loved it for its vivid treatment of the Southern scene I came from, and for the infectious power of the style. At the same time I was influenced by the drier, more restrained style of Flannery O'Connor's *Complete Stories* [1971].

Bell was also inspired by Warren's fellow Agrarians, a group of writers out of Vanderbilt University who were friends with Bell's Vanderbilt alumni parents. The aspiring writer grew up in the company of Allen Tate, Andrew Lytle, and the lesser-known novelist Madison Jones.

By the time he went to college, Bell knew that he wanted to be a writer in the Agrarian vein, but, as he told Bob Summer of *Publishers Weekly,* "What I was doing was writing stuff that was self-consciously Southern." Bell was so aware of the writers he revered, he explains, "their work leaked into mine, and kept it from coming to life." A move to New York City helped break the spell and allowed Bell to discover his own voice. He also avoided the pitfall that hobbles so many writers minted in graduate writing programs as he was, that is, he refused to write minimalist, autobiographical domestic dramas. As he told *Booklist,* in an interview with Donna Seaman: "I think one difference between me and some writers is that I'm not really very interested in writing about my own sensibility. I'm interested in what it would feel like to be somebody else. I'm curious about other people." This penetrating and restless curiosity has driven Bell to write about a parade of intriguing and indelible characters of diverse race and ethnicity, drug dealers, saxophone players, a cell of terrorists, a film editor, an American hypnotist living in London, a Vietnam vet who becomes a bluegrass banjo player, devout Muslims and Russian Orthodox Christians, a devil worshiper, winos, a child psychologist–tae kwon do teacher, and in his most ambitious undertaking, the Haitian military leader and liberator Toussaint-Louverture.

BELL'S CHILDHOOD AND WRITER'S APPRENTICESHIP

Bell's childhood was made-to-order for a writer. Born on August 1, 1957, in Nashville, Tennessee, he was the only child of Henry Denmark Bell and Georgia Allen Bell, who went by her middle name. Henry, an attorney, and Allen, an equestrienne and all-around outdoorswoman, owned a ninety-six-acre farm in Williamson County, Tennessee. Bell's mother taught riding lessons and ran a summer camp, and they grew enough food and kept enough cows, sheep, and hogs to live off the land, thus providing their son with a paradise for rambling and daydreaming. Bell could ride ponies and horses at will and was watched over by the family's much-loved Doberman pinschers. Benjamin Taylor, a black tenant farmer, and his family also lived on the land, and Bell spent so much time in their company he says he was partially raised by them, a profound connection that became the inspiration for the interracial dynamics he so intuitively explores in his fiction. In a piquant autobiographical essay titled "One Art," Bell writes:

> Mine was an atavistic childhood. I knew it at the time, because people told me, and it was obvious anyway. A generation before, it wouldn't have been so unusual to grow up as a child of educated, professional parents who were also real farmers. But at the schools I was driven to in Nashville

there was nobody else who lived the way I did. The town children lived in their backyards, on the sidewalks, in the neighborhoods. For the most part they had less work to do. I might envy them a little, as they would envy me for the horses, the pool, the big territory on which I was free and alone. But mainly I knew I was different from them, and already, in my way, I was proud of it.

By learning to value being "different," Bell recognized the significant roles outsiders, criminals as well as artists, play in society, and he has specialized in portraying renegades and misfits of one persuasion or another with great candor and empathy.

Curiously Bell's body rebelled against the farm's natural wonder and fecundity. He suffered from severe allergies, frequent bronchitis, and chronic asthma, maladies that prevented him from developing the sort of bucolic placidity that would preclude the drive, the need, the hunger necessary for becoming a writer. His mother taught him to read before he began school, and his love of books contributed to his sense of being "different," which was exacerbated by his illnesses. Bell accepted being sick as part of life not only because he knew nothing else but also because it freed him from doing chores and attending school, allowing him to read luxuriously, gluttonously, and gratefully.

Bell has observed that books introduced him to a realm

> in which I realized I could go much further, much faster, than I could in the real world. . . . In bouncing off the books I got some sense of who I was, or might be. . . . I think as soon as I learned to read I wanted to become an author. When I was playing with my friends, I used to punctuate our conversations by mumbling under my breath, "I say," and "he says." Not surprisingly, people thought that was weird, so I dropped it.

Later, just before he graduated from high school, Bell suffered a collapsed lung. During his long convalescence he wrote his first story, thus channeling what he has termed his "habit of fantasy" into an artistic outlet and setting the course for his adult life.

Bell chose not to establish a family tradition by attending his parents' alma mater, Vanderbilt University. He enrolled in Princeton University's undergraduate creative writing program instead. Bell's involvement with the Agrarian writers remained strong, however, becoming an academic focus even as he won four awards for his own fiction. Bell graduated summa cum laude in 1979, and found his mentor, the southern writer George Garrett. Like Bell's father, Garrett's father was an attorney, and the senior Garrett's devotion to justice shaped much of his son's writing, a philosophical and moral orientation Garrett and Bell shared. Garrett also guided Bell toward technical mastery. Both writers have been praised for their exceptional facility with narrative structure. In his introduction to a paperback edition of Garrett's 1996 novel *The King of Babylon Shall Not Come against You,* Bell writes that he "learned from listening to George talk about Faulkner that a truly great writer is also always a great liberator. Each artifact of such a writer opens another door and creates an opportunity for other writers to come along afterward and avail themselves of new freedoms." Garrett is a tremendously prolific, versatile, intellectual, and imaginative writer, as Bell was destined to be, and his trilogy of historical novels helped pave the way for Bell's own bold foray into the field.

Garrett encouraged Bell to follow him to Hollins College in Roanoke, Virginia, to earn his M.F.A. Bell complied, but only after living in New York City from 1979 to 1983, working in film and television as a production assistant and sound man. Unsure of what to write once he arrived in Roanoke, Bell had a dramatic breakthrough: "I suddenly began to have ideas for a story, like voices were talking to me." He began what became his first novel, *The Washington Square Ensemble.* When he had written about three hundred pages, he showed the manuscript to Garrett, who recommended an agent, Jean Gelfman. In no time Bell was on his way to living an ideal literary life. Eventually Bell, again like Garrett, discovered his gift for teaching, which turned out to be the most writing-compatible way for him to earn a living.

THE NEW YORK NOVELS

The Washington Square Ensemble takes the form its title implies. It is a tale told in multiple voices in a jazzy if jangling style. New York City's Washington Square Park has long been famous for its hustlers, buskers, and squatters, especially within the novel's time frame, the feral 1970s and 1980s, when the city was going broke, drugs and sex were peddled everywhere, crime was rampant, and the art and music scenes were gutsy, vibrant, and intense. The park is the epicenter of Bell's thriller-like narrative, the base of operations for the drug dealer Johnny B. Goode and his band of loyal and eccentric employees.

The first and most facile of Bell's tough-guy heroes, Johnny B. (after whom Bell's mother named one of her horses) evinces many of the qualities that continue to fascinate Bell. But he is also a stereotypical young man's macho male fantasy figure: a good-looking, disciplined, solitary, moody, and ironic mastermind. On the lam after a youthful involvement with the mob, he explains that he chose his alias "because I love black people and their music and money, and. . . . When the narco squad comes down looking for Johnny B. Goode, they are not looking for a white Italian." Johnny B. is so cool he lives under yet another false name in a sparsely furnished condo on the elegant Upper East Side, where he conducts his martial arts practice sessions, listens to John Coltrane and Ornette Coleman, contemplates the meaning of life, and personifies cool.

Johnny B. is entirely too stylized, but his cohorts are creations of truly startling power and originality. Among them are the Puerto Rican Santa Barbara, a practitioner of Santeria, a Caribbean-based religion that combines the worship of Yoruba deities with Catholicism; Yusuf Ali, a Black Muslim giant; a junkie called Holy Mother; and Porco Miserio, a boozy down-and-out saxophone player. As Bell fleshes out the troubled pasts of his streetwise characters, he tells wild stories about their searches for God in the direst of circumstances, and beneath the crackle of the frenetic drug dealer–cop plot pulses a passionate inquiry into the nature of the divine and various pathways to revelation. Flashes of wry humor spike the action as events rise to a frenzied and violent climax. After the smoke clears and the blood dries, what remains is a solid foundation composed of nuanced interracial relationships, solitary spiritual quests, a charismatic if misguided leader, the pursuit of artistic endeavors, and violence both purposeful and anarchic on which Bell has built each subsequent novel.

When asked how he came to write so knowingly about the seamy side of urban life, Bell told Seaman of *Booklist* that for much of the seven years he lived in New York City he did not really have a job.

> I wasn't a professional criminal either, but I was somehow getting by without conventional employment. I actually began to make money from writing books and lived on that for a couple of years before I started teaching, which is kind of an unusual pattern for people who write. I didn't have a high standard of living, but I did have a lot of time to stand beside characters like those I've written about without actually being one.

In his second novel, the ferociously apocalyptic *Waiting for the End of the World* (1985), Bell travels even further into the dangerous realm he depicts in his first novel. Dispensing with the superficiality of his first fictional alter ego, Johnny B. Goode, Bell creates a far more complicated and subsequently more human protagonist in Clarence Larkin, a fugitive from the middle class. An epileptic visionary versed in the texts of many religions who creates art works depicting apocalyptic themes and who earns his keep by photographing the disfigured and the deformed for a doctor at Bellevue, Larkin belongs to a secret terrorist cell intent on precipitating Armageddon by detonating an atom bomb beneath the streets of Manhattan. Set in 1982, this eschatological thriller anticipates the apprehension with which Western civilization, striving beneath the pall of nuclear weapons, pollution, and poverty, approached the end of the millennium.

Bell presents dossier-like profiles of each of the terrorists, including the leader, the diabolical and wealthy Simon, who holds a psychology degree from Harvard and who recruited his minions through his anger clinic. Ruben suffered a wretched childhood and a junkie-burglar youth and did prison time. College-boy Mercer becomes a cocaine courier and ends up being tortured in a Mexican jail, and Hutton is a Vietnam vet with serious post-traumatic stress disorder. But the solitary Larkin, who cares little for his cohorts' revengeful motives or infatuation with bloodshed, describing himself as "just a humble servant of the apocalypse," is the heart of the story, and it is his porousness to both beauty and ugliness that imbues this fierce novel with its broken-glass lyricism.

For all his nihilism Larkin is impelled to help the abused and mistreated, including a mute Latino boy with symbols of devil worship carved into his flesh. Larkin takes the boy to a farm in New Jersey to stay with his Russian Orthodox friend Arkady, one of many clues in this story of crazed radicals, crimes and punishments, and epileptic visions that point to the readily acknowledged influence of Bell's "hero," the nineteenth-century Russian novelist Fyodor Dostoyevsky. Bell observes that the plots of Dostoyevsky's novels are basically thrillers in which he intentionally "worked on the edge of that genre." Bell admires and emulates this approach even though many critics continue to malign Dostoyevsky because of it, a rigid attitude that has been applied to Bell's work as well. Bell also praises Elmore Leonard and Joseph Wambaugh, saying: "I like fairly realistic cop and criminal stories. And there is, indeed, deliberately, an element of that in a lot of my books."

But Dostoyevsky's influence goes beyond the manipulation of conventional thriller plot lines. His work has inspired Bell to question the belief that salvation is only found in suffering, to dissect the psychology of terrorism, to refute the notion of progress (human beings are not wiser now than they were in the past), to protest society's rampant materialism and potentially fatal undervaluing of nature, and to analyze our species' inherent perversity.

Waiting for the End of the World is incendiary and furious, a high-octane blend of sheer visceral excitement and a blazing tour through the tenets and paradoxes of radical politics and religions both demonic and sublime. Fueled by rage over the abuse of children and women, the degradation of the environment, and willful obliviousness to the mysteries of existence, it is also a scouting mission into the realm of the apocalypse. As Bell says in an interview with Mary Louise Weaks in the *Southern Review,* the key question of our times is, "Do we have the power to destroy our world completely?" He believes this paradox has such enormous emotional and spiritual implications it will engender a "national literature that turns on that problem. . . . I think that's the big motor that's going to turn out a lot of literary art." Then in one of his characteristic shifts from reflective seriousness to irony, he quips, "In the future it will be interesting to see if there's anyone around to read it."

Bell's bold first novel had been enthusiastically received, and critics praised his second book for its artistry, intelligence, and passion, recognizing the significance of *Waiting for the End of the World*'s cosmological concerns. In a review for the *Atlanta Journal-Constitution,* Bob Summer writes of Bell, "The wonder is that his uncompromising lack of sentimentality—an observant toughness that echoes Dickens . . . is entwined with an ennobled vision that ultimately lifts the reader into the realm of enchantment."

The razor-sharp novel *Straight Cut* (1986) came next, followed by Bell's first short story collection, *Zero db and Other Stories,* but the lyrical, elegiac, and enigmatic book *The Year of Silence* concludes what can be seen as an informal New York trilogy including *The Washington Square Ensemble* and *Waiting for the End of the World. The Year of Silence* is best understood within that framework.

Readers familiar with *Waiting for the End of the World* will be surprised to encounter a character named Larkin in the opening scene of *The Year of Silence,* given the astonishing climax of the earlier novel. An apparently gifted pianist, Larkin is practicing on a carved keyboard of immobile keys rather than on a piano, executing the fingerings of the "Goldberg Variations" in absolute silence. Bell soon reveals his identity. This is Clarence's brother Tom, who has taken a vow of silence after Clarence's inexplicable disappearance as though he could "purchase his brother's return" with this sacrifice. He performs his conceptual music, his prayer, in a typical Bell interior—a mirror-lined apartment as spare as that of Johnny B. Goode's from *The Washington Square Ensemble*—and his roommate, Weber, is, according to Larkin, "a fanatic practitioner of some kind of karate," an art and obsession that Bell assigns to most of his heroes to signify not only the benefit of being able to defend one's self in a hostile, unpredictable world but also and more importantly the value of disciplining both the body and the mind to marshal spiritual powers.

Bell's heroes also share the habit of going on punishingly long walks to outdistance their demons, and as his urban warriors cover miles and miles of pavement, park, and bridge span, Bell transforms the complex cityscape into a map of emotions, memories, and dreams. Parks become chapels, theaters, and proving grounds. The Williamsburg Bridge is a sacred place, where the solitary wanderer can contemplate space and time, alienation and connection, death and the void. Here Weber causes a stir by climbing to the top of the bridge not to jump, as the cops fear, but to "affirm life" in the difficult aftermath of his lover Marian's suicide. In this early scene Bell merely drops Marian's name and moves on, but Marian and her suicide are the kernel of the novel.

Writing, as is his wont, from multiple points of view, Bell portrays an ensemble of men and women affected to varying degrees by Marian's death. At the time of its publication, Bell told Bob Summer of *Publishers Weekly* that he felt *The Year of Silence* was "his best-constructed work," describing its unconventional form as achieving "a ripple effect" with the suicide of his main character, Marian, functioning "like a rock dropped into a pond." Indeed she sits at the heart of the novel like a figure in the center of a mandala, and her enigmatic death becomes a meditation point for the circle of characters that surrounds her. When she dies, they reconsider their hold on life and life's hold on them. Each affirms life in his or her own way, although each affirmation is a variation on letting go, of not clinging to sorrow, fear, or even to the body. To affirm life, Bell suggests, is to be open to its vagaries and mysteries and its twin, death.

One of the most salient differences between *The Year of Silence* and its New York predecessors is the presence of fully realized female characters. Few girls or women appear in the pages of Bell's first two novels, and when they do they are more iconographic than flesh and blood. They are poster girls for surviving the macho brutality of the city or beautiful damsels in distress. By portraying convincing women characters in this exceptionally empathic novel, Bell takes a giant step forward in his maturation as a writer.

Reviewing *The Year of Silence* for the *New York Times Book Review,* Roberta Silman praises the novel's careful construction and concludes that Bell "has an uncanny understanding of the way many people must struggle to live." The fiction writer Jill McCorkle, in a glowing and insightful review in the *Atlanta Journal-Constitution,* marvels at the dynamism and effectiveness of the novel's structure and commends Bell's "dual vision, the ability to see beyond the ugliness of the world at street level, to see the human heart housed within such a wide variety of characters." She concludes, "He has found the glimmers of hope which serve to shroud this world with an overall sense of benevolence."

TRANSITIONAL WORKS

The novel *Straight Cut* and Bell's first short story collection *Zero db* are pivotal books in the progression of his work, testing grounds for his return to his southern roots and the fulfillment of the first great cycle of his spiritual explorations. In *Straight Cut,* Bell's only straightforward, first-person narration, he continues to fill the mold of the thriller with philosophical musings as his hero, the film editor and sometime drug dealer Tracy Bateman, looks to Kierkegaard for guidance. But this novel does not succeed in transcending its form. It stands simply as a sexy, international romp featuring a high-stakes drug deal and a tricky three-way love affair. The writing is lean and sharp-witted, however, achieving a cross between the banter of James Bond and the brooding of Sam Spade. And the opening scene is a breakthrough for Bell. It takes place in a setting much like his family farm in Tennessee, a milieu that he returns to with increasing authority in his short stories and the potent Tennessee novel *Soldier's Joy* (1989).

Taut, smart, and entertaining, *Straight Cut* is a minor work in a major oeuvre. Bell was just flexing his muscles, keeping in shape for the larger works to come, a technique he uses again in *Save Me, Joe Louis* (1993) and *Ten Indians* (1996) with much more meaningful results. He may also have harbored hopes that it would be optioned for film. Bell's novels do have tremendous cinematic potential.

The story collection *Zero db,* published the same year, is on the other hand a veritable fiction laboratory. Each story is a crucible in which Bell, a word alchemist, seeds the visions that later coalesce in the gold of his novels. The collection is divided between stories set in Tennessee and stories set in the New York metropolitan area. The former, each startling in its own way, have a much more organic and intuitive feeling than do the latter, even though they are just as rigorously structured. In "Triptych I," for example, two families, one white, one black, are working contentedly outside on a cold winter day on a Tennessee farm butchering hogs, cooking cracklings, and making sausage until a wholly unforeseen sequence of quietly brutal and absolutely devastating events overturns their lives. Bell's prose is so finely modulated and restrained, however, and his descriptions of the land and the people are so poignant in their specificity that tragedy is tempered by beauty, resulting in the catharsis Bell seeks so passionately in all his work.

Bell illuminates ordinary city life from a much more personal perspective in the New York stories than in his urban novels. The stories exhibit pathos and a deft handling of the absurd as Bell conveys the discomforts and rewards of being in the minority, of being a white man surrounded by people of color, of being an English speaker in a world of Spanish, of being a loner in a welter of large families.

These tales are an important step on the road to writing candidly and imaginatively about race and racism, a path Bell did not at first recognize as his but which he eventually committed himself to with ardor and verve. His eventual journey into historical fiction is even presaged in the riveting "Today Is a Good Day to Die," which takes place just before the battle of Little Big Horn.

After Bell wowed the critics and the reading public alike with the rapid succession of *The Year of Silence, Straight Cut,* and *Zero db,* his mentor Garrett wrote a benedictory essay about his protégé, "Madison Smartt Bell: *The Year of Silence,*" for *My Silk Purse and Yours* (1992), ranking Bell far above his peers, the vastly overrated "Baby Novelists" Brett Easton Ellis, Tama Janowitz, and Jay McInerney. Garrett also offers an intriguing glimpse of the impressively articulate yet enigmatic Bell, whose author photographs are notable for their theatricality:

> Prior to his recent marriage to poet Elizabeth Spires, Bell cultivated an appearance that might have been politely called The Writer as Young Wino or Future Bag Persons of America costume. For a while at Princeton he was something of a cult figure, on account of his karate, his banjo playing, and his writing; and other students dressed like him for good luck. Goodwill stores for miles around Princeton were picked clean.

GOING HOME: *SOLDIER'S JOY*

After writing about New York for ten years, Bell was ready to train his well-honed observational and storytelling skills on his ancestral home, the land that taught him what he loves and what he abhors. The result was *Soldier's Joy.* As the novel opens in 1970, Bell's contemplative yet combat-ready hero Thomas Laidlaw returns to his family's abandoned farm nestled in the hills beyond Nashville with an injured foot and a wounded soul, casualties from a stint in Vietnam. Utterly alone, he plays the banjo for hours at a stretch, just letting his hands work as his mind empties. At night, driven from the kingdom of sleep by dreams he is relieved not to remember, he roams the woods, training himself to learn the pitch and roll of the land, pushing himself to walk and run without a limp.

> It was not only a sharpening of the senses by which he learned to welcome himself into the dark under the trees, but a deeper internal shift, so that he navigated not only what he could see and touch and hear and even smell but by an inner gyroscope which found an increasingly true balance against the rise and fall of the wooded land. Then it was enough for him to step through the fence from the pasture and cross the creek into the trees to utterly, perfectly disappear. A dissolving darkness rose around him, in time to the throb of insect voices; continuous with the woods he passed through like a breeze, he could become invisible, even to himself.

But Laidlaw's invisibility is short-lived. His presence is soon noted by his neighbor, the reticent and decent Mr. Giles, a white farmer who offers to help cut hay and plow the garden. Laidlaw also rescues a starving dog, finds a fiddle player for the band he's decided to put together, and attracts a lover all in one when he meets Adrienne. Then Rodney Redmon, an African American neighbor and intimate boyhood friend, reenters his life. Redmon's father, Wat, worked for Laidlaw's folks, and Laidlaw all but worshiped him when he and Rodney were boys. As the men get reacquainted, Bell explores the tangle of resentment and love that underlies their soon-to-be controversial friendship. He also sensitively elucidates the quandaries faced by Giles as the distressed father of loutish sons who belong to the Ku Klux Klan.

Redmon and Laidlaw's public demonstrations of affection prove to be too much for these hard-drinking racists, and Giles's boys and their cohorts embark on a campaign of increasingly violent harassment and threats. Meanwhile Brother Jacob, a black preacher calling for universal love who attracts large interracial crowds, is coming to town. Laidlaw and his band have been invited to perform, and the Klan has plans to assassinate this proselytizer of black-white love. The stage is set for a major confrontation as the lyricism that shaped the first half of the novel gives way to adrenaline-pumping action in an explosive showdown.

In an interview with Don O'Briant at the *Atlanta Constitution,* Bell said:

> This is my first Southern novel, and although I don't believe in political art, this novel began with a political motive. In 1984, I turned on a radio talk show and heard one of the smooth new breed of Klansmen so glib he made fools of the outraged and comparatively inarticulate people who called in.

The anger aroused by this slick hate monger, disgust over the rise in national prominence of the racist and politically savvy David Duke, and dismay at the arrest of a friend who participated in an anti-Klan demonstration inspired Bell to write a novel that would eviscerate the Klan. Bell explained, "I especially wanted to deny their pretense of representing me or the great majority of other white Southerners—rural or urban, rich or poor—for whom they do not speak and never have." He succeeded in his mission, and *Soldier's Joy,* much praised by critics, garnered the Southern Regional Council's 1989 Lillian Smith Award. One of the competition's judges, the University of Florida professor Anne Jones, noted Bell "invents a new meaning for combat and a new interracial ethic."

A LONDON INTERLUDE: *BARKING MAN AND OTHER STORIES* AND *DOCTOR SLEEP*

After Bell married Elizabeth Spires, the Whiting Writers' Award–winning poet, in 1985, he began accepting a string of itinerant teaching jobs radiating out from their home in Baltimore,

Maryland. He taught at the Ninety-second Street Y in Manhattan, Johns Hopkins University, the Iowa Writers Workshop, and Goucher College in Towson, Maryland, which became his and Spires's permanent base of operations. During this period Bell and Spires also lived in London for a year, a change in venue that proved quite felicitous.

Barking Man and Other Stories (1990) is Bell's second short story collection. Like *Zero db,* it both returns to the settings of his novels and anticipates future works, but it evinces even more versatility, more powerful imaginings, and deeper forays into the human condition. A diverse, passionate, and virtuoso collection, it is held together by a net of poignant underlying themes. Bell's abiding bond with animals surfaces in several tales, as does his interest in how people cope with various forms of entrapment, of being caged, boxed in, abused. Both motifs find surprising expression in "Holding Together," a nimble fable about a highly evolved Chinese mouse who helps his companions survive a terrifying ordeal as unwilling participants in a science experiment, a violation Bell gently parallels with the human torments of exile and slavery. In the title story, a dark and concise drama about the debilitating effects of mindless conformity, a young American living miserably with his anxious brother and sweet sister-in-law in London cracks under the strain and begins to act like a dog. In "Black and Tan" a Tennessean who abruptly loses his entire family finds solace in raising Dobermans and helping troubled boys. One of his best books, *Barking Man and Other Stories* confirms the fact that if Bell had written nothing but short stories he would still be considered a brilliant and important writer.

So much goes on in Bell's boldly orchestrated work that it is possible to overlook his laconically dry humor. Off-handedly self-deprecating in his crisp autobiographical essays and impressively fluent interviews, he injects his heroes with the same highly skeptical view of themselves. This mordant sense of the ludicrousness of the self in particular and life in general is echoed in the structure of his genre-pushing novels as Bell undercuts his metaphysical preoccupation with good and evil with sequences of frenetic suspense and spectacular violence. This wrenching shifting of gears can feel contrived, as though Bell feared that if he didn't crank up the action he would lose readers unwilling to ingest spiritual dialectics. But any reader who gives over to the music of Bell's fiction will recognize that these modulations from contemplation to chaos reflect Bell's perception of the basic reality of life. No matter how disciplined or prayerful an individual is, how careful he or she is to do no harm, or how many people view him or her as a leader, neither that individual nor anyone else can control the thoughts and behavior of others or stop the tides and storms of confusion, desperation, and unadulterated evil that rise up and turn the world insane. Frustration and grief over the individual's inability to stop such tragedies induce Bell to write at a fever pitch and to invent heroes who push themselves to extremes to fight for what is right.

Doctor Sleep, an adroitly composed novel about an American hypnotist living in London on an expired visa, begins with a typical Bell paradox. Adrian Strother, the man who can put people to sleep at a snap, is a chronic insomniac, and the swoops and swings of his sleep-deprived mind infuse this tale with a hallucinogenic quality. Another otherworldly element at work is Adrian's immersion in hermetic gnosticism, specifically the writings of the sixteenth-century Italian philosopher Giordano Bruno, who was burned at the stake for his belief that the divine is manifest in everyone and in all the world—a holistic vision that Bell himself holds in high regard. But as always Bell's protagonist's spiritual focus is challenged by an assault of the mundane—no coffee in the house, no clean clothes—and the horrific—a serial killer preying on London's children. In addition, just to make sure that Adrian is kept completely off-kilter, his lover moves out; his snake will not eat; and Stuart, a man he crossed an ocean to get away from, reenters his life with tumultuous consequences.

Stuart (who debuted in *Barking Man*) is like Adrian a former junkie, and in their New York life they were involved in an unwholesome triangular affair with a woman Adrian nonetheless married. Similarly complicated entanglements emerge in *Straight Cut* and *Save Me, Joe Louis*. Bell uses these tricky romantic configurations to explore the erotic aspects of close male friendships and rivalries and the precariousness of highly sexual but otherwise inarticulate relationships between men and women.

But Stuart's appearance has more than personal repercussions. He is in London to spread his Christian gospel and to set up a center to help drug addicts go clean. Resembling the ripples Brother Jacob's preaching caused in *Soldier's Joy,* Stuart's proselytizing upsets the status quo, and once again Bell explicates often-overlooked nuances of black-white relationships. Ultimately events conspire to force Adrian to put his life at risk as he becomes involved with Scotland Yard, a drug kingpin, a serial killer, and a client burdened by multiple personalities and deeply repressed incidents of childhood sexual abuse.

A great, humming energy is at work on these pages, generated by Adrian's inner monologues, which are spiked with visions brought on by his lack of sleep, preoccupation with gnosticism, musings on the use of drugs to escape the harshness of reality, despair over the pervasiveness of evil and the vulnerability of women and children, and longing for his absent lover. His bright eyes glimmering like planets within dark circles, his flesh bruised and bleeding, Adrian is reaching for revelation, for the light, even if it is just the oncoming headlights of a subway train:

I was the world and the world was I and I felt the unity trembling in my hand. . . . I was the mirror of the universe, so anything that happened to any other person or thing also happened to me personally, and whatever I might do to myself was done to the world and everything in it, which was the meaning of each small act of my self-destruction. A howling began at the bottom of the tunnel, roaring at me again and again that the world itself is the body of God. And so, so long as that holds true, then God Himself can be destroyed—I and my brother humans have gone a long way toward proving that, but not yet all the way, and truly it remains a fearful thing to fall into the hands of the living God.

With this dazzling novel's resolution Bell puts to rest a long chain of philosophical meditations, wrestlings with morality, and searches for spiritual enlightenment. As he told Justin Cronin in 1995:

To my mind, *Doctor Sleep* was the end of a whole trend in my work. . . . After I had finished it, I realized in a way I hadn't before that all the novels I had written up to that time were spiritual pilgrimages of one kind or another. Though they were by and large couched in the form of thrillers, they're essentially experiments in religion.

Many creative writers prefer to leave exegesis of their work to critics, but in the interview with Justin Cronin, Bell is strikingly eloquent on the subject of the evolution of his fiction and brings both acumen and a dash of self-mockery to the discussion as he neatly categorizes each of his novels.

In my first book, *Washington Square Ensemble,* there's a rather complicated argument going on between Islam and Santeria; the next book, *Waiting for the End of the World,* is basically about Eastern Orthodox Christianity; and the next—that's *Straight Cut* I'm speaking of—is about philosophical Christianity under the aegis of Kierkegaard. *The Year of Silence* is a novel about life in a world *without* religion, based on the ideas of French existentialism. In *Soldier's Joy* we're back to primitive Christianity, and then in *Doctor Sleep,* it's hermetic Gnosticism and the writings of Giordano Bruno. To me, this seemed like the answer. I think the idea that the universe *is* divinity is viable as a fundamental precept for a reformed religion of our time.

Because *Doctor Sleep* was the final chapter in a search for a spiritual home that began with his first novel, Bell felt lost and bereft when he completed it. He "experienced some real confusion and depression," and five years later this period still haunted him, prompting him to admit to interviewer Jack Stephens that he worries that after he writes the last page of the last volume in his Haitian trilogy he will face "the same disagreeable options as when I finished *Doctor Sleep*: 1) Suicide (just a rhetorical point, okay). 2) Abandon writing altogether (the Rimbaud/Duchamp solution). 3) Think up a new trick." He claims that thoughts of this ilk plagued him for a long time in the past and kept him from writing, yet Bell's next novel, *Save Me, Joe Louis,* came out less than two years after *Doctor Sleep.* Reminded that not much of a "gap" existed between books, Bell responded in a manner that reveals just how extraordinarily driven and ceaselessly productive he is: "There was though, for me. I usually only take about a week break. That time it was more like six months. In fact, it seems to me now that it was nearly a year, but maybe that's not true; maybe it was just a few months."

STAYING LIMBER: *SAVE ME, JOE LOUIS* AND *TEN INDIANS*

The idea of writing a historical novel about the eighteenth-century Haitian hero Toussaint-Louverture first came to Bell during his research into the Santeria religion for *The Washington Square Ensemble,* when he came across a wealth of information about voodoo. It then was bolstered by his reading about terrorism in preparation for writing *Waiting for the End of the World,* a pursuit that unexpectedly led him to riveting accounts of the Haitian Revolution. "Over the next ten years," he explained in an interview with Jack Stephens, "I kept circling back to the idea, then doing something else instead. Something easier. Until finally there seemed no reason to put it off anymore."

The "something easier" was *Save Me, Joe Louis,* a wild ride of a novel about two outlaws that starts in New York City, whips through Baltimore, and hightails it south to Tennessee. Macrae, who is AWOL, and Charlie, a hard case, as readers who recognize him from *Waiting for the End of the World* can attest, meet on a cold night in Battery Park when each tries to cadge off the other. Seeing that his mark is as destitute as he is, Charlie enlists Macrae as an accomplice in a cash-station mugging, the first of the duo's many crimes, each bloodier than the last. Eventually Macrae and Charlie pick up a third accomplice, Porter, an African American fresh out of prison. After a badly botched armored truck robbery, all three end up hiding out at Macrae's father's Tennessee farm in an interlude that revisits some of the racial conundrums raised in *Soldier's Joy* and introduces one of Bell's more alluring women characters, Lacy, a photographer and Macrae's kissing cousin.

As Bell's violent, live-for-the moment characters, hell-bent on brute survival, wreak havoc across the masterfully rendered countryside, which seethes with the indifferent busyness of nature, Bell transforms their mayhem into an electrifying study in nihilism. His success in infusing a crime spree with metaphysical implications thrilled critics. In a review for the *Chicago Tribune,* Andy Solomon ponders Bell's fascination with lowlife characters and ascribes to him a "Robert Browning empathy that creates no character so defiled that Bell cannot ask, 'What is at the heart of this man that is in me as well?'" When Bell's fellow southern novelist Harry Crews reviewed the novel for the *New York Times Book Review,* Crews praised Bell's "vision of human experience being no more than dust blown in the winds of chance, and finally his determination never to make the life of the novels have more symmetry and sense than flesh and blood normally have."

At one point Macrae and Charlie go crabbing, and Macrae is morbidly intrigued with how the captured crabs were "clawing at each other, angling for position on the backs of the ones below." He says, "They're all against each other, aren't they?" When asked by Donna Seaman in *Booklist* about this vision of nature's aggressiveness, Bell conceded that he "thought crabs were an ideal example of life in the Hobbesian universe where it's the war of all against all. And that's the way these characters are living, like crabs." This vision of "the war of all against all" underlies Bell's subsequent work even when characters attempt to combat life's brutality with compassion and good deeds. This is the theme of *Ten Indians,* the compact and harrowing novel Bell wrote for "fun" after completing *All Souls' Rising* (1995), the first installment of what evolved into a trilogy of historical novels about the Haitian revolution.

Ten Indians provides an intriguing counterbalance to the anarchy of *Save Me, Joe Louis.* Here Bell's characters are flawed but well intentioned. Married and the father of an exceedingly self-possessed seventeen-year-old daughter Michelle, Mike Devlin is a white child psychologist disgusted by the whining of his moneyed patients. A baby boomer who has not lost his rock and roll taste for adventure, he is only at peace with himself when he is practicing tae kwon do. Both he and Michelle hold black belts, and when his instructor approaches him about opening a school deep in the heart of Baltimore's poorest and roughest neighborhood, Devlin decides that this is the challenge he's been waiting for.

In spite of various auguries of disaster, including a drive-by shooting in which a beautiful young African American woman pushing her baby boy in a stroller is killed, Devlin sets up shop. Michelle decides to help out, and while this show of daughter-father solidarity is touching, neither is prepared for the harsh realities of the realm of despair they have naively intruded upon. At first things go smoothly. Devlin's classes fill, and he works hard to convince his students, ardent young men and women on quests for knowledge and salvation, to turn off their beepers and leave their guns and feuds outside. But feelings run high. After one session of ritualized combat mutates into genuine gang warfare, Devlin declares that the school is "a sanctuary. It's not like the rest of the world. It's a place where things make sense." Sadly, an ancient and decorous art of concentrated inner power is no match for guns and the crude laws of the street. As conflicts accelerate and more young people die, it becomes obvious that Devlin, dangerously hubristic, is in way over his head. In addition he has put the person most precious to him, his daughter, in harm's way and is unable to protect her.

Kinetic, suspenseful, and provocative, *Ten Indians* extends Bell's questions regarding an individual's ability to affect change and seems to illustrate that thorny old saying "No good deed goes unpunished." Robert E. Brown, writing in *Library Journal,* recognized the novel's profound themes: "The concept of 'getting involved' applies in a metaphysical as well as a practical sense. 'Boundary crossing' also takes on multiple meanings." Young adult books *Booklist* columnist Michael Cart recommended *Ten Indians* for mature young adult readers, writing that the "novel captures the mix of literary quality and right-on relevance that, if put into the right hands, can change lives."

THE HAITIAN NOVELS

Given Bell's long apprenticeship to various forms of spirituality, it is no surprise that voodoo was the portal through which he entered Haiti's past and present. This African-based religion envisions the soul, or what we call the self, as having a life separate from that of the body. In addition it envisions the souls of the dead as residing in an alternative realm from which various divinities, called the *loa,* take shape. During voodoo ceremonies these spirits, known by their distinctive demeanors and behaviors, displace the consciousness of worshipers and take over their bodies in a phenomenon known as "possession." The *loa* are said to mount initiates, hence the term "divine horsemen."

Bell is profoundly moved by the immediacy and intimacy of voodoo, a religion in which the gods come to Earth and to mankind so tangibly and directly, and his deep appreciation for this extraordinarily accessible manifestation of the divine is one of the most potent themes in his Haitian novels. But he is also drawn to the island's violent history because of his conflicted feelings about his southern heritage. He told Jack Stephens that writing about Haiti, "the only nation on Earth founded by black slaves who freed themselves," has been a "way for me to write about a slave society without involving my own ancestors, some of whom certainly did own slaves. It was just close enough and just far enough away, in that sense."

Bell was also curious, as he wrote in the essay "True Morality," about why, of the "three great revolutions of the eighteenth-century, only the Haitian Revolution carried the ideology of natural human rights to its complete consummation." Neither the French Revolution nor the American Revolution extended civil rights to people of color, a failing that has had enormous consequences. Bell came to see Haiti as a "crucible of all the forces that created our own society," and he also developed a "messianic fascination" with Toussaint-Louverture, whom he described in an interview with Robert Birnbaum as "just an astonishing figure: he was a

military genius, he was very close to being a political genius, he made himself out of nothing . . . he's certainly one of the great men of the world."

As Bell struggled with the tremendous wealth of research material he amassed, much of it in French, and began visualizing all the characters he would need to represent various aspects of eighteenth-century Haiti's color-coded society, he realized that he could not cover it all in one book. So he hatched his master plan of writing three novels, each of which can stand on its own but, when read in sequence as part of a trilogy, becomes part of a larger and more illuminating whole. *All Souls' Rising* came first.

ALL SOULS' RISING

All Souls' Rising, which spans the harrowing years of 1791 through 1793, imaginatively dramatizes the "big bang" that started the Haitian Revolution—a slave uprising that pitched the French colony of Saint Domingue into bloody chaos. Intent on profit rather than colonization, the French had not settled the western half of the island, named Hispaniola by Columbus. Instead the French established ruthlessly managed plantations worked by tens of thousands of enslaved African men and women. So brutal were their lives that they died by the thousands every month, only to be replaced by shiploads more. When the rebellion finally began, inspired in part by the ideology of the French Revolution, it pitted every class and race—white, black, and mulatto—against each other and led to unstable alliances with the competing colonial forces of France, England, and Spain. The powerful attempted to hold on to what they had, and the once powerless fought first for their very survival and then for their freedom. As the revolt rapidly escalated into war, all factions committed atrocities against women and children, and life became an altogether treacherous proposition.

In subject and scope *All Souls' Rising* appears to be a tremendous leap for Bell, whose previous novels explored a past no more distant than the Vietnam War and featured no characters based on historical figures. But his extensive research and profound involvement combined with his finely honed literary skills and Herculean capacity for hard work enabled him to step up from writing tightly constructed contemporary tales to constructing a panoramic historical epic about one of the world's most-complicated and least-examined wars without missing a beat.

All Souls' Rising truly has a cast of thousands, but a constellation of characters of all skin colors, stations in life, and spiritual orientations emerges to form a halo around an adeptly foregrounded trio of major figures. Two are fictional—Doctor Antoine Hebert, a white Frenchman, and Riau, a black runaway slave. The third is Toussaint.

Doctor Hebert, newly arrived in the colony in search of his recently widowed sister Elise, is an archetypal outsider through whose eyes Bell explores this highly volatile, violent, and bewildering world. Keenly observant, resourceful, calm, and without prejudice, Hebert, Bell explains in his essay "Engaging the Past," "serves as a pilot fish for both the reader and the writer: the stranger who arrives in the strange land knowing nothing and needing to learn it all." Indeed Hebert needs to "learn it all" quickly to survive.

In the opening scene Hebert is riding alone on horseback across the vaguely malevolent countryside when he is confronted by a shocking sight emblematic of the hell Saint Domingue has become: a black woman, a slave, has been crucified on a crude cross. This horrific image of extreme cruelty and suffering instantly cues the reader to Bell's refusal to soft-pedal the wrenching truth of the revolution's furious violence. Never one to turn away from the full impact of bloodshed, Bell vividly describes acts of torture, mutilation, rape, and murder throughout this epic tale, a bid for authenticity in depicting the rage loose in the land that moved some reviewers to object to his graphic descriptions as mere sensationalism. Responding, Bell told Jack Stephens:

> In writing this book I came to realize that the real subject of the argument was who counted as being human and who didn't. Those who got categorized as less than human could be butchered. . . . In other words, it is a story about attempted genocide and the inherent violence that goes along with that.

Riau, born in Africa and brought to the island as a slave, is now a maroon, one of many runaway slaves living in clandestine enclaves in the mountains and joining the revolution as a guerrilla force. He is also a practitioner of the then nascent voodoo religion, and the sections he narrates are unusual stylistically, oscillating between first person and third person to reflect how his mode of consciousness is shaped by the experience of possession, of having his self or his ego temporarily erased or moved aside by the spirits who come into his head. This wavering between subject and object is a tricky thing to pull off, and Bell reports that he "had to struggle to preserve this facet of the novel in the published version," overriding his editor's concern that readers would find it confusing. Bell was right to persevere.

Bell met the Haitian historian Michel-Rolphe Trouillot when Trouillot's book, *Silencing the Past: Power and the Production of History* (1995), came out at the same time as *All Souls' Rising*. The men became friends, and Trouillot later contributed an essay titled "Bodies and Souls: The Haitian Revolution and Madison Smartt Bell's *All Souls' Rising*" to an innovative collection created by Mark C. Carnes, *Novel History: Historians and Novelists Confront America's Past (and Each Other)* (2001). Trouillot commends Bell not only for his grasp of history—touting his "Chronology of Historical

Events," a nineteen-page appendix to the 500-plus-page novel, as "better than most such summaries available in English"—but also for his "interiorization" of events and imaginative techniques for bringing them to life. On this score he is particularly taken with Riau, impressed by Bell's empathic conjuring of the life of an eighteenth-century slave, an existence about which practically nothing is known beyond the broadest possible strokes.

Both Hebert and Riau are in awe of Toussaint's great prowess as a leader, and they are mystified by his myriad contradictions. Their nuanced viewpoints reflect Bell's own vision of Toussaint, and Bell has attested to his reluctance to take liberties with the facts in his portrayal of the inscrutable hero he so much admires. A self-educated and multitalented man who was a literate and devout Catholic as well as a voodooist, Toussaint was a loving father and husband, a superb horseman, a healer with great knowledge of medicinal plants, and a wily, self-contained accommodationist adept at playing one group off against another and capable of great ruthlessness and chicanery. Bell's interpretative restraint engenders a narrative highly tolerant of ambiguity, an essential element in any genuinely literary creation, and it also leads to his decision to portray Toussaint from multiple perspectives. "I wanted to try to catch him in the crossfire of many different points of view," Bell explained to Jack Stephens. "So if I can get him intersecting with enough fictional characters, then an image of the complete Toussaint emerges . . . I hope. Sort of like the Invisible Man, caught in the middle of a paintball fight."

As the combatants swell in numbers and switch sides in a bewildering and macabre dance, life goes on, and Bell excels at moving from great sweeping accounts of battles fought on burning city streets and in the secretive mountains to the intimacies of the domestic realm, where people still fall in love and cuddle their children. His adroitness in rendering

meaningful the most minute of details allows him to vividly and pointillistically fill every inch of this grandly panoramic screen, on which every element is in motion physically, intellectually, emotionally, and spiritually. And in the midst of all this bloodshed, Bell has created his most compelling female characters. They include Nanon, a mulatto prostitute with whom Hebert falls in love; a plantation owner's wife, Claudine, who descends into pure evil and then experiences a spiritual rebirth; and Isabelle, seemingly a mere coquette but actually a woman of tremendous depth and fortitude.

All Souls' Rising garnered avid attention. The unexpected subject matter and the extraordinary imagination and energy with which Bell conveys everything from the entanglements of colonial politics to the preparation of a meal, while writing from the viewpoints of blacks, mulattoes, and whites, of soldiers, priests, planters, prostitutes, government officials, smugglers, mothers, and children, amazed critics and journalists alike. A brief but conspicuous *New Yorker* profile by Hal Espen was accompanied by a striking full-page portrait of the author by the celebrity photographer Richard Avedon. John Vernon, writing in the *New York Times Book Review,* objected to the relentless explicitness of the novel's violence, yet he concluded, "*All Souls' Rising,* refreshingly ambitious and maximalist in its approach, takes enormous chances, and consequently will haunt readers long after plenty of flawless books have found their little slots on their narrow shelves." Penelope Mesic, writing in the *Chicago Tribune,* recognized that the brutality at loose in Haiti two hundred years ago is a "nightmare from which we have not yet awoken," a perception shared by Diane Roberts in the *Atlanta Journal-Constitution:* "Like all 'historical novels,' *All Souls' Rising* is really about us, our times, our prejudices, our race wars." Bell wholeheartedly concurs. In a conversation with Ken Ringle of the *Washington Post,* who compares *All Souls' Rising* to William Styron's *Confessions of Nat Turner* (1967), Bell comments: "Haiti's was a full-blown race war over issues we've never really come to terms with in this country. Now we're having our own race war. But it's a slow-motion race war, disguised as crime in the streets. And nobody, black or white, wants to admit what's happening."

MASTER OF THE CROSSROADS

All Souls' Rising won the 1996 PEN/Faulkner Award and the 1996 Annisfield-Wolf Award for the best book of the year dealing with matters of race. It was also a finalist for the National Book Award. These accolades elevated Bell to the top echelon of American writers and raised high expectations for the second installment in the promised trilogy. *Master of the Crossroads* (2000), an even more accomplished novel, was published five years later to even greater critical acclaim. This book relates the extraordinarily complex second phase of the revolution. Toussaint grasped the reins of power and brought the entire island of Hispaniola under his control as he thwarted invasion attempts by both the Spanish and the English. He turned the tide of French policies his way and began laying a foundation for a society that truly embodied universal liberty. Speaking with host Donna Seaman on the radio program "Open Books," Bell said that he

> didn't want *Master of the Crossroads* to be quite so horrific as the first novel. . . . It was important to write about the violence because the magnitude of the atrocities is part of the meaning of the story, but I thought it was a good idea to concentrate less on that in the second book, which is actually more about efforts to stabilize and organize the situation.

Surviving characters from *All Souls' Rising* shine even more brightly as compelling new personas appear. Toussaint in particular acquires

more clearly defined contours as he takes the name of Louverture or "the Opening." Bell has Riau explain the significance of the name: "the understanding came to me, that in calling himself *Toussaint of the Opening* he meant to say it was Legba working through his hands." Since Legba is the voodoo god of the crossroads between the material and spiritual worlds and must be invoked at the beginning of all voodoo ceremonies, Toussaint-Louverture is indeed a powerful and resonant nom de guerre.

One of the most distinctive aspects of the sophisticated structure of *Master of the Crossroads* is Bell's creation of microcosms in the form of love affairs, marriages, friendships, and households that cross racial, class, and religious boundaries to reflect the forces at work in the macrocosm of a colonial society in violent flux. The evolving partnership between Riau and Hebert, for example, stands as a remarkable conflict-transcending relationship, as does Hebert and Nanon's progression from lovers to husband and wife to parents. The erotic thread that runs through *All Souls' Rising* becomes a major element in the lush, multihued weave of the second novel as one set of characters after another asserts life's inherent drive toward union and re-creation. Children are present throughout the novel, offering hope for a saner future since love and the progeny it produces refute genocide. All this is accomplished in prose that is unfailingly precise, lithe, and full of import.

The complex, many-theatered action in the novel's present is punctuated by somber scenes from the future. Toussaint is imprisoned in the isolated snowbound fortress of Fort de Joux, France, a frigid place almost inconceivably remote from the sunny and warm Caribbean, a death trap where our dignified hero nonetheless attempts to negotiate with his captors. These intense vignettes stand in chilling contrast to the great heat of Toussaint's military and diplomatic triumphs at home and point to the myriad twists and turns of a ferocious war that was destined to end with the very sort of apocalyptic act—the massacre of all the whites on the island—that Toussaint idealistically hoped to avoid.

Master of the Crossroads was an immediate critical success. It received starred reviews in *Booklist, Publishers Weekly,* and *Kirkus Reviews,* three highly influential advance-review magazines. In the *Los Angeles Times Book Review,* Malick Ghachem observed that Bell's "exuberant and epic novel is marked throughout by a palpable passion for the troubled Caribbean nation and its contributions to the shaping of the modern democratic world." Writing for the *New York Times Book Review* the novelist, poet, and biographer Jay Parini called the book "a brilliant performance, the work of an accomplished novelist of peculiar energy and courage" and aptly described Bell's motives as "lofty." The third and final novel in Bell's magnificent Haitian trilogy is due out in 2004, the bicentennial of Haiti's independence.

CONCLUSION

The power and majesty of *Master of the Crossroads* is rooted in Bell's ability to write about both the personal and the political, the tightly focused (the texture of a lover's skin, the expression on Toussaint's face as he sits in repose), and the spectacular (the play of shadows across the plain as seen from the mountains above, the massing of troops behind Toussaint as he rides regally on his mount). Every scene is charged with a free-ranging tactile knowledge of the island. This shimmering descriptive richness is even more striking here than in the first novel, an enhancement attributable to the fact that Bell wrote *All Souls' Rising* without ever having set foot in Haiti.

That was not his intention. Bell had received a Guggenheim Fellowship and planned to explore in-depth the country that loomed so large in his mind's eye. But just as he was about to embark on his long-anticipated journey in 1991, the Haitian military seized control of the country and closed it to foreigners. As Bell writes in "Engaging the Past," "Because I am stubborn, I decided to stay home and write the book anyway, solely on the basis of print research." He did not consult with any "professional historians, Haitian or otherwise," and describes this method as writing "in a sort of vacuum sealed by books." However, as he observes, the Haiti he was writing about had vanished long ago under the pressure of the country's population explosion, deforestation, and an entrenched poverty, the result of Haiti's status as a pariah nation in the eyes of the still-racist first world. As it turned out this long-distance approach ended up working to Bell's advantage because, when he was finally able to travel to Haiti, he used *All Souls' Rising* as a calling card, proof that his interest was serious and genuine.

Bell might have found the real Haiti lacking in comparison to the magic of his imaginary version, but instead he fell in love with the island. Not only did his travels bring him in direct contact with the land, the people, the culture, and less pleasingly the politics, all of which he found compelling, his sojourns also carried him into the world of voodoo, which changed his life. Bell has written about his Haitian experiences in a set of stunning essays, and in one, "Sa'm Pèdi," he voices a curious conundrum: "I had come to further my own particular ambitions, but I also had a yearning to have my individual ambitions self-obliterated." He continues later: "My thinking, self-identified *I* had disappeared somewhere. I didn't miss it. Dissolution of the self is a Haitian specialty; the experience can be euphoric, . . . or terrifying."

Moved by the people he met and the sights he saw, Bell was inspired to become a "Vodou pilgrim." As he told Jack Stephens, he also had "what is called *tet lave,* meaning a ritual head washing, something like baptism, which prepares the head to receive the spirit." Bell explained that he underwent this ceremony after experiencing partial possession

> in a hotel room during a blackout in the north of Haiti. Suffice it to say that this was an indelible experience and I have spent a long time since trying to understand it and to come to terms with it. I don't know if the spirit will dance again in my head. What I do feel confident about is that Vodou is one of the great religions of the world.

As Bell observes, the goal of so many religious practices is deliverance from the tyranny of the self and communion with the divine. Vodou, he says,

> will wash your ego right out of your head and leave you cleansed of it, for at least a little while. In Haiti, like nowhere else I've ever been, religious experience is as real as a rock in a field. You can break your toes on it. Or if you stand on it, it will hold you up.

Bell's receptivity to voodoo makes perfect sense given his ardent spiritual inquiry and the intensity of his devotion to his art. Bell is a writer blessed with flow; he writes quickly and precisely and rarely revises. It is almost as though his persona non grata characters—voices usually deemed unworthy in first world mainstream literature because of the color of their skin, their spiritual beliefs, artistic obsessions, outlaw ways, or poverty—were speaking through him, as though he were possessed by their spirits just as voodooists are possessed by the *loa.* His writing spirits ride him hard, and Bell gives body and soul to preserving their messages, motivated by an all-encompassing compassion, an endless quest to understand his fellow persons, and an abiding belief in literature as revelation, stories as forms of enlightenment.

Selected Bibliography

WORKS OF MADISON SMARTT BELL

BOOKS
The Washington Square Ensemble. New York: Viking, 1983.

Waiting for the End of the World. New York: Ticknor & Fields, 1985.

Straight Cut. New York: Ticknor & Fields, 1986.

The Year of Silence. New York: Ticknor & Fields, 1987.

Zero db and Other Stories. New York: Ticknor & Fields, 1987.

Soldier's Joy. New York: Ticknor & Fields, 1989.

Barking Man and Other Stories. New York: Ticknor & Fields, 1990.

Doctor Sleep. San Diego: Harcourt Brace Jovanovich, 1991.

Save Me, Joe Louis. New York: Harcourt Brace, 1993.

All Souls' Rising. New York: Pantheon Books, 1995.

Ten Indians. New York: Pantheon Books, 1996.

Narrative Design: A Writer's Guide to Structure. New York: Norton, 1997.

Master of the Crossroads. New York: Pantheon Books, 2000.

SELECTED UNCOLLECTED STORIES
"Pawnshop." *Vox* 1, no. 1:54–55 (spring 1991).

"Summertime." *Gentlemen's Quarterly,* August 1992, pp. 79–82.

"The Rights of Man." *Ploughshares* 19, no. 4:108–204 (winter 1993–1994).

"Zig Zag Wanderer." *Widener Review* 11:48–63 (summer 1997).

"Leadbelly in Paris." *Oxford American* no. 27/28:58, 69 (1999).

"Top of the World." *Washington Post,* November 12, 2000, pp. E1, E6.

SELECTED UNCOLLECTED ESSAYS
"Less Is Less: The Dwindling American Short Story." *Harper's,* April 1986, pp. 64–69.

"Apocalypse When?" *Chattahoochee Review* 15, no. 1:1–13 (fall 1991).

"One Art." In *My Poor Elephant: 27 Male Writers at Work*. Edited by Eve Shelnutt. Atlanta: Longstreet Press, 1992. Pp. 3–15.

"Bar, None." *New York Times,* March 3, 1996, p. 100.

Foreword to *The King of Babylon Shall Not Come against You,* by George Garrett. New York: Harcourt Brace, 1996.

"True Morality." In *Outside the Law: Narratives on Justice in America.* Edited by Susan Richards Shreve and Porter Shreve. Boston: Beacon Press, 1997. Pp. 32–42.

"Sa'm Pèdi." *Creative Nonfiction* no. 9, 1998. Pp. 100–117.

"Action de Grace." *Creative Nonfiction* no. 10, 1998. Pp. 42–63.

"Soul in a Bottle." *Creative Nonfiction* no. 14, 2000. Pp. 110–134.

"Our Dogs." *Contemporary Authors,* vol. 183. Detroit: Gale Group, 2000. Pp. 17–29.

"Engaging the Past." In *Novel History: Historians and Novelists Confront America's Past (and Each Other).* Edited by Mark C. Carnes. New York: Simon & Schuster, 2001. Pp. 197–208.

BOOK REVIEWS

Bradley, David. "The Battles Didn't End with the War." *New York Times Book Review,* July 2, 1989, pp. 3, 23. (Review of *Soldier's Joy.*)

Brown, Robert E. Review of *Ten Indians. Library Journal,* September 1, 1996, p. 207.

Chappell, Fred. "The Helplessness of Compassion." *Washington Post,* February 1, 1987, p. X07. (Review of *Zero db and Other Stories.*)

Crews, Harry. Review of *Save Me, Joe Louis. New York Times Book Review,* June 20, 1993, p. 8.

DeMarinis, Rick. Review of *Barking Man and Other Stories. New York Times Book Review,* April 8, 1990, p. 11.

Ghachem, Malick. "The Black Jacobins." *Los Angeles Times Book Review,* February 4, 2001, pp. 4–5. (Review of *Master of the Crossroads.*)

Gold, Ivan. Review of *The Washington Square Ensemble. New York Times Book Review,* February 20, 1983, p. 7.

McCorkle, Jill. Review of *The Year of Silence. Atlanta Journal-Constitution,* December 20, 1987, p. J10.

Mesic, Penelope. Review of *All Souls' Rising. Chicago Tribune,* October 22, 1995, pp. 1, 11.

Parini, Jay. "Black Spartacus." *New York Times Book Review,* November 5, 2000, p. 8. (Review of *Master of the Crossroads.*)

Richards, Jeffrey. Review of *Save Me, Joe Louis. Atlanta Journal-Constitution,* June 13, 1993, p. N08.

Roberts, Diane. Review of *All Souls' Rising. Atlanta Journal-Constitution,* November 26, 1995, p. K11.

Silman, Roberta. Review of *The Year of Silence. New York Times Book Review,* November 15, 1987, p. 15.

Skow, John. Review of *Ten Indians. Time,* October 28, 1996, p. 110.

Solomon, Andy. *Chicago Tribune,* May 30, 1993, section 14, p. 1.

Summer, Bob. Review of *Waiting for the End of the World. Atlanta Journal-Constitution,* September 15, 1985, p. J09.

Vaughn, Elizabeth Dewberry. Review of *Doctor Sleep. Atlanta Journal-Constitution,* January 13, 1991, p. N10.

Vernon, John. *The Black Face of Freedom.* Review of *All Souls' Rising. New York Times Book Review,* October 29, 1995, p. 12.

CRITICAL AND BIOGRAPHICAL STUDIES

Cooper, Wyn. "About Madison Smartt Bell: A Profile." *Ploughshares* 25, no. 4:205–209 (winter 1999–2000).

Espen, Hal. "Bell's Epic." *New Yorker,* December 25, 1995/January 1, 1996, pp. 137–139.

Garrett, George. "Madison Smartt Bell: *The Year of Silence.*" In his *My Silk Purse and Yours: The Publishing Scene and American Literary Art.* Columbia, Mo.: University of Missouri Press, 1992. Pp. 208–214.

Ringle, Ken. "Ripples from an Island." *Washington Post,* November 28, 1995, pp. C1–C2.

Summer, Bob. "Madison Smartt Bell." *Publishers Weekly,* December 11, 1987, pp. 45–46.

Trouillot, Michel-Rolph. "Bodies and Souls: The Haitian Revolution and Madison Smartt Bell's *All*

Souls' Rising." In *Novel History: Historians and Novelists Confront America's Past (and Each Other).* Edited by Mark C. Carnes. New York: Simon & Schuster, 2001. Pp. 184–197.

Weintraub, Amy. "Madison Smartt Bell: Seeing in Black and White." *Poets & Writers Magazine,* November/December, 2000, pp. 34–39.

INTERVIEWS

Birnbaum, Robert. "Madison Smartt Bell." *Stuff Magazine,* February 1996, pp. 105–108.

Cronin, Justin. "Interview with Madison Smartt Bell." *Four Quarters* 9, nos. 1–2:13–24 (spring 1995).

O'Briant, Dan. "Anger at Klan Fuels New Novel." *Atlanta Constitution,* June 12, 1989, pp. B1, B4.

Seaman, Donna. "The Booklist Interview: Madison Smartt Bell." *Booklist,* April 15, 1993, pp. 1468–1469.

———. "A Conversation with Madison Smartt Bell." On "Open Books" October 31, 2000, WLUW-FM, Chicago, Illinois.

Stephens, Jack. "Madison Smartt Bell." *BOMB,* no. 73:36–42 (fall 2000).

Weaks, Mary Louise. "An Interview with Madison Smartt Bell." *Southern Review* 30, no. 1:1–12 (January 1994).

—DONNA SEAMAN

Wendell Berry

1934–

*I*N THE AUTOBIOGRAPHICAL essay "A Native Hill" (collected in *The Long-Legged House,* 1969), Wendell Berry commented on the most important decision of his life: "At a time when originality is more emphasized in the arts, maybe, than ever before, I undertook something truly original—I returned to my origins—and it was generally thought by my literary friends that I had worked my ruin." The year was 1964. Berry had already published stories, poems, and his first novel. He had won a Wallace Stegner Fellowship, spent two postgraduate years at Stanford, and traveled in Europe. An assistant professor of English at New York University, he was married, the father of two, and living in Manhattan. His second novel was half finished, and his poems were appearing in *Poetry* and *The Nation.* His career lay all before him, or so it seemed. Why go back? You can't go home again, he was told. Home was rural Kentucky, and that meant—or so his "literary friends" in New York advised him—intellectual death.

Instead, the move back was the beginning of a rebirth. Berry had indeed "worked the ruin" of one kind of literary-academic career. But that cleared the way for a return to what he knew he valued most and what his fiction was about— the land, the families who worked the land, and the complex fate of being a southerner, an agrarian, a descendent of men who owned slaves and, later, depended on tobacco farming for survival. Berry began to understand his life in new terms, and to give it the shape of a symbolic fable or myth.

He wrote, much under the influence of Henry David Thoreau, "The Long-Legged House" (the title essay of his 1969 book), a personal narra-

tive of his fascination with a cabin in the woods built by his Uncle Curran, which had been a site of many family picnics and boyhood escapes. The title of the essay refers to the cabin's position on stilts at the edge of the Kentucky River. "I located a lot of my imaginings in it," he said. But "the Camp," as it was called, became something more when he and a friend first thought of fixing it up and staying there. He recalls this moment when he was fourteen as a metamorphosis: "We had got an idea, and been transformed by it." He acted on the idea again, with more seriousness of purpose, when he and Tanya Amyx were married in 1957, renovating the Camp in preparation for their new life together—although they would only stay one summer. On their return to Kentucky in 1964, Berry rebuilt the camp yet again, this time as "a retreat" for writing, since he expected to live mainly in Lexington and teach English at the University of Kentucky. It was not until the following year that Berry recognized the deeper design of the myth he was engaged in: he was not escaping civilization or retreating to the woods. He was returning to live in that place and become responsible for it full time. To do that well he had to become a farmer, not just a writer and teacher.

He and Tanya bought twelve acres at Lane's Landing Farm and rebuilt Curran's cabin within sight of its original location at the edge of the Kentucky River. It became their joint ambition to reconstruct and restore that house and—even more important, as it turned out—to bring back to health and fruition the neglected farmland that the house stood on. They added forty more acres, some of it damaged by a developer's bulldozer, in 1972. It was from the beginning, as he said in "The Making of a Marginal Farm" (in *Recollected Essays,* 1965–1980), a project of "restoration and healing":

> Most of the scars have now been mended and grassed over, most of the washes stopped, most of the buildings made sound. . . . A great deal of work is still left to do, and some of it—the rebuilding of fertility in the depleted hillsides—will take longer than we will live. But in doing these things we have begun a restoration and a healing in ourselves.

What began as an impulse to cut down weeds and "fix up" a cabin resulted in nothing less than a vocation. As Berry attested in "Reverdure," the concluding poem of his 1977 sequence, *Clearing,* he was driven by the desire to make things green again:

> Though I came here
> by history's ruin, reverdure
> is my calling:
> to make these scars grow grass.
> I survive this fate and labor
> by fascination.

The passage neatly sums up Berry's fundamental myth about himself, his "fate and labor" both as a farmer and a writer. It is above all a story of return: returning to his Kentucky origins, returning to his own family history and to the South's, returning to a particular landscape that he loved, to a place that had been abandoned, neglected, and abused ("history's ruin"), in order to restore and "reverdure" it, returning ultimately to the land itself and to farming as the origin and source of all human sustenance. Like much of Berry's writing, the passage carries a strong sense of responsibility and of a high calling. But it conveys deep pleasure too. The labor may be heavy and some of "history's ruin" irreversible, but "I survive," he says, "by fascination." Watching that natural process of healing and restoration, which can be aided but not ac-

complished by human will, is for Berry the best reward.

It is remarkable how frequently and how variously Berry repeats this narrative of return, whether in his fiction, poetry, or essays. In *The Unsettling of America: Culture and Agriculture* (1977), he locates the myth in a lengthy discussion of Odysseus's return to Penelope and to his homeland at the end of *The Odyssey,* an act which confirms—once he has slaughtered all the suitors—the vital network of responsibilities that links the marriage bed with the land, the nation, and the moral order. "For Odysseus," Berry argues,

> marriage was not merely a legal bond, nor even merely a sacred bond, between himself and Penelope. It was part of a complex practical circumstance involving, in addition to husband and wife, their family of both descendants and forebears, their household, their community, and the sources of all these lives in memory and tradition, in the countryside and in the earth. These things, wedded together in his marriage, he thought of as his home, and it held his love and faith so strongly that sleeping with a goddess could not divert or console him in his exile.

Berry evidently speaks for himself and the "complex practical circumstance" of his own marriage, as well as for that of Odysseus, by insisting on the connections between man and wife, land, community, and history. He rediscovered in Homer what he had learned by coming home from New York in 1964.

In the essay "Poetry and Place" in *Standing by Words* (1983), Berry's fullest statement of the relation between poetry and experience, he discovered another important dimension of his myth. In examples from Wordsworth and Milton, Berry finds warrant for his own departure and homecoming: "Thus in the history of poetry and in the work of some individual poets we find a kind of rhythm of aspiration and descent, of departure and homecoming. This homecoming is always a renewal of both art and earthly vision; it is a return both to 'the very language of men' and to their very world." If Wordsworth returned the language of poetry to ordinary speech, "the very language of men," and if Milton asked his Muse to "return me to my Native Element," why should not Berry's return do likewise? He saw in his return to the land a natural descent in which his words, no less than his whole vision of life, could be grounded and placed.

ORIGINS

Wendell Berry's "native element" was the Berry family homestead in Henry County, Kentucky, where he was born on August 5, 1934. His father, John Marshall Berry, was an attorney in New Castle, the county seat, and one of the founders of the Kentucky Burley Tobacco Growers Cooperative. The family lived near Port Royal, along the Kentucky River, adjacent to the four-hundred-acre farm that Berry's grandfather, Pryor Thomas Berry (1864–1946), worked all his life. The Perry family of his mother, Virginia, had been farmers in Henry County since the eighteenth century. Great-grandparents on both sides of the family held slaves, "a trouble that has lived on to afflict me," Berry wrote in *The Hidden Wound* (1970), his searching study of racism. He came to know well two black workers on his grandfather's farm, Nick Watkins and Aunt Georgie Ashby, whose courage and dignity—as he discovered later—taught him much as a child, but there are few black characters in his fiction just as there were few blacks in the Port Royal community of that time.

As a lawyer and lifelong defender of tobacco farmers, Berry's father came to represent a man of passionate integrity. "He was, in his strength, the most feeling / and the most demanding man / I have ever known," Berry wrote in the poem "In Extremis," included in the 1994 collection *Entries*. That demanding father decided in 1948 that his unruly son Wendell, along with younger brother John junior, needed to attend military school. In a poem addressed "To My Mother," also in *Entries,* Berry confessed, "I was your rebellious son." Four years at Kentucky's Millersburg Military Institute, far from home, seemed only to confirm and harden that behavior. Apparently, he looked to his mother for forgiveness and understanding, to his father for passionate commitment to principle. In another poem collected in *Entries,* "Remembering My Father," the articulate rigor of the man is what he emphasizes first:

> He taught me sentences,
> Outspoken fact for fact,
> In swift coherences
> Discriminate and exact.

Millersburg, on the other hand, represented a mindless authoritarianism that Berry despised: he recalled being reprimanded for such major offenses as reading Balzac and looking up a word in the dictionary during study hall.

At the University of Kentucky at Lexington from 1952 to 1956, Berry's independence and imagination were rewarded. He majored in English, excelled in creative writing and American history, published stories and poems in the campus literary magazine, and became its coeditor in his senior year. He spent his first summer after graduation not at the Camp but taking graduate courses at the University of Indiana, then returned to Lexington to earn an M.A. in English literature from the University of Kentucky in 1957. He had met Tanya Amyx in Lexington as an undergraduate (her father was an art history professor), and they were married on May 29, 1957. Berry spent the following academic year teaching English at Georgetown College, in Georgetown, Kentucky, only fifty miles from home; it was the school from which his father had graduated in 1922. But Berry was ready for bolder ventures.

During the 1950s Wallace Stegner, the novelist and historian of the American West who taught at Stanford, had emerged as a guiding spirit for young writers. His sensitive essay in *The Atlantic Monthly,* "To a Young Writer" (November 1959) demonstrates the sort of nationwide appeal he had come to have. Berry decided in the spring of 1958 to submit chapters of a novel-in-progress for a Wallace Stegner Fellowship, which he won. The Berry's first child, Mary, was born in May, and at the end of the summer they left for California. Berry found himself, over the next two years, among a talented, free-spirited group of writers, including Ken Kesey, Larry McMurtry, Ed McClanahan, Ernest J. Gaines, Gurney Norman, Peter Beagle, and James Baker Hall. Never a maverick writer himself, Stegner was notably sympathetic to writers who were, especially if they criticized a culture intent upon abusing the land and betraying those who depended on it. Berry clearly shared Stegner's values from the start, but his experience at Stanford probably strengthened his later appreciation for more radical critics like Ezra Pound and Edward Abbey. A countercultural fervor in Berry's writing would eventually emerge, akin to but even stronger than that found in Kesey or McClanahan or Abbey.

In his second year at Stanford, Berry taught in the English Department and worked on the novel that became *Nathan Coulter,* published in 1960. The Berrys returned to Port Royal for a year, where he happily divided his time between farming at the Berry homestead and writing. Then he won a Guggenheim Fellowship and traveled in Italy and France, staying mainly in Tuscany and Provence. Before going abroad, Berry was promised a position as assistant professor and director of freshman English at the Heights campus of New York University. The Berrys' second child, Pryor Clifford, was born shortly before they moved to New Rochelle, New York, in the fall of 1962. Despite Berry's immediate dislike of the city, he succeeded in placing his poems in prominent New York journals. When he wrote an elegy for the assassinated president John F. Kennedy, published in *The Nation* (December 21, 1963), the artist Ben Shahn was moved to create illustrations for the poem and George Braziller published the work—*November Twenty Six Nineteen Sixty Three*—as a book in 1964.

Then came his pivotal decision to return to Kentucky. He did not leave the academic world quite so decisively as his personal myth sometimes suggests. He continued to teach at the University of Kentucky from 1964 to 1977, often with reduced teaching loads or time off for grants or visiting appointments. He spent another year at Stanford in 1968–1969, teaching creative writing; he was the Elliston Poet at the University of Cincinnati in 1974, and the writer-in-residence at Centre College in Danville, Kentucky, in 1977–1978. He commented in an interview with Mindy Weinreb (reprinted in *Wendell Berry,* edited by Paul Merchant), "I quit teaching in 1977 with some very strong doubts about my ability to fit into university education as it had come to be, and the years since haven't relieved the doubts. I am a sort of agrarian traditionalist, and the universities are, pretty much without apology, in the service of the military-industrial state." Yet at the time of the interview, 1989, he was about to take up teaching again at his alma mater.

Once Berry returned to his origins and settled—or resettled—where he felt that he needed to be, his life and his work became inseparable. Whether he traveled to Peru (see "An Agricultural Journey in Peru," in *The Gift of Good Land,* 1981) or Ireland (see "An Irish Journal," in *Home Economics,* 1987), he knew himself to be identified and defined by one very particular place. That, he explained in "The Long-Legged House," was his subject:

> As a writer . . . I have had this place as my fate. For me, it was never a question of *finding* a subject, but rather of learning what to do with the subject I had had from the beginning and could

not escape. Whereas most of this country's young writers seem able to relate to no place at all, or to several, I am related absolutely to one.

What then was the meaning of this fateful place that Berry could not escape? His life's work was to explore the answers to that question. And they remained remarkably coherent and consistent answers. Berry's essays, lectures, poems, stories, and novels reflect the same fundamental ideas and feelings. His writings seem closely interconnected—in his words, perhaps, *intimately* connected—just as he sought to be (and argued that others should be) intimately connected with the land.

JEFFERSON AND THE AGRARIANS

In a speech given in 1995, reprinted (under the title "Private Property and the Common Wealth") in *Another Turn of the Crank* (also 1995), Berry declared that his own small rural community was not only "dwindling rapidly" but almost certainly "doomed." He repeated that Faulknerian word: his community was "doomed by the overwhelming victory of industrialism over agrarianism (both North and South) in the Civil War and the history both subsequent and consequent to it." His terms deliberately echo those of the famous manifesto, *I'll Take My Stand: The South and the Agrarian Tradition* (1930), written by twelve southerners who were poets, critics, historians, and professors. They agreed that "Agrarian *versus* Industrial" were the best terms in which to describe the losing battle of their own values beset by the dominant Northern industrial economy. They sought to defend a more Jeffersonian ideal of learning and labor, a more respectful relation between man and nature, and a return to agriculture as the foundation of a more humane culture. They criticized the industrial North for its spiritless and dehumanizing conceptions of work, efficiency, speed, monetary value, and progress.

In *I'll Take My Stand,* John Crowe Ransom wrote, "Our vast industrial machine, with its laboratory centers of experimentation, and its far-flung organs of mass production, is like a Prussianized state which is organized strictly for war and can never consent to peace." Lyle H. Lanier argued that the system of federal subsidies and tariffs had "all but gutted beyond repair the pursuit [of farming] which lies at the base of every social organization." Andrew Lytle argued against slogans like "Industrialize the farm" and "be progressive; drop old-fashioned ways and adopt scientific ways," by saying, "A farm is not a place to grow wealthy; it is a place to grow corn."

Each of these statements could have been written by Berry, so closely do his ideas and feelings match theirs. So could the following, from Robert Penn Warren's contribution concerning African Americans: "If the Southern white man feels that the agrarian life has a certain irreplaceable value in his society, and if he hopes to maintain its integrity in the face of industrialism or its dignity in the face of agricultural depression, he must find a place for the negro in his scheme."

Warren's concerns in 1930 were echoed by Berry in *The Hidden Wound* in 1970. In fact, the Agrarians were not antagonists of the North trying to refight the issues of the Civil War but critics of an industrial system that pervaded and undermined the entire nation. They spoke for agrarians in New England and in the West just as much as for themselves. And Berry sees himself, very consciously, as carrying on their long-standing arguments. He declares in *Another Turn of the Crank,* "I am an agrarian: I think that good farming is a high and difficult art, that it is indispensable, and that it . . . cannot be fostered or maintained under the rule of the presently dominant economic and cultural assumptions of our political parties." No more exact summation of a traditional agrarian view could have been written.

Berry looks back to the writings of Thomas Jefferson, just as the Agrarians did, as the most important source of American agrarian tradition. He writes in chapter 8 of *The Unsettling of America* (1977), "In the mind of Thomas Jefferson, farming, education, and democratic liberty were indissolubly linked." It was Jefferson after all who said in 1785, "Cultivators of the earth are the most valuable citizens. They are the most vigorous, the most independent, the most virtuous, and they are tied to their country and wedded to its liberty and interests by the most lasting bonds." In the same chapter, Berry points out that these bonds are "not merely those of economics and property, but those, at once more feeling and more practical, that come from investment in a place and a community of work, devotion, knowledge, memory, and association." Berry also finds in chapter 9 justification in Jefferson for the idea that "the small" in this country can survive only if "the great" are restrained: "To assume that ordinary citizens can compete successfully with people of wealth and with corporations, as our government presently tends to do," Berry writes, "is simply to abandon the ordinary citizens." Jefferson put it this way in a 1785 letter that Berry quotes:

> Another means of silently lessening the inequality of property is to exempt all from taxation below a certain point. . . . The earth is given as a common stock for man to labor and live on. . . . it is not too soon to provide by every possible means that as few as possible shall be without a little portion of land. The small landholders are the most precious part of a state.

Arguments for that sort of equality and scale run throughout Berry's writings.

RACISM

Berry is not an uncritical defender of the South. He tends to agree with Flannery O'Connor that what southerners have in common is a recogni-

tion of a virtually biblical tragedy enacted by the Civil War: "In the South we have . . . a vision of Moses' face as he pulverized our idols" ("The Regional Writer," in *Mystery and Manners,* 1969). He agrees with Robert Penn Warren that the education of American blacks is a moral necessity, but not if it assumes, as he wrote in *The Hidden Wound* (revised edition, 1989) that they "will be made better or more useful or more secure by becoming as greedy, selfish, wasteful, and thoughtless as affluent American whites." His extended discussion of racism in that book emerged from the civil rights agitations of 1968. It includes a careful scrutiny of his family's complicity in slavery before the war and in a "second-generation" racism after it. Berry's great-grandfather once sold a rebellious slave to a particularly ruthless buyer, "the agent of a horror and an outrage that [Berry's ancestors] had inherited and lived with all their lives, and had never openly faced." That is the "hidden wound," the pain and guilt implicit in family stories told and retold over the generations in unspoken hope "that we will finally tell it to someone who can forgive us."

But Berry's investigation of racism is not just personal or Southern. In *The Hidden Wound,* he finds racism in what he sees as an American willingness to exercise power aggressively, impatient for quick results: "We send a bulldozer or a bomber to do our dirty work as casually, and by the same short-order morality, as once (in the South) we would 'send a nigger,' or (in the North) an Irishman, or (in the West now), a Mexican." Ultimately, Berry locates American racism in an ecological failure, a contempt for the limits nature imposes, an arrogant presumption of white superiority. "That we failed to learn from [native Americans] how to live in this land is a stupidity—a *racial* stupidity," Berry declares. He concludes *The Hidden Wound* in 1970 with these words:

> It is not, I think, a question of when and how the white people will "free" the black and the red

people. It is a condescension to believe that we have the power to do that. Until we have recognized in them the full strength and grace of their distinctive humanity we will be able to set no one free, for we will not be free ourselves. When we realize that they possess a knowledge for the lack of which we are incomplete and in pain, then the wound in our history will be healed. Then they will simply *be* free, among us—and so will we, among ourselves for the first time, and among them.

Nothing here is strident or rhetorical; the passage demonstrates Berry's exceptional ability to transform a quiet personal meditation into the most resonant and far-reaching public utterance.

THOREAU

Berry was inescapably shaped by the values of his family, his region, and its history. He took evident pride in becoming "an agrarian traditionalist" and felt the painful wound of racism "as complex and deep in my flesh as blood and nerves." But both pride and pain were the result of fateful historical forces over which he had little control. The influence of Henry David Thoreau was an altogether different matter. Thoreau provided ideas and a model that Berry could follow selectively, critically, and deliberately. He remembers first reading *Walden* at Curran's camp when he was a teenager, and he kept reading it—and referring his own life to it—as he grew older. In "The Long-Legged House" he imagines his Uncle Curran as a Thoreauvian bachelor, rebuilding his cabin with recycled lumber, ceremonially cleansing the place—as Berry himself would do, more than once, in the years ahead: "It was in his nature to have a house in the woods," Berry speculates. "There was something deep about him, something quiet-loving and solitary and kin to the river and the woods." His uncle is the apparent alter ego here, Thoreau the real one. In fact, Thoreau represented a far more radical and renunciatory self than Berry had imagined for

himself before. Berry probably felt, as did Mahatma Gandhi and Martin Luther King Jr., the influence of Thoreau's essay "Resistance to Civil Government," as well. Of his rebelliousness at military school Berry, in "The Long-Legged House," said, "I was a conscious student of resistance, and got pretty good at it toward the end." In chapter 5 of *Standing by Words* (1983) he describes, again in transparently Thoreauvian terms, how "an individual or a whole nation may be required to go into the wilderness and in that absence from home to learn or relearn something essential." He adds,

> At other times a similar movement is made, and to the same purpose, from high culture to low culture, as when a New England Transcendentalist goes to the woods to live in the rebuilt house of a pauper. The result, either way, is a renewed or corrected understanding of the dependence of human life on its unhuman sources, of the domestic and the wild.

Berry also learned from Thoreau the usefulness of the myth of Antaeus, the giant whose strength was renewed every time his feet touched the earth. In *Walden,* Thoreau had written of growing beans, "They attached me to the earth, and so I got strength like Antaeus." Berry often uses the allusion too, either implicitly, as in poems like "Earth and Fire" (in *Farming: A Hand Book,* 1970) or explicitly, as in *The Hidden Wound,* in his analysis of a "charming" passage from *The Autobiography of Malcolm X,* which describes the young Malcolm lying down between the rows of his garden. Berry comments, "lying there as low as he could get, against the earth, his mind free—filled him with a rich sense of the possibilities of life . . . it is the myth of Antaeus, the giant of Libya, the son of Earth, who could not be conquered so long as he touched the ground."

Berry was even more deeply influenced by a passage from *Walden* (in "Spring") that has spoken eloquently to many another naturalist, environmentalist, and defender of wilderness:

We need the tonic of wildness,—to wade sometimes in marshes where the bittern and the meadow-hen lurk, and hear the booming of the snipe; to smell the whispering sedge, where only some wilder and more solitary fowl builds her nest, and the mink crawls on its belly close to the ground. At the same time that we are earnest to explore and learn all things, we require that all things be mysterious and unexplorable, that land and sea be infinitely wild, unsurveyed and unfathomed by us because unfathomable. . . . We need to witness our own limits transgressed, and some life pasturing freely where we never wander.

That conception of limits pervades most of Berry's writing, his novels no less than his essays. In *Jayber Crow* (2000), for example, the modest farming techniques of old Athey Keith succeed because of his understanding of limits, while those of his ambitious and self-indulgent son-in-law, Troy Chatham, come to ruin. Athey's "nest egg" is a small tract of woods with magnificent old trees set aside for no use whatever—except as a reminder of limits. Similarly, the long essay on "Poetry and Place" in *Standing by Words* comes back repeatedly to the idea of recognizing human limits, admitting what powers we do not and can never have. Berry argues for the decorum and propriety of knowing these limits, which after all means having no illusions about where in nature's scheme of things we really stand.

Another even more direct reference to Thoreau's argument for the "tonic of wildness" comes in Berry's *The Unforeseen Wilderness: An Essay on Kentucky's Red River Gorge* (1971), where he offers the argument that wilderness is not just uninhabited woods or remote landscapes; rather it surrounds and encloses everything:

Wilderness is the element in which we live encased in the fragile enclosure of civilization, as tenuously and precariously as a mollusk lives in his shell in the sea. It is a wilderness that is beautiful, dangerous, abundant, oblivious of us, mysterious, never to be conquered or controlled or second-guessed, or known more than a little.

The purpose of Berry's argument here is exactly like Thoreau's: if we need to preserve and protect our wilderness and its threatened species, that is not because *it* is fragile but because *we* are. Setting wilderness aside, and preserving its "pristine" and "untainted" sublimity, is above all a practical symbolic action. It reminds us to look at the earth apart from ourselves, to "witness our own limits transgressed." Berry echoes Thoreau's idea—and even his syntax—again in "Preserving Wildness," an essay reprinted in *Home Economics*: "We need wilderness of all kinds, large and small, public and private. We need to go now and again into places where our work is disallowed, where our hopes and plans have no standing. We need to come into the presence of the unqualified and mysterious formality of Creation."

Berry nevertheless differs from Thoreau in a number of significant ways. First of all, Thoreau (like most present-day environmentalists) was not a practical farmer, not an agrarian. His bean-field experiment in *Walden* was conducted in a spirit of bemused detachment, not lifelong commitment. He left his cabin at Walden Pond after two and a half years, claiming in *Walden*'s conclusion that "I had several more lives to live, and could not spare any more time for that one." Berry by contrast has lived one life, of farming and writing, grounded in the same place. Thoreau once admitted, in an epigram, that he had failed to do that: "My life has been the poem I would have writ, / But I could not both live and utter it." Berry obviously admired Thoreau's fierce individualism, and would accept his principle in "Civil Disobedience" that, when the government's machine is unjust, "Let your life be a counter-friction to stop the machine" and "any man more right than his neighbors, constitutes a majority of one." But Thoreau carried his individualism further: he asserted that "if *one* HONEST man" in Massachusetts, were to cease holding slaves and be locked up in jail for it, "it would be the abolition of slavery in

America." Berry always argues for communal action and interdependence: "One man alone does not have strength or dignity or joy, but . . . these and all else that is worthy come to him by the grace of the bonds that he has made with his fellows," he writes in *The Hidden Wound,* and in *The Unsettling of America,* "Work that is restorative, convivial, dignified and dignifying" requires "the *enactment* of connections," recognitions of kinship rather than assertions of independence.

Despite such differences, one finds in Berry's writing numerous allusions to Thoreau's ideas and echoes of his style. They both demonstrate a fondness for the lessons taught by etymologies (Thoreau: "a wild man is a willed man" or, "I chiefly fear lest my expression not be *extravagant* enough"); such usage is displayed frequently in Berry's essays, as, for example, in this statement from *The Unsettling of America*: "Ideas of tillage and worship are thus joined in *culture*. . . . To live on the earth, to care for the soil, and to worship, all are bound at the root to the idea of a cycle." Berry's essays are full of pithy generalizations based on phrases such as "the man who" or "a man is," formulations that insistently echo Thoreau's manner: "A man's way through a wilderness he is familiar with has something of the nature of art," writes Berry in *The Unforeseen Wilderness.* "How can a man be a philosopher and not maintain his vital heat by better methods than other men?" writes Thoreau. And like an echo Berry replies in *The Hidden Wound,* "the man who can keep a fire in a stove or on a hearth is not only more durable, but wiser, closer to the meaning of fire, than the man who can only work a thermostat."

LOCATING THE WILD

Unlike the majority of contemporary writers who concern themselves with ecological crises, the preservation of species and habitats, and the creation of "wilderness areas," Berry does not locate the wild in the obvious remote places—in the great deserts of the American West, for example (Mary Austin, Edward Abbey, Ann Zwinger), or in the polar extremes (Barry Lopez, John McPhee), or in the great North American mountain ranges (John Muir, David Brower). In fact, Berry is suspicious of any "nature extremist" or "nature romantic" who wants to preserve nature for purely "scenic," aesthetic, or otherwise disinterested purposes. He argues in chapter 2, "The Ecological Crisis as a Crisis of Character" in *The Unsettling of America* that a "connoisseur of the scenic" does not have any moral concern or substantial responsibility for a particular place: "If the resolve to explore, enjoy and protect does not create a moral energy that will define and enforce responsible use, then organized conservation will prove ultimately futile." Berry even criticizes the slogan of the Sierra Club ("to explore, enjoy, and protect the nation's scenic resources"). "As used here," Berry says in chapter 2, "the word ['scenic'] is a fossil" and befits only a specialized, woefully inadequate conception of what needs to be preserved. Wilderness or the wild should never be confused with mere scenery—however splendid or awe-inspiring it may seem.

For Berry, the actual wilderness is not remote but all around us, residing in natural forces, intertwined with the domestic, thriving at the margins of tilled fields, inherent in our sexuality and in all cycles of growth and decay. In "Preserving Wildness" (in *Home Economics*), Berry reasons that "a forest or a crop, no matter how intentionally husbanded by human foresters or farmers, will be found to be healthy precisely to the extent that it is wild—able to collaborate with earth, air, light, and water in the way common to plants before humans walked the earth." In *The Unsettling of America,* Berry argues for the preservation of margins between fields where a rich diversity of species may thrive. Not only do such margins preserve biodiversity, as he observes in Amish farms in

America as well as in the "primitive" mountain farms in the Peruvian Andes; such margins also—and perhaps even more importantly—become "sacred groves," places "where the Creation is let alone, to serve as instruction, example, refuge; a place for people to go, free of work and presumption, to let themselves alone" (chapter 7, "The Body and the Earth"). It is important to Berry that such places not be physically remote. In a truly sustaining agriculture, Berry sees a "network of wilderness threading through the fields" (chapter 9, "Margins").

In "The Wild" from his first poetry collection, *The Broken Ground* (1964), Berry deromanticizes the idea of wilderness by celebrating its presence in a dreary urban waste:

> In the empty lot—a place
> not natural, but wild—among
> the trash of human absence,
>
> the slough and shamble
> of the city's seasons, a few
> old locusts bloom.

The point here is essentially the same: the view isn't scenic, but its wildness—its sheer irreversible will to exist, utterly apart from us—deserves our recognition and respect. Berry's only work that seems to offer a more conventional view of wilderness is *The Unforeseen Wilderness,* a series of narrative sketches about Kentucky's Red River Gorge, written in 1971 when there was some fear that the area would be dammed and flooded by the Army Corps of Engineers. Berry's text accompanies forty-eight photographs by Gene Meatyard, all somewhat gloomy images in black and white, devoid of human presence. In genre, at least, Berry's narrative of walking and canoeing in a threatened wilderness bears comparison with James Dickey's story in *Deliverance,* with Edward Abbey's chapter in *Desert Solitaire* on canoeing the Colorado River in Glen Canyon, Utah, and

with John McPhee's account of exploring the same now-inundated gorge in *Encounters with the Arch-Druid.* In chapter 5, "The Journey's End," Berry even sounds a bit like Abbey in his criticism of tourists who will use the lake, created by flooding the gorge, for "recreation":

> Relief from the suburbs of brick and bedford stone is to be found in suburbs of canvas and aluminum. Relief from traffic in the streets is to be sought amid traffic on a lake. The harried city dweller, who has for fifty weeks coveted his neighbor's house and his neighbor's wife, may now soothe his nerves for two weeks in coveting his neighbor's trailer and his neighbor's boat—also putting up with his neighbor's children, listening to his neighbor's radio, breathing his neighbor's smoke, walking on his neighbor's broken bottles.

But Berry is not wholly at ease in this sardonic mode. And his low-keyed narrative of a life-threatening experience on the river does not resonate with significance. He concludes with an account of losing his map that smacks too much of Ike McCaslin's experience (relinquishing gun, compass, and watch) in Faulkner's "The Bear": losing the map, writes Berry, "is the symbol of what I have learned here, and of the process: the gradual relinquishment of maps, the yielding of knowledge before the new facts and the mysteries of growth and renewal and change." If this were Berry's only account of a wilderness experience, he would probably not be classed as a great nature writer.

Berry's gift is to be able to find awe and grandeur, mystery and unruly wildness, in immediate and common things—things we may too easily dismiss as ordinary. Perhaps his best statement about the wild emerged in "Christianity and the Survival of Creation," a lecture delivered at the Southern Baptist Theological Seminary in Louisville, Kentucky, in 1992, and included in the collection *Sex, Economy, Freedom and Community* (1993). He spoke about how God should be set apart "from *ideas* about Him":

He is not to be fenced in, under human control, like some domestic creature; He is the wildest being in existence. The presence of His spirit in us is our wildness, our oneness with the wilderness of Creation. That is why subduing the things of nature to human purposes is so dangerous and why it so often results in evil, in separation and desecration.

Nowhere does Berry's fundamental belief ring truer, or with more conviction, than here.

ANIMALS

Another way in which Berry differs interestingly from more typical nature writers is in the way he writes about animals. He seems to have far less curiosity about them than, say, Annie Dillard, Barry Lopez, or Mary Oliver. Even Edward Abbey exhibits more Thoreauvian zeal in naming and studying species than Berry does. Many birds are mentioned in his long autobiographical essay, "The Long-Legged House," but few of them are shown in detail. His eye lingers on two pairs of blue-winged teal, pleasingly at home on the river; a pair of phoebes comes back to nest at the camp, reassuringly; the seven-note song of the sycamore warbler is heard; nineteen coots are counted. If Berry is exuberant at these sightings, or eager to learn more, or concerned about their survival, he does not show it. He mentions, in "Poetry and Place" in *Standing by Words,* the mistaken idea "that animals are always happy, not feelingly involved in chance, suffering, and mortality." But that Jane Goodall–like perception does not lead to much compassionate attention, in his poems and essays, toward animals. His early poem "Sparrow" (in *The Broken Ground)* focuses dispassionately on the thoughtless reflex mechanisms of the bird:

A sparrow is
his hunger organized.
Filled, he flies
before he knows he's going to.

And there is a similar, rather cool detachment in Berry's "The Snake" (in *Openings,* 1968) another short poem of the 1960s.

Berry clearly cares that animals be seen justly, not as symbols or abstractions. In another passage from the same chapter of *Standing by Words* he criticizes Shelley's "To a Sky-Lark" for its failure to represent an actual bird: "Hail to thee, blithe Spirit! / Bird thou never wert." Berry remarks, "to see it *only* as a spirit is to fail to see it as a bird. It is hard not to feel that nature would be safer with Pope, who felt and cared for its materiality, than with so compulsive a spiritualizer as Shelley." Again, Berry seems a little firmer in theory than in practice. In the collection *Farming: A Hand Book,* he included a delightful poem, "To the Unseeable Animal," about a creature just as invisible as Shelley's— yet its materiality is hinted at:

you are always here,
dwelling in the oldest sycamores,
visiting the faithful springs
when they are dark. . . .

Careful reading of the whole poem allows us to realize the existence of what we cannot see, the elusive sycamore warbler. More animals begin to materialize in Berry's later essays and poems. One of the best poems in the *Sabbaths* sequence, (1987, VII) focuses on the winter wren. It concludes,

He makes a gnarled
Root graceful with his airy weight,

Breathes in the great informing breath,
Made little in his wing and eye,
And breathes it out again in deft
Bright links of song, his clarity.

And in a 1982 essay, "Getting Along with Nature," reprinted in *Home Economics,* Berry offers a detailed description of encountering a young red-tailed hawk only twenty feet away from where he was mowing. Here too is close observation in a style that Audubon or Thoreau would have admired. Berry offers some lengthy discussion of the hawk's seeming to mimic or mirror his own curiosity. He concludes that he and his team of horses "furnish hunting ground to the hawk; the hawk serves us by controlling the field-mouse population." Spoken like a practical farmer. Perhaps one reason that Berry rarely lavishes attention on individual species is that he is wary of sentimentality.

In fact he does focus intently on the *relation* between animals and human beings. He argues in "Preserving Wildness," another essay in *Home Economics,* against the popular notion that "the biosphere is an egalitarian system, in which all creatures, including humans, are equal in value and have an equal right to live and flourish." The reality is much more problematic. As Berry puts it, "Humans differ from earthworms, thrushes, and hawks in their capacity to do more—in modern times, a great deal more—in their own behalf than is necessary." In short, animals know their limits and we do not, or at least we have trouble accepting them or understanding them rightly. In Berry's words,

> How much must humans do in their own behalf in order to be fully human? . . . We have no way to work at this question, it seems to me, except by perceiving that, in order to have the world, we must share it, both with each other and with other creatures, . . . [and] in order to live in the world, we must use it somewhat at the expense of other creatures. We must acknowledge both the centrality and the limits of our self-interest.

These are hard things to face squarely. But it is clear that, for Berry, the problem comes back to ourselves, to our desire for more than we need, to our ignorance of what really sustains us. Mere reverence for all other creatures solves nothing.

In "Poetry and Place" in *Standing by Words* Berry suggests that perhaps the old idea of the Great Chain of Being as Alexander Pope understood it would be better than the "egalitarian system" used by some ecologists today. The Great Chain principle, as Berry understands it, protects creatures by emphasizing difference, not equality:

> If humans are responsibly observant of the differences between themselves and the angels above them and the animals below, they will act with respect, restraint, and benevolence toward the subordinate creatures; this is their duty toward the subordinate creatures, and it is part of, inseparable from, their duty to the higher creatures and to God. . . . When humans keep their proper place in the Chain, the connections are unbroken from the microorganisms to God.

Something of this principle emerges in Berry's interesting discussion of the value of draft horses and oxen in *The Unsettling of America.* Nowhere is Berry's compassionate understanding of animals better demonstrated than here, where men and animals work together in harmony with the earth, each dependent on the other. He is of course speaking from long experience in caring for and working with draft horses, having given up using tractors early in his farming life. Rather than congratulate himself for his own enlightened stance, however, Berry ends by describing a farmer in Wales who walked backward before his team of oxen, singing to them as they worked. Thrilled and a bit awestricken by this example Berry concludes, "That seems to me to differ radically from our present customary use of any living thing. The oxen were not used as beasts or machines, but as fellow creatures" (chapter 7, "The Body and the Earth").

LOVE AND MARRIAGE

Berry sees the capacity to care about animals as inseparable from human love, the capacity to care about one another. He believes this not because he's a Christian, but because he sees it as fundamental to survival—a natural law as much as a moral one. In *Standing by Words* he writes that, although it was once "possible to think of 'love one another' as a rule contingent upon faith," that is no longer the case. Now "it may be an absolute law: Love one another or die, individually and as a species" (chapter 5, "Poetry and Place"). Berry himself seems to have been serenely capable of following that dictum. His autobiographical essays show that his love for his wife, Tanya, has been overwhelmingly happy, and the fact of their enduring marriage has been a constant blessing to him. The title poem from his 1973 collection, *The Country of Marriage,* attests to that joy, comparing love to the waters of a deep stream:

> In its abundance it survives our thirst.
> In the evening we come down to the shore
> to drink our fill, and sleep, while it
> flows through the regions of the dark.
> It does not hold us, except we keep returning
> to its rich waters thirsty. We enter,
> willing to die, into the commonwealth of its joy.

Marriage, however, provides a sterner test, and Berry writes much more frequently about it. He clearly felt that his own marriage in 1957 succeeded because it was meaningfully connected with a place, with historical and communal responsibilities, as well as with his work—to write about and care for the land. His extended discussion of Odysseus's return to Penelope in *The Unsettling of America* constitutes perhaps Berry's most searching discussion of marriage. Above all it is the principle of fidelity— Odysseus's consummate action of taking responsibility, not merely asserting authority—that Berry finds compelling: "Fidelity to human order . . . implies fidelity also to natural order. Fidelity to human order makes devotion possible. Fidelity to natural order preserves the possibility of choice, the possibility of the renewal of devotion." Similarly, in *Standing by Words*

Berry finds analogies between poetry and marriage—the speaking of vows, the choosing of forms, and abiding by those choices. Free verse is like courtship; formal verse is like marriage. He concludes:

> Forms join the diverse things that they contain; they join their contents to their context; they join us to themselves; they join us to each other; they join writers and readers; they join the generations together, the young and the old, the living and the dead. Thus, for a couple, marriage is an entrance into a timeless community. So, for a poet (or a reader), is the mastery of poetic form.

Berry clearly believes that one of the causes of failed marriages, unfulfilled relationships, and divorce in the modern world is our assumption that marriage does not require a place, that it can be transported anywhere. As he writes in *A Continuous Harmony: Essays Cultural and Agricultural* (1972), "Modern urban nomads are always moving away from particulars by which they know themselves, and moving into abstraction (*a* house, *a* neighborhood, *a* job)." For Berry, then, love and marriage can only thrive in a particular place.

It is curious to see that this does *not* happen in Berry's fiction, despite the fact that his characters are always grounded in a particular place—Port William, Kentucky, the fictive version of Berry's Port Royal, back in the 1940s and 1950s. From *Nathan Coulter* (1960) onward, marriages and other love relationships in the novels tend to be conflicted, embittered, frustrated, despairing, tragic, or nonexistent. In *A Place on Earth* (1967, revised 1983), for example, the central character, Mat Feltner, grieves so over the death of his son in World War II that he becomes depressed, distant even from his wife, even at times cruel: "She is angry, and hurt, near to crying. Mat sees it, and is sorry but still he exults, as if he would ride his loneliness over her very body." The novel is full of shocking, utterly persuasive moments of pain like this one. Mat and his wife are reconciled at the end, but only because she makes a reconcilation possible. Mat's brother-in-law, Ernest Finley, comes home from the war crippled, fit only (he thinks) for a pitiable marginal existence. When a woman's husband disappears after their child is drowned, Ernest is drawn to her, works at her farm, and cautiously begins to think that love might be possible. Then after many months of hope, the husband returns—and Ernest commits suicide. Berry's delicacy and poignancy here are unforgettable. In *The Memory of Old Jack* (1974) the central frustration of Jack Beecham's life is the abyss between himself and his wife. His climactic realization is of "the great disaster of both their lives":

> She was bound to him by a vision of him that she held above him—that he, in fact, neither understood nor aspired to; and he was bound to her by a vision of her that she would discover, by her own lights, to be beneath her. He bound her to him by disavowing the very energy that bound him to her.

Jack finds some consolation (and further painful conflicts) in a prolonged affair with another woman, and after her death in a fire Jack's only solace comes in his devotion to the land. In *Jayber Crow,* Berry's bachelor protagonist is the town barber, an orphan who returns to Port William where he was born and falls fatefully in love with a high school girl, Mattie Keith. Jayber looks on helplessly as Mattie marries the wrong person, endures his selfishness, supports his wasteful and reckless ambitions, bears his children, and suffers his infidelities. Gradually it dawns on Mattie that Jayber is devoted to her, but neither speaks of their deep and mutual understanding. The novel is crowded with incident, much of it exuberant and celebratory, but its vision of love is anguished. Jayber Crow—like Mat Feltner and Jack Beecham before him—ends up like Thoreau, a bachelor whose only faithful companion is the land itself. In these novels Berry refuses to simplify

the difficulties of love and marriage. They are fragile enterprises, risky, frustrating, imperfect, even dangerous, and they fail more often than not.

Further complicating Berry's conception of marital love is a strong undercurrent of patriarchal traditionalism. He clearly saw in his own father a paragon of virtue that transcended any questions of complicity in the darker aspects of Southern tradition—racism, for example, or the selling of cancer-causing tobacco. In *The Hidden Wound* Berry celebrates his father as a lawyer who "*remained* a farmer," "kept the farmer's passion," and passed those values on "with remarkable insight and foresight" to his sons: "he insisted that I learn to do the hand labor that the land required." This seems all well and good until it appears, uncritically endorsed, in novels like *The Memory of Old Jack* and *A Place on Earth.* Old Jack is remembered not for the domestic tragedy of his life, and not for the contempt with which he treats the women who care for him in later life, but rather for his embodiment of the old agrarian virtues. At Jack's death Mat Feltner "rests his hand briefly on the dead man's shoulder," a touch that connects them with their fathers and grandfathers, sons and grandsons, in what Berry calls a "forever binding salute." Similarly, at the conclusion of *A Place on Earth,* Mat finds peace at last, after a year of suffering, alone "in the great restfulness of that place . . . where death can only give into life." But he has no thought for his wife or his dead son's wife, only that his own sadness has lifted. One critic calls Mat Feltner "the ideal husband to the world," but it is hard to agree with that view without accepting Berry's old-fashioned patriarchal values uncritically.

A LOCAL ECCENTRIC

Berry would probably not agree with the writer in *Contemporary Literary Criticism* who praised his "even-tempered approach to environmental and ecological issues." True, there is considerable detachment in his prose, and a scrupulous effort to be reasonable and just. But he has the mind of a lawyer, as more than one critic has said, and sometimes even the manner of a prosecuting attorney. Being even-tempered plays no part in it. When the cause is important, he is always ready to argue aggressively, thoroughly, and at length. *The Hidden Wound, The Unsettling of America, Standing by Words,* and *Life Is a Miracle: An Essay Against Modern Superstition* (2000) are all book-long arguments. At times in these works his relentless attacks on particular individuals are energized by what can only be called a moral fury. Earl Butz, the U.S. secretary of agriculture when *The Unsettling of America* was written, was the focus of withering criticism; so was W. H. Auden in *Standing by Words* when Berry saw his Yeats elegy as defective; and so too was the biologist E. O. Wilson in Berry's diatribe *Life Is a Miracle,* even though critics have shown that the two fundamentally agree on many ecological issues. To his credit Berry seems well aware of this tendency. He chose to title a 1995 collection of essays *Another Turn of the Crank,* as if willing to admit that he may sound like one. And as an epigraph to this book Berry quotes the biblical prophet Jeremiah, identifying his own melancholy complaints with those ancient lamentations: "For we are left but a few of many" (Jeremiah 42:2). In fact, Berry seems to prefer the role of isolation, resisting and defying the main stream of modern culture, technology, and economics. In *The Hidden Wound* he argues that the best American writing "has been produced by exiles or renegades such as T. S. Eliot and Ezra Pound, or local eccentrics like Henry David Thoreau, Walt Whitman, William Faulkner, and William Carlos Williams." Berry sees himself, evidently, as exiled from the majority, and like Thoreau "a majority of one." And if he cannot claim to be a renegade exact-

ly, he would still proudly be seen as a local eccentric.

In his poetry of the later 1960s Berry invented a persona called the Mad Farmer, a figure that bears some affinity to Yeats's Crazy Jane or the speaker of "Why Should Not Old Men Be Mad?" Berry's logic is that madness, whether it be anger or seeming insanity, is called for by contemporary society. As he puts it in "The Mad Farmer Manifesto: The First Amendment" (in *The Country of Marriage*),

> To be sane in a mad time
> is bad for the brain, worse
> for the heart. . . .

In a poem from *Farming: A Hand Book,* "The Contrariness of the Mad Farmer," he argues for disagreement as one of the better paths to truth: "Going against men, I have heard at times a deep harmony." Some of the Mad Farmer poems are tirades against the status quo, like "The Mad Farmer, Flying the Flag of Rough Branch, Secedes from the Union" (in *Entries*), but others are quieter and more moving. "The Mad Farmer's Love Song" (in *The Country of Marriage*) begins,

> O when the world's at peace
> and every man is free
> then will I go down unto my love.

Then, unwilling to wait that long, the speaker admits that he might see his beloved "several times before that." Behind this persona lies a social critic who is driven sometimes to rage, often toward elegy and lament, frequently to scorn and derision. Nothing could be more characteristic of Berry than the sudden Swiftian anger that erupts in such passages as this, from *Home Economics*: "For our history reveals that . . . humans are not 'natural,' not 'thinking animals' or 'naked apes,' but monsters—indiscriminate and insatiable killers and destroyers." Characteristic too are moments of a quieter, even more scorching contempt, such as the following from *The Unforeseen Wilderness*:

> When I think of the near-perfection of industrial and recreational pollution, or the near-universality of armed hatred and prejudice, of our scientists' ecstatic dance in the light of the first atomic explosion, of the utter destruction of land for its timber or coal—then I feel such a heavy disgust that I look at the so-called lower animals with envy. . . . When I consider that . . . not one of them ever destroyed its own habitat, or poisoned its own food and water, I am astonished at the claims we make for the "higher" human intelligence.

A moralist of Berry's stamp would never be content to sound blandly "even-tempered."

Yet there is much humor in Berry's writing—more than his admirers have usually noticed. Some of it arises simply out of a low-keyed irony. He will mention, unobtrusively, "the infinite human capacity to be wrong," for example, or the fond notion that "people in love are, or ought to be, young—even though love is said to last 'forever.'" Or he will remark, "We are obviously subject to something we do not understand—why else would we be making so many mistakes?" The funniest moments in the novels have a similar rueful subtlety. A character in *A Place on Earth* says that he "never works by the clock, he always rests by it—because . . . it is harder to stop resting than to stop working." Later in that novel it is Old Jack who ruminates, "It is just the truth. And a man who is depending on the truth to console him is sometimes in a hell of a fix." The poems too can be quietly funny. One of the best of these is "Testament," where Berry gives pseudo-solemn instructions for his funeral. Do not call it death when his body is put in the ground, he asks: "Say that my body cannot now / Be improved upon." Or,

> Say that I have found
> A good solution, and am on my way
> To the roots.

Anyone who doubts that Berry can be an exuberantly funny writer—even while he is deadly serious—should turn to "The Joy of Sales Resistance," the essay that prefaces *Sex, Economy, Freedom and Community*.

"THINGS CONNECT"

Berry's achievement is to have become an original writer by going back to his origins and becoming a radical—one who, like Thoreau, goes to the roots to find what is valuable, necessary, spiritually and biologically nourishing. And he has been bold enough to say flatly what is not. That Berry maintained his contrarian independence even while tracing those roots—familial, regional, Southern, agrarian—is a remarkable feat. He has managed to be both a traditional conservative and a scourge to conservatives, a loyal defender of local communities yet a Mad Farmer and local eccentric. He has traced his intellectual roots to writers as diverse as Ezra Pound and John Milton, Walt Whitman and Homer, Edward Abbey and Alexander Pope. He has published his poetry and essays in journals ranging from *The Atlantic Monthly* and *The Hudson Review* to *Organic Gardening, Whole Earth Catalogue,* and *Draft Horse Journal.* He has positioned himself as a major force in the discussion of ecological and environmental issues, partly by being a relentless critic of that movement. In his preface to *Home Economics* Berry explains his enterprise as an attempt begun twenty years earlier to construct an argument: "The subject of the argument is the fact, and ultimately the faith, that things connect—that we are wholly dependent on a pattern, an all-inclusive form, that we partly understand. The argument, therefore, is an effort to describe responsibility."

All of his works, not just his essays, spring from this impulse to understand how "things connect"—not just how death and life, decay and germination, wilderness and domesticity, farming and writing interweave, but also how nothing survives in isolation or separation, how everything interdepends. So there can be no escape from responsibility: what we do to the land, to ourselves, and to others is always connected. Every freedom has its cost, every power its limits, every independent act its web of communal reverberations. Berry's ability to see such connections, and to insist that others see them as well, may be the essence of his extraordinary achievement. His *Home Economics* preface goes on to say, "I keep returning to it, I think, because the study of connections is an endless fascination, and because the understanding of connections seems to me an indispensable part of humanity's self-defense."

Selected Bibliography

WORKS OF WENDELL BERRY

FICTION

Nathan Coulter. Boston: Houghton Mifflin, 1960. Revised edition, San Francisco: North Point, 1985.

A Place on Earth. New York: Harcourt Brace and World, 1967. Revised edition, San Francisco: North Point, 1983.

The Memory of Old Jack. New York: Harcourt Brace Jovanovich, 1974.

The Wild Birds: Six Stories of the Port William Membership. San Francisco: North Point, 1986.

Remembering. San Francisco: North Point, 1988.

Fidelity: Five Stories. New York: Pantheon, 1992.

Watch with Me, and Six Other Stories of the Yet-Remembered Ptolemy Proudfoot and His Wife, Miss Minnie, Née Quinch. New York: Pantheon, 1994.

A World Lost. Washington, D.C.: Counterpoint, 1996.

Two More Stories of the Port William Membership. Frankfort, Ky.: Gnomon, 1997.

Jayber Crow: The Life Story of Jayber Crow, Barber, of the Port William Membership, as Written by Himself. Washington, D.C.: Counterpoint, 2000.

POETRY

The Broken Ground. New York: Harcourt, Brace and World, 1964.

Openings. New York: Harcourt, Brace and World, 1968.

Farming: A Hand Book. New York: Harcourt Brace Jovanovich, 1970.

The Country of Marriage. New York: Harcourt Brace Jovanovich, 1973.

Clearing. New York: Harcourt Brace Jovanovich, 1977.

A Part. San Francisco: North Point, 1980.

The Wheel. San Francisco: North Point, 1982.

Collected Poems 1957–1982. San Francisco: North Point, 1985.

Sabbaths. San Francisco: North Point, 1987.

Traveling At Home. San Francisco: North Point, 1989. (Reprints selected poems from *Collected Poems* and *Sabbaths.*)

Sayings and Doings; and, An Eastward Look. Frankfort, Ky.: Gnomon, 1990.

Entries. New York: Pantheon, 1994.

A Timbered Choir: The Sabbath Poems, 1977–1997. Washington, D.C.: Counterpoint, 1998.

The Selected Poems of Wendell Berry. Washington, D.C.: Counterpoint, 1998.

ESSAYS AND OTHER PROSE

The Long-Legged House. New York: Harcourt, Brace and World, 1969.

The Hidden Wound. Boston: Houghton Mifflin, 1970. Revised edition, San Francisco: North Point, 1989.

The Unforeseen Wilderness: An Essay on Kentucky's Red River Gorge. Photographs by Gene Meatyard. Lexington: University Press of Kentucky, 1971. Revised edition, San Francisco: North Point, 1991.

A Continuous Harmony: Essays Cultural and Agricultural. New York: Harcourt Brace Jovanovich, 1972.

The Unsettling of America: Culture and Agriculture. San Francisco: Sierra Club, 1977.

The Gift of Good Land: Further Essays, Cultural and Agricultural. San Francisco: North Point, 1981.

Recollected Essays, 1965–1980. San Francisco: North Point, 1981.

Standing by Words: Essays. San Francisco: North Point, 1983.

Home Economics: Fourteen Essays. San Francisco: North Point, 1987.

What Are People For? San Francisco: North Point, 1990.

Harlan Hubbard: Life and Work. Lexington: University Press of Kentucky, 1990. New York: Pantheon, 1992.

Sex, Economy, Freedom and Community: Eight Essays. New York: Pantheon, 1993.

Another Turn of the Crank. Washington, D.C.: Counterpoint, 1995.

Life Is a Miracle: An Essay Against Modern Superstition. Washington, D.C.: Counterpoint, 2000.

BIBLIOGRAPHY

Freedman, Russell. *Wendell Berry: A Bibliography.* Lexington: University of Kentucky Libraries, 1998. (Lists all of Berry's publications from 1953 through 1996.)

CRITICAL AND BIOGRAPHICAL STUDIES

Altherr, Thomas L. "'The Country We Have Married': Wendell Berry and the Georgic Tradition of Agriculture." *Southern Studies: An Interdisciplinary Journal of the South* 1:105–115 (summer 1990).

Angyal, Andrew J. *Wendell Berry.* New York: Twayne, 1995.

Askins, Justin. "A Necessary Darkness." *Parnassus* 15:317–330 (1989).

Basney, Lionel. "Wendell Berry: The Grace That Keeps the World." *Other Side* 23:46–48 (January&nash;February 1987).

———. "Having Your Meaning at Hand: Work in Snyder and Berry." In *World, Self, Poem: Essays on Contemporary Poetry from the "Jubilation of Poets."* Edited by Leonard M. Trawick. Kent, Ohio: Kent State University, 1990. Pp. 130–143.

Carruth, Hayden. "Human Authenticity in the Face of Massive Multiplying Error." *Parnassus,* spring/summer 1986, pp. 140–143.

Collins, Robert. "A More Mingled Music: Wendell Berry's Ambivalent View of Language." *Modern Poetry Studies* 11:35–56 (1982).

Cook, Rufus. "Poetry and Place: Wendell Berry's Ecology of Literature." *Centennial Review* 40:503–516 (1996).

Cooley, John, ed. *Earthly Words: Essays on Contemporary American Nature and Environmental Writers.* Ann Arbor: University of Michigan, 1994. (Includes essays on Berry by Wieland, Hicks, and Murphy.)

Cornell, Daniel. "The Country of Marriage: Wendell Berry's Personal Political Vision." *Southern Literary Journal* 15:59–70 (1983).

———. "A Vision of Stewardship: Wendell Berry's Ecological Ethic." *Literature and Belief* 12:13–25 (1992).

Decker, William. "'Practice Resurrection': The Poesis of Wendell Berry." *North Dakota Quarterly* 55:170–184 (fall 1987).

———. "The Wild, the Divine, and the Human World: Rereading Wendell Berry." *North Dakota Quarterly* 59:242–258 (1991).

Ditsky, John. "Wendell Berry's Homage to the Apple Tree." *Modern Poetry Studies* 2:7–15 (1971).

———. "Farming Kentucky: The Fiction of Wendell Berry." *Hollins Critic* 31:1–11 (February 1994).

Fields, Kenneth. "The Hunter's Trail: Poems by Wendell Berry." *Iowa Review* 1:90–99 (1970).

Gamble, David E. "Wendell Berry: The Mad Farmer and Wilderness." *Kentucky Review* 8:40–52 (summer 1988).

Grubbs, Morris, and David Abner. "Helping Us to See: Wendell Berry and the Community of Creation." *Kentucky English Bulletin* 45:43–59 (fall 1995).

Hass, Robert. "Wendell Berry: Finding the Land." *Modern Poetry Studies* 2:16–38 (1971).

Hicks, Jack. "Wendell Berry's Husband to the World: A Place on Earth." *American Literature* 51:238–254 (May 1979).

Hiers, John T. "Wendell Berry: Love Poet." *University of Mississippi Studies in English* 5:100–109 (1984–1987).

Honnighausen, Lothar. "'By Division, Out of Wonder': Gary Snyder, Wendell Berry, and Ecopoetics." *Soundings* 78:279–291 (summer 1995).

———. "Ecopoetical Poetry: The Example of Gary Snyder and Wendell Berry." In *Poetics in the Poem: Critical Essays on American Self-Reflexive Poetry.* Edited by Dorothy Z. Baker. New York: Peter Lang, 1997. Pp. 244–256.

Knott, John R. "Into the Woods with Wendell Berry." *Essays in Literature* 23:124–140 (spring 1996).

Lang, John. "'Close Mystery': Wendell Berry's Poetry of Incarnation." *Renascence* 35:258–268 (1983).

Merchant, Paul, ed. *Wendell Berry.* Lewiston, Id.: Confluence, 1991. (A collection of personal tributes, poems, reminiscences, and interpretive essays by such figures as Wallace Stegner, Hayden Carruth, Terry Tempest Williams, Wes Jackson, and Donald Hall.)

Morgan, Speer. "Wendell Berry: A Fatal Singing." *Southern Review* 10:865–877 (1974).

Murphy, Patrick D. "Penance or Perception: Spirituality and Land in the Poetry of Gary Snyder and Wendell Berry." In *Earthly Words: Essays on Contemporary American Nature and Environmental Writers.* Edited by John Cooley. Ann Arbor: University of Michigan Press, 1994. Pp. 237–249.

Nibbelink, Herman. "Wendell Berry." In *American Nature Writers,* vol. I. Edited by John Elder. New York: Scribners, 1996. Pp. 89–105.

———. "Thoreau and Wendell Berry: Bachelor and Husband of Nature." *Southern Literary Journal* 15:59–70 (1983).

Payne, Warren E. "Wendell Berry and the Natural." *Resonance* 1:5–16 (1969).

Quetchenbach, Bernard. "The Search for Community in the Work of Wendell Berry and Gary Snyder." *Essays in Arts and Sciences* 26:27–40 (October 1997).

Robinson, David M. "Wilderness and the Agrarian Principle: Gary Snyder, Wendell Berry, and the Ethical Definition of the 'Wild.'" *ISLE (Interdisciplinary Studies in Literature and the Environment)* 6:15–27 (winter 1999).

Roorda, Randall. *Dramas of Solitude: Narratives of Retreat in American Nature Writing.* Albany: State University of New York Press, 1998.

Scigaj, Leonard M. "The Long Hunter's Vision: Wendell Berry." In his *Sustainable Poetry: Four American Ecopoets.* Lexington: University Press of Kentucky, 1999.

Slovic, Scott. *Seeking Awareness in American Nature Writing: Henry Thoreau, Annie Dillard, Edward Abbey, Wendell Berry, Barry Lopez.* Salt Lake City: University of Utah Press, 1992.

Triggs, Jeffery Alan. "Moving the Dark to Wholeness: The Elegies of Wendell Berry." *Literary Review: An International Journal of Contemporary Writing* 31:279–292 (spring 1988).

———. "A Kinship of the Fields: Farming in the Poetry of R. S. Thomas and Wendell Berry." *North Dakota Quarterly* 57:92–102 (spring 1989).

Waage, Frederick O. "Wendell Berry's History." *Contemporary Poetry* 3:21–46 (1978).

Whited, Stephen. "On Devotion to the 'Communal Order': Wendell Berry's Record of Fidelity, Interdependence, and Love." *Studies in the Literary Imagination* 27:9–28 (1994).

Wieland, Steven. "Wendell Berry: Culture and Fidelity." *Iowa Review* 10:99–104 (1979).

———. "Wendell Berry Resettles America: Fidelity, Education, and Culture." In *Earthly Words: Essays on Contemporary American Nature and Environmental Writers.* Edited by John Cooley. Ann Arbor: University of Michigan Press, 1994. Pp. 37–49.

INTERVIEWS

Basney, Lionel. "A Conversation with Wendell Berry." *Image: A Journal of the Arts & Religion* 26:45–56 (spring 2000).

Ehrlich, A. W. "Publishers Weekly Interviews Wendell Berry." *Publishers Weekly* 212:10–11 (September 5, 1977).

Pennington, Vince. "Interview with Wendell Berry." *Kentucky Review* 13:57–70 (spring 1996).

Polsgrove, Carol, and Scott Sanders. "Wendell Berry." *Progressive* 54:36 (May 1990).

Weinreb, Mindy. "A Question a Day: A Written Conversation with Wendell Berry." In *Wendell Berry.* Edited by Paul Merchant. Lewiston, Idaho: Confluence, 1991. Pp. 27–43.

—DEAN FLOWER

Kaye Gibbons

1960–

"WHEN I WAS little I would think of ways to kill my daddy." This first line of Kaye Gibbons's first novel, *Ellen Foster: A Novel* (1987), introduces the major themes and techniques that govern her six novels. The opening is characteristically startling and arresting. The reader expects "when I was little" to be followed by a nostalgic, charming childhood memory. For many of Gibbons's narrators, however, childhood is a time of adversity that at once damages and strengthens their characters. They are forced to actions and knowledge well beyond their years. Some face the opposite problem. They are so influenced by strong, sheltering maternal figures that they are slow to mature, separate, and start their own lives. They also "think" or use their reason and imagination in attempts to order and cope with the chaotic world that their dysfunctional families typify. "Ways" of coping do not fortuitously present themselves; Gibbons's protagonists must actively seek them. While not all of Gibbons's narrators plot patricide, these women must find ways to overcome a patriarchal world designed to thwart growth and development through constrictions of class and race as well as gender.

Gibbons's childhood is the source of her heroines' fundamental strength and grace tempered by heartrending tragedy. Gibbons's mother, Alice Batts, was known as "Shine," indicating the qualities of light, love, and direction that governed her daughter's early years. Gibbons remembers the pride and devotion with which her mother dressed her for her first day of school and introduced her to her teacher. This happiness, however, was vulnerable and short-lived. Gibbons's parents were poor tobacco farmers in Nash County in eastern North Carolina. Even as a small child Gibbons was acutely aware of class and monetary rankings. In her story "The First Day of School," she writes: "Undershirts were worn by all decent Southern children from October to April. Common children who lived in the trailer park . . . were not held to this rule." Although her mother's care may have kept her in undershirts and above the "common," Gibbons realized she was not among the local elite, such as the store owner's family in "The First Day of School" who "seemed to have a lot of the best of everything, and I wanted some of it," including a "shingled" roof, not a tin roof, "real grass" in the yard, furniture that "was not solely utilitarian," and "a house that did not smell perpetually of boiled cabbage." Still she recalls in that story, "Before my family life blew apart and nice children couldn't come play with me anymore, I had plenty of friends."

The event that exploded her world at the age of ten was her mother's suicide in 1970 from an overdose of pills. The previous three years, Gibbons remembers in "The First Day of School":

> I would get off the school bus and see one of my aunts' cars in the yard and know that my mother had been taken to the hospital again. She would come home in a few days or weeks, looking older and older. . . . The vision of my mother holding my hand on the school walkway, introducing me to my teacher, is the last one I have of the two of us together that is whole and round and complete.

In contrast, she comments, "The years between ten and thirteen were pretty hard." Two years after her mother's death, Gibbons's father,

Charles Batts, died of alcoholism, and Gibbons lived with a series of relatives and in a foster home until her older, married brother offered her a home in 1973, when she was thirteen.

Like many of her heroines, Gibbons found refuge in education, reading, and writing. School was an island of calm and purpose, as she records in "The First Day of School": "I was in love with the rigid order in which all paints and books and learning toys were kept." One children's story, *The Hollyberrys at the Shore,* remains important to her, she asserts, because it "taught me an early literary lesson about the value of a little surprise in fiction."

> The Hollyberry's dog, named Puppy, barks at the water, and helps Jerry and Jean dig for treasure, which turns out to be a box lunch packed by their clever and attentive parents who, for some reason, are dressed in long-sleeve shirts and slacks. . . . I had started at this stage in my life of reading, to ask questions about stories. Why, for instance, didn't the parents wear bathing suits? Didn't the food get grit in it, buried as it was in the sand? Did they have mustard and mayonnaise? What did they drink: There wasn't a thermos bottle pictured on the green picnic blanket? The father is shown wearing brown pants and loafers and sky-blue socks. Why couldn't he match his socks?

Gibbons's questions demonstrate the relentless realism with which she probes beneath her characters' surfaces and her own meticulous use of compelling and resonant details. In the light of these questions, it is also hardly surprising that the young Gibbons soon eschewed children's books in favor of Poe, Shakespeare, and writing her own poems and stories.

Gibbons's college years set the pattern for the rest of her life, including struggles with mental illness countered by her devotion to her children and her writing. She started college with a scholarship at North Carolina State University and later transferred to the University of North Carolina at Chapel Hill but did not earn a degree. Her studies were interrupted in the early

1980s by bouts of manic depression and hospitalization. In 1985 she married Michael Gibbons, then a student at North Carolina State University. They have three daughters, Mary, Leslie, and Louise, born in 1984, 1987, and 1989 respectively. After her divorce from Michael Gibbons, she married Frank Ward, an attorney, and settled in Raleigh, North Carolina.

Gibbons's career as a professional writer began in 1985, when she enrolled in an English class at Chapel Hill taught by a prominent scholar of southern literature, Louis Rubin. She was inspired by the early twentieth-century African American poet James Weldon Johnson because, as she stated in an interview with Bob Summer for *Publishers Weekly*:

> He seemed to me to be the first poet in the South—not the first writer, since Twain had already done it—to make art out of everyday language. Inspired by him, I wanted to see if I could have a child use her voice to talk about life, death, art, eternity—big things from a little person.

And so she did in *Ellen Foster.* Rubin, the founder of Algonquin Press, sent the manuscript of the novel to the prominent southern novelists Walker Percy and Eudora Welty, who responded enthusiastically, as did the critics and the public when Rubin published the novel.

ELLEN FOSTER

Gibbons staked her claim to a position in American literature and announced a major theme of her works with her epigraph to *Ellen Foster,* the lines with which Ralph Waldo Emerson prefaced his seminal 1841 essay "Self-Reliance":

> Cast the bantling on the rocks,
> Suckle him with the she-wolf's teat,
> Wintered with the hawk and fox,
> Power and speed be hands and feet.

Although these lines seemingly point to the theme of self-reliance, in *Ellen Foster* and in her later novels Gibbons also questions and subverts these lines. Ellen Foster is "cast . . . on the rocks" by her mother's suicide and her father's alcoholism and abuse, but while we admire the ingenuity and grit with which she manages to survive, Ellen is badly damaged by the encounter. Gibbons does not glorify adversity. Even at the end of the novel, living with the foster family she has chosen and named herself after, Ellen is still plagued by "shaking" and needs to put her hands in those of her foster mother. Emerson's exemplar of self-reliance is male and nurtured by nature's tough love. Gibbons's protagonists are women who are often damaged by society and must remain in society to work out their salvation with others. While Ellen is a remarkably resilient and self-reliant child in the way she holds herself together, she can only begin to be cured and to develop when she is helped by the female community of the foster home.

Lack of community, a society fissured by class, gender, and race, is the cause of Ellen's plight. Ellen's mother married beneath her and is disowned by her proud and angry mother, who owns a nearby plantation. In Gibbons's world female "privilege" can do as much damage as adversity. Ellen tells us that her mother's heart was damaged by "romantic fever." While she means "rheumatic" fever, her malapropism is significant. Her mother was too sheltered in a world of romantic fantasy to recognize her father for the mean drunk he is. She is too sick and passive to save herself or her daughter from his abuse and ultimately abandons that daughter through an overdose. Her mother's sisters, two of Ellen's temporary guardians, are similarly feckless. One aunt refuses to see Ellen's plight during a weekend visit and remains with her creature comforts while Ellen returns to her sexually abusive father. The other aunt, who takes Ellen in after Ellen's father's death, eventually throws Ellen out because the unconventional child is a constant reminder of her

selfishness, materialism, and complacency. Ellen's maternal grandmother is an angry and witch-like figure who forces Ellen to work in the blazing sun with her black field hands as she tries to punish Ellen for her parents' transgression against class lines.

Men in Gibbons's novels are often characterized as overgrown children whose dominant position in society gives them the power to abuse others. Ellen's father expects her mother, newly arrived from the hospital, to weed the yard and cook his supper, as Ellen observes, "more like big mean baby than a grown man." The judge, representative of male treatment of people as objects, takes Ellen out of the custody of her countercultural art teacher and her husband, where Ellen has been happy. Because "the family" is "society's cornerstone," he gives Ellen to her grandmother, and Ellen astutely observes that "he had us all mixed up with a different group of folks." The local minister is similarly blinded by his authority and does not deal with the question that is really worrying Ellen at her mother's funeral:

> And what else are you going to say when the Bible comes flat out and says killing yourself is flinging God's gift back in his face and He will not forgive you for it ever? The preacher leaves that out and goes straight to the green valleys and the streets of gold and silver.

For Ellen, God is equally concerned with materialism, ownership, and blaming the victim: "I reminded Jesus that this is not the way a girl needs to be. I told him again to please settle up with me so I could be a pure girl again and somebody good could love me." Ellen has internalized the values of her patriarchal society and judges herself as impure though she is blameless.

At the start of the novel Ellen is also as racist as her southern society. She rightly fears her father's black drinking buddies and their suggestive comments, but she also fears eating a "coloured biscuit" or sleeping under the covers at the home of her African American friend Starletta, whose parents constantly provide Ellen with a refuge and help. By the end of the novel Ellen's trials have taught her how little good her whiteness has done her and how meaningless such racial distinctions are. The novel ends with Ellen watching Starletta and realizing: "And all this time I thought I had the hardest row to hoe. That will always amaze me." Some critics find this ending pat, sentimental, and unrealistic, but it is typical of Gibbons's novels and the works of other contemporary southern women writers in that some African American characters, often female, are idealized and used as the sources of racial and other epiphanies for the white female protagonists. Further this criticism of the ending could also be attributed to the power of Ellen's voice, a voice so compelling that a reader mistakenly tends to equate a child's idealism and hope with the views of the adult author, who has actually presented us with a grim portrait of a racist southern society.

A VIRTUOUS WOMAN

Point of view is an important issue in Gibbons's second novel, *A Virtuous Woman* (1989). The novel is told in alternate chapters by Ruby Pitt Woodrow Stokes and her second husband, Jack Stokes. Ruby is telling her story as she prepares for her death from cancer. Jack is speaking in the aftermath of Ruby's death. Both narratives contain memories of the past that help the narrator explain the present. The final chapter is told by a third-person narrator, an authorial decision decried by some critics, who believe it lessens the intensity of the novel. Gibbons is often compared to William Faulkner, who also uses multiple narrators and in *The Sound and the Fury* (1929) follows the first-person narrations by the three Compson brothers with a third-person narrative. For both Faulkner and Gibbons the first-person narrators indicate the

isolation of the speakers and their difficulty in communicating with others. In both novels the final section's third-person point of view to show a wider social range suggests the possibility of breaking out of solipsism into community. At the end of *A Virtuous Woman,* Jack has lost Ruby to death and has fallen into despair and drinking. But Jack is now helped by his boss Burr and Burr's putative daughter June, whom Ruby and Jack helped raise. As in the foster home at the end of *Ellen Foster,* a hope remains that the ravages of the past can be at least partially mended by a community. As in the F/foster family, this is not conventional blood kin but a family of affinity and choice.

Also like *Ellen Foster, A Virtuous Woman* presents a society disintegrating as it clings to and romanticizes distinctions of race, class, and gender. A number of critics have pointed out that Gibbons is in effect writing the story of Ellen Foster's mother in her second novel. While no literal relationship exists, Ellen's mother and Ruby are certainly sisters under the skin. Ruby is also a victim of "romantic fever" who marries below her class, in her case to a migrant worker named John Woodrow. Like Ellen's mother, she had a sheltered upbringing: "If I had a tough piece of meat on my plate, the minute one of them saw me struggling they'd lean over, take my knife and fork from me and cut the meat up for me." In her idleness and boredom Ruby wants romance so much that she invents it: "I even convinced myself that his idea of courtship, which was sending word up to the house through one of the women in the crew to meet him . . . was romantic."

Ruby's narration concerns her development from a foolish girl who marries the abusive Woodrow into the virtuous woman of the title. After Woodrow is killed in a fight, Ruby does not return to her parents but marries an older tenant farmer, Jack Stokes. Because of a disease she caught from Woodrow, Ruby cannot have children and solaces herself by helping raise

Burr's daughter June, neglected and then abandoned by her own mother. Ruby's narration begins with the words of a virtuous, mature woman, "by Thanksgiving I'll have everything organized," as she prepares meals for the freezer that Jack will eat after her death.

As Gibbons somewhat subversively used Emerson's "Self-Reliance" as an epigraph to *Ellen Foster,* in *A Virtuous Woman* she similarly questions her epigraph, the biblical passage from Proverbs 31:10–25. The lines instruct us that a virtuous woman's "price is far above rubies," and thus points to "Ruby" as the virtuous woman. Gibbons then proceeds to quote the rest of the lengthy passage, in which the virtuous woman is busy day and night, cooking, sewing, planting, performing acts of charity, and selling the products of her industry in the marketplace so that "her husband is known in the gates, / When he sitteth among the elders of the land." The woman finds her constant toil rewarding and "she laugheth at the time to come."

Ruby, like the biblical virtuous woman, enjoys her housework and is proud of the way she takes care of Jack, but she also promotes his dependency on her. As she observes, "Sometimes, I swear, he's just like a child." He is so dependent on her that, when she dies and he runs out of frozen meals, he retreats to his bed, his fantasies, and the bottle. The opening line of Jack's narration is: "She hasn't been dead four months and I've already eaten to the bottom of the deep freeze." While Jack is a decent if limited man and is certainly no villain like Ellen Foster's father or John Woodrow, Gibbons is suggesting that society makes women complicit in and even take pride in the male behavior that oppresses them.

While race is not a prominent issue in *A Virtuous Woman,* its treatment here further calls into question the traditional idea of the virtuous woman. Ruby and her mother are dependent on the services of Sudie Bee, who keeps them sheltered from work and harsh realities, a protection that becomes Ruby's downfall. As Ruby later realizes, "Somebody like Sudie Bee covers for people." After Ruby's death, Jack tries to replace her services with those of Mavis, the African American woman with whom Ellen Foster worked in her grandmother's fields and who helped Ellen when she could not keep up with the rest of the crew. Jack fantasizes Mavis into a stereotype: "I bet that woman can makes biscuits the kind you dream of." Mavis, however, is not Sudie Bee or a mammy figure; she is too concerned with her own ailments and comforts to "slave" for Jack.

Gibbons points out that times have changed and "mammies" no longer exist or should be desired. Similarly she suggests that the role of the virtuous woman has also changed. Ruby is of the generation of Ellen Foster's and Kaye Gibbons's mothers. While the final chapter leaves the points of view of Ruby and Jack, it brings into prominence their "foster" daughter June, who, the reader learns, is good friends with Ellen Foster. June has become an architect but still comes back to help her father get her "foster" father Jack back on his feet by cleaning the house and cheering him. While one might argue that she is merely continuing to promote his dependency, June can also be seen as someone who can move beyond the limited realm of the preceding generation without losing the virtues of caring and compassion that characterized the best of them. June and her friend Ellen may represent the next generation of virtuous women.

A CURE FOR DREAMS AND *CHARMS FOR THE EASY LIFE*

In her next two novels, *A Cure for Dreams: A Novel* (1991) and *Charms for the Easy Life* (1993), Gibbons explores the effect of strong, even heroic maternal figures on a young girl's development. *A Cure for Dreams* is set during the Great Depression and the opening years of World War II on Milk Farm Road, part of a rural North Carolina community. It is Gibbons's first historical novel, and she did research for it among the Federal Writers Project papers at the University of North Carolina at Chapel Hill. The epigraph for the novel comes from W. T. Couch, the regional director of the Federal Writers Project in 1939: "With all our talk of democracy it seems not inappropriate to let the people speak for themselves."

For Gibbons the "people" who now need to be heard are not just the poor and downtrodden of the Great Depression but women. The novel is framed by short sections by Marjorie Polly Randolph, who ends her opening section with the declaration "Talking was my mother's life" and ends the novel with the words "But I wasn't sleeping, not for the sounds of the women talking." Between Marjorie's brief sections her mother, Bette Davies Randolph, talks about her mother, the seemingly larger-than-life Lotte O'Cadhain Davies, who spends much of her time talking.

Lotte leads a rich life despite her withdrawn, workaholic husband. Her talk is not idle chatter but speech with a purpose, helping other women find their voices despite their silencing by men. She organizes card parties so the women of Milk Farm Road can keep up their spirits and exercise their voices despite the exigencies of the depression. She brings Sade Duplin's straying husband back to her by starting "talk" that his mistress has a venereal disease. When Sade finally kills her abusive mate, Lotte and her friends read the domestic clues in a way the sheriff cannot and cover for Sade by promoting "talk" about a wandering vagabond, now long gone, who might have done it. Gibbons revises the plot of Susan Glaspell's 1916 play *Trifles* to emphasize the necessity of female community. Glaspell's Minnie Wright ends up in jail, mad and isolated, but in *A Cure for Dreams,* Sade thrives from the helpful talk of her women friends.

Survival, the goal of *Ellen Foster* and *A Virtuous Woman,* is no longer enough, and women actively seek pleasure in *A Cure for Dreams.* "Hurling oneself at a desire" is now a virtue, not merely enduring suffering. Mothers need to instruct their daughters in the willed pursuit of their own happiness. Emma Garnet Tate's mother in Gibbons's sixth novel, *On the Occasion of My Last Afternoon* (1998), tells Emma: "Live today for memory tomorrow and for pleasure now. Always." It is equally important for mothers to teach their daughters to refuse duties imposed upon them that do not advance their pleasure. Lotte tells Herbert of Bette that "cooking for enlisted men was not my pleasure." The card games, the kitchen table conferences, the walks and visiting up and down Milk Farm Road have the common goals of pleasure and community.

While the novel is in one sense the story of Lotte's heroic efforts to build a female community and to promote women's pleasure, it is also the story of Bette's attempts to become her own person in the shadow of her formidable mother. "All my life, when she rose, I rose." While Bette presents Lotte with great admiration, the reader can see what will ultimately give Bette a little psychological space for growth: Lotte's weaknesses and limitations. Lotte wants to give charity to Trudy, a "trashy" new neighbor from Louisiana, but Trudy refuses to be grateful. She is an abandoned mother but refuses to be pitied or to care what the community thinks, and she advises Bette to get out of town on her own or sink into the mores of the community: "I should do what I wanted to do or give up and fall into having babies." When Bette wants her now widowed mother to leave town with her, Lotte refuses. Bette realizes, "On Milk Farm Road, she'd remade herself into the Queen Bee, more or less organizing life through knowing everything." Away from Milk Farm

Road, when she accompanies her angry crone of a mother, Bridget, on a wretched visit to Ireland and when she is pressed into domestic service at Bridget's house, Lotte loses that power.

When Bette decides to try to widen her own sphere by going to Richmond to take a commercial course, she meets the fate of Gibbons's other sheltered heroines. She gets "romantic fever" and takes up with the wrong man, who turns out to be a drug addict. Unlike Ellen Foster's mother and Ruby Stokes though, Bette does not marry the bounder but returns home to her mother's house, recovered from her romantic fever. She marries Herbert Randolph, a limited and uninteresting man like Jack Stokes, and he conveniently goes off to World War II, leaving her pregnant and living with her mother and the local African American midwife Polly Deal. Bette's labor starts early and she cannot get to the hospital. Polly delivers her baby after urging Bette not to call her mother back from a neighbor's for the birth, saying, "And I think that you as much as anybody needs to do this one thing this time without Miss Lotte." Like Ellen Foster's Starletta, this African American character promotes the growth of the white female protagonist. Bette names the baby Marjorie Polly against her mother's wishes. That, however, appears to the limit of Bette's drive for autonomy. She and Herbert continue to live happily with her mother, "cured" of her foolish "dreams" of romance and self-reliance. In *A Cure for Dreams,* Gibbons comes dangerously close to suggesting that happiness and contentment are incompatible with the challenges that create an intriguing life or plot. Lotte may not be perfect, but her unhappy childhood and marriage caused her to create an interesting and interested life for herself on Milk Farm Road.

Similarly in *Charms for the Easy Life* the narrator, Margaret, tells the story of her larger-than-life grandmother, a self-taught herbal doctor and midwife. Some critics complain that

Charlie Kate's wise handling of every situation becomes boringly predictable, but as in the ending of *Ellen Foster,* it is necessary to consider the narrator of the story. Margaret does worship her grandmother and wants to present her in the light of that love and admiration. While readers share Margaret's conviction that her grandmother is a remarkable woman, readers also can discern her weak points and her increasing irrelevance in the modern world. She is occasionally wrong, for example, when she tells Margaret to invent a letter to a hospitalized soldier's mother supposedly from her son in order to comfort her. Because the son was adopted as a child and the letter sounded like he believed she was his birth mother, the mother was alarmed about her son's mental health.

Charlie Kate cannot save everyone. Her imaginative sympathies are limited by her background and region. She is ignorant of the cancer of her retired African American domestic once she moves out of town and arrives too late to prevent the agonies of her death. Like that of Lotte, Charlie Kate's sphere of influence is limited and local; she cannot understand why she is not obeyed by partying youth when she visits a hotel at the beach. Even though Margaret graduated at the top of her high school class, Charlie Kate does not insist that she go to a good college but allows her to stay home and help her in her practice. By the end of the novel and Charlie Kate's life, people consult doctors and go to hospitals with no need for her services.

Because Margaret worships Charlie Kate, Margaret's relationship to her mother, Sophia, suffers: "Usually I chose my grandmother as I believe she possessed the wisdom of the ages." Margaret blames her mother for marrying her worthless father instead of the noble and enterprising Dr. Charles Nutter, for whom Charlie Kate had advocated. Margaret, however, does not seem to blame Charlie Kate for marrying her grandfather, a man who eventually deserted Charlie Kate and Sophia. Sophia's response to the death of her husband in his sleep indicates that there is more to her than Margaret gives her credit for. She tells Margaret: "He's gone. Start the coffee." Charlie Kate does not want Sophia to remarry, but Sophia marries the kindly Mr. Baines, giving Margaret more psychological space for her own romance.

Unlike Lotte of *A Cure for Dreams,* Charlie Kate realizes that her era is passing, and she wants her granddaughter to find a new life, though not necessarily one of her own. Charlie Kate promotes Margaret's romance with Tom Hawkins III, a soldier recovering from wounds in the hospital at which Margaret volunteers during World War II. This may not lead to Margaret's autonomy since she may be passing from one strong caretaker to another. Margaret notes her increasing attraction to Tom: "I couldn't leave the side of someone described to me in terms I've always applied to my grandmother." At the conclusion of the novel Margaret finds Charlie Kate dead when she returns from a visit to Tom's family. The last line of the novel is: "And then I lay down, rested my head by her feet and waited to be found." While this line indicates Margaret's devotion to her grandmother, it is eerily reminiscent of the child Ellen Foster waiting to be found by the side of her dead mother: "You can rest with me until somebody comes to get you." While Ellen has to get up and struggle to survive, Margaret presumably will be found by Tom and her mother; she can remain passive. As in *A Cure for Dreams,* happiness and community come at the expense of autonomy and adventure. The charm her grandmother gave her for an easy life may make it too easy.

Gibbons's early works were sometimes criticized for their negative portrayal of men. Male characters are monsters of selfishness, like Ellen Foster's father and John Woodrow, or nonentities, like Jack Stokes or Herbert Randolph. In *Charms for an Easy Life,* Gibbons presents a few admirable men. Margaret will marry Tom Hawkins, who has her grandmother's qualities of courage and unconventionality combined with caring. Sophia marries the considerate Mr. Baines, who has the imagination and attention to her pleasure to push her around a frozen lake on a chair, to her great delight. Dr. Charles Nutter, Margaret's grandmother's protégé and Sophia's would-be suitor, becomes a compassionate and inventive surgeon who shows his gratitude to Charlie Kate and her family.

In another departure from Gibbons's earlier novels, *Charms for an Easy Life* is self-consciously literary. Literary allusions are rare in her earlier novels, but in *Charms for an Easy Life* reading and literature are primary topics. Class and race are not important themes, but the ability to imaginatively engage with great literature is. The epigraph to the novel is from Friedrich Nietzsche's *Human, All Too Human*: "Stupidity in a woman is unfeminine." Charlie Kate, Sophia, and Margaret actively combat such stupidity by their avid reading. Margaret comments: "In our house, the point of reading and learning was neither to impress outsiders or to get a job or a husband, nothing like that. It had nothing to do with anybody but the three of us. When a good book was in the house, the place vibrated." They read Sinclair Lewis, Edgar Allan Poe, Marjorie Kinnan Rawlings, Gustave Flaubert, Thomas Hardy, James Fenimore Cooper, Nathaniel Hawthorne, Edith Wharton, James Thurber, Ernest Hemingway, Eudora Welty, and of course William Faulkner. An unworthy suitor for Margaret is unmasked when he displays his inability to appreciate Faulkner. Indeed the ability to appreciate good literature is a touchstone of a character's worth. Tom Hawkins reads Thomas Mann's *The Magic Mountain* (1924) in the hospital and tries to stay in F. Scott Fitzgerald's former room at the Grove Park Inn in Asheville.

SIGHTS UNSEEN

In her fifth novel, *Sights Unseen* (1995), Gibbons returns to a theme she explored in *Ellen Foster,* that of children. Hattie Barnes and her brother Freddy must cope too soon with an adult world of pain and disorder. Hattie Barnes narrates the novel as an adult remembering a childhood dominated by the manic depression of her mother, Maggie. Hattie worries constantly about whether or not something she has done or said could have sent her mother into another cycle of illness. Devastatingly she remarks, "I knew better than to need anything." Hattie even blames herself for getting sick and vomiting, setting off a chain of family events that could upset her mother. At one point she comments, "I was full of anxiety, so full, in fact, that I was weighted down in my seat." She must act like an adult: "Father ended the conversation with his lawyer, then came over to me, sat down and cried on my shoulder, as if I were his mother, or at least a person his size. I patted him on the back." Like Ellen Foster and Kaye Gibbons as a child, Hattie compensates by maintaining order whenever she can: "I processed mother's departure [for a hospital] by locking myself in my room and straightening it thoroughly, obsessively. I separated my construction paper by color, rearranged the furniture in my dollhouse, put a deck of cards in order, and broke, at last, into tears over a missing joker." The missing joker is of course her mother, whose antic behavior, while sometimes comic, is often a tragedy for her young daughter.

Maggie is not successfully treated for her illness until Hattie is twelve years old mainly because the proud family tries keep up appearances and to hide and to cope with Maggie's illness themselves. Hattie remembers, "So much happened in our house that was never to be seen," the "sights unseen" of the title. One reason is patriarchal pride. Hattie's paternal grandfather, Mr. Barnes, is a successful local businessman, a self-made man who feels he must be in complete control of his world. His wife "had no secrets from him and relinquished authority over her sons to him." He keeps Hattie's mother under control and dependent upon him by indulging her whims instead of insisting on getting treatment for her. Hattie observes, "He loved pleasing her, and this urge must have overridden any need he might have seen either to try to adjust her mood himself or to seek professional help for her." When Hattie's mother is well, she defies Mr. Barnes and insists that he show their African American servant Pearl proper respect. Gibbons is equating Maggie's sanity with a sane society, in which racism would be insanity and would not be tolerated.

Mr. Barnes demeans his two sons, including Hattie's father, and they fear him and defer to him. Hattie's father is a good man but ineffectual, wearing himself out between the demands of his father and those of his wife. Not only does he use Hattie for adult comfort but he uses her as a means to help his wife. Hattie knows that she was conceived because her father thought caring for a baby would make Maggie better. The scheme fails of course, and Hattie simply feels more inadequate. Hattie believes herself excluded from her mother because of her mother's intense relationship with and need for her father: "She and I had nothing to compare with her relationship with my father." Because he is so preoccupied with Maggie, he also fails to protect his son Freddy from Mr. Barnes's verbal abuse and even a slap in the face, causing Freddy to further withdraw from family life.

Pearl is another cause of the family's failure to get Maggie treatment, though she is ultimately the catalyst for that treatment. Because Pearl does such a good job of keeping Maggie under control and out of trouble and the public eye, the family can avoid the stigma they attach to institutionalization. Pearl slips one day, and Maggie gets away and hits a woman with her car. Maggie is finally taken to Duke for the treatment that will even out her moods. Pearl, like Sudie Bee in *A Virtuous Woman,* promotes the continued helplessness of a white female protagonist, but like Polly Deal in *A Cure for Dreams,* she is the catalyst for the white female protagonist's change.

While Hattie Barnes resembles Ellen Foster in having adult woes thrust upon her far too early, the tone of *Sights Unseen* is quite distinctive due to the different point of view. Ellen is a child, speaking as a child. Hattie Barnes tells her story from the point of view of an adult. Gibbons uses Katherine Anne Porter's Miranda stories as a model. In an essay in the *Kenyon Review,* Gibbons writes, "Understanding the role of surfaces in the Miranda stories depends on acceptance of the presence of the adult Miranda as their narrator." Hattie presents "surfaces" that are similarly layered since she remembers not only her mother's manic years but also the sane years following her successful treatment when Hattie was twelve. The epigraph from the poet Conrad Aiken's 1941 *Preludes from Memnon* suggests Hattie's adult pity for her mother's lost years of swinging wildly between emotional heat and cold: "For there are dark streams in this dark world, lady, / Gulf Streams and Arctic currents of the soul."

Hattie does not get everything she wants when her mother is well. Some needs will remain unmet. Hattie has accumulated a "backlog of things to say to" her mother and "had accumulated a list of things she and I could do together." The adult Hattie is now willing to accept the loss with the gain. "We never sat down and had a long, constructive and restorative talk." Hattie has learned that "both forgiving and healing are true arts, and in telling my mother's story I have been able to forgive the past without reservation and heal myself without concern over a lapse into acute sorrow over her death." Like Gibbons's other heroines, Hattie can only forgive and heal when she can speak and is no longer silenced by the fear and pity of her early years.

Like the title character of *Ellen Foster* and like June of *A Virtuous Woman,* Hattie is the new woman capable of breaking out of the self-destructive patterns of the women of Gibbons's mother's generation. Hattie believes she has broken the chain of negligent mothering and her children will be nurtured: "My instinct might have been to ignore my responsibility for them the way my mother had initially relinquished responsibility for me." When her mother dies, Hattie is pregnant with her first child and, like her brother, has become a doctor. For Gibbons maternal nurturing, in the best and broadest sense, must take place upon the societal or communal level as well as the family level, and Hattie, a woman of today, is ready to try.

ON THE OCCASION OF MY LAST AFTERNOON

In her sixth novel, *On the Occasion of My Last Afternoon* (1998), Gibbons seeks within the southern past the roots of the problems she has obsessively explored in her earlier novels. *On the Occasion of My Last Afternoon* is set before, during, and after the Civil War. It begins at Seven Oaks, the Virginia plantation of Emma Garnet's father, Samuel Tate, as if Gibbons is exploring the origins of the Old South, and ends in the New South of North Carolina, where Emma Garnet lives and works with her Yankee husband, Quincy Lowell. How Emma Garnet and the South became "new" and at what price are the dominant themes of *On the Occasion of My Last Afternoon.* Emma Garnet Tate Lowell is the first-person narrator, and as an old woman at the end of her life, on the occasion of her last afternoon, she looks back over cataclysmic decades in the South.

Our heroine seems familiar. Like Ellen Foster and Hattie Barnes, Emma Garnet is forced to confront an ugly world too soon. Emma declares, "I did not believe I would ever forgive my father for making me withstand more than I can bear." Also like Ellen and Hattie she feels responsible for her weak mother. Emma Garnet tries to save her mother from her father's verbal and sexual abuse with such ploys as claiming that one of the younger children is sick and needs her mother's attention. When Emma Garnet marries Quincy Lowell and escapes to North Carolina, she takes with her their African American freewoman servant Clarice, the only person her father fears. Emma's mother, left at the mercy of the plantation tyrant, eventually dies of his mistreatment. Emma is happy with Quincy and their daughters, but she continues to have nightmares and will never forgive herself for leaving her mother: "Simply and regrettably, my mother was the price I paid for finally being able to lie down in peace. . . . I am ashamed."

Although Emma Garnet feels shame, Gibbons suggests that the patriarchs of the South, symbolized at their worst by Emma Garnet's father, are the ones who should be ashamed. In characterizing Samuel Tate, Gibbons alludes to the story of Thomas Sutpen in Faulkner's classic novel of the nineteenth-century South, *Absalom, Absalom!* (1936). Like Thomas Sutpen, Tate is a parvenu, shamed and abused by his own "white trash" father as a child. Also like Sutpen, Tate believes he can buy his way into the status of gentleman and into happiness. He buys his slaves and treats them as objects. "I did not mean to kill the nigger!" is the opening line of the novel, a typically startling and arresting Gibbons opening. It also foregrounds Samuel Tate's and the Old South's ability to lie to themselves. Like Sutpen, Tate believes he can buy status with an impoverished but genteel wife and manages to drive her to her grave. Like Sutpen, he furnishes his plantation house with the best of everything except peace and contentment. Gibbons is a bit less critical of Tate than she is of Ellen Foster's father. She

shows that Tate is also a victim of the southern social order based on race and class, though she does not condone his actions.

Essentially Gibbons is suggesting that the Old South was based on lies, lies that required a great deal of effort to maintain and to convince the liars as well as their audiences. The tyrants need their inferiors to be convinced of their greatness. Emma Garnet recalls, "Like the servants, we, his children, were beneath him, and so we were left oftentimes standing with his lies on our hands, like baffling presents." Gibbons apparently shares Mark Twain's view that the novels of Sir Walter Scott were a major cause of the Civil War. Emma Garnet's brother Whateley writes to her, "Beware of Walter Scott, for he is a deceitful man, and his words lull the mind into sweet stupidity." What Twain and Whateley have in mind is the South's tendency to romanticize the slavocracy by comparing it to the aristocracy of the Waverley romances; one only needs to consider the many plantations and children named from Scott's novels. Samuel Tate rationalized an early act of cruelty as necessary for chivalric romance. As a child "he had torn the shell off a live turtle to have a Lancelot shield." Emma Garnet vehemently rejects these lies about the chivalrous, aristocratic nature of southern society, especially after she witnesses the carnage and suffering of the Civil War. No noblesse oblige is found here: "I still hold that it was a conflict perpetrated by rich men and fought by poor boys against hungry women and babies."

Samuel Tate's greatest resemblance to Faulkner's Thomas Sutpen though is his destruction of his sons and hence his failure to found an aristocratic dynasty. His oldest son, Whateley, represents the generation of young southern men destroyed by the southern patriarchs in the service of their pride, racism, and greed. Whateley does not want to inherit his father's plantation and rejects the ideology upon which it is based. When Whateley tells his father of his resolve to abdicate, much in the manner of Faulkner's Ike McCaslin in *Go Down, Moses* (1942), their familial civil war begins. Whateley, exiled from his family, falls in with bad companions and eventually dies alone in an advanced and horrific state of syphilis. The sensitive, caring Whateley finds no place in the South of "the fathers." By naming the family "Tate," Gibbons alludes to the southern renaissance writer Allen Tate's novel *The Fathers* (1938), in which the sins of the fathers are similarly visited upon the heads of their children.

Emma Garnet manages to escape the paternal legacy but not unscathed by guilt and horror. Although she has a monstrous father, she has two women to offer her aid. Her mother is a sweet if passive lady who at least teaches Emma to pursue pleasure and beauty, as she does when she visits the matriarchs of neighboring plantations. Her mother is no longer capable of any depth, as Emma notes, "survival took the place of whatever mind-work she might have accomplished." Clarice, the African American servant, helps Emma Garnet escape her father through her marriage to Quincy. Clarice lives with Emma and Quincy in North Carolina, taking over much of the burden of household management so Emma can continue her life of the mind and can educate her daughters at home.

Emma Garnet owes much of her intellectual life to her brother Whateley and not to her father, autodidact that he was. Emma says of her father, "I cursed him for locking himself in his chambers with Mintus [his valet] as his only listener, hoarding language, excluding me, curious as he knew I was, in his journeys to Carthage, to Rome, to his favorite place and time, Athens in her golden age." Whateley, in contrast, does not exclude Emma from the life of the mind but encourages her by sending her books and reading lists. While he warns against the romantic Scott, Whateley advocates a literature based in a robust realism about human nature, including Washington Irving, Laurence Sterne, Geoffrey Chaucer, William Shakespeare, and James Fenimore Cooper. While Emma Garnet's education undoubtedly enriches and liberates the rest of her life, the subplot in which she educates a poor white girl, Lavina, indicates that class is still paramount, not achievement through learning. Lavina marries above her original station, is abused, and dies. She was unable to recognize the man's quality outside of her own class, the reversal of the "falls" of Ellen Foster's mother and Ruby Pitt Woodrow Stokes, who marry beneath their class in a similarly deluded state of romantic fever.

Through her depiction of Emma Garnet's husband, Quincy Lowell, Gibbons clearly indicates her respect for what seem to be northern values, especially embracing diversity. "Everyone is my own kind," declares Quincy. Unlike her father, Quincy encourages, not suppresses, Emma's voice. He listens, and he responds, rare qualities in Gibbons's male characters. "I am fortunate," states Emma, "to have married a man of splendid liberality of thought who gloried to hear me speak my mind on any subject. Quincy and I were in voice with each other." While it is tempting to interpret being "in voice with each other" as a sort of romance of reconciliation that joins the North and the South in a fruitful union, this is not the case. Quincy is buried in Boston, and all three of their daughters and their spouses live in New England, as if the South is too moribund to cultivate a "splendid liberality of thought."

This contrast between North and South is further reinforced in the epigraphs Gibbons chose for *On the Occasion of My Last Afternoon*. The first is from Allen Tate's poem "Ode to the Confederate Dead" (1930). Tate at this period of his career was a southern advocate and was one of the authors of *I'll Take My Stand* (1930), the title taken from the Confederate anthem "Dixie": "In Dixieland I'll take my stand to live and die for Dixie." When Tate's narrator confronts the past in the form of the

Confederate tombs he contemplates, he finds, "the silence . . . / Smothers you, a mummy in time." The past is not only moribund but death-dealing when carried into the present. The Boston Brahmin poet Robert Lowell, of the same family as the fictional Quincy, is represented by "For the Union Dead" (1964), which he wrote in response to Tate's "Ode." Although Lowell is fearful of the commercialism and "savage servility" he sees in contemporary Boston, he is saved from despair by the example of Robert Gould Shaw, a white Boston Brahmin who led a regiment of African Americans in the Civil War. Shaw died with them and was buried with them in a ditch. The other example of courage is contemporary to Lowell: "the drained faces of Negro school-children rise like balloons." These are the black children who bravely integrated schools.

The epigraphs to *On the Occasion of My Last Afternoon* reinforce the argument of Gibbons's entire body of novels, which finds the values of the Old South pernicious and destructive and looks to salvation from liberal northerners and African Americans. Yet here too the epigraphs read somewhat subversively, since they omit one of Gibbons's principle sources of constructive change: speaking, compassionate, and active southern women. With her attention to women's voices and issues, Gibbons revises the major themes of American and southern literature. She rejects the self-reliant, rugged, and isolationist male hero of the traditional American literary canon for women who know that strength and autonomy are achieved with, not despite, others in a community. She similarly revises the great theme of southern literature, the stifling burden of the past, by imagining women who know how to invent lives that take the past into account but can move beyond it. In *On the Occasion of My Last Afternoon*, Gibbons writes, "That is what so much of this world is anyway, livable chaos." Kaye Gibbons is one of the best of the contemporary generation of southern women writers who show the way to a new American literature based on a community that embraces, not rejects, the diversity of race, class, and gender, transforming them into a synergistic "livable chaos."

Selected Bibliography

WORKS OF KAYE GIBBONS

NOVELS AND SHORT STORIES

Ellen Foster: A Novel. Chapel Hill, N.C.: Algonquin, 1987.

"The Headache." *St. Andrews Review* 32:3–8 (spring/summer 1987).

"The Proof." *Quarterly* 1:60–72 (spring 1987).

A Virtuous Woman. Chapel Hill, N.C.: Algonquin, 1989.

A Cure for Dreams: A Novel. Chapel Hill, N.C.: Algonquin, 1991.

Charms for the Easy Life. New York: Putnam, 1993.

Sights Unseen. New York: Putnam, 1995.

On the Occasion of My Last Afternoon. New York: Putnam, 1998.

OTHER WORKS

"Planes of Language and Time: The Surface of the Miranda Stories." *Kenyon Review* n.s. 10:74–79 (winter 1988).

"Joyner's Store." *Southern Living,* June 1997, p. 204.

"The First Day of School." *Brightleaf: A Southern Review of Books* 1, no. 4:39–42 (fall 1998).

CRITICAL AND BIOGRAPHICAL STUDIES

Barnes, Linda Adams. "Telling Yourself into Existence: The Fiction of Kaye Gibbons." *Tennessee Philological Bulletin* 30:28–35 (1993).

Branan, Tonita. "Women and 'the Gift for Gab': Revisionary Strategies in *A Cure for Dreams.*"

Southern Literary Journal 26, no. 2:91–101 (spring 1994).

Lewis, Nancy. "Kaye Gibbons: Her Full Time Women." In *Southern Writers at Century's End.* Edited by Jeffrey J. Folks and James A. Perkins. Lexington, Ky.: University Press of Kentucky, 1997. Pp. 112–122.

Makowsky, Veronica. "'The Only Hard Part Was the Food': Recipes for Self-Nurture in Kaye Gibbons' Novels." *Southern Quarterly* 30, nos. 2–3:103–112 (winter–spring 1992).

McKee, Kathryn. "Simply Talking: Women and Language in Kaye Gibbons' *A Cure for Dreams.*" *Southern Quarterly* 35, no. 4:97–106 (summer 1997).

Munafo, Giavanna. "'Coloured Biscuits': Reconstructing Whiteness and the Boundaries of 'Home' in Kaye Gibbons's *Ellen Foster.*" In *Women, America, and Movement: Narratives of Relocation.* Edited by Susan L. Robertson. Columbia, Mo.: University of Missouri Press, 1998. Pp. 38–61.

Souris, Stephen. "Kaye Gibbons's *A Virtuous Woman*: A Bakhtinian Iserian Analysis of Conspicuous Agreement." *Southern Studies* 3, no. 2:99–115 (summer 1992).

Summer, Bob. "Kaye Gibbons." *Publishers Weekly,* February 8, 1993, pp. 60–61.

Wagner-Martin, Linda. "Kaye Gibbons' Achievement in *On the Occasion of My Last Afternoon.*" *Notes on Contemporary Literature* 29, no. 3:3–5 (May 1999).

—VERONICA MAKOWSKY

Anthony Hecht

1923–

ANTHONY HECHT IS America's greatest poet of ideological horror. He has written some of the most compelling and unconsoling poetry to have emerged from the primary example of that horror in the last century: the Holocaust. His reputation was founded initially on what has been called the "baroque extravagance" of his poetry. To those unfamiliar with his work, he has the forbidding reputation of a high artist, cool, distanced, and somewhat unsympathetic: a maker of art for art's sake, a poet's poet's poet. (The late Donald Davie wrote that his work appeared as if meant to be "hung on walls"—a criticism that demonstrably stung the poet. Moreover, Davie's onetime acolyte, Michael Schmidt, the editor of England's Carcanet Press, omitted Hecht from his definitive *Harvill Book of 20th Century Poetry in English*.)

Hecht's work, in fact, represents a diamond produced by geological processes under terrific pressure; it indicates what may happen when a somewhat refined, aesthetic, cultured sensibility clashes directly with the most chilling horrors imaginable. Whereas knowledge of those horrors at least in part persuaded the anti-poets of central Europe of the inefficacy of art, Hecht bore witness to them in poems crafted with a jeweler's precision. The dark watermark of the Holocaust is present through much of his work, even in poems not explicitly addressing the subject. He is a saturnine poet, whose humor tends to the sardonic. As an American Jew of German lineage who saw combat in Germany in World War II, he felt the Holocaust impose itself upon him as, in a sense, his subject, and it seems fair to claim that his work would have been entirely different without that experience.

It is legitimate within reason to read his poetry in the light of this crucial biographical fact.

LIFE

Anthony Hecht was born in New York City on January 16, 1923, the first son of parents of German-Jewish origin. (The family on Hecht's father's side was from Bamburg in Bavaria. "Hecht" in German means "pike." The poet's father believed his ancestors to have been fishermen.) His father, Melvyn Hahlo Hecht, was the owner of the New England Enamel Company, and his mother was Dorothea Hecht (née Holzman). His younger brother, Roger, was born two and a half years after Hecht.

The poet's childhood was upper middle class, though Hecht's early years were unhappy, in part because his brother was an invalid requiring constant care from his mother. Hecht's father proved to be an ineffectual businessman who on three occasions went bankrupt and each time attempted suicide. When the poet-to-be was six, the stock market crash of 1929 led to the diminishment of the family's fortunes (they were regularly rescued from impoverishment by Hecht's mother's family); as a youngster Hecht recalled seeing the bodies of those who had committed suicide, covered with blankets, on New York sidewalks. They had thrown themselves from windows as a result of monetary misfortune. When he was young, Hecht later recalled, he regarded his family as vulnerable socially and financially. It was a relative deprivation which provided perhaps a first indication to the child of the force of the external, an awareness that came to be prevalent throughout his poetry.

Hecht attended three distinguished New York City schools—The Dalton School, the Collegiate School, The Horace Mann School for Boys—in his childhood, then, at seventeen, he entered Bard College, an adjunct of Columbia University, in 1940. He majored in music before turning to literature. It was while he was at Bard that Hecht resolved to become a poet. When he announced this ambition to his parents, they called in a family friend, Ted Geisel, the Dr. Seuss of the cartoon and children's books, in an attempt to advise Hecht against this course—an attempt that, fortunately, did not succeed. An inspirational teacher, Larry Leighton, encouraged the young Hecht's early attempts at poetry. The poet has called his three years as an undergraduate at Bard among the happiest of his life.

In 1943, after America entered World War II, Hecht, at the age of twenty, was drafted before graduating from college, trained briefly in Missouri in the 97th Infantry Division, and went with this division to Europe. The wartime period is one of which he has spoken only a little and, by his own admission, never will discuss in detail. Early in his experience of battle, he witnessed the slaughter by machine gun of a small group of German women and children, who were advancing toward the division with flags of surrender. The men involved justified the slaughter on the ground that it may have been a trap. "That morning," Hecht later observed in an interview with Philip Hoy, "left me without the least vestige of patriotism or national pride." Battle, he observed, did not serve in bringing soldiers closer together.

Worse was to come. The poet was in the division that liberated the concentration camp of Flossenbürg. Situated near Buchenwald near the border with Czechoslovakia in the Bavarian forest, it had been set up in 1938. The final death toll was estimated at seventy-three thousand; at

any one time the number of prisoners ranged between five thousand and eighteen thousand; they were held in sixteen huge wooden barracks. The prisoners were forced to work either in a nearby Messerschmidt plant or, for those who were especially persecuted (such as Jews and homosexuals), at stone quarries in the camp. Dietrich Bonhoeffer, the Christian pastor and theologian, also was executed at Flossenbürg on April 9, 1945, two weeks before the camp's liberation on April 23. When Hecht's division arrived at the camp, by his own account five hundred prisoners were dying from typhus every day. The SS personnel had left. (On April 20, fifteen thousand prisoners at the camp had been marched away by the SS as the 97th Division approached.) Hecht, who spoke some French and German, conducted interviews with those French prisoners who were still able to talk. When the SS troops who ran the camp were later captured, Hecht was involved in questioning them and translating their replies back to the French prisoners—a gathering of evidence for possible prosecution. "The place, the suffering, the prisoner's accounts," Hecht later described to Hoy, "were beyond comprehension. For years after I would wake shrieking."

Following a period spent in occupied Japan, where his job was writing journalism intended to show the American military in a worthy light, Hecht was discharged from the Army in 1946. At the recommendation of a former student of the American poet John Crowe Ransom's, Robie Macauley, Hecht spent a year (1947–1948) at Kenyon College, in Ohio. His bachelor's degree had been awarded in absentia in 1944, and he was offered a teaching post by Ransom, a fine poet with some reputation as a social theorist of a conservative bent. The older poet was part of the so-called Southern Agrarians, a grouping of poets whose ideas had undertones of wishing to preserve former white privileges in the southern states; Ransom himself, Hecht was to read to his discomfiture, was not entirely unsympathetic to slavery. The young poet found it necessary to disagree tacitly with the older man, though it was Ransom who published Hecht's early poems in the *Kenyon Review.*

Following his year at Kenyon, Hecht taught for a term at the University of Iowa; there he began suffering post-traumatic stress disorder and had to return to New York. He entered psychoanalysis, taught briefly at New York University, and received his master's degree from Columbia University in 1950; by 1952 he had taken up a full-time teaching post at Bard College, in Annandale-on-Hudson, New York, where he instructed students in poetry writing and English literature. A year earlier Hecht had won a Prix de Rome fellowship, entitling him to a year at the American Academy in Rome. He heard of his award in Ischia, the largest and most populous island in the Bay of Naples, famed for its hot springs, where he was staying in an inexpensive apartment. Ischia was significant for another reason: the British poet W. H. Auden, whose work Hecht had read since he was fourteen, summered in Porto d'Ischia. The two men became reasonably good friends.

Hecht wrote most of his first book, *A Summoning of Stones,* characterized by its relative playfulness, during his year in Rome. The book appeared in 1954, the year in which Hecht also won a Guggenheim Fellowship, which allowed him to return to Rome. There he married his first wife, Patricia Harris. He resigned his post at Bard and did not return to teaching until 1956, when he took a post at Smith College in Northampton, Massachusetts. In 1959, he won his second Guggenheim and separated from his wife, who retained custody of their sons. They divorced in 1961. She later became engaged to a Belgian and left for Europe, taking the couple's sons with her. The effect on Hecht was considerable; clinically depressed, at his own request he was hospitalized for three months in Gracie Square Psychiatric Hospital in New York City—"Crazy Square," as some of the patients called it, and treated with thorazine and other drugs.

He appears to have been teaching at Bard when this hospitalization took place, having taken up his position there in 1961. He continued to teach at Bard until 1967, when he won a Rockefeller Award; in the following year he became an associate professor at the University of Rochester (New York). His second major collection, *The Hard Hours,* was published in 1967. It won the Pulitzer Prize for that year as well as the Russel Loines Award and led to Hecht's promotion to the John H. Deane Professor of Poetry and Rhetoric at the university, a post he held until 1985. Of more lasting importance, the book marked the advance of his poetic voice to one capable of speaking of the horrors within his experience.

In 1971 Hecht married Helen D'Alessandro, a cookery writer and interior designer who, by coincidence, had been a student of his at Smith College in the late 1950s. A Fulbright scholarship awarded in 1969 took him to Brazil, and in 1973 his translation with Helen Bacon of Aeschylus's *Seven against Thebes* appeared—a translation Hecht later expressed dissatisfaction with. This was followed four years later (nine years after *The Hard Hours*) by *Millions of Strange Shadows,* dedicated to his second wife. The book developed themes present in his second collection and was followed, with unusual celerity for Hecht, who is known as a slow and methodical writer, by *The Venetian Vespers* in 1979. The collection marked Hecht's development into a major writer of dramatic monologues.

In 1985 Hecht left Rochester and, attracted by the cultural range of Washington, D. C., took up a professorship at Georgetown University. His book of critical essays, *Obbligati,* appeared the following year. His next collection of verse, *The Transparent Man,* was not published until 1990. In that year Hecht changed publishers, leaving Atheneum and joining Knopf. The latter house published not just *The Transparent Man* but also *Collected Earlier Poems* (1990), including the entire texts of his previous three collections and the fifteen poems he wished to preserve from *A Summoning of Stones*. Hecht's stature became freshly apparent—in 1989 a highly complimentary series of essays on his work, *The Burdens of Formality,* appeared.

In 1993 the poet retired from teaching at the age of seventy, relieved no longer to have to witness the rise of political correctness at the expense of literature in the academy. Since his retirement, he has published two critical works, a study of Auden called *The Hidden Law* (1993), a penetrating critical work on a great poet by his poetic equal, and *On the Laws of the Poetic Art* (1995), part of the Andrew W. Mellon Lectures in the Fine Arts. The *Laws* examines the relationship of poetry to the arts of painting and music, and the volume also includes essays on poetry and morality, among others. (Hecht's criticism is notable, not surprisingly, for its valuing of art above the various ideologies with which contemporary literary criticism is beset. He has written penetratingly of such poets as Elizabeth Bishop, Richard Wilbur, and Robert Lowell, in the first two instances reserving especial praise for their hallowing of the visual world.) In 1996 he published another book of poems, *Flight among the Tombs,* with woodcuts by Leonard Baskin. The poet continued in the early part of the twenty-first century to publish in *The New Yorker* and the British magazine *Stand,* in which appears his remarkable poem "The Hanging Gardens of Tyburn," which is also featured in his collection, *The Darkness and the Light* (2001).

A SUMMONING OF STONES

The thirty poems of *A Summoning of Stones* are prefaced by an epigraph from George Santayana, a philosopher much admired by Hecht for his style. Santayana was a Harvard philoso-

pher who was the subject of three elegies by three poets, one by Hecht himself, one by Wallace Stevens, and one by Robert Lowell. The philosopher was widely admired for his refusal to acknowledge specialisms. The English novelist W. Somerset Maugham said of him in *A Writer's Notebook*: "It was a loss to American literature when Santayana decided to become a philosopher rather than a novelist." Hecht's choice of epigraph from Santayana reads: "to call the stones themselves to their ideal places, and enchant the very substance and skeleton of the world." The epigraph has a certain aptness. As noted in the Hoy interview, Hecht himself later referred to his first volume as the work of an advanced apprentice, though its virtuoso techniques were admired by many critics, including Louise Bogan, a writer for *The New Yorker.* Despite critical admiration, the poems very much have the sense of a young poet still not quite certain of his subject; Hecht was thirty-one years old when the book appeared. Plainly, by this stage, he was more than aware of "the skeleton of the world" but still was attempting to "enchant" it into some ideal through art.

Numerous pieces recall Hecht's models. "Samuel Sewall" is a persona poem much in the manner of John Crowe Ransom's "Tom, Tom, the Piper's Son" or "Miriam Tazewell." "Divisions upon a Ground" (retitled "Le Masseur de Ma Soeur" when the poem was reprinted in Hecht's *Collected Earlier Poems*) is a parody of Stevens's "Le Monocle de Mon Oncle." "A Deep Breath at Dawn" carries distinct echoes of the later works of William Butler Yeats. There is a certain awkwardness, which Hecht himself has commented on, in the elevated register of the poetry, its formal hauteur, and hints of the brutal experiences that the poet may have felt compelled to commemorate or honor but was as yet unable to address directly. Instead, Latinate diction and inverted syntax give many of the poems a mannered quality, a somewhat marmoreal elegance: the contemporary reader admires the surface glitter and flash but is left in the main unmoved. While many critics praised the volume's "baroque exuberance" and "great charm," one dissenting voice was that of the English poet-critic Donald Davie. He referred to the poetry's "insolently perfunctory attitude to subject matter. 'Think of a subject, then verify it,'" he presumed was Hecht's aesthetic procedure. In this he likened the poet to the older W. H. Auden.

While such criticism has its point, it is not entirely fair. *A Summoning of Stones* is, after all, a first book, displaying something of a virtuoso technique on the part of its author. Also, some of its pieces take the mannerisms of the Baroque style and produce delightful verse. "The Gardens of the Villa D'Este," for instance, is a witty, flamboyant celebration of sensuality set in the villa of the poem's title. Formally expert, the poem's eight-line stanzas rhyme *abcddcba,* that is, from the center outward, amusingly echoing the sexual congress of the poem's content. Here he is describing how

> . . . the giggling water drops
> Past haunches, over ledges, out of mouths, and
>   stops
> In a still pool, but, by a plumber's ruse,
> Rises again to laugh and squirt
> At heaven, and is still
>
> Busy descending. White
> Ejaculations leap to teach
> How fertile are these nozzles; the streams run
> Góngora through the garden, channel themselves,
>   and pass
> To lily-padded ease, where insubordinate lass
> And lad can cool their better parts, where sun
> Heats them again to furnace pitch
> To prove his law is light.

Fifteen poems from *A Summoning of Stones* survived Hecht's later scrutiny to be republished in his *Collected Earlier Poems.* They show the young poet as already a considerable talent.

With his next volume, however, he attained poetic maturity; "an insolently perfunctory attitude to subject matter" is an accusation no critic would be able to make, with validity, of that volume's contents.

THE HARD HOURS

The American expatriate poet T. S. Eliot once observed that there are two ways to establish a considerable reputation as a poet. One is to publish as widely as one is able. The other is to publish sparingly, and only work of the highest quality. Hecht's route has been the latter. Thirteen years passed between the appearance of his first book and *The Hard Hours,* which won a Pulitzer Prize in 1968. The book's subject matter is, predominantly, the Holocaust. In his *Collected Earlier Poems,* Hecht significantly placed *The Hard Hours* first, reprinting all its thirty-one pieces. The collection begins with "A Hill," which shows how far his style had come from the ornate and somewhat orotund manner of much of the first book, while not entirely forsaking those qualities. The poem begins, colloquially, even jauntily:

> In Italy, where this sort of thing can occur,
> I had a vision once,—though you understand
> It was nothing at all like Dante's, or the visions of
>   saints,
> And perhaps not a vision at all. . . .

The scene is a market place in a "warm, sunlit piazza." The narrator is with friends near the "great Farnese Palace," one of Rome's most magnificent palaces, which suddenly dissolves, "for all its marble," along with the entire scene, leaving a "mole-colored and bare" hill in its place. The landscape is one of sheer desolation; the trees are "like old ironwork gathered for scrap / Outside a factory wall." There are ominous details: the narrator thinks he hears the "crack of a rifle"; he sees a "ribbon snagged on a hedge." The scene finally dissolves, and the narrator is "restored / To the sunlight and my friends." Giving a reason for the recounting of the episode, the narrator informs us that he has just "today" remembered the location of the hill: "it lies just to the left / Of the road north of Poughkeepsie; and as a boy / I stood before it for hours in wintertime."

The piece is written efficiently in a rather buoyant mix of iambs, trochees, anapests, and dactyls. It has a documentary tone which does not entirely sacrifice lyric elements. The scene is presented without explication, and readers are left to make of it what they will. We have it from the poet's own account, however, that he has always associated emotional barrenness such as he experienced in childhood with desolated landscapes. This may help explain, for instance, why the boy stood before the hill "for hours in wintertime": the hill is not necessarily literal but, as it were, a psychic hill, an image of resonance for the author. The placement of "A Hill," with its contrasting scenes—one of vigor, life, and Italian gaiety and the other of deathly silence and barrenness—is significant in the context of what follows.

The Hard Hours shows Hecht to be a poet of psychological horror whose artistry intensifies rather than diminishes the power of the scenes he sets before the reader. If all mastery in art is joyful, the tension between both the giving of aesthetic pleasure and the sheer pleasure experienced by the poet in writing and the grimness of his subject matter lies at the root of Hecht's difficult art. The so-called anti-poets of World War II, such as the Polish writer Tadeusz Rózewicz, attempted to write poetry from which it would be impossible to derive aesthetic pleasure. In 1960 Rózewicz (as quoted in *The Truth of Poetry,* 1972) wrote:

> I cannot understand that poetry should survive
>   when the men who
> created that poetry are dead. One of the premises
>   and incentives for my
> poetry is a disgust with poetry. What I revolted

against was that it had
survived the end of the world, as though nothing
had happened.

Rózewicz wrote a severely literal, stripped-down poetry, eschewing the art's formal possibilities. Hecht's artistic method was different. While we are appalled by the content of some of his poems, we cannot but admire the skill evident in their construction, and our admiration, at times, is curiously implicating. We become voyeurs of the horrific. The poet presents horror in hammered craftsmanship that, paradoxically, increases its voltage. Throughout his work from this point will be found the distinct note of a poetic master working with the most brutal materials.

A case in point is one of the volume's most singular poems, "'More Light! More Light!'" The poem's title is a translation of the reputed deathbed last words of the German poet Johann Wolfgang von Goethe, who was fascinated by the phenomenon of light and attempted to disprove Sir Isaac Newton's theories on the subject. In the context of the poem itself, its title has a harsh irony. The poem is written in quatrains rhyming *abcb.* It opens by detailing the story of a Christian martyr being burned at the stake after composing in the Tower of London "these moving verses," which we are not shown, almost in illustration of the uselessness of the enterprise. The qualifier "moving" takes on an ironic futility in these circumstances: "Nor was he forsaken of courage, but the death was horrible." The affirming initial clause is balanced by the negation of the second: before what some readers may consider the absolute of death, courage or the lack of it is—almost—irrelevant.

After describing the martyr's brutal end, the poem's content changes rapidly, in the manner of a film and in documentary fashion, with the opening of the fourth stanza. "We move now to outside a German wood," the narrator flatly announces. The poem continues:

> Three men are there commanded to dig a hole
> In which the two Jews are ordered to lie down
> And be buried alive by the third, who is a Pole.
>
> Not light from the shrine at Weimar beyond the
>   hill
> Nor light from heaven appeared. But he did refuse.
> A Luger settled back deeply in its glove.
> He was ordered to change places with the Jews.
>
> Much casual death had drained away their souls.
> The thick dirt mounted toward the quivering chin.
> When only the head was exposed the order came
> To dig him out again and to get back in.
>
> No light, no light in the blue Polish eye.
> When he finished a riding boot packed down the
>   earth.
> The Luger hovered lightly in its glove.
> He was shot in the belly and in three hours bled
>   to death.

The Nazi officer is identified only by a "riding boot" and by the Luger, which is given, as it were, an absolute force by the construction "its glove." The glove, and by extension the Nazi, belongs to the gun, not vice versa. The dehumanization of the Jews and the Pole is emphasized by the use of the definite article instead of the possessive: "*the* quivering chin," "*the* head," "*the* blue Polish eye" [my italics]. The poem presents a tableau of impersonal horror, and the Pole regains "*his* eyes" [my italics] only in the final line of the poem, when he is dead. In complete negation of the poem's title, blocking out the light he can no longer see, the "black soot" of incinerated Jews settles on his face from the chimneys nearby.

The Holocaust and the author's awareness of recent history shadow much of the collection. Poems such as the four-part sequence "Rites and Ceremonies" examine it directly, its opening section with forthright ironic power echoing the beginning of Gerard Manley Hopkins's

"Wreck of the Deutschland," his poem of belief that elegizes five nuns who drowned at sea; such affirmation is unavailable to Hecht. The sequence delineates in harrowing terms the history of Jewish persecution, from medieval times up to the Holocaust.

Even where that event is not explicated directly, it leaves its mark in other poems. "Third Avenue in Sunlight" is a sardonic look at daytime drinking in New York. It opens, flatly, "Third Avenue in sunlight" and continues in a matter of fact tone, "Nature's error." The poem's narrator recounts the life of one of the avenue's drinkers, a former associate called John who is plagued by memories of aggression by his peers in childhood. The poem closes:

> Daily the prowling sunlight whets its knife
> Along the sidewalk. We almost never meet.
> In the Rembrandt dark he lifts his amber life.
> My bar is somewhat further down the street.

There is a movement in the poem involving light. If, at the poem's opening, Nature is held sardonically to be in "error" for shining on Third Avenue, at the close, the sunlight is an assassin. The "we" could refer to a personification of the sunlight and narrator or to the narrator and John or both. How one reads the poem depends upon whether one considers it to have elements of autobiography. If one does, then the narrator may be read as making a bleak comment on the relative mildness of John's experience compared with his own, more grievous experience. John lives in the "Rembrandt dark": he is like a character in a painting. If the poem is seen as autobiographical, one reading is that there is something artistic about John's suffering; it has something of a posture to it. Furthermore, the word "somewhat" in the closing line then becomes freighted with wry sardonicism, and the "down" takes on a punning element, meaning not just distance but depth. Without assuming autobiography, the poem has perhaps less power. It becomes more purely observation.

The volume's closing poem, "'It Out-Herods Herod. Pray You, Avoid It,'" like several other poems in the collection, such as "Adam" and "Jason" (the names of the poet's sons by his first marriage), adopts a more domestic note than the major Holocaust pieces. Here, as a Jew with sons, the narrator of the poem (which it is fair to read as Hecht himself) does not simply become an icily horrified observer but also is implicated with his sons as potential victims of Nazi ideology.

The poem is sparely written in three-beat, or tetrameter, quatrains rhyming *abab,* in predominantly plain language. It opens in familial intimacy:

> Tonight my children hunch
> Toward their Western, and are glad
> As, with a Sunday punch,
> The Good casts out the Bad.
>
> And in their fairy tales
> The warty giant and witch
> Get sealed in doorless jails
> And the match-girl strikes it rich.
>
> I've made myself a drink.
> The giant and witch are set
> To bust out of the clink
> When my children have gone to bed.

While the children live in the world of the fairy tale, the adult narrator's recourse is to make himself a drink, perhaps in preparation for the horrors of memory likely to emerge when the children are in bed. The plain, matter-of-fact nature of the first line of the third stanza undercuts the fanciness of the previous lines. There is an ironic humor about the use of the slang phrase "bust out of the clink." The slanginess is in inverse relationship to the implication behind the statement. Then follow three stanzas in which the register of the poem changes significantly, becoming biblical in timbre. Here is the second of them:

> For the wicked have grown strong,
> Their numbers mock at death,

> Their cow brings forth its young,
> Their bull engendereth.

Here, the repetition of the verbal structure in the final three lines endows the stanza with an air of processional inevitability. The closing three stanzas bring the reader back to the narrator's children, who, "by quite other laws . . . make their case," positing a hero, "Half God, half Santa Claus" but resembling their father, who puts the world to rights. The poem closes with the father's wish that "their sleep be sound" and his admission of helplessness in the face of ideologies larger than the individual.

The Hard Hours was received, understandably, as a major event in American poetry. It established Hecht's as a poetic voice capable of dealing with the bleakest realities, at the same time confirming his reputation for poetic artistry of a high order.

MILLIONS OF STRANGE SHADOWS

After the extremities and power of *The Hard Hours,* which shows Hecht's art at its barest, *Millions of Strange Shadows* contained a number of new elements. The volume is dedicated to the poet's second wife, Helen, and takes its title from the opening lines of Shakespeare's fifty-third sonnet. Some aspects of the poet's playfulness, present in his first book and mainly absent from the second, begin to reappear, and some of the poems turn from an examination of external violence to the poet himself.

The collection opens with "The Cost," a virtuoso performance in a dozen six-line stanzas rhyming *abacbc;* the mix of dactylic and anapestic meters in which the poem is written gives it a bounce and vigor at least partly in keeping with its subject. The poem is set in Rome. The narrator wittily counterpoints a young contemporary couple on a Vespa, a variety of Italian scooter, turning around the base of Trajan's Column, with "two thousand raw recruits," who also turn, in the narrator's historical imagination, "eternally" round it. These recruits are part of the force of the Roman emperor Trajan that fought in the Dacian Wars, which, we are told, "lasted fifteen years." Even Trajan himself (A.D. 52/53–117) is a mere swirl "in the motes kicked up by the cough and spate / Of the Vespa's blue exhaust." The poem's narrator in "The Cost"—the cost here being happiness as the price for knowledge—advises for the couple a blissful ignorance, which he, by dint of greater experience and pensiveness, cannot achieve. The poem ends with the narrator's ironic observation that, in any case, the Dacian Wars, fifteen years in duration, won only "seven years of peace."

It is possible to read this poem with reference to Hecht's own biography, though it also links in sensibility to a translated sonnet in *The Hard Hours,* "The Thoughtful Roisterer Declines the Gambit," in which the speaker states sardonically his reasons for not wishing to fight in another man's war. In "The Cost" both lyric celebrator and realist are present, the former in the vigor and vivacity of the poem's descriptions—it revels in movement—and the latter in the considering voice that recalls the lessons of history. The narrator wishes for the couple a life free of history; his own voice, however, is given gravitas and power by both elements in the poem.

One can see "The Cost" as a gateway into the collection as a whole, as in some ways "A Hill" was to *The Hard Hours.* Many of the poems contain similar counterpoints between a lyric energy and a contemplative gravitas, taking power from each. Some have more of one quality than of the other. "Goliardic Song," for instance, is a witty celebration of sensuality. The poet indulges forgetfulness to write a small hymn of praise to the "classic poise" of Venus Pandemos, "Ur-Satirist of Morals / And Mother of our Joys." The poem takes an added force from its rarity in Hecht's corpus. The Goliards of the poem's title were wandering scholars who

composed the *Carmina Burana,* the "bawdy songs" in German and Latin that were set as a piece of choral music by the German composer Carl Orff. Its three eight-line stanzas, rhyming *ababcdcd,* and tetrameter lines endow it with a pleasing jauntiness. Lyric—and comic—celebrator prevails, regarding indulgently

> We who have been her students,
> Matriculated clerks
> In scholia of imprudence,
> And vast, venereal Works,

These are students who have "Taken and passed our orals." The comedy comes from the contrast between the learned register ("scholia of imprudence")—"scholia" are commentaries or annotations, especially on a classical text—and the shambling, chaotic, gland-prompted reality to which it refers as well as, for example, the pun on "orals." This is a rare instance in Hecht of the unabashedly comic poem.

Elsewhere the poet balances this relative levity. "The Feast of Stephen" extrapolates beyond its opening line from "the coltish horseplay of the locker room," the athleticism of young men in showers and gyms, to the realities of violence perpetrated by gangs of young men on other young men. The poem comprises a four-part sequence of unrhymed sonnets. The sequence sees the large-scale atrocities in the small-scale acts of violence. The language employed ripples with muscularity mimetic of the male figures described. The youth's horseplay is "coltish," and they are "sheathed in glistening light, / flexed and alert." The repetition of the "l" consonant in four of the final five words in that quote, plus the matching pairs of narrow and broad vowels, buttress the line's content. The poem crackles with understated violence, where "blond boys" "flick their live butts into the standing weeds." Even the weather is described in terms of power: "the kilowatts of noon." The sequence derives its title from Boxing Day, a church festival commemorating Saint Stephen, the first Christian martyr, who was stoned to death. The poem takes some of its power from the poet's cool recounting; his noncondemnatory tone; even, in the second sonnet, his willingness to see the exhilaration of the healthy body. The poem ends:

In the kilowatts of noon, they've got one cornered.
The bugs are jumping, and the burly youths
Strip to the waist for the hot work ahead.
They go to arm themselves at the dry-stone wall,
Having flung down their wet and salty garments
At the feet of a young man whose name is Saul.
He watches sharply these superbly tanned
Figures with a swimmer's chest and shoulders,
A miler's thighs, with their self-conscious grace,
And in between their sleek, converging bodies,
Brilliantly oiled and burnished by the sun,
He catches a brief glimpse of bloodied hair
And hears an unintelligible prayer.

Saul was the name of Saint Paul, who converted to Christianity after first persecuting Christians. The "one" may at first appear to be human or animal. The term "one" objectifies and, by doing so, coolly increases the horror. The youths' violence, yet to be committed, is described simply as "hot work," with its ironic implication of something meritorious. In the fourth line quoted, there is an echo of Robert Frost's "Mending Wall," that decidedly ambiguous poem about the value of boundaries. The "prayer" of the poem's closure may be "unintelligible" because it is a shriek, a cry of pain. Or it may be unintelligible because it is in another language, confirming the poem's theme of the victimization of the different. The addition of the religious element in the implied conversion of Saul, in a modern context, offers a barely present redemption.

The volume also saw the continuation of poems concerning family and domesticity that Hecht had begun with "The Vow" and "'It Out-Herods Herod. Pray You, Avoid It,'" in *The Hard Hours*. Among them were "A Birthday Poem," a love poem for the poet's wife, and

"The Odds," dedicated to the poet's third son, Evan. "The Odds" shows various aspects of Hecht's art. Its eight strictly rhymed stanzas open with a breathtaking description of an overnight snowfall:

Three new and matching loaves,
Each set upon a motionless swing seat,
Straight from some elemental stoves
And winter bakeries of unearthly wheat,
In diamonded, smooth pillowings of white
Have risen out of nothing overnight.

In a striking comparison, the snowfall represents, albeit coldly, something creative and nourishing, though the reader is vaguely troubled by those "elemental stoves," which conjure, in passing, the gas ovens of the concentration camps. Throughout the next three stanzas, however, the poet notices increasingly the irregularities and chaos of the winter scene, until at the opening of the fourth stanza, it has become "A sort of stagy show / Put on by a spoiled, eccentric millionaire." By the end of that stanza the scene represents "the spent, / Loose, aimless squanderings of the discontent."

This immediately brings to the poet's mind a bold comparison between these "aimless squanderings" and sperm dying "in dark fallopian canals" or "that wild strew of bodies at My Lai." The poem, we are told, is being written in the eleventh year of the war in Vietnam. (My Lai, one of the grimmer episodes of the Vietnam War, involved the massacre of some five hundred unarmed civilians, including women and children, by American soldiers, on the morning of March 16, 1968.) Then follow four lines beginning "Yet," detailing how, in the midst of these circumstances—snowfall, war—and despite "these incalculable odds" (a reference to the survival rate of sperm), "My son is born, and in his mother's eyes / Turns the whole war and winter into lies."

If "Yet" is a pivotal word in the poem, the phrase "my son is born" acts as a door from the barrenness of war and winter into a room of gratitude for the child's birth. The narrator's, that is, the father's, attitude, however, is contrasted sharply with the mother's. For him, "voices underground / Demand, Who died for him? Who gave him place?" For her, the whole war and winter are "lies." Snow falling in Hecht's work seems to function, in this and later poems, as a motif for natural and, by extension, human chaos. The poem closes with the narrator comparing the snowflakes descending to those small ornaments one knew as a child, in which "Christmas storms of manageable size" settle. They are: "A tiny settlement among those powers / That shape our world, but that are never ours." The "settlement" refers to the controlled snowfall and conjures, too, the idea of "settlement" as a group of dwellings. The qualifier "tiny" emphasizes the settlement's vulnerability. "Those powers" may be taken to be the violent forces of the external world. The narrator concedes a frail tenderness to mother and child but is unable to rescind the harsher knowledge of the force of external reality. To him, birth is not an absolute in this world; "those powers" are.

THE VENETIAN VESPERS

The Venetian Vespers appeared in 1979 and was composed rapidly by Hecht, who is usually a slow writer. The center of the book comprises two dramatic monologues, "The Grapes" and the book's title poem, and two narratives in blank verse, "The Deodand" and "The Short End." Eleven shorter poems, including versions of poems by Joseph Brodsky, Horace, and Pierre de Ronsard, complete the collection.

The volume's longer poems led Langdon Hammer to describe Hecht, in an interview in the *Sewanee Review* of 1996, as "the living master of dramatic monologue." The form has an honorable lineage, from the greatest of its earliest practitioners in English, Shakespeare,

through William Wordsworth, Robert Browning, and Robert Frost. We can discern two varieties, both present in Hecht's book. In the first, a single character speaks in the first person, addressing a silent listener, or listeners, whose identity may or may not be important, as indicated by the tones and subject matter of the speaker. Interpolations by the silent listener may be assumed in the responses of the speaker of the monologue. The second variety is a conventional narrative; the speaker is a godlike narrator informing the reader.

Hecht's book opens with "The Grapes," spoken by a chambermaid at the *Hôtel de l'Univers et Déjeuner*. The character has her origins, we know from the poet himself, in a woman in furs whom he once encountered in a Parisian bar. "She used to be our stripper," he was told, "but then she married a Swiss Millionaire." Hecht's chambermaid has never met her millionaire, and the monologue is the touching—some might say terrifying—account of her realization not only that now such an event is unlikely but also that even more modest hopes are dwindling rapidly.

The poem opens by contrasting the hotel where she works, on a mountainside that is shadowed by the mountain from the early morning light, with the *Beau Rivage* across the valley, which misses the early morning light but receives the light late in the day. (The opening is striking not just for what Hecht makes of this but also because it shows his superb eye.) The maid explains that, for this reason, the *Beau Rivage* appears to attract "the younger set, which likes to get up late"; the patrons of her own hotel tend to be older. The situation permits the poet to utilize his gift for description: "At cocktail time," he writes of the other hotel's inhabitants, "their glasses glint like gems, while we're eclipsed." The maid continues:

Still, it is strange and sad, at cocktail time,
To look across the valley from our shade,
As if from premature death, at all that brilliance

Across which silently on certain days
Shadows of clouds slide past in smooth parade,
While even our daisies and white irises
Are filled with blues and darkened premonitions.

The loveliness of this description shows the accuracy of Hecht's eye. Those white flowers are filled with "blues" because, as any photographer knows, shadowed light has a large blue component. The human brain compensates for this in situ, but the objective lens of a camera records it. And whites, photographed in shade, appear blue when the images are viewed in a separate context. Also hovering at the back of this flower description is the pun on "the blues"; the chambermaid projects her own feelings onto the flowers in a gentle, pathetic fallacy.

The chambermaid—whose name is never divulged, confirming her anonymity—then reveals her dreams at night about Marc-Antoine, a bellboy at the *Beau Rivage*. She is at least ten years older than the bellboy; he has never taken the slightest notice of her and "no doubt" dreams of a young millionairess. The chambermaid desires Marc-Antoine, who desires someone else: the irony of Eros. At the poem's center is the chambermaid's vision of a "crystal bowl of grapes / in ice-water." The grapes are gorgeously described:

They were a sort of pure, unblemished jade,
Like turbulent ocean water, with misted skins,
Their own pale, smoky sweat, or tiny frost.
. . . .
And all those little bags of glassiness,
Those clustered planets, leaned their eastern
    cheeks
Into the sunlight, each one showing a soft
Meridian swelling where the thinning light
Mysteriously tapered into shadow,
To cool recesses, to the tranquil blues
That then were pillowing the *Beau Rivage*.

The grapes seem mimetic of the earth itself. They are described as "clustered planets," and their cheeks are "eastern." The connection of

their own shadows to those of the *Beau Rivage* links them to cosmic processes; the large is seen in the diminutive. This vision is taken by the maid as an intimation: "I seemed to know / In my blood the meaning of sidereal time / And know my little life had somehow crested."

One can compare such a piece with another monologue spoken by a woman, Robert Frost's "A Servant to Servants." Hecht has said he chooses women characters so that they could not possibly be him, perhaps in irritation at a dogged reading of his work by some critics as invariably autobiographical. Frost tends to eschew the opportunity for gorgeous description seized upon by Hecht. In Frost, the character's plight is paramount. His poem is interesting precisely for its narrative content and capturing of the woman's speaking voice. One has the sense, reading "The Grapes," however, that to Hecht the descriptions are as important as the delineation of the chambermaid's character. In this most painterly of poets, to some degree the marvel of description drives the poem.

The book's title poem is also a model of description. Multilayered, it rewards numerous readings. It is nominally a monologue by an expatriate American, living in the latter part of his life on an annuity left him by his uncle. He grew up as the son of Latvian immigrants who settled in Lawrence, Massachusetts, where his father and uncle ran an A & P store. The boy's childhood was tragic. He was only six when his mother died. His father, after traveling to better himself, was mugged and, speaking little English, was incarcerated in Ohio. His uncle, fearing that community scandal would damage his business, ignored three letters from the authorities regarding his brother, who died at the age of forty. During World War II, the narrator enlisted on the day after his father's burial, was considered mentally unsound after two and a half years working as a nurse, and was discharged on psychological grounds. The narrator suspects that the uncle has been sexually involved with his mother, in an echo of Hamlet, and is even unsure of his own provenance, that is, whether his annuity is due to his uncle's guilt over his father or for straightforward biological reasons.

The poem is divided into six sections. The first section comprises mainly a catalogue of disgust: objects, images the narrator finds revolting, recur to him, and he catalogues them obsessively. There is a certain fastidious temperament—sometimes adolescents possess it—that has a heightened sensitivity to the ugly in everyday life, in which images brand themselves on the memory beyond the control of the observer. So it seems with the narrator in Hecht's poem. The second section is set in Venice and is full of Venetian literary history and local color. The third section describes the narrator's life in Venice, ending with an account of his wartime experiences. The fourth section recalls the shop where the narrator was brought up and his mother's death, ending with an epiphany, in the present, of a Venetian rainstorm. The fifth section largely describes the narrator's knowledge of his father's fate and the memory of his burial, and the poem's closing section affects an attempt at a summation of his life, with the narrator cooling his temple at the window glass. The poem's closure is a description of clouds at evening, which reverts to five lines of the narrator's entirely negative view of himself.

"The Venetian Vespers" is an intensely visual poem. (Hecht has commented that he set it in Venice as much to describe the city as to grant his narrator a voice.) The narrator escapes from his predicament and preoccupation with self only through the blessed self-forgetful attentiveness of the eye. Here he is describing part of the interior of the Cathedral of Saint Mark's. Out of the "obscure aquarium dimness,"

> . . . Gradually
> Glories reveal themselves, grave mysteries
> Of the faith cast off their shadows, assume their
>   forms

Against a heaven of coined and sequined light,
A splatter of gilt cobblestones, flung grains
Or crumbs of brilliance, the vast open fields
Of the sky turned intimate and friendly. Patines
And laminae, a vermeil shimmering
Of fish-scaled, cataphracted golden plates.

Such writing is all gorgeous surface; it reminds one of the Irish writer Michael McLaverty's exhortation to the young poet Seamus Heaney: "'Description is revelation!'" (from Heaney's "Fosterage," in *North*, 1975). Hecht here weighs the words with immense care. There is a solid dependability in the use of such terms as "patines," a film or encrustation produced by oxidation on the surface of old bronze; "vermeil," which is gilded silver, bronze, or other metal, here used as an adjective; and "cataphracted," a zoological term referring to the armor of plate covering some fishes.

The narrator's memories of his wartime experiences, however, provide some of the poem's most moving moments, as he recalls

> . . . a corporal I knew in Heavy Weapons,
> Someone who carried with him into combat
> A book of etiquette by Emily Post.
> Most brought with them some token of the past,
> Some emblem of attachment or affection
> Or coddled childhood — bibles and baby booties,
> Harmonicas, love letters, photographs —
> But this was different. I discovered later
> That he had been brought up in an orphanage,
> So the book was his fiction of kindliness,
> A novel in which personages of wealth
> Firmly secure domestic tranquility.
> He'd cite me instances. It seems a boy
> Will not put "Mr." on his calling cards
> Till he leaves school . . .
> . . . .
> This was to him a sort of *Corpus Juris,*
> An ancient piety and governance
> Worthy of constant dream and meditation.
> He haunts me here, that seeker after law
> In a lawless world, in rainsoaked combat boots,
> Oil-stained fatigues and heavy bandoleers.
> He was killed by enemy machine-gun fire.

The character's clinging to some kind of order and pattern is deeply affecting. One finds a similar—if less illusory—quality in Hecht's own devotion to the art of poetry and in the exquisite formality of his craftsmanship.

If the longer narratives form the centerpiece of this collection, the volume is also notable for a number of powerful short poems. These are often stained by the poet's wartime experiences. "Still Life," a beautiful description of rising dawn gracefully written in five six-line stanzas rhyming *abcabc,* leaves the poet—who has identified himself in interview as the speaker in this poem—standing "beneath a pine-tree in the cold, / Just before dawn, somewhere in Germany, / A cold, wet, Garand rifle in my hands." Until the final line, upon which the whole poem is founded, as it were, there is no intimation of anything but pastoral beauty in the piece. The closure entirely transforms the poem. The rifle and Hecht, the soldier holding it, govern the scene with the absolute of potential violence, whether to be committed by or against them; the poem becomes one of waiting menace. It uses a structure common in Hecht's work: he will begin with scenes of often exquisite natural description, only to set them in the context of grimmer realities, even if merely for a line or two.

Thus, "House Sparrows," dedicated to Joe and U. T. Summers (Joe Summers was a colleague of the poet's at Rochester), describes the birds affectionately, their voices enacting "Forsythian spring with primavernal racket." *Passer domesticus* is a common European passerine, gregarious by nature. One hundred birds were introduced into Brooklyn, New York, in 1851, and the species has since settled along the eastern seaboard of America. The poet's characteristic darker shades come after he describes the birds as "Salt of the earth." "The common clay," "meek *émigrés*" they are, he tells us:

> . . . given to nervous flight, the troubled sleep
> Of those who remember terrible events,
> The wide-eyed, anxious haste of the exiled.

He goes on to observe that we have seen such frailty as theirs before, "In pictures of Biafra and Auschwitz." The poem closes:

> Yet here they are, these chipper stratoliners,
> Unsullen, unresentful, full of the grace
> Of cheerfulness, who seem to greet all comers
> With the wild confidence of Forty-Niners,
> And, to the lively honor of their race,
> Rude canticles of "Summers, Summers,
>   Summers."

There is a wry comedy here, of course, in the hyperbole of describing such diminutive birds as "stratoliners," early Boeing aircraft, and in comparing the birds to the hopeful prospectors of the 1849 Californian gold rush. The closing phrase may be read not merely as a pun upon the surname of the poem's dedicatees but also as referring to Jewish and other expatriates who, "full of the grace / of cheerfulness," partake of the unbeatable optimism of nature. The sparrows repeat the same phrase over and over, obsessively, as if willing a different reality. They are the eternal, harrowed optimists. The rhythm of those "canticles" that the birds almost chant is also, from an ornithological point of view, reasonably accurate. The song of the house sparrow is a series of chirps in trochaic meter. And there is a lovely ambiguity in "rude," meaning both "rudimentary" and "defying social convention."

As if placed in the volume in deliberate opposition and implying that the irreducible buoyancy of the sparrows—and, perhaps, of their human counterparts—is beyond him, the preceding poem, "Persistences," describes a bleak winter scene in processional quatrains that grant the poem's movement an air of inevitability (as often with Hecht). Out of this scene emerges, in Hardyesque fashion, "a ghostly equipage,"

> Ancestral deputations
> Wound in the whited air,
> To whom some sentry flings a slight,
> Prescriptive, "Who goes there?"

"Wound in the whited air" recalls Yeats's "Wound in mind's pondering/ As mummies in the mummy-cloth are wound," from "All Souls' Night." The deputations are wrapped in the snowy air, and the narrator wonders about their identity. Are they "loved ones" once offended or the "torturers" of childhood, adults and schoolmates? The poem concludes:

> Who comes here seeking justice,
> Or in its high despite,
> Bent on some hopeless interview
> On wrongs nothing can right?
>
> Those throngs disdain to answer,
> Though numberless as flakes;
> Mine is the task to find out words
> For their memorial sakes
>
> Who press in dense approaches,
> Blue numeral tattoos
> Writ crosswise on their arteries,
> The burning, voiceless Jews.

While, according to Hecht, Nazism is largely considered by the Vatican to have been a pagan phenomenon, Hecht himself has contradicted this in interview, regarding it as a movement with a Christian background. The image of the cross formed by the concentration camp tattoos and the arteries of the Jews in the final stanzas is complex and grievous, implying, as it may, a revenge on Judaism for the crucifixion of Christ. The numberless "flakes" of Jews connect to the "huge helices of snow" that blank out the narrator's view at the poem's opening of the "feathery" Victorian-laced trees. The poet returns to his felt duty of commemoration of the nameless victims of the Holocaust, a theme he later revisited, with singular focus, in his next book, *The Transparent Man.*

THE TRANSPARENT MAN

The Transparent Man was Hecht's first book after eleven years. It is divided into five sec-tions, opening with a somewhat saturnine batch of six poems. These poems are followed by "See Naples and Die," a dramatic monologue spoken by a man about the breakup of his marriage, set against the backdrop of Naples. "A Love for Four Voices," which celebrates love in all its guises and takes four characters from *A Midsummer Night's Dream,* makes up the third section. The piece is a "Homage to Franz Joseph Haydn." The fourth section comprises a series of unusually comic poems, for Hecht, and the book closes with seven poems on more tradition-ally Hechtian themes: there are three elegies, two of them for the poets L. E. Sissman and James Wright, respectively. This last section also includes the title poem, a dramatic mono-logue spoken by a woman fatally ill with leukemia, and "The Book of Yolek," a harrow-ing and eerie sestina that Hoy called "one of the very best poems to have come out of the Holocaust."

Among the centerpieces of the book are once again the dramatic monologues. "The Transpar-ent Man" is spoken by an unnamed thirty-year-old woman who is being visited in a cancer ward on a holiday Sunday by a Mrs. Curtis, making the rounds with a book trolley. The speaker makes it plain that this is her only visi-tor. The poem opens touchingly with the speaker noting how the visitors to other patients, out of kindness, feel it incumbent on them to offer her chocolates and fruitcake; she feels a little "conspicuous and in the way." She considers, however, that "it's better for me without a fam-ily; / It's a great blessing." Her father, who is alive, cannot visit; the daughter looks too much like his dead wife for him to bear observing her terminal illness. The speaker in the poem, Hecht has indicated, is based upon Flannery O'Connor, the Georgia-born novelist and short story writer who died at the age of thirty-nine in 1964 of the chronic autoimmune disease lupus. Hecht, who knew her, was impressed by what struck him as her insouciance and relative unconcern before the fact of her own mortality. "The Transparent Man" is in part his elegy for her; hence its presence among other elegies in the book's closing section.

The speaker in this poem is notable for her lack of self-absorption and self-pity, despite her description of her condition as

> . . . a sort of blizzard in the bloodstream,
> A deep, severe, unseasonable winter,
> Burying everything. The white blood cells
> Multiply crazily and storm around,
> Out of control. . . .

Again we have the image of a snowstorm as symbolic of chaos. The speaker's cool tone increases the poem's plangency. "The Transparent Man" refers to a model of a human being made up of transparent plastic, its "circulatory system all mapped out / In rivers of red and blue," which the speaker and a friend, May Beth Finley, now a Sister of Mercy, used to giggle over as children. She observes the trees beyond her window and compares the structure of their branches and twigs to

> . . . magnificent enlargements
> Of the vascular system of the human brain.
> I see them there like huge discarnate minds,
> Lost in their meditative silences.
> The trunks, branches and twigs compose the
>   vessels
> That feed and nourish vast immortal thoughts.

She imagines one as the brain of Beethoven and another as that of Johannes Kepler. A sense of astonishment at the world, beyond the fact of her own death, is powerfully conveyed. She thinks of how the trees soon will be almost obliterated by simplifying snow, in a bitter image that presages her own coming death, yet their "thickness of particulars" will remain present below the snow's white weight. The poem offers a frail, intellectual consolation in the face of mortality.

"See Naples and Die" charts the end of a marriage, in six sections. The poem contains gorgeous incidentals, lavishly described with Hechtian flourish, but the couple is unable to appreciate fully the spectacular setting of their holiday; instead, it forms an ironic contrast to the barrenness of their emotional life. The poem's speaker starts by reconstructing from his journal the circumstances of a visit to Naples made by him and his wife, Martha. It begins in the present:

> We forget much, of course, and, along with facts,
> Our strong emotions, of pleasure and of pain,
> Fade into stark insensibility.
> For which, perhaps, it need be said, thank God.

Conversely, the disturbing persistence of memory is in part the subject of the penultimate poem in the volume. "The Book of Yolek" is a sestina, a form that uses six six-line stanzas, six terminal words, and a three-line envoy. Hecht's poem is a stunning example of the potentials of the repetition of this form as well as a harrowing account of the Holocaust, refracted through a particular instance—the death of one little boy. We know from the poet's own account that the raw materials for the poem came from *Anthology of Holocaust Literature,* edited by Jacob Glatstein, Israel Knox, and Samuel Margoshes—as well as from his own war experiences. Hecht read in this volume Hanna Markowick-Olczakova's piece about the Jewish educator Janosz Korczak who, refusing to part with children he knew were headed for death camps, went to his death with them. The essay is entitled "Yanosz Korczak's Last Walk" and mentions, among the children, "little Hanka with the lung trouble, Yolek who was ill." Hecht did not remember the account accurately—in his poem he gives Yolek bad lungs. Its German epigraph translates as "We have a law / And by that law he must die"—Martin Luther's translation of a biblical passage, John 19:7.

Hecht uses the repetitions inherent in the standard form of the sestina, which lends itself to a slow buildup of gravity, in a masterly way. The poem's narrator begins with sylvan ease, on holiday, among midsummer hills in the opening stanza. This scene prompts the narrator to remember, "peacefully, an earlier day / In childhood" when he became lost on a nature walk and "thought of home." The terminal words, set up in the opening stanza, are "meal," "walk," "to," "home," "camp," and "day." At the opening of the third stanza, the poem changes register, becoming strictly factual. The languid destination indicated by the "to" in the opening stanza becomes, for instance, a date. Here are the third and fourth stanzas:

> The fifth of August, 1942.
> It was morning and very hot. It was the day
> They came at dawn with rifles to The Home
> For Jewish Children, cutting short the meal
> Of bread and soup, lining them up to walk
> In close formation off to a special camp.

> How often you have thought about that camp,
> As though in some strange way you were driven
> to,
> And about the children, and how they were made
> to walk,
> Yolek who had bad lungs, who wasn't a day
> Over five years old, commanded to leave his meal
> And shamble between armed guards to his long
> home.

In this context, the terminal words take on a sinister tone. The summer "camp" of the opening stanzas becomes the concentration "camp" of the latter stanzas. As a "special camp" in the first stanza quoted, it echoes sardonically the euphemistic language used by the Nazis themselves; the leisurely "walk" becomes the forced "walk."

The final three stanzas deal with the effect, in memory, on an unnamed third person, the "you" of the poem. The relationship between this "you" and the narrator is intriguing. The narrator could be addressing a third party or himself when younger. In any event, the repetition of "you" makes the tone of the poem hover uneasily between accusation—perhaps self-accusation—and obsessiveness. The narrator writes: "Whether on a silent, solitary walk / Or among crowds, far off or safe at home / You will remember, helplessly, that day." The opening "Whether" summons to mind the closure of Samuel Taylor Coleridge's "Frost at Midnight," in which that poet assures his sleeping child that "all seasons shall be sweet to thee, / Whether the summer clothe the general earth / With greenness, or the redbreast sit and sing." The echo lends Hecht's poem both savage irony and sorrow. The "you" addressed in the poem is the helpless prey of his sensibility. The poem ends, chillingly:

> Prepare to receive him in your home some day.
> Though they killed him in the camp they sent him
> to,
> He will walk in as you're sitting down to a meal.

FLIGHT AMONG THE TOMBS

Flight among the Tombs forms in part a collaboration with the artist and engraver Leonard Baskin, well known for the macabre themes and darkness that haunt his work. Twenty-two of his woodcuts accompany the poems in the first section of the book. Represented primarily in skull-like form, the images of death in the woodcuts have a sinister gaiety, an air of the preposterous. The woodcut accompanying "Death as a Society Lady," for instance, portrays the lady as a grinning skull attired in a wide-brimmed hat with a feather boa. Hecht's poems verbally adopt a similar approach. The first five are spoken by Death himself; in the remainder, Death becomes those whom he means to kill—variously, a showman, a whore, a film director, a scholar, among others. It is a tradition that dates back to the medieval "Dance of Death," the danse macabre. Some of the subjects were proposed by the artist and some by the poet, whose main concern was to avoid a monotony of style, a possibility he circumvented by using a range of different verse forms. Hence the opening section contains quatrains rhyming both *abab* and *abba,* blank verse, rhyming pentameter couplets, a villanelle in which the repetitions of the form are used to good effect in conveying the inevitability of Death, a sonnet, a ballade, and rhyming variations on Hecht's often favored six-line stanza.

The section opens with "Death Sauntering About," a three-stanza poem set on a racetrack. The first two stanzas paint a scene of life, color, and vigor, which are debunked and minimized by Death himself in the final stanza. As bets are placed by the "holiday throngs," he, "mute, unremarked, insouciant," saunters, having placed "no premium on haste." In "All Out," a villanelle spoken by Death, the poet impressively contrasts numerous attitudes about how to conduct oneself in the face of the final fact of death: "Some seek the fragile garnitures of fame, / While some drop out, claiming, to salve their pride, / Do what you will, it always ends the same."

"Death the Oxford Don" speaks with a gloomy relish:

Sole heir to a distinguished laureate,
I serve as guardian to his grand estate,
And grudgingly admit the unwashed herds
To the ten point mausoleum of his words.

There is a comic, haughty insouciance in the description of "the unwashed herds" whom he is "reluctant to admit." In "Death the Painter," the arresting of time—the preservation of the representative moment—found in art becomes a metaphor for death. "Death the Painter" has "sought out and arrested everyone"; he converts "all human creatures . . . to a still life." Here Hecht wittily allies the creativity of art with death; from death's perspective, killing, in an ironic twist, becomes a form of creativity. "Death the Judge," on the other hand, already has decided the verdict for everyone; he knows "ahead of time" "that nobody is free of crime or would-be crime." He sentences everyone accordingly.

The difficulty with such a subject, of course, is that the final destination is always the same; to Hecht's artistic credit he varies the method of travel. "Death the Mexican Revolutionary" advises that "the view from here is such / As cannot find a match." We may take the "match" in its obvious sense, meaning "equal," but it also conjures a faint pun on the noun "match," and sardonically implies that the view may be too dark for one to be able to find a match. The poem closes with Death recommending hearty eating before he inaugurates his "brand-new social order / six cold, decisive feet / south of the border." Death and the revolutionary's aims are married seamlessly. In "Death the Film Director," the speaker has designed for the film's "huge cast," humanity itself, "an inevitable plot." The poem cleverly compares the pageant of human life to a filmic process. It begins with a slow zoom into a derelict alley and finds a dead black man under "toppled garbage," emblematic of the only type of scene this particular film director will shoot.

The sequence closes with "Death the Carnival Barker," speaking "*con brio,*" as the poet instructs. He a comic personification of Death as a showman encouraging onlookers to enter his booth:

Step forward please! Make room for those in back!
Come in and see the greatest show on earth!
I promise it will take your breath away!
Something you're sure to call your money's worth!
And bound to last forever and a day!
Softer than down! More powerful than crack!

Such an abundance of exclamation marks in a writer as sparing in their use as Hecht has the effect not simply of conveying the showman's strident tones; even visually, they also function as slight shocks to the eye. The poem's brittle vigor contrasted with the ominous quality of the show in prospect gives the piece a powerful irony.

The second section of the book consists mainly of short poems and includes elegies, as in *The Transparent Man,* this time for the poets James Merrill and Joseph Brodsky. Among the section's most touching poems is "The Mysteries of Caesar." This is an account of boys' Latin lessons with "balding, cologned, mild-manner Mr Sypher"—his name a pun on "cypher," or "a secret message"—who "defied his sentence as a highschool lifer / with a fresh, carefully chosen boutonniere." The poem recounts Mr. Sypher's patience with the haltingly excruciating efforts of the pupils at "pained sight reading from the Gallic Wars." (*De Bello Gallico* was written by Julius Caesar and comprises a detailed description of his war campaigns as a factual report, year by year, of the events from 58 B.C. to 47 B.C.) The baffling tone of inexpertly translated Latin is comically, and yet affectionately, conveyed:

> "Which things being known, when surest things accede,
> He did deem enough of cause . . . ," Jones volunteered.
> Invariably it came out sounding weird,
> The garbled utterance of some lesser breed
>
> Without the law of common intercourse.

At the poem's close, the boys wonder what passes through the teacher's mind as he endures their efforts. Mr. Sypher, the narrator informs us, is imagining "one or another boy" as Antinous, favorite of the emperor Hadrian, who, after Antinous's early death, set up statues in his image throughout the Roman Empire. Such imagining, the narrator informs us, is the result of "the pitiless bliss of solitude." This echo of the closure of Wordsworth's "I Wandered Lonely as a Cloud," in which the "pitiless," with its dry echo of the sibilants in "bliss," qualifies the latter ironically, hints at the suffering undergone by Mr. Sypher.

Hecht has always been a painterly poet, drawn to artists and their work. One of the most striking poems in the second section is "Matisse: Blue Interior with Two Girls—1947." Hecht chose the painting, in the University of Iowa Museum of Art, as a subject to write about from a catalogue sent him as part of a project conducted by the poet Jorie Graham. In *Flight among the Tombs* Hecht quotes a brief passage from the Australian art critic Robert Hughes's *The Shock of the New,* in which that author comments on the French painter Henri Matisse's ability, despite living in a century of ideological horrors, to ignore them within his work. "His studio," notes Hughes, "was a world within a world: a place of equilibrium that, for sixty continuous years, produced images of comfort, refuge, and balanced satisfaction." It is understandable why Hecht should find this passage worth quoting: he was unable to avoid confronting those horrors in his own work. Yet the notion of "pure art," as evidenced by his poetry, is one that he finds beguiling, if impossible.

The Matisse artwork upon which his poem is based shows two girls seated at a table reading in a blue room. Behind their backs is an open window, through which the viewer can make out a garden. Hecht's poem consists of two stanzas, the first of fifteen lines and the second of nineteen. The stanzas act as rooms themselves: the first delineates the world beyond the window and the second, the world of the room where the girls sit. Here, life and art are placed in distinct opposition. The opening stanza presents a world of "Variable May." It is "a world of yearning: we yearn for it, / Its youthful natives yearn for one another." The poet, however, cannot resist pointing out a crucial fact, that the natives, even as they are gloriously alive, are yet mortal. Each is "a lean gnomon / A bone finger with its moral point: / the hour, the minute, the dissolving pleasure." In this, we are informed, "Lies the hot spring of inevitable tears."

Set in contrast is the main scene in the painting, the blue interior. As Hecht observes, "Within is the cool blue perfect cube of thought." The room is a "cool tank of blue."

Blue, the color of contemplation and intellect, contrasts here with the vigorous, organic green present in the first stanza. The girls in the room are reading in the book before them "the pure unchanging text / Of manifold, reverberating depth." The poem ends:

> Deep in their contemplation the two girls,
> Regarding Art, have become Art themselves,
> Once out of nature, they have settled here
> In this blue room of thought, beyond the reach
> Of the small brief sad ambitions of the flesh.

Echoing the Yeats of "Sailing to Byzantium," in "Once out of Nature," the poet opts for the permanence of art. The three abrupt monosyllabic qualifiers to "ambitions" reinforce the content of the phrase. It is an old man's poem; he is no longer "caught in that sensual music" of youth.

It is Anthony Hecht's distinction that, unlike Matisse, he has not been content or able to ignore the ravages of the twentieth century. His refined and polished art has shown itself to be capable of accommodating, if by no means assuaging, the worst horrors. Hecht is surely among the greatest twentieth-century American poets, and his work, in the unfortunate universality of its concerns, is unlikely to date. If, as Robert Frost once intimated, a modern poet is one who can be read at any period in history and still be found contemporary and relevant, Hecht is modern. That is as heartening for the value of art as it is disheartening for what it implies about humanity.

Selected Bibliography

WORKS OF ANTHONY HECHT

POETRY
A Summoning of Stones. New York: Macmillan, 1954.

The Hard Hours. New York: Atheneum, 1967.

Millions of Strange Shadows. New York: Atheneum, 1977.

The Venetian Vespers. New York: Atheneum, 1979.

Collected Earlier Poems. New York: Knopf, 1990.

The Transparent Man. New York: Knopf, 1990.

Flight among the Tombs. New York: Knopf, 1996.

The Darkness and the Light. New York: Knopf, 2001.

PROSE
Obbligati: Essays in Criticism. New York: Atheneum, 1986.

The Hidden Law: The Poetry of W. H. Auden. Cambridge, Mass.: Harvard University Press, 1993.

On the Laws of the Poetic Art, The Andrew Mellon Lectures in the Fine Arts. Princeton, N.J.: Princeton University Press, 1995.

OTHER WORKS
Jiggery-Pokery: A Compendium of Double Dactyls. Edited by Anthony Hecht and John Hollander. Illustrations by Milton Glaser. New York: Atheneum, 1967.

Seven against Thebes. Translated by Anthony Hecht and Helen H. Bacon. New York: Oxford University Press, 1973.

The Essential Herbert. Vol. 5, The Essential Poets Series. Selected and with an introduction by Anthony Hecht. New York: Ecco Press, 1987.

CRITICAL AND BIOGRAPHICAL STUDIES
Atlas, James. "New Voices in American Poetry." *New York Times Magazine,* February 3, 1980, pp. 1–6.

Brown, Ashley. "Anthony Hecht." *Dictionary of Literary Biography,* vol. 5, part 1. Edited by Donald J. Greiner. Detroit: Gale Research, 1980. Pp. 318–324.

Casey, Ellen Miller. "Hecht's 'More Light! More Light!'" *Explicator* 54, no. 2:113–115 (winter 1996).

Davie, Donald. *Shenandoah,* autumn 1956, pp. 43–44.

German, Norman. *Anthony Hecht.* Series 24, vol. 7, American University Studies on American Literature. New York: Peter Lang, 1989.

———. "Anthony Hecht: Contemporary Transcendentalist." *Ball Street University Forum* 30, no. 3: 46–52 (summer 1989).

Hemphill, George. "Anthony Hecht's Nunnery of Art." *Perspective* 12, no. 4:163–171 (1962).

Hoffman, Daniel. "Poetry of Anguish." *Reporter* 38:52–54 (February 22, 1968).

Howard, Richard. "Anthony Hecht: 'What Do We Know of Lasting Since the Fall?'" In his *Alone with America: Essays on the Art of Poetry in the United States Since 1950.* New York: Atheneum, 1980. Pp. 195–208.

Lea, Sydney, ed. *The Burdens of Formality: Essays on the Poetry of Anthony Hecht.* Athens, Georgia: University of Georgia Press, 1989.

Leithauser, Brad. "Poet for a Dark Age." *The New York Review of Books,* February 13, 1986, pp. 11–12, 14.

Miola, Robert. "Anthony Hecht." In *Contemporary Poets,* 6th ed. Edited by Thomas Riggs. New York: St. James Press, 1996. Pp. 463–465.

O'Brien, Timothy D. "Hecht's 'The Dover Bitch.'" *Explicator* 44, no. 2:52–54 (winter 1986).

Spiegelman, Willard. "The Moral Imperative in Anthony Hecht, Allen Ginsberg, and Robert Pinsky." In his *Didactic Muse: Scenes of Instruction in Contemporary American Poetry.* Princeton, N.J.: Princeton University Press, 1989.

INTERVIEWS

Gerber, Philip L., and Robert J. Gemmett. "An Interview with Anthony Hecht." *Mediterranean Review* 1, no. 3:3–9 (1971).

Hammer, Langdon. "Efforts of Attention: An Interview with Anthony Hecht." *Sewanee Review* 104, no. 1: 94–107 (winter 1996).

Hoy, Philip. *Anthony Hecht: In Conversation with Philip Hoy.* London: Between the Lines, 1999.

McClatchy, J. D. "The Art of Poetry XXXX: Anthony Hecht." *Paris Review* 30, no. 108:160–205 (fall 1988).

Smith, Wendy. "Anthony and Helen Hecht." *Publishers Weekly,* July 18, 1986, pp. 70–71.

—GERRY CAMBRIDGE

Alice Hoffman

1952–

*I*N HIS BOOK *The Uses of Enchantment: The Meaning and Importance of Fairy Tales* (1976), Bruno Bettleheim points out that Aristotle said, "The friend of wisdom is also the friend of myth." The contemporary writer Alice Hoffman is a friend of both wisdom and myth. Since the publication of her first novel, *Property Of: A Novel* (1977), Hoffman has been hailed by critics and readers for fiction that seamlessly and lyrically blends the ordinary with the mythic. Words such as "hypnotic," "luminous," "enchanting," "magical," "charming," "daring," and "powerful" have become synonymous with her work. For twenty-four years Hoffman has managed to satisfy the demands of two worlds, garnering both critical literary acclaim and a wide readership as a popular best-selling novelist, a position among serious fiction writers enjoyed by only a few other contemporaries, among them the novelists John Irving, Anne Tyler, and Sue Miller. Hoffman's novels have received mention as notable books of the year by the *New York Times, Entertainment Weekly,* the *Los Angeles Times,* and *Library Journal,* and her twelfth novel, *Here on Earth* (1997), was chosen as an Oprah Book Club selection.

Whether her characters are lonely teenagers, single mothers, imperiled children, angry loners, junkies, aging matriarchs, suburbanites, or men and women bewitched by love, Hoffman infuses their stories with magic, symbolism, and universal archetypes (the antihero, the scapegoat, the outcast). The reader meets Hoffman's troubled characters in a variety settings, from small towns on Long Island, where potato fields are as common as the Southern State Highway; California towns, where earthquakes are both

real threats and symbols of internal disaster; Florida, where gumbo limbo trees host an angel; and small New England villages at the height of summer; to the bustling streets of New York City. In these settings anything imaginable might and usually does happen. The wind, rivers, roses, lemon trees, fireflies, frogs, purple skies, turtles, moon, lightning, trees, constellations, floods and humidity, fire and ice, indeed all the elements of the natural world take on enchanted properties in Hoffman's hands, acting as either ballast or warning for her characters in novels heavily influenced by fairy tale and myth.

Hoffman's skillful blend of myth and archetype with contemporary everyday life is just one of the reasons for the worldwide popularity of novels that have been translated into more than twenty languages and published in more than one hundred foreign editions. In each of her fictions Hoffman incorporates some aspects of the two major myths recognized by literary critics, anthropologists, and psychologists: the seasonal myth and the myth of the hero. The common thread binding these two myths is their cyclical pattern. Both start from an advent or a birth, move to maturity, to death, and finally to a real or symbolic rebirth. In Hoffman's novels as well as in her collection of interrelated short stories, *Local Girls* (1999), as the seasons change so do the characters. In *Fortune's Daughter* (1985) she writes that light coming through the windows "was a sulky color that made you see double," and in *Turtle Moon* (1992) she writes that the "air is so thick . . . sometimes a soul cannot rise and instead attaches itself to a stranger."

Hoffman's knowledge of myth is not accidental. In a brief essay written for Borders Booksellers after the publication of her thirteenth novel, *The River King* (2000), Hoffman reveals that she was a voracious reader as a child, the kind of reader who took a book with her to the movies, on planes and elevators, and even into the bath. The novels Hoffman read were almost exclusively novels of fantasy, science fiction (which draws heavily upon myth), and of course the darker, more complex fairy tales of Jacob Grimm and Wilhelm Grimm (not Hans Christian Andersen). She also admits to the influences of Shakespeare (himself a reteller of myth and fairy tale), Emily Brontë, Nathaniel Hawthorne for his Yankee magical realism, and Edgar Allan Poe.

As a young reader Hoffman searched for the "truth," believing it is in fiction "that the deepest, most soul-searing truths can be found." Agreeing with Plato and Aristotle, who believed the facts were only a part of the true picture, Hoffman says, "Those who write non-fiction must deal with the boundaries of the 'real' and abide by what happened in real time, to real people." Fiction writers can do as they wish and "have bears knock at front doors." For Hoffman reimagining the real world as a fiction is to "take everyday occurrences and turn them inside out getting to the core, the heart, the barest of bones . . . non-fiction writers believe in what happened. But fiction writers believe in what is possible."

At first glance Hoffman's prose style is deceptively simple, and out of context her novels' situations would seem melodramatic. However, Hoffman's accessibility belies work that is riskier, more complicated, and darker than its graceful surfaces indicate. Among contemporary writers Hoffman began exploring taboo (incest and suicide) and the gritty implications of heroin addiction, physical abuse, and alcoholism before these topics emerged in the forefront of the more realistic fiction of the late 1980s and again as bold, confessional memoirs in the 1990s. Death runs through each of the novels; the desire to escape the shadow self or the "double" figures in each. These are not lightweight subjects, but Hoffman's special genius, her impressive knowledge of and affinity with myth led the novelist and critic Frederick Busch to write of Hoffman's work, "Fully aware of the darkness, we end up seeking the light in these stories about the intersection of wounded people who seek to learn where and how to give their love."

Love—too much given for the wrong reasons or the lack of it owing to abandonment, abuse, divorce, or drugs—is the soul force that drives Hoffman's characters. Hoffman's protagonists are vulnerable either by deprivation, for instance, orphans, women who've been deserted by their husbands, widows, men who loved and lost at an early age, men seeking to reunite with or understand their fathers; or they are vulnerable by age, such as young children at the mercy of their parents' whims or fantasies, teenagers straddling the worlds of innocence and experience, and the elderly, whose physical infirmities (decaying eyesight, cancer) frighten them into strange acts of recklessness when death looms close. Because of their vulnerability, Hoffman's characters are easily influenced by external forces. Love confounds them or urges them on toward dangerous yet ultimately transforming emotional-psychological journeys.

For many of Hoffman's heroines, as she writes in *Practical Magic* (1995), a man's attention, even a bad man's attention, "could make it seem as though you were the only person in the universe." Mirroring other literature that draws heavily upon folklore-like stories that mythologize the rites of passage of birth, initiation, death, and rebirth, Hoffman's work adds into the mix the properties of fairy tale, such as the ill king, princess, or outcast who must be restored to health; an act of magic that must be performed; the discovery or gift of a unique talisman; or the necessity to complete a difficult task, which is often the task of self-awareness.

Given these aspects of her novels it is no surprise when a lilac bush grows so large and out of the ordinary that its astonishing blooms draw women from their houses and reawaken their desires. The general decline of a neighbor's house, where crows circle the chimney and a smell grows riper and sweeter each day, draws neighborhood men together to decide what to do, and from that single event an entire subdivision is turned inside out. A single kiss can cast a spell, and for the women who are waiting for love, a man's touch is like fire and often as dangerous.

PORTRAIT OF THE ARTIST

Alice Hoffman was born in New York City on March 16, 1952. She grew up in Franklin Square on Long Island. In 1994, when Ruth Reichl interviewed Hoffman at her home in Brookline, Massachusetts, Reichl recounted, "You get a sense that hidden demons lurk just over her [Hoffman's] shoulder, like the ghosts in one of her novels." Reichl's sense of hidden darkness was not far from the truth. Although Hoffman has been notoriously private throughout her writing career, she admitted to Reichl that her early life was far from perfect. "Unhappiness was trapped in the house like a bubble," she stated, sounding much like one of her heroines, who have been suffocated by the weight of sorrow or loss in their lives.

Hoffman's mother, Mary Hoffman, was a teacher and a social worker; her father, Frederick Hoffman, was a real estate agent. By the time Hoffman was eight years old her father had deserted the family. Hoffman has one brother, who was considered the smart one, "the scientist." Brother-sister duos frequently appear in her work, and similar to her experience, the brother character is often the smarter one.

However, in her fiction the brother is also the character who never reaches his potential.

Despite her reading habit, Hoffman did not entertain the idea of becoming a writer early on. She graduated from high school in 1969 and believed that, regardless of her initial desire to become a veterinarian, she would probably end up becoming a beautician or a secretary. After taking a series of "horrible jobs," in 1970 Hoffman enrolled at Adelphi University in Garden City, New York. She lived at home while commuting to Adelphi and graduated with a bachelor of arts degree in 1973. Her future began to take shape in 1975 when she was awarded the Mirelles Fellowship at Stanford University.

As a fellow in the graduate creative writing program at Stanford, Hoffman came under the mentorship of the writer and teacher Albert Guerard, whom she describes as "one of the greatest writing teachers in the country." Guerard married a talented short story writer, Maclin Bocock. Hoffman credits Bocock with helping her publish her first short story in the magazine *Fiction,* then edited by Ted Solotaroff. Solotaroff was impressed enough to ask Hoffman if she also had a novel. During her time at Stanford, Hoffman, encouraged by Guerard, Bocock, and Solotaroff, wrote *Property Of.* Hoffman also credits Grace Paley's influence on her work. Paley's unique stories and writing voice gave Hoffman a sense that she too had something to say as a writer.

After receiving her master of arts degree from Stanford in 1975, Hoffman enrolled in the post-doctoral program at the State University of New York at Stony Brook, which she did not complete. She then moved to Manhattan, where she met her husband, the teacher and writer Tom Martin. They moved to Boston when Martin enrolled in graduate school there, and they never left the area. They have two sons, Jake and Zach. While Hoffman does not say much about her marriage, it is one of deeply shared interests.

She and Martin have written screenplays together for nearly twenty years. Hoffman authored the original screenplay of the 1983 movie *Independence Day,* the story of an abused housewife that starred Kathleen Quinlan and Dianne Weist. Hoffman's novel *Practical Magic* became a Warner Brothers film featuring Sandra Bullock and Nicole Kidman in 1998.

Hoffman makes her living solely as a writer and does not teach or lecture. What appears to be the perfected artistic life is not without its sorrows, however. Hoffman's struggles inform her novels of the later part of the long and productive career of a gifted and original writer.

AN UNSHAKABLE FOUNDATION

In his *Fables of Identity: Studies in Poetic Mythology* (1963), Northrop Frye maintains that all literature contains phases that correspond to the four seasons and that such "categories" represent the general plots in literature. The critic Leslie Fiedler refined Frye's categories further by insisting that the response of the artist to his archetypal material is what gives the work its uniqueness. In other words, the author's background and how she or he uses it in the work to develop character or to heighten emotion is what gives the author's "signature" to the work. Unlike the New Critics, who eschew biographical facts of the writer's life as irrelevant, Fiedler believes literature is distinguished from pure myth only when the writer's persona is impressed upon the work. Mythology as commonly known has no such personal stamp; it is voiceless, "archetype without signature" (Burrows et al.).

Hoffman's work is myth informed with her unique signature, fully imagined stories that do not shy away from sentiment or passion. Her personal fears (agoraphobia, fear of bridges) and her primary search for "that other person—man, woman, parent or child—who will make us feel whole . . . the search for identity and continuity, and the struggle inherent in that search" (*Contemporary Authors,* vol. 66) fuels each novel.

It is rare when an author's early work holds up over time, but in Hoffman's case the early novels remain some of the best and most complex of her career. In these early novels Hoffman began developing her unique vision of the outcast, the scapegoat, and the double. The archetype of the outcast or the antihero struggling against society, an unloving family, or cruel peers is the archetype Hoffman relies upon the most because "to some extent," she says in her *Contemporary Authors* biography, "we all think of ourselves as outsiders." In an ordinary setting, where other real people move through the world in ordinary ways, Hoffman's characters are singled out for a specific task or journey, and along the way they are beset by the magical, mystical, and exaggerated extremes of weather or nature. This co-mingling of "type" with reality results in the voice and compassion that archetypes in myth do not intend to provide.

The narrator in *Property Of* is an unnamed seventeen-year-old girl who seems to have sprung into being from nowhere. The reader knows nothing about her life before her appearance on "the Avenue" in suburban New York City. The narrator is enamored of a street gang called the Orphans who hang out in a clubhouse. The convincing tawdry details of prostitution, heroin addiction, murder, and violence that Hoffman laces throughout this dark love story between the narrator and the object of her affection, McKay, the heroin-addicted leader of the Orphans, make the novel modern. When the novel opens, the narrator has convinced Danny the Sweet to take her to McKay. She says of the Orphans:

> I fell in love with them on that night, though I suppose I had been even before I knew any names. I could not help it, because the spell was cast, the mood was set, and with the wind on the Avenue

moving around me and the ice shining like a mirror, there was no choice at all.

In many ways the narrator's words describe Hoffman's special gifts as a novelist. The reader tends to fall in love with Hoffman's characters for precisely the same reasons. Similarly this single paragraph sums up the story elements that reverberate in later Hoffman novels as well. The wandering, unparented heroine's desire for love and acceptance, the seemingly magical "casting of a spell," and the natural elements of wind (propelling the narrator regardless of danger) and ice (so shiny it has reflective powers) combine with the narrator's belief that life is beyond her control, that her only choice is to follow. The narrator wants McKay, who does not believe in falling in love, to fall in love with her, which is the difficult task. She has no desire to become one of the Property, the gang members' girlfriends. Her one desire is to experience her sexuality with McKay, to gain experience from him. Over the course of a year she succeeds but at a huge price. Despite his litanies about honor, McKay is a shadow force, the legendary dark double the narrator must descend with fully, much like a hybrid Persephone, before she can reconcile her sexual urges and darker impulses with the better parts of herself.

Hoffman's exaggerated lyrical language and the sophisticated, highly stylized syntax mimic the language of courtly love and myth. As in most myths and nearly all fairy tales, the narrator receives a talisman from the only adult in the novel, the man who owns the corner store where the action begins. He is the voice of reason, and giving her a locket demonstrates his faith in her better judgment. Since Danny the Sweet is the only gang member both too innocent and too dumb to survive the violence of drugs and street life and since he is the arbiter of her initial introduction to McKay, in accordance with archetypal literature, he acts as the scapegoat. His death is the life sacrificed so

that the heroine's vision clears and she sees McKay for what he is, thus freeing her to prevail on her own.

The bad boy in leather and boots who smokes cigarettes and believes he is immune to love but nevertheless is invested with superhuman powers of seduction is the antihero archetype that reappears repeatedly in the novels that follow *Property Of.* Hoffman paints this type as superior in intellect, gifted but unrealized in his potential, and absolutely necessary as a catalyst for growth in the female characters, the representation of the unintegrated self driven by impulse.

Property Of contains a startlingly accomplished passage on the nature of waiting, a hallmark of Hoffman's fiction and one that describes a period similar to the periods of enclosure or waiting in Hindu myth. While McKay is in jail doing time, the narrator notes:

> For six months I did what women do: I waited. This is what women are taught to be good at. It is said that a woman's life is merely preparation for the primal nine month wait. Whatever reason they do it well . . . they count stars and initials and wait: for something to happen, for something to pass, to change, to begin, to end . . . they call fifty men into their bedroom at one time, or they never turn their eyes to men. They watch second hands and suns and moons; they find ways to fill the waiting. And the reason they wait is that they do not know they have a choice . . . mostly they wait to stop waiting.

In myth and fairy tale a period of waiting or enclosure is necessary just before the heroine makes the choice she did not know she had within her all along. Transformation or growth can only occur after the decision to act. In the final scene McKay says, "You wait for me." But his power over the narrator has dissolved. She leaves him and boards a subway knowing that, as she is ferried away, he is rolling up his sleeve, shooting up heroin. As his "dark eyes" close, the narrator, writing her name in the dust on the subway car window, "couldn't help but smile."

Michael Mewshaw, writing for the *New York Times Book Review,* noted that in *Property Of* Hoffman brings a "fierce personal intensity" to her story. Richard Lingeman called the novel "remarkably envisioned, almost mythic in its cadences, hypnotic." Edith Milton, writing for the *Yale Review,* noted that Hoffman "comes close to turning the shoddy values, tarnished ideals and vanishing culture of white, middle-class America into a sort of fairy tale. Her gangs of cutthroats come close to allegory."

With the publication of her second novel, *The Drowning Season* (1979), Hoffman adopted the third-person point of view that she used almost exclusively in succeeding novels. This vantage point allows her the flexibility to enter the minds of even minor characters and gives her books the sweeping feel of mythic saga. Divided into four parts, *The Drowning Season* is a multigenerational novel in which each of the characters has been robbed of family, love, money, and a strong sense of self-worth. Hoffman focuses on two women, eighteen-year-old Esther the Black and her grandmother Esther the White, in a story of reconciliation. Pairs of women who act as foils or doubles reappear in future novels. In *Practical Magic* it would be difficult to ignore the fairy tale influence of the Grimms' "Rose Red and Snow White" played out in the characters of Gillian and Sally Owens and in Sally's daughters Kylie and Antonia.

The two Esthers of *The Drowning Season* live in Esther the White's compound of cottages in St. Frederic's, a Long Island fishing town. Hoffman usually sets her characters in island settings, an outward symbol of their interior sense of isolation. Esther the Black wants to escape, but like the heroines of fairy tales she has no money of her own, and like her alcoholic mother Rose and her suicidal father Philip, who tries to drown himself every August, she is dependent upon Esther the White's money for her existence.

Esther the White is an immigrant Russian. After a series of abusive incidents in her dark past, she vowed to freeze emotion out of herself. Ironically, despite her beauty, elegance, and long, flowing white hair, Esther the White has a blackened heart. She does not love her husband, Misha, and she is incapable of mothering her son Philip, which accounts in part for his suicidal tendencies. Although she has had the custodial care of her granddaughter, Esther the White has never given her heart to the young girl. Only when Esther the White is confronted with her mortality (she is dying of cancer) is she motivated to escape her embittered self as much as Esther the Black longs to escape the compound.

Hoffman draws Esther the White with shades of folklore's old crone and a tint of the wicked stepmother, whose frozen soul can only be thawed by love. Esther the Black differs only slightly from the orphaned narrator of *Property Of.* Esther has family and lives in a protected environment, yet she is alone among these bloodless relatives. Finally, an amulet in the form of a jade pendant, a talisman of renewal, is passed on from Esther the White to Esther the Black by the novel's close. Although Esther the Black has lost her father to a successful drowning, a loss that most likely will haunt her, she moves into the future with the one thing she never believed she could have, her grandmother's love.

Hoffman managed to escape the "sophomore curse" that befalls acclaimed first novelists with their second novels, and she followed *The Drowning Season* with *Angel Landing* (1980). In this book she experimented with alternating first-person and third-person points of view, which enabled her to combine the long narrative passages of *The Drowning Season* with the quick dialogue and scene in *Property Of. Angel Landing* features another pair of women,

Natalie Lansky and her seventy-four-year-old aunt Minnie, but the surprise of this novel is its wit and humor. Natalie is an inept social worker for the crisis center Outreach. Aunt Minnie runs a boardinghouse, and the only boarder lives in the basement, where he is building a raft house. Clearly the characters in this book are not grafted from myth or fairy tale, nevertheless they are endearing and eccentric people hoping for last-minute changes in their lives.

Natalie is plagued by inertia. She clings to a passionless relationship with Carter Sugarland, a rich boy turned anti–nuclear power activist who is content to see her on Wednesday evenings for "lovemaking, marijuana and endless games of hearts." Although Aunt Minnie writes to her congressman, works part-time in an old-age home, drives a Mustang, and points out to Natalie that waiting around for Carter is no way to live, that women do not do that sort of thing anymore, she is lonely and searching for a way to populate her life.

Angel Landing III is the name of the nearby nuclear power plant. When it explodes and colors the sky in a lilac haze, the reader knows it will hover like fog throughout the novel until Natalie and Minnie's lives are transformed. It would not be a Hoffman novel without the leather-clad, scar-faced bad boy. In this book he is Michael Finn, a welder at the power plant. He walks into Outreach one day and announces to Natalie that he is the bomber. Natalie is both drawn to and repelled by Finn, but Aunt Minnie insists that Natalie has fallen in love.

The *Washington Post* reviewer Suzanne Freeman, writing in *Book World,* notes that images from Hoffman's previous two books show up here: "rows of orange daylilies, seashells shaped like angel's wings, men with scarred faces." The dark elements in this book are Finn's relationship with his father and Finn's earlier incarceration, during which Finn experienced a brief homosexual attraction to another inmate. Finn's past is hard-boiled and loveless. Hoffman relates his complicated history in the third-person sections, and they make up some of the most glimmering scenes in the book. With the character of Michael Finn, Hoffman sketches out the truly troublesome, unforgettable Silver, who dominates her next book.

Hoffman's first three books were the warm-up for what might be considered her most difficult, complex, and hypnotic book, *White Horses* (1982). Hoffman took an enormous risk with this psychologically and emotionally demanding story and its exploration of incest between a brother and sister in Santa Rosa, California. The novelist Anne Tyler wrote that *White Horses* marked a significant advancement for Hoffman. Indeed nothing polite, easy, tentative, or coy is in this novel. Peter Prescott accurately described one of the many dimensions of *White Horses* by asking readers to "imagine Emily Bronte alive and writing in California, reworking Sleeping Beauty." "Sleeping Beauty" is also a tale of a sexual awakening. When the prince triumphs over the challenges set before him and finds her, his kiss awakens her to instant love for him and entrance into the world of adulthood. Sleep preserves the purity of the fairy princess, and in *White Horses* sleep becomes the means of escape from the knowledge of a mutual violation.

In *White Horses* the "princess" is the beautiful thirteen-year-old Teresa Connor, who lives in a house that is "darkest in summertime" and where the smell of the river ten miles outside of town summoned children "to the tall yellow fields." Teresa's home life is dark not only because of the drawn curtains but because her father King Connor rules his domestic kingdom with brute force. He's a restless, hard-drinking construction worker who abuses Teresa's mother, Dina, and cannot make himself or his family happy. Dina grows lush gardens, but she cannot nurture her children. Instead she fills Teresa's head with a legend her father used to tell her, the legend of the "Arias." As folklore would have it, Arias are outlaw men so splendid and different from normal men that they appear on white horses under an orange moon and whisk women away. What Dina never realizes as she passes on these stories is that she is casting a dangerous spell. Teresa believes this legend wholeheartedly, a belief that becomes her undoing.

Of Teresa's two brothers, Reuben and Silver, Silver is "special," the mythic shadow. He does not have a white horse, but he is beautiful, lusted after by women, moves by night like a wolf, and always dresses in crisp white shirts—a compelling yet unlikely Aria.

After Teresa witnesses a chilling, violent fight between her parents, she falls into a deep, coma-like sleep. Neither parent is capable of driving her to the hospital, so instead Silver acts as the parent and seeks medical help. When doctors cannot determine the cause of Teresa's fevered sleep, Silver vows that he will always take care of Teresa. In short order King and Rueben desert the family, Dina lapses into despair, symbolized by the decline of her garden, and is rejuvenated only when a new love, Arnie Bergen, enters her life. "We're orphans now," Silver tells Teresa.

Throughout the novel Teresa drops into death-like sleep whenever reality proves too much for her, sleep accompanied by the scent of roses so strong it seems to drift up from the pages of the book. The sleeping sickness worsens as long as Silver is nearby. Silver marries Lee and moves away, and in his absence Teresa struggles to make a productive life while waiting for his return. Silver chooses a life of drug dealing. Like McKay, Silver represents the alluring yet dangerous pleasure-driven aspect of the self. Unlike the unnamed narrator of *Property Of*, who possesses street smarts, Teresa is utterly defenseless. Silver is her brother after all, and much like the Grimms' fairy tales in which Brother and Sister lack parental love or are genuine orphans, these two are dependent upon one another. When Silver defiles her trust in

their first incestuous encounter and insists that "nothing happened," the die has been cast already, and their story becomes a painful, inevitable, yet beautifully choreographed dance between the two disparate parts of the self. It takes four years of changing seasons; Dina's death to cancer; raging weather; the gift of a sapphire pendant from Silver to Teresa, the requisite talisman but in this case one that must be given away; and one last incestuous encounter before Teresa sees Silver for what he is not and relinquishes her hellish wait for rescue from a demonlike brother-lover.

Hoffman's deft combination of fairy tale and myth and her use of rich sensory detail, particularly scent, and scenes of nature run amuck, demonstrating the violent battle between darkness and light, lift the story of Teresa and Silver far enough out of the realistic to allow the reader's suspension of judgment or disbelief and prevent the story from becoming lugubrious. Essentially *White Horses* speaks to the one fear Bettleheim has determined all fairy tales seek to allay, the fear of desertion. Regardless of how many wolves, witches, and demons complicate the tale before its resolution, a fairy tale addresses this fear fancifully. The feeling that justice will be served and all will be well is what puts fear of abandonment to rest. On the other hand, the seasonal and hero myths Hoffman employs reconcile fear of abandonment by virtue of the fact that life's circumstances are not fixed like the quest and the seasons. Change is inevitable in myth; the end of one cycle signals the beginning of the next, allowing the characters to move forward out of darkness.

Hoffman utilizes the incest taboo to show just how far a person will go to assuage loneliness and meet the essential need for love. Throughout the novel Silver keeps moving "west," the direction associated with death in myth, while Teresa moves "east" toward life. The resolution of *White Horses* frees Teresa. Her final words to Silver, "I can't go with you. You're not the one

I love," break the spell and fill the reader with satisfaction. In the aftermath of a storm that had turned the sky "a deep purple," Silver struggles to dig his car out of the mud. "Before long he was covered with mud and he didn't even notice that Teresa had begun to walk east on the River Road." *White Horses* stands apart from the first five novels as the book that heralds the themes and the imagery (roses, the river) Hoffman perfects in *The River King* (2000).

Hoffman's fifth novel, *Fortune's Daughter* (1985), is also set in California and opens with "earthquake weather," with coyotes panicking in the hills. "It was a time when everything you once suspected might go wrong suddenly did." Hoffman's story revolves around two women. Rae is young and lives with Jessup, an angry, leather-jacketed bad boy not meant to possess any of the archetypal characteristics of either McKay or Silver. Jessup is a frustrated dreamer with an attitude. After Jessup leaves her to seek his fortune, Rae discovers she is pregnant. Frightened and uncertain of her future, Rae seeks out Lila, the fortune-teller, for information about the fate of her baby.

Lila, the forty-six-year-old psychic, is married but childless and still is plagued with longing for the illegitimate daughter she gave up twenty years earlier. When Lila meets the pregnant Rae, their encounter opens all of Lila's wounds. *Fortune's Daughter* might be viewed as an ode to female intuition and to motherhood. Two natural events, the violent ice storm in New York City in which Lila delivered her daughter and the earthquake threatening California as Rae faces her pregnancy without Jessup, are the cataclysmic symbols for the power of feminine life-giving force.

For the first time Hoffman in her fiction celebrates the bond between women outside of their relationships to men. In Jessup's absence Rae thrives. After meeting Rae, Lila descends into near-hallucinatory grief, but she gathers enough strength to track down her daughter.

The shock of this novel is that Lila's baby would not have been hers for long even if she had not been forced to give her up. Lila discovers that her daughter died from a congenital heart lesion. This double grief heaped upon one character threatens an otherwise serious examination of grief.

BREAKTHROUGH

Hoffman's personal life and her writing life changed with the publication her sixth novel, *Illumination Night* (1987). Hoffman gave birth to her first son, which made *Illumination Night* the first book she wrote after becoming a mother, a change that sparked her to comment to Ruth Reichl that the books written before it were written by "somebody different." Any novelist looking back at her early work might be provoked to say the same thing, because maturity and seasoned storytelling skill separates apprentice fiction from mature work. It seemed Hoffman was never an apprentice. One might argue that by 1987 the reading public had developed a new appreciation for the kind of fiction Hoffman had been writing all along.

The novels of Tyler, populated with eccentric loners; Irving's Dickensian old-fashioned storytelling in which dancing bears, humor, lovable orphans, and absurdity feel more real than real life; Toni Morrison's folklore-drenched compelling fiction; and Alice Walker's potent, spiritually charged works had moved into the forefront of contemporary literature by this time, taking their places next to Raymond Carver's naturalistic tales of alcoholics, waitresses, ordinary husbands and wives; the biting realism of Russell Banks; and the compellingly drawn domestic crises of Miller.

Readers hankered for Hoffman's richly layered work, and she in turn, always in tune with the core universal experiences of love and loss, was ready to redefine the themes and language of her myth-inspired early work. Formerly her novels viewed the adult world through the prism of the abandoned, confused, or emotionally bereft adolescent, but *Illumination Night* features the married couple Vonny and Andre, their son, Simon, their next-door neighbor Elizabeth Renny and her teenaged granddaughter Jody, and most memorably the Giant, an eight-foot-tall outcast who lives alone in the woods and whose presence becomes the arbiter of change for these characters.

Told in third-person, present tense, this story tells of six intersecting lives in the town of Chilmark on Martha's Vineyard. Opening on the night of the real Oak Bluffs Grand Illumination, the novel sheds light on the undefined terrors of childhood, the uncontrollable heat of adolescence, the fear of death, the death of a child, and most refreshingly a modern marriage threatened by infidelity yet strong enough to withstand the threat. Incapable or absent parents crop up in this novel as well, but Hoffman's heroine Vonny understands as no previous Hoffman heroine has that her own struggles with her distant father "allowed you to know what you are to your own child. You are the person who never dies, you are a parent, not quite human, there only to love him."

Illumination Night cast its magical glow over a new generation of writers in the 1990s as well. Elizabeth Strout's *Amy and Isabelle* (1998) brings to mind the strained mother-daughter relationships of Hoffman's work, and Elizabeth McCracken's *The Giant's House: A Romance* (1996) recalls the tenderhearted, orphaned Giant of *Illumination Night* and his heartbreaking musings on love: "The Giant does not know how other people fall in love. . . . The Giant has never imagined any such possibilities for himself. Who would want him for a lover? Even when he is alone he cannot delude himself into thinking he is like everyone else." Although "chairs are too small for him" and "china breaks in his hands," the Giant voices the doubt anyone in need of love experiences, that he or she is too much, too awkward, too different to be recognized as lovable by another.

In *Boston Review,* Alexandra Johnson praised *Illumination Night* for its depiction of "the hard-won ways in which both parents and children, husbands and wives claim the redemptive power of love in their lives." Jack Sullivan praised Hoffman's technical accomplishments, noting her "unusually fluid form of subjectivity," which allows Hoffman to "glide from one character's consciousness to another . . . sometimes in a single paragraph or sentence."

As Vonny struggles to extinguish the "force field" of her agoraphobia, which like Teresa's sleeping sickness held her a captive of her own fears, she asks: "Who can believe nothing remains? Who does not strain to see the tiny fragments of life that refuse to be extinguished?" Although by the end of this novel Jody leaves for California, Simon's childhood friend Suzanne is dead, and the Giant is once again living alone in the woods, Vonny comes to the understanding that:

> by now you know you will always be afraid. Even when the sky is flat and clear. Even when your husband and son are safely in their beds. You know that every time you drive alone to the store . . . a part of you will expect the earth to swallow you. You will go to the store anyway.

The paragraph reverberates with the Grimms' fairy tale "One Who Went Forth to Feel Fear," in which the hero understands that, unless he knows what it is "to shudder," to be afraid, he will not be able to know how to love either. Of course the fragment of life that "refuses to be extinguished" is love, keeping people afloat through the most terrifying experiences despite fear.

THE WEAK LINK

For any serious writer who produces novels every two years some works are bound to be less than satisfying, novels that feel thinly realized or that overflow with the unresolved odds and ends of the works that preceded them. In Hoffman's career *At Risk* (1988), published a year after *Illumination Night,* lacks her usual certainty and vibrancy.

Clearly the fear Hoffman addressed in *Illumination Night* still held sway with her on an artistic and personal level with *At Risk,* the story of eleven-year-old Amanda Farrell's fight against AIDS. The title eerily announces the "risk" Hoffman was taking in creating a novel out of what had become by 1988 an illness as misunderstood and as feared as the plague.

In *At Risk,* Hoffman's writing is as compelling as it has always been. Hoffman admirably refrains from predictable scenes, and although the reader knows Amanda is dying, Hoffman wisely chooses not to show her death. However, in a novel that is about fear—the parents' fear of losing a child, a community's ignorant fear of AIDS, a younger brother's fear for his sister—the author needs to be fearless. At Risk suffers from Hoffman's visible fear of bringing her usual myth, magic, and sensory detail to a complex subject still so new and daunting to the American culture. The lack of a full understanding reduces the book to polemic regardless of Hoffman's impressive attempts to achieve more.

SEEKERS AND OUTCASTS

In the novels preceding *Illumination Night* the task or challenge for the various heroines was initiation and reconciliation, to move from a state of fragile innocence and dependence to experience and knowledge. But in the second half of her career Hoffman changes the nature of the quest. Most of her heroines are the familiar orphans and products of unhappy homes the reader encountered in the earlier work, but they have moved out of adolescence to womanhood. Some are inching toward middle age. They are world-weary with experience and disappointment, divorced or widowed, and mothers of small children or rebellious teens. Although they know too much about men and sex to "wait to stop waiting," a part of them either secretly hopes for the kind of love they recall from their reckless youths, love that can make them "weak in the knees," or they deny this passionate aspect of their natures, convincing themselves that their roles as mothers, "mother-as-goddess," will keep their more primal desires in check. These heroines are outcasts by virtue of divorce (Nora Silk in *Seventh Heaven,* Robin Moore in *Second Nature*) or by virtue of their histories (Gillian and Sally Owens in *Practical Magic,* March Murray in *Here on Earth*).

These outcasts long to be a part of a "normal" community. For instance, in *Seventh Heaven* (1990) the divorced Nora Silk moves herself and two sons to Hemlock Street, a 1959 suburb where two unspoken rules reign supreme, "mind your own business and keep up your lawn." This is a community in which the surface perfection camouflages a wife beater; a murderer; estranged husbands and wives; and the two McCarthy brothers Ace and Jackie, the Cain and Abel of Hemlock Street. It is also a community on the brink in a chaotic period in American culture. The lovely irony in the novel is that Nora Silk wants what she does not understand that the others only seem to have, that is, security, love, and a simple, perfected life. Nora Silk is the "wise fool" of a fairy tale, a compelling woman in black stretch pants completely unaware that she is already ahead of her time. She is an unwitting feminist who cannot cook, mows her own lawn, and triggers lust and desire in grown men and in her unlikely lover, the outwardly tough Ace McCarthy. In this novel the arrival of the "outcast" transforms a neighborhood.

Turtle Moon (1992), Hoffman's ninth novel, features Lucy Rosen, an obituary writer living in Verity, Florida, an imaginary town Hoffman says appeared in her mind "as if someone had handed her a map" (interview reprinted at the website www.alicehoffman.com). It is a lush setting for a story that is part detective novel, part allegory. Lucy and her son Keith are from Long Island. *Turtle Moon* revolves around a murder; the disappearance of Lucy's son Keith with the victim's baby, Rachel Lee; the detective Julian Cash's guilt over his cousin Bobby's death years ago; Lucy and Julian's love affair; and the love that develops between Julian's dog, appropriately named Arrow, and Keith. These dramas play out in only one month's time, the month of May.

Hoffman writes that Charles Verity "killed off as many of the natives as he could" when he founded the town, but he could not "get rid of the spirits of all the men he'd murdered." Apparently these spirits are as dense as the May humidity, which was "so fierce and sudden it could make grown men cry." Even the sea turtles behave oddly. Mistaking the bright glow of the street lamps for the moon, they leave their natural habitats and crawl out onto the highways. What the talkative residents of Verity fail to tell the "outsiders" Lucy Rosen and her son is that "something is wrong with the month of May." Critics hailed Hoffman for the murder mystery momentum and magic of *Turtle Moon*, but the novel produced the line that became a refrain in Hoffman's next four novels: "It's amazing how many losses a person can bear."

Hoffman followed *Turtle Moon* with *Second Nature* (1994), arguably one of the most affecting, powerful novels in her career. She uses the mythic themes of uniting the primal with reason as she also reconfigures the fairy tale "Beauty and the Beast." In this novel, which critics lauded for its ironies and its exploration of appearance versus reality, the outcast does not seek acceptance in the established community. Instead the protagonist, Robin Moore, finds solace and love by seeking out and protecting another outcast.

Robin Moore is so moved by the vulnerability of a young man who's been raised by wolves that, seeing him at the hospital when he is about to be sent away and locked up forever in a state facility, she impulsively kidnaps the "Wolf Man" and brings him into her home, which she shares with her son Connor. Not since the Giant of *Illumination Night* had Hoffman created a more sympathetic outcast. Stephen, the Wolf Man, thrives under Robin's care, and she falls in love with him. The "second nature" of the title refers to the beast within the "civilized" man and the capacity for love in the "beast."

With her eleventh novel, *Practical Magic* (1995), Hoffman relies more on pure fairy tale than on myth because these "outcasts" probably would not find acceptance in the real world except among their own. They are witches, and this witty, sly story of potions, tricks, and retribution contains all of the requisites of a fairy tale, including the awful two-hundred-year-old curse cast upon the women of the Owens family. Like the opposites portrayed by the two Esthers, Sally Owens and Gillian Owens are as different as night and day. Sally, the young, widowed mother, deadened to the possibility of love, moves away in search of a normal life in another community. Her sister Gillian escapes to a life of thwarted love and nasty, abusive men. But in this novel Sally's three-times divorced sister is swept back into Sally's life. All sense of a "safe" community unravels for Gillian, Sally, and Sally's two daughters when the evil spirit of Gillian's dead boyfriend begins haunting them from his makeshift grave under the lilac bushes in Sally's yard.

Rather than relying on a talisman passed on from the arbiter of transformation, these heroines are marked as "other" by their style of dress, the color of their hair, and the sheer force of their personalities. They may be provoked by olfactory sensations, the scents of jasmine, roses, lilacs; they may receive warnings of impending danger by frogs, a ring around the moon, or a storm brewing; they may wear a bit of "blue for protection," but mostly their best talisman is their own sense of self-worth. In these novels the protagonists, even the lustiest of them, such as Gillian Owens, eventually choose good men.

Hoffman's description of weather in these novels becomes deeply symbolic. The month of August in *Practical Magic* "is the season of reversals, when the birds no longer sing in the morning and the evenings are made up of equal parts golden light and black clouds. The rock-solid and the tenuous can easily exchange places until everything you know can be questioned or put into doubt." August in *Seventh Heaven* can be "so hot you had to keep your eye on the road because all along the Southern State the asphalt had buckled and snapped apart." In *Second Nature* "hallucinations occurred in severe weather; they sprang up from the ground, fully formed."

In the earlier work and even in *Illumination Night* the most striking aspect rested in Hoffman's rich characterizations. Critics spoke of the two Esthers, Lila, Vonny, and Silver as though they were truly alive, not fictional creations. Hoffman is the star of her next four books. Hoffman's exquisite writing, her use of imagery, and her visible creative hand, particularly in *Practical Magic,* provoked Mark Childress to point out that in her eleventh novel Hoffman "plays tricks with the reader's expectations by suddenly shifting tenses or passing the point of view around the room like a football."

The same visible authorship occurs in *Here on Earth* (1997), Hoffman's homage to Emily Brontë's *Wuthering Heights* (1847). Hoffman grafts a riveting contemporary love story onto the Gothic Brontë classic and, as she did in *Practical Magic,* provides unexpected, fresh turns, focusing her version on the second rather than the Catherine-Heathcliff generation of lovers. Once again Hoffman, like Brontë before her, explores taboo, unbridled passion in battle with reason and the consequences of explosive love. The critics praised Hoffman's bravura performance, and the novel, steeped as it and its predecessor are in mood, powerful landscapes, ancient myth, and symbolism, was an immediate success.

Taken altogether the five novels in the later part of Hoffman's career reveal significant experimentation with point of view, setting, the alternating use of the optimistic tone of fairy tale (*Turtle Moon, Practical Magic, Seventh Heaven*) and the more mutable, subtle tone of myth (*Second Nature, Here on Earth*). The novels also reveal an interesting reversal from Hoffman's first five books in the way she imbues the heroines' children, Billy Silk, Connor Moore, and Kylie Owens, with the ability to read people's minds, sense their moods, or feel their pain acutely. In Hoffman's early work childhood is pure innocence. The protagonists of those novels are limited in their emotional resources. In the later set of novels their gifts permit them to see and hear the invisible, a power their divorced, perhaps cynical mothers must be reawakened to. In a sense the children and teens become the parents, the spell casters, the fairy godmothers to the adults, reviving their parents' faith in love and possibility.

LOCAL GIRLS AND *THE RIVER KING:* ORIGINAL NATURE

In the late 1990s Hoffman's personal life was riddled with loss and sorrow. Her sister-in-law Jo-Ann lost a battle with brain cancer; Hoffman's mother suffered a severe stroke then was diagnosed with breast cancer. For two years Hoffman divided her time among family members needing care. By the time *Here on Earth* was chosen as an Oprah Book Club selection, Hoffman herself wasn't feeling well. On a hot July afternoon Hoffman was informed that she had breast cancer. Several weeks after Hoffman's diagnosis, she learned that her other sister-in-law had been diagnosed with breast cancer as well.

"That ill people become more themselves, as if once the excess is stripped away only the truest core of themselves remained," is a particular truth Hoffman expressed several times in her novels that had now become a fact of her life. In an elegant essay for the *New York Times,* "Sustained by Fiction," Hoffman stated that the deaths and her own illness urged her to create, that once she started writing she "believed anything was possible."

Ironically the sorrow and pain of real life infused both *Local Girls* (1999) and *The River King* (2000) with Hoffman's original themes. With these two books Hoffman slithered deep inside the skins of her characters to reenter the worlds of orphaned children, suicide, and myth.

Local Girls is a collection of fifteen interrelated stories centered around the Samuelson family in which Hoffman, at her edgy best, captures the scope of a novel within the flash fires of short fiction. In this collection a cat speaks, and a bolt of lightning plays Cupid. But the deeper strangeness is the main character Gretel's growing awareness that her parents' marriage is about to explode. In a series of offhandedly and wryly delivered diary entries, Gretel introduces her world. Her brother Jason is a doomed genius; her mother, Franny, is at love's desperate end; her grandmother Frieda is a wise, comic figure; her friend Jill is a soul mate; and Margot is her mother's cousin, neighbor, and best friend and one of love's shell-shocked victims. "When a marriage breaks up, it's the children who suffer," Margot says. Hoffman sets out unsentimentally and with surprising humor to explore this truth from various points of view.

Gretel Samuelson narrates eight of the stories. Unfettered by the novel's narrative demands, Hoffman is free to move wherever she likes in point of view and time. The gems of this collection are stunning in their emotional immediacy. The story "Gretel" resumes the brother-sister motif of *White Horses,* replacing the incest taboo with a mutual sense of fear, devotion, and helplessness. Gretel and Jason's visit to their father's new digs is short-circuited by their stepmother Thea, who calls Gretel "a little bitch" and tosses both Jason and Gretel out of the car. Stranded and bereft of the family they once had, Jason tells Gretel: "Face it. We're lost." Gretel's mother, Franny, is diagnosed with cancer, and in the story "Devotion," Hoffman dreamily records a mother's conflicted thoughts before death as she is caught between her desire to live for Gretel's sake and her personal wish to "let go."

The most profound and the darkest of the stories is "The Boy Who Wrestled with Angels," in which the ghosts of McKay and Silver are called up in the character of Gretel's brother Jason, the gifted, compelling antihero whom Gretel adores. Jason is plagued by a sense of failure, is seduced by heroin, and is led inevitably to his death.

In the title story "Local Girls," Hoffman follows the cyclical seasonal myth and takes the reader full circle to a summer night years later, when Gretel is visiting her Long Island home, the ghosts of her past, and her best friend Jill before moving on to California. In the dark Jill points to a house where two teenage girls have recently committed suicide. "Boy problems. Family problems. The same exact troubles we had," Jill says. With fireflies blinking and a history thick with friendship and shared sorrows, Hoffman sure-handedly reclaims the mythic mold in which endings become beginnings.

Some critics complained that the form of *Local Girls* created too many repetitions. Others were stunned by the book's sheer unabashed expression of sentiment, which by 1999 was a quality in American fiction tamped down in favor of strident, sassy, ironic stories and novels. *Local Girls* represents a significant experiment. A writer as prolific and successful as Hoffman is usually loathe to tamper with her readers' expectations, but with *Local Girls,* Hoffman offers readers and critics the opportunity to hear a compelling, intimate first-person voice again and to move through narrative time randomly rather than in a connected linear arc.

In *The River King* (2000) Hoffman dove completely into the marvelously rendered world of Haddan, Massachusetts, with a story of cruel teenagers, magic, misguided adults, suicide, death, guilt, and love, in which appearances deceive, fishermen prove themselves kings, and "kings" reveal their weaknesses. The novel opens with raging weather and a cautionary tale about crossing the boundaries between classes. The Haddan residents harbor resentment toward the rich Haddan School students, and the townies are of interest to the Haddan faculty and students only as long as they can be of use.

Roses, swans, death, and magic converge when two "outsiders," Carlin Leander, a beautiful, talented fifteen-year-old swimmer from Florida with hair "the color of stars," and August "Gus" Pierce, a boy who "viewed his own life as a prison sentence and experienced his existence much as a condemned man might have," arrive in Haddan. Gus immediately charms Carlin, winning her friendship and love with a magic trick.

Mirroring Gus and Carlin are Betsy Chase, a photography instructor at Haddan, an orphan, and a beautiful woman "in possession of survivor's guilt," and Abel Grey, Haddan's former bad boy turned cop. Because Abel's brother committed suicide years ago, he too carts a hefty bag of guilt. Carlin, Gus, Abel, and Betsy are as vulnerable as they are individual.

Vulnerability as Hoffman renders it is what villains like the senior Haddan School student Harry McKenna prey upon. McKenna is the ringleader at Chalk House, where the boys pursue hazing with diabolical zeal. Dressed in an emblematic black coat, "marked" for otherness and death, Gus is their favorite scapegoat.

In the manner of all mythic scapegoats whose lives must eventually be sacrificed for the greater good, Gus offers up passive resistance, which only escalates his torturers' fury. Carlin angrily tells Gus to stand up for himself, and Gus accepts the Chalk boys' challenge: to change a white rose into a red one. With his talent for magic, Gus accomplishes this feat with ease. The following morning he is found dead in the river.

Haddan officials want to dismiss the death as a suicide, but Abel Grey is not convinced. As he investigates, a wealth of Haddan secrets floats to the surface of this complex story about death and rebirth. Carlin begins wearing Gus's black coat whether it is hot or cold; she grows paler and thinner as her grief threatens to swallow her up. She discovers stones and minnows from the river in her pockets and always feels an odd presence around her, especially when she is in the water swimming laps. Carlin wonders, "Was it possible for a soul to linger . . . right at the edge of our commonplace world, substantial enough to catch minnows in the river?"

Betsy Chase's photographs of Gus's room reveal a vaporous figure sitting on the bed. Carlin, Abel, and Betsy depend upon Gus's restive soul to point Abel toward the real cause of Gus's death, to urge Betsy toward love for Abel, and finally to grant release to Carlin and return her from the depths of grief to her rightful place in the kingdom of the living.

Woven within this intricate story are subplots involving an abandoned baby found by the river, revelations of town corruption, and the old story turned legend of George Howe, as cruel as any vicious king in a fairy tale, who refuses to grant his wife, Annie Jordan, a divorce. Annie is capable of making "swans line up like gentlemen," at the sound of her "sweet voice." She also has a gift for growing roses so spectacular that their scent fills the air even in February. The relationship between George Howe and Annie most mirrors the devastating and painful relationship between Teresa and Silver in *White Horses,* only in this novel George Howe's cruelty drives Annie to suicide.

The river that splits the town in two is Hoffman's most fully realized symbol of the life force. From the beginning to the end of this iridescent story the river is kept in as sharp a focus as the characters. The Haddan river floods, rushes, freezes; it flows through this book like blood coursing through veins. With this novel Hoffman culled the best scenes, legends, archetypes, and motifs from an entire career, refined and reenvisioned them, and created a potent story of love, death, and rebirth. It is fitting that *The River King* ends on a note of quiet, subtle rest: on a June night Carlin swims in the river alongside the fish, "all the way home."

In an interview after the publication of *The River King,* which critics applauded, Hoffman stated that her next book would be a collection of modern fairy tales for adults and that she was also hard at work on a novel that would be based on a controversial fairy tale, the name of which she did not reveal. After ten months of successful chemotherapy, Alice Hoffman the woman has fared well. As a gesture of gratitude and support, she donated the royalties from *Local Girls* to breast cancer research.

And what of Alice Hoffman the writer? Her goals and passions as a novelist do not seem to have changed despite all of the changes and losses in her life. In the essay "Sustained by Fiction," Hoffman says that, at the height of her draining chemotherapy,

> I wrote to find beauty and purpose, to know that love is possible and lasting and real, to see day lilies and swimming pools, loyalty and devotion. . . . I wrote because that's who I was at the core, and if I was too damaged to walk around the block, I was lucky all the same.

Like the most memorable of her protagonists, women, men, and children walloped hard by the vicissitudes of life, no situation seems so horrible, no loss seems so unbearable, no room seems so dark to hold back Alice Hoffman, "the friend of wisdom and myth," from seeking and believing in the light.

Selected Bibliography

WORKS OF ALICE HOFFMAN

NOVELS AND SHORT STORY COLLECTIONS

Property Of: A Novel. New York: Farrar, Straus & Giroux, 1977.

The Drowning Season. New York: Dutton, 1979.

Angel Landing. New York: Putnam, 1980.

White Horses. New York: Putnam, 1982.

Fortune's Daughter. New York: Putnam, 1985.

Illumination Night. New York: Putnam, 1987.

At Risk. New York: Putnam, 1988.

Seventh Heaven. New York: Putnam, 1990.

Turtle Moon. New York: Putnam, 1992.

Second Nature. New York: Putnam, 1994.

Practical Magic. New York: Putnam, 1995.

Here on Earth. New York: Putnam, 1997.

Local Girls. New York: Putnam, 1999.

The River King. New York: Putnam, 2000.

UNCOLLECTED SHORT STORIES

"Blue Tea." *Redbook,* June 1982.

"Sweet Young Things." *Mademoiselle,* June 1983.

"Sleep Tight." *Ploughshares* 15, nos. 2–3 (1989).

"Provider." *New York Times Magazine,* November 1, 1992, pp. 22–23.

"True Confessions." *Southwest Review* 82, no. 4:531–542 (1997).

CHILDREN'S BOOKS

Fireflies. New York: Hyperion Books for Children, 1997.

Horsefly. New York: Hyperion Books for Children, 2000.

Aquamarine. New York: Scholastic, 2001.

SCREENPLAYS

Independence Day. Warner Brothers, 1983.

Practical Magic. With Robin Swicord, Akiva Golds-man, and Adam Brooks. Warner Brothers, 1998.

OTHER WORKS

"The Book That Wouldn't Die: A Writer's Last and Longest Voyage." *New York Times,* July 22, 1990, p. 14.

"Reviving the Spirit of a Cape Cod Farmhouse." With Richard Mandlekorn. *Architectural Digest,* February 1997, pp. 36–40.

"Hot Potato Wisdom." *Utne Reader,* November 1998, pp. 37–38.

"Sustained by Fiction While Facing Life's Facts." *New York Times,* October 14, 2000, p. El.

BIOGRAPHICAL AND CRITICAL STUDIES

BOOKS

Bettleheim, Bruno. *The Uses of Enchantment: The Meaning and Importance of Fairy Tales.* New York: Vintage Books, 1989.

Burrows, David J., Frederick R. Lapides, and John T. Shawcross, eds. *Myths and Motifs in Literature.* New York: Free Press, 1973.

Contemporary Authors New Revision Series, vols. 34, 66. Detroit, Mich.: Gale Research, 1981–.

Contemporary Literary Criticism, vols. 7, 25, 51. Detroit, Mich.: Gale Research, 1977–.

Current Biography, vol. 53. New York: Wilson, 1992. Pp. 14–15.

Cyclopedia of Literary Characters II. Rev. 3d ed., Pasadena, Calif.: Salem Press, 1990.

Dewey, Joseph. "Music for a Closing: Responses to AIDS in Three American Novels." In *AIDS—The Literary Response.* Edited by Emmanuel S. Nelson. New York: Twayne, 1992.

Dictionary of Literary Biography. Vol. 52, *American Writers for Children since 1960: Fiction.* Detroit, Mich.: Gale Research, 1986. Pp. 192–202.

Frye, Northrop. *Anatomy of Criticism: Four Essays.* Princeton, N.J.: Princeton University Press, 1957.

———. *Fables of Identity: Studies in Poetic Mythology.* New York: Harcourt, Brace & World, 1963.

Leeming, David Adams. *Mythology: The Voyage of the Hero.* Philadelphia, Pa.: Lippincott, 1973.

Linkon, Sherry Lee. "Turtle Moon." In *Masterplots II: Women's Literature Series.* Edited by Frank M. Magill. Pasadena, Calif.: Salem Press, 1995.

PERIODICALS

Becker, Alida. "Trouble on Hemlock Street." *New York Times,* August 5, 1990, section 7, p. 2.

Brown-Davidson, Terri. "To Build Is to Dwell: The Beautiful, Strange Architectures of Alice Hoffman's Novels." *Hollins Critic* 33:1–15 (December 1996).

Busch, Frederick. "The Soul Is Part of the Action." *New York Times,* April 26, 1992, p. 1ff.

Charyn, Jerome. "The Witches' Tale." *New York Times,* July 15, 1979, p. 13.

Childress, Mark. "The Witches of Magnolia Street." *New York Times,* June 25, 1995, p. 25.

Cravens, Gwyneth. "Flying from the Windows, Biking down the Stairs." *New York Times,* August 9, 1987, section 7, p. 7.

Dooley, Susan. "Mothers and Daughters." *Book World,* May 19, 1985, p. 11.

Ferguson, Sarah. "Islanders." *New York Times,* July 13, 1999, p. 31.

Fortini, Amanda. "The Spirit Moves Him." *New York Times,* July 16, 2000, p. 12.

Freeman, Suzanne. "Love at the Crisis Center." *Book World,* December 21, 1980, p. 4.

Haupt-Lehmann, Christopher. "Lights of the Vineyard." *New York Times,* July 25, 1987, p. 19.

Hogan, Katie. "Speculations on Women and AIDS." *Minnesota Review: A Journal of Committed Writing* 40:84–93 (spring–summer 1993).

Jefferson, Margo. "A Tale of Two Esthers." *Ms,* August 1979, pp. 34–35, 37.

Johnson, Alexandra. Review of *Illumination Night. Boston Review,* October 1987, p. 31.

Klass, Perri. "Childbirth with Fire and Ice." *New York Times,* March 24, 1985, p. 7.

Lardner, Susan. "Complications." *The New Yorker,* July 15, 1985, pp. 83–85.

Leader, Zachary. "Cool as a Cobra." *Times Literary Supplement,* no. 3968:432 April 21, 1978.

Lingeman, Richard R. "*Property Of.*" *New York Times,* July 14, 1977, p. 25.

Maryles, D. "May Is a Good Month for Hoffman." *Publishers Weekly,* May 11, 1992, p. 16.

Mewshaw, Michael. Review of *Property Of. New York Times Book Review,* July 10, 1977, p. 10.

Milton, Edith. Review of *Property Of. Yale Review* 65, no. 2:267–268 (winter 1978).

Mosher, Howard Frank. "Love Conquers Wolf." *New York Times,* February 6, 1994, p. 13.

Pinsker, Standford. "The Grip of Family in the Novels of Alice Hoffman and David Small." *Critique Studies in Contemporary Fiction* 38:251–261 (summer 1997).

Prescott, Peter S. "Night Moves." *Newsweek,* April 12, 1982, p. 82.

Prose, Francine. "*Here on Earth.*" *People Magazine,* October 20, 1997.

Seaman, Donna. "*The River King.*" *Booklist,* April 15, 2000.

Strouse, Jean. "Esther the White, Esther the Black." *Newsweek,* August 20, 1979, p. 72.

Sullivan, Jack. "Better to Have Loved." *Book World,* August 2, 1987, pp. 8, 13.

Tyler, Ann. "Ordinary Family, with a Difference." *New York Times Book Review,* March 28, 1982, pp. 11, 38.

INTERVIEWS

James, Caryn. "*At Risk* Author Discusses Fears about AIDS." *New York Times,* July 18, 1988, p. 15.

Reichl, Ruth. "At Home with Alice Hoffman: A Writer Set Free by Magic." *New York Times,* February 10, 1994, p. C1.

—DENISE GESS

Anne LaBastille

1938–

ANNE LaBASTILLE HAS lived for nearly thirty years in the log cabin she built on Black Bear Lake in the heart of New York State's Adirondack wilderness. It has been the center of her adult life and the place where she has written most of her books, including her widely popular wilderness autobiographies *Woodswoman* (1976), *Beyond Black Bear Lake* (1987), and *Woodswoman III: Book Three of the Woodswoman's Adventures* (1997). Her published output, which also includes 125 articles for conservation publications and the popular *Ranger Rick* magazine, has contributed richly to public understanding of ecology and has encouraged women to seek wilderness experiences and careers. Her backcountry trek has been a difficult one. It has forced her, by trial and error, to draw her own maps and to overcome personal barriers. LaBastille's autobiographical books focus on feminist issues of gender identity and personal freedom and their points of intersection with issues of ecological research and environmental activism. LaBastille's thirty-year saga encapsulates some of the central issues of the contemporary feminist and environmental movements, both of which gained public attention in the early 1970s, just as she was beginning her career as a wildlife ecologist and establishing her retreat in a remote corner of the Adirondack Park. A woman living for extended periods in isolation from her society, LaBastille has waged a campaign for an enlarged, more embracing definition of femaleness, proving that women can live and work in backcountry settings and that women can write about nature and environmental concerns despite the fact that at the outset of her career men dominated the fields of wildlife ecology and nature writing.

Few writers can claim a more dramatic life transformation than LaBastille's. She was born in New York City in 1938 and was raised in Montclair and East Orange, New Jersey. But despite her urban environs, her heart yearned from an early age for wildness and freedom. She received no encouragement in this regard from either her father, Ferdinand LaBastille, a professor of languages, or her mother, Irma Goebel, a writer and concert pianist. As if in early revolt against the restrictions and artificiality of suburban living, she camped out in her backyard and read wilderness and adventure literature voraciously.

With dreams of becoming a biologist, LaBastille attended the University of Miami in Florida, attracted to their marine biology program, but graduated with a B.S. in Natural Resources from Cornell University. At the conclusion of her undergraduate years, LaBastille found employment at an Adirondack mountain lodge. Before long she married the owner of the lodge, and with her husband's guidance she dedicated herself to becoming knowledgeable about her newfound home, the six-million-acre Adirondack Park. During the 1960s she divided her time between the demands of the Adirondack Inn, wildlife tours to the Caribbean and Latin America, and completion of a master's degree in Big Game Management from Colorado State University in 1960. On one of her winter trips to Guatemala's Lake Atitlán she became fascinated with a flightless bird, the giant pied-billed grebe. This little-known and unstudied species became a research subject for her Ph.D. in Ecology at Cornell University, which she completed in 1970. The grebe continued as an important element in her research and writing for the next twenty years. In 1964 LaBastille published her first book, *Birds of the Mayas,* an attractive collection of essays, illustrations, folktales, and natural history. She provided a field guide to Maya birds useful for both amateurs and specialists, combined with translations of traditional Maya stories and myths in which bird life figures prominently. The book appealed to both specialists and lay readers. During this busy period LaBastille's seven-year marriage came to its end, and she began looking for a new home in the Adirondacks. Her search resulted in the purchase of twenty-two acres of old-growth forest on a body of water bordering state wilderness land she refers to as Black Bear Lake. The story of this purchase and of establishing her cabin and Thoreau-like life there, as narrated in *Woodswoman,* has become legendary.

WOODSWOMAN

In *Woodswoman* (1976), the first book of her autobiographical trilogy, LaBastille narrates the fascinating story of her withdrawal from metropolitan and academic life for a Walden-like existence in a self-constructed log cabin in remote Adirondack country. Attempting perhaps to make a sizable splash and to gain a readership sympathetic to her life choices and concerns, LaBastille writes with feisty combativeness for her newfound place in the wilderness. Although her often-strident and emotional tone becomes muted and balanced in her later work as her thinking and writing mature, her stridency matches the dynamics of the 1970s and doubtless endeared her to a new readership.

LaBastille can be seen as both victim and proponent in the struggle for gender equality. She recalls in *Woodswoman* that as a "tomboyish" sixteen-year-old she asked her parents for hiking boots and a .22 rifle only to receive silk stockings and a dictionary. Throughout her adolescent years her parents tried their best to feminize LaBastille, dragging her to dancing and art lessons, while she secretly dreamed of becoming a Wyoming wrangler or a trapper in Saskatchewan. Her mother in particular seems to have been anguished by her "boyish" desires and repeated the litany "girls don't go camping" and "you mustn't walk in the woods alone."

Although LaBastille takes credit for building her own wilderness cabin in defiance of parents and social convention, she also credits the several lumbermen who helped her with the heaviest work of positioning the logs and then moving the completed cabin twelve feet when she was later informed she had built too close to the shore of Black Bear Lake. This act initiates a series of clashes and collisions with nonparental authority, a force LaBastille repeatedly identifies as patriarchal. She hates going to New York City to deal with male lawyers and their technicalities during the purchase process, and now another male in a position of power insists that she cut back her own stand of tall spruces and move her cabin the requisite twelve feet. Even though she complies with the "preposterous demand," LaBastille admits that with this conflict she "acquired a deep contempt for the 'letter of the law.'" She is enraged by this "unfair attack" upon her rights to build her own cabin where she chooses, presumably outside the reach of male authority, but she discovers "big brother is watching" even in the heart of the country. She appears unable to concede the possibility that "big brother" might have been working from sound ecological and aesthetic principles in insisting that all buildings be placed at least fifty feet from the shores of lakes within the park. Later, when she could tell that an inspector had visited the site to see if she had complied, she foamed in anger: "If I had caught him in the act [of measuring] I would have smeared that man with . . . grease and tied him to one of those stumps for the bears and black flies to devour. I couldn't have cared which!"

After completing basic work on her cabin, dock, outhouse, and woodpile, LaBastille posts her property against human invaders and arms herself with a bit more than the .22 rifle her parents had denied her. She purchases a pistol, a .300 Savage rifle, and a sixteen-gauge shotgun. Her conception of survival insists on not just backcountry skills and the necessary equipment but also that she must be a "pistol-packing woodswoman" with a reputation scary enough to keep even the most threatening men away.

Thus the gender wars commence, and as her several autobiographies tell it, LaBastille outdraws and outfoxes all male invaders with the exception of two wilderness-compliance inspectors. She relishes in relating incidents in which she has intercepted male trespassers, announcing "Gentlemen, this land is posted." On one such occasion, when a group of probably drunken male hunters approaches her dock at night and by boat, she declares, shotgun in hand, "If any one of you sets foot on my land or even comes close to my dock without an invitation, I'll shoot first and ask his name after." Even though Adirondackers seldom fence or post their lands and relish the freedom of open woods in which to roam, hunt, and fish, they view with concern the tendency of outsiders like LaBastille to close their lands. The added fact of a woman living alone in the woods no doubt heightens the tension and increases the incidents of trespassing or baiting. The result is a gender battle in which LaBastille views all unidentified males as potential enemies—threats to her body, her property, and the environment. Given the ample evidence of threatening male behavior in her books, readers may well be sympathetic to her defensiveness.

During the 1970s LaBastille makes no direct reference to the feminist movement, yet *Woodswoman* represents in practice many of the same gender conflicts and redefinitions that feminist critics such as Annette Kolodny and Elaine Showalter were writing about during this period. LaBastille appears to be writing in isolation from the feminist movement, waging her private war for gender transformation and equality, until the publication of *Women and Wilderness* (1980), in which she quotes from feminist critics and acknowledges the pioneering efforts of other women to live and work in wild country settings. Showalter wrote the essay "Feminist Criticism in the Wilderness," in *The New Feminist Criticism: Essays on Women, Literature, and Theory* (1985), as if with knowledge of LaBastille's travails. She suggests that the situation of women, certainly including woodswomen, who pursue traditionally male activities is analogous to the plight of a lost hiker trying to find her way in a pathless wilderness. Kolodny develops this idea further, arguing in *The Lay of the Land: Metaphor as Experience and History in American Life and Letters* (1975) that since settlement the American landscape has been repeatedly feminized by paternalistic concepts of penetration, domination, conquest, and ownership of the body of the woman-land. As Kolodny expresses it, before the power of the masculine, the feminine (including nature) "is always both vulnerable and victimized." She further asserts that, while women are often symbolically associated with nature, they have been discouraged from entering the backcountry and are frequently warned of its dangers to their well-being. As *Woodswoman* makes abundantly clear, LaBastille suffers through all these oppositions yet perseveres toward the accomplishment of her personal and career goals of living in and working for better understanding and protection of our wild human heritage.

Perhaps this makes understandable LaBastille's initial impulses to build her fortress in the woods and to protect her tiny wilderness kingdom. Her writing powerfully conveys the importance of property rights and boundaries.

Her fortress mentality finds expression in the language of ownership rather than of stewardship. Her prose is filled with possessive references to "my fir forest," "my giant spruce trunks," "my pond," "my little swamp" ad infinitum. The possessive language prominent in *Woodswoman* more closely resembles the egocentrism of the "rugged individualist" than the philosophy of land stewardship with its values of humility, responsibility, and community.

Toward the end of *Woodswoman,* LaBastille admits that all her life she has wanted to avoid being seen as a "dumb blond," a "helpless female." Although she decisively disproves such fears, the text also reveals a women anxious about her femininity, her friendships with men, and her image as a physically and sexually attractive woman. This is not to say that LaBastille has lived in isolation from all men. To the contrary, men seem to be ever-ready to help with the heavier tasks, including two state troopers, whom she persuades to carry a thousand pounds of propane gas tanks to her roadless cabin. Regarding those men she cares about, LaBastille confesses, "The more competent I became, the more insecure certain men acted or the more aggressive others behaved toward me." Far from acting the role of the "helpless female" in the woods, she of necessity becomes an androgynous personality, so complete and independent that her male friends express "inferiority complexes." Her closest friendship is with Nick, a naturalist whose professional interests coincide with her own. After an extended live-in friendship, Nick leaves to take a teaching job in Alaska, admitting to her, "You can do everything so well around here, it makes me feel like a dunce."

A number of the photographic illustrations in *Woodswoman* further this theme of the androgynous woodswoman or more precisely of a woman split between socially constructed feminine and masculine personality traits. The net effect is a curious blend of mixed impulses, as LaBastille poses in stereotypically male settings with a snowmobile, with a chainsaw, with a seaplane, and in mountain clothing with a backpack, then in stereotypically female settings in short shorts, or a bikini, cooking in her cabin kitchen, or reading on her dock. She often uses domestic and traditionally feminine metaphors, forming comfortable language bridges that facilitate the passage of her readers from city to wilderness.

While clothed in decidedly female summer wear, she also seems to take pleasure in flaunting if not violating traditional backcountry wisdom and regulations of the Adirondack high peaks. In one photo we see LaBastille in a bikini washing her hair in Black Bear Lake with her dog Pitzi. The caption reads, "Pitzi licks shampoo off my head whenever I wash my hair in the lake." When she becomes concerned about the water quality of her lake, she avoids mention of possible phosphate contamination, however. In another dramatic photo she is cooking on an open fire atop Mt. Marcy, the highest peak in the Adirondacks, on which open fires have been forbidden for years and all dogs (except perhaps hers) are to be leashed. Even more poignant is her overnight camp on the summit of Mt. Algonquin, the second highest mountain in the Adirondacks. Like Mt. Marcy, its summit contains rare and fragile alpine plants. The pertinent photo shows LaBastille's tent sitting, one has to assume, atop an alpine garden, while, in short shorts and displaying her shapely figure, she is cutting a sizable pile of "brush" from this fragile ecosystem for her evening fire. Where is her camp stove, and why is she not camped well below the summit in a protected col? one might ask. This event follows on the heels of her conversation with a veteran male backpacker who complains of the adverse pressures of hikers on the fragile soil and alpine plant life of the high peaks. The hiker adds: "You'll find Algonquin almost as bad as

Marcy. Its delicate soil and tiny plants have been pounded down by hikers' feet." Earlier on her pack trip LaBastille counted 450 hikers who had signed the backcountry register, but she does not ask what would happen if each had camped on the summits of Mt. Marcy or Mt. Algonquin.

In *Woodswoman*, LaBastille asserts that she is her own woman; she will do things her way. Given the continuing popularity of the book, it is apparent her readers appreciate her feisty independence, even from conservation rules and policy, and her unusual mix of confessional candor and scientific knowledge. LaBastille has learned to survive, even to thrive in her harsh environment. With disarming honesty she has revealed an unresolved bundle of conflicts between property rights and stewardship, between egocentrism and biocentrism, between confession, even exposé and the need for privacy. *Woodswoman* remains in print and had sold some 170,000 copies by the end of the twentieth century, including several foreign-language editions. With its eruptions of energy and emotion, its seething and unresolved conflicts, it has become a beacon of northern light, bringing a significant readership to La-Bastille and her wilderness way of life.

ASSIGNMENT, WILDLIFE

Assignment, Wildlife (1980), a companion volume to *Woodswoman,* emphasizes LaBastille's activities as a wildlife ecologist engaged in fieldwork primarily in Latin America and the Caribbean. She establishes here a personal style that serves her ably and becomes a hallmark of her field studies. She balances her scientific interest in flora, fauna, and ecosystems with her warm response to native and local people and her confessional narrative of her own feelings, fears, loves, and losses. Her growing command of Spanish allows her to connect individually with people living in and dependent on the habi-

tats she studies and seeks to preserve, allowing an infectious warmth few other visiting biologists seem to match. The opening section of *Assignment, Wildlife* deals with her winter sojourns in Guatemala, during which she surveys and seeks help to preserve the dwindling giant grebe of Lake Atitlán. The most dramatic lesson La-Bastille learns in these adventures, one not taught in any classroom, is how intimately and complexly conservation work is connected with social and cultural issues. The preservation of endangered species becomes difficult if not impossible when surrounding villagers are desperate for food, fuel, and natural resources. Their poaching often comes more from desperation than from malicious intent. Many setbacks during her field adventures only make her all the more certain of Rachel Carson's message that humans are totally dependent on a healthy ecosystem for physical and spiritual well-being. Because the essays in this volume are reprinted and updated in *Mama Poc* (1990) and *Jaguar Totem* (1999), they will receive fuller discussion under those headings.

BEYOND BLACK BEAR LAKE

Beyond Black Bear Lake (1987) both continues the saga of LaBastille's life in the wilderness and marks a significant departure from the own-build-post-protect-defy impulses ever-present in *Woodswoman.* Here a more experienced LaBastille draws from twenty years of living in the Adirondacks and crafts a more introspective, retrospective, and biocentric narrative. This is not to say that the territorial and gender skirmishes do not continue, but they take back seats to her growing concern about acid rain, nuclear waste disposal, water and noise pollution, development pressures, habitat protection, and the wilderness character of the Adirondacks.

With passing years LaBastille becomes aware of one assault after another on her pristine and secluded environment at Black Bear Lake. New houses and cottages emerge each year, bringing with them more speedboats and concerns about septic systems and water quality. Acting from her concerns, LaBastille provides occasional boat transportation to the state water quality team as they check potential pollution sites. The day after one such volunteer act she discovers a cut fuel line on her small outboard motor. This action is seriously malicious when a boat is the only means of transportation around a roadless lake, and it all but openly declares a backlash against environmental activists.

How the tables have turned from LaBastille's first year on the lake, when she boasted she would tie up the regulation enforcement official who insisted she move her cabin back from the lake and leave him for bears to devour. Although she started her wilderness adventure as a woman living and writing in seclusion, LaBastille comes to admit the need for more, not fewer, regulations and enforcers to preserve the quality of the Adirondack environment. During the 1980s she becomes increasingly involved as an environmental activist both in her own "backyard" and in international fieldwork, writing, and personal appearances. Having seemingly made her peace with regulations and government bureaucracy, LaBastille furthers her commitment to regional planning and environmental protection by accepting an appointment as a commissioner of the Adirondack Park Authority.

But the greatest peril to Black Bear Lake and the entire Adirondack bioregion comes to light when in the mid-1970s LaBastille tests the waters of her lake for acidity. By comparing the results with available records, she discovers that the lake was one hundred times more acidic than it was fifty years earlier. She begins testing other relatively high-altitude lakes and ponds and gets about the same results. By snorkeling in these same lakes, she realizes they have "the eerie feeling of a cemetery. . . . There were no rising fish, stalking herons, swimming mergansers, or plopping frogs."

As LaBastille continues to study the lakes of the Adirondacks, she also begins to publish articles in periodicals, such as *Outdoor Life* and *National Geographic,* about the devastating impact of acid rain. The enormity of the damage to marine life, bird life, and other wildlife from excess acidity disheartens LaBastille, for she realizes that even with remediation and massive changes in fossil fuel abatement technology, she will not live to see the lakes restored to the conditions she witnessed when she first came to the Adirondacks.

Acid precipitation is not the only new and adverse impact on the region. Low-flying military aircraft shatter the silence of the mountains, and all-terrain vehicles (ATVs) and snowmobiles bring additional noise and, perhaps worse, more people further into the deepest recesses of the Adirondack wilderness. But the worst threat of all comes from a U.S. Department of Energy team surveying the rock formations of the Adirondacks for a possible high-level nuclear disposal site. The Adirondacks are attractive for this purpose because of the massive presence of thick and stable Canadian Shield granite formations. LaBastille and many others work through the park agency to convince the Department of Energy that the Adirondacks should be excluded from site consideration and placed in the same category with national parks. While the impulse to protect one's own nest, neighborhood, town, and region is understandable and even commendable, LaBastille never questions the wisdom of the "not in my backyard" approach or admits that at best it can serve as a desperate, last-gasp environmental tactic. The larger perspective, which her writing perhaps implies, is "not in anybody's backyard." The elimination of environmental contamination at its point source plus energy conservation and a shift to renewable energy sources is the direction of nearly all long-term solutions, yet

LaBastille gives little attention to such front-end changes. Her reaction to mounting environmental assaults, an understandable one, is, "All I could do was fight small holding actions . . . not an easy conclusion for a woodswoman and ecologist to have to come to."

Perhaps because of the assault and threats upon her immediate environment, LaBastille decides to build a retreat on Lilypad Lake, a small body of water at the back boundary of her twenty-two acres surrounded by state wilderness lands. If any place could give her peace and privacy, making her days and nights once again pure encounters with nature, this little lake close to the heart of the wilderness should be that place. As she warms to the project LaBastille decides to model her cabin after Henry David Thoreau's, to compare her experience with his, and to call her retreat Thoreau II. If she had called it Walden II the comparison might conceivably have been limited to their cabins, but stated this way she invokes a comparison between her wilderness experience and his. It is a fair analogy, for during this period in her life and career she enjoyed the celebrity of high name and face recognition. Her publications were widely read, and she appeared on numerous television talks shows as an attractive and intelligent oddity, a woman living a self-chosen Thoreauvian existence and doing so for a lifetime, not merely for a two-year experiment. In constructing her retreat LaBastille followed Thoreau's example with care, attempting to "simplify, simplify, simplify" her life, paring it down to the necessities that she might, as Thoreau puts it in *Walden,* "front only the essential facts of life." Since no trails or buildings exist on Lilypad Lake, LaBastille's approach is that of a first settler, felling trees, splitting logs, and building with what she had cut down.

As work progresses LaBastille decides she had better check with the legal office of the Adirondack Park Authority, since she is after all a commissioner, to make sure she is building in compliance with backcountry requirements. For the second time in her wilderness life she is told her structure is not in compliance with Adirondack Park regulations. The maximum size allowable is ten feet by ten feet, and such a structure can exist only for "occasional occupancy." Her reaction is instructive to all who support a principle yet are shocked when it restricts their own freedom of action. After reading the opinion and the new restrictions regarding cabin size, temporary residency, tree cutting, and brush clearing, she rails against governmental imposition:

> What irony! As a commissioner who dealt monthly with the applications, permits, variances, approvals, and denials of *other* people's projects, I was being told what and how to conduct *my* business. This made me froth at the mouth, even as I knew these environmental and developmental controls were basically for the good of the Adirondacks. What a dilemma!

The difference this time is that LaBastille can no longer categorize this clash as one of female independence being hamstrung by a patriarchal "big brother," since she has become her own adversary. Perhaps symbolically LaBastille desires to own wilderness property and to remove it from public access precisely because of the recently won right (in a historic sense) of women to own property and to live, work, and travel independently in wilderness areas. Even though she can conceptualize the wisdom of the policies designed to preserve the rural and wild character of the Adirondack Park, they collide heavily with her personal values of ownership, self-protection, and individual property rights, reducing her discourse, briefly, to foaming, inarticulate anger. Her confessional honesty and agonizing clash of conflicted values are among the qualities that her readers seem to admire in LaBastille, as she dramatizes the debates, including self-conflicts, within the environmental community. Reinventing herself as a guide to and protector of the Adirondacks as Arcadia, LaBastille meets unexpected complications at each turning in her trail.

In *Beyond Black Bear Lake,* LaBastille also admits to the dilemma faced by all artists who win a sizable following: "I've created a two-edged sword; my readers nourish me through sales, yet they threaten to devour me through over attention." Her difficulty stems from wishing to encourage her readers, especially women, to have direct wilderness experiences while needing to protect her own privacy from their invasive interests. LaBastille transposes the usual wilderness gender orientation, proving time and again that she is a happy survivor in the wilderness and that her unwished-for male visitors are the outsiders.

Beyond Black Bear Lake is both a sequel to *Woodswoman,* a continuation of her saga, and an expression of the author's new concerns for the protection of her immediate environment and her cherished Adirondack Park from environmental degradation on many fronts. She also records several heartfelt personal losses, including the deaths of Rob, one of her guiding mentors, and of Condor, her canine companion. Her search for both inner wholeness and a secure retreat further away from public intrusion are no doubt a reaction to personal losses and environmental assaults. As she walks about her new cabin, Thoreau II, she thinks of Thoreau sauntering the environs of Walden Pond. Like Thoreau she also finds meaning and centeredness by ritualizing her pilgrimages, her morning swims, her prayerful meditations with the towering ancestral trees. Careful readers will find ample evidence of a uniquely personal pantheism. Although this volume places more emphasis on her circle of friends and her attachments to the human prospect, her core values and sense of the sacred seem to emanate from her worshipful relations with pristine, unaltered nature.

WOMEN AND WILDERNESS

In response to the needs of female readers, LaBastille begins to offer wilderness workshops and backpacking trips for women and turns her pen to the subject of women and wilderness. By doing so she more than answers Hélène Cixoux's declaration in *Coming Into Writing,* "Woman must write her self; must write about women and bring women into writing." LaBastille writes about women in the forbidden landscape, opening to women the possibility of entrance into the wild. Cixoux's further observation, "Your continent is dark. Dark and dangerous," speaks to LaBastille's new enterprise as a writer and licensed wilderness guide: to introduce groups of women to wilderness travel, to encourage women to pursue careers in backcountry work, and to tell their stories of work and life in the wild. The fruit of this project is displayed in *Women and Wilderness* (1980), which profiles the lives of fifteen contemporary wilderness women. In this book she not only tells of the trickle then flow of women into the "traditionally male bastions" of wilderness life and work but also explores the reasons why in earlier decades and centuries women were kept from the dark forests of the continent and from their own identities. She quotes a convenient opening line from Louise Bogan's poem "Woman" (1954), "Women have no wilderness in them," as a way of expressing the contrasting sea change in thinking about the place of women in wilderness. She expresses this change, "across our continent women are entering the traditionally male bastions of wilderness work and life." In addition to writing on this new topic, LaBastille begins to take groups of women on wilderness trips. Some of her participants bring with them fears of the wild and self-doubt, yet she reports that nearly all gain strength and confidence and "come to value a place where they could go safely without fear of rape, robbery or harassment."

With *Women and Wilderness,* LaBastille turns from gender conflicts, environmental degradation, and conflicts over her own property rights to draw a historical and contemporary sketch of the relationship of American women to wilderness. *Women and Wilderness* reveals that La-Bastille had not been living in intellectual isolation from the impact of the feminist movement and women's studies, although that assumption could have been drawn from her autobiographies. In her new role LaBastille presents a short history of American women in wilderness settings during the colonial, pioneer, and settlement periods. She recognizes that in earlier decades few women had any choice about wilderness life; with few exceptions they followed husbands. She summarizes the findings of the feminist critic and historian Annette Kolodny that for most women wilderness contact was confining rather than liberating.

In her chapter on frontier women LaBastille profiles the lives of women who challenged and sometimes rose above the gender constraints of their times to work as teachers in frontier and Native American settlements, women like Elaine Goodale Eastman, who became known as the "Little Sister of the Sioux," and Catherine Beecher. LaBastille points out that some nineteenth-century frontier women became so adventuresome, defiant, and freedom loving as to challenge the wildest of their male counterparts, women like Calamity Jane, Lille Hitchcock Coit, Isabella Bird, Nellie Cashman, and Pearl Hart. Calamity Jane stands out for her rare combination of masculine and feminine traits, a combination that may have been instructive to LaBastille in her personal and professional search for new amalgamations of socially constructed feminine and masculine traits. La-Bastille reports that, during Calamity Jane's checkered career, she was a "bartender, scout, gambler, drinker, cowgirl, sharp-shooter, prospector, stage driver, cook, stunt woman [in Bill Cody's Wild West Show], sometime prostitute,

and wife [to Wild Bill Hickock]." LaBastille includes lengthy passages from several of Calamity Jane's moving letters to her daughter, conveying her humor and generosity, her deep love of nature, and a personality capable of felicity and tenderness yet alternatively as assertive and combative as any man in the frontier camps. LaBastille also examines literary portraits of frontier women in the novels of A. B. Guthrie, Conrad Richter, and Willa Cather.

The main body of the book is a series of fifteen portraits of women who have chosen to work and live in backcountry. For these portraits she contacted several hundred women and narrowed her selection to fifteen who would represent the variety of professions, lifestyles, and viewpoints she encountered. Unlike the experiences of frontier and pioneer women, who had little choice in shaping their experiences, the women LaBastille profiles report few gender-related difficulties. She also reports that wilderness women "lack the militancy and hostility toward men that some women's liberation groups display." The characteristics of a good woodswoman, as reported by her interviewees, are not gender specific. They include an appreciation of the natural world, wilderness survival skills, and a self-sufficient and independent nature. One of LaBastille's codirectors of wilderness workshops, Jon Fairbanks, comments that, although men are often physically stronger than women, "it is the individual spirit that is critical, and this I have observed certainly as much in women as in men." The one gender-specific concern reported to LaBastille is "the deep-seated fear of being raped or molested while alone outdoors." Although her wilderness sisters did not comment on the idea of carrying a gun for personal protection in backcountry, that has often been LaBastille's hidden source of confidence and protection.

In contrast to the discouragement she received from her mother, LaBastille shares her new knowledge of her environmental foremothers and reveals to a largely unsuspecting 1980 audience the work of her wilderness sisters. A notable change from the autobiographical emphasis of her previous books, here she celebrates the work of others and engages in a discernible feminist project: a direct, nontheoretical revelation of the lives of women living and working in the outdoors. She proves that women and men bring equal skills and abilities to outdoor work, although she recognizes that childbearing places almost impossible demands on women living and working in remote locations. As Kate Winter comments in *American Nature Writers* (1996), "The social change effected by feminism not only brought women into the wild but freed the wild in them." Knowledge of shared commitments has given LaBastille and many other women with similar professions or lifestyles courage to assert their rights and to demand equality with males in all dimensions of their lives.

MAMA POC

Mama Poc: An Ecologist's Account of the Extinction of a Species is a compelling saga of LaBastille's two-decade commitment to understanding and protecting the giant pied-billed grebe, a flightless bird whose habitat was limited to the waters of Guatemala's Lake Atitlán. LaBastille shares some of this remarkable story with readers in the first four chapters of *Assignment, Wildlife. Mama Poc* reprints those chapters and adds others, presenting the many facets of this complex, twenty-four-year effort to save a species from extinction. The title refers to a name affectionately given to LaBastille by villagers as they realize her dedication to their imperiled grebe—the passion and dedication of a mother fighting for the lives of her children.

In 1960 the estimated grebe population at Lake Atitlán was over two hundred birds, but five years later the census results had plummeted to eighty. Grebe hunting has been prohibited by the Guatemalan government since 1959, but local police never enforce the ordinance, and they lack the means to do so. Surprised at her concern, one official says to LaBastille, "And what difference does it make. . . . I'm sorry, senorita, there's nothing that can be done about the *pocs*." ("*Poc*" is the local Guatemalan name for the giant grebe.) After completing her initial survey and realizing the dangerous decline in numbers, LaBastille looks into the causes. One is the overharvesting of reeds by local people. The grebes nest and find cover in reed beds, but villagers also need the reeds for woven products, including mats and furniture. Not only is their nesting ground disappearing, the *poc*'s food source also is declining. In an effort to promote North American tourism, the Guatemalan government introduced bass to Lake Atitlán for sport fishing. The local fishermen do not own the necessary equipment to fish for the bass, which grow rapidly in size and numbers. The smaller fish population of Lake Atitlán, on which both the grebes and the local fishermen depend, declines.

Undefeated by these setbacks, LaBastille is instrumental in establishing a grebe refuge on the lake, which includes reed habitat protection and a captive breeding program to jump-start the process of recovery from the brink of extinction. By the end of 1975 grebe numbers rise to over two hundred, and recovery appears to be under control—that is, until a natural disaster puts all LaBastille's efforts in jeopardy again. In February 1976 Guatemala is devastated by an earthquake that takes the lives of about two hundred Guatemalans and leaves hundreds of thousands of people homeless. The water level of Lake Atitlán drops four feet as a result of the quake, creating a new shoreline and leaving the essential reed beds to dry and die out. LaBastille works with the Guatemalan Department of Forestry to reestablish the grebe refuge in deeper water and to transplant some of the reed beds. Meanwhile, perhaps in response to the excellent sport fishing on the lake, more and more chalets and condominiums are built, slowly converting a wild lake shore into docks and beaches largely devoid of natural vegetation.

Unfortunately, the work of LaBastille and many other conservationists in Guatemala is curtailed in the 1980s by the civil war between guerrillas and government forces. Edgar Bauer, a game warden responsible for grebe protection, is murdered in 1982. By the mid-1980s the grebe population is dwindling rapidly, and La-Bastille and others can do little, given the dangerous military situation, to continue the recovery program. In November 1987, twenty-two years after her first trip to Lake Atitlán, La-Bastille presides at a sizable gathering in Guatemala City and officially announces the extinction of the giant grebe. Refusing to signal total defeat, she urges those in attendance and their public officials to dedicate their efforts to saving Lake Atitlán itself. She can draw satisfaction from the limited success of a refuge and captive-breeding program that might have succeeded in the absence of catastrophic natural and political upheavals.

By the conclusion of this heartbreaking process LaBastille expresses the limitations of her scientific education in addressing environmental problems: "I now realize that a good scientist must recognize social and political issues." *Mama Poc* is the dramatic story of a monumental conservation effort and the death of an endangered species. But it is also the story of an ecologist's evolution.

THE WILDERNESS WORLD OF ANNE LaBASTILLE

The first book published by LaBastille's own publishing company, West of the Wind Publications, *The Wilderness World of Anne LaBastille* (1992) is her contribution to the centennial celebration of the Adirondack Park. It is also a sampler of the range and diversity of La-Bastille's interests and writing styles, including poetry, essays, short stories, and striking color photographs.

In the introduction LaBastille writes about the often unrecognized value of wilderness to humanity, providing opportunities for solitude and the absence of human-made sounds. Wilderness for LaBastille plays vital roles in buffering the corrosive tensions and stresses of urban living and in psychological healing and spiritual centering. Reconnecting with nature in its near-pristine state can supplant the need for therapists, ministers, and in some cases for medical attention. In LaBastille's view nature is a remarkable healer and restorer.

Through description, irony, and juxtaposition, LaBastille's poetry dramatizes the birds and wildlife of her world. In one of her most dramatic poems, "Requiem," she adopts the point of view of a manatee swimming in Florida's tropical waters. She helps readers feel the terror of this gentle, slow-moving creature as a high-speed power boat approaches. The reader sees the fatal wounding as the boat's propeller rips through the manatee's belly. The reader smells the stink of the manatee washed ashore, treated as garbage by the owners of posh seaside villas. LaBastille's poetry is less notable in style than in content, especially in comparison to masters of the nature poetry form, such as Mary Oliver and Pattyann Rogers. Nonetheless the freshness and energy in her voice and chosen subjects is welcome relief from the solipsism characteristic of contemporary poetry.

In the essay section of the book LaBastille reprints previously published short articles on the value of silence, the impact of acid deposition on Adirondack lakes, and on flying squirrels. The concluding section includes four autobiographical stories. One is a tribute to the old-time Adirondack guide Rodney Ainsworth, another tells of LaBastille's adventures on an outclassed motor yacht in a serious Caribbean storm, and a final essay compares her wilderness living with Thoreau's.

WOODSWOMAN III

This third book of LaBastille's autobiographical trilogy, *Woodswoman III: Book Three of the Woodswoman's Adventures* (1997) tells of her third decade of living in the Adirondacks and gravitates between continuity and change. At the advent of her fourth decade in her log cabin on Black Bear Lake, she looks back with pleasure at the choices she made as a young woodswoman and at her many accomplishments and wide public recognition. In addition to her awards for international conservation work, she received the Roger Tory Peterson Award as a National Nature Educator in 1994, a Gold Medal from the Society of Women Geographers in 1993, an honorary doctorate, and distinguished alumna awards. Although *Woodswoman III* overlaps much of what she has written previously, she reveals several new directions and dimensions to her life during her third decade in the wilderness.

After the publication of *Mama Poc* in 1990 by a commercial publisher, LaBastille decided to launch her own company, West of the Wind Publications, to self-publish her future books. She produced *The Wilderness World of Anne LaBastille, Woodswoman III,* and *Jaguar Totem* through her company. As president of her own press, LaBastille is no longer at the whimsy and mercy of commercial publishers, which allows her relative freedom to approve of copy, illustration, and design, choices most writers would envy. Since she has illustrated her books for years with her photographs and drawings, these books do not have a radical new look, but she now has full artistic and design control. She is her own copy and production editor, in charge of her own marketing and sales. One drawback is that a skilled copy editor would detect occasional peccadilloes, such as this line from *Jaguar Totem*: "This generous and helpful man died in the late 1970's of a fatal disease." In spite of some risk that her readership will decline to a regional audience, the move to self-publishing is in keeping with her career-long approach to life and work. Each of her previous books portrayed her as a whole person, mixing the personal, even confessional Anne LaBastille with the professional woman. Through self-publishing and distribution, LaBastille creates a seamless process from writer to reader. The result is exactly what this author wishes to give, even with a signed copy to reinforce the point. LaBastille reaffirms here the rightness of her decision to pursue independence and freedom from as many institutions and restraints as possible. As in the previous autobiographies, she also relishes in reminding readers she is a "pistol packing Mama." Her announcement of a concealed weapon doubtless gives the author a modicum of security from assault but may cause confusion for her readers. Does she recommend that all women or all backcountry hikers carry concealed weapons? Given the number of fatalities and injuries caused by gun accidents and impetuous over-responses, the wider implications of LaBastille's practice may create problems, even if the firearm gives LaBastille and her women clients added confidence as she leads them on wilderness camping and canoeing trips. Most of her clients come to the Adirondacks from fast-paced and stressful urban jobs and lives. They come seeking physical and spiritual rejuvenation. LaBastille teaches them to identify Adirondack flora and fauna, to use a compass, to overcome childhood fears, and to travel more confidently in her wilderness world. At the end of each trip she asks her clients to help her care for the Adirondack Park and the environment. "Maybe I've made two new converts to protect our planet. That's what my guiding is all about."

A combination of factors, including the year-around demands of her publishing business, the nearly impossible living conditions at her cabin during the heart of the winters, and the dawning recognition that she is no longer a youngster, motivates LaBastille to buy a "ramshackle homestead" farm still within the Adirondack

Park but sheltered by the milder climate of the Lake Champlain valley. Captivated by the kestrels that nest and hunt in her new farm meadow, she names the place Kestrel Crest Farm. In addition to a handsome old farmhouse and barn, both of which need restoration, LaBastille purchases a mixed landscape of meadows, woods, wetlands, and a pond. Given the redundant proximity of food and water, her farm supports a more numerous and more diverse wildlife population than her conifer-forested wilderness property. Along with the new pleasures are new dilemmas to weigh in the context of her lifetime experiment with simple, "small footprint" living. She has become a user of electricity, natural gas, a riding mower, and a host of electrical appliances and tools. Life has become easier, especially during those harsh winter months, but it has also become different. Will her readers still think of her as the "woodswoman"? Will life on a farm be as interesting to readers as life in a wilderness cabin? Can she mix the two landscapes successfully in her life narrative? Such questions will doubtless receive answers with future LaBastille publications. Meanwhile, as an ex-commissioner of Adirondack Park, living on a homestead farm is not a panacea; it too has its challenges and disasters. In May 1992, while LaBastille and many others celebrate the one hundredth anniversary of the Adirondack Park, the barn at Kestrel Crest Farm burns completely to the ground, the apparent work of an arsonist. Although no one has ever been arrested in connection with the fire, LaBastille feels it was clearly the work of someone angered by her work on the park commission, perhaps for placing environmental restrictions upon the use of his property.

At the end of *Woodswoman III,* LaBastille describes the death and disintegration of her "companion tree," a stately old spruce that towered over her wilderness cabin for three decades. From feelings of loss she takes heart in the "botanical reincarnation" as mosses, mushrooms, lichens, and other decomposers spring forth from its defiant bulk to make new soil for the forest floor. Mindful of our common fate, she begins to face "old age, weakness, death, oblivion." She can look ahead with acceptance of her own inevitable passing, and as if writing her last will, she expresses the desire to be buried on her own land and to join the biological process, as have her beloved German shepherds and companion trees before her. Her final words on the subject are: "Someday I too will live again."

JAGUAR TOTEM

Jaguar Totem (1999) continues the narrative of LaBastille's many field experiences, primarily in the Caribbean and Latin America, initiated in *Assignment, Wildlife.* Not included here is the saga of her two-decade effort to save the giant grebe of Lake Atitlán, Guatemala, which she narrates in *Mama Poc. Jaguar Totem* begins on the cloud-forested slopes of Volcan Atitlán, high above Lake Atitlán, where LaBastille and a photographer are looking for the resplendent quetzal, Guatemala's national bird. Although it has been protected since 1875, this striking bird (the green tail feathers of the male often measure a yard long) is under increasing pressure throughout Central America. At elevations above nine thousand feet LaBastille's team encounters local crews cutting and burning forests that had been prime quetzal habitat. Although her field project is a success and her quetzal article appears in the January 1969 issue of *National Geographic,* she feels compelled to return the following year to work for habitat protection.

LaBastille admits she falls in love with more than Guatemala and its quetzals. She also falls in love with a strong, attractive, and affectionate young ranger named Armando. As she travels through the villages and farms surrounding Volcan Atitlán, this blond, young wildlife ecologist causes many heads to turn and jaws to drop. But her compelling combination of Spanish-language proficiency, warmth of personality, and professionalism apparently convinces the Guatemalans she works with that she is dedicated to the welfare of the Guatemalan national bird. By the end of this second trip her mission is partially accomplished. One thousand acres of prime habitat have been set aside as a quetzal reserve. As to her future with Armando, she chooses to pursue her career and maintain her independence.

As one field project leads to another during the 1970s and her reputation grows as a hardworking field biologist, she is invited to join larger and better-financed projects. One such assignment is an ecological survey for Panama's first national park conducted under the auspices of the International Union of Conservation of Nature and Natural Resources (IUCN). At one point during the survey LaBastille finds herself in a village of a remote tribe of Guaymí. The contrast between the young scientist and the Guaymí cannot be more pronounced. The tribal chief breaks the tense silence by donning his quetzal-feathered headdress and painting LaBastille's face with a jaguar design reserved for special visitors. The villagers receive her warmly and come to understand her purpose for being there. LaBastille learns from her contact with the Guaymí and other tribal peoples how to become an effective field ambassador as well as an advocate for wildlife protection. She discovers during this and other field assignments that a scientist has to understand the cultural traditions and life needs of indigenous peoples whose traditional homelands will become incorporated within or will surround a park or reserve.

LaBastille's work toward establishing national parks and biological reserves in developing nations is quickly noticed by international conservation organizations. In 1974 she is awarded the Gold Medal for Conservationist of the Year by the World Wildlife Fund with a sizable cash prize donated by J. Paul Getty. During the award ceremony and its aftermath, she meets world conservation elites, including Getty, Thomas Lovejoy, Sir Julian Huxley, Prince Philip, Indira Gandhi, and Lawrence Durrell. As LaBastille expresses the challenge: "Nature has no defense against modern high technology, man-made pollution, and the human population explosions. No place is safe anymore." LaBastille is a reminder that one person can make a significant difference and that conservation teams and organizations can affect positive change on many fronts.

LaBastille's confessional narratives in her autobiographical trilogy reveal her struggles between a desire for personal freedom and the restrictions inherent in environmental protection. In *Woodswoman* her initial response to each new ecological crisis is to protect her own backyard, to accuse men of violating her property or the environment, and to retreat to the wild heart of her acreage. This impulse to flight is augmented in *Beyond Black Bear Lake* with a desire to fight. She develops a growing recognition that the not-in-my-backyard response, while often required, signals emergency intervention when altered policies and practices are also needed. It is not enough to retreat from civilization into even the most remote wilderness regions, she comes to see, because city problems (acid rain, personal violence, waste disposal) soon become backcountry problems. Her thinking and actions move from an earlier confrontational style to a more holistic and embracing philosophy, influenced, she admits, by Aldo Leopold's "land ethic" and maxim that we must each become "a plain member and citizen of the land community" (*A Sand County Almanac*).

Her field experiences as a wildlife ecologist working in many regions and lands, primarily in developing nations, are characterized by efforts to understand the interplay between culture and ecology. In addition to her struggles as an embattled commissioner and defender of her backyard and much-loved Adirondack Park,

LaBastille learns to approach ecological problems in other regions with fresh and innovative thinking. She comes to realize that field ecologists can ill afford to ignore population pressures and local needs for natural resources. Conservationists may have to help improve desperate social conditions to preserve a quetzal reserve, a flamingo reserve, or a national park. In each of her field projects LaBastille reaches out with warmth and understanding to the people she encounters. Through three decades of work as a wildlife biologist, she has grown in her understanding of the complex relationship between the needs of people and the needs of natural species and ecosystems.

LaBastille consistently defies the tendency in science toward specialization and objectivity, always assuring her readers they are encountering an individual, a woman, as well as a scientist. Leaving behind parents, a marriage, and an academic career, she embraces freedom, individualism, and eco-feminism. In her own words in *Jaguar Totem,* "The growth in the women's and the environmental movement happened in parallel, and I benefitted from both." She more than benefited from the proximity of these movements; she contributed significantly to each. Although the impact of her contributions can at this point only be guessed at, her conservation work has resulted in protection for wildlife in many developing countries. Her publications and her workshops for women have inspired many to take up the environmental cause and work to promote beneficial change.

Selected Bibliography

WORKS OF ANNE LABASTILLE

BOOKS

Birds of the Mayas. Big Moose, N.Y.: West-of-the-Wind Publications, 1964.

Bird Kingdom of the Mayas. Princeton, N.J.: Van Norstrand, 1967.

Whitetail Deer. Bobcat. Opossum. Seals. New York: Dutton, 1974.

Woodswoman. New York: Dutton, 1976.

Assignment, Wildlife. New York: Dutton, 1980.

Women and Wilderness. San Francisco: Sierra Club Books, 1980.

Beyond Black Bear Lake. New York: Norton, 1987.

Mama Poc: An Ecologist's Account of the Extinction of a Species. New York: Norton, 1990.

The Wilderness World of Anne LaBastille. Westport, N.Y.: West of the Wind Publications, 1992.

Birds of the Mayas: Maya Folk Tales: Field Guide to Birds of the Maya World: Complete Check List of Birds. Westport, N.Y.: West of the Wind Publications, 1993.

Woodswoman III: Book Three of the Woodswoman's Adventures. Westport, N.Y.: West of the Wind Publications, 1997.

Jaguar Totem. Westport, N.Y.: West of the Wind Publications, 1999.

ESSAYS

"My Backyard: The Adirondacks." *National Geographic* May 1960.

"The Quetzal, Fabulous Bird of Maya Land." *National Geographic,* January 1969, pp. 140–150.

"How Fares the *Poc?*" *Audubon,* March 1972, pp. 36–43.

"Panama Practices the Art of the Possible." *Audubon,* September 1973, pp. 64–77.

"A Delicate Balance; with a Biographical Sketch." *National Wildlife,* June 1976, pp. 28–32.

"On the Trail of Wisconsin's Ice Age." *National Geographic,* August 1977, pp. 182–205.

"Heaven, Not Hell." *Audubon,* November 1979, pp. 68–103.

"Acid Rain: How Great a Menace?" *National Geographic,* November 1981, pp. 652–681.

"Goodbye, Giant Grebe?" *Natural History,* February 1983.

"And Now They Are Gone." *International Wildlife,* July–August 1990, pp. 18–23.

"Doctors of the Wilderness." *Natural History,* May 1992, pp. 42–47.

"How the King of the Birds Was Chosen and Other Mayan Folk Tales." *International Wildlife,* March–April 1997, pp. 30–35.

MANUSCRIPTS

LaBastille's manuscripts are held in the reference collection at Old Forge Library, Old Forge, New York.

CRITICAL AND BIOGRAPHICAL STUDIES

Kolodny, Annette. *The Lay of the Land: Metaphor as Experience and History in American Life and Letters.* Chapel Hill, N.C.: University of North Carolina Press, 1975.

Kunsler, James Howard. "Wild Thing." *Adirondack Life,* July–August 1989.

Showalter, Elaine. "Feminist Criticism in the Wilderness." In her *The New Feminist Criticism: Essays on Women, Literature, and Theory.* New York: Pantheon, 1985. Pp. 243–270.

Winter, Kate H. "Anne LaBastille." In her *The Woman in the Mountain: Reconstructions of Self and Land by Adirondack Women Writers.* Albany, N.Y.: State University of New York Press, 1989. Pp. 125–133.

———. "Anne LaBastille." In *American Nature Writers.* Edited by John Elder. New York: Scribners, 1996. Pp. 499–511.

—JOHN COOLEY

Thomas McGrath

1916–1990

EARLY IN PART Two of his extraordinary long poem *Letter to an Imaginary Friend* (1970), Thomas McGrath describes a village on the island of Skyros in Greece, and in one fluid gesture he moves from that locale to his own place of origin:

> Honeysuckle, lavender, oleander, osiers, olive
>   trees, acanthus—
> All leafsplit, seedshaken, buckling under the drive
> Of the living orient red wind
>   constant abrasive
> North Dakota
>   is everywhere.
>   This town where Theseus
>   sleeps on his hill—
> Dead like Crazy Horse.
>   This poverty.
>   This dialectic of money—
> Dakota is everywhere.
>   A condition.

The passage has both fascinated and baffled commentators on McGrath's poetry. It seems emblematic of the poet's strengths as well as the reasons for his neglect by the American poetry establishment. "Neglect" is a relative term here. By the time of his death on September 30, 1990, from complications following a stroke, McGrath had won numerous awards and honors and had several times benefited from the financial largess of establishment institutions. But major prizes such as the Pulitzer, which might have brought his art to the wider audience it so richly deserved, eluded him, and this injustice has left an aura of defensiveness in much that has been written about him. The fact that McGrath's poetry has gone virtually unnoticed by some prominent East Coast critics

only adds to this defensiveness. As is evident in the passage above, McGrath's vision of the human condition was rooted in his region. "Dakota is everywhere" because it contains the same essential realities that define this condition in all places: mythologies and histories in symbiotic relationships, the troubled marriage of humanity and environment, the economic conditions of the status quo and resistance to it.

Unsympathetic readers might see only Dakota, an empty state they drove through once, where the land is flat and the winters are harsh. But that would be like looking at Manhattan and seeing only the Trump Tower. Such blinkered views miss the storied quality of place. As it happens "Dakota" is an important landscape of the American West or the western edge of the Middle West. It is Gatsby's birthplace. The dreams and atrocities of this region are important aspects of American culture. McGrath was one of the great poets of the West, and neglect of his work during his lifetime may have stemmed from a broad literary prejudice against Western writers that no longer exists in quite the same way.

His politics are another matter. A revolutionary leftist—part of what he eventually called "the unaffiliated far left"—McGrath was for some years a member of the Communist Party and even lost an academic position in Los Angeles for refusing to cooperate with the House Un-American Activities Committee in 1953. This one brave gesture, nobly expressed in his statement to the committee, made McGrath a hero in some circles and a pariah in others. By compromising his academic career for a number of years, eventually leaving him to teach in "remote" universities in North Dakota and Minnesota, the gesture probably kept him from the networks of literary allies who would have been helpful reputation builders. Though his talent was at least equal to that of any poet of his generation, McGrath's temperament was impatient with such notions as career success. He proudly made friends with people who could do nothing to further his career because he believed in the revolutionary commune, in what the Marxist critic Christopher Caudwell had called "the collective festival, where poetry is born."

McGrath was a populist with a Joycean vocabulary, a revolutionary poet comparable to Hugh MacDiarmid in Scotland, Bertolt Brecht in Germany, Yannis Ritsos in Greece, and Pablo Neruda in Chile, a bona fide Marxist-Leninist thinker impatient with the party line. In the United States after World War II the dominant trends in literary criticism from the New Criticism to poststructuralism made it difficult to extol poetry engaged with real social issues. This was also a period in which American poetry was dominated by facile autobiography. It became almost a truism that poets wrote about themselves and their own feelings at all times. Critics like E. P. Thompson and Dale Jacobson have pointed out that McGrath bucked these trends. While most of American poetry became private, McGrath spoke in a public voice. While the minimalism of William Carlos Williams began to take hold in poetic theory and practice, McGrath remained a poet of rhetorical flourishes, lyrical excesses, puns, jokes, bawdiness, invective—a range of inventiveness and reference, of sound, fury, and hilarity, that makes most of the American poetic landscape look as flat as the Red River Valley bordering North Dakota and Minnesota.

To be sure some critics have found a "sameness" in McGrath. In "The Imaginary Friendships of Tom McGrath" (1994) Marty Cohen writes, "Throughout the work are scattered promising poems whose impact is lessened by an appeal to dogma, by allusions to popular styles or common measures that dip into bathos." No doubt this remark holds some justice. One often wishes to edit McGrath, and his politics sometimes make it easy to disagree with him, just as politics complicate reading Ezra Pound. In his long lines and large voice McGrath is often compared to Walt Whitman, but like William Carlos Williams he at first found Whitman not to his taste. A more accurate comparison of McGrath's technique would be to that of Robinson Jeffers, the once-popular poet of California who has suffered neglect at the hands of literary tastemakers and another poet with a big, public voice. McGrath discovered Jeffers early, as he says in several interviews, and found Jeffers's long line attractive. In a 1982 letter to Sam Hamill, McGrath lists other influences:

> Big Bill Haywood, Wm. Z. Foster, E. Gurley Flynn, Debs, and (right here) the Non-Partisan League and Townley. But the *poets* who really showed me most were Crane, Neruda + B. Brecht and I was lucky to read the last two because they were published by left and Communist magazines. Then I found their books and read them while 'the poets of my generation' (tho I was between generations) were deep in their academic slumbers. Not all, of course: Rexroth, Rukeyser, [Don] Gordon—others as well.

Perhaps the fact that his two most supportive publishers were Alan Swallow and Sam Hamill, both important small publishers in the West, was another symptom of his "outsider" status.

Ultimately McGrath will have to be understood as a crusty individualist, neither academic nor beat, a poet without peer who, despite his lesser work, deserves a place of honor in the American canon. At the end of the passage in Part Two of *Letter to an Imaginary Friend,* he writes:

And I am only a device of memory
To call forth into this Present the flowering dead
  and the living
To enter the labyrinth and blaze the trail for the
  enduring journey
Toward the round dance and commune of light . . .
                  to dive through
     the night of rock
(In which the statues of heroes sleep) beyond
  history to Origin
To build that Legend where all journeys are one
                where Identity
Exists
     where speech becomes song . . .

For McGrath the act of making the poem was tribal. Though he lived much of his life in isolation, his poetry assumed a public, and it continues to find one.

EARLY YEARS

Thomas Matthew McGrath was born on November 20, 1916, on a farm near Sheldon, North Dakota. This is a place of gently rolling hills where cottonwoods line the Sheyenne River to the south, the Maple River to the north, with occasional groves of box elders, shelter belts of evergreens, and a few Russian olives. It is wide-open country, though not as flat as the valley of the Red River to the east, a river that flows north through Fargo and Grand Forks to Winnipeg. Rivers were always important to McGrath, associated with the sources of poetry itself.

Both sets of McGrath's grandparents had emigrated from Ireland. In an interview with Reginald Gibbons and Terrence Des Pres, McGrath recalled that his maternal grandfather, whose name was Shea, homesteaded in what is now Fargo:

around the tail end of the '70s, maybe it was '80. . . . But he was broke, so he got a job freighting from Fargo to Winnipeg, and according to him, he used to drive these old Red River ox carts with the wheels about as high as the ceiling, because it was a gumbo mud there.

Eventually this grandfather moved to a farm on the Maple River. "He sent back to Ireland and he got a wife who was about three times his size from over the Shannon, where the English said they would drive the Irish to hell or Connacht. . . . She was a Gaelic speaker, whereas his Gaelic was very, very little." On the other side, "my father's father came from Ireland to Canada, and from Canada came down and eventually wound up at a little place called Fort Ransom, homesteaded, got killed by a runaway team, the farm went under, and everybody went every which way." The poet's father could recall being told to run for Fort Ransom during a time of Indian trouble, and McGrath reasoned that this would have been the era of the Ghost Dance, culminating in the massacre at Wounded Knee in South Dakota in December 1890.

These details provide the rudiments of McGrath's early consciousness. He grew up in a family that, in contrast to the predominantly Scandinavian culture of the region, was Irish Catholic. Their life was textured by the Latin rituals of itinerant priests and by the languages and folk culture of Ireland, with its resentment of empire and class. James McGrath, Thomas McGrath's father, had worked as a lumberjack and encountered the labor politics of the Wobblies (the Industrial Workers of the World). Thomas McGrath's mother, Catherine Shea, had grown up in a prosperous farming family but had seen her father's fortunes fall. Consequently from both sides of the family came a mistrust of banks and other powerful economic interests. In the late nineteenth century North Dakota had been a hotbed of radical politics, sympathetic to the Farmer's Alliance, which had attempted to form a national third party. A year before the poet's birth another political insurgency formed the Nonpartisan League, which with its socialist agenda dominated state politics until just after World War I. The atmosphere of McGrath's childhood was heavily politicized in terms that pitted labor, including farm labor, against the robber barons and captains of industry. When his parents married and began to farm, they were not landowners but renters. McGrath remembered his father not as a politically active man but as one who had a basic mistrust of the rich.

The element of Irish identity should also be stressed. McGrath would surely have been aware that he was born in the year of the Easter Rebellion in Ireland. Irish identity carries with it a history in which vigorous language becomes a form of revolt. (James Joyce's Stephen Dedalus said that his soul fretted in the shadow of the English language, yet few have ever written English as well as Joyce.) In an interview with Frederick C. Stern, McGrath recalls his father:

> as a wonderful storyteller who had memorized the whole *McGuffey's Readers*. He hadn't gone to more than the fourth or fifth grade, though he was probably older than people would be in those grades now. I remember many Saturday nights, when all he would do is sing, or tell stories or recite poems.

From his earliest years then McGrath would have known to respect language as the stuff of life.

He was the eldest of six children. The others were Jim (killed in World War II), Joe, Kathleen, Martin, and Jack. In *A Memoir of Thomas McGrath* (1993) McGrath's English friend Jack Beeching recalls a visit to the family farm with McGrath in the late 1960s:

> Charlotte and I shared Thanksgiving with Tom's widowed mother on the farm at Sheldon. A serious front room, with large old photos and the pious mementos of a Catholic household—a family shrine. Alive or killed on active service, Tom's brothers were an invisible strong presence. Old objects and new comforts filled a warm house— her sons looked after her, and Tom himself wore all day a different face, his seldom-revealed, underneath face, tender.

Beeching had first known McGrath in England and Greece as a man of the world. Now he was afforded a rare glimpse of McGrath at home. McGrath's parents had eventually become owners of the farm, referred to in his poem "The Old McGrath Place." He grew up with this close-knit family, aware of his Irish heritage and the history of injustices on the land surrounding him, and through reading he became aware of the larger world. He recalled the bookshelf in his small country school, no larger than a filing cabinet, where he found the *Iliad* and the *Odyssey* and the Norse *Edda*. He read the Irish songwriter Thomas Moore, the novels of Sir Walter Scott, and the Border Ballads. While a student at Sheldon High School he bought a copy of James Joyce's *Ulysses* (1922), which became a hugely important influence on his own work. McGrath was a voracious reader with a powerful memory. Years later he recalled his incredulity at meeting young, would-be poets who had no desire to read the great literature of the past. For him such knowledge was precious and hard-earned. After all, he was thirteen when the Great Depression began, and much of his consciousness was formed by the political and economic conditions of the 1930s. It is most important to note about McGrath's early years that he could remember a happy, pastoral beginning as well as a Fall from Grace and that Catholicism, folklore, politics, and literature contributed to his broad sympathies and real erudition as well as his modesty, his perspective on the human condition. He knew firsthand the farm life of manual labor, and he conceived of the larger world in terms of a revolutionary struggle, a tension of ideas and actions—a place in which words mattered.

THE FIRST BOOKS OF POEMS

After a brief period of study at Moorhead State in Minnesota, which he left due to financial difficulties in the depression, McGrath entered the

University of North Dakota in Grand Forks, graduating with a bachelor's degree in 1939. There his interest in poetry deepened. In the interview with Stern he particularly mentions the influences of Hart Crane, Conrad Aiken, and T. S. Eliot, all poets who attracted him through the rich aural textures of their poems. McGrath was drawn first and foremost to poets of linguistic and formal intensity. The rich musicality of Crane and the early Eliot appealed to his almost genetic predisposition to lyricism. From his family life and his study McGrath knew such popular literary traditions as the Scottish Border Ballads and Irish and American folk songs, and with time he also became an aficionado of jazz. Unlike many poets of later generations, he never associated politics with poetic form. He was intrigued by modernism and its free verse experiments, but he had a gift for meter and rhyme and saw no reason why serious poetry should not also give pleasure. The aural richness of Gerard Manley Hopkins and Dylan Thomas were becoming better known, and McGrath was lured as much by such sonic possibilities as by the earthiness of Joyce.

When he graduated with his B.A. in 1939, McGrath was also awarded a Rhodes Scholarship to Oxford, but the advent of war forced him to postpone overseas travel. Instead he entered a master's degree program in English at Louisiana State University (LSU) in Baton Rouge. By now a member of the Communist Party, he distributed leaflets in black neighborhoods and seems to have felt ambivalent about the priesthood of literary scholarship, even as practiced by professors he respected, like Cleanth Brooks. At LSU McGrath met his fellow westerner Alan Swallow, who later became one of the most important independent publishers of the twentieth century, when they were both students in Brooks's class on the history of criticism. Swallow had acquired a hand letterpress and was printing a book of student

poems in his garage. McGrath helped him out on a few occasions, and one day Swallow declared that he would like to publish McGrath's first collection. The result was a pamphlet called *First Manifesto* (1940). It is much better than journeyman work, and it was favorably reviewed by the poet Selden Rodman. A letter from McGrath to Swallow dated July 1, 1940 (a copy of which is among the McGrath papers at Copper Canyon Press), reveals a great deal about McGrath's early literary experience and his view of the war:

Dear Swallow,

I am sending you the review from the *Saturday Review of Literature*. Rodman did the review of *First Manifesto*, along with books by Kimball Flaccus, Oscar Williams (*The Man Coming Toward You*), and Eugene Jolas. You can see for yourself that, while the review is pretty kindly, it is also pretty stupid, a typically bourgeois affair. Earlier in the article, when he is just shadowboxing with himself, and preparing to get started, he suggests that I must have been influenced by Kenneth Patchen. If this is so, it must be a retroactive influence, since, until I borrowed the Patchen book from you, I had read only about five or ten lines of his. It's marvelous the way these things work.

With luck, I should finish the thesis this week. After that, I hope never to have to look at it again. I have to keep it in the ice box at night, or the smell will kill off the neighbors.

I am still hoping to get out there [Swallow was in New Mexico at that time], although I'm not sure I shall make it. Anyway, I'll try. I am glad that Russia is moving into Rumania. In that case, she should be fairly well set. It looks as if the words of the International were true—the stage seems to be getting set for the "final conflict."

Mac

It is not only the party line politics that are of interest here but also McGrath's denial of a literary influence attributed to him by the critic. In fact some of the poets who most influenced him at this time were the British leftists W. H.

Auden, Louis MacNeice, and Stephen Spender. Over the next decade McGrath certainly composed poems that can be called "gritty" and "American," but he also displayed a fondness for accentual meters and slant rhymes much like the 1930s poetry of Auden and MacNeice. A case in point is his "Jig Tune: Not for Love," obviously modeled on Auden's "O Where Are You Going?"

> Where are you going? asked Manny the Mayor.
> What are you doing? asked President Jane.
> I'll bet you're a bastard, said Daniel the Deacon;
> We'll put you away where you'll never be seen.

Indeed in a letter written earlier on June 18, 1940, he notes that he had been reading book reviews by Auden and Spender for his thesis. The Auden generation poets attracted him for good reason. They combined social conscience with linguistic variety. Auden and MacNeice especially brought intriguing new images and a sense of urgency to poetic idiom.

The same letter of June 18 reveals that McGrath intended to marry—"more or less secretly"—his girlfriend Marion Points, who was working at the time in Springfield, Missouri. They were married a week later, a date commemorated in McGrath's poem "Celebration for June 24th." The couple soon moved to Waterville, Maine, where McGrath had accepted a teaching position at Colby College. While there, thinking of Crane and perhaps the landscape of his own childhood, McGrath wrote one of his longer early poems, "The Drowned Man: Death between Two Rivers," in which he tried out ambitious symbolic structures. McGrath did not feel suited to teaching at that point in his life, or not when the world appeared to be so full of important action. In a letter to Swallow dated May 24, 1941, McGrath expresses a commitment to clarity in poetry, saying he is working on "another fairly big poem" and planning to move with Marion to New York.

Having left his teaching position that year, McGrath held a number of jobs in New York as a labor organizer, a research assistant for lawyers working for leftist causes, and a welder at the Kearney Shipyards. "The Dialectics of Love," another small collection of his poems, was published as part of a larger book, *Three Young Poets,* edited by Alan Swallow, in 1942. That year, with the permission of the Communist Party, McGrath entered the U.S. Army. Colorblindness kept him from flight school, and he was lucky enough not to be shipped to Europe or the South Pacific. Instead, as a member of the army air force, McGrath spent two years, 1943 to 1945, in the Aleutians, most of it on the island of Amchitka. The United States had already been attacked by Japanese planes at Dutch Harbor to the east, and at the end of the war U.S. troops staged a bloody recapture of Attu to the west. But on Amchitka, McGrath had to endure the boredom of a treeless landscape, the horizontal rain, and the absurdity of military life. When in one poem, "A Letter for Marion," he wrote, "I sit musing, ten minutes from the Jap," he was nearly being literal. He alluded sardonically to Edna St. Vincent Millay, "My candle is burning at both ends and the middle." In addition he made a sort of Audenesque allegory out of the lousy weather: "Am going on instruments, my private weather / Socked in zero zero." (Another American poet doing similar work at the time, but in a more dangerous theater, was Karl Shapiro.) McGrath's poems dealing directly with the war include "Blues for Warren," "Crash Report" and "Homecoming." The Aleutians later reappeared in "Remembering that Island" and *Letter to an Imaginary Friend.*

Despite his absence from combat, the war took a huge personal toll on McGrath. The worst blow came in 1945, when his brother Jimmy was killed in a plane crash. Later poems that deal with this event include "Blues for Jimmy" and "The World of the Perfect Tear." McGrath also blamed his absence during the war for the eventual failure of his marriage to Marion. In his novel *This Coffin Has No Handles* (written in France in 1948), McGrath's narrator arrives in New York after the war and gets involved in labor struggles but finds himself unable to return to the woman he had loved. Perhaps McGrath was wrestling with thinly disguised autobiography. He and Marion remained married for a few years after the war, but they had already begun to drift apart emotionally.

The war's end also meant that McGrath could at last take advantage of his Rhodes Scholarship. He spent the academic year of 1947–1948 at New College, Oxford. In the interview with Stern he recalls, "I wrote most of *Longshot O'Leary['s Garland of Practical Poesie]* there, some of it up at Scotland during the winter Christmas vacation." These are some of McGrath's jauntiest, songlike poems, including "Ars Poetica; or, Who Lives in the Ivory Tower" (imitating MacNeice's "Bagpipe Music") and "A Real Gone Guy," his lyric to the tune of "The Streets of Laredo":

> As I walked out in the streets of Chicago,
> As I stopped in a bar in Manhattan one day,
> I saw a poor weedhead dressed up like a sharpie,
> Dressed up like a sharpie all muggled and fey.

The popular techniques employed in *Longshot O'Leary* (1949), with its rhymes and rollicking meters, endeared McGrath to many of his nonliterary readers, but these poems were often dismissed by those who wanted their poetry to be serious. In the United States, Auden suffered the same dismissals from critics who thought him frivolous. The often comic sensibilities of Auden and McGrath have been consistently misunderstood by readers who want purity in poetry—purity of diction or form or politics. Auden and McGrath were, in their different ways, too irrepressible to fit easily into the categories of others. McGrath wanted impurity and explicitly said so many times. He also wanted breadth and variety. So it is not surprising that he wrote *Longshot O'Leary* in the same year that Swallow published his more somber first full-length book, *To Walk a Crooked Mile* (1947), which begins with the meditative "The Seekers," subtitled "Pueblo, Colorado 1940," and includes many of the early poems of military experience and the love poems to Marion.

McGrath's idea of political poetry had never been simplistic, and he formulated a theory of "tactical and strategic" poetries, usefully summarized by Mark Vinz in his memoir "Thomas McGrath: Words for a Vanished Age":

> As Tom explains it, "tactical poetry" is immediate, practical, and tied to issues as they arise— written as an artist might make a banner or a sign, to appeal to a wide audience and often drawing on the vernacular and oral traditions (and in some ways parallel to the work of such writers as Woody Guthrie or Joe Hill). "Strategic" poetry, on the other hand, is not as interested in clarity, familiarity, or immediacy, even though it might make the same kind of political statement. Most of McGrath's work is clearly "strategic" in nature, very often (especially in parts of *Letter*) relentlessly experimental, working on several levels at once.

At Oxford, McGrath learned a great deal and formed strong friendships with leftist writers in the London literary scene, such as Thompson and Beeching, but his plans for a thesis on Eliot were rejected—dead poets were preferred. At the end of the year McGrath abandoned his Rhodes Scholarship, went to a fishing village in the south of France, and wrote his novel. Though *This Coffin Has No Handles* (1984) contains powerful descriptive passages, some of its dialogue and plotting are clumsy, and it failed to find a publisher until the 1980s. World War II and the advent of the Cold War had made literature about labor struggles and American Communists unfashionable to say the least.

After traveling in Europe, McGrath returned to the United States in 1949, where he worked odd jobs and wrote pulp fiction in New York. His marriage to Marion ended in 1950, and in

1951 he accepted a teaching position at Los Angeles State College. His relationship to the Communist Party was also increasingly complicated due to his objections to party hierarchy and tactics as well as to policies of compromise with mainstream Democrats. McGrath detested political expediency. While he was never officially expelled from the party, he drifted away from it and at one point cofounded his own whimsical alternative, the Ramshackle Socialist Victory Party or RSVP. He also cofounded a literary magazine, the *California Quarterly* (1951–1954), served on the editorial board of *Mainstream* (1955–1957), and wrote new poems of his own.

This relatively stable life in southern California included marriage in 1952 to Alice Greenfield, but that life did not last long. In 1953 the House Un-American Activities Committee called McGrath before its hearings in Los Angeles. His statement to the committee gave three rational grounds for refusing to cooperate: 1) his responsibility to his students precluded cooperation with any force that would interfere with their education, 2) his responsibility to the profession prevented his interfering in any way with academic freedom, and 3) as a poet he refused to cooperate "on aesthetic grounds," adding that "poets have been notorious noncooperators where committees of this sort are concerned. As a traditionalist, I would prefer to take my stand with Marvell, Blake, Shelley and Garcia Lorca." By the spring of 1954 McGrath was out of a job and blacklisted. He worked a series of jobs at the Los Angeles Stock Exchange, laying mosaic tile, carving wooden animals for a toy maker, and gardening. He also began to write film scripts, mostly documentary. But for the rest of the decade his academic career was over. In commemoration and protest his students privately printed a book of his poems, *Witness to the Times!* (1953). Later he satirized this period in *The Gates of Ivory, the Gates of Horn* (1957), another novel.

THE DOUBLE WORLD

Beeching's memoir describes the life of a blacklisted academic:

> The nervous strain for Tom must at times have been past a joke—his face aged. Yet unlikely as it sounded, the unequivocal and crazy world of witch hunt California turned out to be a milieu in which for the time being his genius could thrive. Out of glum years which for those less clearsighted might have been destructive emerged the brilliantly sardonic poems collected in *Figures from a Double World* (1955).

The book Beeching refers to was important in several ways. With its arch portraits of a variety of characters, it may have carried McGrath's impersonal style as far as he could take it and thus may have helped engender the personal recollections of *Letter*. *Figures* contains important personal poems, especially "The World of the Perfect Tear" in memory of his brother Jimmy. But much of the book reads something like the "Robinson" poems of Weldon Kees, though McGrath's anger is perhaps less autobiographical and more allegorical, turned outward at the mendacity of American life. "Mr. Carson Death on His Nights Out" concludes:

> It is the world he wants. It is the world
> He hates: Is it too early to depart
> In the dark prime of hope and of despair?
> The contradiction chills the morning air
> As again the ritual of dionysian art
> Starts clocks in all his condominiums.

The contradictory life depicted here reflects a sense of doubleness that McGrath had always felt, which was also expressed by Auden in books like *The Double Man* (1941).

In numerous writings, including reviews McGrath avidly read, Auden suggests that human beings remember a kind of Eden in the womb, a wholeness lost at birth when, over time, people become divided by self-consciousness. Alien to essential wholeness, people are doomed to despondency and desire. For Auden in the 1940s this psychological allegory was increasingly understood in religious terms, heavily influenced by Kierkegaard. For McGrath a decade later this Fall from Grace and desire for the lost Eden was best explained by Karl Marx. In "McGrath on McGrath" (1973), he speaks of "the Angel in the form of the class struggle" who "blocks the way" to Eden "with a flaming sword." The "general production of false consciousness even by men who think they are men of good will" necessitates the engagement of a poetry that is not merely navel-gazing or frivolous. McGrath was serious about revolution.

But perhaps again like Auden, McGrath understood that even for the politically engaged poet a split, a division existed between the real world and representations of it. If it is true that some of McGrath's poems appear merely dogmatic, like leftist alternatives to William Butler Yeats's fascist marching songs, what saved him in his best work from mere propaganda was his love of the word, the delightful intoxication of poetry itself. The doubleness of human consciousness, which Karl Marx describes as a dialectic of necessity and freedom, materialism and choice, left McGrath free to find fulfillment not only in sober notions of "reality" but also in the multiple pleasures of poetry. In "McGrath on McGrath" he says:

> I sometimes dream of writing couplets when I'm old. An acceptance of form solves, or seems to solve, many problems, and I have always admired and envied J. V. Cunningham [another poet published by Swallow] who seems always to know exactly what he is doing. But I also like Lorca. My old age will not be an easy one.

The most powerful poem in *Figures from the Double World* (he preferred the definite article in the title) is his "Ode for the American Dead in Asia," a sequence of three sonnets memorializing the Korean War. It memorably begins:

> God love you now, if no one else will ever,
> Corpse in the paddy, or dead on a high hill
> In the fine and ruinous summer of a war
> You never wanted.

It is significant that this Marxist poet could liberate himself sufficiently from materialism to evoke God with simultaneous ritual and irony. When poetry takes on a ritual voice, as McGrath's could do very well, its elevation creates awareness that such language is not at the level of our daily muddle. One of McGrath's richest later lyrics is called "The Bread of This World," but its diction is hardly ordinary. McGrath could write with the ritual voice because he held a double view of poetry itself. It served purposes, and it was itself a purpose, a way of being in the world.

LETTER TO AN IMAGINARY FRIEND

"The poem began one afternoon in 1954 at the house of the poet Don Gordon, in Los Angeles." So begins an elucidation of *Letter* in "McGrath on McGrath." After praising such "Lost Poets" as Gordon and Naomi Replansky, McGrath refers to his own trepidation at writing a long poem. "I suppose Don knew instantly that it was more lack of nerve than anything else that was stopping me. He gave me the obvious advice: Begin and see what happens." McGrath went home, as indicated in line two of the poem, and made his start:

> I am in Los Angeles, at 2714 Marsh Street,
> Writing, rolling east with the earth, drifting toward
>   Scorpio, thinking,
> Hoping toward laughter and indifference.

Here is the anxiety of the blacklisted teacher starting over, as Yeats put it, "In the foul rag and bone shop of the heart."

Line one of the poem is in quotes as if overheard from conversation: "From here it is necessary to ship all bodies east." Most commentators point out that McGrath was aware of the end of manifest destiny or, as Louis Simpson later put it in his ironic take on Whitman, "the end of the Open Road." The mysterious ruefulness of McGrath's opening alludes to American myths gone wrong and is composed with the thoughtful fragmentation of Eliot. Of the American journey west McGrath simply writes, "I do not know what end that journey was toward." He records the process of writing as he writes himself back in time, "On a mission of armed revolutionary memory!" It will not be merely a nostalgic backward look, for, as he writes later, "Nostalgia is decayed dynamite." It will be the long poem that attempts to contain the whole man. McGrath could never have been the great lyric poet of the perfectionist sort, like Robert Frost or Richard Wilbur. Instead McGrath's lyric gifts most frequently emerge in larger structures. Amy Clampitt, writing in the *Nation,* calls his long poem, "By turns fierce, somber, rollicking, and outrageous—a simmering *olla podrida* of an epic, from which there is the urge at moments, perhaps, to turn away. Only one doesn't, much as one can't tear oneself away from a party that is getting out of hand." Terrence Des Pres, in *Praises and Dispraises* (1988), uses the carnival image derived from Mikhail Bakhtin's *Rabelais and His World* to describe the poem's structure and worldview.

Letter to an Imaginary Friend evolved over more than thirty years of McGrath's life, from the blacklisted 1950s to his teaching years at North Dakota State University (1962–1967) and Moorhead State University (1969–1983). Part One was published by Swallow in 1962 and Parts One and Two together in 1970. Parts Three and Four were published by Copper Canyon Press in 1985. In the intervening years Alan Swallow died of a heart attack in Denver. His second marriage having ended in divorce in 1957, McGrath married the Greek American Eugenia Johnson in 1960, and in 1969 they had

a son, often called Tomasito in the poems. To find himself a father at age fifty-three gave McGrath an unanticipated delight. He experienced other changes and developments, some of which were recorded in the completed poem, and by the time its final sections were published McGrath's own health was severely compromised.

Any thorough discussion of a poem as big, significant, and unruly as *Letter* would require volumes, but it is possible in less space to at least touch upon its themes and high points. McGrath himself discussed its shape in terms of spirals, like the diagram of DNA he prints in Part Four, and its technique by comparison in terms of cuts in a film (remember that he was an experienced, professional writer of scripts). In "McGrath on McGrath" he makes it clear that he gave a great deal of thought to the problem of the long poem:

> Poe was 100% wrong. It is the *"short"* poem which is a contradiction in terms. In reality there are only *long* poems and the void. It is true that what we appear to get are "aphorisms, epigrams, songs, song-like poems" and so on. But these are only fragments of the long poem which the poet somehow failed to write, that long poem which he will go on trying to write by fits and starts his whole life long.

This is the theory by which the collected poems of Yeats, for example, can be read the same way as *Leaves of Grass*—as one lifelong project in multiple versions. McGrath's statement goes on to consider the examples of long poems by Crane, Homer, MacLeish, Pound, Williams, and Allen Ginsberg—all of which he found unhelpful as models. Dante too was a source for images in *Letter,* along with William Wordsworth and William Blake. But McGrath's long poem is ultimately sui generis. By turns narrative and fragmentary, lyrical and prosaic, historical, mythical, autobiographical, surrealistic, and visionary, riddled with puns, allusions, neologisms, high and low humor, revolutionary but in some of its attitudes "politically incorrect," it is the kind of broad creation that invites comparison to great writers of the past.

Parts One and Two contain the most realistic and accessible sections, though the same could be said of some of the Christmas section in Part Three. Generally the shorter final sections are wilder, more difficult, at times even trying the patience of sympathetic readers. The central metaphor of Part One is Eden, the Fall from Grace spelled out in the young McGrath's dawning awareness of political struggle. Significantly the crucial scene is a communal one, a harvest-time in North Dakota sometime in the mid-1920s. These were the last years of the steam threshers, some of which remain on display in communities like Rollag, Minnesota, east of Fargo-Moorhead. So McGrath's vision of an ideal community carries with it the image of a technology predating Marx:

> Feathered in steam like a great tormented beast
> The engine roared and laughed, dreamed and
>   complained,
> And the petcocks dripped and sizzled; and under
>   its fiery gut
> Stalactites formed from the handhold's rheumy
>   slobbers.
> —Mane of sparks, metallic spike of its voice,
> The mile-long bacony crackle of burning grease!
> There the engineer sat, on the high drivers,
> Aloof as a God. Filthy. A hunk of waste
> Clutched in one gauntleted hand, in the other the
>   oilcan
> Beaked and long-necked as some exotic bird;
> Wreathed in smoke, in the clatter of loose
>   eccentrics.
> And the water-monkey, back from the green quiet
>   of the river
> With a full tank, was rolling a brown quirly,
> (A high school boy) hunkered in the dripping
>   shade
> Of the water tender, in the tall talk and acrid sweat
> Of the circle of spitting stiffs whose cloud-topped
>   bundle-racks
> Waited their turns at the feeder.
> And the fireman: goggled, shirtless, a flashing
>   three-tined fork,

> Its handle charred, stuck through the shiny
>   metallic
> Lip of the engine, into the flame, smoky
> Firebox of its heart.
> Myself: straw-monkey. Jester at court.

In what is surely one of the great descriptive passages in American poetry, McGrath mythologizes the machine and the workers, makes them figures from a primordial world. And the whole long description funnels down to the small boy called out to work because one of the men was missing. "Was it hard?" he asks later. "No. Everyone wanted to help me." This is what McGrath means by the commune, the community united in work.

McGrath began the poem far from home, alone, working odd jobs with no future. The title speaks volumes here. The public world of profession had rejected him, and he was far from famous even as a poet. The gesture of writing a letter to an imaginary friend seems childlike in its simplicity, evoking the despair of so many poets who wonder what became of their audience. In interviews, however, McGrath was fond of echoing Ralph Waldo Emerson, saying that each of us lives two lives, once as a private self, then as a Representative Man. His method in *Letter* is to begin with autobiography and move toward allegory. The boy working as straw-monkey out in the fields is the man writing the poem, who recalls, "My father took me as far as he could that summer, / Those midnights, mostly, back from his long haul." Another man, McGrath informs us, could take the boy further:

> But mostly Cal, one of the bundle teamsters,
> Sun-blackened Virgil of the spitting circle,
> Led me from depth to depth.

The literary self-consciousness of the allusion to Dante brings with it images of journey, harrowing hell, and tribal identity. Even the six-beat line, the basic line for many of his strongest passages, seems almost a borrowing from Homer. (Later poets like Seamus Heaney and Derek Walcott, both Nobel Prize winners, used such allusive structures for their longer poems. McGrath deserves at least to be in their company.) But if Cal is his Virgil, it is only for a time. Cal is a Wobbly:

> He read *The Industrial Worker,*
> Though I didn't know what the paper was at the time.
> The last of the real Wobs—.

Cal teaches him to shoot and to handle horses. "He wanted me to grow without growing too fast for myself. / A good teacher, a brother."

In a crucial scene, Cal gets into a fight over labor issues with one of McGrath's uncles and is severely beaten. The scene has an almost biblical force:

> Cal spoke for the men and my uncle cursed him.
> I remember that ugly sound, like some animal cry touching me
> Deep and cold, and I ran toward them
> And the fighting started.
> My uncle punched him. I heard the breaking crunch
> Of his teeth going and the blood leaped out of his mouth
> Over his neck and shirt—I heard their gruntings and strainings
> Like love at night or men working hard together,
> And heard the meaty thumpings, like beating a grain sack
> As my uncle punched his body—I remember the dust
> Jumped from his shirt.

In the wake of this violence, which seems to upset everyone in McGrath's family, the boy runs off alone to the river. There, among the trees, "Runeless I stood in the green rain / Of the leaves." Away from people he seeks a kind of solace. These lines might be compared to Whitman's "Out of the Cradle Endlessly Rocking." The scene ends when he is back with his family, hears from his mother that Cal will not eat, and hears from his father: "Hard times, Old Timer."

> I sat in the lantern's circle, the world of men,
> And heard Cal breathe in his stall.
>
> An army of crickets
> Rasped in my ear.
>
> "Don't hate anybody,"
> My father said.
> I went toward the house in the dark.

When chapter 3 of Part One ends, the community has been broken.

Chapter 4 is McGrath's paean to budding sexuality: "O great kingdom of Fuck! And myself: plenipotentiary!" These passages evoke adolescence's hyperbolic obsessions, while chapter 5 begins, "Love and hunger!—that is my whole story." But the hunger here is for learning and self-improvement. The depression was on when McGrath went away to college, first to Moorhead:

> And the first man I met was some kind of dean.
> O excellent title!
> What did it mean? Did the tumbleweed
> Blowing out of Saskatchewan know it?
> A man, anyhow, thin as a rail and mean
> As a cross-barred barbwire gate, with a flat face to him
> Like Picasso's Vallauris plates; all piss and moment,
> A pithy, pursy bastard, like a quidnunc espaliered
> Against the ass of the North Wind.
> He sat there like a chilly Lutheran Buddha,
> All two dimensions of him—

McGrath has moved far from lyrical remembrance deep into invective and satire. Like Auden he shows a fondness for mixing high and low diction—the Latin of quidnunc set "Against the ass of the North Wind"—but McGrath's macaronic language has a fully American flavor to it, a gruffness akin to Pound's. He delights in sending readers to the dictionary, and the breadth and depth of his word hoard is part of his poem's carnival spirit.

His education interrupted by "hard times," he returns home, where in chapter 7 he gives us a Frostian woodcutting scene:

> And did we burn?
> We burned with a cold flame.
> And did we freeze?
> We froze in bunches of five.
> And did we complain?
> We did, we did, we did.

Chapters 8 through 11 are fairly straight autobiography, vividly written, the bildungsroman of "Tom Fool," still a jester. We follow his Marxist education, his university years in Grand Forks and Baton Rouge, his meetings with Marion Points, Alan Swallow, and Cleanth Brooks, then the war and the Aleutians. Part One of *Letter* ends in chapter 12 at the level of song or chant. These are McGrath's pagan beatitudes:

> Blesséd be the blood hung like a bell in my body's
>   branching tree;
> Blesséd be dung and honey;
> Blesséd be the strong key of my sex in her womb,
>   by cock and cunt blesséd
> The electric bird of desire, dropped in the locked-
>   room mysteries of country charm;
> Blesséd be my writing hand and arm and the black
>   lands of my secret heart.

The passage goes on for three large-format pages, a strong rhythmic conclusion signed *"Los Angeles, 1955."* It was the year before Ginsberg's *Howl and Other Poems,* but McGrath had begun, on his own and with far less fanfare, what his friend Beeching later called, "His quiet lifelong counterattack."

Part Two begins where Part One left off, with song, but it finds McGrath in Greece, thinking "Dakota is everywhere." Rather than forwarding the plot in strict chronological fashion,

McGrath circles back over Part One in an "eccentric spiral." The "present" of the opening—his life in Greece with Eugenia in the 1960s—contains the past the way a tree's rings are its former skins inside its present one. The poem also reflects all of the places in which it was written. Part Two is signed, *"—North Dakota—Skyros—Ibiza—Agaete—Guadalajara, 1968."* He recalls the poem's genesis with the liberating advice of Gordon. He recalls his work as a labor organizer in New York. And he recalls the feeling of waiting for the revolution, the great change to come upon the world.

Also in Part Two McGrath introduces his next major symbol:

> Wait for the Angel.
>   SAQUASOHUH:
>   the blue star
> Far off, but coming.
>   Invisible yet.
>   Announcing the Fifth
> World
>   (Hopi prophecy)
>   world we shall enter soon:
> When the Blue Star Kachina, its manifested spirit,
> Shall dance the *kisonvi* for the first time.

McGrath's appropriation of Native American mythology may put some readers off, but they should know that it is not done in the spirit of liberal sentimentality. In 1960 he married Eugenia, and the same year they founded the journal *Crazy Horse,* announcing later in a manifesto, "We the Irregulars of Crazy Horse, Ghost Dancers of the essential existential Solidarity, now summon into being the hosts of the new resistance. Give up those bird-cages built for lions! Alienation is not enough! Jawsmiths, nightwalkers, moonbirds: Unite!" Whimsical, dismissive of academic formalism, and well beyond mere politics, the manifesto compares McGrath's own resistance to that of the eradicated Ghost Dancers his father had heard about at Fort Ransom. (McGrath returned to this vision in "You Can Start the Poetry Now; or, News from Crazy

Horse.") By the time he wrote Part Two of *Letter,* the United States had not yet seen the movies that equated the Indian Wars and Vietnam in the popular imagination, such as *Soldier Blue* (1970) and *Little Big Man* (1971), and certainly nothing like the later sentimentality of *Dances with Wolves* (1990). Readers might assume that McGrath was a "wannabe," a white man yearning to be Indian, but he was not. He was a westerner, which meant that he grew up with Indians in proximity, and he could not escape the fact that their story was part of his own. It was one of the deep national wounds of America.

McGrath's use of Hopi ceremony and story is no less legitimate than Eliot's use of *The Golden Bough.* Furthermore it is intelligently based upon Frank Waters's important *Book of the Hopi* (1963), which like most studies of ceremony also demonstrates the universality of narrative sources. According to Waters, Hopi narratives describe at first a progress through three worlds: "The Fourth World, the present one, is the full expression of man's ruthless materialism and imperialistic will; and man himself reflects the overriding gross appetites of the flesh." But the Fifth World will come

> when a *kachina* [an embodied spirit] removes his mask during a dance in the plaza before uninitiated children. For a while there will be no more ceremonies, no more faith. Then Oraibi [the Rock on High] will be rejuvenated with its faith and ceremonies, marking the start of a new cycle of Hopi life.

While it is not surprising that a now-unaffiliated Marxist poet would be attracted to millennial images of revolutionary change, it is interesting that the images McGrath uses for his vision of communal solidarity derive from religious systems (the other principal image comes later in his "Christmas Oratorio," another borrowing from Auden). The blue star kachina, Saquasohuh, is not the Angel of Class Struggle barring the gate to Eden with a flaming sword but the Angel of a new Annunciation. In the interview

with Gibbons and Des Pres, McGrath had a difficult time maintaining that he was still a materialist in Marxist terms precisely because of the visionary leap he makes in the latter half of *Letter.*

Part Two then shifts away from linear narrative and works instead by thematic association, replaying scenes like the woodcutting from Part One, building on images of women in the story of Jenny, a real or fictional lover and fellow worker from his early years. In both present and past, with Eugenia and Jenny, Part Two is dominated by a feminine principle, just as Part One was often masculine. Also present is an effort to see Jenny as she really was and not merely as a sex object:

> ENOUGH!
>   Even then I could see it was not that way.
>   She was no
> Gongshagging lamewit.
>   But then what was she?
>   Easy: merely
> Lost.
>   And what did she want?
>   To enter.
>   To burn
> Alive.

Something prevents many people from feeling fully alive, and McGrath resembles other poets in wanting all readers to feel more fully. Indians are important here not because they are morally superior but because they remind whites of how "We learned the pious and patriotic art of extermination," perfecting whites' own callousness. Part Two is also about displacement, about standing outside the Garden, trying to make the kachina.

In the new, definitive edition of the complete *Letter,* published in 1997 by Copper Canyon Press with the help of Jacobson, Part One and Part Two take up 271 pages, Part Three and Part Four take up just over 130. Completed in 1984, the whole poem does have a feeling of rushing to its conclusion. Now living in Moorhead, teaching at Moorhead State University, and the father of a young son, McGrath harked back to his Catholic childhood for an image of community. Catholicism also gave McGrath a language, Latin, and an image of charity. The star of Jesus and the blue star of Saquasohuh are both important symbols in *Letter*. But as if to be certain readers understand it is not the institution of the church he extols, McGrath gives in Part Three a magnificently Joycean confession scene. In its vocabulary alone it is one of the most outrageous and inventive passages in the entire poem.

> "I am guilty of chrestomathy, Father."
>
> He lets out a grunt in
> Gaelic,
> Shifting out of the Latin to get a fresh purchase
> on sin.
> "And?"
> "Barratry, Father.
> "And mineralogy . . .
> "Agatism and summer elements . . .
> "Skepticism about tooth fairies . . .
> "Catachresis and pseudogogy . . . ."

From the unity of family at Christmas to the absurdity of this confession, McGrath moves to the camaraderie of poets, mostly male, living and dead, listing his father the storyteller among them. Then he circles back to the family "gathered now by the river of Latin in our little church." As Part One ended with song or chanted beatitudes, Part Three ends with an oratorio in musical parts, dissolving finally in fragmentation that echoes Eliot's *The Waste Land* (1922). Part Four makes a great heave toward conclusion, beginning with the line "NOW MOVE ALL SYMBOLS THREE LEAPS TO THE LEFT!" From there it flows on through a speedy lyrical deconstruction of family history, the spirals of DNA, and so forth. These fragments though are not shored against anyone's ruins. They are rushed through, headlong, as McGrath recaps the Hopi journey through the Four Worlds toward the Fifth, the blue star kachina. The critic Jack Foley has

remarked upon how little of McGrath's hopeful vision arises from images of adult life, how much of it from childhood and youth, and has wondered whether he really succeeds in avoiding nostalgia. It might be said that McGrath throws coherence to the winds in these final pages but his vision is not merely fanciful, and possesses the gravitas of hard experience. Perhaps at the end of the poem he is like Dante coming, finally, up to the shimmering limits of the word.

ECHOES AND PASSAGES

When Beeching went to Fargo in the late 1960s, he witnessed McGrath's difficulties with certain aspects of academic life. He tells of a party where they met a psychologist just back from aiding the war effort in Vietnam, having experimented with such techniques as dropping broken glass into rice paddies to break Vietnamese morale.

> In a deceptively quiet voice McGrath, who in his day had seen the wartime Aleutians, the jim crow South and the New York dock strike, asked him, "Just what did you thinking you were doing?"
>
> "Fighting Communism."
>
> "Then come outside and fight me."

McGrath was unusual in the consistency of his convictions. In 1974 he met Sam Hamill, who became his friend and, at Copper Canyon, the primary publisher of his poetry. It was typical of McGrath that such matters as writing and publishing were related more to friendship than to commerce and career.

Despite the relative stability of his job, McGrath's personal life was troubled. Though he loved teaching and was good at it, he complained in letters about the constant grading of student writing. The workload for faculty at Moorhead State University was heavy, often eight or nine classes per year, two-thirds of them in composition, and faculty burnout was not unheard of. McGrath could be quietly gregarious and had always loved drinking. Some of his former colleagues at Moorhead have suggested that alcohol was taking a toll on his marriage. In the summer of 1975, at a time when he and Eugenia were living separately and often arguing about Tomasito, McGrath killed a man named Fred Nickaboine, with whom Eugenia was having an affair. He wrote to Hamill about the event roughly two weeks after it occurred:

> [He] was breaking into my wife's house where she and my little son were at. He was crazy drunk, with a history of this kind of violence and it was his intention to kill my wife—maybe all of us. Or to get himself killed. He had been warned off by police during the day, by my wife in the evening when he called, very drunk, and by myself as he tried to break down first the back and then the front door. I fired a warning shot and then as the door was caving in—I thought he had an ax—I fired at random thru the door.

The letter soon takes a strange turn, especially considering McGrath's long-standing sympathies for Native Americans:

> What makes it hard: he was an Indian + the white law is terrified of the power of the nearby reservation. . . . So: instead of a coroner's inquiry + a verdict of justifiable homicide I was charged with 3rd degree murder and manslaughter, jailed + am now out on $10,000 bail.

As if his personal dilemma were not difficult enough, McGrath now found himself "in a scapegoat situation," having enraged the Reservation community.

Beeching was in New York when he learned of the shooting, and he immediately flew to Minnesota to help his friend. His memoir gives sketchy details of the shooting, more about the subsequent grand jury trial, which he witnessed himself. He describes the difficulty Tom's family and friends had in getting him to prepare himself to appear before a jury, to dress properly and watch his words. He also describes in detail the defense put on by McGrath's attorney, climaxing in a moment of drama when "the actual shot-perforated door" was carried into court "to prove Tom had fired blind." In the end the charges were dropped. But these events certainly clouded McGrath's life, while his marriage to Eugenia remained troubled by continued fighting over "Little T."

McGrath's health was also breaking down. A letter of October 10, 1980, reports a "semi-diabetic condition" necessitating a change of diet. It also details some work done toward a new book of poems eventually titled *Passages toward the Dark* (1982). McGrath ruefully jokes about getting the Pulitzer for it, knowing it will not happen. And he mentions work on a film script, one of fourteen McGrath wrote, including his unfilmed adaptation of Frederick Manfred's novel *Conquering Horse* (1959) for the director Michael Cimino, who quoted McGrath in his film *Thunderbolt and Lightfoot* (1974). The letters to Hamill in the early 1980s record feelings of depression, isolation, the burden of work, and more fights over custody of Tomasito. In 1979 McGrath was in a car accident that gave him whiplash, and over time the pain in his neck and shoulder became unbearable. After he retired from teaching in 1983, he underwent surgery to correct the condition, but the operation went terribly wrong. "I'm now about 60% paralyzed + in worse pain, wheel chair etc.," he wrote in August. It was the beginning of a run of bad luck. While he regained mobility and much of his old vitality, he would sometimes use a cane. Nerve damage in his left hand was such that he often wore a heavy glove to keep it warm. For the last six years of his life he referred to himself as a cripple, suffering chronic pain, though some of his friends report that he exaggerated his ailments and was often remarkably cheerful.

Whatever his condition, McGrath was publishing poems and gaining recognition. He had moved to the Twin Cities in 1983, to be closer to Tomasito and to more of Minnesota's cultural life. There he lived alone in an apartment near the Loft, an arts organization that was beginning to recognize his work. Once he had been championed mostly by leftist magazines and small journals like California's *kayak,* a feisty periodical edited by George Hitchcock, who had himself performed with comic aplomb before the House Un-American Activities Committee. Now McGrath's work appeared regularly in the *American Poetry Review* and other prominent journals. He had already won an Amy Lowell Traveling Poetry Fellowship, followed by a Guggenheim Fellowship, various arts board fellowships, and an award from the Academy of American Poets that allowed him to travel to Nicaragua. His new books, *Passages toward the Dark* (1982) and *Echoes inside the Labyrinth* (1983), both contained important poems mixed in with lesser work. *Passages* includes "The Bread of This World," while *Echoes* begins with "Trinc," McGrath's exuberant paean to beer, and such fine lyrics as "Remembering the Children of Auschwitz." But both books also include an increasing number of short poems, some of them reading like the deep image work of McGrath's friends Robert Bly and James Wright. Often these short poems are comic, in the tradition of Japanese senryu.

In 1980 Swallow had brought out a paperback of *The Movie at the End of the World,* the collected poems first published in 1972, but McGrath's productivity and publishing history were such that a new, comprehensive selection was called for. *Selected Poems, 1938–1988* (1988), edited and introduced by Hamill, was published by Copper Canyon and won both the Shelley Memorial Award and the Lenore Marshall/*Nation* Award. McGrath was gratified by his growing reputation, but his health had deteriorated to the point where he could no longer write comfortably, and he required the assistance of friends like Abigail Jensen, a young woman who handled much of his last correspondence. In and out of hospitals for his last years, with the help of friends, former students, and family McGrath began to compile a final collection, *Death Song,* which appeared posthumously in 1991. *Death Song* also contains a mixture of mid-length poems and shorter ones, including his "Song of the Open Road," dedicated to Reginald Gibbons:

> Protected from all running dogs
> Through Hell and through Gone I go:
> Guided by the great Saint Yes
> And his master: great Saint No.

After McGrath's death, memorials for him were held in Chicago and Minneapolis as well as in the college towns on the Red River of the North. His colleagues at Moorhead State University planted a cottonwood in the quad with a small plaque bearing one of McGrath's most touching short poems:

> You out there, so secret.
> What makes you think you're alone?

Selected Bibliography

Note: I wish to thank Sam Hamill, Thomas McGrath's literary executor, for permission to quote from letters in the files of Copper Canyon Press. I also benefited from reading the unpublished dissertation of McGrath's former student, David Pink.

WORKS OF THOMAS McGRATH

POETRY
First Manifesto. Baton Rouge, La.: Alan Swallow, 1940.
Three Young Poets: Thomas McGrath, William Peterson, James Franklin Lewis. Selected by Alan Swallow. Prairie City, Ill.: J. A. Decker, 1942.
To Walk a Crooked Mile. New York: Swallow Press and William Morrow, 1947.

Longshot O'Leary's Garland of Practical Poesie. New York: International Publishers, 1949.

Witness to the Times! Los Angeles: Students of Thomas McGrath, 1953.

Figures from a Double World. Denver, Colo.: Alan Swallow, 1955.

Letter to an Imaginary Friend. Denver, Colo.: Alan Swallow, 1962.

New and Selected Poems. Denver, Colo.: Alan Swallow, 1964.

Letter to an Imaginary Friend, Parts One and Two. Chicago: Swallow Press, 1970.

The Movie at the End of the World: Collected Poems. Chicago: Swallow Press, 1973.

Voices from Beyond the Wall. Moorhead, Minn.: The Territorial Press, 1974.

Trinc: Praises II: A Poem. Port Townsend, Wash.: Copper Canyon Press, 1979.

Passages toward the Dark. Port Townsend, Wash.: Copper Canyon Press, 1982.

Echoes inside the Labyrinth. New York: Thunder's Mouth Press, 1983.

Longshot O'Leary Counsels Direct Action: Poems. Minneapolis, Minn.: West End Press, 1983.

Selected Poems, 1938–1988. Edited by Sam Hamill. Port Townsend, Wash.: Copper Canyon Press, 1988.

Death Song. Edited by Sam Hamill. Port Townsend, Wash.: Copper Canyon Press, 1991.

Letter to an Imaginary Friend. Corrected and complete edition. Preface by Sam Hamill. Concluding essay by Dale Jacobson. Port Townsend, Wash.: Copper Canyon Press, 1997.

PROSE

McGrath's papers at Copper Canyon Press, Port Townsend, Wash. Statement. U.S. House of Representatives. *Hearings before the Committee on Un-American Activities.*, 83d Cong., 1st sess., 1953, pp. 862–863. 83 H1428-2-E. Reprinted in Fred Whitehead, ed. "Dream Champ—A Festschrift in Honor of Thomas McGrath." *North Dakota Quarterly* 50, no. 4:8–9 (1982).

The Gates of Ivory, the Gates of Horn. New York: Mainstream Publishers, 1957; Reprint, Chicago: Another Chicago Press, 1987.

Clouds. Illustrations by Chris Jenkyns. Los Angeles: Melmont Publishers, 1959. (Juvenile)

The Beautiful Things. Illustrations by Chris Jenkyns. New York: Vanguard, 1960. (Juvenile)

"Manifesto: No More Cattlemen or Sheepmen—We Want Outlaws!!" *Crazy Horse* 2 (1961). Reprint, "Dream Champ—A Festschrift in Honor of Thomas McGrath." *North Dakota Quarterly* 50, no. 4:10 (1982).

"McGrath on McGrath." Edited by James Bertolino. *Epoch* 22:207–219 (1973). Reprint, "Dream Champ—A Festschrift in Honor of Thomas McGrath." *North Dakota Quarterly* 50, no. 4:11–26 (1982).

"On My Work." *American Poetry Review* 3, no. 1:26 (1974).

The Movie at the End of the World. CIE, St. Paul, Minn., 1981. (Film.)

"Language, Power, and Dream." In *Claims for Poetry.* Edited by Donald Hall. Ann Arbor: University of Michigan Press, 1982. Pp. 286–295.

"North Dakota Is Everywhere." *North Dakota Quarterly* 50, no. 3:6–7 (summer 1982).

This Coffin Has No Handles. North Dakota Quarterly 52, no. 4:1–244 (autumn 1984). Reprint, New York: Thunder's Mouth Press, 1988.

CRITICAL AND BIOGRAPHICAL STUDIES

Beeching, Jack. *A Memoir of Thomas McGrath.* East Grand Forks, Minn.: Spirit Horse Press, 1993.

Bly, Robert. "Helmsmen." *Hungry Mind Review,* summer 1988, pp. 3, 23.

———. "In Praise of Thomas McGrath." In his *American Poetry: Wildness and Domesticity.* New York: Harper & Row, 1990. Pp.130–145.

Butwin, Joseph. "The Winter Count: Politics in the Poetry of Thomas McGrath." *North Dakota Quarterly* 50, 4:59–67 (fall 1982).

———. "The Last Laugh: Thomas McGrath's Comedy." *North Dakota Quarterly* 55, no. 1:31–40 (winter 1987).

Carruth, Hayden. "Tom McGrath Is Harvesting the Snow." *Poetry East* 23 & 24:89–92 (1987).

Clampitt, Amy. Citation for the Lenore Marshall/ *Nation* Poetry Prize 1989. *Nation,* November 6, 1989, pp. 534–536.

Cohen, Marty. "The Imaginary Friendships of Tom McGrath." *Parnassus: Poetry in Review* 19, no. 2:193–209 (1994).

Des Pres, Terrence. "Thomas McGrath." *TriQuarterly* 70:158–192 (fall 1987). Reprinted in his *Praises and Dispraises: Poetry and Politics, the Twentieth Century.* New York: Viking Penguin, 1988. Pp. 151–186.

Doyle, Joe. "*Longshot O'Leary*: Tom McGrath's Years on the Waterfront." *North Dakota Quarterly* 50, no. 4:32–40 (fall 1987).

Foley, Jack. "Thomas McGrath, *Letter to an Imaginary Friend.*" *Alsop Review* (http://www.alsopreview.com/foley/jfmcgrath.html), July 15, 2000.

Gibbons, Reginald, and Terrence Des Pres. "A Personal Introduction." *TriQuarterly* 70:7–221 (fall 1987).

———, eds. "Thomas McGrath: Life and the Poem." *TriQuarterly* 70:7–221 (fall 1987). Reprint, Urbana: University of Illinois Press, 1992.

Hall, Donald. "McGrath's Invective." In his *Goatfoot, Milktongue, Twinbird: Interviews, Essays, and Notes on Poetry,* 1970–76. Ann Arbor: University of Michigan Press, 1978. Pp. 50–52.

Hamill, Sam. "The Problem of Thomas McGrath." *North Dakota Quarterly* 50, no. 4:92–94 (fall 1982).

———. "The Justice of Poetry." In his *A Poet's Work: The Other Side of Poetry.* Seattle, Wash.: Broken Moon Press, 1990. Pp. 175–184.

Hazard, Mike. "Movie Moonlighting; or, the Other Career of Tom McGrath." *North Dakota Quarterly* 50, no. 4:101–106 (fall 1982).

Jacobson, Dale. "The Mythical Element in *Letter to an Imaginary Friend.*" *North Dakota Quarterly* 50, no. 4:71–82 (fall 1982).

———. "The Journey to Celebration in McGrath's Poetry." *American Poetry Review,* May–June 1989, pp. 27–30.

Levine, Philip. "Small Tribute to Tom McGrath." *TriQuarterly* 70:103–105 (fall 1987).

Mason, David. "Thomas McGrath." In his *The Poetry of Life and the Life of Poetry: Essays and Reviews.* Ashland, Oreg.: Story Line Press, 2000. Pp. 143–145.

Stern, Frederick C. "'The Delegate for Poetry': McGrath as Communist Poet." In *Where the West Begins: Essays on Middle Border and Siouxland Writing, in Honor of Herbert Krause.* Edited by Arthur R. Huseboe and William Geyer. Sioux Falls, S.Dak.: Center for Western Studies Press, 1978. Pp. 119–127. Reprinted in "Dream Champ—A Festschrift in Honor of Thomas McGrath." *North Dakota Quarterly* 50, no. 4:107–115 (1982).

———. "Thomas McGrath." In *A Literary History of the American West.* Sponsored by the Western Literature Association. Edited by Thomas J. Lyons. Fort Worth, Tex.: Texas Christian University Press, 1987. Pp. 806–812.

Stern, Frederick C., ed. *The Revolutionary Poet in the United States: The Poetry of Thomas McGrath.* Columbia: University of Missouri Press, 1988.

Vinz, Mark. "Thomas McGrath: Words for a Vanished Age: A Memoir." *Great River Review* 4, no. 2:167–175 (1983). Reprinted in "Dream Champ—A Festschrift in Honor of Thomas McGrath." *North Dakota Quarterly* 50, no. 4:131–138 (1982).

Whitehead, Fred, ed. "Dream Champ—A Festschrift in Honor of Thomas McGrath." *North Dakota Quarterly* 50, no. 4:5–146 (1982).

INTERVIEWS

Gibbons, Reginald, and Terrence Des Pres. "An Interview with Thomas McGrath, January 30–February 1, 1987." *TriQuarterly* 70:38–102 (fall 1987).

Stern, Frederick C. "An Interview with Thomas McGrath." In his *The Revolutionary Poet in the United States: The Poetry of Thomas McGrath.* Columbia: University of Missouri Press, 1988. Pp. 150–179.

Vinz, Mark. "Poetry and Place." *Voyage to the Inland Sea* 3:33–48 (1973).

Weiner, Joshua. "More Questions: An Interview with Thomas McGrath." *TriQuarterly* 70:193–210 (fall 1987).

ADDITIONAL SOURCES

Caudwell, Christopher. *Illusion and Reality: A Study of the Sources of Poetry.* London: Lawrence & Wishart, 1977. (First published in 1937.)

Waters, Frank. *Book of the Hopi*. New York: Viking Penguin, 1963.

—*DAVID MASON*

Claude McKay

1889–1948

THE JAMAICAN-BORN Claude McKay was one of the most influential African American writers of the twentieth century. As a prolific poet, political essayist, novelist, and short story writer, McKay helped initiate the Harlem Renaissance and the African and West Indian literary movement Negritude. He was also an involved socialist who participated in the Russian Revolution. He traveled extensively in Europe and North Africa, where he wrote books about working-class blacks. During the Great Depression he wrote important works on Harlem and its religious and political figures for the Federal Works Project. McKay overcame many obstacles, including racism, poverty, political ostracism, neglect, and illness, to write some of the most memorable African American literature.

McKay first earned recognition in his native Jamaica for his socially aware dialect poetry. Two volumes of his poetry, *Songs of Jamaica* and *Constab Ballads,* were published in 1912, when he was only twenty-two years old. The dialect poems written from the perspective of the rural Jamaican peasants were of pioneering importance in the development of West Indian literature.

McKay immigrated to the United States in 1912 and attended the Tuskegee Institute and Kansas State College, where he studied agriculture. After quitting school and moving to Harlem, he worked in a variety of low-paying jobs while writing poetry. His only marriage failed, and McKay never met his daughter from that union. In New York, McKay was involved in early labor and socialist groups, including the Industrial Workers of the World. During World War I he worked as a dining car waiter on the railroad.

McKay's militant protest poetry, written in the United States after World War I, helped launch the intense black literary movement known as the Harlem Renaissance (1925–1939). McKay's radical efforts to create solidarity and afrocentric consciousness in America's black population inspired other writers, like Langston Hughes, Zora Neale Hurston, and Richard Wright.

In 1919 McKay went to England, where he became further involved with radical politics. He attracted the attention of the conservative authorities with his articles on communism, English colonialism, and African nationalism. He was critical of England's treatment of its black immigrants. Before leaving to go back to the United States, McKay published *Spring in New Hampshire and Other Poems* (1920), a collection of the poems he wrote in Harlem and in England.

Although perhaps most famous as a poet and novelist, McKay also was a well-respected essayist and political theorist. He was a proto–black nationalist, whose indictment of modern colonialism anticipated such later West Indian expatriates as Franz Fanon, Derek Walcott, and V. S. Naipaul.

Upon returning to the United States, McKay became an editor of the *Liberator,* a well-known socialist newspaper that had replaced the banned *Masses.* His lifelong and influential friendship with Max Eastman, chief editor of the *Liberator,* began at this time. McKay helped organize black radicals and intellectuals in New York. In the spring of 1922 he published *Harlem*

Shadows, his most famous book of poetry, which contains the often anthologized poem "If We Must Die."

In the fall of 1922 McKay worked his way to the Soviet Union. In Moscow he became a well-recognized figure and gave speeches at the Third Party International representing the viewpoint of the American black working class. He also wrote his first nonfiction, *The Negroes in America,* published in the Soviet Union in 1923. This short study on the working conditions of African Americans in the United States was commissioned by the Communist International and was published in Russian translation.

McKay left Russia in May 1923, and traveled to Germany, France, Spain, and Morocco. He wrote his two most famous novels about working-class blacks and expatriate black Americans during this time. *Home to Harlem* (1928) and *Banjo: A Story without a Plot* (1929) influenced West Indian and West African writers, such as Aimé Césaire from Martinique and Leopold Sedar Senghor from Senegal, in their development of the important literary movement called Negritude. Ironically, most of McKay's best fiction, including *Gingertown* (1932), *Banana Bottom* (1933), and the unpublished "Romance in Marseilles," was written while he lived as an expatriate in France and Morocco.

Largely because of the success of *Home to Harlem,* McKay returned to the United States in 1934 a famous author, but he was soon engulfed in the misery of the Great Depression. Having lost faith in the communist movement, his essays now critiqued its totalitarianism. Reduced to poverty, McKay joined the Federal Writers Project. Evidence of a slowly progressive heart disease began to appear.

McKay's political articles about Harlem were published in many magazines and newspapers. He also wrote an autobiography, *A Long Way from Home* (1937). His book *Harlem: Negro Metropolis* (1940) gave a detailed account of the culture and political life of the depressed black urban community of the 1930s. While writing this book McKay also worked on an unfinished novel entitled *Harlem Glory,* which was published posthumously in 1990. The work of fiction dealt with many of Harlem's most famous religious and political figures.

In June 1943 McKay collapsed from a disabling stroke while working on a riveting job in New Jersey. His heart illness threatened his life, but he was nursed back to health by the Catholic-sponsored Friendship House. He later joined this group in Chicago and converted to Catholicism. He spent his last years in Chicago and New Mexico, where he worked on a book of Jamaican memoirs entitled *My Green Hills of Jamaica* (1979). He died in Chicago on May 22, 1948 of heart disease at the age of fifty-eight and was buried in New York City.

EARLY LIFE

Claude McKay was born on September 15, 1890, in the Jamaican village of Sunny Ville in Clarendon Parish. He was the youngest of eight children. His parents, Thomas Francis McKay and Ann Elizabeth McKay, were Baptists and respected leaders of the black community. Thomas McKay was a descendant of the West African nation of Ashanti, and he told stories of African traditions and customs.

During his early adolescence McKay lived with his oldest brother U'Theo near Montego Bay in the northwestern part of the island. U'Theo possessed an impressive library, which helped develop McKay's literary background. McKay was also influenced by Walter Jekyll, a transplanted English aristocrat. Jekyll, who had known Robert Louis Stevenson, collected and studied the folk music and songs of the Jamaican farmers. Jekyll was particularly interested in stories of the trickster spider man Annancy, which had West African origins. He urged

McKay to write in peasant dialect rather than in formalized English.

In 1906 McKay received a three-year stipend to enter trade school in Kingston, but in 1907 Kingston was destroyed by an earthquake. McKay left to work as a wheelwright in the country. His mother died soon after he moved to the country, and he returned to Kingston, where he worked in a match factory and on the police force (constabulary). At this time he began writing poems.

McKay's early poems often gave voice to the island's poor and expressed the vitality of the Jamaican common folk. The Kingston *Daily Gleaner* on January 27, 1912, published a long poem in native dialect entitled "Peasants' Way O' Thinkin'," which evokes the immense problem of economic inequality:

> We wouldn' mind ef dem could try
> Mek calico cheaper fe buy;
> Tek duty off o' we blue shirt
> An also off o' we t'atch hut.

"Passive Resistance," published in the *Daily Gleaner* on April 6, 1912, urges solidarity among the poor:

> We will show an alien trust
> Dat Jamaicans too can fight
> An' dat while our blood is hot,
> They won't crush us wi' deir might.

These and other poems anticipate McKay's militant protest writings, whose influence helped alter race relations around the world.

McKay's first collection of poems, *Songs of Jamaica,* was quickly followed by *Constab Ballads,* which received the Jamaica Institute's Musgrave Silver Medal for distinguished achievement. McKay achieved popular recognition immediately with these publications. He was highly lauded for his courage in using Jamaican dialect or patois, which was actually a language unto itself with discernible African language retention.

However, the collections as a whole were uneven. His reliance on nineteenth-century English Romantic poetry structure and tropes indicated a sentimentality that plagued McKay for the rest of his life. In fact a duality in McKay manifested itself in many ways. His outraged side gravitated to poems of protest and militancy written in original verse. His sentimental side proffered poems of lost love and disillusionment rife with clichés. He later abandoned innovative dialect poetry, but his militant appeal for justice continued unabated in other forms.

McKay left Jamaica in 1912 to attend school in the United States, and he never returned to the island. McKay spent only six months at Booker T. Washington's Tuskegee Institute because he found the regimentation of student life personally intolerable and was unnerved by the racism prevalent in Alabama. He transferred to Kansas State College, where he studied for two years. W. E. B. Du Bois's *The Souls of Black Folk* (1912) affected McKay deeply, and he decided to leave school for New York City in the summer of 1914. On July 30, McKay married Eulalie Imelda Lewars, who had emigrated from Jamaica to be with him. The marriage lasted six months. The couple never divorced lawfully, but Eulalie returned to Jamaica, where she gave birth to McKay's only child, Rhue Hope McKay, a daughter he never met.

Over the next few years McKay worked as a porter, a janitor, a butler, a factory worker, and a kitchen helper. He was employed as a dining car waiter on the Pennsylvania Railroad during World War I. He later drew much material for the characters of his working-class novels from these years.

Although McKay did not publicly acknowledge his homosexuality, it was an important theme in his published novels and short stories. Throughout a life of almost constant movement, he was often alone and in foreign lands. His search for companionship and community deeply affected his life decisions. An intensely spiritual and morally committed individual, McKay found little rest in his quest to better the human condition.

In Harlem, McKay made contact with the National Association for the Advancement of Colored People (NAACP) and the National Urban League. He met the great leaders of the new African American awareness, including Du Bois, with whom McKay later quarreled. In fact throughout his career McKay retained a contentious relationship with middle-class black intellectuals, such as Du Bois, Arthur Schomburg, and Alain Locke.

In October 1917 the magazine *Seven Arts* published two sonnets by McKay written under the name of "Eli Edwards." "Invocation" and "The Harlem Dancer" suggest that African Americans are alienated in white civilization and have lost touch with their African heritage. He writes in "Invocation":

> Bring ancient music to my modern heart,
> Let fall the light upon my sable face
> That once gleamed upon the Ethiopian's art
> Lift me to thee out of this alien place.

In 1919 black soldiers returned from World War I to face prejudice and discrimination at home. Twenty-five race riots occurred in urban centers that summer, later called the "red summer of 1919," and many blacks were hung. The riots and racial warfare affected McKay deeply.

Eastman encouraged McKay to write and offered to publish his work. In April 1919 the *Liberator* printed McKay's poem "The Dominant White," which attacks racial superiority. In July 1919 the *Liberator* published seven more poems, in which McKay proclaims his own growing political and revolutionary attitudes. Among these was his most famous poem, "If We Must Die." A well-crafted poem with a foreshadowing message of black power, "If We Must Die" is more than a political statement.

The poem sums up the desperation and outrage of a whole race while exhorting its members to triumph over their oppressors:

> If we must die, let it not be like hogs
> Hunted and penned in an inglorious spot,
> . . . .
> If we must die, O let us nobly die,
> So that our precious blood may not be shed
> In vain. . . .
> . . . .
> Like men we'll face the murderous, cowardly
>   pack,
> Pressed to the wall, dying, but fighting back!

The poem was widely reprinted in the nation's black newspapers, and it rapidly became both an anthem of defiance and a moving testament to the unquenchable spirit of disfranchised blacks everywhere. It launched McKay's writing career like a rocket going off in the night.

In 1919, while working a factory job in New York, McKay joined the International Workers of the World, a progressive worker's union that respected black rights. McKay naturally gravitated to working-class politics and socialist ideals that were congruous with his own highly developed egalitarian principles. Convinced that a total social revolution was the only solution for racism, McKay became a member of the African Blood Brotherhood, a diverse group of African Americans who advocated international socialism. This group later merged with the American Communist Party.

ENGLAND, 1919–1921

In late 1919 McKay left the United States for England. During his short stay in Britain he made friends with many radical leftists, read Karl Marx, and continued his exploration of communist politics. In 1920 he attended the Communist Unity Conference, which established the Communist Party of Great Britain. He also joined the International Socialist Club. McKay later denied that he ever became a Communist Party member, but the evidence of his involvement in the cause seems to suggest otherwise. Recognized as one of the few black Americans writing about communism at that time, he was asked to contribute to alternative periodicals. Over the course of 1920 and into 1921 he published sixteen poems, twenty articles and letters, and five book reviews in the *Dreadnought*.

Many of McKay's contributions were written anonymously to escape political prosecution. For example, "Socialism and the Negro" (1920) is a strongly worded advocation of black nationalism. It praises the radical Jamaican, Marcus Garvey, who was living in New York at that time. Garvey's Back to Africa movement was an extremely popular grassroots black pride and black power organization flourishing in Harlem.

McKay's *Spring in New Hampshire and Other Poems* (1920) was his first collection of poems published since 1912. The title derived from the winter of 1915, when McKay worked at a resort hotel in Hanover, New Hampshire. This collection contains no verses in Jamaican dialect, but many of the poems explore the themes of economic injustice and rebellion against racial oppression and were written while McKay worked in New York. The other verses in *Spring* run the familiar gamut of lost love and nostalgic reminiscence and are written in stilted language.

McKay remained unemployed in England, and English conservatives suspected him of being a communist spy. This false accusation followed him across many borders. McKay had already been spotlighted by the FBI for his revolutionary activity in New York. His file continued to grow throughout his travels in the Soviet Union, Europe, and North Africa.

In the end England proved inhospitable. McKay made many friends but deplored the English intolerance for black immigrants. McKay was the first black socialist to write for the English press, and his legacy changed the world in the coming years. In England he published "Exhortation," which was later included in *Spring in New Hampshire*. Replete with new Russian-inspired revolutionary attitudes, "Exhortation" urged black men to revolt against the old British order. McKay's ideas on black nationalism and socialist brotherhood influenced the black African nationalist independence movements against colonialism led by the Africans Kwame Nkrumah, Julius Nyerere, and Jomo Kenyatta.

NEW YORK, 1921–1922

McKay arrived in New York in the winter of 1921, and Eastman asked him to join the *Liberator* staff as an associate editor. Eastman advocated communist social change and V. I. Lenin's Russian Revolution. McKay also was extremely excited by radical politics and worked intensely both as an organizer and writer. He respected the working class and advocated black participation in socialist unions. However, the socialist theories of people around him were constantly changing as various communist ideologues vied for control of the paper. Many of their arguments were confusing and self-serving and eventually proved dangerously blind to Joseph Stalin's subsequent excesses.

Within McKay's own sphere the ideological differences between white and black radicals became unbridgeable. The only black editor on a predominantly white radical magazine, McKay was in constant battles over black proletarian issues. When Eastman left his chief editorship in 1921, McKay soon found himself at odds with the new acting editor. He decided to leave when the intellectual frenzy began to take its toll on his health.

McKay continued to write poems and to seek publishers. Some of the poems from this period manifest the pain and loneliness he was feeling. "Outcast" from 1922 speaks of "Something in me is lost, forever lost, / Some vital thing has gone out of my heart" (*Selected Poems*).

Besides his poems McKay contributed eleven articles and book reviews to the *Liberator.* These included ringing appreciation for the pioneering black musical *Shuffle Along* (1922) and a bitter denunciation of segregation in New York theaters. He also wrote another commentary on Garvey, comparing him to a "Negro Moses," but he tempered his assessment with a critique of Garvey's lack of modern social ideas. In "How Black Sees Green and Red" McKay declares, "It is with the proletarian revolutionists of the world that my whole spirit revolts."

In 1922 a comprehensive collection of McKay's best poetry was published as *Harlem Shadows,* his most famous book of poetry. These seventy poems mirror the familiar duality of McKay's spirit. Love poems and nostalgic poems of Jamaica account for two-thirds of the contents. The other third consists of his protest poetry based on his racial experiences. The alienation, anger, and rebellion of blacks dominated by a white culture find a full voice. Not until James Baldwin's prose essays of the 1950s and 1960s would a black writer speak this forcefully again.

Critics such as James Weldon Johnson considered McKay the best black poet since Paul Laurence Dunbar. His protest poems influenced a new generation of black American writers, such as Langston Hughes, Countee Cullen, and Wallace Thurman. McKay's work helped awaken the black creativity that produced the Harlem Renaissance.

In August 1922 McKay published his last article in the *Liberator,* "Birthright." The essay rails against socialist shortsightedness regarding the African American cause and marks the end of McKay's most active political years in United States. He never found a comfortable niche as a writer, a poet, or a political intellectual in New York.

RUSSIA, 1922–1923

In September 1922, when he was thirty-two years old, McKay worked his way back to England as a coal stoker on a merchant freighter. He traveled first to London, then to Berlin, and arrived in Moscow in time for the Communist Party's Fourth Congress. He spoke in front of the Fourth Congress as an African American writer representing the potential for all blacks to work within the International Communist movement. McKay's speech influenced the Fourth Congress's "Resolutions on the Negro Question."

McKay was a sudden celebrity in the Soviet Union by virtue of his skin color and his cogent remarks on African American disfranchisement. During the May Day celebration of 1923 he held an honored place in the reviewing stand along with the highest officials of the Soviet Republic.

While in the Soviet Union, McKay met the American radicals John Reed and Louise Bryant. Reed later wrote an eyewitness account of the revolution, *Ten Days that Shook the World* (1919). McKay also busily wrote articles for the Russian press. At the request of Communist officials McKay expanded his articles into an overview of black conditions in the United States. McKay wrote *The Negroes in America* (1923) in English, and it was then translated into Russian. Some of the book is a revisionist interpretation of black American history showing how economics condition race relations. While McKay focuses on marginalized African American workers, he also criticizes working conditions for all laborers and makes an appeal to connect black civil rights arguments with women's rights. *Negroes in America* remained unpublished in English until 1979.

In writings from this period McKay makes many observations that predate the 1960s Black Power movement in the United States. He praises African American culture, including vernacular field songs, blues, folktales, and spirituals, and urges black pride in their Afro-centric origins.

McKay's participation in the constantly changing Russian Revolution was an opportunity to further his understanding of socialism. It was perhaps the first and only time he really felt himself a respected member of society with an appreciative audience for his ideas. But McKay was aware that his color added to the exoticism of his role in the Soviet Union. The tumult and attention soon proved too much for the physically depleted McKay. Before he left the Soviet Union he attempted to sell articles on his experience to the American press. Only *Crisis,* a magazine founded by Du Bois, published an account in two installments in 1923 and 1924. McKay had no luck in placing other articles with white American publishers.

1923–1925

In 1923 McKay left the Soviet Union and returned to Berlin, where he met the satirical cartoonist George Grosz and the American modernist painter Marsden Hartley. In October McKay traveled to Paris, where he collapsed into a severe depression and fell ill with syphilis. During this period he read Ernest Hemingway, James Joyce, and D. H. Lawrence, whom McKay particularly admired.

In January 1924 McKay left Paris for the French Mediterranean coast, where he settled in Toulon and lived on a monthly stipend of $50 from the Garland Fund. The Garland Fund, also known as the American Fund for Personal Service, supported individuals working creatively for society along radical lines. McKay made friends with black sailors and workers in both Toulon and Marseilles. Their lively lifestyle and celebration of music, dancing, language, and food reminded McKay of his working-class struggles in New York.

Around this time McKay met Sinclair Lewis, who supported McKay's bid to have his Garland grant extended. Also Alain Locke published several of McKay's poems in *Survey Graphics* (1924), a special edition devoted to black arts and letters. Locke used his *Survey Graphics* selections as the basis for his influential anthology *The New Negro* (1925).

During a visit to Nice, McKay met the African American actor and singer Paul Robeson, whose radical sympathies had resulted in his political persecution. But even with these high spots, McKay's life was a constant struggle of grinding poverty and continuous movement. Over the next several years he lived in Toulon, Marseilles, Nice, Barcelona, Tangiers, and Casablanca.

While in Cap d'Antibes, a resort on the Mediterranean, McKay reunited with Eastman and Eastman's new Russian wife. For many months McKay had been struggling with his political consciousness. Long conversations with Eastman, who had lived in the Soviet Union, helped McKay vocalize his growing dissatisfaction with communism. To McKay's perceptive eye and intuitive grasp of human nature, the whole system appeared unworkable. McKay understood the danger of totalitarianism, which was fermenting in communism's constantly changing face. McKay's romance with communism was coming to an end.

But McKay's proletarian consciousness remained and now engendered perhaps his biggest literary breakthrough. He decided to write about the urban black working-class vagabonds he had lived with in Harlem and France. McKay wanted to capture their vibrant worldview and their folk expressions in everyday language.

McKay's first novel, "Color Scheme," went through many drafts and was never published. Described as a realistic comedy of life among blacks on the railroad and in Harlem, it was rejected by American publishers in part because of its raw use of black language. McKay suffered severe disappointment and destroyed the manuscript, but a second attempt, *Home to Harlem* (1928), soon followed.

Encouraged to expand one of his short stories into a novel, McKay worked hard under limited resources to finish the novel in May 1927. While living in Marseilles and Barcelona, he finished a second novel, *Banjo,* with similar themes and which drew characters from the black Africans, West Indians, and African Americans he had lived with in the old port of Marseilles.

HOME TO HARLEM AND BANJO: A STORY WITHOUT A PLOT

Although *Home to Harlem* takes place in the United States and *Banjo* is set in Marseilles, the two books share many of the same themes and techniques. The novels are written in episodic style and champion working-class blacks in their everyday lives. The loose structures of both books reflect the nomadic aspect of the black working class. The books celebrate the free black vagabond who reacts to life with spontaneous improvisation. In this view working-class blacks are closer to nature and are spiritually healthier than whites and middle-class blacks. The books are also indictments against racism and economic enslavement. The characters are at war with all aspects of white civilization and the corruption at its heart.

Home to Harlem centers on the exploits of the African Americans Jake and Ray. Jake goes AWOL during World War I and returns home to Harlem. On his first night back he meets the beautiful Felice, who mysteriously disappears in the night. The plot is structured around Jake's efforts to find Felice again.

Jake meets Ray while working as a waiter on a railroad dining car. Ray is a young Haitian immigrant who wants to write about the vibrant life of black workers, but he is inhibited and full of self-doubts about himself and his place in the world. Jake's uncorrupted nature is presented as a positive example of living in the moment. But Ray is a visionary with a desire for universal brotherhood and egalitarian ideas.

Banjo has an international cast of characters with names like Malty, Bugsy, Taloufa, and Goosey. But in the second part of the book Jake and Ray from *Home* run into each other in the old port of Marseilles. "Banjo," Lincoln Agrippa Daily, is a southern black drifter and banjo player. He is happily stranded in Marseilles between seafaring jobs. As a popular member of the dockside family of black expatriates, he enjoys a carefree life.

McKay evokes the old port of Marseilles as a place where anything can be bought for a price. It can be a dangerous port with its undercurrent of desperation and poverty and its spooky alleyways and sinister clubs. But it is also an environment where the pleasure-seeking joys of the healthy black man can be accessed with innocence. The black drifters thrive on the bustling nightlife's music, wild dancing, and sensual aura.

Banjo is a natural man living in the immediacy of the moment. "I'm just a right-there, right-here baby, yestiday and today and tomorrow and forevah. All right-there right-here for me now." This hedonistic philosophy glosses over some hard problems of survival. But McKay insists that the rhythm, music, and dance of blacks like Banjo and Jake provide the fundamental durability that gives blacks the strength to survive.

A political consciousness also is engendered in part by the way the French government mistreats it black immigrants. Bugsy in *Banjo* is consumed by a fierce hatred for all whites. Capitalism and its economic policies are critiqued. The black workers in *Home* have been touched by the Garvey movement, by radical labor agitation, and by the growing voice of anticolonial protest in West Africa and the West Indies.

Both books end urging resistance to assimilation into Western civilization. Instead blacks should nurture pride in their African roots. Ray, the wandering black intellectual, continues to search for a way to combine political brotherhood and social meaning with the spirit of immediacy. The books reflect the duality of McKay's own existence, as he lived the lifestyles of both Jake and Ray.

The publication of *Home to Harlem* coincided with a growing interest in African American writing developing from the Harlem Renaissance. Selling beyond expectations, the book was McKay's most popular and most successful work. He won the Harmon Gold Award for literature. But the book was also the center of a controversy among black writers in Harlem. The older racial leaders, such as Du Bois and Locke, argued that *Home* encouraged the stereotype of the primitive happy-go-lucky black. Du Bois felt McKay's treatment glorified the lowest class of African American life. The younger generation of black writers, including Zora Neale Hurston, Rudolph Fisher, Wallace Thurman, and Langston Hughes, saw the expression of common black folk in a positive light, and they explored some of these same motifs in their own work.

Although *Banjo* was not successful in the United States, it made an overwhelming impression on African writers, like Leópold Sédar Senghor, Aimé Césaire, and Leon Damas, and on Paulette Nardal from Martinique. McKay's writing was an inspiration for the Negritude movement, which encouraged black Africans and West Indians to rediscover their folk cultures. Senghor remarked in his *An Intellectual History* (1971), "Claude McKay can be considered . . . as the veritable inventor of Negritude . . . of the values of Negritude."

1929–1934

In 1929 McKay traveled to Tangiers and Casablanca and was intrigued by the people of Morocco, who lived with a balance among diverse ethnic groups. It seemed an ideal African Americans could strive for, and McKay began to develop new concepts about community interaction and black nationalism.

McKay worked on short stories, many of them harking back to his Jamaican childhood. "The Agricultural Show" from this period was a re-creation of the wonder and joy he felt in the pastoral country. This story eventually was included in his collection *Gingertown* (1932), which contains four stories of Jamaican country life evocative of a rapidly vanishing black rural heritage and its racial harmony and social health.

Gingertown also holds six Harlem stories and two other stories, one set in a Mediterranean port similar to Marseilles and the other in an Arab city resembling Tangier. When *Gingertown* appeared in the United States, reviews were favorable, but sales were poor. Fisher felt that McKay was out touch with Harlem as a locale and that the Jamaican stories were more authentic.

Living comfortably in his own house near Tangiers, McKay set to work on *Banana Bottom* (1933). The book was lauded as his best by those who found its Jamaican setting and characters less threatening than his earlier working-class novels. *Banana Bottom* is the story of a young black woman's successful efforts to reintegrate into the peasant culture of her youth. At the age of twelve Bita Plant had been raped. With her parents' consent, Bita was sent to England for formal education and redemption.

Bita Plant returns to Jamaica an accomplished pianist and a highly literate and civilized young lady. But she finds the lifestyle of Christian piety and service restrictive to her spirit. Slowly she follows her natural inclination to embrace the black folk and their settled, steady sensibilities. She chooses to marry the traditional farmer Jubban over a local black clergyman.

The book is a graceful depiction of the Jamaican mountain culture's relaxed lifestyle connected to the land. Bita says, "I take pride in being coloured and different." She rejects Western culture for the rustic simplicity of Jamaican peasant life. Participating in an Obeah ceremony, she is possessed by the healing spirit. Finally she sheds all aspects of Western culture and returns to the folk lifestyle she was born into.

Banana Bottom was McKay's last novel, and it failed to attract an audience. He spent his remaining months in Morocco trying to sell to publishers a book he had been working on for years. First titled "The Jungle and the Bottoms," then "Savage Loving," and finally "Romance in Marseilles," it is a story of passionate love set in the old port city. A stowaway African named Lafala has his legs amputated, and with the money he receives in compensation, he sets out to win the love of Ashima. Although it focuses more on this tragic love affair, the book again presents the case for working-class black characters in their struggle against oppression. One chapter deals with homosexual characters who live near the docks. Their plight is frankly and sympathetically presented. McKay had no luck in finding a publisher.

RETURN TO THE UNITED STATES

In February 1934 McKay returned to the United States after twelve years abroad. The severity of the Great Depression had finished the Harlem Renaissance, and white patrons and downtown publishers no longer sought out black writers. By 1934 McKay's novels, which had celebrated African American vitality, seemed dated and irrelevant.

McKay found Harlem changed. The American Communist Party was enlisting many black intellectuals, who ignored McKay's warnings against scientific socialism. The inevitability of Marxist revolution was looking unlikely, and McKay's new theories called for meaningful equality for African Americans as a powerful ethnic group within the American nation. He was against assimilation, and his criticism of the integrationist orientation of the NAACP led to many arguments. McKay wanted a more developed spirit of communal self-help among blacks, and he defended the largely discredited programs of Booker T. Washington. His uncompromising attitudes and sharp conflicts with black leaders left him isolated in his poverty.

The Universal Ethiopian Students' Association launched a monthly magazine in October 1937 entitled the *African: A Journal of African Affairs* that dealt with European imperialism in Africa and encouraged an international perspective for black Americans. McKay and Countee Cullen made a bid to take over the magazine in April 1938 and wanted to rename it the *African: A Journal of Literary and Social Progress*. Negotiations failed, however, and the magazine never appeared.

After joining a New Deal work camp in upper New York State, McKay reached the end of his rope. In 1936 he moved back to Harlem and was accepted into the Federal Writers Project. He worked on a history of New York's black population, including a number of biographical sketches of Harlem figures subsequently preserved in the Schomburg Collection of Negro History and Literature in Harlem. He published an article in the *Nation* entitled "Harlem Runs Wild" that describes the rioting and looting of stores along 125th Street on March 19, 1935, prompted by resentment toward white merchants. The protesters demanded clerical jobs for Harlem's unemployed blacks.

McKay received a $500 grant from the Julius Rosenwall Fund in Chicago to write a memoir in which he hoped to clarify his social, political, and artistic evolution. Unfortunately, the autobiography, *A Long Way from Home* (1937), failed to meet his criteria. In this hastily written work McKay describes himself as a literary artist in the Romantic mold and focuses on his encounters with political and literary figures. He avoids close examination of the deep inner conflicts and motivations that propelled his long and fascinating journey. He particularly side-steps any honest appraisal of his affair with communism between 1919 and 1923.

From 1937 to 1940 McKay wrote numerous articles for the *New Leader,* the *American Mercury, Common Sense, Opportunity,* and the *Amsterdam News,* which printed his regular weekly column. Many of these articles indicate a new attitude. McKay tried to convince his fellow blacks to organize and improve their lives through self-help groups and an integrated communal life. His life abroad convinced him of the importance of a cohesive group culture for survival. He wrote several perceptive articles on North Africa and French colonialism that antedated Franz Fanon's important work on colonialism in the 1960s.

McKay also argued against communism as a divisive political movement that deluded and used African Americans in its campaign for world dominance. He left a meeting of the League of American Writers in 1937 in protest against their party line rhetoric. His emphasis was now on concentrated black unity within the larger American nation. In April 1940 he received his final U.S. citizenship certificate and published his last book.

Harlem: Negro Metropolis (1940) was drawn out of McKay's experiences in Harlem following his return to the United States. It is in a way a factual portrait of Harlem composed of ideas and portraits of Harlem figures drawn from articles and essays he had already written. McKay depicted a demoralized Harlem community torn apart by religious divisions and economic insecurity. Labor organizations fell far short of coping with actual problems. Furthermore the American Communist Party misled many blacks into supporting the Soviet Union.

The phenomenon of Father Divine, the popular Harlem religious figure, is analyzed in depth, and the grassroots labor movement led by Sufi

Abdul Hamid is presented as an example of local activism that works. Hamid led a boycott and a protest against Harlem merchants' refusal to hire black employees that proved effective, at least for the short term. In the book McKay also shows how Garvey's Black Star Back-to-Africa movement galvanized Harlem blacks and gave them hope and pride in themselves. Other activities, such as the numbers racket and the amusement and entertainment business, are criticized for their debilitating effects on the black struggle. In addition a chapter discusses West Indian and Hispanic social relations.

McKay elaborates on his arguments for a stronger community development program and maintains that less emphasis upon integration and assimilation for blacks in the United States would create a healthier atmosphere. African Americans should take direct social responsibility for their communities and the education of their children. He advocates solidarity, self-help, and self-pride. Overall the book is perceptive and novel in its arguments, and McKay's concepts and attitude predate the Black Power movement of the 1960s.

McKay worked on one more book-length manuscript before he left New York in April 1944. Entitled *Harlem Glory: A Fragment of Aframerican Life* (1990), it dramatizes some of the characters and incidents from his work in *Harlem: Negro Metropolis.* But it also provides a more cohesive look at McKay's evolving social ideas.

Buster South returns to Harlem after a long European expatriation, and lonely and poor, he has to work in a labor camp. He also gets involved with Glory Savior, whose religious self-help message has influenced thousands in Harlem. The political movement Yeoman of Labor led by Omar, a Muslim of African American origin, proves successful in organizing Harlem's poor blacks. Omar's slogan, "Defend Black America," rings with power in the text.

The American Communist Party is the enemy along with American capitalism. McKay wants a radical transformation of society, but it needs to come from within, not without. Black-white working-class solidarity is advocated as the way to defeat capitalist labor practices without resorting to enlistment in an international political movement.

Although McKay left *Harlem Glory* unfinished, the book shows McKay still had a powerful vision for a radical transformation of society. His portrayal of social unrest among African Americans and his determined fight against institutionalized racism continued to be interesting.

Harlem Glory was not picked up by publishers, and *Harlem: Negro Metropolis* failed to sell well. McKay lost his last chance to reestablish himself as a popular and financially successful creative writer. Since 1929 he had struggled long and hard for recognition and literary success. His energies were running out, and time was no longer with him. From this point on his accomplishments and his name went into an eclipse.

In September 1942 McKay got a job with the Office of War Information in New York City, but he lost it after three months. He took a job as a riveter at the federal shipyard in Port Newark, but the work was too strenuous for a man in his depleted physical condition. On June 25, 1943, he suffered a disabling stroke while on the job site.

McKay was living alone in a Harlem basement apartment at the time. Friendship House, a Catholic lay organization in Harlem, helped nurse him back to semihealth. While recuperating he wrote a series of unpublished sonnets called his "Cycle Manuscript," which summarize much of his disillusionment with the nation's myopic approach to black America. McKay's disgust with political ideologies and the opportunism of political figures verged on despair.

McKay was drawn to the Catholic Church as represented by Friendship House, attracted by the church's efforts to establish a society based on Christian principles through organizations like this one. In 1944 he was offered a job as adviser to Bishop Bernard J. Sheil in Chicago. McKay taught a course on black literature at the Sheil School, and he lectured at various midwestern universities. He was attracted to Dorothy Day, a Catholic activist and editor of the socialist-pacifist *Catholic Worker.*

In October 1944 McKay was baptized a Catholic. By the spring of 1945 he was ill again and had to spend a month in bed. He decided he should leave for a warmer climate. In Albuquerque, New Mexico, he completed a short memoir of his Jamaican childhood, *My Green Hills of Jamaica* (1979). In this work he returns in thoughts to his quiet pastoral childhood.

In July 1947 McKay returned to Chicago, and his last year there was fraught with anxiety and ill health. McKay's daughter, Hope, was in New York City attending Columbia Teachers College. In April 1948 McKay and Hope made plans to meet for the first time, but it never happened. On May 22, 1948, at age fifty-eight, Claude McKay died of congestive heart failure in Chicago. He was buried in New York after a service in Harlem.

Selected Bibliography

WORKS BY CLAUDE McKAY

BOOKS PUBLISHED DURING McKAY'S LIFETIME
Constab Ballads. London: Watts, 1912.

Songs of Jamaica. London: Gardener, 1912. Reprint, Miami, Fla.: Mnemosyne, 1969.

Spring in New Hampshire and Other Poems. London: Grant Richards, 1920.

Harlem Shadows. New York: Harcourt Brace, 1922.

Four Negro Poets. Edited by Alain Locke. New York: Simon & Schuster, 1927.

Home to Harlem. New York: Harper & Brothers, 1928; New York: Pocket Books, 1965.

Banjo: A Story without a Plot. New York: Harper & Brothers, 1929. Reprint, New York: Harcourt, Brace, Jovanovich, 1970.

Gingertown. New York: Harper & Brothers, 1932; Freeport, N.Y.: Books for Libraries Press, 1972.

Banana Bottom. New York: Harper & Brothers, 1933. Reprint, Chatham, N.J.: Chatham Bookseller, 1970.

A Long Way from Home. New York: Lee Furman, 1937. Reprint, New York: Harcourt Brace, 1979.

Harlem: Negro Metropolis. New York: E. P. Dutton, 1940. Reprint, New York: Harcourt Brace Jovanovich, 1972.

BOOKS PUBLISHED POSTHUMOUSLY

Selected Poems. New York: Bookman Associates, 1953. Reprint, New York: Harcourt Brace and World, 1969.

The Dialect Poetry of Claude McKay. Freeport, N.Y.: Books for Libraries Press, 1972.

The Passion of Claude McKay: Selected Prose and Poetry, 1912–1948. Edited by Wayne F. Cooper. New York: Schocken Books, 1973.

Trial by Lynching: Stories about Negro Life in North America. Edited by A. L. McLeod. Translated by Robert Winter. Mysore, India: Centre for Commonwealth Literature and Research, University of Mysore, 1977.

My Green Hills of Jamaica and Five Jamaican Short Stories. Kingston, Jamaica: Heinemann Educational Books, 1979.

The Negroes in America. Edited by Alan L. McLeod. Port Washington, N.Y.: Kennikat Press, 1979. (Originally published as *Negry v Amerike.* USSR, 1923.)

Harlem Glory: A Fragment of Aframerican Life. Chicago: Charles H. Kerr, 1990.

ESSAYS, ARTICLES, AND POEMS

"Peasants' Way O' Thinkin'." *Kingston Daily Gleaner,* January 27, 1912, p. 8.

"Passive Resistance." *Kingston Daily Gleaner,* April 6, 1912, n.p.

Eli Edwards, pseud. "The Harlem Dancer." *Seven Arts,* October 1917, p. 741.

Eli Edwards, pseud. "Invocation." *Seven Arts,* October 1917, p. 741.

"If We Mus Die." *Liberator* 2:21 (July 1919).

"Socialism and the Negro." *Worker's Dreadnought,* January 31, 1920, pp. 1–2.

"How Black Sees Green and Red." *Liberator* 4:17–21 (June 1921). (Essay.)

"He Who Gets Slapped." *Liberator* 5:24–25 (May 1922). (Essay.)

"Birthright." *Liberator,* August 1922, pp. 15–16.

"A Negro to His Critics." *New York Herald Tribune Books,* March 6, 1932, pp. 1, 6. (Essay.)

"Harlem Runs Wild." *Nation,* April 3, 1935, pp. 382–383.

"Lest We Forget." *Jewish Frontier* 7:9–11 (January 1940). (Essay.)

"Look Within." *Cambridge Magazine* 11:8 (January 1945).

"On Becoming a Roman Catholic." *Epistle* 2:43–45 (spring 1945). (Essay.)

"The Middle Ages." *Catholic Worker* 13:5 (May 1946). (Poem.)

"The New Day." *Interracial Review* 19:37 (March 6, 1946). (Poem.)

CRITICAL AND BIOGRAPHICAL STUDIES

Bone, Robert. *The Negro Novel in America.* New Haven, Conn.: Yale University Press, 1958. Revised ed., 1965.

Cooper, Wayne. "Claude McKay and the New Negro of the 1920's." *Phylon* 25:297–306 (1964). (Valuable treatment of McKay's relationship to the Harlem Renaissance.)

———. *Claude McKay: Rebel Sojourner in the Harlem Renaissance: A Biography.* Baton Rouge: Louisiana State University Press, 1987.

Du Bois, W. E. B. "The Browsing Reader." *Crisis* 35:202 (June 1928). (Famous hostile review of *Home to Harlem.*)

Gayle, Addison, Jr. *The Way of the New World: The Black Novel in America.* Garden City, N.Y.: Anchor Press, 1975.

Giles, James R. *Claude McKay.* Boston: Twayne Publishers, 1976.

Hathaway, Heather. *Caribbean Waves: Relocating Claude McKay and Paule Marshall.* Bloomington: Indiana University Press, 1999.

Huggins, Nathan Irvin. *Harlem Renaissance.* New York: Oxford University Press, 1971.

Jackson, Blyden. "The Essential McKay." *Phylon* 14:216–217 (1953). (Largely sympathetic review of *Selected Poems*.)

Kaye, Jacqueline. "Claude McKay's *Banjo.*"*Présence Africaine* 73:165–169 (1970). (Important analysis of *Banjo*'s contribution to the concept of Negritude.)

Ramchand, Kenneth. *The West Indian Novel and Its Background.* New York: Barnes & Noble, 1970.

Tillery, Tyrone. *Claude McKay: A Black Poet's Struggle for Identity.* Amherst: University of Massachusetts Press, 1992.

—STEPHEN SOITOS

Paul Monette

1945–1995

ONE OF THE most arresting moments in Paul Monette's best-known work, *Borrowed Time: An AIDS Memoir* (1988), occurs when Monette's lover, Roger, is diagnosed with *Pneumocystis carinii* infection of the lungs, the infection that killed many patients with acquired immunodeficiency syndrome, or AIDS, in the mid-1980s, before any effective treatment became available. Roger's doctor turns to Monette and says, "You're a writer? . . . Why don't you write about this? Nobody else does." This comment brings a reader up short today. It is at first difficult to remember a time when no one wrote about AIDS. Monette's *Borrowed Time* documents this period, when AIDS, then considered a disease of Haitians and gay men, was referred to by the acronym GRID, for "gay-related immune deficiency." *Borrowed Time* is the most famous AIDS narrative, the first and perhaps the only one to become a national bestseller.

Borrowed Time had the effect of garnering sympathy both for AIDS sufferers and for the Gay Pride movement, which had been threatened by the disease. The Gay Pride movement had been born in the wake of an incident now called "Stonewall," which refers to a hot summer night in 1969 when the Stonewall Inn, a gay bar in New York's Greenwich Village, was besieged by police officers and the vice squad. This was a frequent occurrence, but this time the bar's patrons fought back, achieving a certain media attention. Homosexual acts were at that point technically illegal, and homosexuals were harassed by the police. After the Stonewall rebellion, the movement grew, until AIDS threatened to shove many homosexuals back into the closet.

In 1988, the year that saw the publication of *Borrowed Time,* anger and activism by ACT UP (AIDS Coalition to Unleash Power) and other groups who were tired of being ignored by the Reagan government increased. It was still possible at that time for a mainstream newspaper columnist like James K. Kilpatrick to pose what he called a "hard question" about AIDS, namely, "What's the big deal?" (quoted in Bob Sipchen, *Los Angeles Times*). It was still noteworthy for a sympathetic reporter interviewing Paul Monette to point out that Monette finds the word "tragedy" to be "too weak a term to describe what he has seen. *Calamity, nightmare, holocaust* are among the words he chooses." The contemporary student may feel that such terms are standard for describing AIDS, but, in fact, Monette was among the first to use them.

Especially because of the terror invoked by AIDS and the housing and job discrimination frequently inflicted upon men assumed to be infected, few homosexuals dared to tell any of their stories—about AIDS, about "coming out," about political issues germane to gay lives. It is important to remember that Monette's memoirs were among the first. Randy Shilts's book, *And the Band Played On,* had been published in 1987, one year before *Borrowed Time,* but it is essentially an exposé of the AIDS epidemic rather than a personal history. Monette's book, as Sipchen observed in the same *Los Angeles Times* article, "uses that ghastly landscape only as the backdrop for his intimate close-up of one gay couple and one small circle of friends contending with a very personal crisis." Comparing his own work with that of Shilts, Monette remarked, "I don't want to appropriate the term from the Jewish people, but I feel that this is our holocaust. . . . If Randy Shilts has written 'The Rise and Fall of the Third Reich,' I think what I wanted to write is 'Anne Frank's Diary.'" Norman René's movie *Longtime Companion*—the title of which refers to the euphemism employed by the *New York Times* and other major newspapers in obituaries for the surviving man whose partner had died of AIDS—did not appear until 1990, two years after the publication of *Borrowed Time.* The movie followed the lives of seven gay men in vignettes dramatizing the impact of AIDS.

"Until I was twenty-five, I was the only man I knew who had no story at all," Monette observes in *Becoming a Man: Half a Life Story* (1992), his autobiographical memoir of growing up in the closet and finding the courage to emerge from it. His experience of feeling isolated and alone because of the need to hide the secret of his sexuality seems less typical of gay men and women now, growing up in a world deluged with memoirs, novels, and stories about gay life and about AIDS.

In 1988, when Monette went on an eight-city tour to publicize *Borrowed Time,* he faced a tidal wave of hatred fueled by ignorant fear of infection with AIDS. At that time he already had heard of camera crews refusing to be in the same studio as a person with AIDS. As he puts it in *Borrowed Time,* "The country was in full-scale panic, no amount of reassurance convincing the populace that the virus couldn't be passed by mosquito and toilet seat." Monette tells us that a radio interviewer once glanced at him and said, "You look all right. How much time do you think you have?" Callers called in to the show and told Monette that he had gotten what he deserved, that, in his words, "the nation would soon be rid of the whole lot of us Sodomites."

In his preface to a collection of poems, *Love Alone: 18 Elegies for Rog* (1988), which he wrote during the five months after Roger died,

one right after the other, with "hardly a half day's pause between," Monette invokes the World War I poet Wilfred Owen. He claims not to be setting his poems in the context of the generation of young men destroyed by "the great war," as it was then known, but that context is nevertheless apt:

> Wilfred Owen's *Preface* to the poems he wrote in 1917 and 1918 is the best caution I know against beauty and eloquence. He begs us not to read his anthem for the doomed youth of his generation as a decorous celebration of heroes. Decorum is the contemptible pose of the politicians and preachers, the hypocrite slime whose grinning hatred slicks this dying land like rotten morning dew. I do not presume on the nightmare of Owen's war—may the boys of Flanders be spared all comparison—and I don't pretend to have written the anthem of my people. But I would rather have this volume filed under AIDS than under Poetry, because if these words speak to anyone they are for those who are mad with loss, to let them know they are not alone.

In fact, the doomed generation of soldiers seems particularly appropriate, especially since neither a literature about AIDS nor any pretence of a cure existed by the time Monette—"dying by inches" as he writes in his autobiography—wrote these poems. Monette's desire to be filed under "AIDS" rather than under "Poetry" is shared by some of his critics, who feel that his politics intrudes into his art.

Bereft when he realized that his lover was on the verge of death, Monette asked one of Roger's doctors, "What am I going to do without him?" He got this answer: "Write about him, Paul. . . . That's what you have to do." Paul Monette was a writer created by a crisis—the AIDS epidemic and its devastating impact on gay men in the 1980s. At that time, a diagnosis of AIDS led to a life expectancy of a few months; a horrible, painful death; and, often, total rejection by disapproving parents or terrified lovers fearing infection. The situation has changed in western industrial countries, where new drugs are available and many patients now live for years. Monette, who made a living writing movie scripts in Hollywood after having achieved respect as a poet, might have continued in that vein had he, his lover, or his community not been afflicted by AIDS. He wrote six entertaining, but slight and often melodramatic, novels for a gay audience and three collections of verse. His lover's illness and death galvanized him to write his memoir of the epidemic, *Borrowed Time,* which was nominated for the National Book Critics Circle Award in 1989 and was the winner of the 1989 PEN Center USA West Literary Award for best nonfiction work. He also was moved to write his autobiography about life in the closet and coming out, *Becoming a Man.*

By 1993, two years before he died, Monette had produced a third volume of autobiographical writings, the essay collection *Last Watch of the Night: Essays Too Personal and Otherwise* (1994), devoted to the various elements of his life and to gay and lesbian concerns that he wanted to address before succumbing to AIDS. The best of these essays include meditative self-analyses, like his reflections on refusing a young Italian monk's efforts to seduce him, a lone sightseer, at the Basilica of Saint Francis in Assisi:

> He lounged against the banister, coquettish and yet oddly passive, a virgin tramp. Giving him nothing back, I left by the opposite staircase, as huffy as a Puritan divine. . . .

> But as I lay there waiting to sleep, long after midnight, restless from the drumming of the rain on the red tile roofs, I berated myself for having been so icily aloof. I could have ignored his clumsy advance and still been kind, acknowledging we were brothers somehow. I even knew what it was that had made me cruel: how much his awkward pose and tentative pass had called back my own ineffectual moves at twenty-five, eyeing men from a hopeless distance. Always terrified that one of them would respond in kind, giving me back what I wanted and dared not have. I had acted out instead the affronted pride of a straight man.

When they succeed, these essays, along with Monette's other work, present psychological realities of specifically gay concerns and delineate the isolation and despair felt by many gay men of his generation. In his autobiographical writings, the two memoirs, and the book of essays, Monette is truest to himself, able to be direct about being gay at last. The writing is artistically superior to much of his earlier work. He confessed in *Becoming a Man* that "until I came out . . . clear was the last thing I wanted my writing to be. Poetry served as a sort of intellectual wallpaper to brighten up the closet." Author of six novels and four collections of poetry, Monette most likely will be remembered primarily as a memoirist, for it is in his autobiographical writings that he finally combines artistry and honesty with a consistency lacking in much of his other work.

CRITICISM AND CONTROVERSY

In a 1996 review of AIDS memoirs that appeared in the *New Statesman,* Richard Canning remarked,

> AIDS literature needs no aesthetic. Theories about art can come later; and must, if they are to take into account the subgenre of AIDS memoirs (some fictionalised) emerging out of the epidemic. To postpone conclusions about AIDS and art should not mean suspending judgment, however. AIDS literature will not achieve greatness through pity alone. Naturally, aesthetic judgments feel inappropriate. It is hard to keep in mind the dynamics of prose when a writer—or his lover . . . is dying. Objecting to a turn of phrase feels bogus, or surplus; like criticising a man's handwriting as he writes his will. Perhaps this is why critics have said little of importance about AIDS art.

Although the Modern Language Association index lists only three entries for Paul Monette—

two of them primarily biographical and bibliographical entries in general surveys of gay and lesbian literature—many journalists interviewed Monette and wrote about his work. Monette acknowledged during his life that controversy existed about how artistically successful his highly politicized writings could be, remarking that he would rather be known for loving well than writing well.

In two of his essays in *Last Watch of the Night* he alludes to denigrations of himself as a writer in the gay press and takes issue with the denigrators. In "3275"—the title refers to the number of the lot Monette purchased for graves for himself and his lover Roger—Monette writes of his desire to inscribe his own grave with the words

DIED OF HOMOPHOBIA
MURDERED BY HIS GOVERNMENT

He adds, "My heart is too exhausted to sustain the bitterness anymore, not even against the calumnies of my enemies," a sentence that disproves itself. "The writer who trashed me twelve years ago in the *Native* [the *New York Native,* a gay newspaper] has kept up his campaign," Monette adds. He recounts that this enemy remarked of Monette's prose to one interviewer, "It isn't even English." He goes on to say that the same writer "has a friend who calls him . . . and reads whole paragraphs of me, reducing them both to whinnies of laughter."

Any writer can sympathize, because all writers worth their salt at some point endure bad reviews, especially if whatever they have to say is new or controversial. Monette might have considered the wise words of one of the heroes of Gay Pride, the Irish playwright and wit Oscar Wilde, who remarked that "there is only one thing in the world worse than being talked about, and that is not being talked about." Certainly "not being talked about" is the kiss of death for a writer, quite literally for one writing about AIDS, who needs to keep the illness in

the limelight in order to stimulate political and medical interest in finding cures. Monette also might have regarded angry and belittling reviews as the signs of envy they probably were. The fact that his better-known work has received little critical attention, however, perhaps points to a flaw that critics have discussed and that Monette alludes to without accepting it in his essay "The Politics of Silence." He writes,

> A friend of mine suggested to me last week that *Becoming a Man* would have been a better book without the diatribe of the first five pages. A more seasoned writer, he seemed to imply, would have tossed those pages out before submitting the book for publication. We talked at some length about whether art should be political or not. His own sister is a novelist, a very fine one, and it was she who'd heaved my book across the room after feeling assaulted by those five pages.

Monette goes on to recount that he asked his friend whether the sister was political and that the friend replied no, that she was an artist, a distinction to which Monette no longer subscribes. In defense of his position he remarks that "if you live in political times . . . then all art is political," and on his terms, bad art fails to be consciously political.

It is understandable that a man who had cared for, had gone to extreme lengths to barter medication for, and, by the time he wrote this essay, had buried two lovers in the knowledge that he, too, would die a similar painful death would be bitter. It is even more understandable that such a man would feel extreme rage toward the government of Ronald Reagan and its indifference toward the need for medical research into AIDS and the necessity for distribution of available medications. But an artist finds a way to transcend or transmute the rage. What makes art is, in part, the ability not just to record the rage (that qualifies as journalism) but also to lead readers toward the emotional or philosophical resolution the artist has forged. Monette frequently compares the Reagan government's indifference to AIDS to the Nazi murder of Jews. It is therefore well to remember that the best literature to emerge from the European Holocaust—for instance, the work of Anne Frank, Primo Levi, and Paul Celan— transcended the embittered rage of loss and pain. This transcendence was sometimes achieved philosophically (Anne Frank's "I still believe that people are really good at heart"), sometimes through a painstaking recording of events (Levi), and sometimes through lyrical homage to the memorialization of details of forgotten lives (as in Celan's poem "Alchemical," which includes the lines "All these names / All these names / burnt with the rest"). Monette does not attempt to transcend his rage, feeling that to do so would blight his art; this was a feeling not shared by many of his critics.

LIFE AND DEATH

Paul Landry Monette was born on October 16, 1945, in Lawrence, Massachusetts, an industrial town on the Merrimack River known for textile mills in the nineteenth century and as the conductor and composer Leonard Bernstein's birthplace in the twentieth century. Monette grew up in Andover, Massachusetts, the home of Phillips Academy, the academically demanding boarding school that he attended for high school. While he was a student there, his lower-caste status as a mere "townie" initially protected him somewhat from exposure as a homosexual, since at first he felt automatically excluded from social situations that might have made it difficult for him to hide his sexuality.

His parents, Paul Monette and Jackie Lamb, had been high school sweethearts. In 1951, when he was six, a brother, Robert, was born with spina bifida, a congenital defect in which one or more vertebrae fails to develop completely, leaving a portion of the spinal cord exposed. Children born with this condition are, Monette writes bitterly in *Becoming a Man,*

'crippled.' From here I see how the word is rotten with judgment, obscenely Biblical, hissing curses. *Your brother will never walk. He will forfeit his boyhood shuttling back and forth to a hospital for crippled children, where they will break his legs and try to reassemble them, over and over in a jigsaw of pain. Damn you all.*

His brother's condition of abnormality had particular resonance for Monette, who began early in life to view himself as abnormal. As he describes it in *Becoming a Man,* one day, his mother caught the nine-and-a-half-year-old Paul masturbating with a boy his age and demanded to know what they had been doing. "Nothing," said young Paul, repeating the answer several days later when she repeated the question:

I was right, of course—it *had* been nothing. Yet I knew as I walked lead-footed to my bedroom that the high-wire act of passion was over, because it was somehow wrong. Even if I'd had the wherewithal to challenge her confusion, it wasn't worth the fight. There had already been enough damage to our family, more than enough of the pain of being different. The last thing they needed was something weird from me. Thus did the subtext of my growing-up get set in stone: *I had to be the normal one.* To compensate for the family curse, my brother, whose laughing demeanor and scrappiness were already at odds with the tragic whispering of neighbors and gawkers.

Compensating for his brother by trying to be "the normal one" put young Paul in an impossible situation. Only by excelling academically—at least, in his elementary and junior high school years—could he offer his stricken parents some illusion that at least one of their children approximated the longed-for normality that typified the conformist 1950s. "Paul is perfect," a teacher gushed on one of his second-grade report cards. Thus did the boy who saw himself as worse than imperfect, as a one-of-a-kind grotesque, struggle to fit in.

Family strains continued, since at the time when his brother was born treatments for children with his condition remained limited at best and public schools were "wholly undesigned for the handicapped," Monette writes. Many parents did not even bring such children home from the hospital, but left them to be warehoused in Willowbrook-like institutions where no one ever saw them, least of all family members. Monette's brother, Robert, "was going to a school out of *David Copperfield,*" Monette writes, exaggeratedly, for no child was beaten or tormented in the school—as they are in Charles Dickens's Victorian novel—but only neglected. Bobby's school, a single schoolroom "behind a rickety gift shop on Main Street" was run by one of three spinster sisters who lived in a state of genteel poverty. The children—most of whom were mentally retarded—sang hymns every morning, and Monette's brother, "his brain untapped, whiled away the time trading ball scores" with one of the boarders in the sisters' home. The brother's education amounted to nothing more than "day care in a madhouse," Monette reports.

In different ways, Monette and his brother were segregated from the other children in the town of Andover the older they grew, for Monette's brother was hardly able to walk—transporting himself with a "bare-bones iron chassis" cart that friends had built for him—and Monette early on was recognized by other children as gay. Having had the harrowing experience of watching a gang of bullies torment a gay boy he knew, Monette tried hard to hide his sexuality behind the role of courtier—amusing everyone, laughing when he felt like crying, imagining that he could conceal himself "in the role of the clown sophisticate," he writes.

At this point Monette took entrance exams, applying at the same time for a fellowship to Phillips Academy, the bastion of privilege and separateness that prepared the children of the rich for life in the professions and the leisured classes. Long known as a feeder for such Ivy League colleges as Princeton, Yale, and Harvard, the school boasted many highly successful and famous graduates. Paul's teachers egged him on, and although he felt frightened of "that brick utopia on the hill, with its lofty porticoes and endless carpets of lawn," he wanted to go. He wanted to go even though, and also because, as a local boy, passing "through its wrought-iron portals . . . meant that ever afterwards he would lose his citizen status in the village." Beneath his parents' and teachers' and even his own dreams of academic advantages lay his own far more pressing need to escape the local high school:

Because what was really left for me in the town, as my courtier's dance grew ever more frenetic, the boys and girls increasingly distinct from each other, no whisper of androgyny allowed? How long could I pass for straight among these kids who'd known me since first grade?

Hindsight drove Monette to the realization that he probably did not pass for straight at all:

My brother tells an excruciating story from this era. He was pumping his cart up Chestnut Street and suddenly found himself surrounded by a pack of thugs, probably from the housing project across the way. "His brother's a queer," announced their leader, the rest baring their teeth as they grunted in disgust. Bobby quaked in fear that he was about to be pulverized. Then the whole thing turned around. "We know *you're* okay," said the leader. "And if anyone tries to hurt you, you just tell us. 'Cause we'll wipe the street with 'em."

Bobby went home disturbed and confused by the incident. Six years younger than Paul, he failed to understand the slurs on his brother's name and told their mother what had happened, asking what the boys had meant. She said, "Nothing" and then urged him not to mention the incident to anyone. "Secrets upon secrets," comments Monette. "Thus by inexorable degrees does the love that dares not speak its name build walls instead, till a house is nothing but closets."

Monette borrows the phrase "the love that dare not speak its name," from the trials of Oscar Wilde, who dared to parade his gay lover in the staid London of the 1890s. In 1895, he was convicted in London for so-called indecent acts, as sexual behavior excluding sexual intercourse between men was known. This was enough to condemn him to two years at hard labor in an English prison, at that time almost equivalent to a death sentence. (A conviction for sodomy would have brought him seven years in prison.) Wilde, who has become a hero and martyr of the Gay Pride movement for going public with his love life when such an act remained unimaginable, had appropriated the phrase from a poem ("Two Loves") written by his lover, Lord Alfred Douglas, and published in Oxford's undergraduate magazine, *The Chameleon,* in 1894. When asked in court to state what the line meant, Wilde dared to define it as something beautiful, fine, and noble. Although court spectators felt moved to give Wilde a standing ovation, neither their sympathy nor his status as an important writer saved him from the ruinous prison term or from the ranting judge's visceral disgust.

A century later, by the time of Monette's death from AIDS in 1995 in Los Angeles, things had changed enough so that homosexuals in England and America could boast legal protections. As all of Monette's autobiographical writings reiterate, such protections often meant little in the face of a homophobic crowd's fury. Although they are understandable, interesting, and also historically important as an index of a time in which homosexual men had almost no political clout with which to protect themselves, Monette's raging indictments of wholesale discrimination against homosexuals reveal his writing as far from his lyrical, observant best. Writing about homophobia, he often sounds melodramatic, cliché-ridden, and almost indis-

criminate in the range of his fury. In *Becoming a Man,* he interrupts with a torrent of invective an exultation about being able to celebrate gayness after a life in the closet:

> When we laugh together . . . and dance in the giddy circle of freedom, we are children for real at last, because we have finally grown up. And every time we dance, our enemies writhe like the Witch in *Oz,* melting, melting—the Nazi Popes and all their brocaded minions, the rat-brain politicians, the wacko fundamentalists and their Book of Lies. . . .
>
> Genocide is still the national sport of straight men, especially in this century of nightmares.

At Phillips Academy Andover, Monette continued to live deeply in the closet, and although life in an all-male academy afforded the possibility of avoiding the pretence of being heterosexual, it gave him small relief. His close friends became the other two closeted gay boys, and none of them ever dared to breathe a word of their burdensome secrets. "We never spoke of sex, *ever,* not even in puns." Self-hatred as much as fear muzzled them. Monette observes that what stuns him the most about his brother's story of the thugs is that it still pains him as he writes his memoir, some twenty years later. He feels shame at not having been able to conceal who he was and also something "that still winces that I wasn't enough of a man."

Depressed, lonely, and isolated by his scholarship boy status as well as by his efforts to hide his sexuality, Monette identifies a lingering self-pity in his miseries. As a writer he rightly disapproves but indulges these feelings: "I must add here that I understand that being a nerd in prep school doesn't rank high on the scale of human suffering. I didn't have to look any further than my brother to know what a life of struggle was." Yet the pressures he faced, especially the indirect ones, proved daunting. One of the schoolmasters found him chatting with his gay, but chaste and closeted classmates and rebuked him in a report card, referring to his behavior as silly and "not healthy." He damned Monette with the cutting remark "He's got a lot of growing up to do if he wants to be a man." Monette's parents missed the implication, which tormented Monette but ultimately probably provided the focus and the title for *Becoming a Man,* in which he describes manhood on his own terms. The book remains an open and, at its best, honest argument with himself about the achievement of manhood and masculinity as a gay man: Monette's openness about his despair and doubts are among the book's great strengths. Describing these doubts and his partial and intermittent victories over them, he offers the best of autobiography as a genre, that is, the story of an individual transcending a crisis of life or identity.

Considering the pressures afflicting Monette—his outsider status as a day student and his secret identity—it is amazing that he achieved decent grades at Andover. Adolescence by itself, let alone an entirely new way of life among persons of completely different (that is, far more socially prominent) standing, might have been enough to derail any young person. Monette persevered, winning admittance to Yale University, where he received a bachelor of arts degree in 1967. He began his prolific writing career not long after finishing college, writing poetry exclusively for eight years. During these years he taught at Milton Academy and Pine Manor College.

While he was in his late twenties, Monette experimented with the free love mores of the times, having half-hearted affairs with various women and men and trying to change his sexuality through psychotherapy. He finally did come out of the closet, and his life changed dramatically when he met the great love of his life, Roger Horwitz, on September 4, 1974, in Boston at a dinner party hosted by the poet Richard Howard. Monette was twenty-eight, and Horwitz was thirty-two. They moved to Los Angeles in November 1977. There, Roger practiced law, and Paul wrote novels and screenplays. Their whirlwind romance had developed into a lifelong companionship halted only by Roger's death from AIDS on October 22, 1986.

Another personal culmination occurred for Monette when he was able to attend the Gay March on Washington, D.C., despite the fact that he was already severely ill with AIDS, and then give a speech for the National Book Award ceremony at the Library of Congress. About his experience of participating in this celebration of gay life, Monette writes:

> What we would take away with us from Washington was also . . . personal. For me it began in a small town in Massachusetts forty years ago—a sickness of the soul about being different. And nothing more important, not breath itself, than the need to keep it secret. The stillborn journey of my life took off at last, the moment I opened the closet door. To know how dark a place you come from into the light of self-acceptance—it is to enact a sort of survivorship that leaves a trail for those who come after. But you carry that kid with you the rest of your life—wounded as he is by hate and lies—a shadow companion who needs you to free him.

Monette succumbed to complications from AIDS in Los Angeles on February 10, 1995. He was forty-nine years old. A ninety-minute documentary film, "Paul Monette: The Brink of Summer's End," was made of his life. Directed by Monte Bramer, it has been called a "nonfiction version of Norman René's *Longtime Companion*" (*The Austin Chronicle Movie Guide*).

MAJOR WORK

Borrowed Time is indeed a landmark in reporting about AIDS. The book's chief subject is the final years in the life of Monette's lover Roger, who died of complications from AIDS exactly nineteen months after the disease was diagnosed.

It has been praised widely by journalists, but there is little literary criticism about it. William M. Hoffman, writing in *The New York Times Book Review,* praises the work as "a magnificent monument to his lover's bravery, their commitment to each other and the plague of hatred and ignorance they had to endure." Significantly, he lingers on the journalistic virtues of the memoir rather than its literary importance:

> The memoir has the leanness and urgency of war reporting, sparing the reader none of the details of the illness or the emotional state of the principals. Just as Roger learns how to cope with increasing weakness, fevers, and the toxic drug reactions, he goes blind. . . . Understandably, Mr. Monette feels a great deal of rage, especially at an Administration whose chief spokesman was Patrick Buchanan, "one of whose major qualifications for the job was his . . . remark that nature was finally exacting her price on homosexuals." . . . As in war reporting, there is much black humor, especially when the author tries to earn some sorely needed cash by writing a comedy for Whoopi Goldberg while his lover is in intensive care.

Reading between the lines, Hoffman admires Monette's strength under pressure but excuses the book's literary failings without saying directly that they exist. Many reviewers may not have wanted to criticize the writing style, because they knew that a book regarded as inflammatory by the far right of the political spectrum (who thought, How dare homosexuals tell their story? How dare they exist?) might sink under the weight of any comments about rage that overwhelmed the narrative or the prose style. Monette himself joked about the Christian right wing. When Senator Sam Nunn proposed the "Don't Ask. Don't Tell" policy for Gays in the Military, Monette wondered, "Why couldn't we see they could live with us—Baptists and generals and pundits all—if we'd just stay in the closet? We can live with you if you'll just play dead."

In a review of Monette's novel *Afterlife* (1990), which picks up where *Borrowed Time* leaves off, with the problem of the AIDS "widower," Judith Viorst describes *Borrowed Time* as a "gallant and wrenching account of his lover's doomed struggle with AIDS." Viorst appraises Monette's writing almost exclusively in emotional, rather than critical terms, for instance, characterizing *Afterlife* as a "tough, painful book about gay sex and love." This tendency to laud Monette's aims and honesty rather than the literary qualities of his work appears in nearly every mainstream press review of his work.

Liberal affinities or perhaps the guilt of the unafflicted may explain the disinclination of mainstream press writers to mention infelicities in Monette's style, but as Monette himself mentions, this was not the case with the gay press. Daniel Mendelsohn, identified in his byline as writing "regularly about gay culture," gives Monette a sympathetic review in the *Nation* but also address problems with his writing. Of Monette's essay collection, *Last Watch of the Night,* Mendelsohn observes,

> It's a far from perfect work—like much of Monette's writing, it's overstuffed and tends to be impulsive, characteristics that are least desirable in the essay as a genre—but it is ultimately moving, precisely because, even in extremis, Monette [who was very ill with AIDS when he wrote these essays] still won't compromise any component of his identity—political, sexual, or personal.

Mendelsohn goes on the remark that Monette's "refusal to depersonalize has been the source both of the greatest pleasures and of the most egregious failings" in his work. His personality is "all over" his writing, and, for this reason, how readers feel about *him* defines how they feel about his work. Mendelsohn writes fondly of Monette's early "pre-plague" novels, such as *Taking Care of Mrs. Carroll* (1978) and *The Gold Diggers* (1979), and Monette's delight in writing in an "unabashedly gay mode," but he mentions his "weakness for melodrama," which "manages to be engaging," and his "Benzedrinelaced B-movie plotting." Bringing home these qualities, Mendelsohn summaries a section of Monette's novel *Halfway Home* (1991):

> In the opening pages . . . the story of a perfor-mance artist with AIDS who retreats to a friend's California estate to confront his mortality, Mo-nette first reunites two estranged brothers, one gay, one straight; a few pages later, the straight one gets blown up, the victim of an organized crime hit, his demise witnessed by the gay brother on the nightly news; and a few pages after *that,* it all turns out to be a case of mistaken identity, and they're reunited again. All this, I should add, comes well before you even get to the steamy revelations of sibling incest.

Generally, Mendelsohn admires Monette's ir-repressibility but feels that it "too often curdles into self-indulgence." This is the case, he believes, with Monette's poetry as much as it is with his prose. Of the collection *Love Alone,* Mendelsohn writes that even though some poems hit the mark, in many of them "the poet is so intent on his own feelings that he can't consider yours, and you can't help feeling a bit left out. . . . You can't shake the prurient feeling that you're eavesdropping." This seems a matter of taste; some might admire precisely the raw quality that Mendelsohn dislikes. His comments on Monette's rage seem justified:

> In [Monette's essay] "My Priests". . . Monette lets loose at "the Vatican Nazis," "bloodsucker con-vents" and Cardinal Ratzinger, "the Vatican's Minister of Hate." This stuff is unfortunate, and never rings as true as the moments when Monette trains his poet's eye and sentimentalist's ear on small details. When a cancer-ridden physician and friend steps out of bed and feels her ankle "snap like a leafless twig," the sound echoes in your mind far longer than does the noise of Monette's artillery.

This captures the highly disparate qualities of Monette's writing, which vary with his moods and especially with his degree of despair.

As journalism and as a historic record, the value of *Borrowed Time* remains unquestion-able, but as memoir it leaves much to be desired. Emotions are evaded through cliché or the oft-repeated line "I can't express," as in the following passage, in which Monette berates his lover's brother for refusing to discuss AIDS: "I can't express how icy cold I went inside. This was the asshole who'd fenced us into our secret, and now he wouldn't share it with us? It's a battle scar I can still feel." A writer's job is to express how icy cold he or she felt, without cli-ché and easy rage.

When Monette describes his first meeting with Roger Horwitz, his language is anything but original, which seems a significant failing in a book devoted to Roger as the most important love relationship of Monette's life: "Summer has always been good to me, even the bit-tersweet end, with the slant of yellow light, and I for one was in love before the night was done. I suppose we'd been waiting for each other all our lives." This sounds like formula writing for a romance novel or melodrama, and certainly Monette did his share of Hollywood film scripts. A reader wants to learn the particulars. What made him fall in love? Was it Roger's eyes or the smell of his skin or the way his hair fell on the back of his neck? What exactly *were* those irrational reasons, difficult to pinpoint, that constituted the feeling of love? Why did he feel that he and Roger were made for each other, to use another cliché, and what would the phrase mean in this instance? Why doesn't Monette the writer make his readers see, hear, smell, touch, and taste his experience of love?

This point should be raised, because Monette discourses at length on the self-hatred caused by life in the closet in virtually all of his writ-ing and also on the difficulty of ridding himself of this self-hatred. It is possible that a sad remnant of self-disgust made it impossible for him to conjure up the love of his life in language that could make that love believable.

Self-hatred perhaps overpowers his feelings of love. To take one of many instances, in *Borrowed Time,* Monette discusses plans for his local gay and lesbian center's annual dinner and how it will help with the crisis of AIDS. "For once we would not internalize the homophobia," he writes. Reading his writing is a revelation concerning how constant and difficult a battle he waged not to do this. As it stands, the writing remains flat. Hatred for homophobes rivals self-hatred in much of his work.

The inability to transcend is a flaw in the writing, but thankfully not an ever-present flaw. Monette's wit, charm, and lyrical style enhance much of his work. He is particularly good at conveying the experience of crisis, as, for instance, where he describes a point of no return in Roger's illness, when it is clear that it will soon be impossible to hide the nature of his condition from family and friends:

> I have virtually no record of the next three months. Except for a few doctors' appointments, Roger's calendar is completely blank for the rest of the year, and he wouldn't even bother with a calendar for '86. Between then and the end of January there is a single five-line entry in my journal, and my daily calendar is as empty as Roger's, because I ceased to write my appointments down. I kept the ones I could remember. Indeed, we both went on working as long as we could, struggling into November, but it was as if the whole idea of calendars had become a horrible mockery.
>
> I wish I had an account of just the meals we ate, or a log of the calls that came in, for there was where we lived. . . . When you live so utterly in the present, the yearning to record it goes away. To write in a diary you have to hope to read it later—or last long enough to make the appointment two weeks down the road.

His melodrama in *Borrowed Time* has been praised as a conscious literary strategy by one critic, Douglas Eisner, who writes in an article for *College Literature:*

Monette's autobiography is, understandably, obsessed with memory and with desire. His strategy is to articulate his memories and his desires with heightened rhetoric; for example, Monette writes, "Now we would learn to borrow time in earnest, day by day, making what brief stays we could against the downward spiral from which all our wasted brothers did not return.". . . As a writer of movie novelizations and screenplays, Monette uses his skills as a melodramatist to construct a story that will heighten the effects of normalcy by which he defines his and his lover's relationship and the effects of AIDS' "invasion" of this normalcy.

In the absence of criticism about Monette—Eisner's is one of the three essays listed in the Modern Language Association's bibliography—it is hard to say whether his views constitute a trend among literary critics. His first sentence seems merely to define autobiography, in general, as opposed to autobiography dealing with AIDS or, more to the point, any autobiography concerned with a traumatic loss of life. Eisner does not say why he considers Monette's melodrama to be a strategy for "normalizing" his way of life, bringing homosexual couples into the fold and giving them, in the words of the prominent gay social critic Bruce Bawer, "a place at the table."

An alternate and perhaps a more realistic view might be that Monette's melodrama was no conscious strategy. Instead, his melodrama is possibly the unknowing defense of a mind so reeling with fear and sadness that it could not bear to face the emotions that writers must endure in order to write well about pain. Cliché and melodrama are nothing if not the avoidance of real emotions, especially strong ones.

BECOMING A MAN: HALF A LIFE STORY

Monette's autobiography begins with a longing for the freedom and ease of heterosexuals and a grim description of life in the closet:

Everybody else had a childhood, for one thing. . . . First they had their shining boyhood, which made them strong and psyched them up for the leap across the chasm to adolescence, where the real rites of manhood began. . . .

And every year they leaped further ahead, leaving me in the dust with all my doors closed, and each with a new and better deadbolt.

The book describes the ways in which the closet walls went up and the ways in which Monette kept them up for years, tentatively emerging from the closet and then putting his head back in again, before finally coming out in his twenties. The first chapters cover his boyhood and show a developing pattern of furtive contacts with other boys like himself that get broken off abruptly because of shame and guilt. After Monette's mother repeatedly asks him what he was doing with the first boy he loved, Kite, and Monette replies, "Nothing," he begins to pray at night. He asks "for it to be taken away, not knowing that 'it' was love. *Forgive me for what I did with Kite, and don't let it happen again.*"

Scenes like this—and there are many—effectively reveal the imprisonment within himself that Monette felt as a young child. Unfortunately, he does not let them speak for themselves, perhaps not comprehending his own eloquence. Interrupting the memories are moralizing distractions:

I don't know when hate starts. Bigotry has to be taught, that much is clear, because babies and small children don't think in vicious epithets. . . .

I've come to see the church of the Polish pope as a sort of Greenwich Mean of moral rot—thus in my small way returning the compliment of Sturmführer Ratzinger.

These outbursts reveal how deeply Monette has been injured by those who hate, but they leave the impression that he has not found a way to cope with the hatred, because he cannot help but accept it and feels a great deal of self-hatred that he recognizes only intermittently:

There's a whine in every memory I call up from the prep school years that is so deeply unappealing, even to me, that I find myself wanting to slap the faceless boy I was. . . . But how else to explain the closet I built except to describe the unrelieved perception of being *less than*? My failure to achieve the school's idea of manhood proved to me I was no man at all.

The question he raises about how to explain the closet he built is one he never really answers, perhaps because to do so would require that he experience once again the hatred of homophobes as well as his self-hatred. He implies an equation of the two, but the situation is far more complex and remains incompletely addressed. For instance, describing his love of art, which developed in adolescence, he recounts an incident in which a sculpture by Alexander Calder was knocked to the floor of the Addison Gallery of American Art. The staff picked it up "tenderly," Monette relates. "At least I could feel for art what the laws of desire and my own self-hatred prevented me from feeling for another man." The word "self-hatred" does not explain the particulars of that feeling for his personality, the ways in which the feeling manifested itself.

Among his rueful memories of the closet are his thoughts on marriage. The young Monette develops a gimlet eye for the secretly gay husband:

It would be a while yet before I could spot one of those shuttered unions across a dance floor. The dumpy wife with her gray ponytail, like an old little girl, the smile on her face as strained and pale as the sherry in her glass. The husband a bit too natty in his plaids, his bloodless charm on automatic, and one eye hungering after the barman. Yet even a decade later, foiled at finding a man to love me back, I was still weighing the devil's bargain. Still debating if this woman or that would have me above the waist, and then we could both eat pheasant till it came out of our ears. The closet is all about compartments.

In Monette's fine depiction of these sad unions, his own frustration and sadness emerge much more effectively than they do in his moral tirades.

Toward the end of his Yale education, Monette made a now or never decision. Funded by a Yale fellowship, he went to England, where he read the letters of the Victorian poet Alfred, Lord Tennyson at Cambridge University. As he describes it, angered by Tennyson's never-declared love for his friend Arthur Hallam, who died, Monette determines to force his own way out of the closet. He remains extremely ambivalent even as he does so. One minute he walks the streets of London in the direction of gay bars, still thinking, *Change me, change me* [into a heterosexual man]," and the next he lets a man pick him up. He goes home with the man, where he enjoys himself until the man wants anal sex, which turns out to be excruciating. All Monette's self-loathing returns: "Hating myself for acceding to the *woman's* role, when what I had been so desperate for was to prove I was a man." Loathing himself for feeling less masculine after an incident that he assumes will make him feel more masculine, he leaves the man's house abruptly, despite the fact that, or even because, he likes him.

A pattern of rejecting those who expressed romantic and erotic interest in him was to continue for years. His struggle to define the nature of manhood on his own terms is a moving, but incomplete part of his story. His disgust with himself at taking what he perceived as a woman's role reveals how trapped he was at this point in his life in stereotypic ideas about masculinity. Masculinity is aggressive, and femininity is passive; even to assume that the receiving role he took was "passive" reveals a certain naïveté. He attempted to recover from the feelings of self-doubt that this episode raised by going on his own private gay European tour, talking to anyone and everyone and having the time of his life.

He finished his education at Yale and began work as a teacher in a boys' boarding school, but his problems returned when one of the boys developed a crush on him and succeeded in seducing him. Fortunately for Monette, the affair was resolved in his favor, and the student, who, according to the headmaster, had a penchant for "turning on" those who helped him, was sent packing. The event left Monette shaken. He still had a strong desire to control his sexuality and to change it, and he began therapy with the expressed desire to be transformed into a heterosexual. The therapist agrees, one suspects only as a ploy for keeping Monette in treatment and eventually inducing him to accept who he is. Gradually, Monette moves from trying to be "not that gay" to trying to be bisexual to realizing—almost the moment that he first meets his life's companion, Roger—that he is gay.

LAST WATCH OF THE NIGHT

The essays in *Last Watch of the Night,* the third and final volume of Monette's autobiographical writings, feature travel more than any other theme. The idea of transcending the fear of death by transmuting it into an exotic journey unifies the collection as a whole. The first essay, "Puck," concerning Monette's happy and irrepressible dog named after Shakespeare's sprite in *A Midsummer Night's Dream,* opens with a comment by Monette's dying companion, Stephen Kolzak, a TV executive whom he met in 1988 and who died in 1990. Kolzak was the second of Monette's lovers to die: "I miss Puck," he remarks from his hospital bed. As if to underscore the tentativeness of their survival, Monette replies with a question: "You think Puck's going to survive me?"

Monette raises the question in the context of new medical developments in fighting AIDS that had occurred by 1990, and which led him to hope that the disease was on the verge of becoming a chronic, manageable one rather than one that was invariably fatal. His dying boyfriend, Stephen, sensed otherwise, telling him that, of course, the dog would outlive him. The rest of the essay is a meditation on the dog as a child to be abandoned by Monette's death. Puck is a family member who helped him endure the pain of losing Roger by grieving with him and the only living being who would really know Monette's story when Monette was gone, "guarding the world for dear life anyway. . . . Noble beast."

The next essay, "Gert," captures little-known slices of life in lesbian history. Gert, the greataunt of a former student of Monette's, had been both the stage manager and the lover of the Broadway actress Katharine Cornell, and she had known the ever-mysterious Greta Garbo, who also had been a lover of Cornell's. The essay provides a series of fascinating anecdotes and a strong sense of what it meant to be a lesbian in closeted days. Despite his disagreement with Gert's sense of discretion (she prefers the word "friend" to "lover" for gays), he finds her an inspiration: "Gert was my pioneer, a link to the dreams that made me different, the push I needed to go my own way."

Describing her as a cross between the American playwright Lillian Hellman and the British poet W. H. Auden, Monette remarks that the seventy-five-year-old Gert "kept to a rigorous code of silence when it came to the proclivities of the theater girls of her generation." But she apparently told Monette her life story, which offers amusing glimpses at Garbo's life story as well. Once, when Garbo arrived on the set of one of Cornell's plays, Gert was packed off with Cornell's gay husband to supper at the "21" club, where the two glumly downed caviar and stiff martinis:

> When Gert and Guthrie came lurching home to Beekman Place, they found that Kit had brought Garbo to the house. The two actresses sat in the parlor before the fire, eating soup and sharing a torn baguette. As Gert came in, Garbo was laughing (Garbo laughs!) and waving her bare feet in the air. "See how big they are!" she announced with glee. "Like a fishwife's!"

Monette remarks that when he told the story to friends old enough to know the cast of characters, all of them had known about Gert and Katharine Cornell. It "seemed like a secret that nobody kept," although it was "protected by a wall of glamour that the press wouldn't have dreamed of trying to vault. It was a separate life conducted on the higher slopes of Olympus. . . . A bohemian aristocracy."

Another anecdote that Monette provides in the essays concerns a day when the aging Garbo came to lunch at Sneden's Landing—a fashionable spot on the Hudson River—with Gert and another friend of hers. This was thirty or forty years after the foot incident with Katharine Cornell. Garbo preferred not to remember and muttered while "staring moodily at the river" that she hated it "when somebody calls me Gigi." No one had done so, but Gert then observed, "Well, you don't have to worry about that, because everyone in the *world* calls you Garbo." Offended dignity warred with satisfaction on Garbo's face.

One other tale worth telling emerges from Gert's treasure trove. In 1944, Katharine Cornell and Gert were performing for the Allied troops in France and Italy and arrived in Paris thinking that they would be stuck with another cold water hotel. Then they were invited to Marlene Dietrich's room at the Ritz. After enjoying a hot soak and climbing back into their dirty uniforms,

> Dietrich cast a disapproving look at the olive-drab uniforms sported by Kit and Gert. Then she flung open the imperial closet, revealing a whole Savile Row tailor's line of officers' uniforms, one for every branch of the Allied powers, and each one fitted to Dietrich's svelte form. . . .

For the next couple of hours the women played dress-up with the military gear—Gert a general, Kit an admiral, Dietrich a Marine commandant.

When Gert told Monette her stories, she also delighted in hearing his, but she was not happy with the ways in which "the Stonewall generation changed the rules forever" and feared the backlash from the religious right. In one of their last meetings, Gert revealed that she had known the gay (but closeted) English dramatist and actor Noel Coward as well. Coward had once stood in the spot Monette was standing on and had sighed, "I don't know that I ever really had love in my life. Not the way I wanted it."

The next essay, "My Priests," concerns closeted priests whom Monette has known, some of them good friends who died of AIDS. It includes many diatribes against the Catholic Church, referred to as the "Vatican Nazis." When he regains his humor, Monette is best on private lives, as when he recounts the tales of a former Trappist monk who regales him with insider stories:

> "I loved being a monk," he would say. "The hot lunch program was fabulous. And every Easter we'd all go over to Rome for the parties. I always stuck with the Kennedys, because they got invited *everywhere*."
>
> So how many priests and monks are gay? I'd ask. . . . What did he think the percentages were? He'd flutter his pudgy hands. . . . "Oh my dear, who can say? A hundred and ten percent. No wonder it took me so long to decide—I really wanted to be a *nun*, not a priest."
>
> And so he was on special occasions. . . . He had a closetful of habits.

In the end, the atheistic Monette, loving the servants, not the institution, remarks: "We need the people of God, especially if He isn't there." The next essay, "3275," offers a tour of scenic and historically interesting gravesites, like that of Robert Louis Stevenson in Samoa. The essay veers between sadness and rage, the evanescence of life and the ravages of AIDS. Longing for an epitaph in which he proclaims himself a victim of homophobia murdered by his government, Monette writes, "I can't tell anymore whom I am addressing with my epitaph. The accidental tourist? Or my own grieving friends who can't even parse their losses anymore, who don't need bronze to recall me." He wants his gravesite to spur visitors to act against governments and medical systems that fail to provide available drugs to AIDS patients: "Tell yourself: *None of this ever had to happen.* . . . Grief is a sword, or it is nothing."

THE POETRY

As in all his work, Monette ranges in his poetry from the very good to what some have called the "regrettable." Among his successful poems is "Gardenias," from *West of Yesterday, East of Summer: New and Selected Poems, 1973–1993* (1994), in which AIDS becomes a monstrous underground root system:

> pain is not a flower pain is a root
> and its work is underground where the moldering
> proceeds the bones of all our joy winded
> and rained and nothing grows a whole life's love
> that longed to be an orchard forced to lie
> like an onion secret sour in the mine of pain
> the ore veined out there's just these tunnels shot
> with roots but then we were never gardeners
> were we planters waterers cleanup crew
> more yard boys three bucks an hour than rose
>   queens

In "Bones and Jewels," from the same collection, Monette personifies Time:

> Time has simply got to shut up. Or else
> I'll beat him senseless, bind his hands, and saucer
> his fat bachelor's face like a discus
> on the wind. Then let him try to talk of me
> as if I had manners and must make do.

Despite Monette's belief that art had to be overtly political in the age of AIDS, his best poems are subtle: the politics can be inferred.

CONCLUSION

Monette's work paved the way for other writers, setting a standard for reportage and emotional honesty. The deluge of AIDS memoirs that have followed from both patients and doctors—among the best are those of Harold Brodkey, Abraham Verghese, and Abigail Zuger—have been shaped by his pain, his humor, and his energy. Each of these writers has, like Monette, told an unknown story about AIDS: Brodkey's tale is that of an older patient who thought of himself as heterosexual, though some youthful homosexual adventures infected him. Verghese, a doctor in a small southern town, treats young men who have come home to die and must face their families. Zuger, also a doctor, treats intravenous drug abusers and their partners, many of them women, at an inner city clinic.

Selected Bibliography

WORKS OF PAUL MONETTE

POETRY

The Carpenter at the Asylum. Boston: Little, Brown, 1975.

No Witnesses. With drawings by David Schorr. New York: Avon, 1981.

Love Alone: 18 Elegies for Rog. New York: St. Martin's Press, 1988.

West of Yesterday, East of Summer: New and Selected Poems, 1973–1993. New York: St. Martin's, 1994.

NOVELS

Taking Care of Mrs. Carroll. Boston: Little, Brown, 1978.

The Gold Diggers. New York: Avon, 1979.

The Long Shot. New York: Avon, 1981.

Lightfall. New York: Avon, 1982.

Afterlife. New York: Crown, 1990.

Halfway Home. New York: Crown, 1991.

MEMOIRS

Borrowed Time: An AIDS Memoir. New York: Harcourt, Brace, Jovanovich, 1988.

Becoming a Man: Half a Life Story. San Diego: Harcourt, Brace, Jovanovich, 1992.

NOVELIZATIONS

Nosferatu: The Vampire. New York: Avon, 1979. (Adaptation of a screenplay by Werner Herzog.)

Scarface. New York: Berkeley, 1986. (Adaptation of a screenplay by Oliver Stone.)

OTHER WORKS

Predator. New York: Berkeley, 1986. (Movie novelization.)

Midnight Run. New York: Berkeley, 1990. (Movie novelization.)

Havana. New York: Ivy Books, 1991. (Movie novelization.)

Last Watch of the Night: Essays Too Personal and Otherwise. New York: Harcourt Brace, 1994.

Sanctuary: A Tale of Life in the Woods. Illustrated by Vivienne Flesher. New York: Scribners, 1997. (Gay fable.)

ARCHIVES

Monette's papers are collected at the University of California at Los Angeles, which maintains a website devoted to Monette's work (http://www.oac.cdlib.org:28008/dynaweb/ead/ucla/mss/monette).

CRITICAL AND BIOGRAPHICAL STUDIES

Borawski, Walta. Review of *Halfway Home. Gay Community News,* April 21–May 4, 1991, p. 7.

Canning, Richard. "Looking AIDS in the Face," *New Statesman,* November 22, 1996.

Clum, John M. "'The Time Before the War': AIDS, Memory, and Desire." *American Literature* 62, no. 2:648–667 (1990).

Davis, Christopher. Review of *Afterlife. Lamda Book Report* 2, no. 3:20–21 (1990).

Eisner, Douglas. "Liberating Narrative: AIDS and the Limits of Melodrama in Monette and Weir." *College Literature* 24, no. 1:213–226 (1997).

Feinberg, David B. Review of *Afterlife. Outweek,* April 4, 1990, p. 59.

Hoffman, William M. "Dispatches from Aphrodite's War," *New York Times Book Review,* September, 1990, p. 3.

Kaufman, David. "All in the Family." *Nation,* July 1, 1991, pp. 21–25.

Labonte, Richard. "Fire and Ice." *Advocate,* September 13, 1988, pp. 65–66.

Longcope, Kay. "Leaving a Legacy for the Gay Community." *Boston Globe,* March 5, 1990, p. 30.

Maggenti, Maria. "No Half Measures." *Outweek,* May 8, 1991, pp. 56–58.

Mendelsohn, Daniel. "Embracing between the Bombs." *Nation,* September 19, 1994, pp. 276–280. (Review of *Last Watch of the Night.*)

Monteagudo, Jesse. Review of *Afterlife. TWN,* April 25, 1990, p. 6.

Newtown, George. "From St. Augustine to Paul Monette: Sex and Salvation in the Age of AIDS." In *True Relations: Essays on Autobiography and the Postmodern.* Edited by Thomas G. Crouser and Joseph Fichtelberg. Westport, Conn.: Greenwood Press, 1998.

Román, David. "Tropical Fruit?: Latino 'Gay' Men in Three Resistance Novels of the Americas." In *Tropicalizations: Transcultural Representations of Latinidad.* Edited by Frances Aparicio and Susana Chávez-Silverman. Philadelphia: Temple University Press, 1993.

———. "Paul Monette (1945–)." In *Contemporary Gay American Novelists: A Bio-Bibliographical Critical Sourcebook.* Edited by Emmanuel S. Nelson. Westport, Conn.: Greenwood Press, 1993.

Shaw, Marv. Review of *Halfway Home. Bay Area Reporter,* May 23, 1991, p. 30.

Simpson, Janice C. Review of *Halfway Home. Time,* May 6, 1991, p. 72.

Viorst, Judith. "The AIDS Widowers' Club: Review of *Afterlife.*" *New York Times Book Review,* March 4, 1990, p. 7.

Weir, John. Review of *Afterlife. Washington Post,* April 26, 1990, p. 3.

Williams, K. Orton. Review of *Halfway Home. San Francisco Sentinel,* May 9, 1991, p. 21.

—MELISSA KNOX

Lorrie Moore

1957–

WHEN ASKED WHY her characters are such losers, Lorrie Moore responded, "It's not that they are losers exactly; I see them more as being aggressively *not* winners." Moore's wry response is typical of the syntactical surprise and wit that have become synonymous with her fiction. Lorrie Moore is the much-acclaimed author of three short story collections, *Self-Help: Stories* (1985), *Like Life: Stories* (1990), and *Birds of America* (1998), and two novels, *Anagrams: A Novel* (1986) and *Who Will Run the Frog Hospital?: A Novel* (1994). Her stories have received O. Henry Awards and the National Magazine Award for Fiction. In 1999 Moore was the only American writer to win the International Fiction Prize in the Irish Times Literature Prizes, awarded in Dublin. The inclusion of her work in *Best American Short Stories of the Century,* edited by John Updike in 1999, cemented her growing reputation as one of the most clever, sophisticated, and accomplished short story writers.

Taken altogether Moore's stories and novels might be described as the fiction of the faithless moderns, stories in which the characters' ardent desires for emotional connection and lasting shelter are stymied by their own awkwardness and fear and the flotsam of ordinary life. As Moore expressed in the short story, "Like Life," mostly her characters hold out for the possibility that "Life was long enough so that you could keep re-learning things, think and feel and realize again what you used to know."

Moore's protagonists are well educated, savvy, philosophical, culturally aware, and in many cases ambitious individuals: artists, musicians, historians, lawyers, writers, teachers, and professors.

Despite their intellectual prowess or perhaps because of it, Moore's characters are often perplexed about how their lives have turned out. In some stories the regret of the road not taken hovers over them like a garish flashing neon sign. At other times, even when they are certain they have chosen the correct road, the one they truly wanted, a shadowy disenchantment accompanies them on their journeys.

In Moore's fiction it is not so much that life is terrible as that it is complicated, filled with sorrow and joy, friendship and loneliness, marriage and divorce, sex and infidelity, imperiled children, and ultimately death. Likewise all shelter (literal and metaphorical) is temporary and love is often elusive. In the story "Starving Again," Moore has her characters thinking about love and food: "You went out on a limb for food, but not for love. Love was not food." Moore's characters persistently question love's power to sustain them. In fact they constantly question the very definition of the word because definition is also a major part of Moore's artistry. Language itself, its slipperiness, its idiosyncrasies, its absurdities, its contradictions, and the deeply personal ways in which people attach value to words, is always a character in the stories.

The following are several of Moore's perspectives on the word "love." In the short story "The Jewish Hunter" love is menacing. The protagonist, a poet named Odette, believes, "All love is a truck on the interstate roaring up from the left, a thing she must let pass." On the other hand, for a dying woman who has wasted her life married to a cold man in "What Is Seized," love has remained careful and gentle. "Love is art," she tells her daughter. "It's like painting scenery." And for Benna Carpenter, the protagonist of the novel *Anagrams,* love is imagination, where invention compensates for lack of connection.

Given the difficulty Moore's characters encounter sustaining a level of satisfaction, it would seem that Moore's fictional world is a depressing place populated with self-absorbed, insatiable neurotics who think too much and are their own worst enemies when it comes to living a contented life. Nothing could be further from the truth because, even when things turn out badly, Moore celebrates "the beauty or value of gesture," and she renders enough of them throughout the body of her work to keep her characters and the reader from nihilistic despair. In addition Moore understands the absolute necessity for and value of humor in all of its forms, everything from the Tom Swifty, to deflective wordplay, to the good joke told in a bad situation. This accounts for why John Casey among others compared Moore to Woody Allen. Humor is ballast in the fiction even though Moore, a self-professed pessimist, believes the essence of her work is sad.

Although her work poses the question of how to live life and maintain a sense of humor about it, it quickly becomes obvious why Moore believes her work is essentially sad. Repeatedly the gnarled and deeply embedded knot at the heart of Moore's short stories and novels is actually an exploration of the essential solitariness of human existence. In this sense Moore's chief artistic concern most closely echoes what the poet Rainer Maria Rilke stated in his meditations *Rilke on Love and Other Difficulties* (1975):

> To speak of solitude again, it becomes always clearer that this is at bottom not something that one can take or leave. We *are* solitary. We may delude ourselves and act as though this were not

so. That is all. But how much better it is to realize that we are so, yes, even to begin assuming it.

Whenever Moore's characters are faced with the slightest possibility of a preordained, eternal connection to another person, much as they long to embrace it, they are skeptical. They balk at joy not because they do not value it but because they value it so much. Moore and the characters she creates are so painfully aware of the transitory nature of both the good and bad events of ordinary life that the challenge for them is: How can I make meaning if I am alone and nothing is certain?

In the history of American literature the belief in God calms the characters' violent psychic churnings. Moore's fictive world is not a godless world, but her characters are a self-directed lot. They are as disinclined to expect rescue, or for that matter punishment, from a heavenly force as they are disinclined to turn toward a standard religion to allay their solitariness. Self-awareness is next to godliness for most of them.

Great changes or transformations, the kind associated with the more traditional Joycean epiphany, rarely occur for the characters in Moore's work. Instead, the stories build and then turn on the characters' quiet resolve to embrace what they may have suspected but were reluctant until forced by circumstance or their own intelligence to accept.

As a short story writer Moore is most frequently compared to Grace Paley and Dorothy Parker. She shares with these writers a distinct vision of the world, an instantly recognizable narrative voice, but above all else a mordant, irrepressible sense of humor that at times is either so antic or caustic that its effect is always bracing and might sometimes strike the reader as rude, even pugnacious in the overtly sadder stories.

Moore's use of language, which is more syntactically complex than that of her predecessors, separates Moore from both Paley and Parker. She combines ferocious wordplay and pun with a talent for arranging a sentence the way a poet might, layering startling image upon image with a sense of structure and rhythm that never interferes with her gift for compelling narration. Whether a character is a woman diagnosed with cancer planning an "aesthetic suicide" in the story "Go Like This" or Berie Carr, the heroine of the novel *Who Will Run the Frog Hospital?* who once sang "*Frere Jacques*" "with the bewildering line 'Sonny lay my Tina,'" Moore's characters are never as motivated to change as they are motivated to grapple with their circumstances by rigorously questioning and dissecting the descriptive language usually associated with their particular mood or their moral or emotional dilemma. Graced and cursed with formidable, tireless imaginations and linguistic skill, Moore's characters are thinkers, men and women whose armor and comfort is often (but not exclusively) found in the language of comedy.

"I don't have a love life. I have a like life," a character quips in "Like Life." It is a line that elicits a laugh first before its full weight is felt. In one swift stroke Moore subtly implores the reader to examine what it truly means to speak of a "love life," a term tossed around loosely in the course of colloquial conversation.

The pithy one-liner, the wisecrack, the bad joke, and the good joke are the means through which her characters approximate connection or delay pain when they are faced with an inevitable ending through death, change, or affection-numbing stasis. Although she is acclaimed for her razor-sharp wit, sense of irony, and hilarious humor, Moore makes it clear that for her characters the joke is mere pretense, the most palatable antidote for their saddened hearts and incisive intellects.

"I don't know why I joke. I hurt," says the mistress to her married lover in "How to Be an Other Woman." "Nothing's a joke with me. It just all comes out like one," Odette tells her lover in "The Jewish Hunter." And in Moore's

1998 collection *Birds of America,* the protagonist in "Agnes of Iowa" remembers that a good joke "made any given day seem bearable. . . . It had been a determined sort of humor, an intensity mirroring the intensity of the city, and it seemed to embrace and alleviate the hard sadness of people having used one another and marred the earth the way they had." Moore's wit is never far behind. "It was like brains having sex," Agnes tells her husband.

THE LIFE BEHIND THE ART

It is a long-held assumption, mainly because in many instances it is based in truth, that writers like Moore, whose situations and characters reflect real life so trenchantly, must surely be writing from deep personal wounds and lived experience. What else would explain her unerring ability to render the talk, the unfailingly fresh observation, the precise detail, and the interior downward spiral of emotion associated with real life's traumas—divorce, death of a parent, unsuccessful love lives, mental illness, cancer, and betrayal?

In an interview for *New Letters on the Air: Contemporary Writers on Radio,* recorded after the publication of her second short story collection *Like Life,* Moore responds to the question "Where do your stories come from?" Moore says she does not write from the "facts" of her life but writes instead from "the energy and imagination" of her experiences. First and foremost Moore is an observer. And she keeps notebooks.

Moore says she is more inclined to take a notebook with her on a vacation than a camera, and she makes notes on what she sees and hears rather than relying on either her skills or her memory. Some notes, she explains might "never be used," and she might discover later that some of the notes were "stupid." Nevertheless she is reluctant to trust her brain alone and adds: "If our memories were so good why would anyone have the need to write anything down at all?"

Similarities between Moore's life and her characters' lives are superficial at best. Clearly the author is as smart as those people who inhabit her fictions. Moore skipped ahead in elementary school, won a New York regents scholarship upon high school graduation, and graduated summa cum laude from college. She is as witty as her characters, but Moore has remained intensely private about her personal life. While the temptation to plumb the work for autobiographical parallels is strong, succumbing to that temptation is futile and a disservice to the imaginative power of Moore's writing.

Marie Lorena Moore was born on January 13, 1957, in Glens Falls, New York, a relatively small town in the Adirondack Mountains. She is the second of four children born to Henry T. Moore, an insurance executive, and Jeanne Day Moore, a nurse who gave up the practice of nursing to become a housewife. In Moore's fiction parents make unhappy appearances, but her own parents are not divorced. Unlike those mothers Moore writes about who suffer from mental breakdowns or cancer, Moore's mother is alive and well. In fact at one time both of her parents entertained the idea of pursing writing careers. Her mother wanted to become a journalist; her father shared a writing class with the literary luminary Evan S. Connell and the critic Vincent Canby. Still Moore's parents' aspirations did not directly propel her toward a writing career.

After her high school graduation Moore attended St. Lawrence University in 1974, where she majored in English, was the editor of the literary magazine, won *Seventeen* magazine's fiction contest when she was nineteen years old, and graduated with distinction in English in 1978. Such early accomplishments and recognition may have been undeniable signals that a writing career was hers for the taking, yet after her graduation from St. Lawrence University, Moore was still undecided about her life's direction. In addition to her writing ability and outstanding academic achievements, Moore is musically gifted. Her instrument is the piano. She was still attached to her first love, music, and not yet fully committed to writing after graduation, so she took some time to sort out her options. She moved to Manhattan, where she worked as a paralegal for two years. Not until 1980, when writing won her affections over playing piano or being a paralegal, did she enroll in the M.F.A. program at Cornell University. At Cornell one of her teachers, the novelist Alison Lurie, took a special interest in Moore's work.

Between the years 1980 and 1983 Moore worked on a series of short stories she finally submitted as her master's thesis. Lurie suggested Moore submit the short stories to her own agent, Melanie Jackson. Jackson then sent the manuscript to Victoria Wilson, an editor at Alfred A. Knopf. In 1985 Knopf published the first of Moore's books, a short story collection entitled *Self-Help* that garnered immediate, enthusiastic critical acclaim.

In his review for the *New York Times Book Review,* Jay McInerney wrote that in *Self-Help* Moore employs "a distinctive, scalpel-sharp fictional voice" to produce "cohesive and moving" stories. He adamantly added that after reading the collection anyone who "doesn't like it should consult a doctor." Most of the reviews of Moore's debut collection reflect similar excitement. Since the publication of *Self-Help,* the trajectory of Moore's writing career has read like something wished for.

In 1984 Moore accepted the position of assistant professor of English at the University of Wisconsin, Madison, where she has remained. She subsequently became a professor of English and creative writing. In the earlier part of her teaching career, when the Midwest proved slightly more isolated than she was used to,

Moore traveled between Madison, Wisconsin, and Manhattan for brief stints during the summers, perhaps part of the reason many of her stories capture East Coast urban life so well. With the exception of her first novel *Anagrams,* which met mixed reviews, the critical reception to her work continued to be generous and laudatory.

If the characters in Moore's work find themselves perennially disappointed in love and incapable of sustaining long-term relationships, such has not been the case for Moore. Moore jokes that even as a younger woman, she had the same boyfriend until she was twenty-four. The author married a lawyer, and the couple has a son named Benjamin.

SELF-HELP AND ANAGRAMS

The most insightful critics sensed that the manic jokes, the structural gimmicks, and the shoulder shrug of resignation limning both *Self-Help* and *Anagrams* were mere foils for a much deeper range of emotion. Moore was relatively young, only twenty-six, when *Self-Help* was published, an apprentice writer fashioning her art. Nevertheless the depth and range of emotion, especially as it appears in her later collection *Birds of America,* was already in evidence in this debut collection.

In a long, thoughtful essay for *Harper's* that traces the changes in the American short story in general and Moore's work among others in particular, the author Vince Passaro notes that the closer the American short story hugged realism, as it had in the 1930s and again in the 1950s and 1980s, the more it met with popular interest. Passaro cites the Ernest Hemingway short story as one of the reasons, since Hemingway was the most imitated model for short story writers given his "stoical, serious, pared-down approach." But Passaro also unapologetically writes that Hemingway "was almost never funny, and he was almost never right—never,

that is, about what we might call the full nuances of human relations, human frailty, and in the face of that frailty, human morality."

Therefore by 1985, as minimalism seemed to die with the master most frequently compared to Hemingway, Raymond Carver, the appearance of Moore's *Self-Help* signaled a much-needed shift in the emotional terrain and shape of the American short story. Nothing could be more different from Hemingway (Moore is always funny) or closer to the bone in *Self-Help* than the nuances of human relations and human frailty.

With *Self-Help,* Moore took a calculated risk. The nine stories that make up the collection contain three qualities her contemporaries lacked: biting humor, intellectual sophistication, and trust in the reader's intelligence. Six of the nine stories dare to offer something else to readers. They unfold around a central, controlling conceit that further distinguishes Moore from her peers: a second-person, mock imperative voice. These six stories—"How to Be an Other Woman," "How to Become a Writer," "How," "How to Talk to Your Mother," "The Kid's Guide to Divorce," and "Amahl and the Night Visitors: A Guide to the Tenor of Love"—use the rhetorical mode of process analysis, more commonly known as the how-to, a categorical process commonly reserved for technical writing and guide books.

Samuel Smiles authored the first of these guides to personal fulfillment in 1859, but unlike Moore's, his *Self-Help* is far from tongue in cheek. Smiles's compendium of sketches and biographies of the most successful men and women of the industrial revolution is an earnest attempt to instruct readers in how they might model themselves on these idealized successes to achieve similar contentment in their own lives.

By the mid-1980s the belief that life's more niggling problems could be approached or solved by reading self-help books had become part of American contemporary culture. People flocked to bookstores to buy the latest self-help guide, searching for the most efficient ways to repair a marriage, to divorce with minimal pain, to love better, or to raise a happy child. A keen observer of modern trends and personalities, Moore seized upon this cultural phenomenon, then transformed a mostly utilitarian rhetorical mode into art by combining process analysis with the imperative second-person voice. The result is a collection of astute, satirical, and sly short stories. The narrators' intention is to guide, but the result is guidance by default. For instance, "How to Be an Other Woman" is actually a story about how not to become one and why.

In an interview with *Contemporary Authors,* Moore says the stories in *Self-Help* were written as "stylistic experiments," as a way to see what kind of tension would result if she "foisted fictional experience off of the 'I' of the first person and onto the more generalized 'you' of the second—the vernacular 'one.'"

Moore's experimentation with tension yields a supple interplay between laughter and tears. For instance, in "How to Become a Writer," Moore begins humorously enough: "First, try to be something, anything else."

The beleaguered speaker receives a laconic response from her mother when she announces her intentions to be a writer; her English teacher faults her stories for their lack of plot; she declares herself a psychology major but stumbles accidentally into a creative writing class; her peers fault her work for its lack of plot. The more she tries to follow the rules to become a writer of course the more success eludes her. This double-bind is hilarious, skittering along brightly on the surface of the story. To heighten its effect Moore uses short, clipped sentences for deadpan delivery. When asked if writers get discouraged, Francie replies: "Say sometimes they do and sometimes they do. Say it's a lot like having polio." Francie is always

raising deeper questions: "Why write? Where does writing come from? These are questions to ask yourself. They are like: Where does dust come from? Or: Why is there war? Or: If there's a God, then why is my brother now a cripple?"

Although Francie's wounded Vietnam veteran brother, who returned from the Cambodian border "missing half a thigh, a permanent smirk nestled into one corner of his mouth," is only mentioned twice, it becomes clear that this tragedy and Francie's determined, tamped anger regarding it in part fuels her quest to be a writer, to find the right words to make a story from this painful event and its meaning to her. Francie it turns out may joke all she wants, but her pursuit is serious, forcing her to conclude that "there are no words for this." That line also implies that for Francie and for Moore the act of writing is always artifice, a "like life." The belief that some tragedies exist on a plane beyond words and even the phrase "there are no words" are reiterated later in Moore's career in a story from her collection *Birds of America,* "People Like That Are the Only People Here: Canonical Babbling in Peed Onk."

The seriousness of Moore's subjects— solitude, mortality, the artifice of writing, and the power of language—is closer to the surface in her later, more accomplished work. Still the reader senses the seriousness as the foundation of the weakest stories in *Self-Help,* even those in which it is drowned out by the young writer's loud, lacerating humor.

The most successful stories in *Self-Help* eschew the mock-imperative voice altogether, take on a more traditional shape, and employ a first-person narrator whose interior life the reader accesses. In two of these stories, "What Is Seized" and the final story "To Fill," the protagonists are more willing to display their emotions without the protective tarp of jokes. Although the trademark Moore humor is not absent from either of these stories, it is far less antic and more measured. Moore exercises the lyric qualities of writing, moving her natural elegance into the foreground whenever she drops the quips in favor of the purer emotion behind them.

In "What Is Seized," Moore creates unforgettable, original images using her musical knowledge. "The rooms in our house were like songs," the narrator says. Moore then extends the metaphor in a long, elegant paragraph. Taken out of context the passage reads like a prose poem as she introduces each room: "It was the bookcase in the living room that seemed particularly symphonic, the books all friendly with one another, a huge chorus of them in a hum." Later she describes her father, "An icy anger tucked behind his face, locked up like a store after hours, a face laced tight as a shoe." Not one simile but two. Initially this feels like an unnecessary simile pile up, yet it evolves into the image of not one but dozens of faces laced tight that amplifies the feeling of implacable coldness. Along with Moore's humor, this type of image loading has become a signature of her writing.

"To Fill" is the story of a nearly middle-aged woman's rickety descent into madness. Riva is a wife, a mother, and a thief who begins embezzling from the store where she works "for no other reason than this nameless, bullying ache." Aware that her husband, Tom, is having an affair, Riva tries to maintain her sanity by remembering Phil, a man who once loved her deeply, but the trick does not work. Essentially a story about emotional starvation, "There is no dignity in appetites," Riva laments, it is also the prototype for Moore's novel *Who Will Run the Frog Hospital?* In that book the protagonist, Berie, is married to a philanderer, and the memories of her first passionate attachment to her best friend, Sils, acts as a sharp contrast to and comfort for her present emptiness. "To Fill" does not offer Riva the redemption Moore offers to Berie in *Hospital,* but the story does serve up a familiar Moore refrain: the belief in

happiness is the source of most unhappiness. In a review of *Self-Help* for *New Statesman,* Geoff Dyer concludes: "Reading Lorrie Moore you simultaneously recognize and realize for the first time these stories hurt . . . like bumping your face in a mirror, they're funny as well."

Benna Carpenter, the main character of Moore's first novel, *Anagrams,* is another unhappy, hungry, incurably funny character bumping into not one but many mirrors in Moore's stylistically experimental work. *Anagrams* was published in 1986, only a year after the publication of *Self-Help.*

In an interview with *New Letters on the Air,* Moore quite bluntly calls *Anagrams* "an amphibious thing." She describes her second book as "a short story writer's novel." She adds that one of the challenges still before her as an artist is to experiment with the novelist's preexisting literary forms more extensively.

Anagrams was published to less than resounding reviews. The criticism was split into two valid camps: those who maintained that less experimentation and more control over the inrushing tumble of wisecracks would have yielded a far more engaging novel, permitting the reader to linger with and absorb emotions rather than dash by them; and those who were thoroughly engaged precisely because of the random, cubistic structure of the book as an anagram. In an interview with Barbara Lovenheim for the *New York Times,* Moore says she was inspired by "the idea of an anagram . . . the rearrangement of characters to make a new word. What I did was to rearrange characters to make new worlds."

The heroine of *Anagrams,* Benna Carpenter, is one of Moore's most enchantingly aggressive "non-winners," a young woman who realizes that everything other women have and she does not, "grandchildren, stability, a postmenopausal grace, some mysterious, hard-won truce with men," are finally "the only thing anyone really wants in life: someone to hold your hand when you die." In her attempts to secure such a connection, Benna Carpenter is perhaps Moore's most solitary but also her most resourceful character.

Moore structures the book in five chapters. The first four chapters read as self-contained short stories featuring the same set of characters. These chapters have the loose, playful feel of the novelist's shape-shifting drafts, in which occupations and relationships continuously flip-flop until the novelist finally hits the combination that yields a cohesive story. That is what the fifth chapter, titled "The Nun of That," finally provides. This final section is long, novella-like, taking up almost two-thirds of the book. It is prefaced by a new trio of epigraphs, Moore's method of indicating a fresh start a third of the way into the novel. At its weakest the structure is needlessly self-conscious, but this complexity and wordplay are what make *Anagrams* a novel as much about creating art as it is about isolation.

In the first chapter Benna is presented as a young widow and a nightclub singer who lives next door to Gerard, a preschool aerobics instructor and Benna's sometime lover. The bathrooms in their adjacent apartments are separated by a wall so thin Benna and Gerard can talk to each through the barrier of tiles. Benna and Gerard are together yet separate, a familiar Moore dynamic. But in the second chapter Benna and Gerard's circumstances change, and the point of view switches from third person to Benna's first-person narration. In this version of Benna's life she is between jobs, she is Gerard's lover, and Gerard is a musician. Her best friend, Eleanor, who shares Benna's tic for relentless puns and jokes, betrays Benna by sleeping with Gerard. Benna discovers a lump in her breast, becomes pregnant with Gerard's child, and has an abortion.

Throughout the costume changes Benna Carpenter's character remains fixed: she is funny, vulnerable, and stubborn. In fact she is funny because she is so vulnerable and stubborn. Benna says for the longest time she insisted upon trying to make anagrams from words that could not be made into anagrams. Her self-deprecating admission supports Moore's belief that relationships, love, the perfect life may not be possible. "Between large and small, between near and far," Benna says, "there was no wisdom or truce to be had. To be near was to be blind; to be one among so many was to own no shape or say." In essence Benna Carpenter has no "anagram" for her real self. No matter how many life revisions she invents, she cannot escape the one word that defines her life: solitary.

When Moore settles into the final long chapter, the real Benna and Gerard are revealed. Benna is indeed childless, and she is a widow. Her husband left her, then died, possibly a suicide, in a car accident.

But she is not the singer; Gerard is. Benna is a poet teaching "The Reading and Writing of Poetry" at a community college, FVCC, in Fitchville, USA. She and Gerard have never been lovers. They are good friends who meet daily at Hank's coffee shop, engage in witty repartee, and hold each other's hand through life's disappointments, one of them being Benna's ill-fated love affair with her student Darrell. Benna also confesses in this chapter that the Eleanor of the preceding four chapters was an imaginary friend. The invented Eleanor is an instructor at FVCC, Benna's comedic colleague, an alter ego, and one of the symbols of Benna's resourcefulness. Without a husband or a lover to satiate her hunger for a child, Benna provides her own solace by inventing an imaginary six-year-old daughter, Georgianne Michele. Therefore what seems disjointed in the first four chapters of *Anagrams* transforms itself into an exciting exploration of and argument for the positive power of imagination and perception.

In some ways *Anagrams* resembles Renata Adler's *Speedboat* (1976), a novel that also intrigued and confounded readers and critics when it was published. Adler's book features a narrator who blurs the boundaries between fact and fiction in short, episodic scenes. In *American Fictions* (1999), a collection of Elizabeth Hardwick's literary criticism, Hardwick calls *Speedboat* remarkable for its randomness, suggesting that perhaps the rearranging of the facts coupled with the movement from one set of circumstances to another is the valid, unifying experience of a novel that does not adhere to the traditional, plotted narrative. In *Anagrams* Benna's dominant character trait is her perception, what Hardwick calls "a precocious alertness to incongruity."

Moore has Benna express her alertness in myriad ways, most of them funny. Benna hears every slip of the tongue and notices the immense gaps in logic between what people say and what they mean. But in the following description of birds, Benna's "precocious alertness" leads the reader to contemplation: "The flock had a kind of group life, a recognizable intelligence; no doubt in its random flutters there were patterns, but alone any one of those black birds would not have known what was up. Alone, as people live, they would crash their heads against walls."

Here Benna's insight does the work of more directly rendered emotion. Birds are a metaphor for human connection and dislocation. In fact birds as symbols of transition, flight, and lightness have been present in Moore's work all along. The bird imagery floats through *Anagrams,* a hint of Moore's mastery with this metaphor in *Birds of America.*

Perception, not plot, is the driving wheel of *Anagrams.* When Benna imagines herself as Gerard's lover or as a mother, she supplies herself with energy. Georgianne is "a gift I have given myself, a lozenge of pretend." The word "lozenge," a small, temporary analgesic, is powerfully appropriate, an example of Moore's consistent precision. The word makes all the difference between a character like Riva, who has relinquished her grip on reality, and Benna Carpenter, whose acute awareness inspires her (between bouts of sadness and sarcasm) to act, to give herself one small positive thing to cherish that cannot be wrested from her. Benna alone chooses to hold on to Georgianne or to relinquish her.

Benna Carpenter genuinely loves Gerard. If unconditional love is possible between adults, Benna and Gerard's relationship is one of Moore's finest examples of it. Their friendship is characterized as so comfortable that nothing—time apart, arguments, or Benna's preoccupation with the imaginary parts of her life—seems to disturb the bottomless well of mutual goodwill they extend to one another. Benna and Gerard always circle back to each other, birds returning to the flock. Gerard dies from complications of a freak accident, and Benna's resilience is the reward at end of the novel. Benna's resilience heralds the beginning of a new texture for Moore that permits a thread of unmasked sorrow without bitterness in the fabric of her next three books.

LIKE LIFE: A TURNING POINT

The short story collection *Like Life* represents the first shift away from the conceit that molded *Self-Help* and the self-conscious scaffolding of *Anagrams.* Critics who were less than charmed by the strategies of *Anagrams* expressed surprise and exuberance for the new collection. Ralph Sassone, writing for the *Voice Literary Supplement,* called *Like Life* Moore's "toughest work" because of its "heightened sympathy." Michiko Kakutani praised the collection for its passages of "lyrical meditation" in between the passages of signature banter and wit.

The collection contains eight stories, including "You're Ugly, Too," the first of many Moore published in *The New Yorker.* Just as Moore's work was developing, so was her career. At this juncture Moore had received grants from the Rockefeller Foundation, the National Endowment for the Arts, the Wisconsin Arts Board, and the Corporation of Yaddo, the external signs of growing recognition and acceptance.

Although the criticism up to this point focused on Moore's wit and style, little if any attention had been given to Moore's use of epigraphs. They are as integral to reading her stories as an allegro or a fortissimo is to a piece of music, indicating as the signatures do how the work should be heard and with what emphasis. Moore usually chooses two to three epigraphs, in *Anagrams* she used a total of six, juxtaposing the earnest with the droll. A quote from the comedian Jerry Lewis takes its place alongside a line from Robert Frost, and a line from *The Wizard of Oz* shares amiable space with Roy Chapman Andrews's explanation of the derivation of the word "mammoth."

Like Life is a departure for Moore in this area. The collection is prefaced by a single, surprising epigraph from a source not usually associated with Moore's work. The line was written by Zelda Fitzgerald in a 1932 letter to her husband, the novelist F. Scott Fitzgerald. It is simple, direct, and personal: "It seemed very sad to see you going off in your shoes alone." For the first time Moore's selection of epigraph is aligned with her own belief in the basic sadness of her work. She resists the impulse to counter wistfulness by pitting the line against the acerbic. If this particular epigraph were a signature to a piece of music, Moore's direction would be: Play it with deep feeling.

Thus the stories in *Like Life* are nothing if not deeply felt. Moore is as confident hitting the mournful minor keys as she always has been delivering the rueful one-liner. Solitude and love remain Moore's central concerns, but the jokes no longer leap from the page as distractions from depth and consequence. Instead, Moore's

humor is better timed, organic, and in service to the serious aspects of these stories. The stories are lengthier and broader both in style and in subject matter than the stories in *Self-Help.*

A natural maturation in Moore herself may account for some of the success of these stories. It is believed and hoped that an older, wiser writer will create more sophisticated work. In *Like Life* the wisdom is achieved because Moore widens her lens. Her first two books focused on the urban, young, single heroine not quite comfortable in the modern world or her own skin. The early stories settled on a narrower population in a specific setting, New York City. The reader met parents only through the filters of their daughters' eyes, as in the stories "What Is Seized," "How to Talk to Your Mother," and "The Kid's Guide to Divorce."

The stories in *Like Life* include an older married couple whose son simply left one day and never returned, a couple married for fourteen years, a woman who works in a cheese shop in the Midwest, and a fully rendered male hero instead of the cipher-like men who made cameo appearances in Moore's first short story collection. All eight stories are told in the third-person point of view, which lends a capaciousness to the fiction, allowing Moore the room to showcase her gifts for creating atmosphere. A stylized unity of time, place, and mood courses through each story. With the exception of "Starving Again," the stories are luxurious in length. They lure the reader in easily through a single character's consciousness or situation, then move languidly, exploring all the twists and turns of a particular situation in unpredictable but inevitable ways. The "precocious alertness" of *Anagrams* is evident in these stories as well, but this time the insights feel more earned and emerge naturally from these invented people. Moore herself does not intrude upon them.

The title story, "Like Life," was the first begun and the last completed. In the interview with *New Letters,* Moore calls it a "cursed story," the only one she felt could have evolved into a novel, an idea she toyed with while writing it, and the only one she still considers not quite what she hoped for. Regardless of its placement at the end of the collection, "Like Life" is the centerpiece, the thread that links the eight stories thematically. More than any of the others, this story posits the wager that informs the collection:

> There was only this world, this looted, ventriloquized earth. . . . She was afraid, and the afraid, she knew finally, sought opportunities for bravery in love. She tucked the flower in her blouse. Life or death. Something or nothing. *You want something or nothing?* She stepped toward him with a heart she'd someday tear the terror from.
>
> Here. But not now.

"Something or nothing?" It is a simple question with enormous consequences for the characters, especially for Mamie in "Like Life," who is trying to decide whether she should remain married to Rudy, a struggling, angry painter who has yet to meet with success at age thirty-five. Rudy and Mamie live in Brooklyn in a neighborhood that has deteriorated. Mamie reasons that in the marriage perhaps they have been "too dreamy and inconsistent." She thinks that for love to survive "you had to have illusions or have no illusions at all," something or nothing, but the nether world of in between would "endanger things."

Something or nothing? This question holds the answer the characters fear the most: when one chooses, there is a risk. The bigger the risk the more there is to fear. For these characters the "pay-off" for high risk will always be either high yield or a deflating, disastrous disappointment. The loftiest risk is love.

In "Two Boys," Mary tries to stall choice as long as possible. For the first time in her life she is seeing two men, known only as Number One and Number Two. Number One is married, and Number Two loves her. Of course Mary wants Number One more. With Number Two she feels "a mix of gratitude and disappointment settled in her joints like the beginnings of flu." And with Number One "there was always so much to keep back . . . you tried to shoo things away, a broomed woman with a porch to protect." Dressed in white, she leaves her apartment over a meat-packing company, where every day she tries "not to step in the blood that ran off the sidewalk." Mary's white "unsullied" clothing and the alarming puddles of blood create a terrific tension between the heart that is pure and the one that is carnivorous, wants more perhaps than it is entitled to. Each day Mary observes the same group of little girls in the park, a reminder of her former state of innocence.

Moore's careful sensory detail transforms a clichéd situation into a compelling one because Mary is neither overly glib nor naively sentimental about her situation. In fact Mary's guilt is a new emotion in Moore territory, one she later explores in depth in the story "Terrific Mother."

In "Vissi d'Arte," the first of Moore's stories to focus on a male character, Harry's choices are murkier than Mary's. Harry is a playwright living in an awful apartment near Times Square. At one time one of Harry's plays was produced, and his picture appeared in the *New York Times* with an article trumpeting him as one of the up-and-coming playwrights under thirty. Since that time Harry has been working on the play he believes is his masterpiece, a play he lets no one see, not even his live-in lover Breckie, because the "material felt so powerful to him . . . that a premature glimpse by the wrong person might curse it forever."

Harry's real problem is fear of taking another risk. The wager, something or nothing, does not enter Harry's mind. In a sense he is bewitched by his own past accomplishment, too fearful to test his "masterpiece" in the real world. Breckie leaves him, trucks park on the street outside his apartment at night sending noxious fumes into his home, the bathtub backs up spewing garbage. Daily Harry hopes for a call from Glen Scarp, an oily television producer who expressed interest in Harry. When Scarp finally does call and they meet for drinks, Harry is worn down by the physical deterioration of the neighborhood, its effects on him, and his own myopic allegiance to his former successful self. He unwittingly spills the contents of his masterpiece over drinks with Glen. Will Scarp use the material? Yes.

The sadness of the story does not hinge on this plot point, however, as much as on the more isolating truth about longing and success, about art and commerce. Between something and nothing lies the vast canyon of risk and self-protection. Ironically, Harry's fervent desire to protect his play becomes the source of his ruin and solitude.

Self-protection and lack of confidence motivate the poet Odette in "The Jewish Hunter." The characters Odette and Pinky Eliot are well developed and affection winning, and the reader roots for them as if he or she is a friend who matched them up and wants to toast them at their hoped for wedding. No such wedding occurs, but if love is possible Moore suggests that Pinky and Odette might be as good as it gets, even when it does not last.

Odette is Moore's most elegant bird, the swan. The story begins with a fairy tale or the ballet Swan Lake's tone, "This was in a faraway land." But the opening line is swiftly followed up with vintage Moore: "There were gyms but no irony or coffee shops. People took things literally—without drugs." Odette is forty years old, a poet from New York who supplements her income by accepting library fellowships that pay for her to live in a town for a six-week period, during which she gives a reading at the local library. Odette is on a fellowship in one of these "boonie" towns when her gym partner Laird fixes her up with his former grade school friend Pinky Eliot, a lawyer who represents farmers.

All Odette wants is to be kissed. She is not looking for love because she believes wholeheartedly that she is "bad at love." Pinky convinces her that she loves quite well. The story is pleasurably tense and tender, but it is imbued with a dark subtext. Pinky's parents are Holocaust survivors, and he ritually watches a film about the Holocaust every night. Unlike the Self-Help stories, in which the barrier to love hinges on the characters' awkwardness or pessimism, the chasm between Odette and Pinky involves a moral-historical context of magnitude. Odette is not Jewish.

Whether or not she loves Pinky matters less than the realization that she will not be able to understand the depth of his anguish. Moore's unvarnished sensitivity to the real versus the invented terrors in life marks a profound maturity in her sensibility.

When Odette starts thinking that one "had to build shelters . . . she should live where there were trees . . . where there were birds. No bird, no tree had ever made her unhappy," the reader's heart leaps. But Odette does return to her solitary life. However, unlike the previous Moore heroines, Odette leaves feeling "like someone of whom she was fond, an old and future friend of herself . . . like a light that moves." Her self-knowledge compensates for whatever act of bravery in love she cannot muster.

Like Life is laced with unexpected gestures of kindness, unpredictable moments of gratitude and insight. In "Joy," Jane, who works in cheese shop, takes pleasure in a moment she shares with Heffie, a co-worker who snacks on the cheeses throughout her shift. At the end of the story they are reconciled to their unfulfilled expectations; they drink champagne together and make a toast to "their little lives." In "Places to Look for Your Mind," Hane and Millie, a couple who agree to host their daughter's friend on his first visit from England, try unsuccessfully to make him into the son who left them, whom they have not heard from in years. Their attempts at make-believe reveal the spaces of their empty nest. Initially Hane appears as cool and detached as the husband in "What Is Seized," but Moore's story shows a new willingness to open outward, and this story opens to aching poignancy after the visitor has returned to England. Alone and awkward together in their suburban home, Hane whispers to his wife, "You are my only friend."

The shortest story, "Starving Again," shows friendship in a different light. Moore said the story was commissioned by the *New York Times,* who asked her write a story containing some health issue. Written mostly as dialogue, "Starving Again" has the urban crackle of the *Self-Help* stories. Dennis is lovelorn, reading a book called *Why I Hate Myself* to figure out why his love affair has gone bad. He and his friend Mave are in a health food restaurant, starving literally and emotionally. Like all people who require sustenance desperately, they cannot see or hear beyond their own needs; their conversation is a dialogue of missed connection. The story builds to the moment of Dennis's surprise that Mave may not be listening to him at all. In this story starvation becomes solipsism.

Generally speaking a balanced collection of short stories, equally weighted for their over-all effect, is rare. Often the hit story in a collection, like the hit song on an album, renders the other stories less satisfying than they would be standing alone. But *Like Life* is a balanced collection. Each story fully develops the emotional landscape of the characters. Their motivations are clearly depicted; their conflicts resolve organically; they include no gratuitous dissections and analyses of language. Every element is orchestrated to blend voice, character, setting, and mood in a harmonious whole. These qualities are what distinguish *Like Life* from the fiction that preceded it.

WHO WILL RUN THE FROG HOSPITAL?: THE SHORT STORY WRITER AS NOVELIST

In the years between the publication of *Like Life* and her next major book, Moore garnered more awards, the Guggenheim Fellowship and the Academy of Arts and Letters, and her short stories were regularly anthologized. She also published a book for children, *The Forgotten Helper: A Story for Children* (1987). In 1992 she edited the anthology *I Know Some Things: Stories about Childhood by Contemporary Writers.*

In 1994 Moore's second novel *Who Will Run the Frog Hospital?* was published to nearly unanimous praise. Some critics believed Moore's new novel was her richest work yet, combining the pace and compression of her short fiction with lush language and an exquisitely controlled first-person voice, elegiac on the one hand, funny and ironic on the other. In all it is a beguiling gem among contemporary novels.

The critical reaction stood in marked contrast to the reaction Moore received for her first attempt as a novelist with *Anagrams*. The novels differed in their narrative strategies. This time Moore decided on a single voice and linearity. While the book has two narrative lines, each line moves forward directly rather than in the random circles of *Anagrams*. Berie Carr is a well-developed narrator, confidential in tone, reflective, mature, and although she is troubled, she inspires trust in the reader. Her self-awareness and her willingness to poke fun at herself and to articulate uncomfortable feelings make her more reliable than Benna Carpenter. The settings, a small town called Horsehearts on the Canadian border and the city of Paris, are also precisely rendered and symbolize the contrast between adolescence and adulthood. Like Fitzgerald's *The Great Gatsby* (1925), which is compact without sacrificing intricacy or complexity, Moore's diminutive *Who Will*

Run the Frog Hospital? weighs in at a slim 148 pages but is not a lightweight novel despite its size.

The title for the book is taken from an illustration by Nancy Mladenoff that pictures two little girls ministering to bandaged frogs wounded by too many kisses. Moore places the illustration inside the novel by having the character Sils paint the same Mladenoff illustration. The frog calls up a wealth of fairy-tale images for the reader that are appropriate in the context of this story. *Frog Hospital* is part reflective meditation on youth, part longing for the magic that can transform a frog into a prince, and part letting go of a waning adult marriage.

The heroine Berie Carr is a thirty-seven-year-old photography curator visiting Paris with her doctor husband, who is there to attend a medical conference. The novel opens with a lean, direct power: "In Paris we eat brains every night. My husband likes the vaporous, fishy mousse of them. . . . Me I'm eating for a flashback. . . . I'm hoping for something Proustian, all that forgotten childhood." In the space of only two pages Moore paints the portrait of a troubled marriage from which neither spouse has yet decided to let go.

> My husband pronounces tirez as if it were Spanish, pére as if it were pier. The affectionate farce I make of him ignores the ways I feel his lack of love for me. But we are managing. . . . We say, "Look at that!" wanting our eyes to merge, our minds to be one.

Berie's ailing marriage acts as a frame, the present point from which Berie looks backward and replays the summer of 1972, when she is fifteen and works as a cashier at a theme park called Storyland. Berie's best friend, the beautiful Silsby Chaussee, works at Storyland too; her job is impersonating Cinderella. Of all the people in Berie's adolescent life, she loves Sils the best, admires Sils for her sexiness, her worldliness, which Berie realizes later was more the result of her perception than objective reality. Like the Cinderella character Sils impersonates, Berie believes the happy ending is a fait accompli for Sils. Berie is not sure what lies ahead for herself, only that getting out of Horsehearts will be necessary.

Berie's other youthful desire is to be able to split her voice. Berie says:

> I wanted to make chords, to splinter my throat into harmonies—floreted as a field. . . . I felt, I might be able to people myself, unleash the crowd in my voice box, give birth, set free all the moods and nuances, all the lovely and mystical inhabitants of my mind's speech . . . there must have been pain in me. I wanted to howl and fly and break apart.

The split, the "breaking apart" accounts for the structure of the book, a dual narrative, the double voice of Berie in the present and of Berie nostalgic, one foot, one eye, one ear still focused on the past. This passage also highlights Moore's chief artistic theme, the recognition of individual solitude coupled with the desire to "people" oneself, to expose the secret longings inside, which is the root finally of the "pain" inside Berie. It is significant that Berie and her husband are childless, the echo of Benna Carpenter's same unsatisfied longing in *Anagrams*.

The challenge before all of Moore's characters remains to find language, "the crowd in the voice box," and to be heard and appreciated as a plentiful, fulfilling piece of human music.

For Berie and Sils the fantasies and dreams spun from their summer of passionate attachment gives way to the reality that all things, even their inconceivably unbreakable friendship, must pass. Before that summer ends Sils becomes pregnant, and Berie comes to her rescue. Berie ingeniously finds a way to embezzle money from the cash register at Storyland to pay for Sils's abortion. But Berie is caught and punished. Her parents send her off to a Bible camp to reconsider and to make amends for the error of her ways. Sils and Berie meet only once again in the novel, at a high school reunion that shows the spaces between them where they once believed none existed.

If it is true that one special relationship is the key that unlocks one's impacted past, then Sils represents that key. Remembering Sils is a means for Berie to safely revisit a part of herself. Memory also provides the impetus for Berie to move forward. In effect Moore makes the novel as "floreted" as Berie wishes her voice to be.

The reader visits the whole landscape of Berie's past, her relationships with her parents, her brother Claude, and her foster sister LaRoue. The close-up of her present reveals an unfaithful, callous husband Daniel, but Berie is a heroine for whom the reader feels an intimacy and an affinity.

The fact that Berie tells the story of that adolescent summer from such a distance in a foreign country, where nothing belongs to her, not even the language, heightens the elegiac tone and irony. In an essay for the *Writer's Chronicle* the novelist Debra Sparks points out that one of the lovely ironies of Moore's novel is that Berie and Sils are simultaneously the caretakers and the wounded frogs of the novel. The men they have kissed in their lives have not turned into princes at all but have remained their essential toady selves with regard to Sils and Berie.

Moore's intent with *Who Will Run the Frog Hospital?* is to tell the story of that time in life before a person is fully formed. By depicting it Moore also returns the reader to a similar place in his or her own youth. This universality of experience and desire reveals new levels of mastery and sensitivity. The power arises from her elegant language and fully developed characterization without a shred of sentimentality. In *Frog Hospital* the language is more finely honed than in *Like Life,* as if Moore were

sharpening the skills she would need to compose the complicated stories of her next collection, *Birds of America.*

BIRDS OF AMERICA: THE AUTHOR TAKES FLIGHT

Moore's third collection of short stories, *Birds of America,* was published in 1998 to nearly hyperbolic praise, which earned her a National Book Critics Circle Award nomination for the best work of fiction. She did not win the award, but the collection has won her the respect of literary critics and the reading public.

Titled after the Mary McCarthy novel of the same name and John James Audubon's *Birds of North America* (1983), the collection is Moore's biggest book. Each of the twelve stories demonstrates what the epigraph from Charlie Smith's poem "The Meaning of Birds" suggests:

> We are often far
> from home in a dark town
> and our griefs are difficult to translate into a
>   language
> understood by others.

That Moore did find a language for these "griefs" is one of the reasons the collection is considered remarkable.

Bats, crows, flamingos, performing ducks, and bird feeders crop up in the stories. Many of these stories first appeared in *The New Yorker.* They are woven of the painful irony that continues to support Moore's vision that the desire to bridge the canyon between isolation and intimacy is still the bravest act between people. In "Which Is More Than I Can Say for Some People," the protagonist thinks, "No matter what terror or loveliness the world could produce . . . there was nothing as complex in the world . . . as a single hello from a human being." Throughout the collection Moore depicts the complexity of that hello; in these stories the simple two-syllable word becomes as explosive as dynamite.

In 1995 Moore became a mother, a change in her personal life bound to increase her already heightened sensitivity to the nuances of human emotion and mortality. If *Like Life* represents a widening of the aperture, *Birds of America* opens the aperture fully, allowing all manner of terrors and infirmities to enter.

Like the birds who symbolize them, many of the characters have migrated far from home and feel their estrangement keenly. Some are in ill-fated relationships, like the aging actress Sidra in "Willing" and the tormented foreigner Olena in "Community Life." Some are longing for friendship or consolation, like the homosexual couple Mack and Quilty. Some are longing for lightness through laughter, as in "Agnes of Iowa," or through family connection, as in "Charades" and "Which Is More Than I Can Say for Some People." The settings are varied, global, and carefully rendered, including Tuscany, New Orleans, Ireland, and the Midwest. And the quintessential Moore sentences appear throughout, such as, "He was thinking, but she could tell he wasn't good at it"; "I'm going to marry you, whether you like it or not"; and "I don't have talent. I have willingness."

However, "People Like That Are the Only People Here: Canonical Babbling in Peed Onk" is critically regarded as the tour de force of this collection and of Moore's career. The story is touted for its structure, a metafiction; its prose style, elegant, openly passionate, ferociously funny; and its terrifying subject matter, an infant with cancer. In a rare act of revelation, Moore let it be known that her son, Benjamin, was diagnosed with a kidney tumor similar to the Baby's in the story. "Peed Onk," as it is commonly called, is the story of a Mother/Writer married to a lawyer, referred to as "The Husband," who discovers blood in her baby's diaper. It is a harrowing opening, indeed a melodramatic one, but Moore never plays to the expected. Because of its dark humor, "Peed Onk" becomes a story as much about making a story as it is about mortality. Moore's selection of metafiction rather than straight realism as a narrative technique allows her to engage her most caustic humor—"Take notes," the Writer's Husband urges—and simultaneously to invent language for the unspeakable:

> You turn just slightly and there it is: the death of your child. It is part symbol, part devil, and in your blind spot all along, until if you are unlucky it is completely upon you. Then it is a fierce little country abducting you; it holds you squarely inside itself like a cellar room—the best boundaries of you are the boundaries of it.

The passage, with its "blind spot," recalls Odette's thinking of love as the menacing truck she must let pass. Now the menacing object in the blind spot is not love but death.

The boundaries Moore's characters have tried to maintain or to cross to no avail are blurred utterly in only one relationship, a mother and her child. Moore revisits the certainty of death in "Real Estate," a story about a woman with cancer whose marriage is simultaneously dying with her. In "Terrific Mother," Moore confronts Adrienne's grief, guilt, and self-forgiveness after she accidentally falls while holding a friend's baby and the baby dies.

Of these three stories "Peed Onk" is the boldest example of the fiction writer's attempt to give voice and shape to what cannot be shaped or apprehended in reality. It also stands as the best argument for what Moore's fiction has always implied about the differences between reality and artifice. The narrator of "Peed Onk" points to these differences quite plainly:

> The trip and the story of the trip are two different things. The narrator is the one who has stayed home, but then, afterward, presses her mouth upon the traveler's mouth, in order to make the mouth work, to make the mouth say, say, say . . . all that unsayable life!

Moore's knowledge about the world and the world of making art and her vibrating awareness of the distances between the two—vaster than any of the distances between the characters she depicts—rumbles beneath each of her fictions. Such searing intelligence and insight would be unbearable without humor. In Moore's work the humor prevents the whole from erupting and spewing out the raw, unsynthesized emotion and easy situation that would yield only melodrama. However, Moore never intends for the humor to obscure the ache in the work. Rather, her intention is to supply the reader with a walking stick so to speak, a crutch with which to navigate the treacherous terrain of sadness and solitude. As the Mother in "Peed Onk" recognizes, "In a life where there is only the bearable and the unbearable, a sigh of relief is an ecstasy." Lorrie Moore has continued to produce such literary ecstasies.

Selected Bibliography

WORKS OF LORRIE MOORE

NOVELS
Anagrams: A Novel. New York: Knopf, 1986.
Who Will Run the Frog Hospital? A Novel. New York: Knopf, 1994.

SHORT STORIES
Self-Help: Stories. New York: Knopf, 1985.
Like Life: Stories. New York: Knopf, 1990.
Birds of America. New York: Knopf, 1998.

OTHER WORKS
The Forgotten Helper. New York: Kipling Press, 1987.
"Trashing Women, Trashing Books." *New York Times,* December 5, 1990, p. 23.
"Imagining What You Don't Know." In *The Best Writing on Writing.* Edited by Jack Heffron. Cincinnati, Ohio: Story Press, 1994.

CRITICAL AND BIOGRAPHICAL STUDIES

Bernard, April. "The Whiny White Whine." *Nation,* November 15, 1986, pp. 525–527.
Brockway, Michelle. "The Art of Reading Lorrie Moore." *Poets & Writers,* September/October 2000, pp. 16–19.
Casey, John. "Eloquent Solitudes." *Chicago Tribune—Books,* May 20, 1990, p. 3.
Crichton, Jennifer. "*Self-Help.*" *Ms.,* June 1985, p. 68.
Dyer, Geoff. "Clear-Sighted." *New Statesman,* September 27, 1985, p. 34.
Dzarl, Dawn Ann. "An Assemblage of Trifles." *Commonweal,* September 20, 1985, pp. 505–507.
Gilbert, Matthew. "*Anagrams.*" *Boston Review,* December 1986, p. 30.
Hardwick, Elizabeth. *American Fictions.* New York: Modern Library, 1999.
Hill, Carol. "Sestinas and Wisecracks." *New York Times Book Review,* November 2, 1986, p. 15.
Hornby, Nick. "The Tricky Ouch of It." *Listener,* September 6, 1990, p. 27.
Kakutani, Michiko. "Observations on Failures in Passion and Intimacy." *New York Times,* June 8, 1990, p. C28.
"Lorrie Moore." In *Contemporary Literary Criticism,* vol. 39. Edited by Sharon K. Hall. Detroit, Mich.: Gale Research, 1986. Pp. 82–85.
"Lorrie Moore." In *Contemporary Literary Criticism,* vol. 45. Edited by Daniel G. Marowski and Roger Matuz. Detroit, Mich.: Gale Research, 1987. Pp. 279–284.
"Lorrie Moore." In *Contemporary Literary Criticism,* vol. 68. Edited by Roger Matuz. Detroit, Mich.: Gale Research, 1991. Pp. 295–302.
McCauley, Stephen. "Love Is Like a Truck on the Interstate." *New York Times Book Review,* May 20, 1990, p. 7.
McInerney, Jay. "New and Improved Lives." *New York Times Book Review,* March 24, 1985, p. 32.
"Moore, Marie Lorena (Lorrie Moore)." In *Contemporary Authors,* vol. 116. Edited by Hal May. Detroit, Mich.: Gale Research, 1986. Pp. 330–331.
Passaro, Vince. "*Birds of America.*" *Harper's,* August 1, 1999, pp. 1–12.

Rilke, Rainer Maria. *Rilke on Love and Other Difficulties. Translations and considerations of Rainer Maria Rilke by John J. L. Mood.* New York: Norton, 1975.

Sassone, Ralph. "This Side of Parody." *Voice Literary Supplement,* June 1990, p. 15.

Sparks, Debra. "Aspects of the Short Novel." *Writer's Chronicle,* May/Summer 1999, p. 26.

INTERVIEWS

Lovenheim, Barbara. "In a Constant State of Surprise." *New York Times,* November 2, 1986, p. 15.

Share, Linda. *New Letters on the Air: Contemporary Writers on Radio.* Kansas City, Mo.: University of Missouri, 1990.

—*DENISE GESS*

Anaïs Nin

1903–1977

"*I* HAVE ALWAYS been tormented by the image of multiplicity of selves," the diarist Anaïs Nin announced in her first of many volumes. The self she presents initially is revealing, since she later claimed to be a voice for women. "Louveciennes resembles the village where Madame Bovary lived and died," she writes of the suburb of Paris in which she was living. "Unlike Madame Bovary, I am not going to take poison." Like the ill-fated heroine of Gustave Flaubert's 1857 masterpiece, Nin was married to a man she found sexually dull. Also like Emma Bovary she lived dangerously: "Ordinary life does not interest me. I seek only the high moments. I am in accord with the surrealists, searching for the marvelous." Like Emma Bovary, Nin's search for the marvelous led her to what she herself repeatedly described as poison. At the age of thirty she sought out and seduced the father who had abandoned her family when she was eleven years old.

The event proved the focal point of her life. Her diary began as a letter of longing to her father at the point in her young life when he, who purportedly had beaten and sexually abused her for years, left the family. For the rest of her life she tried to replace him with her diary, imagining it listening as she wanted him to listen, scolding and beating her as she had been scolded and beaten before. Any interpretation of this torturously contradictory document, filled indeed with a "multiplicity of selves" as Nin wrote, must begin with the father-daughter relationship and the ways Nin, who aspired to be a "Donna Juana" like him, tried to find peace by identifying with him. "Women see themselves as in a mirror, in the eyes of the men who love them. I have seen in each man a different woman—and a different life," she wrote in her early diary. She never escaped her father's gaze or her own compulsion to conjure it up.

Nin was born on February 21, 1903. Baptized Angela Anaïs Juana Antolina Rosa Edelmira Nin y Culmell, her extravagant name fit her extravagant personality. She often remarked that her name was seldom pronounced correctly, the correct pronunciation being "Ah-nah-ees" (not "Uh-*nay*-is," as it is typically pronounced). Her father, Joaquin Nin y Castellanos, a handsome, penniless Spanish Catalan, was a talented pianist. Her mother, Rosa Culmell y Vaurigaud, a singer, was the daughter of a conveniently wealthy Danish merchant and his French Cuban wife. With no assets apart from his gargantuan ego, Joaquin Nin (as he was later known) believed himself a genius, a belief his devoted daughter Anaïs appears to have adopted about herself later in life, when her many surrealist novels received ridiculing reviews.

Nin remained, in the words of her brother Joaquin Nin recorded by Deirdre Bair, "a steel hummingbird . . . determined to be famous." When publishers turned down Nin's novels, she printed them herself. In the course of her life she purchased three printing presses. Not until 1966, by which time she was in her sixties, did she finally achieve the fame for which she had longed and then not for her novels but for *The Diary of Anaïs Nin (1931–1974)* (1966–1980). After she spent over thirty years of publishing little-known fiction and essays, the diaries brought her hundreds of requests for lectures and interviews, and she became especially well known on the college circuit. She was once described as "undoubtedly one of the most frequently interviewed of twentieth-century authors."

In her dark days of badly reviewed novels, Nin persevered, writing lines like this one from *Cities of the Interior* (1974), first published in 1961: "She awakened unfree, as if laden with the seeds of his being." The opacity of this line, the lack of directness typical of her fiction and of many passages in her diary though not of her criticism, suggests her hidden fear of revealing herself, a great paradox in a diarist who was initially celebrated for telling all. As much scholarship has demonstrated, however, Nin's famous diary is largely an invention, at least regarding many of the events reported. As a record of a woman's emotional reactions to the real and imagined experiences of her life, which seems what Nin intended it to be, it has few parallels. It is a portrait of a soul tortured by fear, frustration, and inhibition, which she attempts to shake off with arrogance, recklessly self-endangering sexual adventures, and single-minded hard work. She is indeed a profile in courage, if a perverse one. A remark made in her criticism, in a 1947 essay entitled "On Writing," sums up the central difficulty she encountered whenever she attempted what readers thought of as confession in her diaries:

There is [a] great danger for the writer, perhaps the greatest one of all: his consciousness of the multiple taboos society has imposed on literature, and his inner censor. In the diary I found a devious (a woman's) way to evade this outer and inner censor. It is surprising how well one writes if one thinks no one will read you.

In fact she produced the diary with an audience in mind, but this apparently disingenuous remark may throw light on her obscure essays and fiction. It is surprising indeed how clearly she did write in those essays, possibly because she thought at the time that hardly anyone would read them.

Adopting the age-old view of woman as a devious being, she identifies her well-grounded need to be devious because of her unconventional behavior, which included the incestuous affair with her father, as well as her justifiable feeling that as a woman she dare not write openly about incest, abortion, sexual arousal, multiple sexual partners, and masturbation, some of the important topics of her diary that she only hints at in much of her fiction. Her fiction, she once admitted, was only an extension of the *Diary*.

In the *Diary*'s original form, which exists only in manuscript, these topics are discussed in great detail. Nin or her editor Gunther Stuhlmann excised much of the sexual material from the highly expurgated, indeed bowdlerized, first version of her published *Diary*. Thus the central event of her life, her relationship with her father, which influenced her descriptions of herself, her interests, and all her relationships, shaping her ability to tell her story at all, remains invisible in all published versions of the diary until fifteen years after her death. When in 1992 the volume entitled *Incest: From "A Journal of Love," the Unexpurgated Diary of Anaïs Nin, 1932–1934* appeared, it represented far from the complete story. (The complicated publishing history of Nin's *Diary* is discussed below in a separate section.)

For glimpses at Nin's inner life, a reader can turn to some of her interesting literary criticism, in particular a work she wrote at the age of twenty-three, *D. H. Lawrence: An Unprofessional Study* (1932). As much an autobiography as it is a prescient study of D. H. Lawrence, it reveals the intensity, impulsiveness, and turbulence of her own mind. To "begin to realize Lawrence is to begin immediately to realize philosophy not merely as an intellectual edifice but as a passionate blood-experience," she writes, very much in search of such an experience herself at the time. Having just moved to Paris, she was in the midst of a personal crisis spurred by a confluence of events: a sexually dissatisfying marriage, the accidental discovery of a closetful of pornography (where else but in Paris?), and an almost-consummated affair with her husband's much-admired college professor John Erskine. When she was thinking about writing the study, she confided to her diary that her crude working title was "When D. H. Lawrence Found Himself." Her lifelong project to find herself as a writer and as a sexually satisfied woman began with Lawrence.

One of the themes of the book, reading between the lines, is Nin's total identification with Lawrence and with the version of her father that she had internalized. In a chapter entitled "In Controversy," the word most applied to her life, she writes:

> Certain of Lawrence's readers were so struck by the first wave of his sensuousness that they could go no further. No ideas, no poetry, no philosophy could exist outside of the appalling fact of "pornography." Lawrence, they said, was enslaved by sex. Meanwhile, *they* were smothered, overwhelmed, subjugated by sex. And here they remained, arguing in defense of purity, and against the slavery of sex—of Lawrence's slavery, I mean.

She meant her own slavery as well. Enslaved indeed by her many conflicted feelings about sex, she might have been writing her own epitaph.

Although she could write straightforwardly about the process of writing and about various literary figures, the style of her diary instead constantly entices, seductively implying that a detailed erotic passage is just a paragraph away. Only, in the diary as originally published, it never is. Passages like the following, however, from the first (highly expurgated) volume of her diary ensured that she would be remembered more for her writings on sex than for her many other perceptive insights into the psychology of women and of various writers: "I want to live only for ecstasy. Small doses, moderate loves, all half-shades, leave me cold. I like extrava-

gance. Letters which give the postman a stiff back to carry, books which overflow from their covers, sexuality which bursts the thermometers. I am aware also that I am becoming June." She refers to June Mansfield, the wife of Henry Miller, a prominent writer known for novels about sex. In the *Diary,* Nin portrays June as constantly drunk and highly promiscuous.

In purportedly "unexpurgated" versions of the diary first released in the mid-1980s, Nin produced numerous passages like the following:

> We spent another day in his room. . . .
>
> At night—caresses. He begs me to undress and lie at his side. His caressing suppleness and mine, the feelings which run from head to toes—vibrations of all the senses, a thousand new vibrations . . . a new union, a unison of delicacies, subtleties, exaltations, keener awareness . . . .
>
> Endless stories about women. Exploits. Teaching me at the same time the last expertness in love. . . . I had at moments the feeling that here was Don Juan indeed. . . .
>
> When I walked down the dark hall to my room—with a handkerchief between my legs because his sperm is overabundant—the mistral was blowing.

This passage concerns her father. He always presented himself to her as a man who had "possessed more than a thousand women." She followed suit, seducing as many men as she could, among them Miller; Otto Rank, a psychoanalyst who had been a member of Sigmund Freud's inner circle and who analyzed Nin; and René Allendy, her first psychoanalyst.

Nin's birthplace, Neuilly-sur-Seine, a fashionable suburb of Paris, suited her father's social snobbery but not her mother's pocketbook. Living on her mother's small inheritance, the family moved soon after Anaïs's birth and continued to move frequently: Havana, Berlin, Uccle (a suburb of Brussels), Arcachon, a small town on the Atlantic seacoast of France, back to Uccle in the wake of her father's desertion of the family in 1914, when Nin was eleven. Then they moved to Barcelona, to New York City, and finally to Richmond Hill, Queens, where Anaïs attended but never completed high school. Somewhere between Paris and Berlin two brothers were born. The youngest, Joaquin, was destined for a distinguished career in music. Nin worked as an artist's model in New York, frequently posing for Charles Dana Gibson and other prominent artists. After she married Hugh Guiler on March 3, 1923 (in Havana, Cuba), she moved to Paris, returning to the United States when World War II broke out. She traveled extensively, and many of her writings catch the soul of the exotic locales she visited.

Nin died of cancer in Los Angeles a few weeks before her seventy-fourth birthday. In the course of her nearly seventy-four years she produced novels, tales, erotica, letters, an "unprofessional" study of Lawrence, as she called it, and the thirty-five-thousand-page diary that transformed her into either a religion or a laughingstock, depending upon which critics a reader finds congenial. It remains a curious part of Nin's legacy that she provokes extreme reactions, inspiring two schools of critical thought, the fans and the incredulous. What she wrote as a young woman about Lawrence offers a pertinent commentary on her own reputation as a writer and personality:

> D. H. Lawrence has been difficult to measure because he is the kind of writer who rouses either enthusiasm or hate. No one can hold a neutral opinion of him; he is too definite a personality, and the world he created in his books is too vigorous and unique to be overlooked.

When the first installment of Nin's diary was published in 1966, it received almost nothing but praise. It was hailed on the dust jacket as "a feminine confessional, displaying the inner life of a woman" and "a daring advance into the psychology of female being." It was greeted as "among the outstanding literary works of this century . . . the diary examines human personal-

ity with a depth and understanding seldom surpassed since Proust" and "one of the most remarkable [diaries] in the history of letters . . . a literary accomplishment." Nin's diaries begin in 1914 as a letter to her absent father and end in the summer of 1974, two and a half years before her death in January 1977. Her father is the central, unstated concern of all the diaries published during her lifetime and shortly thereafter, though often this theme appears under the guise of interest in women, especially the emotional and erotic life of women, and human relationships generally.

PUBLISHING HISTORY

All students of Nin need to be aware that the diary has never been published in its original form. The version of the *Diary* that first attracted critical acclaim—the six volumes published during her lifetime, between 1966 and 1974—are, as mentioned, known to have been heavily edited and expurgated by Nin or her editor and literary agent Stuhlmann. Volume seven appeared in 1980, followed by four volumes of *The Early Diary of Anaïs Nin* (1978–1985). These volumes of *The Early Diary of Anaïs Nin* for the years 1914 through 1931 concern her adolescence in the United States, where she never felt at home, and her meeting and courtship with Guiler, the banker who married her and whose money supported all her erotic and literary liaisons with Miller and others. The purportedly unexpurgated supplements—entitled *Henry and June: From the Unexpurgated Diary of Anaïs Nin* (1986); *Incest: From "A Journal of Love," the Unexpurgated Diary of Anaïs Nin, 1932–1934* (1992); *Fire: From "A Journal of Love," the Unexpurgated Diary of Anaïs Nin, 1934–1937* (1995); and *Nearer the Moon: From "A Journal of Love," the Unexpurgated Diary of Anaïs Nin, 1937–1939* (1996)—appeared posthumously. (In reality all so-called "unexpurgated" portions of the diary have been edited, rearranged, and expurgated by one of her widowers, Rupert Pole. To see the diary as it was written, a would-be reader must visit several rare book rooms in major libraries.) *Henry and June* concerns Nin's meeting, friendship, and affair with Miller and his wife, Mansfield. *Incest* reveals the affair with her father. *Fire* explores her affairs with her psychoanalyst Rank, with Miller, and with an impoverished Spanish Marxist named Gonzalo Moré. *Nearer the Moon* goes into yet more detail about Miller and Moré and describes Nin's erotic reactions to them.

The first of seven edited volumes of *The Diary of Anaïs Nin* presented, her editor Stuhlmann remarks, "what could be told at the time about her life as an artist and the world she created for herself and others between 1932 and 1974." The censorship was quietly acknowledged, but the degree of distortion of her life never became apparent until the "unexpurgated" versions of the *Diary* were published. As of January 2001, fourteen volumes drawn from heavily edited diary pages were in print. The diaries themselves are housed in the rare book room of the University of California at Los Angeles, many letters and other papers are at the Gleeson Library of the University of San Francisco, and still others are at the University of California at Berkeley. Other papers and manuscripts are scattered in various libraries and research centers, among them the Lilly Library, Indiana University at Bloomington; the Anaïs Nin archive at Northwestern University; and the Harry Ransome Humanities Research Center at the University of Texas, Austin. A diary, especially one of this length, cannot be summarized, but below some of the chief topics of the seven volumes initially published are mentioned.

Volume one (1931–1934) is often described as the best or most readable, perhaps because in it Nin struggles to understand whom she would like to become. "The struggle of Diary I is for

birth," writes Sharon Spencer. It recounts as well the relationships Nin formed with a series of men who are father figures, including Miller; the novelist René Allendy; and her first psychoanalyst Rank, who broke with Freud, theorizing that birth itself rather than the Oedipus complex is the psyche's first trauma.

Volume two (1934–1939), published in 1967, begins with Nin sailing to the United States to work as a psychoanalyst with Rank. It includes moments of humor, as when she coaxes the staid and somewhat inhibited Rank to a dance hall in Harlem. The mood of the second diary is one of sadness and loss: "The death of houses, how they seem to collapse as soon as we leave them, as soon as we prepare ourselves to leave them." It closes with the outbreak of World War II and the need to leave France and return to the United States combined with other losses, including, though not discussed recognizably as such here, her traumatic abortion when six-months pregnant.

Volume three (1939–1944), published in 1969, laments the loss of Europe and the behavior of the numerous "children," that is, various artists and writers whom Nin has undertaken to support and her feeling that they have destroyed her as a mother. Volume four (1944–1947), published in 1971, concerns Nin's efforts to publish her fiction. At this phase she had founded the Gemor Press, where she and Gonzalo Moré printed one of her novels, *This Hunger* (1945). This novel subsequently became part one of her lengthy collection *Ladders to Fire,* published in October 1946 by Dutton. Now she begins to deal with characteristically ridiculing reviews of her work, complaining about the "painful cheap burlesque of the *New York Times* review, entitled 'Surrealist Soap Opera.'" Volume five (1947–1955), published in 1974, includes a gorgeously described trip to Mexico along with further struggles and some success with her novel writing. Volume six (1955–1966), published in 1976, reports the success of the publication of volume one. Invitations to interviews and talks as well as financial security follow. Volume seven (1966–1974), published in 1980, relishes success and complains about hostile interviewers with a familiar cry of not being understood.

THE DIARY

One of Nin's biographers refers to her *Diary* as a "literary striptease," which describes its essential ambiguities, its constant tension between a compulsion to expose everything and a desire to conceal it all. A sympathetic critic, Sharon Spencer, writes:

> In spite of the ongoing denigration of Nin's work in the U.S., her books have been translated into at least twenty-five languages, including Russian, Lithuanian, Icelandic, and Romanian. Her artistry is highly respected in countries as distant as Sweden and Japan. In Japan, Anaïs has attracted more than a dozen dedicated translators and critics.

Certainly Nin's *Diary* has spawned a veritable industry. The Doors wrote a song based on *A Spy in the House of Love* (1954), one of her novels. The eighteen-volume journal *Anaïs: An International Journal,* disseminates memories of her, tidbits from unpublished sections of her diary, and fiction inspired by her fiction or by her life. According to Noël Riley Fitch, the French house of Cacharel concocted Anaïs, Anaïs, a scent devoted to her, "Le Premier Parfum de Cacharel" as it was first marketed in 1981. A 1990 movie *Henry and June* tells the story of her complicated affair with Miller and his wife. Miller is one among scores of lovers she describes in the unexpurgated volumes of her diaries. Other scalps on her belt, as she sometimes thought of them, included Hanns Sachs, another distinguished psychoanalyst from Freud's inner circle; and Edmund Wilson, the dean of American literary critics who, Anatole

Broyard suggested, was struggling between his desire and his taste when he wrote a glowing review of her novel *Under a Glass Bell* (1944). She wanted to try for Carl Jung, but the venture failed.

Nin tended toward extremes in her own life, writing, for example, when she met Miller's wife, June, "As June walked towards me from the darkness of the garden into the light of the door, I saw for the first time the most beautiful woman on earth." When at age thirty Nin meets the father who had abandoned her family, she mentions his "supreme, open egotism," a term along with "Donna Juana" some biographers have found appropriate to describe her life and writings. Like her father she flitted from bed to bed, once writing, according to Bair, that her "recipe for happiness" was to "mix well the sperm of four men in one day."

Nin's admirers almost invariably worship her; her detractors, who call the admirers "Ninnies," love to hate her. Yet the passion of some detractors suggests an extreme but unwilling admiration. Gore Vidal, who conducted a long friendship with Nin, later devoted five novels to unflattering portrayals of her. Incidentally his 1995 memoir *Palimpsest* includes photos of his mother and photos of Nin that bear a remarkable resemblance. Along similar lines, the poet Katha Pollitt writes:

> My idea of hell is to be stranded on a desert island with nothing to read but Anaïs Nin's diaries, but some people, apparently, can't get enough of them . . . her publishers, for instance. . . . But no question about it, Nin is much more readable as a female Don Juan than she was as the dreamy princess in the tower depicted in the earlier series of diaries. When she is not rhapsodizing about her feelings, she can write earthily and entertainingly about sex, although unfortunately not in a way that can be quoted in a family newspaper.

This mixture of fascinated disgust and reluctant admiration is not unusual in criticism of Nin.

Since virtually all of Nin's writing concerns the erotic life of women, a student seeking thumbnail sketches of her will find her depicted as "Madonna of St. Clitoris" and "Venus with an over-bite," yet at the same time she seemed, according to Lawrence Durrell, a "diva" with "a shy, virginal side." According to Fitch, a radio announcer from the BBC remarked on the contradictions: "Anaïs wears a necklace of imaginary foreskins emblematic of make-believe conquests . . . but Anaïs never gets piked. She entices us to the shadowy fringes of Lesbos and then pulls down the shade." Something of the prudish libertine always lingered about her. Despite the apparent freedom and unbounded desire in sexual relationships she broadcasts in the so-called "unexpurgated" versions of her diary, she reveals a frenetic urgency in her writing that belies the sense of satisfaction she hoped for from her sexual encounters.

CONTROVERSY

To some a fount of truth, to others "the liary," Nin's diaries have found their way into women's studies curricula and have received high literary praise from Miller, who wrote in a frequently quoted article of late 1937 in T. S. Eliot's magazine the *Criterion* that Nin's "monumental confession" would one day take its place "beside the revelations of St. Augustine, Petronius, Abelard, Rousseau, Proust." This must be taken with a grain of salt, since Miller's existence depended at the time on Nin's handouts. After meeting in Paris in 1931, these gurus of sexual liberation conducted a clandestine romance, each producing some of his or her best-known writing, including what became Nin's first two diaries and her novel *House of Incest* (1936) and Miller's novels *Tropic of Cancer* (1934) and *Black Spring* (1936). However, Nin's writings won her France's Prix Sévigné for autobiography in 1971, election to the National Institute of Arts and Letters in 1974, the distinction of being named Woman of the Year by the *Los Angeles Times* in 1976, and most of a column in *Bartlett's Familiar Quotations,* more space than André Gide and about the same amount as Arthur Schopenhauer. New York University's Graduate School in Comparative Literature has a fellowship in her name. Praised by her admirers for her exceptional candor and sensitivity in writing about women's inner lives and sexual experiences, she is criticized as a compulsive liar by her detractors.

Two biographers, Deirdre Bair and Noël Riley Fitch, have documented that the diary is "a work of fiction," "an act of self-invention," filled with untrue confessions, self-censorships, reworked versions of the diary that Nin copied out and rewrote many times. But as Nin's editor Gunther Stuhlmann remarks in the introduction to her first published diary, "Miss Nin's truth is . . . psychological." By this he apparently means that truth, on her terms, reveals a genuine human desire or need, not necessarily an actual event in her life. Reviewing Bair's biography of Nin for the *New York Times Book Review,* Bruce Bawer comments that letters, interviews, and the expurgated diary that appeared between 1966 and 1985 reveal "that the published *Diary* is in many ways fictional, that the supposedly 'unexpurgated' diary volumes published as *Henry and June* (1986) and *Incest* (1992) were heavily edited, and that Nin's self-portrait in the *Diary* represented a serious distortion."

Certainly the spontaneous outpourings implied by the term "diary" never existed in any published form of Nin's *Diary,* but many published diaries and confessions (Oscar Wilde's *De Profundis,* for example) show signs of considerable revision. Nin took pains to construct a public persona in the published versions of her diary. Whether that invalidates their stated purpose of revealing a woman's development remains a point of heated critical debate. Observing that, although Nin's novels are taught in women's studies courses, professors "tend to shun the diaries as 'untruthful' or 'unreliable,'" Bair remarks, "One wonders . . . why 'truth' is the primary criterion for judging diaries, especially those such as Nin's, which were intended from the beginning to represent one woman's view of herself and her life." Nin meant for the diaries to reveal emotional realities, not the facts of her life. These realities included her wish to feel confident, to have experiences she never had, and to meet persons whom it now seems she never met, André Gide for example.

Nin's observations in an essay she wrote at age twenty-eight, "The Mystic of Sex—A First Look at D. H. Lawrence" (1930), seem to explain the kind of truth she originally had in mind for all her writing: "If you are terribly truthful the ground will always move from under you, you will have to shift with shifting truth. You will crave a definite idea (that is our hell), you may worship one, but you will also shift with shifting truth, as Lawrence did." Part of her shifting occurred as a result of her experiencing separate and conflicting truths and selves at the same time. In 1920 she wrote in her *Diary* that she had been at a social gathering, where a "gentleman" had told her: "If one knows two languages, then one is two people. If one knows three, one is three people." She then asked, "So then, what am I?" She could never answer the question in a way that relieved the agony behind this urgent question, for she never felt satisfied with herself. A child of warring parents from different cultures, she never reconciled their languages or their ways and attempted to create her own private culture separate from all others. In a talk given in 1971 she said:

> Why one writes is a question I can answer easily, having so often asked it of myself. I believe one writes because one has to create a world in which one can live. I could not live in any of the worlds offered to me—the world of my parents, the world of war, the world of politics. I had to create a world of my own, like a climate, a country, an atmosphere in which I could breathe, reign, and re-create myself when destroyed by living. That I believe is the reason for every work of art.

In December 1946 Leo Lerman, a friend, asked Nin for a short autobiography. Her response reveals that she had thought seriously about the concept of truth and how possible it is to tell it in emotional, literary, and philosophical contexts and that her essential view remained that truth was protean:

> I see myself and my life each day differently. What can I say? The facts lie. I have been Don Quixote, always creating a world of my own. . . . It took me more than sixty diary volumes until now to tell about my life. Like Oscar Wilde I put only my art into my work and my genius into my life. My life is not possible to tell. I change every day, change my patterns, my concepts, my interpretations. I am a series of moods and sensations. I play a thousand roles. . . . My real self is unknown. . . . I create a myth and a legend, a lie, a fairy tale, a magical world, and one that collapses every day and makes me feel like going the way of Virginia Woolf. I have tried not to be neurotic, not romantic, not destructive, but may be all of these in disguises.

Her narcissism is evident here in her comparison of Wilde's genius to what she only imagines is her own. She once admitted: "It's true I can't write, but I can live. I can create life around me, give strength, stimulate, defend, love, save." Her depiction of herself as constantly changing her mind and finding her real self to be "unknown" is tragically true. She reveals her awareness of a destructive artificiality in her everyday life, but it is in her criticism, where she can hide behind the mask of writing about others, that insights into herself creep into her writing. If a diary consists of spontaneous outbursts of insight about the self, then in a sense the real diary is tucked away or scattered about in writings she considered only as literary criticism. Revealingly she appropriated exactly the same

Wilde quotation to describe her father in volume one of her *Diary*:

> Like Oscar Wilde, he put his genius in his life, his talent in music. He has created a personality. There is also a Spartan quality in him; he abstains from drink and overeating to remain slender. He lives with great discipline. He has a passion for perfection. Even his lies are to embellish, to improve on reality. . . . His only indulgence is love-making.

Like father, like daughter. The extremes she adopted, Spartan and all-indulgent, compelled her to duplicate the pattern of her father's life in every detail. The idea of copying and duplicating dominated her to the last detail, for she often adopted two identities and two different names to go with two different versions of the diary she was writing at any given moment.

Nin's comparison of herself to Wilde is nonetheless suggestive, since Wilde held similar ideas about truth as an unstable, ever-changing thing: "To know the truth one must imagine myriads of falsehoods. For what is Truth? In matters of religion, it is simply the opinion that has survived. In matters of science, it is the ultimate sensation. In matters of art, it is one's last mood," he wrote in an essay titled "The Critic as Artist." His ideas about literary criticism as a form of autobiography seem particularly germane to Nin's life and writings. In "The Critic as Artist," (1890) one of Wilde's best-known essay-dialogues, he defined "the highest criticism" as "the record of one's own soul." Anaïs Nin's criticism of Lawrence and other figures may be read as a fount of self-revelation, whereas in many of her other writings, especially the diary, she seems immersed in a dreamy, avant-garde style. Consequently she produced passages of consummate vagueness, for example, this one from *Fire*:

> The mouth alone touches the womb. Clouds of dreams, mist of diamond and sulfur from the eyes, but the mouth alone touches the womb, the mouth stirs, moves, flowers, the lips open, and there flows the breath of life and breathlessness of desire. The shape of the mouth shapes the currents of the blood, stirs, lifts, dissolves.

No wonder Miller said to her, according to *Fire*, "I believe in your vagueness."

INCEST: THE CENTRAL THEME OF NIN'S WRITINGS

A diary cannot be summarized the way a novel or a poem can. Nevertheless, the careful reader of all of Nin's diaries perceives a dominant theme, unstated but influencing all events in the original published versions, revealed graphically yet incompletely in the so-called "unexpurgated" diaries, that is, her lifelong preoccupation with her father. She has always been controversial, partly for discussing sexual experience in ways that few had before her. The biographer who called her diaries "a literary striptease" referred to the popular but unjustified view of all of her work as pornography of one kind or another. So it is worth remarking that some of her well-earned controversy stems not from the sexual content of the *Diary* but from considerations of whether or not the diary form may be deemed a literary genre. Diaries until comparatively recently did not receive serious scholarly consideration. For a variety of reasons they, like biographies, have remained stepchildren of literature, typically not among works canonized as major or "classic" literature. Scholarly studies of life writing have typically considered autobiography as distinct from diary—perhaps a dubious distinction. Felicity A. Nussbaum, in Elizabeth Podnieks's *Daily Modernism* (2000), writes: "Diaries often remain unpublished documents; their length may make reading tedious and difficult; they lack the formal cohesiveness that lends itself to New Critical readings; and, despite their articulation of human chronology, diaries are not classic realist texts."

The prevailing feeling of much criticism seems to be that the relatively low status of diaries as literature stems from several factors. Diaries are, as Podnieks notes, perceived as "either a spontaneously uncrafted document or a carefully crafted text. The crisis that obtains is this: a definition of the diary as literature necessarily hinges on its conception as an aesthetic work; but if the diary in question is artistically motivated, it cannot be a diary per se." In other words, if the diarist writes for an audience instead of pouring thoughts and events on the page without censorship, like some Platonic ideal of a psychoanalytic patient, then the diary is not really a diary. This Catch-22 distinction belies the reality that probably no diary ignores audience or exists uninfluenced by craftsmanship.

The greatest of Nin's confessions, which appears only in the posthumous *Incest,* was that she had seduced and carried on an affair with her father when she was thirty. His sexual abuse of her as a child, her unconscious compulsion to repeat the pain she had then suffered, and her conscious zeal to punish him by seducing and then abandoning him as he had abandoned her mother and her family had an enormous impact on the content, style, and self-censorship of the *Diary* and on Nin's many other writings. This remains a fertile field for Nin scholars, scholars of women's writing and of diary writing, and psychologists who study sexual abuse. Podnieks has suggested that the *Diary*, which began as a letter to her father, came in Nin's psychic world to represent the man himself:

> She spoke to it and feared it just as she would her father, asking it "to pardon me for writing in pencil but I am in bed"; and she worried that "My dear diary will scold me and judge me severely." Words such as "pardon," "scold," and "judge" are associated more with a figure of authority than with the secret "confidant" that the diary also served as.

This brilliant insight reveals the source of Nin's extreme conflict about writing. She transferred her feelings of incestuous love and guilt onto the father she imagined figured in her *Diary,* and the result was a massive case of writer's block, which she combated with surrealist attempts at automatic writing, unintelligible except as a code, a palliative attempt to hide her feelings from herself.

The desire to hide but at the same time display her feelings is particularly obvious in her novel *House of Incest.* This book has no real signs of incest anywhere but the title, apart from a mention of "Lot with his hand upon his daughter's breast while the city burned behind them," and in block letters "I LOVE MY BROTHER" after the narrator's confession that she "could not bear to attend my own wedding, could not bear to be married to man, because, because, because." The novel is characterized by purple, windy passages like the following:

> I carry white sponges of knowledge on strings of nerves.
>
> As I move within my book I am cut by pointed glass and broken bottles in which there is still the odor of sperm and perfume.
>
> More pages added to the book but pages like a prisoner's walking back and forth over the space allotted to him. What is it allotted me to say?

Whatever it was, Nin could not say it. The incest taboo had penetrated her writing. What the novel does reveal occasionally is her extreme fear and guilt and her dread that she had disfigured and destroyed herself through her incestuous experiences and lifelong incestuous desires that infected every relationship.

> I came upon a forest of decapitated trees, women carved out of bamboo, flesh slatted like that of slaves in joyless slavery, faces cut in two by the sculptor's knife, sowing two sides forever separate, eternally two-faced, and it was I who had to shift about to behold the entire woman. Truncated undecagon figures.

The prose shields her from emotions she found unbearable, particularly fears of having been mutilated, but at the same time offers glimpses of them.

In the version of the *Diary* that appeared during Nin's lifetime, she seems a self-possessed, daring woman making friends with leading artists and intellectuals as well as down-and-out musicians and poets. In this guise she appealed to many, especially women so trapped by marriages or poverty that none of the self-fulfillment described by Nin seemed remotely possible for them. At that time none of her readers knew that Nin was herself anything but the icon of liberated independence she conjures up in the *Diary*. She was instead trapped in a marriage riddled with ambivalence but blessed by her husband's large salary. She suffered constantly from feelings of guilt and feelings of sexual frustration as well as her need to suffer. Only in the posthumously published volume *Incest* did she admit to being "a prisoner of material necessity" and reveal the sexual disgust and pain she endured with her husband:

> I submit to his caresses. My body is so indifferent. But before his desire, then, I am in revolt. I hate his mouth on mine. And the pain, the big, clumsy ravages, always like a violation. My face is twisted with pain. . . . Fortunately, he is swift, like a heavy-clawed bird.

As Podnieks has pointed out, here Nin envisions herself as Leda being raped by the "heavy-clawed" Zeus disguised as a swan. Since Zeus was the father of the other gods, and since he tended to appear in disguise to mortal women (as a bull to Europa, as a rain of gold to Danae), the myth of Leda suggests the incest taboo, sexual desire for the father, which must be concealed by disguises. One reason for Nin's sexual revulsion for her (first) husband, Hugh Guiler, appears to have been that she saw him as a father. When she married her second husband, Rupert Pole, without pausing to divorce her first, she confessed to a friend that

her life was divided between Hugh the father and Rupert the son.

When Nin literally committed incest, her feelings as depicted in the volume *Incest* reveal similar guilt and anxiety. She describes herself as the seducer, mounting her father, as if to assert the existence of the control, indeed the self-control, that she lacked, largely because the possibility of developing it was robbed from her by her father's own lack of self-control when he repeatedly photographed her naked and spanked her sadistically as well as erotically when she was a young child. Now lifting her negligée and climbing on top of him, she envisions herself at last as a real femme fatale, seizing with the intention of abandoning the man who more than twenty years earlier had terrorized her. Calling her an "ugly little girl," he thereby thrust her into a lifelong frantic attempt to display an absolute, alluring beauty, which she never really thought she had, no matter now many men she managed to seduce.

Nin describes their kiss, adding that it unleashed "a wave of desire. . . . Another kiss. More terror than joy. The joy of something unnamable, obscure." She feels a strange combination of extreme sexual arousal combined with fear: "All the while some part of me was hard and terrified." In the end she declares repeatedly her feeling that she has been "poisoned by this union." No other well-known female writer has so poignantly depicted the dilemma of incest, with the possible exception of Kathryn Harrison in *The Kiss* (1997), a memoir of Harrison's affair as a young woman with a father who, like Nin's, had abandoned the family when she was still a child.

Some critics have reasoned that the adult Nin sought out her father in a combined thrill-seeking and revenge-inspired expectation of some ultimate sexual experience. Pollitt, for example, remarks that the incest was not "quite as horrifying" as it sounds, since she had seen him only once in the twenty years following his desertion of their family and since both of them were "equally self-infatuated and self-mythologizing." This underestimates the impact of Nin's early sexual experiences on her ability to make rational judgments. Similarly Podnieks reads Nin's seduction of her father as self-empowerment. Thrill-seeking may indeed have been the motive uppermost in Nin's own mind, but to assume that her conscious aims dominated her in a particular sexual choice and in her sexual tastes would be to assume in her a completely different emotional makeup from every other human being. The sexual feelings stirred up in her as a child by her father exercised an overpowering influence on her when she returned to him as an adult, supposedly knowing better, and damaged her judgment. Wanting to exploit him rather than be exploited by him again, she probably had the (fleeting) illusion that she was the one in charge. Instead, by completing the sexual act she condemned herself to greater guilts and terrors. Hoping to resolve conflicts and to redress old injuries, she only intensified both.

As her *Diary* reveals, in virtually every sexual relationship Nin sought exploitation or exploited others. A lover of legions of men, she writes graphically about extreme arousal but often hints or even confesses that sexual release escapes her. She funded all her projects and supported down-and-out artists with household money given to her by her banker husband, one of many facts not revealed by the diaries. The unmentioned Guiler sympathized with her literary ambitions, hiring a full-time housekeeper early in their marriage: "Due to the thoughtfulness of my Pussy, I am going to be free," she writes in the *Early Diary,* which appeared long after her counterfeit identity as an independent woman had been established.

As originally published between 1966 and 1980, the diary hovered around the introspections and erotic life of Nin without going into more than a few tantalizing details. Later volumes vacillate between extremely graphic and surprisingly opaque explorations of mental and sensual states. "*Incest,* the second volume of the unexpurgated edition of the diary, reveals that she was having affairs with, basically, all the men who had deemed worthy of mention back in the expurgated volumes, excepting Antonin Artaud, whose impotence proved something of a relief, given the laudanum stains around his mouth," comments Claudia Roth Pierpont. Although Nin wrote a number of novels and essays on literary and psychological topics and on the concerns of women, she became far better known for the *Diary,* for her personal charm and dramatic style as a lecturer, and for two collections of her erotica, *Delta of Venus: Erotica* (1977) and *Little Birds: Erotica* (1979). These were written for a dollar a page in 1940 for a wealthy collector but were not published until 1977 and 1979 respectively.

CRITICAL APPRAISALS AND CULTURAL IMPACT

By the 1990s a majority of critics appeared to find earlier claims for Nin's literary greatness exaggerated. Her major biographer, Bair, steers deftly between those who ridicule Nin and those who worship her, suggesting that she is a minor writer, but insists on calling her "a *major* minor writer." Drawing on Cynthia Ozick's essay about the role of another minor writer, the novelist Alfred Chester, Bair follows Ozick's point that if readers could all agree on what makes a writer minor, it "would bring us a little nearer to defining a culture," for "the tone of a culture cannot depend only on the occasional genius, or the illusion of one; the prevailing temper of a society and time is situated in its minor voices, in their variegated chorus."

Prevailing cultural interests of the twentieth century include increasing open-mindedness about sex, new concepts of the self, and psychoanalysis. Nin emerges as a figure in the vanguard of those who transformed the way readers think about these things. In his preface to her early diary *Linotte: 1914–1920* (1978), her brother Joaquin Nin hints at her introspective abilities and at the therapeutic role of the diary for her, qualities that must have predisposed her toward the psychoanalytic treatments she received later in life. Joaquin writes:

> Above all, [her early diary] stemmed from her overwhelming vocation to observe, comment and set down. Her laughter, her tears, her sadness, her enthusiasm, come to the surface like bubbles of oxygen from the deep waters of her introspection. She was a deep-sea diver from the start, and the diary was her indispensable lifeline.

The desire to plunge into the depths of the unconscious mind led her to surrealism in her writing, to Lawrence, Marcel Proust, Freud, Jung, and Rank in her reading, and ultimately to writing her first serious novel, in her terms a "modernist" novel, *House of Incest*. Although it often does not show in the diary, Nin was an extraordinarily well-read woman.

The timing of the first appearance of her diary, the late 1960s and the 1970s, enhanced their appeal because the burgeoning women's movement sought prominent female voices to authenticate its claims and to highlight the importance of women in literature and culture. Although she was criticized for her silence concerning important feminist issues, such as economic equity and the need for legislative changes, Nin's charm and tact and her seeming personal interest in women seeking self-development rendered her an important voice in the movement.

Nin was frequently suspect, was sometimes derided, and even endured catcalls and hissing because of her ultrafeminine appearance, including flowing, exotic robes and heavy make-up, and her refusal to answer questions about her source of income or the ultrasecret private life the *Diary* pretends to reveal. She was lauded

for remarks like the following from the introduction to volume one of the *Diary*:

> What I have to say is really distinct from the artist and art. *It is the woman who has to speak.* And it is not only the woman Anaïs who has to speak, but I who have to speak for many woman. As I discover myself, I feel I am merely one of many, a symbol. I begin to understand women of yesterday and today. The mute ones of the past, the inarticulate, who took refuge behind wordless intuitions, and the women of today, all action, and copies of men. And I, in between.

The remark seems to express the needs and desires of many women who were at the time frustrated with their lives and with cultural restrictions placed on women. The prominent feminist Kate Millett hailed Nin as "the mother to us all."

Nin liked to portray herself and to be portrayed as a savior or a resurrecter of voices she perceived as silenced through fear or lack of courage. But her revolutionary fervor seems to have failed her whenever it would have come into conflict with her romantic image. Pollitt, discussing Nin's late-term abortion that was disguised in early published versions of the *Diary* as a miscarriage, notes:

> That Nin would have disguised this fact when she published the passage in 1966 is, I think, significant: it shows that she was hardly the bold-truth-teller of women's secret experiences that she claimed to be. She knew just how far she could go without risking real controversy and calling into question her image of ethereal femininity and selfless nurturance. In the 1960's, when abortion was illegal, it would have done some good for a well-known older woman to have gone public about her abortion. Now, no thanks to Nin, it's old news.

It is a small wonder that the critic Pierpont characterizes Nin as being at "the forefront of the rearguard of the women's movement."

An ideology Nin perpetuated, that of the woman as victim, may well have increased her enormous popularity. In a 1970 interview on women's liberation, Nin remarked:

> The aspect of the diary which has been helpful to other women is that I noted the patterns of which I was the unconscious victim (which analysis helped me to realize). These patterns included racial, religious, those made by the father or the family, the ideals of the family, the mythological saintly grandmother.

She went on to discuss the "more difficult" time women have had because of the "role playing" imposed upon them as "wife, companion, mistress, mother—a little more difficult for woman than the man's confrontation with the world. He wasn't so concerned with the personal world."

FIRE AND FRIGIDITY

In December 1936 Nin wrote in *Fire*: "The symbolism of small traits: I have never lit a fire that has gone out." She then ignores fire as a symbol and instead details actual fires she has lit, at a beach party, for example. Yet if one considers the obvious symbolism, this seems a sad revelation. It suggests a haunted hungering in a woman who became a symbol of sexual liberation and satisfaction. In reality she seems to have been a Flying Dutchman of the bed because no bed ever brought what she really wanted. In March 1932, caught up in her affair with Miller and his wife, Mansfield, Nin admitted, "It is like a forest fire, to be with him. New places of my body are aroused and burnt. . . . I leave him in an unquenchable fever." "Unquenchable" implies strong arousal with no orgasmic release. In an analytic session with René Allendy, her analyst at the time, she pleads, "If I were frigid, would I be so preoccupied with sex?" Allendy replies, "All the more so." Nin's response—to herself, not to Allendy—is characteristic in that she dares not reveal her innermost thoughts to any human being, not even to the analyst. *Henry and June* conceals the secrets:

> I am thinking that with all the tremendous joys Henry has given me I have not yet felt a real orgasm. My response does not seem to lead to a true climax but is disseminated in a spasm that is less centered, more diffuse. I have felt an orgasm occasionally with Hugo, and when I have masturbated, but perhaps that is because Hugo likes me to close my legs, and Henry makes me open them so much. But this, I would not tell Allendy.

Although her words on the page are graphic, she hides the crucial material from the analyst from whom she purportedly seeks help for sexual problems. These words, it is worth reminding the reader, also never found their way into the original published version of her diary. Only in 1985 did they appear in the (still edited and expurgated volume) entitled *Henry and June*. Striking is this self-censorship in a woman inspired personally and professionally by Lawrence, enthralled by her reading of James Joyce, Freud, and Proust, and handmaiden to the birthing of Miller's lustiest novels. Bair, commenting on the failure of Nin's fiction, remarked in an interview with Cynthia Joyce:

> Most fiction writers take the stuff of their lives and the lives of the people around them and convert it into a form of fiction, but they somehow convert it into art. . . . Nin was always so afraid of being discovered for this transgression or that transgression, that she was never able to do that . . . [except with] the erotica [which] was going into a private collector's hands, it was never to be seen again in the world.

Nin could write graphic erotic fiction, that is, on the condition that only one person, the mysterious collector whom she never met, would read it. Ironically, her two volumes of erotica became her first best-sellers and the sole works of hers that are practically universally known.

The reasons behind this self-censorship deserve far more literary and psychological exploration than they have received thus far. Traditional feminist appeals to a female sense of shame and need for secrecy as a result of sexual oppression or exploitation by men do not go far enough. The specifics of Nin's unconscious defenses need to be known, especially since she attempted to delve into the Freudian, Jungian, and Rankian versions of the unconscious by a myriad of methods, from various forms of psychoanalytic treatment to surrealist experiments in automatic writing and misguided and random sexual adventures that she hoped would make her feel less inhibited. In the late 1950s, Bair records, she finally confessed to her psychoanalyst, Inge Bogner, that the only way she had been able to feel passion with all her many lovers was to fantasize that her father was "lifting my dress, pulling down my panties, spanking me—no, not spanking me, he is caressing me, he is making love to me. My mother will catch me."

The pathological role of her father in her life has gone underestimated as a definite influence on her literary style, specifically on her puzzling vacillations between the pornographic and the shyly reticent and on the compulsion to lie that seems to have frequently rendered inert her fine observational powers and critical abilities. When, however, the *Diary* is recognized as a lifelong expression of her torturously conflicted relationship with her father, her oddities of style become more understandable, psychologically and sometimes literarily interesting. In March 1935 she confesses in *Fire,* "Lying is the only way I have found to be true to myself, to do what I want, to be what I want with the least possible pain to others."

The identification with her father cost her emotional agony and sexual frustration. She was impressed by her father's assertion that he had bedded thousands of women. Idealizing him as a Don Juan, identifying with the aggressor who had stirred up her sexual responses so prematurely, Nin, Gore Vidal reports in Bair's book, "frequently referred to herself as 'Dona Giovanna,' a woman who could fuck men the way they fucked women." Only she could not. In the essay "Eroticism in Women," written several decades after her adult affair with her father, Nin writes: "From my personal observation, I would say that woman has not made the separation between love and sensuality which man has made. The two are usually combined in woman; she needs either to love the man she gives herself to or to be loved by him." The highly traditional language, "gives herself," for example, suggests a woman intent on satisfying the man rather than on achieving satisfaction herself.

THE EROTICA

Toward the end of her life, knowing that she was gravely ill, Nin's publishers persuaded her to publish the erotic tales she had written with Miller in the late 1930s and early 1940s for a wealthy collector. Two collections, *Delta of Venus* and *Little Birds* appeared in 1977 and 1979 respectively. She had not wanted to publish them, claiming that she feared her "style [in the erotica] was derived from a reading of men's works. For this reason I long felt that I had compromised my feminine self." However, rereading the stories after many years, she changed her mind, as recorded by Spencer: "I see that my own voice was not completely suppressed. In numerous passages I was intuitively using a woman's language, seeing sexual experience from a woman's point of view." In the interview with Joyce, Bair adds, "It's really the first time that a woman was able to express her own command of her own sexuality in a lyrical, beautiful form."

Critical response to these stories, like critical response to much of Nin, seems diametrically opposed. Typical among positive appraisers, Spencer writes in *Collage of Dreams*:

> The stories . . . are rendered in vivid sensuous prose, a prose that is poetic, filled with imagery, and yet plainer and more direct than the musical improvisatory style of Nin's fiction. . . .
>
> [She] portrays the pleasures of the senses with playfulness and joy. . . .
>
> Nin strikes . . . a characteristic blend of lyricism and humor as she explores a woman's discovery of the delicious variations on bodily pleasure.

Typical of negative responses to Nin's erotica, Pierpont writes, "What one notices, reading these stories from beginning to end, is that far from manifesting a new female freedom, or a 'joyous display of the erotic imagination,' as a cover quote promises, they are, in disconcerting proportion, tales of harrowing female frustration." Pierpont goes on to observe the frequency with which men in Nin's erotic tales are "passive," "wilted," "frightened," put off by the woman's desires, or leave her "unsatisfied" with "desire unanswered." Pierpont adds, "All the last-minute happily-ever-after 'submissions' are no match for the pages of sexual suffering and humiliation these women undergo." The exception perhaps is a woman damaged by early experience as is Nin, who relied on fantasies of humiliation for the only erotic gratification she ever received, as she confessed to her analyst.

Nin's idea that she was writing in a woman's voice for women did strike a chord with many women. Her erotica contains an immense variety of experience, including developed scenes of erotic flagellation, pedophilia, homoerotic lovemaking, and incest. The humiliation of women in many of these stories and their resentful endurance of men who do not complete intercourse at the moment they seem to want it may be aimed at an audience of women who, like Nin, felt arousal primarily from masochistic situations. In the interview with Joyce, Bair observes that many women she knew "left their partners, changed their sexual identity, just totally changed their lives, and in many instances really messed up their lives" in the wake of reading Nin's diary in the version originally published in the 1960s. When these women found out that Nin was not independent, especially not financially, and not at all in control of her sexual experiences, they angrily blamed Nin, Bair adds. Perhaps they blamed her for getting across the idea, both subtly and graphically, that most women know far less about their sexuality than most men do.

DEATH

Nin died on January 14, 1977, at Cedars of Lebanon Hospital in Los Angeles of cancer beginning in the vagina. Her cause of death seems chilling considering her popular appeal as a high priestess of sex and a seducer of many men. A woman driven, indeed tormented, by a craving for secrets and by her need to hide them, a bigamist who successfully concealed each husband from the other, she divided much of the last half of her life between her Los Angeles husband Pole and the man she had married at age twenty, the banker Guiler, who shared an apartment with her in New York's Greenwich Village. At her death the *Los Angeles Times* listed her husband as Pole, while the *New York Times* said she was married to Guiler. Neither marriage is mentioned in her world-famous diary. What she left out of her diary has attracted more scholarly and prurient attention than what she put into it. Kate Millett admires Nin's *Diary* and remarks, "Not since Henry James has an American laid claim to such fine perceptions, such exquisite discernments." Millett also observes: "There is a lot she leaves out. The *Diary* is as discreet as a maiden lady."

"What does the future hold for me?" Nin asked her diary, *Linotte,* at age sixteen. Part of her answer seems to prophesy the controversy that later surrounded her world-famous diary: "Each of us is a book without an Epilogue, an unfinished book whose Author reserves the right to write the ending, since He wrote the beginning." At that age Nin was already the author of her own life, merging the reporting of life with the imagining of it in her diary, proficient at telling whoppers, her most scholarly biographer Bair notes. Nin sensed that she was beginning a remarkable journey as a writer. "I am traveling in a country that has no landmarks," she observes in *Linotte*.

Selected Bibliography

WORKS OF ANAÏS NIN

DIARIES

The Diary of Anaïs Nin. Edited by Gunther Stuhlmann. Vol. 1, 1931–1934. New York: Harcourt, Brace and World, 1966. (Copublished with Swallow Press.) Vol. 2, 1934–1939. New York: Harcourt, Brace and World, 1967. (Copublished with Swallow Press.) Vol. 3, 1939–1944. New York: Harcourt, Brace and World, 1969. Vol. 4, 1944–1947. New York: Harcourt Brace Jovanovich, 1971. Vol. 5, 1947–1955. New York: Harcourt Brace Jovanovich, 1974. Vol. 6, 1955–1966. New York: Harcourt Brace Jovanovich, 1976. Vol. 7, 1966–1974. New York: Harcourt Brace Jovanovich, 1980.

The Early Diary of Anaïs Nin. Preface by Joaquin Nin-Culmell. Vol. 1, *Linotte: 1914–1920.* Translated from the French by Jean L. Sherman. New York: Harcourt Brace Jovanovich, 1978. Vol. 2, 1920–1923. New York: Harcourt Brace Jovanovich, 1982. Vol. 3, 1923–1927. San Diego, Calif.: Harcourt Brace Jovanovich, 1983. (Published as *Journal of a Wife.* London: Peter Owen, 1984.) Vol. 4, 1927–1931. San Diego, Calif.: Harcourt Brace Jovanovich, 1985.

Henry and June: From the Unexpurgated Diary of Anaïs Nin. San Diego, Calif.: Harcourt Brace Jovanovich, 1986.

Incest: From "A Journal of Love," The Unexpurgated Diary of Anaïs Nin, 1932–1934. New York: Harcourt Brace Jovanovich, 1992.

Fire: From "A Journal of Love," the Unexpurgated Diary of Anaïs Nin, 1934–1937. New York: Harcourt Brace, 1995.

Nearer the Moon: From "A Journal of Love," The Unexpurgated Diary of Anaïs Nin, 1937–1939. Harcourt Brace, 1996.

FICTION

House of Incest. Paris: Siana Éditions, 1936; Denver, Colo.: Swallow Press, 1958.

The Winter of Artifice. Paris: Obelisk Press, 1939.

Winter of Artifice: Three Novelettes. New York: Gemor Press, 1942; revised ed. Denver, Colo.: Swallow Press, 1961. (In the revised ed. the first story, "Djuna," is replaced by "Stella.")

The All-Seeing. New York: Gemor Press, 1944. (Chapbook, 40 copies). (Most Gemor Press editions include woodcuts by "Ian Hugo," the name adopted by Hugh Guiler, Nin's first husband.)

Under a Glass Bell, and Other Stories. New York: Gemor Press, 1944; New York: E. P. Dutton, 1948.

This Hunger. New York: Gemor Press, 1945. (Part 1 of *Ladders to Fire,* 1946.)

Ladders to Fire. New York: E. P. Dutton, 1946; Denver, Colo.: Swallow Press, 1966.

A Child Born out of the Fog. New York: Gemor Press, 1947. (Pamphlet.)

Children of the Albatross. New York: E. P. Dutton, 1947; Denver, Colo.: Swallow Press, 1966. (Swallow Press books are now published in Athens, Ohio, by the Ohio University Press.)

The Four-Chambered Heart. New York: Duell, Sloan and Pearce, 1950; Denver, Colo.: Swallow Press, 1966.

A Spy in the House of Love. Paris and New York: British Book Centre, 1954; Denver, Colo.: Swallow Press, 1966.

Solar Barque. New York: Anaïs Nin, 1958. (Expanded as *Seduction of the Minotaur,* 1961.)

Seduction of the Minotaur. Denver, Colo.: Swallow Press, 1961.

Collages. Denver, Colo.: Swallow Press, 1964.

Waste of Timelessness, and Other Early Stories. Weston, Conn.: Magic Circle Press, 1977.

EROTICA

Auletris. Carmel, Calif.: Press of the Sunken Eye, 1950. (Five typed, bound copies.)

Delta of Venus: Erotica. New York: Harcourt Brace Jovanovich, 1977. (Abridged as *The Illustrated Delta of Venus.* London: Allen, 1980.)

Little Birds: Erotica. New York: Harcourt Brace Jovanovich, 1979.

COLLECTIONS

Anaïs Nin Reader. Edited by Philip K. Jason. Introduction by Anna Balakian. Chicago: Swallow Press, 1973.

Cities of the Interior. Denver, Colo.: Swallow Press, 1961; with introduction by Sharon Spencer and preface by Anaïs Nin, Chicago: Swallow Press, 1974. (Includes *Ladders to Fire, Children of the Albatross, The Four-Chambered Heart, Spy in the House of Love,* and *Solar Barque.*)

SELECTED NONFICTION

(Excluding excerpts and reprints of the *Diary.*)

"The Mystic of Sex." In *Canadian Forum* 11, no 121:15–17 (October 1930). (On D. H. Lawrence.)

D. H. Lawrence: An Unprofessional Study. Paris: Edward W. Titus, 1932; with introduction by Harry T. Moore, Denver, Colo.: Swallow Press, 1964; London: Black Spring Press, 1964.

Preface to *Tropic of Cancer.* By Henry Miller. Paris: Obelisk Press, 1934.

Realism and Reality. New York: Alicat Book Store, 1946. (Reprinted in *The White Blackbird,* 1985 [chapbook].)

On Writing. Hanover, N.H.: Daniel Oliver Associates, 1947; revised with an essay on Nin's art by William Burford, Yonkers, N.Y.: O. Baradinsky, 1947.

"Alan Swallow." *Denver Quarterly* 2, no. 1:11–14 (spring 1967). (Reprinted in *Publishing in the West: Alan Swallow: Some Letters and Commentaries.* Edited by William F. Claire. Santa Fe, N.Mex.: Lightning Tree, 1974. Pp. 12–15.)

The Novel of the Future. New York: Macmillan, 1968.

Unpublished Selections from the Diary. Athens, Ohio: Duane Schneider Press, 1968.

Nuances. Cambridge, Mass.: Sans Souci Press, 1970.

"Dear Djuna Barnes (1937), with a Note (1971)." In *A Festschrift for Djuna Barnes on Her 80th Birthday.* Kent, Ohio: Kent State University Libraries, 1972. P. 12.

In Favor of the Sensitive Man, and Other Essays. New York: Harcourt Brace Jovanovich, 1976.

"Magic in Los Angeles." *Westways* 66, no. 1:28–31, 63 (January 1974). (Reprinted in *A Western Harvest: The Gatherings of an Editor.* Edited by Frances Ring. Santa Barbara, Calif.: John Daniel, 1991. Pp. 47–53.)

Portrait in Three Dimensions. Colored plates by Renate Druks. Los Angeles: Concentric Circle Press, 1979.

Preface to *My Sister, My Spouse: A Biography of Lou Andreas-Salomé,* by H. F. Peters. New York: Norton, 1974.

A Woman Speaks: The Lectures, Seminars, and Interviews of Anaïs Nin. Edited by Evelyn J. Hinz. Chicago: Swallow Press, 1975.

The White Blackbird and Other Writings. Santa Barbara, Calif.: Capra Press, 1985.

Conversations with Anaïs Nin. Edited by Wendy M. DuBow. Jackson, Miss.: University Press of Mississippi, 1994.

The Mystic of Sex: And Other Writings. Edited with a preface by Gunther Stuhlmann. Santa Barbara, Calif.: Capra Press, 1995. (Uncollected writings, 1931–1974.)

LETTERS

A Literate Passion: Letters of Anaïs Nin and Henry Miller, 1932–1953. Edited by Gunther Stuhlmann. San Diego, Calif.: Harcourt Brace Jovanovich, 1987.

Arrows of Longing: The Correspondence between Anaïs Nin and Felix Pollak, 1952–1976. Edited by Gregory H. Mason. Athens, Ohio: Swallow/Ohio University Press, 1998.

SOUND RECORDINGS BY ANAÏS NIN

Anaïs Nin, Contemporary Classics. Sound Portraits. Issued by Louis and Bebe Barron, 1949.

Anaïs Nin in Recital: Diary Excerpts and Comments. Caedmon TC 1613. 1979.

The Diary of Anaïs Nin, Volume One: 1931–1934 and Volume Two: 1934–1939. Spoken Arts SA995–996. 1968.

BIBLIOGRAPHIES

Cutting, Rose Marie. *Anaïs Nin: A Reference Guide.* Boston: G. K. Hall, 1978. (Fourteen supplements compiled by Richard R. Centing and published in *Under the Sign of Pisces: Anaïs Nin and Her Circle* 11, no. 2 [spring 1980] and 12, no. 2 [spring 1981] and in *Seahorse: The Anaïs Nin/Henry Miller Journal* 1 [1982] and 2 [1983].)

Franklin, Benjamin, V. *Anaïs Nin: A Bibliography.* Kent, Ohio: Kent State University Press, 1973.

————. "Anaïs Nin." In *Facts on File Bibliography of American Fiction, 1919–1988.* Edited by Matthew J. Bruccoli and Judith S. Baughman. New York: Facts on File, 1991. Pp. 379–381.

Goldsworthy, Joan. "Nin, Anaïs 1903–1977." In *Contemporary Authors, New Revision Series,* vol. 22. Edited by Deborah A. Straub. Detroit, Mich.: Gale Research, 1988. Pp. 340–345.

CRITICAL AND BIOGRAPHICAL STUDIES

Bair, Deirdre. *Anaïs Nin: A Biography.* New York: Putnam's, 1995.

Bawer, Bruce. Review of *Anaïs Nin: A Biography. New York Times Book Review,* March 5, 1995, p. 10.

Boyce, John. *Aphrodisiac: Erotic Drawings.* Introduction by Anaïs Nin. New York: Crown, 1976. (For selected passages from the works of *Anaïs Nin.*)

Fitch, Noël Riley. *Anaïs: The Erotic Life of Anaïs Nin.* Boston: Little, Brown, 1993.

Franklin, Benjamin, V., ed. *Recollections of Anaïs Nin.* Athens. Ohio: Ohio State University Press, 1996.

Joyce, Cynthia. "Dear Diary: Deirdre Bair on the Secret Life of Anaïs Nin." *Salon* (http://www.salon.com/weekly/bair960729.html), April 18, 1996.

Millett, Kate. "Anaïs: A Mother to Us All." In *Anaïs: An International Journal* 9:3–8 (1991).

Pierpont, Claudia Roth. "Sex, Lies, and Thirty-five Thousand Pages." In *Passionate Minds: Women Rewriting the World.* New York: Knopf, 2000.

Podnieks, Elizabeth. *Daily Modernism: The Literary Diaries of Virginia Woolf, Antonia White, Elizabeth Smart, and Anaïs Nin.* Montreal, Canada: McGill-Queen's University Press, 2000.

Pollitt, Katha. "Sins of the Nins." *New York Times Book Review,* November 22, 1992, p. 3. (Review of *Incest: From "A Journal of Love," The Unexpurgated Diary of Anaïs Nin, 1932–1934.*)

Richard-Allerdyce, Diane. *Anaïs Nin and the Remaking of Self: Gender, Modernism, and Narrative Identity.* De Kalb: Northern Illinois University Press, 1998.

Schneider, Duane. *An Interview with Anaïs Nin.* Athens, Ohio: Duane Schneider Press, 1970.

Spencer, Sharon. *Collage of Dreams: The Writings of Anaïs Nin.* Expanded ed., New York: Harcourt Brace Jovanovich, 1981.

PERIODICALS DEVOTED TO ANAÏS NIN

Anaïs: An International Journal. Edited by Gunther Stuhlmann. Becket, Mass. Annual. Vols. 1–18 (1983–2000).

Seahorse: The Anaïs Nin/Henry Miller Journal. Edited by Richard R. Centing. Columbus, Ohio: Ohio State University Libraries. Quarterly. Vols. 1–2. (1982–1983).

Under the Sign of Pisces: Anaïs Nin and Her Circle. Edited by Richard R. Centing and until 1973 Benjamin Franklin V. Columbus, Ohio: Ohio State University Libraries. Quarterly. Vols. 1–12 (1970–1981).

FILMS ABOUT ANAÏS NIN

Snyder, Robert. *Anaïs Nin Observed: Portrait of a Woman as Artist.* 60 min. 1974. Documentary film.

Kaufman, Philip. *Henry and June.* 1990. Feature film based on Anaïs Nin's *Diary.*

FILMS FEATURING ANAÏS NIN

Anger, Kenneth. *Inauguration of the Pleasure Dome.* 1950.

Deren, Maya. *Ritual in Transfigured Time.* 1946.

Hugo, Ian [Hugo Guiler]. *Apertura.* 1970.

Hugo, Ian [Hugh Guiler]. *Bells of Atlantis.* 1953.

Hugo, Ian [Hugo Guiler]. *Jazz of Lights.* 1954.

Hugo, Ian [Hugo Guiler]. *Melodic Inversion.* 1958.

Hugo, Ian [Hugo Guiler]. *Through the Magicscope.* 1968.

Snyder, Robert. *The Henry Miller Odyssey.* 1969.

—*MELISSA KNOX*

Sharon Olds

1942–

THE PHILOSOPHY OF Sharon Olds is "Flinch not. Tell the truth about it," and this credo has been evident in her work since the publication of her first book, *Satan Says,* in 1980. She has addressed issues such as domestic violence, sexuality, religion, and death with the kind of intimacy normally reserved for the confessional. Whether or not readers appreciate this stance is another matter and has been at the center of an ongoing controversy about her poetry.

Since the appearance of *Satan Says,* which won the inaugural San Francisco Poetry Center Award, Olds's detractors have been as passionate as her advocates. Readers are seldom lukewarm about her poetry. Members of the audience have been known to leave her readings offended; others have given her standing ovations. This range of response helps to explain her large following as one of the best-selling poets in the United States. Most readers find her intense. As G. E. Murray remarked in a 1981 review of *Satan Says,* "Olds makes poetry as if she were lancing boils and enjoying it." In a review of the same book in 1983, William Logan stated that "her images are powerful . . . but. . . . they establish so quickly an economy of violence, where one horrible effect can only be succeeded, or exceeded, by another, that the poems soon depend on violence for vitality." Others praise her for being a highly readable poet. As Michael Bugeja stressed in a 1985 review of Olds's second collection, *The Dead and the Living* (1984), "If universality were the main criterion—the ability to appeal to baker and bricklayer, as well as to scholar and fellow poet—then . . . one name, above all, stands out: Sharon Olds."

Olds was born in San Francisco on November 19, 1942. She received a B.A. from Stanford University in 1964 (cum laude), a Ph.D. from Columbia University in 1972, and has taught at such institutions as Sarah Lawrence College, Columbia University, and Brandeis University. From 1992 she has worked as a professor of English at New York University, where she teaches in the graduate writing program. The recipient of a Lila Wallace–Reader's Digest Writer's Award from 1993–1996, she was recognized for founding a creative writing program at Goldwater Hospital on Roosevelt Island in New York, where she and NYU student volunteers work with patients with physical challenges. Her literary prizes include a Guggenheim, 1981–1982, and a National Endowment for the Arts fellowship, 1982–1983; she was named New York State Poet from 1998–2000. Married, with two grown children, at the start of the twenty-first century, she lived in New York City. Olds has made a decision not to disclose information about her personal life. This reticence, combined with the startling candor of her poems, has created an air of mystery, adding to her popularity.

OLDS AS CONFESSIONAL POET

From the beginning of her career, Olds has been linked with the confessional poets of the mid-twentieth century, especially Anne Sexton and Sylvia Plath, although some find her less technically interesting than her predecessors. In 2001 Kathleen Ossip pointed out the difficulty in writing confessional poetry at the turn of the twenty-first century:

> In 1959, the literary community represented by the Boston-centered, WASP-Identified confessional poets had considerable allure . . . that can be seen in retrospect as problematic. . . . Poets have every reason to question the first-person narrative centered around a single self. The heterogeneity of society and omnipresence of material from all corners of the globe can seem to make the individual voice less significant than it ever has been.

Not only is it difficult to assert the primacy of the self in a global age, but the threshold for shock value is now higher. Plath and Sexton's mental illness and Plath's rage, directed toward both her dead father and her estranged husband, now seem commonplace. Olds, who writes about topics ranging from a slippery diaphragm to the pope's penis, prompted the critic James Finn Cotter to quip that "confessional poetry becomes *True Confessions* in Sharon Olds." A measure of voyeurism is unavoidable in reading her work. As the speaker of "The Indispensability of the Eyes," from *Satan Says,* laments, "What went on at home / I couldn't bear to see." Yet Olds writes about the unbearable, and readers strain to look.

One important question raised in Olds's work—and in that of all confessional poets—is whether the work is literally true. Olds, like Sexton, has sidestepped the issue. In an interview for the online magazine *Salon,* she told Dwight Garner that she wishes to be "accurate," but then stated: "I don't just mean mathematically accurate. But to get it right according to my vision." She added, "To me the difference between the paper world and the flesh world is so great that I don't think we could put ourselves in our poems if we wanted to." Yet if the speaker of the poems is not Olds, she shares Olds's personal concerns, as well as her troubled family history.

SATAN SAYS

The title poem of *Satan Says* presents the struggle that has informed Olds's work since the beginning of her career: How does one address a troubled family history without being consumed by anger, even hatred? What price is there to pay for truth, and is there a price that one is not willing to pay? In "Satan Says" the speaker addresses "the pain of the locked past." Pictured as locked inside a cedar box and "trying to write [her] / way out," the speaker is tempted by Satan, who offers hate as a way to open the "heart-shaped lock," the way out of the self, as defined by the past, and to the necessary catharsis. "*Say / My father is a shit,*" says Satan. "*Say your mother is a pimp,*" adding, "*Say shit, say death, say fuck the father.*" This dismantling of the family promises freedom from former suffering:

> The pain of the locked past buzzes
> in the child's box on her bureau, under
> the terrible round pond eye
> etched with roses, where
> self-loathing gazed at sorrow.

The speaker is torn, stating, "I love them but / I'm trying to say what happened to us in the lost past." Satan gives her a view of life before her birth—her parents making love—and invites her to "come out" and thus erase history. Yet she cannot; she cannot take "the exit . . . through Satan's mouth." When she refuses to take his words and accepts her own, he seals her in, and she must deal with the suffocating pain and beauty of her past. Even if, as Satan asserts, this choice, to engage and come to terms with the past, may be her "coffin," she accepts the risk and "warms . . . her hands / in . . . the suddenly discovered knowledge of love."

Satan Says is organized around the motif of a journey. While the first poem in the book emphasizes an inward path, the book itself illustrates a parallel outward path, with its four sections, "Daughter," "Woman," "Mother," and "Journey," emphasizing growth. The simplicity of such an organizational strategy belies the difficulty of the emotional struggle that the book presents, and seems to amount to a statement on the author's part in the vein of, "I at least know this much to be true." Ironically, this book, which is anchored in female labels, is heavily informed by fathers, both literal and poetic.

For Olds, the most important figure is the literal father, and like Plath, whose father is viewed as both "the Colossus" and a Nazi, she uses imagery of vastness and emotional amplitude to make her point. In "Love Fossil," she faces the otherness of her father in the shape of a dinosaur, the "super sleazy extinct beast my heart dug for." What separates father and daughter is not only the fact that the father is huge, but that he is vegetarian; by contrast, the speaker, a carnivore, longs for his "meat": "I did not understand his doom or my taste for the big dangerous body." She acknowledges his faults, and yet she is fascinated by him; watching him, she is always the helpless voyeur. Like a scientist digging for fossils, she digs for love.

Olds, like Plath, is not afraid to link the suffering of her speakers to the suffering of millions in the Holocaust. In "That Year" the speaker sees her individual suffering mirrored first in the rape and death of a classmate and then in the experience of the Jews during World War II:

> The year of the mask of blood, my father
> hammering on the glass door to get in
>
> was the year they found her body in the hills,
> in a shallow grave, naked, white as
> mushroom, partially decomposed,
> raped, murdered, the girl from my class.
>
> That was the year my mother took us and
> hid us so he could not get at us
> when she told him to leave.

She moves through her personal family to the human family:

> in Social Studies, we came at last
> to Auschwitz. I recognized it
> like my father's face, the face of the guard
> turning away—or worse yet
> turning toward me.

While the speaker has this horrifying vision of her father, what she ultimately takes away from the experience is that she survived it. In this sense, Olds deflects the criticism that Irving Howe and others have made about Plath's use of the concentration camps as poetic devices. The speaker has "survived"; indeed, much of Olds's poetry is about what it means to be a survivor: living through difficult experiences, becoming empowered as a result, and returning to the past as a new, strong person.

Olds links herself with the literary past as well, particularly with Walt Whitman, who nursed the dying during the Civil War. This makes sense, given Whitman's candor, his open sexuality, and his long, breathless poetic lines; in "Nurse Whitman," the speaker makes allusions to her personal civil war, admitting, "You move between the soldiers' cots / the way I move among my dead, / their white bodies laid out in lines." She blurs the sexual and temporal boundaries between herself and Whitman, recognizing that they are both "conceiving" poems through their relationships with men.

While women are not as important as men in this book, the mother figure plays a crucial, if problematic, role. In "Quake Theory" Olds writes, "When two plates of earth scrape along each other / like a mother and a daughter / it is called a fault." Bitterness arises because of the mother's role in the household and raises important questions. Can the mother prevent the abuse of the father? Can she will herself not to see what is happening in the home? In fact, in "Tricks," the mother goes so far as to take out her eyes, replacing them with "oil . . . bourbon and feces." It is the mother's sexual relationship with the father that is the critical point:

> In the grand finale
> she draws my father
> slowly out of her cunt and puts him
> in a tall hat
> and he disappears.

Her mother is "a hole in space"; she can also make things "whole." If we conflate the speaker and Olds, the daughter too becomes something of a magician, by writing the poem and manipulating her mother's image. From this position of power, she draws up from the past her earlier, victimized self. She goes on to assert her power in "The Rising Daughter," saying, "I would be / for myself, then, an enemy / to all who do not wish me to rise."

The next two sections of the book, "Woman" and "Mother," explore a female world that the speaker of these poems seems to find alien; Olds, at least early on in her work, seems more comfortable writing about men. "The Language of the Brag" asserts her desires for achievement and links her not only with Walt Whitman but with Allen Ginsberg, whom she admires for the same reasons. The speaker admits, "I have wanted some epic use for my excellent body, / some heroism, some American achievement / beyond the ordinary for my extraordinary self." Here, though, Olds takes the idea of literary conception and wrings it out through the female body. Her argument is that men have wanted to give birth and cannot; she can do that: "I have / passed the new person out." She as woman has trumped both poets and men.

The last section of *Satan Says* illustrates the extent of the journey, traveling back from the past to the present. In the first poem of the section, the speaker, having grown up, can approach her father through "time travel," choosing the best memories: "He belongs to me forever like this." In the last poem of the section, the speaker has her own life, as she says

in "Prayer," "Let me be faithful to the central meanings." She has moved from Satan to prayer in the course of the book, saying about the birth of her daughter and her own rebirth as a mother, "let me not forget: / each action, each word / taking its beginning from these." The book effects a reconciliation with the past, allowing the speaker to "take [her] beginning" not from the injurious past but from her moment of rebirth.

THE DEAD AND THE LIVING

Olds's second book, *The Dead and the Living* (1984), which was the Lamont Poetry Selection for 1983 and the National Book Critics' Circle Award for Poetry in 1984, explores some of the same themes as *Satan Says,* but frames them differently. The cover of the book—which, like all the covers of her books published by Knopf, was chosen by Olds—helps to set the tone: a 1910 photograph by Frank Eugene titled "Adam and Eve." In the photograph, the couple are naked, with Adam turned away from the camera and Eve facing it; they are innocent no longer. Stephen Behrendt stresses "their displacement into a wilderness both material and psychological." This loss of innocence is important to Olds, as is the idea of exile. With her focus on innocence versus experience, Olds once again returns to the personal. As Linda McCarriston points out, Olds, in a variation of William Carlos Williams's famous line, believes that there are "No ideas but in beings." The critical consensus at the time of its publication was that *The Dead and the Living* was a better book than *Satan Says,* revealing her earlier promise and unveiling her characteristic themes with more craft.

The book is divided into two parts: "Poems for the Dead," subdivided into "Public" and "Private," and "Poems for the Living." In organizing the first section this way, Olds expands her scope by personalizing historical events. Linda Gregerson adds, "The 'public' poems wish to cast off all issues but those of human suffering and its deep counter-argument, the stubborn faith and sublime intelligence of the human body, its survival and its eloquent representation (in children, in photographs, and in imagination)." Yet the personal or "private" poems take up three-quarters of the book. Gregerson argues that these poems are even more effective as political arguments because here Olds illustrates the workings of power though the dynamics she knows best: family. In addition, Olds is able to make her case outside established public opinion on the issues.

In the book's public poems, Olds addresses topics such as execution ("Ideographs," "Nevsky Prospekt," and "Aesthetics of the Shah"), race ("Race Riot, Tulsa, 1921"), drought ("Photograph of the Girl"), and celebrity ("The Death of Marilyn Monroe"). Because these poems are often written in the third person and based on photographs, they might be described as more objective than Olds's former works. Yet the overall feel to them is personal. The suffering that infuses her earlier poems surfaces in a dying man's look, transmitting the message, *Save me, there is time* ("Ideographs"); a dead man's "face tilted up / toward the sky, to get the sun on it, to / darken it more and more toward the color of the human" ("Race Riot, Tulsa, 1921"); an ambulance driver's transformation after transporting an American icon:

> . . . listening to a
> woman breathing, just an ordinary
> woman
> breathing.
>
> ("The Death of Marilyn Monroe")

The ending of the poem "The Issues" underscores her attitude that what is public is understood only through the personal: "Don't speak to me about / politics. I've got eyes, man."

In the section's "private" poems, Olds addresses grandparents, friends, miscarriage, and abortion. A common theme is loss of innocence.

In "The End" a couple decides to terminate a pregnancy, but subsequent events intervene. An automobile accident occurs outside the couple's home, and their guilt about their decision to end the pregnancy makes them feel somehow responsible for the carnage they view out their window. The description of the bodies being removed from the wreckage parallels the abortion procedure: "Cops pulled the bodies out / bloody as births from the small, smoking aperture of the door." After this event, the woman gets her period:

> The next morning I had to kneel
> an hour on that floor, to clean up my blood,
> rubbing with wet cloths at those dark
> translucent spots, as one has to soak
> a long time to deglaze the pan
> when the feast is over.

The original feast of the relationship is over, and the couple cannot return to their former "innocent" state. Martin Kich is troubled, however, by the series of events needed to make that point: "While it is possible that the stress caused by, first, deciding to abort, and, second, witnessing a horrible wreck might trigger the woman's menstruation, one wonders what would have happened had the accident not occurred." He feels that a preoccupation with these issues lessens the impact of the poem's "more profound implications."

The second section, "Poems for the Living," is divided into three subsections: "The Family," "The Men," and "The Children." All of these extend the theme of loss of innocence, highlighting such topics as victimization, sexuality, and rebirth.

Ideas of victimization and power are prevalent, often conveyed through Holocaust imagery. These images are not only associated with the father, but with other family members: the sister as the führer—"Hitler entered Paris the way my / sister entered my room at night" ("The Takers"); the sister as protector or shield ("The

Elder Sister"); the brother assuming his own self-punishment:

> I can see you
> sending your body to hell as they sent us to
> bed without supper. . . .
> .   .   .   .
> Please, don't. Please, don't
> do their work for them.
>   ("Late Speech with My Brother")

Relationships are examined, severed, reformed, reenvisioned, lost. Family is never seen as whole, but broken, for which a tremendous price has been paid.

Loss of innocence is also revealed through sex, one of Olds's signature topics. She delves into a first sexual relationship ("Poem to My First Lover"), sex after childbirth ("New Mother"), lovers faced with illness ("The Line"), and casual sex: "How do they do it?" ("Sex Without Love"). The poems emphasize the moment, illustrated best in the final poem in the section on men, "Ecstasy":

> As we made love for the third day,
> . . . we did not stop
> but went into it and into it and
> did not hesitate. . . .

In such poems, sex makes it possible for Olds to adopt a carpe diem philosophy; she meaningfully admits, "We did not turn back."

Children make it possible to start over; in addition, they are a way to reexamine one's own childhood, which for the speaker involves an examination of gender roles. Against the backdrop of earlier fear and victimization, the speaker says of her daughter, in "Exclusive," I am "memorizing you / against the time when you will not be with me." In these poems about the physical and emotional development of children, there is acute awareness of sexual difference, as well as of sexuality itself, underscoring the speaker's abusive background. Thus, the son, at six years old, lifts his penis, "hard as a heavy-duty canvas fire-hose" and urinates on the lawn ("Six-Year-Old Boy"); the daughter "moans" in protest of having eggs for breakfast as she approaches adolescence ("Eggs"), and begins to prepare for adulthood ("Bread"). The speaker contemplates her daughter's future sex life ("For My Daughter"), and the six- and seven-year-old warriors who attend her son's birthday party ("Rite of Passage"), particularly their potential for violence as men. At the same time, Olds uses the image of the chrysalis for both children as the two outgrow their childhood clothes ("Size and Sheer Will," "Pajamas"). As they mature, they reflect characteristics of the speaker's family members—"my daughter looks at me with an / amber black look, like my father / about to pass out from disgust" ("The Sign of Saturn")—and the speaker's wish is to pull her children away from the past's negative influence. Eventually, as she did from her parents, the children will go on without her—whatever their history, good or bad; however much the speaker regrets this inevitability, she admits, "It's an old / story— the oldest we have on our planet— / the story of replacement" ("35/10"). The last poem in the book leaves the reader with an image of the two children having fallen asleep in the car, and the speaker "finding their only union in sleep, in the dark solitary / power of the dream—the dream of ruling the world" ("The Couple").

THE GOLD CELL

The Gold Cell (1987) cemented Olds's reputation as an intimate and often shocking poet, or, as Peter Harris remarked in a 1998 review of the book, as a poet of "make-you-squirm explicitness." Andrew Hudgins, while taking issue with Olds in terms of her narrative development (in his opinion, the bodies of the poems are not as effective as their beginnings and endings), admitted that "she's a lot of fun to read" and that the poems are "hypnotic."

The Gold Cell recalls Olds's previous book, *The Dead and the Living,* with a public part prefacing three personal sections. The revisiting of this organization acknowledges the human compulsion to rewrite history until it makes emotional sense. As Alicia Ostriker pointed out in a 1995 essay, "Olds is never represented in isolation but always in relation, penetrated and penetrating, glued by memory and gaze to others." Yet, for some, the central issue with regard to the book is less one of relationship than of repetition. In a 1998 review of *The Gold Cell,* Peter Harris stated that "the poems too often seem in the same voice, searching for the same kinds of insights with the same rhythm of acceleration as her last book." Yet he went on to write, "That should not obscure the fact that she writes with great flair and often shows a resonant dramatic intelligence in searching out the contexts, or the frameworks of implication, in which to lodge and justify her dark witness-bearing."

While Satan frames Olds's first book and Adam and Eve set the tone for her second, here the dominant image is the cell. The cover features a gold circle, with a snake coiled around it. In a 1987 review of the book, Ostriker described the paradox of the image: "'The gold cell' as a figure for life's primary unit implies both entrapment . . . and pure treasure." Elsewhere, Stephen Yenser expanded upon the image: "This gold cell is . . . protean and recurrent. . . . If among other things the gold cell is the gamete, it can also be understood as the very principle of life." He added,

> The jacket illustration . . . acknowledges Jung's study, *The Archetypes and the Collective Unconscious,* where the source turns out to be the section entitled "Concerning Mandala Symbolism," in which the plate is described as "an Indian picture of *Shiva-bindu,* the unextended point," or Shiva in the primordial state, encircled by Shakti,

the snake that "signifies extension, the mother of Becoming, the creation of the world of forms." At the moment that Shakti embraces the extended point, known also as the "golden germ" or "golden egg," creation begins.

In her public poems there is this assertion of life over death, often illustrated through a moment of recognition. Olds deals with dramatic public topics—a potential suicide ("Summer Solstice, New York City"), race ("On the Subway"), an abandoned baby ("The Abandoned Newborn"), Siamese twins ("The Twin"), a rape and murder ("The Girl"). She asserts life over death more fancifully—and some might say sacrilegiously—in her poem "The Pope's Penis," where the Pope's penis "stands up / in praise of God." In a startling poem about nuclear war, a mother holds her small daughter, and the two, rather than exhibiting fear or horror, see only the beauty of the bomb ("When").

Olds moves from this point, the end of the world, to the start of her own life, and contemplates never having been born. "I Go Back to May 1937" revisits the devil's invitation in "Satan Says" to disown the parents and erase them:

> I want to go up to them and say Stop,
> don't do it—she's the wrong woman,
> he's the wrong man, you are going to do things
> you cannot imagine you would ever do,
> you are going to do bad things to children,
> you are going to suffer in ways you never heard
> of,
> you are going to want to die.

However, eliminating this past means eliminating the self. The speaker admits, "I want to live," then addresses her parents: "Do what you are going to do, and I will tell about it." Both in this book and across Olds's career, the child as witness becomes increasingly empowered by the writer as witness.

Not only is Olds's speaker empowered by Olds as writer, she is empowered by the knowledge and experience she gains as an adult. In "What if God" the speaker questions a God who will allow a mother to be complicit in her own daughter's victimization. God is compared to a masturbating buffalo, a curious squirrel, a biology student, and a rapist. In a twist of events, the speaker longs to go back to save her mother, since God couldn't save either one of them. The speaker, as an adult woman, will provide the solace she couldn't give her mother as a child:

Is there a God in the house? Then reach down and
take that woman off that child's body,
take that woman by the nape of the neck like a
   young cat and
lift her up and deliver her over to me.

She will not only be her own parent, she will be her own God.

A poem that may stand as a microcosm of Olds's work as a whole is "Now I Lay Me," which explores domestic abuse through the familiar childhood prayer beginning "Now I lay me down to sleep," and once again focuses on witnessing. The child, who is praying throughout the poem, feels lost, surrounded by parents whom she sees as beasts, with "their / fur and their thick varnished hairs." She envisions God wrestling the father for her soul and possibly losing. Most telling about the poem is its earnestness, with the child going through the cycle of prayer each night, as if one day the story will turn out differently; such revisiting is familiar in Olds's work. Ironically, "Now I Lay Me" is one of the few personal poems not written in the first person; this uncharacteristic distancing illustrates, perhaps, the poet's difficulty in directly revisiting this particular subject.

The possibility and implications of forgiveness are at stake here. In "After 37 Years My Mother Apologizes for My Childhood," the mother's apology for her complicity in the sexual abuse by the father redefines the speaker's worldview: "I could not / see what I would do with the rest of my life." She admits, "I hardly knew what I / said or who I would be now that I had forgiven you." After looking for a way out of her locked box, she finds it, but now what? What can it mean to open the box oneself?

In *The Gold Cell,* Olds's mature style is evident, the poems without stanza breaks, the breathlessness of presentation, the comma splices and unnatural line breaks. In "First Sex" the speaker describes watching her lover reaching sexual climax:

. . . he gathered and shook and the actual
flood like milk came out of his body, I
saw it glow on his belly, all they had
said and more, I rubbed it into my
hands like lotion, I signed on for the duration.

Yenser, for one, finds that the unnatural line breaks create a feeling of "erasure," while Ostriker finds them "puzzling." In any event, they allow her poems to move swiftly down the page, so that some critics, like Yenser, claim that it is impossible to quote Sharon Olds without quoting her at length, so intertwined are her style and content.

Olds's preoccupation with sexuality deepens in *The Gold Cell.* The poem titled "It" captures a range of feelings about sex: from "fit[ting] together like the . . . body of the banana," to being "comb[ed]" by glass, to being left in a state of awe: "I / sit on my bed the next day with my mouth open and think of it." "Topography" uses geographic entities to playfully illustrate the joining of bodies: "my / San Francisco against your New York, your / Fire Island against my Sonoma."

Ultimately *The Gold Cell* stresses the importance of loving and appreciating life, and usually children help to make this point. In "Little Things" the speaker admits, "I am doing something I learned early to do, I am / paying attention to small beauties, whatever I have." Thus, the speaker in other poems in the section studies the way her daughter eats a piece of fruit ("Liddy's Orange"), and the way her son's shirt captures his vulnerability ("The Green Shirt"). The speaker is sensitive to the fragility of the world—her son's susceptibility to harm ("The Latest Injury") and the death of a mouse ("Mouse Elegy"). There is such specificity of detail concerning the smallest of gestures that we believe the speaker when she says, in "That Moment," "It is almost too long ago to remember— / when I was a woman without children." In the poems about her children Olds does everything she can to remember, whereas in many of her poems about the past she remembers in spite of herself.

THE FATHER

The Father (1992), which was short-listed for England's T. S. Eliot prize, chronicles the death of Olds's father from cancer. Brian Dillon points out that, up until *The Father,* "Rather than one full-length *Prelude*-like account, Olds offers snapshots, literally dozens of short poems, a few which metaphorically delineate the father damaging the family structure, and others which narrate in specific detail the father's brutal presence." Here the plot about the father is extended. The book faces many of the difficult issues of Olds's work—the influence of the father, the difficulty of loving an abusive person—and traces in a painful series of poems the last days of the father's life. Lee Upton remarked that readers "will be battered by it." Laura E. Tanner emphasized the importance of the witness—or, the "gaze"—in this book: "The death-watcher dissolves the subject/object dynamics of the gaze until the healthy subject is forced to acknowledge its own mortality, and the watcher becomes the watched." Many critics found this collection repetitive, with too much dwelling on the minutiae of death. Louise Gluck found that Olds had not grown as a poet. At the same time, no reader questioned the intensity of the poems.

Olds does not use the possessive "my father" as the title of the book but the indefinite "the father," as if acknowledging the layering of male influence—both personal and poetic—upon her work. The book is not broken up into sections, and there is no cover picture. The typeface throughout is plain, as if setting the tone for the serious matter of the collection.

The first poem, "The Waiting," with its emphasis on the daughter approaching the father, is typical of the poems in the book:

> No matter how early I would get up
> and come out of the guest room, and look down
>   the hall, there between the wings of the wing-
>   back chair
> my father would be sitting. . . .
> · · · · · · · · · · · · · · ·
>   . . . like something someone has made.

At issue is the speaker's desire for the father to come to her, to make a gesture that will make sense of the complicated past. He does perform small actions, like clipping a loose thread off her bathrobe in "Nullipara," but throughout the book the speaker is waiting for more. Meanwhile, the speaker is contemplating her father's transformation. He is bulging with growths "like a stocking stuffed with things" ("The Picture I Want"), and he "shines" as he moves toward death ("The Lumens"). Part of this change involves forgetfulness about the past. When the father looks at a portable altar, brought to his hospital room by a minister, the daughter is reminded of her childhood and her jewelry box, with its

>   ballerina who un-
> bent . . . she
> rose and twirled like the dead. Then the lid
> folded her down, bowing, in the dark,
> the way I would wait, under my bed,
> for morning.
>   ("His Terror")

As the father moves toward death, it is difficult for the two of them to acknowledge the past, and so there is only the present.

The speaker lives with contradictory emotions. On the one hand, she remembers her father's cruel comments—"*Women yakking. . . / Women are so / stupid it destroys your mind*" ("The Want"). On the other hand, she is receiving the tenderness and intimacy she has wanted from her father all her life. When he shows her his cancerous body, she is in awe:

> . . . If anyone had ever told me
> I would sit by him and he would pull up his
>   nightie
> and I would look at him, at his naked body,
> at the thick bud of his penis in all that
> dark hair, look at him
> in affection and uneasy wonder
> I would not have believed it.
>
> ("The Lifting")

She gives him a back rub ("The Look"); she would like to wash him ("Last Acts"); and she is extravagantly pleased by his request for a kiss ("Last Words"). She sums up her feelings movingly in "Wonder":

> . . . I would have traded
> places with anyone raised on love,
> but how would anyone raised on love
> bear this death?

As Harold Schweizer has suggested, the speaker focuses on the father as a body, not as someone through whom it is possible to receive a larger "spiritual" understanding. In "The Dead Body" she admits,

> . . . I stood by him
> in the hospital and stroked him, touched his
> arm, his hair, I did not think he was there
> but this was the one I had known anyway.

After his death, she is taken by the fact that in some ways she is glad that he's gone, because he won't be able to take his last acts of affection away from her ("Beyond Harm"). One year later, she lies down on his grave and falls asleep, kissing his gravestone and licking the dirt surrounding his body ("One Year"). Still, one memory snakes around another, as in her poem "Natural History," where she remembers her terror at being held up by her father in front of an eel at the aquarium and offered as food. She remembers her father, like an eel, passed out on the couch, and then later she offers herself to the dead eel of her father underground.

Certain longings of the speaker are never satisfied. She admits,

> I wanted to watch my father die
> because I hated him. Oh, I loved him,
> my hands cherished him, laying him out,
> but I had feared him so.
> ("I Wanted to Be There When My Father Died")

Some of the most moving poems in the book include those in which the speaker imagines her father saying loving things about her. In "When the Dead Ask My Father about Me" the father says, "I liked her exaggerated passions. . . . She was a dream to tease. . . . I liked that she was bad." The last poem in the book, "My Father Speaks to Me from the Dead," which Peter Scheponik suggests "taunts"—like Olds's other work—with the idea of incest, is the clearest example of the speaker's attempt to "rewrite" history. The father speaks lovingly about the daughter, finally, from the grave:

> I love your bony shoulders and you know I
> love your hair, thick and live
> as earth. . . .
> .   .   .   .   .
> I love your brain.

He speaks of what to him matters most—matter itself:

> I understand this life, I am matter,
> your father, I made you, when I say now that I
>   love you
> I mean look down at your hand, move it,
> that action is matter's love, for human
> love go elsewhere.

An offering is made, beyond the human grave, by the daughter, who has always wanted human love from her father.

THE WELLSPRING

In turning from *The Father* to *The Wellspring* (1996) Olds moves from Thanatos to Eros. The cover of the latter book, blue with a rush of white, evoking ripples on water, suggests that here the emphasis is on renewal.

While *The Wellspring* develops along the lines of her previous books, divided according to stages of life, this volume does not end with the subject of children but with sex. James Sutherland-Smith, in a 1998 essay, pointed out that "the divisions are an occasion for a surface decorum and cordon off erotic recollection from the recollections of her children." At the same time, Sutherland-Smith emphasized that these poems about children are nevertheless erotic.

The poems addressing the past often convey a sense of shame. In "The Lisp" the speaker admits, "Sometimes they liked me," and proceeds to explain the way her family made fun of her inability to make the *s* sound. Her pain drives her to her own cruelty, emphasized in "Dirty Memories":

> . . . I'm talking about the power of putting
> poison into the bowl with my sister's
> fish. My chest was hot as I poured,
> I'm saying I was *glad*.

Yet it is only when one is guilty, lost, and shamed that redemption is possible. "Mrs. Krikorian" concerns a sixth-grade teacher who becomes a savior. She shows the speaker kindness and offers her books as release from the pain of her life. The speaker unravels Mrs. Krikorian's past, speculating on what forces and events are responsible for bringing this good woman to her rescue. The speaker postulates,

> I end up owing my soul to so many,
> to the Armenian nation, one more soul someone

jammed behind a stove, drove
deep into a crack in a wall,
shoved under a bed.

This image of being under the bed is a segue to the speaker's personal history, her own experience in childhood of finding herself under the bed upon waking in the morning. She is reduced to dust in this state, and Mrs. Krikorian teaches her to breathe in the world of ideas.

Release in the next section is achieved through sexuality. "Adolescence" is about first sexual encounters, involving a dirty hotel room and experimentation with birth control. In these poems there is an air of discovery, of humor, and of vulnerability:

> . . . And I could not learn to get that
> diaphragm in, I'd decorate it
> like a cake, with glistening spermicide,
> and lean over, and it would leap from my fingers.

She discloses in "The Source" that sexuality "became the deep spring of my life." The poems, though written from an adult perspective, continue to communicate discovery. The speaker says in "The Source,"

> To reach around both sides of a man,
> one palm to one buttock,
> the other palm to the other, the way we are split,
> to grasp that band of muscle on the male
> haunch and help guide the massed
> heavy nerve down my throat until it
> stoppers the hold behind the breastbone that is
>   always
> hungry, then I feel complete.

Yet in the last poem in the section ("May 1968"), it is the child that the speaker is carrying that has weight, both literally and figuratively. In the middle of a student protest in 1968, the speaker realizes that her involvement in this activity has put both herself and her child at risk. She thinks that she will die:

I looked at the steel arc of the horse's
shoe, the curve of its belly, the cop's
nightstick, the buildings streaming up
away from the earth.

Her wish is to keep the police at bay, and
miraculously they keep their distance, the horses
lying down like the lion with the lamb. In the
meantime, she has promised her life to her
daughter.

Part 3 of *The Wellspring* opens Olds to the
criticism, as noted by Sutherland-Smith, that the
poems sexualize children and the experience of
motherhood. The first poem of the section,
"First Birth," describes the birthing experience
as inverse sexual intercourse:

> . . . my eyes
> rounded in shock and awe, it was like being
> entered for the first time, but entered
> from the inside, the child coming in
> from the other world.

The language of the poem is sexual: "Each
thing / I did, then, I did for the first / time,
touched the flesh of our flesh." While readers
may find this element in Olds's work disturbing, the poems assert that our most intimate
experiences are sensory and erotic.

In their physical development, the children
allow Olds to explore her own sexuality. The
speaker shows how far she and her children
have come; there are poems of escape and
transformation. Suddenly her son is like Hou-
dini, escaping from his boy's body:

> . . . I cannot imagine him
> no longer a child, and I know I must get ready,
> get over my fear of men now my son
> is going to be one.
>
> ("My Son the Man")

Her daughter attends her first dance ("First
Formal") and gets ready to go to college ("High
School Senior"). In every moment, both birth

and death are present. No emotion has weight
unless it is informed by history.

Olds ends this book with an emphasis on
adults and their sex lives, yet the participants
exhibit a knowledge and way of being beyond
the physical. In "This Hour" the speaker asserts, "We could never really say what it is
like, / this hour of drinking wine together." She
continues,

> . . . we know we will make love, but we're
> not getting ready to make love,
> nor are we getting over making love,
> love is simply our element,
> it is the summer night, we are in it.

Wisdom and shared experience are important
throughout this section.

The speaker uses specific physical images in
speaking about sex: "I began to lick you, the
foreskin lightly / stuck in one spot, like a petal,
I love / to free it—just so—in joy" ("Full
Summer"). The same is true in "Last Night"
and "Am and Am Not," where the speaker talks
about the stages of her lovemaking and the feeling of being the penis' "twin." Sexual history
informs the last poem in the book, which
emphasizes the relationship between the speaker
and her husband. In "True Love" the speaker
admits,

> . . . I know where you are
> with my eyes closed, we are bound to each other
> with huge invisible threads, our sexes
> muted, exhausted, crushed, the whole
> body a sex—surely this
> is the most blessed time of my life.

The speaker has traveled far to feel this way, to
have this positive wellspring of emotion inform
her experience.

BLOOD, TIN, STRAW

Olds's 1999 book, *Blood, Tin, Straw*, while it
deals with the personal as most of Olds's work

does, is organized in a way to capture the mood of the framing object. The cover is based on Mary Frank's "Elements," 1995–1996. The design is divided into six sections on both the front and back covers. On the front, water and absence predominate; on the back, sunlight and human activity. If the book is unfolded so that the front and back covers are viewed at once, there is a stunning view of human beings interacting with nature.

The book, divided into five sections— "Blood," "Tin," "Straw," "Fire," "Light"—has an emphasis on transformation not suggested by the title. There is a mingling of time frames in this book, as if Olds has moved away from the clear divides of her earlier books as somehow limiting.

Critical response to the book resembled that for earlier works by Olds, although the voices on each side were more emphatic. William Logan, one of her harshest critics, wrote in a 1999 review, "If you want to know what it's like for Sharon Olds to menstruate, or squeeze her oil-filled pores, or discover her naked father shitting, *Blood, Tin, Straw* will tell you." By contrast, Donna Seaman in another review of the book, averred, "If the body is the temple of the soul, then Sharon Olds is the priestess."

Initially, blood is the defining element, with the first poem in the book, "The Promise," being about the price of blood, or the sacrifices we must make for family. The speaker and her husband are making a pact to kill each other, should a mercy killing be necessary if they are ever incapacitated by illness, injury, or old age. The speaker explains, "I tell you you do not / know me if you think I will not / kill you." This dedication to the beloved—whatever the cost—is the promise of the book.

Blood is also literally displayed in the book, as in "When It Comes," a poem about the menstrual cycle. Olds's attention to the biological workings of the body is reminiscent of Anne Sexton. Olds wants to glorify the moment as

well as the cycle, writing, "It's lovely when it comes, and it's a sexual loveliness. / . . . you make a dazzling trail, the petals / the flower-girl scatters under the feet of the bride." The "dazzling trail" of blood is what Olds focuses on throughout her work, both literally and figuratively.

She questions her family blood ties—and thus her childhood—in "Aspic and Buttermilk," with the poem addressing two foods that her father would force her to eat. She did not then nor does she now understand his intentions. She concludes that

> . . . A family is a mystery,
> the human a mystery—beauty and cruelty,
> more passion for life on any
> terms than death.

In "Poem to the Reader," the speaker ponders her identity as a writer and a person. The child of parents who took more than they gave, she admits, "I was a craving spirit." And yet even acknowledging that she takes at the same time that she gives, she wonders if we are all takers, and if we may even like—the way the beloved does—to be taken. In short, she believes that the compulsion to take is what makes us human.

The "Tin" section emphasizes both the strong assertion of the self and the diminishment of the self. "Take the I Out" is about the former, as learned through the father. Her father sold I beams, and while that is a cold image, it is one the speaker holds on to, perhaps in spite of herself: "I, I, I, I, / girders of identity, head on, / embedded in the poem." Interestingly, this poem precedes "After Punishment Was Done with Me," in which the speaker, after having been beaten, lies down amid the dust and detritus of the house. This interplay between strength and weakness is important, if we consider that tin is both strong and common. The last poem in the section, "What Is the Earth?" where "earth is a homeless person," reinforces the paradox.

The "Straw" section says something about the ineffable quality of relationships, as rooted in common objects and experiences. "A Vision," the first poem of the section, describes the evolution of detail that describes the transcendent: the speaker's husband's honor is illustrated through a flower that becomes a baby, then becomes the human genitals—male and female—joined. To say that this is all "straw" defies what the speaker is talking about, and that is precisely the point. It is through the straw that the speaker discovers something holy like the soul.

The section goes on to describe more of the straw of human life, the intimacy of dailiness: the daughter's singing ("The Sound"), the speaker and her husband dancing ("Mortal Eternal"), even taking a shower ("Outdoor Shower"). Olds invites the reader to partake in these experiences not only through her direct speech, but goes so far in "Outdoor Shower" as to invite the reader to

Turn and turn in hot water,
column of heat in the cool wind
and sunny air, squeeze your eyes and then
open them again—look, it is still there,
the world as heaven, your body at the edge of it.

This is not to say that there is not pain in ordinary experience, and in "Leaving the Island" the speaker plays out her past through a father-and-son dynamic. A boy drops a cup of coffee he is carrying to his mother, thus incurring his father's wrath: "*I carry four things, / and I only give you one, and you drop it, / what are you, a baby?*" When the speaker offers consolation to the boy, "*I spilled my coffee on the deck, last trip, / it happens to us all,*" the boy responds with "*Shut up,*" protecting his father. Here, in the moment, the transcendent relationship of father and son turns to mud, to straw, and yet there is a connection, even though painful, in the muck.

At the end of the section the speaker envisions herself dead, mere straw, in her coffin in front of a church ("By Earth"). Imagining the dead self is a common fantasy, but here it is a vehicle for the speaker to look back on her life, rather than attempting to erase her life. Here she muses about what her mother criticized about her: her femaleness, her eye color, her hair. Yet the speaker realizes that her friends will forgive her everything and will accept—and have accepted—her the way she is. They are a family too. The speaker says with some ease: "I will lie in my coffin easy as a baby / asleep at the center of a family."

"Fire" in section four becomes a symbol of defiance. The speaker of "By Fire" prefers cremation over burial because "I want, dead, to / pull up my hands in fists, I want / to go out as a pugilist." This poem is followed by "Warrior: 5th Grade" with the speaker eager to fight, "to hit someone." The anticipation of violence draws upon memories of the speaker being hit by her mother. She says, "I wanted to be / like her, and hit, and hit, and hit." She buries these memories until she is having sex in her twenties and realizes that she wants her lover to be less gentle: "I wanted to be / fucked blind, pummeled half dead with it." This realization, suffice it to say, gives her pause.

The title of the book comes from the poem "Culture and Religion," where there is an interplay between Jesus and the Wicked Witch of the West. This unlikely combination is joined in the speaker's mind, because the two characters, Jesus and the Wicked Witch, respectively, appeared in the only two movies the speaker, in her girlhood, had ever seen. The speaker focuses on the punishment in each movie:

. . . And the witch wanted
to torture them to death, like Jesus
—blood, tin, straw—what they
were made of was to be used to kill them.

The focus on a vulnerable essence is at the heart of Olds's work, and ironically, if one follows *The Wizard of Oz* ramifications to their conclusion, where does the journey to Oz lead finally? Does the journey, upon which Olds as a poet has embarked, lead to the nothingness at the center of power? Or is her simple truth like Dorothy's: Whatever she does, she ultimately finds herself returning home? Complicating this parallel is the fact that at the end of "Culture and Religion" Olds has the Wicked Witch of the West disappear over the Crucifixion, upon which we gaze with guilt and complicity.

"The Burned Diary," about a girl killed in her building by evicted tenants, stresses the recording of experience, after death by fire. While she is killed, her diary survives, and her innermost thoughts are shared with the readers of a newspaper. In the poem readers feel that they know the girl, perhaps better than they ever could have imagined, because they have her words. This evidence of the burned diary—the lost, or pained, or suffering self—is naturally important to Olds, who has used words to save herself, to bring herself, like Plath's Lady Lazarus, "out of the ashes."

The last section of the book, "Light," emphasizes seeing and realization. The pivotal poem is "The Falls," in which the speaker recalls her father saving her from being "whisked" away into the Falls. In this moment everything is changed. The speaker admits, "I could have been / their middle child who died." Yet she is the one who tells their story, who *sees*: "No one would have written of them. / They would have died unsung—and they would have / preferred that." Ironically much of Olds's work is about what has saved her from her parents, and yet here she has been saved by one of them—at least for now.

In this last section—linked by the light, by seeing, by knowing—many of Olds's preoccupations come together—a longing for the mother, but not her own ("These Days"); a fascination with her son's interests ("Electricity Saviour"); the intimacy of lovemaking ("Ssshh").

The last few poems of the collection are sexual, and they emphasize one of the reasons the speaker sees for being born, the light she has had in her life. In "The Native" the speaker admits, "it feels to me like the most real thing." At the end of the poem she returns to her preoccupations from the beginning of *Satan Says,* addressing Satan:

> Satan, I do not want to rule,
> only to praise. I think I did not
> want to be born,
> I did not want to be conceived,
> I held to nothing, to its dense parental
> fur. Slowly I was pulled away,
> but I would not let go.

The last poem in the book, "The Knowing," focuses on the gaze, the gaze of the lover, the gaze of the human. After this long journey of the self, Olds is brought to the transcendent moment, one involving love and supreme connection. From Satan at the beginning of her work, she has moved to the "paradise coma" of love. The speaker watches the beloved, and she watches him watching her. She says, "I am so lucky that I can know him. / This is the only way to know him. / I am the only one who knows him." Just as Olds does in her work, poem by poem, experience by experience, here the lovers are

> entering,
> deeper and deeper, gaze by gaze,
> this place beyond the other places,
> beyond the body itself.

Although she could have chosen hate, she has always found a way to love.

Selected Bibliography

WORKS OF SHARON OLDS

POETRY
Satan Says. Pittsburgh, Penn.: University of Pittsburgh Press, 1980.

The Dead and the Living. New York: Knopf, 1984.

The Gold Cell. New York: Knopf, 1987.

The Matter of This World: New and Selected Poems. Nottingham, Great Britain: Slow Dancer Press, 1987.

The Sign of Saturn: Poems 1980–1987. London, Great Britain: Secker and Warburg, 1991.

The Father. New York: Knopf, 1992.

The Wellspring. New York: Knopf, 1996.

Blood, Tin, Straw. New York: Knopf, 1999.

OTHER

Four Contemporary Poets: Sharon Olds, Eleanor Wilner, Maddie Gomez, Juanita Tobin. Flushing, N.Y.: La Vida Press, 1984. (Contains one new poem by Olds, "The Bond.")

UNCOLLECTED PROSE

Foreword to *What Silence Equals: Poems,* by Tory Dent. New York: Persea Books, 1993.

"George and Mary Oppen: Poetry and Friendship." *Ironwood* 26:73–80 (1985).

"Ruth Stone and Her Poems." *The House Is Made of Poetry: The Art of Ruth Stone.* Edited by Wendy Barker and Sandra M. Gilbert. Carbondale: Southern Illinois University Press, 1996.

CRITICAL AND BIOGRAPHICAL STUDIES

Bedient, Calvin. "Sentencing Eros." *Salmagundi* 97:169–175. (1993). (Review of *The Father.*)

Behrendt, Stephen. Review of *The Dead and the Living. Prairie Schooner* 59, no 1:100–103 (1995).

Brown-Davidson, Terri. "The Belabored Scene, the Subtlest Detail: How Craft Affects Heat in the Poetry of Sharon Olds and Sandra McPherson." *Hollins Critic* 29, no. 1:1–9 (1992).

Bugeja, Michael. Review of *The Dead and the Living. Open Places* 40:61–65 (1985).

Cotter, James Finn. "Poetry Marathon." *Hudson Review* 37, no. 3:503 (1984). (Review of *The Dead and the Living.*)

Dillon, Brian. "'Never Having Had You, I Cannot Let You Go': Sharon Olds's Poems of a Father-Daughter Relationship." *Literary Review* 37, no. 1:108–118 (1993).

Garner, Dwight. "Sharon Olds: The Salon Interview." *Salon* (http://www.salon.com/weekly/interview96070.html), July 2001.

Gilbert, Sandra M. "Family Values." *Poetry* 164, no. 1:50–53 (1994). (Review of *The Father.*)

Gluck, Louise. "The Forbidden." *Proofs and Theories: Essays on Poetry.* New York: Ecco, 1994. Pp. 53–63.

Gregerson, Linda. "Short Reviews." *Poetry* 145, no. 1:36–37 (1984). (Review of *The Dead and the Living.*)

Harris, Peter. "Four Salvagers Salvaging: New Work by Voigt, Olds, Dove and McHugh." *Virginia Quarterly Review* 64, no. 2:265–269 (1998). (Review of *The Gold Cell.*)

Hudgins, Andrew. "What's My Line? A Poetry Chronicle." *Hudson Review* 40, no. 3:524–526 (1987). (Review of *The Gold Cell.*)

Kich, Martin. "Analysis of 'The Sisters of Sexual Treasure' and 'The End.'" *Notes on Contemporary Literature* 26, no. 1:6–7 (1996).

Logan, William. "First Books, Fellow Travelers." *Parnassus: Poetry in Review* 11, no. 1:211–216 (1983). (Review of *Satan Says.*)

———. "No Mercy." *New Criterion* 18, no. 4:60–61 (1999). (Review of *Blood, Tin, Straw.*)

McCarriston, Linda. "Book Briefs." *Georgia Review* 38, no. 4:899–900 (1984). (Review of *The Dead and the Living.*)

McFarland, Ron. "With Sharon Olds in Idaho." *Weber Studies: Voices and Viewpoints of the Contemporary West* 17:44–53 (1999). (Available online at http://weberstudies.weber.edu.)

Murray, G. E. "Seven Poets." *Hudson Review* 34, no. 1:158–159 (1981). (Review of *Satan Says.*)

Ossip, Kathleen. "No Room in the Booth?: An Appreciation of Confessional Poetry." *Writers' Chronicle* 33, no. 1:45–53 (2001).

Ostriker, Alicia. "The Tune of Crisis." *Poetry* 149, no. 4:234–236 (1987). (Review of *The Gold Cell.*)

———. "I Am (Not) This: Erotic Discourse in Bishop, Olds, and Stevens." *Wallace Stevens Journal* 19, no. 2:234–254 (1995).

Plath, Sara. Review of *Satan Says. Booklist,* September 1, 1980, p. 26.

Pybus, Rodney. "Poetry Chronicle." *Stand* 30, no. 1:74–75 (1998–1999). (Review of *The Matter of This World.*)

Scheponick, Peter C. "Sharon Olds's 'My Father Speaks to Me from the Dead.'" *Explicator* 57, no. 1:59–62 (1998).

Schweizer, Harold. "The Matter and Spirit of Death: Sharon Olds' *The Father*." In *Suffering and the Remedy of Art*. Albany: State University of New York Press, 1997. Pp. 171–177.

Seaman, Donna. Review of *Blood, Tin, Straw. Booklist*, October 1, 1999, p. 339.

Sutherland-Smith, James. "Death and the Unmaidenly: An Exploration of Sharon Olds' *The Wellspring* with Reference to Georges Bataille." *PN Review* 24, no. 4:42–46 (1998).

Sutton, Brian. "Olds' 'Sex Without Love.'" *Explicator* 55, no. 3:177–180 (1997).

Tanner, Laura E. "Death-Watch: Terminal Illness and the Gaze in Sharon Olds's *The Father*." *Mosaic: A Journal for the Interdisciplinary Study of Literature* 29, no. 1:103–121 (1996).

Upton, Lee. "Mortal Ordeals." *Belles Lettres* 8, no. 1:30 (1992). (Review of *The Father*.)

Wright, Carolyne. Review of *The Dead and the Living. Iowa Review* 15, no. 1:151–161 (1985).

Yenser, Stephen. "Bright Sources." *Yale Review* 77, no. 1:140–147 (1987). (Review of *The Gold Cell*.)

—*KIM BRIDGFORD*

Marjorie Kinnan Rawlings
1896–1953

Enchantment lies in different things for each of us. For me, it is in this: to step out of the bright sunlight into the shade of orange trees; to walk under the arched canopy of their jadelike leaves; to see the long aisles of lichened trunks stretch ahead in a geometric rhythm; to feel the mystery of a seclusion that yet has shafts of light striking through it. This is the essence of an ancient and secret magic. . . . And after long years of spiritual homelessness, of nostalgia, here is that mystic loveliness of childhood again. Here is home. An old thread, long tangled, comes straight again.

THE LONG-TANGLED thread of Marjorie Kinnan Rawlings's writing life finally came straight when she moved to Cross Creek, Florida, in 1928, at the age of thirty-two. During the ten years between her graduation from college and that momentous move to Florida, virtually every story she sent out for publication was returned with a rejection slip. In fact, though she had enjoyed some success writing for newspapers, none of Rawlings's published work before she moved to Cross Creek indicated that the future author of *The Yearling* (1938) and other important works of American fiction was in the making.

Indeed, it seems that Florida itself, with its "ancient and secret magic," transformed a minor journalist of feature stories and light verse into a major novelist. The primeval landscape of Florida and the precarious lives of its rural settlers provided the raw materials that Rawlings needed to fashion great art.

CHILDHOOD

Marjorie Kinnan (pronounced Kin-NAN) was born on August 8, 1896, in Washington, D.C., to Arthur Frank Kinnan and Ida Traphagen Kinnan, their first child. At the time of his daughter's birth, Arthur Kinnan worked for the U.S. Patent Office in charge of the Division of Electricity. Through his interest in politics, he formed a close friendship with the congressman Robert La Follette, a future governor of Wisconsin. The relationship between the La Follettes and the Kinnans influenced the family's later move to Wisconsin, where Marjorie attended college.

Although Arthur Kinnan rose rapidly and performed well in his position with the patent office, his real love was reserved for the dairy farm he owned in Rock Creek, Maryland, just outside of D.C. This farm, Marjorie later said in a letter to Max Perkins, was where her father's heart and mind lived. Rawlings and her father had a close and loving relationship; "Peaches" was his nickname for her, and many members of her family called her that all her life. Like her father, Marjorie loved visits to the farm. Not so her mother, Ida, who had grown up on a working farm in Michigan; Ida preferred their well-run home in D.C., where she presided over elaborate dinner parties.

Given the different temperaments of her parents, Marjorie enjoyed a greater kinship with her father, with his warmth and love of nature. When she was four, she gravitated equally easily to her new baby brother, Arthur Houston Kinnan. Her relationship with this handsome and scapegrace younger brother was always close and maternal. Indeed, Marjorie's lifelong love of boys (and men) was no doubt linked to her early bonds with her father and her younger brother. Meanwhile, her relationship with her mother was always somewhat strained, a quality that some critics have found reflected in the cold and emotionally distant mothers that frequent her novels and stories.

Meanwhile, even as a young child, Marjorie displayed skill as a storyteller. According to Elizabeth Silverthorne, in *Marjorie Kinnan Rawlings: Sojourner at Cross Creek* (1988), "Marjorie's quick imagination and dramatic flair combined to make her the source for dramatic entertainment in her neighborhood." The neighborhood boys (she did not allow girls to participate) gathered at twilight to hear Marjorie tell tales, and by first grade she was an avid writer of poems (all of them dedicated to her father). At age eleven, Marjorie won a prize for a story published on the Sunday children's page of the *Washington Post,* and as a junior at Western High School in D.C., she won second prize in a youth fiction contest sponsored by *McCall's* magazine.

Marjorie felt herself destined to be a writer from a young age, but she was also growing up in a culture just opening its doors to women professionals. Her childhood coincided with the end of the socially repressed Victorian era and the beginning of the technologically advanced twentieth century. In the first twenty-five years of her life, automobiles and radio transformed travel and communication in America, and suffragettes moved women ever closer to achieving the vote (which they finally won in the late 1920s).

Of course, the same superior technology that led to the invention of cars and radios was also responsible for the devastating weaponry of World War I (1914–1919), the world's first "modern" war, which decimated the male population of Europe and, to a lesser degree, America. Advances in travel led to the rapid

global spread of an influenza pandemic in 1918–1919 (American soldiers incubating the virus when they left for Britain killed—through contagion—many of the Allied troops they had come to help). And while Henry Ford revolutionized American transportation with his new flivvers, the much-touted and supposedly unsinkable *Titanic* went to the floor of the Atlantic Ocean in 1912.

Personal tragedy struck the Kinnan family in 1913: Arthur Kinnan Sr. died of a kidney infection. Marjorie, a senior in high school, was devastated by the death of her beloved father. Later she described the "great and terrible stillness" that descended upon her the day he died (quoted in Harry Evans, *Family Circle*).

COLLEGE AND MARRIAGE

Arthur Kinnan Sr.'s friendship with Robert La Follette had made him, as he'd once remarked, "Wisconscious." Therefore, it was to Wisconsin that Ida Kinnan moved her two children after Marjorie graduated from high school. In the fall of 1914 Marjorie Kinnan enrolled at the University of Wisconsin in Madison, as an English major.

When Marjorie entered college, she was an attractive, slender young woman with dark wavy hair, rosy cheeks, and bright blue eyes. She possessed a lively personality and good sense of humor as well as high intelligence, and she quickly made friends, such as Beatrice Humiston (later McNeil), that she would keep all of her life. With Bee, she appeared in several plays—both had a flair for the theatrical. Marjorie also had a gift for playwriting; she wrote a successful script, "Into the Nowhere," that was performed not only at Wisconsin but also by drama groups at other universities. Another among her circle of thespian friends was Freddy Bickel, later the movie star Fredric March.

In her junior year, Marjorie was elected to Phi Beta Kappa and became an editor of the school's literary magazine. Here she met Charles Rawlings of Rochester, New York, a handsome fraternity boy and avid bridge player. Chuck Rawlings loved water and boats and wrote well about yachting events—a subject that became his specialty later as a newspaperman and occasional contributor to *The Atlantic* and other national magazines.

Both were good-looking and popular students, and Marjorie and Chuck had many interests in common, in particular a love of literature and a desire to make their fortunes as creative writers. If the United States' entrance into World War I in April 1917 darkened their last years of college, it also gave them a reason to move to the East Coast, the mecca of the American literary establishment: after enlisting in the army, Chuck was stationed on Long Island. Marjorie moved to New York City (with her mother as chaperone for the first several weeks) with the hope of finding work in the publishing world.

Lovelorn letters flew between Chuck and Marjorie, but he could rarely get leave to visit her and she was unable to find a suitable job in the city (she later settled for a low-level public relations position with the YWCA). As her letters from those days reveal, her passionate love for Chuck occasionally gave way to bursts of rage if he did not write her frequently enough or with enough depth of emotion. Marjorie would send Chuck angry, wounding letters, and then follow them with placating and repentant missives. In one of the latter (quoted in Silverthorne), she wrote, "I wish I was normal and cow-like and grass chewingly contented, no matter what happened. But the trouble with me is, I act like a nut *when nothing* happens! . . . It's bad enough to live with yourself when you're a nut—but it must be awful for someone else!"

Despite the disapproval of Marjorie's mother, Chuck and Marjorie were married in May of 1919. The war in Europe was over, Charles had been mustered out of the army, and they thought their future in New York City looked bright. Unfortunately, Marjorie continued to be unable to sell any of her short stories to magazines, and Chuck quickly lost a promising job with an export firm when it went bankrupt.

Although Chuck enjoyed a close relationship with his parents and two brothers, Marjorie resisted the notion of moving to Rochester to live near his family (his father had once told her that in retirement, he and his wife planned to live with her and Chuck), nor did she have any desire to put herself back in the sphere of her mother's influence in Wisconsin. To avoid giving up their young independence, the couple moved to Louisville, Kentucky, and took jobs on the *Courier-Journal*.

Marjorie wrote feature stories for the newspaper while Chuck worked as a reporter. Here Marjorie learned to tighten her prose by cutting unnecessary adverbs and adjectives, and both Marjorie and Chuck began to engage in regular drinking (despite Prohibition) and heavy smoking, two vices that Marjorie indulged in for the rest of her life. Still, after two years of hard work on the paper, both of them realized that their careers were going nowhere and their finances had not improved. Reluctantly, they packed their bags and moved to Rochester.

In January 1922, Charles took a job with his father's shoe factory as a traveling salesman and left on his first monthlong trip. Marjorie settled down again to revising her short stories, but by fall, with nothing but rejection slips to show for her efforts, she once again turned to journalism and began to write features for the *Rochester Times-Union*.

"SONGS OF A HOUSEWIFE"

As with her contributions to the Louisville paper, Marjorie specialized in articles about women in the marketplace. For a brief period, she also wrote a society column under the pseudonym Lady Alicia Thwaite for the Rochester magazine *5 O'Clock*. These columns show the first evidence of the satiric wit that she displayed more fully in her best fiction.

In 1926 Marjorie tried a new idea on the *Rochester Times-Union*: a poetry column dedicated to the trials and tribulations of housewives. She proposed to assume the persona of a wife and mother of four children and pen a poem five days a week under the title "Songs of a Housewife." Not surprisingly, the male editor of the paper was dubious—the audience for the *Times-Union* was largely working-class and, he figured, not particularly interested in poetry. Marjorie's persistence finally won out, and the column began on May 24, 1926 and ran until February 29, 1928.

To the amazement of the editors, the column was hugely successful, and not just in Rochester. Shortly into its run it was syndicated in fifty papers all over the United States. Rodger L. Tarr, who edited the first published collection of these poems in 1997, makes the case that Rawlings, by celebrating the "romance of housework," was validating the role of the housewife as essential and "founded upon a rich and enduring tradition." He adds, however, that this was far from an antifeminist position; the feminist suffragettes that preceded the 1920s generation had succeeded in creating "a new class of American women" who were "asserting their rights, demanding equality not only in the workplace but in the home as well." Certainly, women readers responded enthusiastically to Rawlings's poems. In fact, many of her verses were written directly in response to a letter from a reader (printed at the top of the column), and the poet encouraged her readers to send in their suggestions.

The themes of the poems generally fall into four categories: cooking, nature, friends and family, and motherhood. A verse from one of the representative cooking poems (from her February 25, 1927 column) shows that these were hardly feminist screeds:

The woman who can make good pie
   Stands on her own Gibraltar,
And men will always hover by,
   To lead her to the altar.

Rawlings's poems about motherhood are poignant in light of the fact that she died childless and yet loved children, particularly boys. In "All Boy" (May 26, 1926), about Tom, the poet-persona's scamp of a son, she concludes, "But would I change him? Not for pearls / His muddy footsteps bring me joy / I wouldn't trade him for ten girls— / I'm sinful proud that he's 'all boy'!" Clearly these poems have cultural and historical importance, because they found such a receptive audience in the 1920s, but it is hard to make a case for them as enduring art— although Rodger Tarr certainly tries, despite the politely dismissive comments of other major Rawlings scholars, including Gordon Bigelow (author of *Frontier Eden: The Literary Career of Marjorie Kinnan Rawlings* and coeditor of the *Selected Letters*) and Elizabeth Silverthorne, Rawlings's primary biographer. What the poems do show are the main concerns of Rawlings's later work and life: they highlight the importance for her of friendship; the enduring delight of cooking and enjoying good food with beloved companions; her acute sense of nature as the fabric into which humanity is inextricably woven; and her lifelong conviction that any work done well is noble. As she told the editor of the *Times-Union*, "Most people who amount to anything do work hard, at whatever their job happens to be" (June 8, 1924).

"FOR THIS IS AN ENCHANTED LAND"

By 1928, hard work had availed Marjorie Kinnan Rawlings very little in terms of literary recognition. Her success as a journalist did not fulfill her need to publish serious fiction, and Chuck Rawlings had long since given up on selling shoes for his father's company. Both worked for the *Times-Union* and felt, once again, that their careers were at an impasse.

Meanwhile, Chuck's two brothers, Jim and Wray Rawlings, were working in Florida. In the northern interior of the state, the brothers ran a filling station and dabbled in real estate. In March, Chuck and Marjorie went down to visit the men and were immediately charmed by the natural beauty of the area, the dark loveliness of spring-fed lakes and rivers, the tall palm trees and spreading live oaks festooned with Spanish moss, fragrant orange groves, and the simple but self-reliant country people who populated the area and pieced together a living from fishing, hunting, trapping, and farming the land.

"Let's sell everything and move South!" Marjorie urged Chuck. "How we could write!" Chuck agreed, and thanks to a legacy from her mother, who had died in 1923, Marjorie had the means to take out a mortgage on a seventy-four-acre orange grove with dilapidated farmhouse and tenant house in Cross Creek, Florida. In November, they left Rochester for good and moved to their new home on the creek connecting Orange and Lochloosa Lakes. In the section of *Cross Creek* titled "For This Is an Enchanted Land," Rawlings explains that she "knew the old grove and farmhouse at once as home" and felt a thrill of terror because "the joining of person to place as of person to person, is a commitment to shared sorrow, even as to shared joy." Thus emerged the idea that would inform her best writing: humans can only reach fulfillment in a place where their spirits can live in harmony, frightening though that commitment might prove to be. For Rawlings, Cross Creek was such a place. She stayed on, working the grove and writing, long after Jim and Wray Rawlings departed (in 1930), followed by Chuck, from whom she was divorced in 1933.

According to Anne E. Rowe, the author of *The Idea of Florida in the American Literary Imagination* (1992), Florida has always held an Edenic appeal for northern American writers, just as the Mediterranean has for northern European writers. The notion of Florida as a tropical Garden of Eden is a motif that runs through the work of visiting writers of the past three centuries, from William Bartram the eighteenth-century naturalist (he renamed the state "Elysium" in his *Travels*), to Ralph Waldo Emerson, Harriet Beecher Stowe, and Stephen Crane, who came to Florida for their health in the nineteenth century, and on to James Branch Cabell, Ernest Hemingway, and Rawlings, who made the state their home and a subject of their fiction in the twentieth.

Florida's natural charms are a mixture of the lovely and the lethal, its abundance of tropical flowers, mellifluous songbirds, and pristine beaches matched by its acres of swamps, ferocious mosquitoes, alligators, and snakes. Rawlings moved to Cross Creek the same year that Ernest Hemingway moved to Key West, and both encountered a landscape still in a relatively undeveloped, and thus largely unspoiled, condition. As Rawlings quickly discovered when she met her "Cracker" neighbors (a term that refers to the descendants of the first English settlers of Georgia and Florida, who herded cattle around the St. Johns River with the "crack" of their whips), they represented "an authentic, living remnant of the American frontier, surviving into the twentieth century."

Within the first two years of her life in Florida, Rawlings made the notes that formed the basis for all of her later Florida writing. She found the Florida Crackers "elemental folk," possessing a vitality lacking in their more civilized counterparts elsewhere in America. She jotted down detailed examples of their dialect and speech mannerisms. She also studied the birds, learning all of their calls and flight patterns. She described every tree, shrub, and flower with a naturalist's eye to detail; her notebooks overflowed with descriptions of sunsets and sunrises, encounters with the voracious insect life of Florida, and struggles with the orange grove, including the desperate efforts required to save it from winter freezes. Mostly, however, she wrote about her neighbors, the colorful people who lived near her in the village of Cross Creek, and those who lived further out, in the wilderness known as "the Big Scrub."

After years of rejection for her "slick" stories, she finally began to write about the simple, tenacious people she had discovered in the interior of Florida. In 1930 she sent a group of Florida sketches, titled "Cracker Chidlings," to the editor of *Scribner's Magazine*. To her amazement, the piece was accepted and she was asked to provide a biographical note for publication. She replied in a letter Alfred Dashell, editor of *Scribner's Magazine,* that the years before 1928 meant little to her. "They are a shadow, against the substance that is our life in the heart of . . . Florida," she wrote.

REAL TALES FROM THE FLORIDA INTERIOR

The subtitle Rawlings appended to "Cracker Chidlings" was "Real Tales from the Florida Interior." However, a brief definition of the word "chidlings" might help readers understand how much the author admired the people of whom she wrote. "Chidlings" is Cracker for "chitterlings" which are—bluntly put—hog guts. Florida Crackers have guts, and that's what Rawlings intended to show here and in her other works about rural Floridians. As the subtitle announces, these were indeed "real tales," based on real people whom Rawlings had met in and around Cross Creek.

The sketches include the antics of Tim the moonshiner, Fatty Blake, whose "big doin's" include enough free squirrel pilau (squirrel parts and rice) and Brunswick stew for two counties, and Sam Whitman, who "hates a Georgian worse than most Florida Crackers, because he married one." The success of the sketches prompted Marjorie to write a longer short story for *Scribner's,* "Jacob's Ladder," a poignant romantic tale of a shy Cracker couple named Mart and Florry, whose love enables them to endure hurricanes, hunger, and other disasters, with stoic patience.

Rawlings's ear for dialect is evident here (Mart tells Florry, "Leave me tell you . . . I ain't studyin' none on quittin' you, no ways, no how—no time—"), as is her sense of the impermanence of anything existing in time. In one of their brief periods of abundance, Mart and Florry live in a cabin that Mart rents for a percentage of the hides he gets from trapping. The cabin is on a lake, where

> frogs piped up and down the length of their small silver song. Hoot owls over the marsh boomed with the vibrancy of a bass viol. The cranes and loons cried dissonant, not quite inharmonious. . . . The palms were silver in the moonlight. The new growth of the oaks was white as candles. An odor grew in the stillness, sweeter than breath could endure. . . .Yellow jasmine was in bloom.

To the lushness of these sensory details, Rawlings adds the depth of emotion that binds human nature to the natural world: "Florry put out her hand to Mart with a quick, awkward motion. In the richness of her content, it was vital to her to touch him. . . . Deep-sunk in her was a wisdom warning her that beauty was impermanent—safety was not secure. . . . Nothing good stayed forever."

As Rodger Tarr explains in his introduction to Rawlings's collected *Short Stories,* "In her Cracker stories she was able to capture the human drama found in a life of deprivation and alienation, to locate tragic heroes in the coarseness of life in the formidable scrub." Rawlings captured this human drama in "Jacob's Ladder" and it brought her to the attention of Charles Scribner's Sons' famous editor, Maxwell Perkins. Perkins immediately recognized the breadth of Rawlings's talent and, with an editorial gift all his own, improved her fiction with expert advice, gently given. Perkins always said that his chief duty as an editor was to help writers "realize themselves," and this he did with several major American writers in the 1920s and 1930s: Hemingway, Thomas Wolfe, and F. Scott Fitzgerald among them. Rawlings was his protégée from 1931 on, and to her Perkins became not only a mentor but a beloved friend.

It was Max Perkins who urged Rawlings to write a full-length work of fiction and, after several more of her Cracker short stories appeared to acclaim in *Scribner's Magazine,* she began the research that would culminate in her first novel, *South Moon Under* (1933).

THE BIG SCRUB

In order to gather firsthand her material for a full-length novel about a Florida Cracker family, Rawlings made arrangements to move in with the Fiddia family, who lived in a cabin in the Big Scrub, a wild area of Florida that is now part of the Ocala National Forest. Insofar as this region figures in all of her longer Florida stories, it is worth quoting the description of it that she sent to Max Perkins, in a letter of November 4, 1931.

> The scrub is a silent stretch enclosed by two rivers, deeply forested with Southern spruce (almost valueless), scrub oak, scrub myrtle and ti-ti, occasional gall-berry and black-jack and a few specialized shrubs and flowers, with "islands" of long-leaf yellow pine. There is an occasional small lake with its attendant marsh or "prairie." The only settlement is here and there on these bodies of water, and along the river edges, where the natural hammock growth has been bitten into by the settlers' clearings. It is a fringe of life, following the waterways. The scrub is a vast wall, keeping out the timid and the alien.

From August until October 1931, Rawlings entered wholeheartedly into the lives of the Fiddias in their cabin on a high bluff above the Ocklawaha River. The Fiddia family consisted of two individuals: a tiny but powerful old lady named Piety and her tall, gangly son, Leonard.

Rawlings helped Piety wash heavy quilts by stomping them in washtubs full of lye soap; she also learned to make lye soap from ashes and grease, and brooms from branches of sage bush. In the company of Leonard, she hunted squirrel and deer, dynamited mullet out of the water, and shot limpkins (an indigenous bird) for food. Much of this hunting was illegal, but Rawlings defended the food-gathering practices of the Crackers to Perkins by noting that they only killed what they could eat, not for sport.

The greatest acquisition to the store of her knowledge about Cracker life, however, came from her experiences with Leonard at his moonshine still. Like the character Lant Jacklin in the novel *South Moon Under,* Leonard had been betrayed to federal agents by a cousin; the agents smashed and burned his still, though they did not quench his desire to continue making and selling "'shine." He built a new still and hid it even farther out in the Scrub.

In many ways, *South Moon Under* echoes the facts of Leonard and Piety Fiddia's lives. The main characters of the novel are Lant and Piety Jacklin, also a son and his mother, and they live, just as the Fiddias do, in a cabin in the Big Scrub. In fact, Rawlings almost titled the novel after the scrub country, except that "big scrub" had a football connotation for readers outside of Florida. Instead she settled on *South Moon Under,* a phrase that refers to the time of night when the moon is invisible, or under the earth, and yet has a pull on certain nocturnal animals, such as deer, owls, and rabbits. Lant, hunting in the scrub at this hour, contemplates the invisible power of the moon to move the forest creatures:

> He wondered if it might be so with men. Perhaps all men were moved against their will. A man ordered his life, and then an obscurity of circumstance sent him down a road that was not of his own desire or choosing. Something beyond a man's immediate choice and will reached through the earth and stirred him. He did not see how any man might escape it.

South Moon Under had the same power to stir readers when it appeared in 1933. It was a Book-of-the-Month-Club selection and garnered numerous reviews similar to the one from the *New York Times* that observed, "It glows with the breath of life" (March 5, 1933). But Rawlings was most delighted with the response of Leonard Fiddia, her model for Lant Jacklin, who told a mutual friend, "It's a good thing she didn't tell no more'n she did about my huntin'—she'd of had the game warden on my neck shore" (quoted in a letter dated April 1933, *Max and Marjorie*).

Meanwhile, the success of Rawlings's first novel corresponded with the failure of her marriage to Chuck Rawlings. As she described it to her college friend Bee McNeil, "The first five years I cried; the next five years I fought; the last four years I didn't give a damn" (quoted in Silverthorne). Rawlings craved emotional support and approval from her husband but, as their happiness dwindled, she received only his criticisms (some Rawlings scholars, such as Tarr, suggest that his verbal aggression toward her became physical abuse in the last months of the marriage). Rawlings later referred to Chuck's "mental cruelty," a comment echoed by his next two wives when they divorced him. Nevertheless, Marjorie surely contributed to their unhappiness with her volatile mood swings and increasing abuse of alcohol.

These characteristics would also strain her second, far happier, marriage, to Norton Baskin, but that was many years away. Instead, from 1933 to 1941, Rawlings embraced life as a single woman, the owner and manager of an orange grove and a full-time writer. This period of her life was her most productive.

"BEAUTY IS PERVASIVE"

In one of her lectures on creative writing, called "The Relativity of Beauty," Rawlings told her listeners, "No one is immune to beauty." Hap-pily, neither was she; otherwise, she might not have survived the depression that descended upon her in the first weeks after Chuck moved out. That period of her life she chronicled in a story titled "Hyacinth Drift," first published in *Scribner's Magazine* and later reprinted as the penultimate chapter of *Cross Creek*.

"Hyacinth Drift" is the narrative of her journey up the St. Johns River (which, like the Nile, flows from south to north), with her intrepid friend Dessie Smith Vinson. Of course, the boat journey is also a spiritual journey for Rawlings. Local men warn the two women that they'll get lost, that the river winds through "some of the wildest country in Florida." Rawlings is so miserable that this threat has little impact: "Life was a nightmare. The river was at least of my own choosing."

Early in the trip, the women do lose their way. Rawlings has the compass and map, but these tools are useless—the river winds through a marsh choked with hyacinths and a drought has evaporated many of the channels on the chart. Lost at dusk, they make camp in a desolate place, "a few square yards of . . . black muck" a foot above the water line. They have no dry wood for a fire and, when they lie down on cots to sleep, mosquitoes descend on them in swarms. Dessie manages to keep the bugs from their bodies by propping up a mosquito net with her .22 rifle.

However, from this night of physical and spiritual desolation, Rawlings awakes to a vibrant morning, to the sight of cranes and herons walking near her on the shore and Dessie casting for bass from their rowboat.

> Marsh and water glittered iridescent in the sun. The tropical March air was fresh and wind-washed. I was suddenly excited. I made campfire with fatwood splinters and cooked bacon and toast and coffee. Their fragrance eddied across the water and I saw Dess lift her nose and put down her rod and reel. She too was excited.

"Young un," she called. "Where's the channel?"

I pointed to the northeast and she nodded vehemently. It had come to both of us like a revelation that the water hyacinths were drifting faintly faster in that direction.

From that moment on, they never lose their way again; they quit fighting the river and give themselves up to its current. Rawlings feels "a tremendous exhilaration, an abandoning of fear," a parallel of what she must have felt relinquishing the "safety" of marriage and giving herself up to the current of her new life as a single woman writer. She muses upon the revelation of the hyacinths, a revelation that suggests her personal epiphany, "It was very simple. Like all simple facts, it was necessary to discover it for oneself."

The rest of "Hyacinth Drift" treats the pleasure of the women's time on the river, then Rawlings's fear as the journey comes to an end that she'll "never be happy on land again." This proves not to be true; the fluid world is lovely, but dry ground also enjoys nature's artistry:

> Beauty is pervasive, and fills, like perfume, more than the object that contains it. Because I had known intimately a river, the earth pulsed under me. The Creek was home. Oleanders were sweet past bearing, and my own shabby fields, weed-tangled, were newly dear. I knew, for a moment, that the only nightmare is the masochistic human mind.

As the critic Edna Saffy, writing about Rawlings's theory of composition, explains it, "Beauty was the effect [she] attempted to convey to her audience." Although Rawlings always took pains to make her descriptions of the people and their activities in the Florida backwoods accurate, it is her infusion of imagination that made them beautiful.

For Rawlings, the effect of beauty can be authenticated, whereas truth can never be validated aesthetically. Therefore, as she said in a lecture on creative writing, "Beauty is more valid, more important, more trustworthy than truth, because while we cannot be sure of truth, we know with our own minds and senses when we are aesthetically or spiritually stirred, and by what."

Gordon Bigelow, whose *Frontier Eden* is the first major study of Rawlings's work, observed that she discovered in Cross Creek "a subject matter that appealed powerfully to her imagination and allowed her romantic sensibilities fullest exercise, but which was at the same time anchored in a living reality. The result was a kind of delayed explosion."

Rawlings's great gift as a writer was her ability to impart to readers the natural beauty of Florida and its people. She settled in Cross Creek, keenly observed her surroundings, then drenched those observations in the light of her distinctive imagination. The result was fiction based on "real" tales but infused with the archetypal power of myth.

A LOCAL COLORIST, A REGIONAL WRITER

Perhaps it was inevitable that Rawlings's faithful depictions of the speech and habits of Florida Crackers would equate her, in many critics' minds, with that genre of writing known as "local color." In general, the tag "local colorist," has a pejorative connotation. It refers to writers who focus on specific characters in a distinct region and describe them in a humorous, though often sympathetic, fashion. Such writing often turns the characters into stereotypes, and perhaps this is why the term is used dismissively. On the other hand, local-color writing has a long history in American literature. Much of the South's nineteenth-century literature—by authors such as Mark Twain, Augustus Baldwin Longstreet, and Kate Chopin—has at one time or another been categorized as such by literary scholars.

"Regional writing" is a larger category containing the local colorists as a subset.

Regional writers closely align their characters with a particular place and its history, but the characters are not primarily described from the viewpoint of an external observer; instead, their motivations and interior vision are integral to the work; they act as subjects in their own stories rather than objects described by an outside narrator. This country's best-known regional writers are also by and large Southern, and they include William Faulkner, Alice Walker, and Flannery O'Connor.

Rawlings herself moved progressively through these categories and perhaps beyond them. Her first story for *Scribner's,* "Cracker Chidlings," does have the qualities associated with local color. The story is composed of sketches of characters, seen from the outside, whose dialect and doings are sympathetically portrayed but also humorous to readers outside the region. However, by her second published *Scribner's* story, "Jacob's Ladder," Rawlings had transcended the outsider's perspective and given her Cracker characters profound interior lives and motivations. Her stories from that point on, whether primarily humorous (such as the Quincey Dover stories, told from the point of view of a three-hundred-pound Cracker woman known for her wit and wisdom) or tragic (such as "Gal Young 'Un," about an older Cracker widow who is duped by a young fortune hunter, who marries her to get her money and then has his girlfriend, "gal young 'un," move in), retained the inner vision and hence the innate dignity of their characters.

Nevertheless, Rawlings wrestled with the concept of herself as a regional writer, a label book critics often plastered on their reviews of her work. In November 1939, Rawlings gave a lecture on the topic of "Regional Literature of the South" to the National Council of English Teachers (this lecture was later published as an article in the February 1940 issue of the journal *College English*). She noted that local color "written on purpose is perhaps as spurious a form of literary expression as ever reaches print." To hold up the speech and customs of people from a certain area, simply to gain the stares of the curious, "is a betrayal of the people of that region." However, Rawlings went on, "many of the greatest books of all time are regional books, in which the author has used, for his own artistic purpose, a background that he loved and understood." Into this group, Rawlings placed Thomas Hardy and her contemporary in America, Ellen Glasgow.

Rawlings probably could not have imagined then that the project she would be working on when she died would be a biography of Ellen Glasgow (1873–1945), a novelist whose best books, such as *Barren Ground* (1925), depict the social and political conflicts of the post–Civil War South, specifically those of her native region, Richmond, Virginia.

Rawlings may have felt an affinity for Glasgow because of their shared focus on a distinct region and their admiration for each other's writing (Glasgow told Rawlings that *Cross Creek* reminded her of "a luminous web which captures and holds some vital essence of a particular place and moment of time"), but there is yet another similarity between the women that neither seems to have noted (*Letters of Ellen Glasgow,* 1958). Both enjoyed their greatest success as writers while independent women; both championed the rights of women in the workplace and elsewhere; and both often cast strong, independent women as the heroines of their fiction (Piety Lantry in *South Moon Under*; Dorinda Oakley in *Barren Ground*).

Perhaps, then, it is not surprising that much of the critical attention now given to Rawlings focuses on her not as a regional writer, but as a *woman* writer.

A WOMAN WRITER

The second novel Rawlings published was ultimately titled *Golden Apples* and appeared as a book in 1935 after running as a serial in *Cosmopolitan* magazine, a treatment that Rawlings called "cheapening," though she needed the money. After Chuck's departure in March 1933, and a poor orange crop, Rawlings felt a pinch in her finances that linked her to people all over the country; America was in the midst of the Great Depression.

Fortunately, Max Perkins sent her advances on her royalties for *South Moon Under* and she continued to publish short stories regularly in *Scribner's Magazine.* This gave her the wherewithal to go to England for two months in the summer of 1933 to conduct the research for the novel that would eventually become *Golden Apples.* The plot concerns a young Englishman named Tordell, who is exiled by his family to Florida. There he takes over the family's abandoned orange grove. Throughout the story, his disdain for the Cracker brother and sister, Luke and Allie, who have been squatting on the land, is balanced by their love for the wild beauty of the region and Luke's commitment "to merge himself with the earth, to follow the seasons and let the sun and rain unite the sweat of his body with the soil he tended."

This novel, generally considered the least successful of Rawlings's books (*Time* called it a "dull melodrama," and Bigelow deems it "ill-starred from the beginning"), nevertheless contains a powerful heroine, Camilla Van Dyne. Camilla, on horseback, oversees her own orange grove, and is, in general, a capable, authoritative, and independent woman. She is, in fact, a great deal like Rawlings in the years she single-handedly tended to the grove at Cross Creek. Indeed, Camilla relishes her strength and fears being perceived as soft. "Soft women," she observes, "they go down."

Although she is hardly soft, Camilla is, like Marjorie, tremendously generous to her neighbors, including Luke and Tordell. It is to his credit that Perkins liked this character, though he thought her not quite realistic; *Cosmopolitan,* however, thought Rawlings should tone down Camilla's masculine attributes of strength and independence, which Rawlings refused to do. She told Perkins, "If I finish up with something that old women read in their rockers and think 'too sweet,' I'll never write another word as long as I live" (quoted in a letter dated January 15, 1935, *Max and Marjorie*).

Janet L. Boyd, a feminist scholar who looks at Rawlings as "a strong woman in a patriarchal society" who "strove to please the critics who create the canon," sees Camilla Van Dyne as a strong female character who subverts the male plot structure of the book. Boyd quotes feminist scholars such as Annette Kolodny, Nina Baym, and Margaret Homans, who scrutinize a theory of American literature shaped by male critics to favor a male protagonist, outcast from society, who manages to tame, or conquer, some portion of the wilderness. Boyd goes on to show that both Tordell and Luke see the hammock landscape in feminine terms and both long to possess and tame it; the difference is that Tordell sees it as a threatening jungle whereas Luke sees it as "virgin" ground that he would like to seed and nurture.

In sharp contrast to these male viewpoints, Rawlings presents Camilla Van Dyne as the finest grower in the district, the true guardian of the "golden apples" of myth, which may have been oranges. Her relationship with the grove she tends is symbiotic as opposed to overmastering, but her role in the story is minor (she doesn't even appear until Chapter 25) compared to that of Luke and Tordell. Meanwhile Allie, the other major female in the story, is hardly a strong heroine: she is a shy Cracker girl akin to Florry of "Jacob's Ladder."

Boyd believes that "writing against the grain of her life" to please male critics made Rawlings both physically ill upon the completion of each novel and prompted her to downplay strong heroines, like Camilla, who so closely resembled herself. Peggy Whitman Prenshaw, another important Rawlings scholar, takes this idea further and suggests that Rawlings's discovery of Florida and its engaging inhabitants "was not nearly so crucial to her literary career as was the ending of an unhappy and enervating marriage and the courageous decision to go it alone at Cross Creek." Prenshaw stresses that her newfound freedom and "a place of her own" enabled Rawlings to produce her best writing.

THE YEARLING

Rawlings's most successful and best-known novel is *The Yearling,* the story of a lonely boy growing up in a cabin in the Florida scrub country. Jody Baxter is an isolated only child; his daily human companionship consists of his father—a kind, indulgent, hardworking farmer named Penny—and his mother, a cold, distant woman whose maternal instincts have been effectively quenched by the deaths of several children before Jody. Not until Jody rescues and then raises a fawn, which he names Flag, does he finally lose his sense of isolation. Unfortunately, when the fawn becomes a yearling—just as Jody is a human yearling, on the cusp between boyhood and manhood—it begins to destroy the Baxter's crops.

In order for the family to survive, Jody's father orders him to shoot Flag. Jody feels betrayed by his father, a feeling that is compounded when he must himself betray Flag and kill the companion who loves and trusts him, the being that has eased his loneliness. Jody runs away, goes hungry, and finally realizes that there is nowhere to go but home. When he returns, his father delivers the essence of the novel's wisdom: "'Ever' man wants life to be a fine thing, and a easy. 'Tis fine, boy, powerful fine, but 'tain't easy. Life knocks a man down and he gits up and it knocks him down again." Jody, who has seen death and endured hunger, is a boy no longer. "He did not believe he should ever love anything, man or woman or his own child, as he had loved the yearling. He would be lonely all his life. But a man took it for his share and went on."

The Yearling appeared in the spring of 1938, but the idea for the novel was first put into Rawlings's mind by Perkins in June 1933 when he suggested that she consider writing about the life of a boy or a girl growing up "in the scrub." Rawlings had already begun the notes for *Golden Apples,* but she was intrigued by his suggestion and they corresponded about it for the next several months. On October 27, 1933, Perkins wrote, "The idea is really perfectly simple to me. I am thinking of a book about a boy, but his age is not important." Perkins goes on to list several popular boys' books, including Rudyard Kipling's *Kim,* Twain's *Huckleberry Finn,* and Robert Louis Stevenson's *Treasure Island.* "All these books are primarily *for boys.* All of them are read by men and they are the favorite books of some men. The truth is the best part of a man is a boy."

By this time Rawlings had learned to trust Perkins's instincts. On the other hand, she respected his idea enough not to "toss off a . . . simple boy's story of the scrub." She knew, she told him, that she couldn't do a good book casually. "There is more fine material to be gotten for it, that will have to come slowly. . . . A boy's mind is really too sacred a responsibility just to flip crumbs at it." Instead she first wrote *Golden Apples* and, with Perkins's always kind and insightful advice, it was better than it otherwise would have been.

Maxwell Perkins played a signal role in Rawlings's sense of herself as a worthy human being. He gave her the emotional and professional support that she had craved, but not received, from her husband. As her mentor, Perkins filled the role of the warm and nurturing father that she had lost. As her editor, he helped her to produce her best writing and she knew it. She told him, "What a prodigious genius I feel you have for getting inside a writer's mind and judging absolutely from the inside; for making the incoherent, coherent. Frankly, I could not endure the thought of having to get along without your help, and I hope no circumstance ever deprives me of it" (quoted in a letter dated December 1934, *Max and Marjorie*).

When *The Yearling* appeared in April 1938, it immediately earned rave reviews in all the major magazines and newspapers. It quickly rose to the top of American best-seller lists, where it remained for ninety-three weeks, and Rawlings's agent sold the movie rights for $30,000, an enormous sum in those days. For the first time in her life, Rawlings did not have to worry about money. What she did have to worry about was her health.

SUCCESS AND SUFFERING

Rawlings had suffered for years from diverticulosis, an abnormality in the walls of the colon that can lead to severe inflammation (diverticulitis), accompanied by abscesses and excruciating pain. In 1931 doctors had removed her appendix only to discover that that organ was healthy but her colon was diseased. Since then, recurring bouts of inflammation left Rawlings vulnerable to peritonitis, an internal infection that could kill her. By June of 1938, when her success with *The Yearling* was assured, she suffered a particularly severe bout of diverticulitis.

Dr. Vinson (Dessie's husband), her surgeon in Tampa, advised her to have an operation that would remove the lower section of her colon. The operation had only a 30 percent survival rate, but she decided to risk it, writing Perkins that she didn't fear death, because "I have lived so full and rich a life, with so much more than my share of everything" (quoted in a letter dated June 8, 1938, *Max and Marjorie*). Perkins, however, was alarmed, as was Norton Baskin,

her close friend and companion since her divorce in 1933.

Baskin, who had been in Alabama on family business, returned to Florida to talk Rawlings out of the surgery. He insisted that she get a second opinion, which she did, and the operation was called off. Instead she was prescribed a rigid diet (diverticulosis is a disease of the Western world, related to a low-roughage diet) and sent home.

At this point, Rawlings began to realize just how much she depended on Baskin's concern for her welfare, his steady affection and reliability in a crisis. A busy owner/manager of hotels, Baskin liked his own independence as much as Rawlings did hers, but he came through for her when she needed him. He had already asked her to marry him several times and she'd refused, but during this period of her life she began to think seriously of making a permanent commitment. In 1941 she and Baskin were married.

Meanwhile, the enormous success of *The Yearling*—it was awarded the Pulitzer Prize in 1939—brought requests from all over the world for more information about the author and her region. Perkins encouraged her to write a nonfiction book about her life in Florida, a suggestion that she found "uncanny," for by that time she had already begun work on what would become *Cross Creek*.

CROSS CREEK

Cross Creek, a collection of short vignettes about her life in Florida, appeared in 1942. Many critics consider this semiautobiography to be Rawlings's best work; it certainly contains her best nature writing, prompting many reviewers to dub her a "female Thoreau." Like *The Yearling*, *Cross Creek* quickly rose to the top of the best-seller lists. The book is a paean to place and to the inevitable affinity between people and the natural world:

We were bred of earth before we were born of our mothers. Once born, we can live without mother or father, or any other kin, or any friend, or any human love. We cannot live without the earth or apart from it, and something is shrivelled in a man's heart when he turns away from it and concerns himself only with the affairs of men.

Rawlings goes on to describe the relationship she shares with her neighbors at the Creek. Despite quarrels and occasional serious feuds, "when the great enemies of Old Starvation and Old Death come skulking down on us, we put up a united front and fight them side by side, as we fight the woods fires."

Rawlings's anecdotes are filled with wit and wisdom about the primitive living conditions of the Creek (she has a bathroom installed with the proceeds from her story "Jacob's Ladder"), her experiences with poisonous snakes (she faces her fears by going on a rattler hunting expedition with Ross Allen, a famous Florida herpetologist), "varmints" of all varieties, her battles to save the orange grove from freezes, and her chronic trouble finding and keeping "hired help."

In these sections about the black population of the Creek, Rawlings reflects the racism of her era. The black maids she hires are almost all portrayed negatively as drunkards, nymphomaniacs, and/or lazy incompetents. Rawlings is guilty of the worst kind of "local color" writing in this instance, for she makes laughable caricatures of most of her black neighbors, ennobling only the Martha Mickens character as the wise old matriarch of the Creek's extended black family—and this portrayal, too, is a stereotype.

To her credit, Rawlings's attitudes about race altered dramatically when she met the author Zora Neale Hurston (author of *Their Eyes Were Watching God*). Rawlings entertained Hurston at the Creek farmhouse and apparently much enjoyed her company and her writing. However, according to Idella Parker, Rawlings's maid at the time, Hurston stayed in the tenant house, even though there were empty bedrooms available in the main house. At that moment in the American South, it seems that Rawlings simply could not transcend the social code that prevented a white woman from treating a black woman as her equal.

She came closer to achieving a sense of racial justice in her later life when her association with Hurston led her to publicly condemn the evils of segregation. She fought the local school board of Cross Creek to allow a black child to ride the all-white school bus, and she wrote a piece advocating equality in the armed forces during World War II that was so controversial, the publisher refused to print it. Her eyes may have opened to the shamefulness of racism later than her admirers today would wish, but they nevertheless opened well ahead of the civil rights movement of the 1960s. If her attitudes were retrograde in 1942, they were advanced by the time of her death in 1953.

INVASION OF PRIVACY

Rawlings described *Cross Creek* as "a love story," but at least one person depicted in the book, Zelma Cason, found it a personal attack: she sued Rawlings for "invasion of privacy." One of the lawsuit's many ironies is that Zelma Cason was the first person Rawlings met when she came to Florida and, of all the people she worried might resent her depiction of them in *Cross Creek,* Rawlings did not think Cason would be one of them. In fact, when one of the locals had become outraged at her earliest depiction of the region's inhabitants in "Cracker Chidlings," it was Zelma Cason who had defended and protected Rawlings from the irate party.

The passage that Cason found offensive occurs in the chapter of *Cross Creek* titled "The Census," in which Rawlings describes accompanying Zelma on horseback to take the local census. Zelma, she wrote, "is an ageless spinster resembling an angry and efficient canary," an amusing and, according to Cason's contemporaries, accurate portrait of her. The chapter goes on to portray Cason as a warm, maternal figure with a large heart and an extraordinary capacity for colorful cursing. Although Rawlings apologized to Zelma, the damage was done: Cason brought a lawsuit that dragged through the courts for over five years, culminating in a famous trial held in Gainesville, Florida, in May 1946.

Rawlings found herself defending an author's right to publish the truth, while Cason defended a subject's right not to be ridiculed publicly. In the end, after almost all of the witnesses from Cross Creek testified on her behalf, the jury found Marjorie Rawlings Baskin not guilty. However, Cason appealed the verdict and the Florida Supreme Court agreed that invasion of privacy had occurred. However, they only permitted the plaintiff to collect "nominal damages and costs." Marjorie and Norton paid Zelma $1.00 in damages and court costs of $1,015.10, but the trial took an incalculable toll on the author.

Patricia Nassif Acton, author of *Invasion of Privacy: The Cross Creek Trial of Marjorie Kinnan Rawlings* (1988), believes that the lawsuit sapped Rawlings's creative energies and contributed to the serious decline in her writing abilities during the last decade of her life. Certainly the trial, finally concluded in 1948, put an enormous emotional strain on Rawlings during the five years it lasted, but heavy drinking also took its toll, as did worry about her husband— Norton Baskin joined the American Field Service during World War II and she wrote him daily, as she did many other American soldiers. Baskin drove an ambulance and, at the end of his service, was lost in enemy territory. When the army finally found him, he was suffering from malarial dysentery and came home extremely ill. Surely, however, the worst effect on

her writing stemmed from the death of Maxwell Perkins in 1947. Marjorie's reaction was one of "unspeakable grief" and the quality of her writing, certainly, never recovered from the blow.

During the Cross Creek trial, Rawlings's main contribution to literature was a cookbook, *Cross Creek Cookery* (1942), which Perkins had urged her to put together. It is a compilation of her favorite Florida recipes, some of which were initially mentioned in the "Our Daily Bread" chapter of *Cross Creek*. Rawlings was an accomplished cook and hostess and the cookbook served to express, in yet another way, the connection of the local people to the land and its bounty, the link between a place and its food.

The last book Rawlings and Perkins worked on together was *The Secret River* (published posthumously in 1955), a children's book with a black girl, Calpurnia, as its heroine. Rawlings avoided using any "Negro dialect" in this story because, as she told Perkins, she wanted to give complete dignity to all the black characters in the book.

At the time of Perkins' death, Rawlings had just begun work on her final novel, *The Sojourner*, set in upstate New York and based on the life of her maternal grandfather, Abram Traphagen, whose farm in Michigan she had frequently visited as a child and young adult. The writing was tortuous and slow and, without Perkins to help her, it was also substandard. She wrote to a friend, "I should not be in such anguish if Max were here. He could have told me long ago whether or not I am on the right track" (quoted in Silverthorne).

The novel contained all of the author's beliefs about time and the universe, human relationships and loneliness, and the enduring quality of the land, where humans begin and end their short "sojourn" on earth. Unfortunately, these concepts, which she had wrought so finely in *South Moon Under, The Yearling,* and *Cross Creek,* become tedious platitudes in this final novel. *The Sojourner* reaped mixed reviews in its time and today it is rated with *Golden Apples* as one of her lesser books.

After the publication of *The Sojourner*, Rawlings immediately plunged into work on a full-scale biography of Ellen Glasgow. This was what she was working on at the time of her death from cerebral hemorrhage on December 14, 1953. Her death contained one final irony: Norton Baskin mistook the cemetery where she wanted to be buried and she was accidentally interred in Antioch Cemetery—a short distance from the grave of Zelma Cason.

CONCLUSION

Perhaps because Rawlings's best writing was about her life and that of the people she lived with in Florida, the best of the scholarship devoted to her also focuses primarily on her life. In addition to Elizabeth Silverthorne's biography, *Sojourner at Cross Creek,* three memoirs of Rawlings, one by her former neighbor J. T. Glisson (*The Creek,* 1993) and two by Idella Parker, her former maid (*Idella: Marjorie Rawlings' "Perfect Maid,"* 1992, and its sequel, *Idella Parker: From Reddick to Cross Creek,* 1999), provide intriguing glimpses of Rawlings as a person, a neighbor, and an employer.

In the chapter of his memoir titled "That Woman Next Door," J. T. Glisson gives a memorable portrait of Rawlings in witty and vivid prose that measures well against her own. Glisson, who remembers Chuck Rawlings, Marjorie's first husband, gives him a far kinder treatment than the feminist critics who have studied the author's life and work. "Charles," Glisson writes, "was a personable man with a quick wit and a love of satire. He clearly enjoyed feeling akin to the other Creek men and found great satisfaction in physical labor." Charles helped Tom Glisson prune their orange grove, and the two men fished together. When Marjorie and Charles came to the Glisson house on a spring day in 1933 to say goodbye—Chuck was leaving, for good—the Glissons were sorry to see him go.

As far as Rawlings's impact on her neighbors goes, Glisson observes that "she was of little or no real consequence in the daily lives of the Crackers at the Creek, although they felt a neighborly responsibility to her." He then expands on the impression she made on the neighborhood:

> She exuded an aura of energy and controversy. She was charismatic, antisocial and unyielding, a force that could not be ignored. She smoked in public at a time when most women smoked in secret and publicized her taste for good liquor when most of the county buried their empty bottles. Her fast driving, reckless accusations, and occasional profanity all created an image not always admired but never ignored.

J. T. Glisson remembers Rawlings as a good friend, particularly to him. He showed her how to make a "flutter wheel" (a toy water-wheel made out of palm fronds), a device that serves an important symbolic purpose in *The Yearling.* J. T. Glisson's ardent avoidance of chores in his boyhood reminds one of Jody in Rawlings's story and, though he does not say it, his memoir suggests that Rawlings may have had him in mind when she created this character. As for *Cross Creek,* "Mrs. Rawlings's version . . . was in some ways more vibrant, yet more simplified, than the real-life Creek. . . . The book was a gift of a time and a place that was passing, though I was too young to know it."

If Glisson provides a neighbor's viewpoint on Rawlings, Idella Parker, "the perfect maid" Rawlings mentions in *Cross Creek,* provides that of an employee. Recalling the saying that "No one is a hero to his valet," Rawlings certainly was no heroine to Idella Parker. Their relationship was further complicated by the fact that Parker was not only Rawlings's maid but her *black* maid. In her first memoir, Parker remembers her days with Rawlings as days of segregation, when blacks feared whites. "Fear caused us to be obedient and do as we were told," and Rawlings, she adds, never asked, she *told.*

Parker's portrait of Rawlings says a great deal about her own life after 1953. Idella Parker lived to see the civil rights movement and integration, but Rawlings will forever remain trapped in the early 1950s. As an employer, Rawlings was described by Parker as generous and kind for the most part, though she could be savage when drunk (which was most of the time, according to Parker), and "she was often sad, sometimes to the point where she couldn't get out of bed in the morning." She adored Norton Baskin who, Parker says, did his best to make her happy, but happiness seemed always just out of her reach.

Parker's reiterated theme is that Rawlings "was a good, kind woman who never meant anybody harm. The person she hurt most was herself." Her second memoir, published after the death of Baskin, tells even harsher stories of Rawlings's drinking and cursing, as if Parker seems less and less able—or willing—to remember the generous aspects of her former boss.

In the end, of course, it is not Rawlings's life that will matter most, but her work. The work, like the land of Cross Creek, is indifferent to human opinion. Her best writing, in fact, treats this idea, and it appears at the conclusion of *Cross Creek*:

> After I am dead, who am childless, the human ownership of grove and field and hammock is hypothetical. . . . [The earth] gives itself in response to love and tending, offers its seasonal flowering and fruiting. But we are tenants and not possessors, lovers and not masters. Cross Creek belongs to the wind and the rain, to the sun and the seasons, to the cosmic secrecy of seed, and beyond all, to time.

Selected Bibliography

WORKS OF MARJORIE KINNAN RAWLINGS

FICTION
South Moon Under. New York: Scribners, 1933.

Golden Apples. New York: Scribners, 1935.

The Yearling. New York: Scribners, 1938.

When the Whippoorwill. New York: Scribners, 1940. (Short stories.)

The Sojourner. New York: Scribners, 1953.

The Secret River. New York: Scribners, 1955. (Children's book.)

NONFICTION
Cross Creek. New York: Scribners, 1942.

Cross Creek Cookery. New York: Scribners, 1942.

COLLECTED WORKS
The Marjorie Rawlings Reader. Edited by Julia Scribner Bigham. New York: Scribners, 1956.

Short Stories. Edited by Rodger L. Tarr. Gainesville: University Press of Florida, 1994. (Contains all of Rawlings's short stories published after 1930 with the exception of "Mountain Prelude.")

Poems by Marjorie Kinnan Rawlings: Songs of a Housewife. Edited by Rodger L. Tarr. Gainesville: University Press of Florida, 1997. (Contains 250 out of 495 poems that Rawlings wrote for the *Rochester Times-Union* between May 1926 and February 1928.)

UNCOLLECTED FICTION, POETRY, ESSAYS, AND ARTICLES
"The Reincarnation of Miss Hetty." *McCall's Magazine,* August 1912, pp. 27, 72. (Short story.)

"The Miracle." *Wisconsin Literary Magazine* 17:7 (October 17, 1917). (Poem.)

Editorial on Vachel Lindsay. *Wisconsin Literary Magazine* 17:169–170 (April 1918).

"Having Left Cities Behind Me." *Scribner's Magazine* 98:246 (October 1935).

"Mountain Rain." *Scribner's Magazine* 104:63 (July 1938).

"I Sing While I Cook." *Vogue,* February 15, 1939, pp. 48–49.

"In the Heart." *Collier's,* February, 3 1940, pp. 19, 39. (Reprinted in altered form in *Cross Creek.*)

"Regional Literature of the South." *College English* 1:381–388 (February 1940).

"Cross Creek Breakfasts." *Woman's Home Companion,* November 1942, pp. 72–73.

"Sweet Talk, Honey!" *Vogue,* December 1, 1942, pp. 77, 116–118.

"Trees for Tomorrow." *Collier's,* May 8, 1943, pp. 14–15, 24–25.

"Florida: A Land of Contrasts." *Transatlantic* 14:12–17 (October 1944).

Introduction to *Katherine Mansfield Collection.* Edited by John Middleton Murray. Cleveland: World, 1946.

"Mountain Prelude." *Saturday Evening Post,* April 26, 1947–May 31, 1947. (Serialized novel in six parts.)

"About Fabulous Florida." *New York Herald Tribune Book Review,* November 30, 1947. (Review of Marjorie Stoneman Douglas' *The Everglades: River of Grass.*)

"Portrait of a Magnificent Editor, as Seen in His Letters." *Publishers Weekly* 157:1573–1574 (April 1, 1950).

CORRESPONDENCE AND PAPERS

Selected Letters of Marjorie Kinnan Rawlings. Edited by Gordon E. Bigelow and Laura V. Monti. Gainesville: University Press of Florida, 1983.

Max and Marjorie: The Correspondence between Maxwell E. Perkins and Marjorie Kinnan Rawlings. Edited by Rodger L. Tarr. Gainesville: University Press of Florida, 1999.

The largest collection of Rawlings material is housed in the Marjorie Kinnan Rawlings Collection, Special Collections, University of Florida Libraries, Gainesville, Florida. This collection includes her manuscripts, correspondence, "autobiographical sketches," and lecture notes, in addition to miscellaneous papers and her published works. Other holdings of Rawlings's material may be found in the Scribners' Archives of the Princeton University Firestone Library, and smaller collections exist at Yale University, the University of Virginia at Charlottesville, and the University of Georgia at Athens.

BIBLIOGRAPHY

Tarr, Rodger L., ed. *Marjorie Kinnan Rawlings: A Descriptive Bibliography.* Pittsburgh: University of Pittsburgh Press, 1996.

CRITICAL AND BIOGRAPHICAL STUDIES

Acton, Patricia Nassif. *Invasion of Privacy: The Cross Creek Trial of Marjorie Kinnan Rawlings.* Gainesville: University of Florida Press, 1988.

Bellman, Samuel I. *Marjorie Kinnan Rawlings.* Boston: Twayne, 1974.

Berg, A. Scott. *Max Perkins: Editor of Genius.* New York: Dutton, 1978.

Bigelow, Gordon E. *Frontier Eden: The Literary Career of Marjorie Kinnan Rawlings.* Gainesville: University of Florida Press, 1966, 1989.

Boyd, Janet L. "'More Than Meets the Eye': Camilla Van Dyne as the Inversion of the American Myth in Golden Apples." *Marjorie Kinnan Rawlings Journal of Florida Literature* 3:41–48 (1991).

Evans, Harry. "Marjorie Kinnan Rawlings." *Family Circle,* May 7 and 14, 1943.

Glisson, J. T. *The Creek.* Gainesville: University Press of Florida, 1993.

Jones, Carolyn M. "Nature, Spirituality, and Home-making in Marjorie Kinnan Rawlings' Cross Creek." In *Homemaking: Women Writers and the Politics and Poetics of Home.* Edited by Catherine Wiley. New York: Garland, 1996.

Morris, Lloyd. "A New Classicist." *North American Review* 246 (September 1938).

Morrison, Sally. *Cross Creek Kitchens.* Gainesville: Triad Books, 1983.

Parker, Idella, with Mary Keating. *Idella: Marjorie Rawlings' "Perfect Maid."* Gainesville: University Press of Florida, 1992.

———, with Bud and Liz Crussell. *From Reddick to Cross Creek.* Gainesville: University Press of Florida, 1999.

Marjorie Kinnan Rawlings Journal of Florida Literature. Rollins College, Winter Park, Florida. (Complete index of article titles available online at http://fox.rollins.edu/~jcjones/toc.htm.)

"Marjorie Kinnan Rawlings." *Los Angeles Times,* April 24 and May 3, 4, 10, 17, and 24, 1953. (Rawlings's answers to a questionnaire were reconstructed as an "autobiographical" account.)

Prenshaw, Peggy Whitman. "Marjorie Kinnan Rawlings: Woman, Writer, and Resident of Cross Creek." *Marjorie Kinnan Rawlings Journal of Florida Literature* 1:1–18 (1988).

Rowe, Anne E. *The Idea of Florida in the American Literary Imagination.* Gainesville: University Press of Florida, 1992.

Rubin, Louis D., Jr., ed. *The History of Southern Literature.* Baton Rouge: Louisiana State University Press, 1985.

Saffy, Edna. "Marjorie Kinnan Rawlings' Theory of Composition." *Marjorie Kinnan Rawlings Journal of Florida Literature* 2:109–130 (1989–1990).

Silverthorne, Elizabeth. *Marjorie Kinnan Rawlings: Sojourner at Cross Creek.* Woodstock, N.Y.: Overlook Press, 1988.

Trefzer, Annette. "Floating Homes and Signifiers in Hurston's and Rawlings' Autobiographies." *Southern Quarterly* 36 (spring 1998).

Turk, Janet K. "Marjorie Kinnan Rawlings: Forgotten Woman of the American Canon." *Conference of College Teachers of English Studies* 64 (September 1999).

York, Lamar. "Marjorie Kinnan Rawlings' Rivers." *Southern Literary Journal* 9 (1977).

FILMS AND PLAYS BASED ON RAWLINGS'S WORKS

The Yearling. Produced by Sidney Franklin; directed by Clarence Brown. MGM Studios, 1946.

The Sun Comes Up (based on "Mountain Prelude"). Directed by Richard Thorpe. MGM TV, 1949.

The Yearling. Broadway musical adapted by Herbert E. Martin and Lore Noto; music by Michael Leonard, lyrics by Herbert Martin. (A flop—it opened December 10, 1965, and closed after three performances.)

Gal Young 'Un. Directed by Victor Nunez for television. Independently produced, 1979.

Cross Creek. Produced by Robert Radnitz; directed by Martin Ritt. Universal Studios, 1983.

A Tea with Zora and Marjorie. Play by Barbara Speisman. Performed in various locales and published in *The Marjorie Kinnan Rawlings Journal of Florida Literature* 1:67–100 (1988).

The Yearling. Television movie produced for CBS in 1994 by Robert Halmi Sr.; directed by Clarence Brown.

—SUSAN BALÉE

Ishmael Reed

1938–

PERHAPS NO OTHER writer has sparked as much controversy and debate in the past few decades as Ishmael Reed. Never afraid to back down from a good fight, Reed could be accused of "reckless eyeballing," the title of one of his most infamous novels. Instead, Reed provides serious readers and critics of American culture with a steady and unflinching look at American history, cultural genocide, and the sometimes terrorist practices of arbiters of artistic taste. There appear to be few people whom Reed has not agitated, inflamed, or at least exasperated. Even his most ardent critics find themselves having to defend his style and his vision. Truly, he seems to be a writer you either love or hate—or at least wish would just shut up and leave you alone.

Of course, almost every writer who has ever considered himself or herself a satirist has suffered the slings and arrows of the reading public. At a time when satire is increasingly a misunderstood art, Reed is an easy target for pundits and critics. Since some of Reed's targets include the very people who would read, study, and write about his work, it is not surprising that many of the reviews and essays about Reed say little about the work and more about the man's "problems" with society. Some critics have argued that Reed fans the flames in his numerous interviews, where he discusses his work and directly responds to his critics, usually by name. All of this obscures the art and the "message" of the work. A concentrated study of his writing reveals an artist deeply devoted to his faith in the word. The manifestation of that devotion is Reed's self-realized "Neo-HooDoo Aesthetic," which embraces and cel-

ebrates multicultural, multilingual, multidisciplinary visions of art. Kinetic, infectious, playful, soulful, innovative, and "possessed of the spirit," Reed's style has been compared to jazz. Its bebop rhythms and philosophy capture on the page the essence of that music, so much so that the jazz drummer Max Roach called Reed the "Charlie Parker of American fiction."

In an interview with John O'Brien, Reed said that one of the goals of his work is to help "create our own fictions" and that his novels are really "guerrilla warfare against the Historical Establishment. . . . So this is what we want: to sabotage history." Neo-hoodoo is an instrument in the modern world of ancestral voices that Reed uses to hear and remember the past—not as it has been recorded but as an African American voice, unheard at the time, might have written it. Reed's intent is to undermine the accepted version of history that limits the stories of African American life. This salient feature of his writing mirrors the purposes of many of his contemporaries, including Charles Johnson, John Edgar Wideman, and Toni Morrison. His hybrid, intertextual, and multivoiced narratives also mark his work as postmodern and echo the work of such twentieth-century literary theorists as the Russian Mikhail Bakhtin. To varying degrees, each of Reed's nine novels, four collections of essays, five plays, five collections of poetry, and edited anthologies display his "Neo-HooDoo Aesthetic" sensibility.

LIFE

Born on February 22, 1938, to Thelma Coleman and Henry Lenoir, Ishmael Scott Reed spent his early years in Chattanooga, Tennessee. This was the only significant time that Reed spent living in the South. Reed's parents were divorced before he was four. He moved to Buffalo, New York, following the marriage of his mother to Bennie Reed in 1942. A precocious child, Reed displayed an early writing talent and the ability to hold an audience with his words. He often was called on to write poems for family, friends, and school. By age fourteen, he was writing a jazz column for Buffalo's African American newspaper, the *Empire Star Weekly*. Reed's interest in music has been lifelong and is one of his sources for the formation of the neo-hoodoo aesthetic. A songwriter and saxophonist, Reed captures in his work his interest in a multidisciplinary approach to art. A "renaissance man" (an appellation that Reed himself would satirize), he also acted in his youth.

In 1956 Reed graduated from East High in Buffalo. Between 1956 and 1960, he attended Millard Fillmore College and the University of Buffalo but then left school because he no longer wanted to be a "slave" to someone's "reading lists." In 1960 he married Priscilla Rose Thompson; their daughter Timothy was born that same year. Meeting the American civil rights leader Malcolm X in the early 1960s inspired Reed to move to New York City in 1962, where he seriously pursued writing as a career. He joined a writing workshop with other writers, such as Al Young and Calvin Hernton. In 1963 he started writing for *Umbra* magazine. It was there that Reed says he began formulating ideas that later became neo-hoodooism. In the same year he separated from his wife. Reed became the editor for the Newark newspaper *Advance* two years later.

Reed's work gained national attention with the publication of the novel *The Free-Lance Pallbearers* in 1967. Also in 1967, he moved to California and began teaching at Berkeley. Over the next few years, Reed became a prolific and successful writer. He published *Yellow Back Radio Broke-Down* in 1969. In the following year, Reed divorced Priscilla Rose and married Carla Blank. He also published his first collection of poems, *catechism of d neoamerican hoodoo church* (1970). This collection includes some of his seminal writings on the neo-hoodoo aesthetic. In 1970 he edited the anthology *19 Necromancers from Now*. The following year he helped found the journal *Yardbird*—the name is an allusion to the jazz musician Charlie Parker.

Two of Reed's most influential and remarkable works, the novel *Mumbo Jumbo* and the collection of poetry *Conjure* were published in 1972. The same year saw the establishment of Reed's publishing company, Reed, Cannon, and Johnson. The culmination of Reed's growing literary achievements was the double nomination he received for the National Book Award. *Mumbo Jumbo* and *Conjure* were selected as choices for fiction and poetry, respectively. While neither book won, the nomination was noteworthy for solidifying Reed's stature as a writer and for being the only time in the history of the award when a single author had two nominations for a book in two different categories in the same year. *Conjure* also received a Pulitzer Prize nomination the following year. In 1974, Reed published a sequel of sorts to *Mumbo Jumbo*, *The Last Days of Louisiana Red*. In the same year, Reed was honored with the John Simon Guggenheim Fellowship and a National Endowment Fellowship for writing.

In 1975 Reed returned to Buffalo, where he accepted a visiting teaching position at the State University of New York (SUNY) at Buffalo. He also received the National Institute of Arts and Letters Award for *The Last Days of Louisiana Red*. The next year was also momentous for Reed's work. He published the critically acclaimed *Flight to Canada* and established the Before Columbus Foundation.

Since 1967 Reed had been teaching at the University of California, Berkeley. In 1976 he was encouraged to pursue tenure in the English department, but he was denied tenure the following year. "The Great Tenure Battle" (as the event in Reed's life was later called) is, for some critics, the impetus for many of Reed's later satirical attacks on universities, but Reed's criticism of academic systems, philosophies, and personnel can be found even in his earliest novel. While the well-publicized denial seemed to the outside world the most newsworthy event of this year in Reed's life, no doubt the birth of his daughter Tennessee took precedence.

The late 1970s still saw a considerable flurry of activity from Reed. Within a few years, he organized the American Book Awards; published two books of poetry; won the American Civil Liberties Award; had an opera based on his poetry produced; taught at Yale, Dartmouth, Columbia University, Harvard, and the University of California at Santa Barbara; and was made an associate fellow of the Harvard Signet Society.

In the following ten years, Reed continued to show his artistic versatility. His play *Mother Hubbard* (1981), which has not been published, received a reading at the famed Actors Studio in New York City. He wrote and published the novels *The Terrible Twos* (1982), *Reckless Eyeballing* (1986), *The Terrible Threes* (1989), and *Japanese by Spring* (1993) as well as collections of essays, including *God Made Alaska for the Indians* (1982), *Writin' Is Fightin'* (1988), and *Airing Dirty Laundry* (1993). He also wrote two, as yet unpublished, plays *Hubba City* (1988) and *Savage Wilds* (1989), and published *New and Collected Poems* (1988). Reed recorded an album of his poetry collection *Conjure* in 1983.

The several editions of multicultural texts that Reed has edited are evidence of his commitment to young authors and marginalized writers. At the end of the twentieth century, Reed received several significant awards that speak directly to his body of work, his dedication to the African American tradition, and his critical

eye. He was awarded the Langston Hughes Medal for lifetime achievement in 1994. In 1995 SUNY–Buffalo gave him an honorary doctorate. Three years later, the MacArthur Fellowship, one of the most prestigious awards for an artist, was bestowed on him. This last achievement signals Reed's place as a writer who does not simply buck trends but who creates them. His current projects include the third book in the "terribles" trilogy, "The Terrible Fours," and a satirical novel based on the O. J. Simpson trial. This work promises to be classic Ishmael Reed.

THE POETRY

There is little critical work that focuses primarily on Reed's poetry. Most references or reviews see the poems as windows to the novels. A more helpful way of analyzing Reed's poetry is to consider it in jazz terms. The novels and the poems act as point and counterpoint in Reed's canon. Both the novels and the poems are variations on a theme, call-and-response moments. This could be said of all of Reed's work. Each genre and text seems to speak to another, revising the standards already set. Like a good jazz musician, Reed does not play it the same way every time. Many of the themes of the novels are expressed in the poems, but the poems should not be seen as separate stepping stones to the larger works. It could be argued just as easily that the novels explain the poetry.

Reed's first book of poetry, *catechism of d neoamerican hoodoo church,* establishes many of the ideas of his neo-hoodoo aesthetic, but the poems also offer us a glimpse of a more intimate Reed and a sense of his cultural philosophy. Just as important, we find in the poems Reed's concern with history and how this concern helps distinguish his style and develops his postmodern desire to deconstruct historiography and historical assumptions that drive American culture.

One of the primary images in Reed's works is duality. One instance of this is seen in the dual strands of cultural interplay in America between European and African tradition. The writer W. E. B. Du Bois describes this duality as double consciousness, which Reed revises in the novels. The poem "Dualism" suggests some of these ideas. The poem's subtitle is "in ralph ellison's invisible man." Reed's "response" to Ellison's novel, what the critic Henry Louis Gates Jr. has noted elsewhere as Reed's "signifying" on the tradition, draws our attention to the place of that novel in African American literature and its own characterization of double consciousness. At the same time, we comprehend that the place of African Americans in American history is dual and oppositional. The speaker is both "inside" and "outside" history. The figure does not find comfort in either position. He is "hungry" for acceptance in both places. The complex space that African Americans inhabit in the American historical spectrum is recognized in the allusion to *Invisible Man* in the subtitle. No matter where they are in the poem's image of history, African Americans will not stop being invisible until they have control over their own history. This theme reverberates in many of Reed's novels.

The poem "I am a cowboy in the boat of Ra," works as a connection between *Yellow Back Radio Broke-Down* (1968) and *Mumbo Jumbo* (1972), two novels that come before and after the poem, respectively, in the chronology of Reed's work. Like a musical bridge, the poem extends and flows into the pieces that proceed and follow it. The cowboy is a figure from *Yellow Back Radio Broke-Down* known as the Loop Garoo Kid. The "Kid" is also a symbol of neo-hoodoo and ancient art. He is a magician with words. He is linked directly with the Egyptian images of Osiris, a god also associated with magic and creativity. In both novels to which the poem alludes, the "villain" is a figure who tries to control or destroy the earthy

and creative magic that these characters and figures represent.

"The Neo-HooDoo Manifesto," a prose poem in *Conjure,* is one of the most direct representations of Reed's aesthetic. Neo-hoodoo is magic, voodoo, and dance; it is shape-shifting. The writer Zora Neale Hurston is the "theoretician" of the aesthetic, and the musician Charlie Parker is one neo-hoodoo artist, as is the poet Quincy Troupe. Reed lists other musicians who embody the aesthetic, such as the jazz pianist and composer Jelly Roll Morton, the blues vocalist Etta James, and the soul group The Temptations. Reed includes not just African American figures from jazz, the blues, and soul; he also suggests that the rock music groups Procol Harum and Credence Clearwater Revival exemplify the sensibility. It also is found in Native American poetry and South American dances. Reed stresses the multicultural, multiracial, and multinational flavor of the aesthetic. In fact, he uses the metaphor of gumbo to explain the qualities of the aesthetic and the artist's role in its creation. There are varied ingredients, and the signature and style of each "cook" determine the "taste" of the work. Each bowl of gumbo, like each work of art, is unique and has been given its taste by many different elements, not just one. Reed extends this image to argue that no one voice, no one "taste" (especially literary "tastes" or judgments), should be considered the most important. The neo-hoodoo aesthetic is an essential ingredient in understanding Reed's novels, as are his notions of individuality and the need to write one's own history.

THE FREE-LANCE PALLBEARERS

Reed's first novel, *The Free-Lance Pallbearers,* exhibits many of the characteristics and themes of his later novels. Its fantastic plot, characters, and satire are a direct reaction to the neorealism of many of his literary contemporaries in the 1960s. They also are a conscious recalling and revising of earlier African American traditions, notably the African American autobiography, one of the earliest and most prevalent literary forms in the tradition. Henry Louis Gates Jr. develops much of his theory about African American literature and signifying around the works of Ishmael Reed. In *The Signifying Monkey,* Gates asserts that *The Free-Lance Pallbearers* is a self-conscious "parody of the confessional mode which is the fundamental, undergirding convention of Afro-American narrative." To signify, Gates suggests, is to recall, revise, and satirize or parody a work, a form, or a genre. With his first work, Reed drives to the heart of the tradition, its beginnings and its essence. Along the way, Reed also pokes fun at everything—*Ebony* magazine, the American physicist J. Robert Oppenheimer, academia, the Roman Catholic Church, Du Bois, and even Richard Nixon's dog, Checkers.

The main character, Bukka Doopeyduk, lives in the projects of Soulsville (a version of Harlem) in the country of HARRY SAM. Married to Fannie Mae, Doopeyduk's life changes when HARRY SAM, the dictator for whom the country is named, asks him to replace Eclair Porkchop as head bishop. The names of Reed's characters resemble Warner Brothers and Disney cartoon figures. Like cartoon figures, Doopeyduk and others are drawn with exaggerated features and act as though they and their actions are prescribed by the rules that govern that medium. Doopeyduk, however, begins a transformation that alters his role in the work and in society. No longer content to fit the fictions that society has written for him, he plans a revolt against HARRY SAM.

We have seen all along Doopeyduk's potential for change. His mother-in-law gives him several names, all of them derogatory and many of which are plays on his own. The names suggest his ability to be more than one figure or at least to have the potential for multiple identities beyond the limited ones he has always known.

At one point, he is "hooDooed" and changed into a werewolf—a shape-shifter. This ability to transform and the folkloric figure illustrate Doopeyduk's need and capacity to shape his own destiny.

Other scenes in the novel imply that Doopeyduk is not the only one controlled by images. HARRY SAM runs the country through television. Visual images exert his power and impose his desires throughout the society. In a sense, SAM merely has to advertise how to feel and how to think on television, and the society follows along. The images of illness and decay associated with SAM maintain Reed's idea that the old western forms are dying. This also is demonstrated by one of the central metaphors of the book, the academic paper on the Egyptian dung beetle, and the numerous scatological images found throughout the novel (most of which are applied to people in power or to institutions). Unlike many other African American autobiographers, Doopeyduk does not, Reed suggests, become a mouthpiece for the very institutions that have helped enslave or oppress him. By refusing to accept without criticism the form of his narrative, Doopeyduk (and Reed) resist the fixed and monolithic versions of African American life. Doopeyduk's death, the critic Neil Schmitz believes, indicates Reed's desire to "murder a style." The style has only imprisoned African American authors in certain modes of expression.

YELLOW BACK RADIO BROKE-DOWN

Another formula that Reed attempts to deregulate with *Yellow Back Radio Broke-Down* is the western. Reed presents not only the traditional western as a target of his parody but also any forms produced by "western" civilization and culture. The novel is populated with cowboys, gunfights, cattle, frontier justice—all the elements of a "horse opera" or dime western, also known as "yellow" paperbacks (hence the title).

In Reed's own entry in *Conversations with Ishmael Reed,* he explains further that the title denotes his desire to parody the form and that the novel is "the dismantling of a genre done in an oral way like radio."

One way in which Reed "dismantles" the genre is through the violation of time and space, a characteristic of the neo-hoodoo aesthetic. Anachronisms abound in the work. Historical figures, such as Thomas Jefferson, the frontier explorers Meriwether Lewis and William Clark, the nineteenth-century "voodoo queen" Marie Laveau, the outlaw and gunslinger John Wesley Hardin, and the fifteenth-century pope Innocent VIII, are presented in a world populated with radios and airplanes. The violations of the western genre and of the notions of linear history remind us that such forms of knowledge and expression are not static or stable. We are reminded that similar to neo-hoodoo shape-shifting, writing, too, is a "shape-shifting" process, as is history. This idea echoes in the beginning of the novel, where we are told that the town Yellow Back Radio has been taken over by the younger generation. The "youth," for a time, are free of the constraints of the "older, western" traditions: "For three hours a day we went to school to hear teachers praise the old. Made us learn facts by rote. Lies really bent upon making us behave. We decided to create our own fictions." As we have seen in *The Free-Lance Pallbearers,* Reed asserts the need for new writers to clear their own space to speak and create, revising former traditions. Moreover, it is incumbent upon African American writers to address the limited stories constructed by the "western tradition" that have defined African Americans rather than letting African American writers, artists, and historians do so themselves.

The power of flexibility and the magic of creation are embodied in the hero of the novel, the Loop Garoo Kid. He is a black cowboy, and his name plays on the nicknames often given to characters in westerns, but it also is related etymologically to a "garou," or a werewolf. The conflation of identities in the single name revises the notion of the traditional cowboy hero. Even the fact that Loop Garoo is African American is a reworking of the generally accepted notion of cowboy heroes in the popular culture imagination. Historically, of course, African Americans were significantly instrumental in the westward movement, but the media and Hollywood present a limited vision of life in the west. These "fictions," in many people's minds, assert that there was no such thing as an African American cowboy, because they never saw one in a John Wayne movie.

Loop is not merely a folklore figure; he is also a neo-hoodoo "operative." Garoo has multiple identities, each seemingly contradictory, and Reed and his neo-hoodoo sensibility never see the need to reconcile the multiplicity. In the interview with John O'Brien, Reed says of his creations that Bo Shmo (the leader of the "neo-social realist gang" in the novel) is a "guy who has two minds. Garoo has an infinite variety." Part of that variety includes Garoo's claim that he is Christ's twin. He is God's eldest son, "booted out of his father's house after a quarrel." This description suggests that he is a Satan figure as well, a fallen god. At other times in the novel, he is an African American version of a Haitian deity, or loa, and he has abilities and characteristics reminiscent of the "bad man" figure of African American folklore, Stagolee. The beauty of neo-hoodoo is that Garoo takes all of these identities at once, a symbol of artistic freedom and creative magic. The name Garoo connects him to a shape-shifting identity, and Garoo's position in the novel reminds the reader once again of the need for flexibility in writing style, as well as readings of history.

Garoo's freedom and multiplicity are reflected in his own art. When Bo Shmo buries him up to his neck in the desert (a classic trope of the American western), punishing him for being a "crazy dada nigger," Loop responds, "What if I write circuses? No one says that a novel has to be one thing. It can be anything it wants to be, a vaudeville show, the six o'clock news, the mumbling of wild men saddled by demons." Garoo then questions Shmo's philosophy, wondering why he believes that "all art must be for the end of liberating the masses." Shmo's writing is the most extreme form of limiting fiction. All African American fiction in his view would portray African American life as nothing but miserable.

Reed seems to be alluding specifically here to writers like Richard Wright, who was championed by such white critics as Irving Howe, who celebrated the "realistic" portrait of the bleak life of African Americans. That version of art does not interest Loop Garoo. It does not dance or sing. It does not embrace the seemingly paradoxical relationship between individuality and diversity that is neo-hoodoo. It is the multiple and shifting and even conflicting selves that give Garoo his power and that Reed implies is the source of art, especially African American art. Again, because Garoo can be all of these characters, no one "story" can define him, especially if someone else (other than he) designs it. Reed also emphasizes that it does not matter whether that definition comes from a "western" (that is, European) source or an African American one.

Chief Showcase rescues Loop Garoo (in a helicopter). Showcase's name is an allusion to the Apache chief Cochise, but it also implies that he is a "showcase." His culture has been removed from him, placed in museums. He exists only to entertain others. This is the worst form of cultural genocide in Reed's eyes. Showcase is one of the few people who recognize Garoo's true powers, and he also exhibits one of neo-hoodoo's characteristics, verbal wordplay and parody. At times, Showcase seems to capitulate to Drag Gibson, Loop Garoo's arch-nemesis, when he is actually criticizing

him. Showcase's tricksterism is an example of the oral qualities of neo-hoodoo that are almost impossible to destroy as long as their spirit is kept alive.

MUMBO JUMBO

The immutable power of neo-hoodoo is one of the defining characteristics of Reed's next novel, *Mumbo Jumbo*. Reed's most critically successful work to date, *Mumbo Jumbo* has achieved a cult status with readers throughout the world. Gates calls the work the "great black intertext," citing its layering of many stories, traditions, and genres. He theorizes that Reed's novel is a parody or an act of signifying on the entire African American literary tradition. "Jes Grew," the manifestation of neo-hoodoo in the text, is the essence of African American culture. Its power derives from the fact that it cannot be contained; it cannot be measured or destroyed. Just when you think it has disappeared, it pops up somewhere else.

Mumbo Jumbo is the story of the search for Jes Grew, for the authentic text or literary tradition. The novel is Reed's parody of the detective story. Reed successfully accomplished a parody of the western, and it is fitting that one of the other most formulaic western (European) cultural forms should be exemplified in Reed's most complex artistic achievement. Not only does Reed deconstruct the detective's narrative, he also parodies the very nature of western thought and reasoning. The detective story enshrines deductive reasoning, linear thinking, and the search for a singular, stable truth. There is a definite and unchangeable conclusion to the traditional detective story. It is the emphasis on the rational that keeps most of the society in *Mumbo Jumbo* from understanding Jes Grew. But Jes Grew refuses to be analyzed or categorized; "once we call it one thing it forms into something else."

The classic detective searches for the facts. Reed suggests throughout his work that we must question our assumptions regarding "the facts." Facts are often manipulated to say what someone else wants them to mean. Often, it has been statistics about African American life that have been sold as history or sociology, when, as Reed has revealed, history is a fiction itself. Reed's parody of the detective novel resists closure. It resists the idea that clues lead to a single truth. The detective in *Mumbo Jumbo,* PaPa LaBas, is more interested in recovering the unknown history that is hidden by the cultural guardians of America. His office is the Mumbo Jumbo Kathedral, and he is most concerned with sizing up "clients to fit their souls." We also are told that he is a "descendant from a long line of people who made their pact with nature long ago." He is characterized by his intuition and his prophecy, which run counter to the rational designs of the typical detective story. He rejects the western mode of thinking when he tells his assistant, "Evidence? Woman, I dream about it, I feel it, I use my 2 heads."

Reason is more the companion of the Wallflower Order, PaPa LaBas's chief nemesis in the novel. The Order represents the "order" of western civilization itself. It is defined by its adherence to rigid paradigms, reflected especially in its historiography and linear thought. PaPa LaBas's name connotes an association with Esu-Elegbara (also known as Legba), the Yoruba god of indeterminancy, the guardian of the crossroads, where past, present, and future intersect and exist. It is clear that we have seen such figures in Reed's other novels. The crossroads imply a way of thinking about reality that is the antithesis of the standard, linear western model.

Music pervades *Mumbo Jumbo,* representing not only Jes Grew but also neo-hoodoo. The writer James Weldon Johnson used the term "jes grew" to describe ragtime and early jazz in the 1920s. It is also an allusion to the character Topsy in Harriet Beecher Stowe's novel *Uncle Tom's Cabin* (a work that would become a significant target of satire in *Flight to Canada*). Music, too, affects the style of *Mumbo Jumbo.* More so than any other of Reed's works, this book is influenced by his interest in jazz. The novel reads like a bebop composition, and it is clear that one of the founders of that innovative musical style, Charlie Parker, is one of Reed's neo-hoodoo priests. We are told that Jes Grew was the "Something or Other that led Charlie Parker to scale the Everests of the Chord. . . . Jes Grew that touched John Coltrane's Tenor."

Bebop as a musical movement was a reaction against the "fixed" and formulaic jazz popularized by big bands in the 1930s. Jazz, an African American cultural development, was mainstreamed by Euro-American artists and corporations. We see this reflected in much of the action of the novel. Bebop, often called the "revolt against the museum," is echoed here in the Mu'tafikah, the group whose mission is to free cultural artifacts of indigenous or third world cultures from museums, the agents of western civilization. The Mu'tafikah want to return the art to its rightful owners. In a sense, that is what Parker and other musicians of the bebop movement attempted to do—free African American musical traditions from cultural constraints imposed on them from the outside. We have seen this previously in Reed's work. He steadfastly attacks any attempts to limit the possibilities of either African American art or African American existence.

The range of Reed's objects of satire in the novel is too broad to outline, but one of his primary targets is the "museums," those people or institutions that designate themselves the arbiters of artistic taste. Such groups are responsible for a monocultural view of the world. Reed extends this criticism to theorists and artists connected to the black aesthetic and the black arts movement of the 1960s, who, he argues, tried to place limits on African American creativity. As he told Reginald Martin in an interview: "The black aesthetic crowd came in and writers were required to perform to their Marxist blueprints. But that's happened to Afro-American artists throughout history." The black aestheticians are as guilty as white theorists, in Reed's view, in creating a monocultural society. Reed uses *Mumbo Jumbo* to destabilize the traditions of America and Europe to their very core: through language, form, and the conception of reality. Like a neo-hoodoo magician, he conjures up a new form through his parody of the detective genre, satire, verbal puns, and intertextuality to attack the marginalization and cultural genocide of African American art by the academic hierarchy. Reed uses many of the rhetorical weapons of the western tradition against itself.

Marked by its postmodern hybrid nature and neo-hoodoo qualities, the new form not only destabilizes history but also redefines it. The violation of form and linear time emphasizes the fiction of history. The discourse of *Mumbo Jumbo* takes place in the 1920s and the 1960s as well as in the pre-Christian era in ancient Egypt and medieval Europe. The "primary" text is interrupted continually by "secondary" texts (photos, illustrations, bibliographies, dictionary entries, announcements, and other items). One should hesitate, however, to consider these other texts as ancillary. They serve to layer the work as a whole with Reed's multidisciplinary artistic sensibility, and, more important, they violate the artificial boundaries that were designed by the western tradition. Those boundaries have established hierarchies of art and thought for centuries, arguing that one type of writing is more acceptable or more truthful than another. Such hierarchies notoriously placed the art of non-western cultures at the bottom of the pile. Folklore or any other oral forms, for example, fell to the work of anthropologists, while works produced by European authors were considered "high art," worthy of study and imitation. As

Gates points out, Reed parodies these assumptions most clearly through his use of bibliographies, secondary sources, and footnotes, as a way to mimic the "fictions of documentation and history which claim to order the ways societies live."

Language itself is a possible threat to Jes Grew. Woodrow Wilson Jefferson likes the style of the *New York Tribune* because it is "objective, scientific," and uses the "collective We, Our." He never realizes that the "We" and the "Our" are meant to exclude him from the tradition or force him into assimilation (a dilemma that will face the hero of *Japanese by Spring*). Reed's playing with language, his verbal puns and signifying, emulate the spirit of Jes Grew and its resistance to scientific discourse. The Wallflower Order alludes to other groups in academia, especially those that use rational discourse to discuss art. Again, this works as another way to exclude certain artists from the discussion. Biff Musclewhite, one of the agents of the Order, argues against multiculturalism: "They are the ones that must change, not us. They . . . must adopt our ways, producing Elizabethan poets; they should have Stravinskys and Mozarts in the wings, they must become civilized." The Order (that is, the academy) brings out its "goons" with "letters after their names," which are their weapons against diversity. Their God is Milton, whom "English professors like because he's their amulet . . . keeping niggers out of their departments and stamping out Jes Grew before it invades their careers."

Hinkle Von Vampton, a satirical portrait of the white Harlem Renaissance patron and writer Carl Van Vechten, is in charge of controlling Jes Grew. One way in which he attempts to do this is by recruiting African Americans who will act as mouthpieces for his cause. Nathan Brown, a young intellectual and activist, sees through the offer to be a representative of the "Negro Experience." Brown accuses Von Vampton of implying that African Americans experience the world all in the same way.

The white academy, of course, is not the only group that wants to keep Jes Grew under control or that suggests limits on African American experience. Abdul Hamid, a representative of the black aesthete, denounces PaPa for his jungle ways and superstitions and burns the Jes Grew text (the Book of Thoth) when he decides that it is immoral and would influence the race negatively. His moral "superiority" makes him the sole arbiter. Luckily, Jes Grew cannot be destroyed; otherwise, Abdul's censorship would have been akin to a race's self-immolation. Just as Abdul has destroyed the text, black aesthetics threatens to destroy creative freedom, leaving no room for diversity. Reed seems tired of being confined to the false and accepted fictions (proposed by the western and the African American traditions) that African American history and literature are primitive, insignificant, or a mere catalog of degradation and human suffering. Reed parodies these conceptions in a text that is vibrant, mystical, and expansive.

The ending of the work has been a source of debate for critics and scholars, but if readers consider the conclusion in light of the neo-hoodoo aesthetic, Reed's intention is clear. When PaPa LaBas opens the box to reveal that Jes Grew has vanished, we should not assume its destruction. The scene reaffirms Reed's contention throughout his writing that there cannot be a single authority, not even the Jes Grew text. The essence of Jes Grew is process and change and its ability to adapt to each age and environment. Like the slaves that brought Jes Grew to the American shores, Jes Grew survives because of its ability to revise itself and because of its creative response to suffering and threats of destruction. PaPa LaBas summarizes the once and future Jes Grew text: "Jes Grew is life. . . . We will make our own future text. A future generation of artists will accomplish this." LaBas, however, realizes that each new generation will need to revise its traditions and texts, just as Reed has done in *Mumbo Jumbo*.

THE LAST DAYS OF LOUISIANA RED

Less critically successful was the sequel to *Mumbo Jumbo, The Last Days of Louisiana Red.* This novel continues many of the same themes presented in *Mumbo Jumbo.* PaPa LaBas returns as the detective assigned to discover who has killed Ed Yellings. The gumbo recipe in the preface alerts the reader that this is also a work of neo-hoodoo and that it will be a mix of styles and tastes. Gumbo is a stronger metaphor in this work than in Reed's other novels. Yellings's business was the SGW, or Solid Gumbo Works. His real "business" was voodoo. "Business" often has been used to refer to the work of voodoo priests. Yellings apparently had found a cure for several diseases before he was murdered, most notably the cure for Louisiana Red, which is the pathological ignorance of your past and your history. In the novel, it takes the form of mass amnesia. Gumbo, or neo-hoodoo, is the only way to help people who have forgotten their heritage or who are ignorant of their historical context.

Most of the novel deals specifically with Yellings's children rather than the mystery or the solution to his murder. Minnie, his daughter, is the focus of Reed's satire. She belongs to a quasi-political/social group known as the Moochers. Her name is an allusion to the Cab Calloway song "Minnie the Moocher," the story of a wanton and irresponsible female. These characteristics could be applied to Minnie in *The Last Days of Louisiana Red,* but less in terms of Minnie's physical desires. In the novel it is her obsessive and single-minded pursuit of political power that is the target of Reed's satire. What is particularly irresponsible about Minnie is that she has no concrete political philosophy other than Mooching. Her political machinations have no direction other than to serve her own ego, and they pose a danger to her community and her family. Her sister accuses her of "sloganism." Minnie has no solutions to the problems of the community. Many critics and scholars have argued that Moochers are African American intellectuals or members of the black arts movement or black nationalism (figures such as Eldridge Cleaver and Angela Davis are satirized in the work), who are ultimately, in Reed's portrait, interested only in serving their own needs and not the community's. Moochers, Reed writes, are

> people who, when they are to blame, say it's the other fellow's fault for bringing it up. Moochers don't return stuff they borrow. Moochers ask you to share when they have nothing to share. Moochers kill their enemies like the South American insect which kills its foe by squirting it with its own blood. God, do they suffer. "Look at all of the suffering I'm going through because of you." Moochers talk and don't do.

In the interview with Reginald Martin, Reed says that Minnie is also a representation of the feminist movement. Like the Greek tragic figure Antigone, she is a "single issue female. That was my attitude toward the feminist movement."

Sophocles' play *Antigone* also is parodied in the work (as are other versions of *Antigone*), once again showing Reed's penchant for satirizing forms, especially western ones. Here, the elements of Greek tragedy are used to comment on the similarity between the original place of Greek drama in its society and the attitudes of Moocher-types in the 1960s. Greek tragedy developed out of burial rites and sacrifices to the gods. Reed suggests that the African American Moochers he is satirizing also have sacrificed their own people, but their sacrifices are to the gods of money, public opinion, and political ideology. Amos Jones, who works for PaPa LaBas, chides George Kingfish Stevens and Andy Brown for their actions, "You Moochers always intimidating us, extorting us because we're the same skin color; even insects and

animals have a higher criterion than that for comradeship." Both Stevens and Brown have transformed themselves into stereotypical portraits of "Black Power" political advocates. The image is a false one for them, however. They embrace the image because they see it as an easy opportunity to get more power and money in the community, to mooch off of others' work. Minnie's actions, like those of her Greek counterpart, run counter to what is good for the community. In the case of Antigone, however, her deeds and their consequences emanate from a strong moral conviction that opposes the state. Minnie has no such conviction, other than Mooching. She is also willing to be the pawn of the white Machiavellian character Max Kasavubu. As in the Greek tragedy, Minnie's actions lead to her brothers' fratricide. The murder is the novel's symbolic foretelling of black-on-black crime and the "moochering" by African American intellectuals of their community.

FLIGHT TO CANADA

After *Mumbo Jumbo,* Reed's *Flight to Canada* is his most critically successful novel. The work follows the adventures of Raven Quickskill, an escaped slave and writer in the tradition of Frederick Douglass and William Wells Brown. Brown is, in fact, a character in the novel and a hero of Quickskill's. Brown and Douglass, and all slave narrators and their narratives, are parodied by Reed. Reed seems most interested that this novel bring attention to the flaws of the slave narrative form. Those flaws are primarily the result of white abolitionists' control of the narrative, as a form, and of its appropriation by such writers as Harriet Beecher Stowe in such books as *Uncle Tom's Cabin.* The voice of African Americans, in Reed's argument, is regulated and limited by the white "masters." Escaped slave narrators merely exchanged one form of control for another.

Because of its formulaic structure and purpose, the slave narrative constrained not only what African Americans could say but also how they could say it. Reed revisits the form to question this history and also so that he can open the form up to new possibilities. Reed is not alone as a contemporary author who returns to slave narratives. Such writers as Toni Morrison, Ernest Gaines, and John Edgar Wideman also have used slave narratives to reclaim historical African American voices. Reed, however, is one of the first to write a "neo-slave narrative."

According to Ashraf Rushdy in his critical study *Neo-Slave Narratives,* Reed's *Flight to Canada* is the "first of the Neo-slave narratives mobilized by the new discourse on slavery." The new discourse on slavery is the result of numerous events, most notably the civil rights movement, the black arts movement, and the publication of William Styron's *Confessions of Nat Turner.* The 1960s and its political climate brought new attention to African American history and its portrayal in American culture. Many writers revisited the slave past to give African Americans voices in a period when they were most brutally silenced. The publication of *The Confessions of Nat Turner,* written by the Euro-American author Styron, persuaded many writers, including Reed, that if African Americans were not careful, white writers once again would appropriate the historical voices of African Americans. Styron was the new Stowe. Reed and others returned to the slave narrative in its contemporary form as a means to combat such appropriation as well to recover African American history.

The neo-slave narrative is a popular form for many contemporary writers, including Reed, because it reminds its audience of the inexorable connections between America's past and its present. The problems of racism today have their roots in the slave past. Only by confronting the legacy of this past is art able to transcend it. The neo-slave narrative is one of the most

effective ways to bring to light the "hidden history of the black experience" in contemporary African American writing, according to Rushdy. Reed's violations of time frames in the novel (Raven, for example, takes a plane to escape the plantation) emphasize the relationship between the past and the present.

In *Flight to Canada,* as we have seen elsewhere, Reed highlights the need to control one's own fictions. This need is heightened in a parody of a form that was politically controlled by white abolitionists. That need also is exacerbated by Styron's novel and the climate of the late 1960s and early 1970s, when *Flight to Canada* was written. Reed focuses our attention on this need by his parody of Harriet Beecher Stowe in the novel. In *Uncle Tom's Cabin,* Stowe herself appropriated the story of Josiah Henson, a slave who escaped his master in Maryland and ran away to Canada in the early nineteenth century. Here, she wants to write the story of Uncle Robin, one of the slaves in Reed's novel. Reed sees appropriation as dangerous: "A man's story is his gris-gris, you know. Taking his story is like taking his gris-gris. The thing that is himself. It's like robbing a man of his Etheric Double." By taking Henson's story, Stowe, in a sense, took his life and once again enslaved him. In addition, she created stereotypes, "fictions," such as Uncle Tom, that persist today. By parodying Stowe, Reed resists and dismantles the "master narratives" that control much of the American cultural and historical imagination.

Turner and other historical figures, such as Douglass, Brown, and Uncle Tom, are given a new perspective in the novel. Most of the slaves in the work are portrayed as intelligent, creative, and forceful in their own way. Uncle Robin, especially, is a trickster, who seems passive on the surface. We later discover, however, that he has rewritten his master's will to change his own destiny. Uncle Robin's "rewriting" is a sign not only of his intelligence and creativity but also of the need for all African Americans, especially artists, to control their own stories and rewrite the fictions that others have designed for them. In a sense, Reed even suggests that Uncle Robin has more control over his destiny than did someone like Douglass, who, because of his position as the leading African American abolitionist voice, often had to suppress his creative impulses and voice to accommodate the needs of politics and history.

The anachronisms of the novel are numerous and serve to remind the audience that much has not changed for African Americans since the end of slavery. Quickskill uses a calculator, men drink CoffeeMate, the slaves have cable television, and Abraham Lincoln is assassinated on live television. Reed highlights the "fiction" of history here through these violations. Quickskill asks, as Reed might, "Who is to say what is fact and what is fiction?" The difference lies in who is telling the story. In the novel, Stowe's work is placed in the literature section of the library and Quickskill's work in the section on anthropology. The "arbiters of taste" determine how writing is defined. They also decide what is truth and what is fiction. More than in any of his other works, Reed questions here our very notions of these "ideas" and the nature of historiography. Quickskill ponders the nature of history: "Strange, history. Complicated, too. It will always be a mystery, history. New disclosures are as bizarre as the most bizarre fantasy." Reed points out that any fiction is as viable and as "truthful" as anything that we accept as fact. He also examines throughout the novel what happens when one group writes the "history" of another group.

In particular, Quickskill's former girlfriend and a Native American, Quaw Quaw, represents this focus in the novel. Her brother is buried alive in the Metropolitan Museum of Art. As in *Mumbo Jumbo,* Reed argues that the "museum" is a sign of cultural appropriation and is, in *Flight to Canada,* a deadly reminder of what cultural loss can mean for a people. In the novel Reed says, "There are more types of slavery than merely material slavery. There's a cultural slavery." This idea also is suggested by the figure of Yankee Jack, who, as a capitalist, has the most power in the book. He decides what "books, films, even what kind of cheese, no less, will reach the market." It is not always the academics and "taste" police who determine the fictions that we read. The economy is another decisive factor in determining who is heard and who is not. We are told that Jack is a "pirate," and the image focuses our attention on the ways that Europe and America have "pirated" cultures.

Reed concludes that the piracy of history and others' stories makes everyone vulnerable. The flight to Canada is less a physical journey to an actual place of freedom than the freedom to express oneself as one sees fit and as one wishes. Unless people can control their own stories, they will never be free. As Reed argues at the end of the novel, "Canada, like freedom, is a state of mind." Raven is the dismantler of the fictions that control him and his people. He is the neo-hoodoo representative of the text and a "scavenger to some, a bringer of new light to others." His name, like others in the novel, alludes to bird imagery and flight, an image that was common in slave narratives and slave poetry. But the novel begins with Raven's escape; it does not end, as the slave narratives did, with the flight to freedom. Instead, *Flight to Canada* concludes at the plantation, where Uncle Robin, having received the land from his master's will, has set aside a space for Raven to write. Uncle Robin has asked Raven to help him write his narrative, so that Stowe will not be able to do so. He knows that Raven will not "steal" his story. Uncle Robin's desire to make a community for artists and Raven's help in bringing his voice to the world are evidence of Reed's purpose in much of his work: to allow writers the narrative space to create and to give each writer the freedom to have his or her own voice.

RECKLESS EYEBALLING

Reed's most controversial novel is doubtless *Reckless Eyeballing.* Read by feminists as a vitriolic attack on women (especially feminists) and on Alice Walker's book *The Color Purple,* the novel is, on the most basic level, an examination of the effects of a politically correct climate on a writer's art. Ian Ball, an African American playwright, is having trouble getting his most recent play produced, because his last play outraged feminists. Now he finds that he must work with Tremonisha Smarts, an African American female playwright, whose play "Wrong-Headed Man" is a lampoon of *The Color Purple.* His producer, Becky French, is a white feminist. Ball is a man headed for trouble with women long before his play is produced. He is a chauvinist and womanizer, and even after he "changes his spots" to curry favor with Smarts and French, he has sexual fantasies about them.

Ball's new play is about Ham Hill, an allusion to and revision of a historical figure—fourteen-year-old Emmett Till, who was murdered in the South in 1955 for whistling at a white woman (or "recklessly eyeballing"). French wants Ball to rewrite his ending so that Hill can be resurrected and put on trial (as a decomposed skeleton) and found guilty of his crime. The ridiculousness of this act emphasizes the hysteria that Reed believes women exhibit about the image of the "black male as rapist." Peripherally, a man named the Flower Phantom is attacking feminists in the theater district, shaving their heads and accusing them of collaborating with the enemy. Smarts has suffered one of these attacks. Ian's "head told him that this man was a lunatic who should be put away for a long time, but his gut was cheering the man on. His head was Dr. Jekyll, but his gut was Mr. Hyde."

Real-life people again are the targets of Reed's satire, including the white feminist Susan Brownmiller. African American intellectual radicals are represented in the work by the playwrights Jake Brashford and Randy Shank. Reed's most disturbing vision, however, is the ritual sacrifice of Ball's friend Jim Minsk, who is murdered at Mary Phagan College. As the critic Jeffrey Melnick has argued persuasively, the allusion is specific for Reed. The murder of Mary Phagan, an employee of a pencil factory, in 1913 sparked waves of anti-Semitism in the South, when Leo Frank, her employer and accused killer, was sentenced for the crime. When his sentence was commuted, Frank was kidnapped from prison and lynched. Reed's purpose is not perfectly clear here, but he is directing the readers to reconsider, and possibly revise, the historical relationships between Jews and African Americans in this country.

THE TERRIBLE TWOS AND THE TERRIBLE THREES

Reed's "terrible" series has received less critical attention than other of his novels. The first work in the series, *The Terrible Twos* is a parody of several artistic forms and stories as well as a look at Reagan-era economics and the greed that drove the eighties. Reed published the work in 1982, yet he clearly predicts the decade's emphasis on materialism and conservative politics. At the center of Reed's parody is Charles Dickens's *Christmas Carol.* The metaphor of Scrooge permeates the novel. Institutions and corporations act in a greedy manner toward the citizens of the society, acquiring money while sacrificing humanity. They even co-opt Santa Claus for their own benefit. We are told it is "grand times for white men."

Reed also parodies the form of Dickens's work and other nineteenth-century novels. Reed uses the realism and sentimentality of these works to argue against limited artistic forms and also as a political tool. Realism and sentimentalism in the nineteenth-century novel, Reed suggests, did little to change the political climate; they merely reinforced the attitudes and situations upon which they were trying to shed light. Reed extends the satire of nineteenth-century realism to include the neorealism of the 1960s, which, we have seen elsewhere, he finds less than satisfactory.

The Terrible Twos and *The Terrible Threes* follows the stories of Saint Nicholas, Black Peter, and President Dean Clift. President Clift is a former model who campaigned as a cowboy. The allusion is clearly to Ronald Reagan. References to *A Christmas Carol* continue in such scenes as the day that Clift spends with his butler and the butler's crippled son. The events of the day begin to transform Clift as Scrooge is transformed in the Dickens's work.

Another intertext in *The Terrible Twos* is Dante's *Divine Comedy*. Clift is taken on a journey to hell, where he sees the circle known as President's Hell. Here, past presidents repeat the mistakes that have been costly to humanity. Clift's experiences change him, and he returns a transformed man. He decides that America must finally take responsibility for its actions. He announces that he will help the poor and weak. Rivals have him declared insane and remove him from office.

Reed alludes to the toddler years in the title *The Terrible Twos*. The image implies that America is irresponsible and, worse, greedy and petulant; everything is "mine, mine." We demand constant attention and gratification, just like a two-year-old. The novel supports this idea with numerous images of toys and tricycles. It is only Black Peter who has a mature vision of America and attempts to help us develop before it is too late. *The Terrible Threes* continues the story of the 1980s and its corruption, indicating that America still has not grown up. "The Ter-

rible Fours," which will be Reed's conclusion to the trilogy, is not yet finished.

JAPANESE BY SPRING

Two of Reed's favorite targets, the literary tradition of western culture and the academics that police it, receive some of his most biting attacks in his most commercially successful novel to date, *Japanese by Spring*. A postmodern work of a different breed than *Mumbo Jumbo* and *Flight to Canada*, *Japanese by Spring* still retains its multiplicity. Diversity comes through the need to accept many traditions and cultures. Reed sharpens his sword in the "Battle of the Books" still happening on college campuses today. He has expanded his view of the enemy in *Mumbo Jumbo* to include all "ethnic chauvinists," who secretively guard their own cultures and work to exterminate the validity of other traditions rather than support a collective, multicultural America. The enemy, especially here, lives in the ivy halls of academia. Academics, Reed insists, should know better. The goings-on at Jack London College are less than humane, and one is reminded of the brutal beasts that populate Jack London's novels. These beasts have an excuse, of course: they are animals. In his discussion of his own tenure battles, Reed notes in an interview with Jon Ewing that "King Kong is probably more civilized than some of these people teaching in these English departments. Gorillas are very fastidious, very aware of hygiene, they're vegetarians."

A literary theory mercenary, Benjamin "Chappie" Puttbutt, drives the novel. In the case of Puttbutt, "multiplicity" is a criticism. Puttbutt's many versions of his theoretical stance and of himself is not a sign that he embraces neo-hoodooism. Puttbutt does not occupy multiple visions at once, in celebration of multiculturalism; he merely changes his mind often, shifting with the political winds on his campus. The reader begins to understand that Puttbutt has sold his soul for a "mess of pottage," to quote James Weldon Johnson. Puttbutt's desire to be accepted in his department so that he can be awarded tenure separates him from his own talents and traditions and ultimately from himself. He is reminiscent of another Reed character, Ian Ball. Puttbutt has traded his convictions for a stable, fixed position at the university. We have seen earlier what Reed thinks of "fixed, stable positions." While Puttbutt is not a text, so to speak, he does represent someone closed off to neo-hoodoo. Reed's satire suggests that Puttbutt's middle-class desires have orphaned him from his heritage. He no longer suffers from the "double consciousness that Du Bois spoke of. The black part of him had been completely annihilated."

Puttbutt's theory du jour is New Criticism. He has decided that it will be the one that ensures his place in the "inner circle" (an allusion to the Wallflower Order of *Mumbo Jumbo*). Puttbutt naively believes that this group of theorists (who, Reed argues, are elitist) will accept him because he has adopted their voice. In an extension and revision of the earlier picture of Miltonists presented in *Mumbo Jumbo* Puttbutt is denied tenure by Dr. Crabtree, a Milton scholar. Crabtree keeps Puttbutt out of the inner circle because early in his career Puttbutt called Shakespeare a racist. Crabtree is reformed (or revised) at the end of the novel by his forced immersion in Yoruba language and poetry. Crabtree might now be called a Yorubist; he seems capable of celebrating only one tradition at a time.

Each of the academics in the novel is a monolithic observer. Among them are Dr. Milch, a white man who has become a black feminist ideologue because it is trendy and secures his position in the department; Marsha Marx, a feminist who sees gender oppression in Marxist terms; Dr. Charles Obi, who echoes the character of Dr. Bledsoe in *Invisible Man,* a former black nationalist who has traded his principles for his position; and Yamato, a Japanese imperialist. These are all characters who merely serve as cultural theory mouthpieces. They are types that Reed uses to flesh out his feelings about academia and the culture wars. As characters in the novel (another postmodern violation of fact and fiction), Reed calls these types "cause pimps." They are willing to further any principle as long as it gets them to where they want to go. They also judge the world by one aesthetic standard and do so in a rigid and very non-neohoodoo manner. The dean of the university is even more rigid in applying his rules. He sees all humanities professors as "losers," because they do not bring a profit into the university machine.

Later in the novel, when Puttbutt works for Yamato, his former colleagues call him "black fang." While the nickname sounds attractive to Puttbutt, who has heretofore been powerless, as usual the joke is on him. The inversion of Jack London's "White Fang" character does not represent freedom or power; it represents animalistic nature. "Black fang" is still controlled by either a master (now the Japanese imperialist machine and industry) or the forces of society. Puttbutt's father tells him that he joins "whatever side advances him," and like the "White Fang," dog of the north, he must adapt to its environment to survive. Puttbutt is caught in the grip of nature.

Reed echoes the image of naturalism as a literary trend here as well, especially in the figure of the naturalist Richard Wright, who for years held the position of the African American writer whom others were encouraged to emulate. Reed argues that the academy tries to control how we write and who we are, and until Puttbutt can forge his own identity, rather than accept the tags that others give him, he will remain completely lost as an individual, and, by extension, so will African American artists. It is the Reed character in the story who reminds the reader that the only way to achieve such freedom ultimately is to fight the D'Gun ga Dinzas (a parody of the name of neoconservative scholar and writer Dinesh D'Souza) of the world. The allusion to "Gunga Din" also reminds us of writers and thinkers like Rudyard Kipling (who wrote the poem) and Dinesh D'Souza, a staunch opponent of multiculturalism, who Reed feels, were and are servants to cultural massacres.

By embracing diversity, paradoxically, we are more free to choose our style and our identity (the two are inexorably connected for Reed). One of the final scenes at the temple illustrates this: "They dance. Sun Eagle Drummers & Fancy Dancers, Zydeco Flames, Salsa, Charanga Tumbao Y Cuerda, Cuban Salsa, Soca/Calypso/ Reggae, Kotoja, Modern Afro Beat. Flamenco. Traditional Flamenco. Rumba Flamenco. Vietnamese Music Ensemble." The diversity of the dance is the embodiment of the rhythms and freedom of neo-hoodoo. In this passage Reed also suggests by repetition, revision, and variation that these different art forms share a common ancestry.

CRITICAL RECEPTION

Despite Reed's "female troubles" and his problems with other critics who misunderstand or misread his work, he continues to be one of the most studied and written about contemporary novelists. His numerous awards and the scholarly debate that he ignites are a testament to his craft and his keen intelligence. If Reed were not striking nerves, no one would be talking about him. His desire to revise the past and its literary forms to suggest that there are many ways of seeing is as old as the work of African griots. These oral storytellers transmit the entire history and literature of a people, and from earlier eras to the present have given each story they tell its own distinction and situate oral epics and songs in the community to entertain, amuse, and instruct.

Reed has garnered a position as one of the most satirical and innovative artisans in the traditions of American and African American literature, one who is always fearless in his experiments with language, form, and content. His assaults are so wickedly pointed that the reader (and, it is hoped, society at large) feels compelled, in the words of the song made popular by Nat King Cole, to "straighten up and fly right."

Selected Bibliography

WORKS OF ISHMAEL REED

NOVELS
The Free-Lance Pallbearers. Garden City, N.Y.: Doubleday, 1967.
Yellow Back Radio Broke-Down. Garden City, N.Y.: Doubleday, 1969.
Mumbo Jumbo. Garden City, N.Y.: Doubleday, 1972.
The Last Days of Louisiana Red. New York: Random House, 1974.
Flight to Canada. New York: Random House, 1976.
The Terrible Twos. New York: St. Martin's, 1982.
Reckless Eyeballing. New York: St. Martin's, 1986.
The Terrible Threes. New York: Atheneum, 1989.
Japanese by Spring. New York: Atheneum, 1993.

ESSAYS
Shrovetide in Old New Orleans. Garden City, N.Y.: Doubleday, 1978.
God Made Alaska for the Indians: Selected Essays. New York: Garland, 1982.
Writin' Is Fightin': Thirty-Seven Years of Boxing on Paper. New York: Atheneum, 1988.
Airing Dirty Laundry. Reading, Mass.: Addison-Wesley, 1993.

POETRY
catechism of d neoamerican hoodoo church. London: Paul Breman, 1970.

Conjure: Selected Poems, 1963–1970. Amherst: University of Massachusetts Press, 1972.

Chattanooga. New York: Random House, 1973.

A Secretary to the Spirits. New York: NOK, 1978.

New and Collected Poems. New York: Atheneum, 1988.

EDITED WORKS

19 Necromancers from Now. Garden City, N.Y.: Anchor Books, 1970.

The Before Columbus Foundation Poetry Anthology: Selection from the American Book Awards. New York: W.W. Norton, 1992.

MANUSCRIPTS

A large collection of Reed's papers, artwork, sound recordings, unpublished plays, correspondence, interviews, and essays is located at the University of Delaware, Special Collections Department.

CRITICAL AND BIOGRAPHICAL STUDIES

Butler, Robert. "Ishmael Reed's *Flight to Canada*: Artistic Process as Endless Voyage." In his *Contemporary African American Fiction: The Open Journey*. Madison: Fairleigh Dickinson University Press, 1998. Pp. 103–114.

Cowley, Julian. "'What If I Write Circuses?': The Space of Ishmael Reed's Fiction." *Callaloo* 17, no. 4:1236–1244 (fall 1994).

Davis, Matthew R. "'Strange, History. Complicated, Too': Ishmael Reed's Use of African-American History in *Flight to Canada*." *Mississippi Quarterly* 49, no. 4:734–744 (fall 1996).

Dick, Bruce Allen, ed. *The Critical Response to Ishmael Reed*. Westport, Conn.: Greenwood Press, 1999.

Fabre, Michel. "Ishmael Reed's *Free-Lance Pallbearers*: On the Dialectics of Shit." *Obsidian* 3, no. 3:5–19 (winter 1977).

———. "Postmodernist Rhetoric in Ishmael Reed's *Yellow Back Radio Broke-Down*." In *The Afro-American Novel Since 1960*. Edited by Peter Bruck and Wolfgang Karrer. Amsterdam: Grüner, 1982. Pp.167–189.

Fox, Robert Elliot. *Conscientious Sorcerers: The Black Postmodernist Fiction of LeRoi Jones (Amiri Baraka), Ishmael Reed, and Samuel R. Delaney*. Westport, Conn.: Greenwood Press, 1987.

Gates, Henry Louis, Jr. *The Signifying Monkey: A Theory of Afro-American Literary Criticism*. New York: Oxford University Press, 1988.

Harris, Norman. "*The Last Days of Louisiana Red*: The HooDoo Solution." In *Connecting Times: The Sixties in Afro-American Fiction*. Jackson: University Press of Mississippi, 1988. Pp. 166–188.

Hoffman, Donald. "A Darker Shade of Grail: Questing at the Crossroads in Ishmael Reed's *Mumbo Jumbo*." *Callaloo* 17, no. 4:1245–1256 (fall 1994).

Jessee, Sharon A. "Laughter and Identity in Ishmael Reed's *Mumbo Jumbo*." *MELUS* 21, no. 4:127–139 (winter 1996).

Joyce, Joyce Ann. "Falling through the Minefields of Black Feminist Criticism: Ishmael Reed, a Case in Point." In her *Warriors, Conjurers, and Priests: Defining African-Centered Literary Criticism*. Chicago: Third World Press, 1994. Pp. 243–272.

Lindroth, James. "Images of Subversion: Ishmael Reed and the HooDoo Trickster." *African American Review* 30, no. 2:185–196 (summer 1996).

Ludwig, Sami. "Dialogic Possession in Ishmael Reed's *Mumbo Jumbo*: Bakhtin, Voodoo, and the Materiality of Multicultural Discourse." In *The Black Columbiad: Defining Moments in African American Literature and Culture*. Edited by Werner Sollors and Maria Diedrich. Cambridge, Mass.: Harvard University Press, 1994. Pp. 325–336.

———. "Ishmael Reed's Inductive Narratology of Detection." *African American Review* 32, no. 3:435–444 (fall 1998).

Martin, Reginald. *Ishmael Reed and the New Black Aesthetic Critics*. New York: St. Martin's, 1988.

Mason, Theodore O., Jr., "Performance, History, and Myth: The Problem of Ishmael Reed's *Mumbo Jumbo*." *Modern Fiction Studies* 34, no. 1:97–109 (spring 1988).

McGee, Patrick. *Ishmael Reed and the Ends of Race*. New York: St. Martin's, 1997.

Melnick, Jeffrey. "'What You Lookin' At?' Ishmael Reed's *Reckless Eyeballing*." In *The Black Columbiad: Defining Moments in African American Literature and Culture*. Edited by Werner Sollors and Maria Diedrich. Cambridge, Mass.: Harvard University Press, 1994. Pp. 298–311.

Rushdy, Ashraf. *Neo-Slave Narratives: Studies in the Social Logic of a Literary Form.* New York: Oxford University Press, 1999.

Schmitz, Neil. "Neo-HooDoo: The Experimental Fiction of Ishmael Reed." *Twentieth-Century Literature* 20:126–140 (April 1974).

Soitos, Stephen F. "The Black Anti-Detective Novel." In *The Blues Detective: A Study of African American Detective Fiction.* Amherst: University of Massachusetts Press, 1996. Pp. 179–219.

Weixlmann, Joe. "Culture Clash, Survival, and Transformation: A Study of Some Innovative Afro-American Novels of Detection." *Mississippi Quarterly* 38, no. 1:21–32 (winter 1984–1985).

———. "African American Deconstruction of the Novel in the Work of Ishmael Reed and Clarence Major." *MELUS* 17, no. 4:57–79 (winter 1991–1992).

Zamir, Shamoon. "The Artist as Prophet, Priest, and Gunslinger: Ishmael Reed's 'Cowboy in the Boat of Ra.'" *Callaloo* 17, no. 4:1205–1235 (fall 1994).

INTERVIEWS

Dick, Bruce Allen, and Amritjit Singh, eds. *Conversations with Ishmael Reed.* Jackson: University Press of Mississippi, 1995. (Includes interviews conducted by Jon Ewing, John O'Brien, and Reed himself.)

Martin, Reginald. "Interview with Ishmael Reed." *Review of Contemporary Fiction* 4, no. 2176–2187 (summer 1984).

—TRACIE CHURCH GUZZIO

Tom Robbins

1936–

When Tom Robbins's sixth novel, *Half Asleep in Frog Pajamas,* appeared in 1994, Karen Karbo led her review of it for the *New York Times Book Review* with a supposition about who it is exactly that reads Tom Robbins novels: "My theory on Tom Robbins is that unless his work was imprinted on you when you were 19 and stoned, you'll find him forever unreadable." Karbo's remark reveals how novelists like Robbins, whose fictional approaches include heavy doses of joy and mysticism, often find themselves shunted off into the drug-crazed, brain-fried intellectual discount bin of American letters. "A sober 21-year-old," Karbo continued, "is already too steely-eyed and seasoned to frolic in Mr. Robbins's trademark cuckoo plots, woo-woo philosophizing, overwrought metaphors and cheerful misogyny." The last of these perceived characteristics is interesting, given that a large proportion of Tom Robbins's readership is women, or at least that is how things started out when *Another Roadside Attraction* (1971) and *Even Cowgirls Get the Blues* (1976) entered the lives of so many wasted nineteen-year-olds back in the 1970s. This discussion will get to the women issue shortly, but Karbo's diminution of Robbins's abilities with plot, philosophy, and language represents a persistent strain in critical reactions to his work—that he just does not take things seriously enough to be taken seriously himself as a writer.

A look back at the critical responses to Robbins's novels shows that some reviewers have approached them with admiration and respect, but it also shows that for each published book one can count on the inevitable comparison to some philosophically lightweight icon of popular culture (Erma Bombeck and the Muppets come to mind). One of the more cryptic comments came from a British critic who quipped, "Tom Robbins writes like Dolly Parton looks" (*Still Life with Woodpecker*). In many instances of course such comparisons simply mask a political or philosophical objection on the part of the reviewer to Robbins's own outlook. But in other cases the message is that the very nature of Robbins's approach—one based on joy and positivism, one that believes in the transforming capabilities of laughter, and one that is skeptical of the cultural hegemony granted to the rational and intellectual over more mystical forms of experience—precludes him from being considered a serious artist.

Robbins attacks this line of thinking directly both in his novels and in interviews and articles about his work. As early as his second book, *Even Cowgirls Get the Blues,* he records the following when describing the fortune-teller Madame Zoe as she peers into Sissy Hankshaw's future:

> Over the years, like those literary critics who are forced to read so many books that they begin to read hurriedly, superficially and with buried resentment, she had become disengaged. And like those same dulled book reviewers, she was most resentful of a subject that did not take *her* values seriously, that was slow to reveal itself or that failed to reveal itself in a predictable manner.

Robbins's mission throughout his career has been to explode the expectations of accepted values and predictable manners, looking for new connections, new patterns of meaning, and alternative ways of perceiving reality and thus of living our lives.

In *Cowgirls* the narrator makes an important distinction between mysticism and magic by noting that magic can "be *made,* wholly and willfully, from the most obvious and mundane. . . . It is a matter of cause and effect. The seemingly unrealistic or supernatural ('magic') act occurs through *the acting of one thing upon another thing through a secret link.*" That secret link is a matter of perception. Robbins celebrates the transforming power of the individual view. If magic exists through the action of a secret link—or our ability to recognize the connections that appear all around us, all of the time— then magic also provides the basis for what Robbins sees as the Great Secret: that "one has not only the ability to perceive the world but an ability to alter her perception of it; or, more simply, one can change things by the manner in which one looks at them." This in turn creates an environment of limitless possibility and constant change, a fertile mixture for promoting individual freedom and that most profound of human attributes: choice. All of which, in Robbins's view, is cause for joy.

Reviewers and critics often characterize Robbins's "happy gospel" (in the words of reviewer Frank McConnell) as a facile brand of whimsy, suggesting that it ignores the evil, depressing realities of contemporary existence. They point to the ending of *Still Life with Woodpecker* (1980)—"It's never too late to have a happy childhood"—as naive and simplistic in its refusal to acknowledge the power of human suffering. Quite to the contrary, Robbins would argue, the joy embodied in his fiction is hard-earned. "My characters suffer," he maintained in a 1978 *New York Times Magazine* interview with Mitchell S. Ross, "they die, they look the beast of totalitarianism straight in the chops, and still opt for joy. . . . joy in spite of everything."

The philosophical thread that unites all of his novels is the belief that, when it comes to a fundamental view of existence, everyone has to figure things out for himself or herself. But the intriguing element of Robbins's preoccupation with individual perception is that it leads to stronger and more meaningful connections *between* people, particularly lovers. Once characters allow themselves the intellectual and emotional space free from public roles to figure out what gives their lives meaning, they can then interact with others from a position of freedom and strength.

The trick then is to give the power of perception free reign. Robbins's novels are exercises in identifying and breaking through the dimensions of contemporary life that block the capacity for individual and creative perception, which inhibits the ability to act independently and to establish a joyful relationship to the world. His primary means for conveying this process is comedy. But unlike other comedic writers— Thomas Pynchon and Kurt Vonnegut often appear as benchmarks for comparison—Robbins's comedy contains a bedrock positivism that makes him suspect in the eyes of critics who believe his humor and whimsy belie serious intent. Robbins typically greets such suspicion with sentiments akin to Bernard Mickey Wrangle's in *Still Life*: "Those who shun the whimsy of things will experience rigor mortis before death."

Yet Robbins is also deadly serious when it comes to his ambitions as a novelist and his comic view of life. In *Alive and Writing: Interviews with American Authors of the 1980s* (1987) Robbins told interviewers Larry McCaffery and Sinda Gregory:

Comic writing is not only more profound than tragedy, it's a hell of a lot more difficult to write. There seems to be almost a conspiracy against exploring joy in this culture; to explore pain is considered not only worthy but heroic, while exploring joy is considered slight. This kind of attitude strikes me as nearly insane.

Robbins's fiction attempts both to expose the conspiracy and to offer an example of just how meaningful an exploration of joy might be.

THE TAO OF ROBBINS

The plots of Robbins's seven novels revolve around what he identifies as the "veils" to human understanding and freedom. Of course to think of them as plots in the traditional sense is to ignore their frequent trespassing of the boundaries ordinarily assigned to time, space, and reality. As goofy as the goings-on may sometimes appear, however, Robbins's approach frequently reflects an intense interest in the intricacies of modern physics, which sees all things—human and otherwise—as both connected and in constant motion. The organization of events in Robbins's novels, particularly the early novels, also demonstrates his awareness of the relative nature of our normal conceptions of time and space.

In the late 1970s Robert Nadeau made a convincing case for the role contemporary physics plays in Tom Robbins's worldview and explained how that manifests itself in *Another Roadside Attraction* and *Even Cowgirls Get the Blues*. Nadeau also established the link between the new physics and Robbins's predilection for Eastern religious philosophy, which seemed better able to accommodate the underlying relatedness of all things and the relative nature of time and space than traditional Western religious systems. Robbins's playful and garrulous narrators, often thinly disguised personas for the author himself, offer a mishmash of Eastern metaphysical musings tempered with an awareness of Western pagan beliefs and rituals. Characters too are not afraid to go off on philosophical rambles that reflect a spiritual outlook far removed from and frequently quite

hostile to the American Judeo-Christian tradition. The combination of new physics and Eastern mysticism in Robbins's work (a combination that has prompted more than one critic to recommend Fritjof Capra's *The Tao of Physics* [1975] as a helpful primer for Robbins's fiction) provides a philosophical framework for his primary task as an author—to get readers to see other possibilities for how to view life than those provided by family, by society, by government, by all external entities that seek to exert influence over individual consciousness.

As readers first made their way to Tom Robbins's paperbacks in the mid-1970s, it is doubtful they responded to the books on the basis of Robbins's integration of new physics with old philosophy. What they discovered instead was a voice that reflected their own counterculture leanings with its celebration of nontraditional lifestyles; its rejection of authoritarian social structures, like government and the church; its playful rejoicing in the physical and emotional pleasures of human sexuality; and its reassertion of individual consciousness as ultimate arbiter of reality. They also found in Robbins someone who knew something about drugs.

Some of the critical hostility or indifference to Robbins's fiction can probably be attributed to his status as countercultural shaman, stubbornly holding to a belief in the potency of illegal substances to help individuals break from standard-issue views of reality. One of the most important days in his creative life, both as an artist and as an individual being, came in the early 1960s, when he first experienced the effects of LSD. Since then Robbins has not wavered in his insistence that drugs with mind-expanding properties can open the door to a more creative understanding of purpose in both life and death. And thus they can be an important first step in escaping the stranglehold of contemporary ideology and orthodoxy. In no less a bastion of middle-class American values than *People* magazine, Robbins declared in a 1985 interview with Steve Dougherty, "I still regard LSD as right up there with the microscope and the telescope as an instrument of exploration."

Another of the problem areas for critics responding to Robbins's attempt to confound orthodoxy is his approach to women. He considers himself an ardent feminist, yet many readers who consider themselves the same find little to appreciate in what they view as Robbins's treatment of women primarily as sexual playthings. For his part Robbins maintains a belief in masculine and feminine principles, though he would argue that men and women can embody either or both. His goal as a writer has been to foster a return to a more loving and intuitive relationship with the world and with each other, a relationship he believes existed in matriarchal societies of the past. Where he runs afoul of some feminists is in their sense that what Robbins really means by the feminine principle is the *female* principle, a conception that limits women's potential for self-definition. One indication of this, they argue, is his reliance on sex as a primary means for achieving a more harmonious and independent existence.

Vivid sexual escapades and female protagonists are mainstays of Robbins's fiction. The former often assert independence or signal self-discovery in the latter. But most of all sex brings the element of play into characters' lives, an element Robbins thinks is sorely lacking in Western civilized society. Robbins devotes some of his most energetic descriptions to the touches, tastes, sights, sounds, and smells of bodies at sexual play or, as is sometimes the case, the singular body at play. Such episodes invariably appear as moments of physical joy and emotional freedom for Robbins's characters. But as Karbo's comment about Robbins's "cheerful misogyny" suggests, some readers, women readers in particular, have wondered how much really separates Robbins's bodies at play from

traditional male fantasies, where the message is that all women really need to be happy is a good fuck.

THE MANY-TONGUED BEAST

The fact that Robbins's novels often seem to be a grab bag of loony characters set loose on farcical adventures in pursuit of some otherworldly pot of gold at the end of his philosophical rainbow illustrates the importance he attaches to alternative points of view, but it also testifies to his faith in style over content. As Amanda notes in *Another Roadside Attraction,* we

> must use style to alter content. If our style is masterful, if it is fluid and at the same time complete, then we can re-create ourselves, or rather, we can re-create the Infinite Goof within us. We can live *on top* of content, float above the predictable responses, social programming and hereditary circuitry, letting the bits of color and electricity and light filter up to us, where we may incorporate them at will into our actions.

Robbins attempts always, through a masterful style, to self-consciously conjure a reading environment that fosters imaginative re-creation. Of course the tool for that conjuring, the tool that creates consciousness itself, is language. Robbins addressed his commitment to language in a 1984 article in *fiction international*: "A writer's first obligation is not to the many-bellied beast but to the many-tongued beast, not to Society but to Language. Everyone has a stake in the husbandry of Society, but Language is the writer's special charge."

More than anything Robbins likes to play around with language. And his approach is neither subtle nor obscure in this regard. He wants readers to be conscious of the fact that they are reading an artificial configuration of words. He wants readers, as he puts it, to appreciate fully the essential "bookness" of the novel they hold in their hands. The following often-quoted passage from *Even Cowgirls Get the Blues* shows exactly how self-conscious he can be when it comes to matters of language:

> This sentence is made of lead (and a sentence of lead gives a reader an entirely different sensation from one made of magnesium). This sentence is made of yak wool. This sentence is made of sunlight and plums. This sentence is made of ice. This sentence is made from the blood of the poet. This sentence was made in Japan. This sentence has a crush on Norman Mailer. This sentence is a wino and doesn't care who knows it. . . . This sentence is proud to be part of the team here at *Even Cowgirls Get the Blues*. This sentence is rather confounded by the whole damn thing.

Such playful stylizing places Robbins within the metafictional camp alongside writers like John Barth or Donald Barthelme. But where readers of the others sometimes get lost in the funhouse of language and technique their novels both construct and embody, Robbins is careful to keep readers' interests pinned to at least some semblance of a recognizable plot and to clearly discernible albeit outlandish characters. Robbins's narrators frequently help hold things together as well by reporting on chronological or other kinds of narrative disruptions in a novel as it progresses. Although Robbins's prose has become less wildly self-referential over the years, it always finds a way to acknowledge the writer's special charge.

Given his penchant for rambling digressions, Robbins's style may initially strike a reader as having a baroque quality to it. But as Jerome Klinkowitz points out, Robbins is actually "a master of plain American speech." Klinkowitz adds, however, that Robbins frequently bends such speech into wacky combinations that, through metaphorical, suprarational connections, recompose the world inside a reader's head. Using simile and metaphor, Robbins often juxtaposes incongruous elements in a highly entertaining and edifying manner, once again forcing readers to acknowledge the artificial construct of language itself and how *it*, ultimately, is what

a book amounts to. One can find in any Robbins novel examples of linguistic tomfoolery that nonetheless give readers pause for contemplation. That pause offers the opportunity to *participate* in making meaningful connections rather than simply to observe the author doing so.

A related feature of Robbins's love affair with words is the extended riffs he ventures into in order, through the sheer accumulation of sounds and syntax or through puns and one-liners, to drive home a point relative to his or his character's overall outlook and sometimes just for the pure pointless fun of it. Robbins's description of Plucky Purcell's grin in *Another Roadside Attraction* offers a sampling of both Robbins's diabolical combinations and his jazz-like tendency to improvise:

> Man, Purcell has a grin like the beer barrel polka. A ding-dong daddy grin. A Brooklyn Dodger grin. A grin you could wear to a Polish wedding. His smile walks in in wooly socks and suspenders and asks to borrow the funny papers. You could trap rabbits with it. Teeth line up inside like cartridges in a Mexican bandit's gunbelt. It is the skunk in his rosebush, the crack in his cathedral.

The exuberance Robbins displays in matters of language is another expression of the energy and positivism his work represents overall. An unabashed, unapologetic romantic who favors the transformational power of magic over the plodding consistencies of logic and rationalism, Robbins believes too much of what is sanctified great American literature simply reflects the bitter neuroses of its creators and is therefore self-pitying and destructive. He advocates instead for a literature of joy, one that places full responsibility for individual happiness on individuals themselves.

IT'S NEVER TOO LATE TO HAVE A HAPPY CHILDHOOD

The fact that Robbins serves as literary poster boy for magic and freedom can be considered either ironic or inevitable given that he is the product of a conservative Baptist upbringing. Born on July 22, 1936, in Blowing Rock, North Carolina, Thomas Eugene Robbins was the first of four children. A younger sister died at age four, when Robbins himself was only seven, and twin sisters arrived later. Both parents were the children of Baptist ministers. Robbins's mother, Katherine Robinson Robbins, wrote children's stories for Southern Baptist magazines; his father, a book lover, ascended the executive hierarchy at a regional power company. Robbins's family background ensured that early on he was obsessed with reading and was steeped in conservative religion. Jesus quite naturally became one of his first heroes, a worship he says lasted until Johnny Weismuller exposed him to the sensual primitivism of Tarzan. He treats the supplanting of his personal Savior by the loinclothed vine-swinger in characteristically comic yet intellectual fashion near the end of his first novel, *Another Roadside Attraction*.

When Robbins was still a young boy, the family moved to Burnsville, North Carolina, where, according to Peter Whitmer, "magic" first entered his life in the form of the Barnes and Beers Traveling Circus. By the time Robbins attended the public high school in Warsaw, Virginia, where the family had once again relocated in the mid-1940s, Robbins had become enough of a hell-raiser to eventually land himself in the Hargrave Military Academy. From there he moved on to Washington and Lee University in 1954, an academic stint that included working on the school newspaper briefly with an upperclassman, Tom Wolfe. Booted out of his fraternity in 1956 and recognizing the subsequent social pariahism as tantamount to expulsion, Robbins left Washington and Lee to do odd jobs and to hitch-hike around the country, winding up in Greenwich Village in 1956 as a twenty-year-old would-be poet.

While in New York, Robbins received his draft notice and promptly enlisted in the air force. He studied meteorology and wound up teaching it to South Korean air force pilots. Being stationed in Korea gave him the opportunity to periodically hitch rides on air force planes to Tokyo, where he first studied Eastern philosophy. After air force officials made it clear to him that he would be a better civilian than soldier, Robbins returned to Richmond and enrolled in art school at the Richmond Professional Institute, now known as Virginia Commonwealth University. He did well there and graduated with a degree in art in 1960; then he worked as a copy editor at the *Richmond-Times Dispatch*.

One of his duties at the conservative *Dispatch* was seeing that photos accompanied the text of the local entertainment columnist Earl Wilson. Robbins inadvertently angered both Wilson and the paper when he published a photo of Louis Armstrong, a no-no in the Jim Crow South. After a warning, he then not-so-inadvertently repeated the blunder by running a picture of Nat King Cole. Robbins finally sabotaged his short career at the *Dispatch* by slipping in a photo of Sammy Davis Jr., with his Scandinavian wife. Exacting that small measure of revenge, Robbins left Richmond for Seattle with his first wife, Susan, and her daughter from a previous marriage. The feelings Robbins harbored for Richmond later burst forth blisteringly in his presentation of that city as Sissy Hankshaw's birthplace in *Even Cowgirls Get the Blues*.

Robbins likes to tell interviewers that he picked Seattle because it was the place in the lower forty-eight states farthest from Richmond. Actually an interest in the "mystic" school of painters, which he had studied while at the Richmond Professional Institute, brought him to the Northwest, where artists like Guy Anderson, Mark Tobey, and Morris Graves lived and worked. Once in Seattle, Robbins enrolled briefly in the Far Eastern Institute of the University of Washington to further his growing preoccupation with Asian philosophy. To help pay for his studies, he worked as a copy editor and sometimes art critic for the *Seattle Times*. After two-and-a-half years of less than satisfying work, a pivotal moment occurred for Robbins's life and career—he dropped acid.

Perhaps appropriately, the exact day has been variously recorded as July 16 and July 19, 1963. Robbins tells of the event in a 1977 *Rolling Stone* feature by Michael Rogers. He had read an article in *Holiday* magazine about the consciousness-expanding properties of mushrooms and, while seeking further information, linked up with a University of Washington pharmacology professor who was working with the then virtually unknown (and legal) substance LSD. He took his first dose at an art gallery and, Robbins surmises, did not move for eight hours.

Once the doors of his perception had been so violently blown open, it was not long before Robbins "called in well" to the *Seattle Times* (a scenario he would use to comic effect in *Cowgirls*) and headed to the East Village in New York. Ostensibly Robbins headed east to do research for a book he planned to write on Jackson Pollock, a book that never really got under way, though he did publish a short biography of Guy Anderson in 1965. An equally compelling reason for returning to New York was Robbins's desire to explore more fully what he had discovered through his experiments with LSD by being around others who might share his new enthusiasm for expanding consciousness. His first marriage had failed, and Robbins headed to New York to find his own people.

Robbins hung around New York for a year or so, a period during which he encountered Timothy Leary giving a speech at Cooper Union in December 1964. The two did not meet then, but they eventually became good friends. Robbins then made his way back to Seattle. His

travels during this time followed a 1960s triangle between New York, San Francisco, and Seattle. To some extent he chased the zeitgeist as much as anyone of his solitary nature could, even showing up at one of Ken Kesey's famous acid tests at the Avalon Ballroom in June 1966. As Robbins recalled for Whitmer: "I followed it all, and in a certain sense I participated in it, right at a very core level, but I was never really a part of that scene. It was just not in my nature to be part of a scene." Despite that sense of remove, however, Robbins absorbed thoroughly the intellectual and emotional vibe of late-1960s romanticism.

Once firmly settled back in Seattle in the late 1960s, Robbins returned to copyediting, this time at the *Seattle Post-Intelligencer.* He also hosted an FM rock music radio program and did some writing for the underground newspaper the *Helix*. His output as a writer soon expanded to include an art column for the weekly *Seattle* magazine. Robbins sees these columns as his first good criticism, where his own voice became clearly discernible. That voice caught the attention of a Doubleday West Coast editor named Luther Nichols, who contacted Robbins about the possibility of writing a book—about art. When the two met, Robbins quickly dispensed with the art book idea in favor of a novel he had been batting around in his head that somehow involved the corpse of Jesus being unearthed to rattle the foundations of institutionalized religion. Receiving cautious encouragement from Nichols for this new story idea (Nichols being under the impression the book was already under way), Robbins promptly set out to write what was until then only a loose collection of ideas. The result was *Another Roadside Attraction.*

Doubleday rejected the *Roadside* manuscript twice before deciding, with some trepidation, to publish it in 1971. One might forgive them their reluctance since it was probably unlike any novel they had seen before. Initial sales did little to allay their fears. A little over 2,000 of a 5,000-copy first run sold when the hardcover appeared, despite the book being generally admired by reviewers. When *Roadside* came out in paperback, however, it slowly but steadily found its audience, mostly young people, particularly college students. In 1983 Roger Sutton, in *School Library Journal,* tapped into the reason for *Roadside*'s success with young, often adolescent, readers by noting that "cult books" like Robbins's are

> their first introduction to the idea that a work of fiction can be an inspiration for a new way of looking at the world, validating and extending one's perception. . . . Cult books seem to say to their readers, "You are the first, I've been waiting for you." The readers believe they are unique, that no one has felt this way about this book before. Of course, the irony is that other young adults across the country, and often across generations, believe precisely the same thing.

The growing popularity of *Another Roadside Attraction* testified to that very irony in Robbins's case.

Feeling less than satisfied with Doubleday's effort on *Roadside*'s behalf, Robbins negotiated his release from the publisher and secured the services of a new agent, Phoebe Larmore, who rightly sensed where Robbins's potential audience lay and therefore took the unusual step of selling the paperback rights for his second novel, *Even Cowgirls Get the Blues,* to Bantam and allowing Bantam to make a hardcover deal. In 1976 Houghton Mifflin published *Cowgirls* simultaneously in hardcover and trade paperback editions, the latter of which sold extremely well. A year later Bantam's mass-market paperback was a phenomenal success.

Robbins became a star of the literary underground. Long pieces on him and his work appeared in *Rolling Stone* and *New York Times Magazine.* A reluctant and surprisingly nonverbal interview subject, Robbins nevertheless conveyed the same playful and genial personality that came across so engagingly in the novels. He also proved prescient about his own cult status, telling Michael Rogers in *Rolling Stone,* "I want to be permanently corruptive and subversive, but it's really hard." Later novels show Robbins confronting that conundrum, but with *Even Cowgirls Get the Blues* he confirmed and enhanced the outlaw credentials he earned with *Another Roadside Attraction.*

After his *Cowgirls* windfall, Robbins published a novel every four to six years. Working at a painstaking rate and considering himself lucky to complete two pages a day, he generally tinkers with his sentences and paragraphs until they please him. When he finishes a draft he in fact has finished a book. An adopted son of the American Northwest, Robbins has lived and worked in LaConner, Washington, north of Seattle. After spending three to fours years writing a book then another year editing and promoting it, he usually opts for a year off to travel and rejuvenate. Reports of his journeys sometimes show up in *Esquire.* Additionally he contributes short nonfiction pieces to popular magazines on a regular basis and occasionally lectures. Invited to speak at Yale in October 1994, Robbins delivered an address entitled, "Writing from the Inside Out: Style Is Not the Frosting; It's the Cake."

Despite the changing social climate in the United States over the past three decades, Robbins has held doggedly to the outlook he first espoused in *Roadside* and *Cowgirls.* For the most part his original readers have stayed with him through those decades as well. And although adolescents still find Robbins liberating, the author acknowledged in a 1990 interview with Mari Edlin that he has lost the group between the sixteen-to-eighteen-year-olds and the baby-boomers, largely because he is no longer considered subversive. Given Robbins's increasingly old-fashioned love for the written word in an image-laden cyberculture that can fuel the subversive fantasies of young adults at the click of a mouse (a transformation in consciousness Robbins addresses in *Fierce Invalids Home from Hot Climates* [2000]), it is not surprising that those in their twenties might find Robbins's gentle prodding passé.

THE NOVELS: A DANCE OF SEVEN VEILS

A reader coming new to Tom Robbins would do well to begin with his fifth novel *Skinny Legs and All* (1990), because in it Robbins explores directly the most pervasive manifestations of contemporary ideology and orthodoxy, individual examples of which appear as primary elements in all his novels and serve as impetus for the authorial digressions that are so prominent and compelling a feature of Robbins's prose. The climactic Dance of the Seven Veils in *Skinny Legs* presents Salome shedding her veils during the ritual celebration of Super Bowl Sunday and in the process revealing the seven principal obstructions to a free and autonomous existence: 1) a hypocritical and unhealthy attitude toward sexuality; 2) a misguided belief in the dominion of human beings over other inhabitants of their planet; 3) a futile and foolhardy trust in political solutions to human problems; 4) the corrupting influence of organized religion as a response to the divine; 5) a debilitating emphasis on money and material success in human endeavor; 6) a limited and self-limiting conception of time, history, and the afterlife; and 7) resistance to the fundamental principle of life—that everyone must establish a one-on-one relationship with reality. Remarkable in their combination of philosophical consistency with narrative variety, Robbins's seven novels to date present characters who must confront any or all of these "veils" to human understanding and freedom.

ANOTHER ROADSIDE ATTRACTION

Another Roadside Attraction (1971) belongs to its spiritual center, the sensual, independent,

new age Earth goddess Amanda. As a child her fascination with butterflies and her dismay at their too-brief life span led her to the discovery that "the life-span of the butterfly is precisely the right length," an early acceptance of the natural processes and constant flux of existence. After a larger youthful study of the Earth and life around her, Amanda emerged from childhood believing in birth, death, and copulation and convinced that humans need to live according to the rhythms of nature, accepting that a Great Mystery underlies all.

But if *Roadside* ultimately belongs to Amanda, it does so because the story, the narrative itself, belongs to Marx Marvelous, a scientific genius who has been whiling away the years at an eastern think tank but is currently AWOL from the East River Institute and in search of America's spiritual future. Marx believes the social climate in the United States demonstrates that Christianity is at its nadir in terms of its practical influence on citizens and that some new religious or spiritual movement must be waiting in the wings to capitalize on the inevitable religious vacancy in Americans' lives. After hearing about Amanda, her husband John Paul Ziller, and the Captain Kendrick Memorial Hot Dog and Wildlife Preserve (complete with Flea Circus), Marvelous senses they are onto whatever the next spiritual "something" will turn out to be and seeks them out.

Amanda ends the novel pretty much as she begins it, at least in terms of the identity she projects through the narrator. But Marx undergoes profound personal change. He comes to the Captain Kendrick preserve a rationalist who believes in the methods of science, although he also has always demonstrated a streak of "whimsical ambivalence" about those methods that has prevented him from fulfilling his great scientific potential. Marx leaves the East River Institute to search as much for himself as for the next great awakening, although he is clearly skeptical about the romantic impulse Amanda and John Paul embody when he first meets them. In fact Marx attempts to argue Amanda out of her reliance on such romantic notions as magic and freedom, but Amanda refuses be trapped by his appeals to rationalism and logic. Amanda wins Marx over not through debate but by example.

Marx's transformation, his surrender to the possibilities of mysticism, is embodied in his telling of *Another Roadside Attraction*. Although the book might appear to depend on the narrative fireworks of Plucky Purcell's adventures with a brotherhood of sadistic monks and his absconding with the mortal remains of the son of God, Marx makes it clear that it is really about the girl, about his love for Amanda and its effect on him, about her ability to transform his relationship to the world simply by virtue of her own peace and harmony within that world. He thereby emphasizes the utterly subjective nature of his presumably "historical" report on the missing-Christ caper. Robbins ends *Roadside* with a brief description of a pine cone striking a tent and waking its inhabitant to a new day. Amanda serves that awakening purpose for Marx Marvelous, and through his report she might do the same for readers, as Robbins suggests in his closing: "Let Amanda be your pine cone."

Roadside's cast of primary characters also includes the aforementioned Plucky Purcell, a friend of the Zillers from their circus days, whose adventures and letters serve primarily to expose the corrupt underbelly of organized religion, particularly Catholicism, and its pernicious influence over individual lives. A case of mistaken identity lands Plucky in a rural monastery and eventually in Rome at the Vatican. When an earthquake rocks the catacombs at St. Peter's Cathedral, where Plucky happens to be when it hits, he uncovers the corpse of Jesus Christ. Seeing an opportunity, he swipes the holy remains, then smuggles them out of Italy and back to the Captain Kendrick, where the gathered crew must decide what to do with them.

Plucky's exploits set the stage for numerous philosophical rants against the church. Yet Plucky discovers even the church is ultimately composed of individuals, which leads him to a recognition of the larger social evil:

> What I hate in the Church was what I hated in society. Namely, authoritarians. Power freaks. Those greedy, underloved, undersexed twits who want to run everything. While the rest of us are busy living—busy tasting and testing and hugging and kissing and goofing and growing—they are busy taking over. Soon their sour tentacles are around everything: our governments, our economies, our schools, our publications, our arts and our religious institutions. . . . they fear all that is chaotic and unruly and free-moving and changing—thus, as Amanda has said, they fear nature and fear life itself.

Although outlining the events of the novel might indicate the fantastic nature of Robbins's plot, it does not do justice to the organizational monkey business of *Roadside* overall. Descriptions of the book often call attention to its formlessness, but Robbins argues that it was carefully structured on a psychedelic model. "Its structure *radiates* in many directions at once," he told McCaffery and Gregory, "rather than progressing gradually up an inclined plane. . . . There are lots of little *flashes* of illumination strung together like beads. Some of these flashes illuminate the plot; others merely illuminate the reader."

The novel begins in fact with the FBI and CIA descending on the Captain Kendrick and the narrator informing us that John Paul and Plucky have disappeared with the corpse. Once establishing these vital facts, the unidentified reporter who serves as narrator feels no compunction to follow any kind of chronological narrative sequence, opting instead to periodically return to unfolding events concerning the abducted corpse, while filling in important background information about the characters in no particularly logical order. He also supplements his narrative perspective with past entries from his own journals, excerpts from Plucky's letters, newspaper stories, and various other external sources inserted into his report.

Roadside's events therefore are self-consciously manipulated by the narrator, who readers discover near the end is Marx Marvelous, something careful readers might discern before Marx reveals himself. The Marx Marvelous who tells the story, however, has already been transformed by his exposure to Amanda and the Captain Kendrick. The end result is a novel that never lets a reader get comfortable with time and place as it shifts continually between its multiple contexts. All events appear to occur simultaneously, which, in Robbins's psychedelic model, forces readers to push open a door of perception, if only a crack, to the light of a new sensibility.

EVEN COWGIRLS GET THE BLUES

Like its predecessor, *Even Cowgirls Get the Blues* (1976) focuses on an independent, freedom-loving, attractive female who breaks through the boundaries imposed on young women growing up in the United States. But Amanda displays an identity fully realized from start to finish, while Sissy still has much to learn about herself. Born into a working-class family in Richmond, Virginia, Sissy is cursed or blessed, depending on who in the story is consulted, with remarkably overgrown thumbs, a nod to Dean Moriarity's magnificent bandaged thumb in Jack Kerouac's *On the Road* (1957). In her family's view the offending appendages mark her as handicapped. Sissy herself, however, refuses to accept invalidism, choosing instead to celebrate the uniqueness bestowed upon her by her unusual physical gift. She even develops a talent for hitchhiking, cultivating a

sense of freedom through movement via her innate and infallible ability to flag down passing vehicles. Driven from Richmond by the limiting assumptions of her family and by the cruel or indifferent behavior of her classmates, Sissy takes to the road, hitchhiking back and forth across the United States. By the novel's end she achieves a much richer sense of what it means to live a free and autonomous life.

To pay for her nomadic lifestyle, Sissy periodically models for the owner of a feminine hygiene products company. The Countess, an over-the-top effete born and raised in Ohio but with pretenses to Russian nobility and an inveterate hatred of female smells, made his fortune with the best-selling Yoni Yum douche bag. Sissy sees the Countess as her employer and friend, not recognizing him for what he really embodies in the novel—a misogynistic exploiter of women who would deny them their true sexual natures.

The Countess sends Sissy on a modeling assignment to the Rubber Rose Ranch in North Dakota, where a gang of female ranch hands has been stirring up trouble on his beauty farm dude ranch. Led by Bonanza Jellybean, the cowgirls want to replace the Countess's regimen of beauty tips with a more natural program that meets the *real* needs and desires of women rather than male projections of those needs and desires. The battle for control at the Rubber Rose allows Robbins to explore dimensions of the feminist movement, most importantly what kind of spirit will guide it.

Delores del Ruby, a whip-toting, peyote-munching she-devil, leads one faction. The Mother Goddess spoke to her in a vision and helped to convince her that "the natural enemy of the daughters were the fathers and the sons." She advocates meeting male aggression with violence and force if necessary. Her counterpart Debbie believes that to succeed women must be different from men, as Bonanza Jellybean explains to Sissy:

Debbie says that if women are to take charge again, they must do it in the feminine way; they mustn't resort to aggressive and violent masculine methods. She says it is up to women to show themselves *better* than men, to love men, set good examples for them and guide them tenderly toward the new New Age.

After a violent confrontation with federal authorities over the cowgirls' interference with the migratory behavior of a flock of whooping cranes, Delores has a peyote-induced Third Vision, during which she discovers that the natural enemy of women is not men after all but "the tyranny of a dull mind." Violence, she learns, will not help women achieve freedom. Instead, a Fourth Vision telling women what to do will come "to every cowgirl in the land, when you have overcome that in your own self which is dull."

The struggle over the direction the cowgirls' revolution should take strikes a responsive chord in Sissy, who is at the ranch partly to escape a marriage to a New York artist that has thrown her identity into question. Not long after arriving at the Rubber Rose and meeting Bonanza Jellybean, she finds herself in a sexually charged relationship with the cowgirl, which adds to the confusion she feels about her marriage to Julian. Like her family back in Richmond, Julian views her thumbs as an abnormality to be overcome rather than a source of independence and freedom.

Sissy learns a great deal from the philosophical skirmish among the cowgirls and from loving conversations with the idealistic Jelly. But her real intellectual and spiritual education begins when she runs into the Chink, who lives in a mountain cave overlooking the Rubber Rose. Just as Amanda does for *Another Roadside Attraction,* the Chink provides the philosophical heartbeat for *Even Cowgirls Get the Blues* as he slowly and reluctantly reveals to Sissy his belief that freedom is an internal condition and that the primary problems facing men and women are philosophical, not political.

The most anyone can do to change things for the better is to set a good example:

> If you believe in peace, act peacefully; if you believe in love, act lovingly; if you believe every which way, than act every which way, that's perfectly valid—but don't go out trying to sell your beliefs to the System. You end up contradicting what you profess to believe in, and you set a bum example. If you want to change the world, change yourself.

Although sought out as a spiritual guru, the Chink chases away would-be disciples seeking wisdom, believing it is everyone's individual responsibility to come to terms with matters of life, death, and spiritual enlightenment. The biggest obstacle to confronting that responsibility is the traditional conception of time and its inevitable by-product, the debilitating notion that time is running out. The Chink has thus derived his own means for calculating time, one that acknowledges a balance between order and disorder, predictability and randomness. A collection of garbage can lids, old saucepans, car fenders, and various other bits of refuse from civilized society all wired together, the Clockworks at random moments catches a rock falling or a bird flying through it or adjusts itself to wind or rain or rust, and with each such unpredictable occurrence it chimes or echoes a "poing!" or "bonk!"

The Clockworks thus recognizes intervals of time, and yet those intervals are random and unpredictable, sometimes occurring only after months have passed, sometimes sounding three times within ten minutes. As Robert Nadeau argues in "Physics and Cosmology in the Fiction of Tom Robbins," the Clockworks represents a tension between opposites consistent with contemporary understanding of the physical world and is designed to help the Chink "sustain an awareness of the randomness or indeterminacy of natural process that makes freedom a human possibility." This runs counter to the classical belief in "laws" governing nature and thus determining the quality of human existence. The Chink's refusal to accept the narrow confines of received conceptions and his willingness to embrace instead the freedom inherent in randomness and indeterminacy helps explain the paradoxical nature of his creed:

I believe in everything; nothing is sacred
I believe in nothing; everything is sacred.

The structure of *Even Cowgirls Get the Blues* also recognizes the need to break from the traditional understanding of time. The manipulation of time contexts even prompts the narrator to intrude and deal with readers' expected confusion or impatience by informing them that some of the events in parts 1, 2, and 3 of the novel occurred *after* Sissy "had come to the Rubber Rose and gone again." The narrator both justifies the book's arrangement of events and sympathizes with readers' need for order:

Even though we agree that time is relative; that most subjective notions of it are inaccurate just as most objective expressions of it are arbitrary; even though we may seek to extirpate ourselves from the terrible flow of it . . . even though we pledge allegiance to the "here and now," or view time as an empty box to fill with our genius, or restructure our concepts of it to conform with those wild tickings of the clockworks; even so, we have come to expect, for better or worse, some sort of chronological order in the books we read, for it is the function of literature to provide what life does not.

Although Robbins's novels after *Cowgirls* always acknowledge in some manner the arbitrariness and artificiality of time and order in human affairs, they also increasingly adhere to the sentiment expressed at the end of the preceding passage.

When Sissy returns to New York, not surprisingly she experiences tension with Julian, who sends her to a therapist. As it turns out, however, Dr. Robbins has misgivings of his own about the benefits of normality, arguing with his boss Dr. Goldman that people should seek to transform not transcend the circumstances of their lives. Sissy's confusion over her own identity after her exposure to Bonanza Jellybean, the Chink, and all the cowgirls at the Rubber Rose eventually erupts in violence directed at the Countess. Her feelings of remorse lead to the amputation of one of her magnificent thumbs before she heads back to the Rubber Rose for the whooping crane showdown with the feds. That showdown leaves Bonanza Jellybean dead, the Chink injured, Sissy pregnant, the cowgirls in possession of the Rubber Rose, and Dr. Robbins making his way up Siwash Ridge as the reader discovers he is the chronicler of this tale.

Although the bizarre and melodramatic plot of *Cowgirls* has its own appeal for many Robbins fans, the novel's success really rests on its philosophical outlook and on the manner in which that outlook is conveyed through the narrator. At chapter 100 the narrator uncorks and shares with the reader a bottle of champagne to celebrate the century mark. After a Robbins riff on the number 100, he writes, "There also are a hundred ways to successfully write a novel, but this is probably not one of them." The irony of that statement of course is that it is precisely why the book succeeds. The novel's style is its point; through it, as Robbins indicates in his next paragraph, "*Even Cowgirls Get the Blues* can still teach you a thing or two."

STILL LIFE WITH WOODPECKER

Although remarkable in the publishing world as the first hardcover book issued (simultaneously with a trade paperback edition) by Bantam, *Still Life with Woodpecker* ranks as Robbins's least remarkable novel in terms of its characters and plot. This could be due to the fact that Robbins had a more particular ax to grind in *Still Life* than in any of his other novels. Whereas his attacks on authority and dull-mindedness in *Roadside* and *Cowgirls* respond to large social forces that inhibit individual freedom, in *Still Life* the enemy seems more personal—to Robbins's philosophical outlook if not to Robbins himself. And in a surprising display of appearing to bite the hand that feeds him, Robbins's targets this time around are liberal do-gooders who align themselves with political and social organizations, which to his mind means turning a spiritual impulse into a political one and in the process converting white magic to black.

Robbins published a revealing prelude to *Still Life* in Seattle's *Weekly* in June 1978 entitled "Notes on Nukes, Nookie, and Neo-Romanticism" (retitled "Feminismo" or "Move over Macho, Here Comes Feminismo" when syndicated to newspapers throughout the United States that summer). In the article Robbins describes his appearance at an antinuclear benefit in Seattle, where he told a few sex-related jokes that some of the more politically correct of the event's organizers found offensive and sexist. Robbins uses the occurrence to launch an attack against what he sees as "the soft *yin* of feminism . . . appropriating the harsh *yang* of machismo." Political androids, according to Robbins, had drained feminism of its spirituality, had adopted many of the dubious tactics of men, and had transformed the possibility of genuine revolution into the reality of low-grade political power games.

To some extent this represents the same battle for hearts and minds embodied in the cowgirl factions led by Delores del Ruby and Debbie in *Even Cowgirls Get the Blues*. But the tone is decidedly more urgent, as Robbins seeks to make clear that the tyranny of the dull mind afflicts organizations and movements of all kinds, not just those to the right on the political spectrum. "There are no group solutions," he writes in "Notes." "There are only individual solutions, individual liberations." Robbins applies this idea to *Still Life with Woodpecker,* using the main character Leigh-Cheri's desire to do good works and her attendance at the Geo-Therapy Care Fest in Hawaii as means to demonstrate that, in its own highly organized, self-righteous fashion, "good can be as banal as evil."

Still Life is presented in fable or fairy tale form. Princess Leigh-Cheri is the daughter of King Max and Queen Tilli Furstenberg-Barcalona, whose homeland is now ruled by a U.S.–backed right wing military junta. The CIA has set up a palace-in-exile for the Furstenberg-Barcalonas on the shore of Puget Sound, where Max now spends his days playing poker and watching American sports, while Tilli attends society teas and registers moments of surprise with the phrase, "Oh-Oh, spaghetti-o." Leigh-Cheri grows up in a fairly typical (for a princess), pampered manner, doted on by her nurse Gulietta, but her fairy tale existence takes a dark turn as a young adult after one abortion, a disastrous love affair, and the miscarriage of her second pregnancy. The princess retires to her childhood attic playroom, furnished with only a cot, a chamber pot, and a pack of Camel cigarettes.

In her attic seclusion, after swearing off romance for good, Leigh-Cheri develops a purpose for her life—she will help humanity. She henceforth adopts Ralph Nader as her hero (and fantasy lover). Following this epiphany, news of the Geo-Therapy Care Fest entices her from her attic hermitage and sends her to Hawaii to help rescue the world from itself. On the flight to Maui she meets Bernard Mickey Wrangle, alias the Woodpecker, famous both for his red hair and his bombing expertise. Bernard has been on the lam and has lived underground for years, having busted out of prison, where he had been sent for a bombing he masterminded in Madison, Wisconsin, during the days of the Vietnam War protests. The Woodpecker has been inactive during his period underground, but the Geo-Therapy Care Fest has brought him out of retirement.

Bernard sees himself as an outlaw, someone who stands for "uncertainty, insecurity, surprise, disorder, unlawfulness, bad taste, fun, and things that go boom in the night." He targets the Care Fest because it represents the fate of outlaw forces co-opted by organization and politics and suffering from the "discouragingly common affliction called tunnel vision":

> a disease in which perception is restricted by ignorance and distorted by vested interest. Tunnel vision is caused by an optic fungus that multiplies when the brain is less energetic than the ego. It is complicated by exposure to politics. When a good idea is run through the filters and compressors of ordinary tunnel vision, it not only comes out reduced in scale and value but in its new dogmatic configuration produces effects the opposite of those for which it originally was intended.

Bernard disrupts but does not shut down the Care Fest after bombing its principal location, the Pioneer Inn. The progress of Leigh-Cheri and Bernard's love affair—the climax of which appears in six pages of sensory-laden erotic detail interspersed with samplings of leftist platitudes from a Nader keynote speech—parallels their struggle and debate over Leigh-Cheri's brand of collective do-goodism versus Bernard's outlaw individualism. Not surprisingly Bernard gets all the best lines. By the novel's end, however, both have surrendered their larger social missions to a more private concern for each other and for themselves individually, spending some days together and some alone.

Amidst the social and political implications of Robbins's fairy tale, when Bernard is arrested the two lovers must also confront the more personal question: Who knows how to make love stay? As an act of homage to their love, Leigh-Cheri returns to her attic hideout. While there she becomes intrigued by the design on the pack of Camels and builds around it her own mythology concerning a long lost tribe of redheads from the planet Argon. She is also drawn to the one-word message on the pack that reads the same way even when reflected in a mirror: CHOICE.

In Leigh-Cheri's ruminations on the Camel pack, Robbins combines the insights derived from his own psychotropic travels with his understanding of physics to emphasize the significant roles objects play in our daily lives and can play in our understanding of the nature of existence:

> The fabric of even those objects that seem densest is, in actual fact, a loose weaving of particles and waves. The differences and interactions between objects have their roots in the interference patterns produced along combined frequencies of vibration. What it amounted to was that Leigh-Cheri was exerting force on the Camel pack. And it on her. . . . Leigh-Cheri found herself in a relationship with the Camel pack as an object.

Leigh-Cheri's sensitivity to the pack of cigarettes manifests itself when she returns to the world outside her attic cured of her "animate chauvinism" and displaying a new casual affection for the objects surrounding her, recognizing now how they might "minister to the silent zones of man as an individual . . . [and] form a bond between the autistic vision and the experiential world."

In his next novel, *Jitterbug Perfume* (1984), Robbins addresses the import of this bond more fully:

> Life is largely material, and there is no small heroism in the full and open enjoyment of material things. The accumulation of material things is shallow and vain, but to have a genuine relationship with such things is to have a relationship with life and, by extension, a relationship with the divine.

And he takes up the cause of animate chauvinism in even more striking fashion in *Skinny Legs and All,* where objects become characters in their own right.

The events in *Still Life* are brought to readers by a narrator who signals a change in Robbins's narrative approach. While he still shares the philosophical and humorous garrulousness of Marx Marvelous in *Another Roadside Attraction* and Dr. Robbins in *Even Cowgirls Get the Blues,* the unidentified controlling voice in *Still Life* remains outside the activity of the novel itself, not participating in the lives of its characters as Marx and Dr. Robbins do. Yet in periodic interludes the narrator does report on his ongoing battle with a new typewriter, the Remington SL3, that does not appear to be communicating *Still Life*'s story to the author's satisfaction. Finally, after enunciating in the epilogue the morals to be drawn from this tale, the narrator realizes this is "the very kind of analytical, after-the-fact goose gunk the Remington SL3 cut its teeth on" and pulls the plug, finishing up the novel in longhand.

In reviewing *Still Life* for *Commonweal,* Frank McConnell recognized something in the narrator's troubles with the typewriter that has interesting implications for *Roadside* and *Cowgirls* as well:

> In that distance between the rationalizing, distraught novelist and his wonderfully liberated creations lies Robbins's real strength and brilliance. His stories insist that everything is all right, that everything rightly perceived is beautiful, is part of the Tao. . . . But his *storytellers* incarnate his, and our, difficulty in accepting such a simple, pacific, happy gospel. So that the real plot of a Robbins novel is very like the real plot of our learning to trust his fiction.

McConnell wrote this as the 1970s and its vestiges of 1960s' idealism combined with therapeutic self-exploration were receding into the harder, more cynical decade of the 1980s. Robbins's neo-romanticism was becoming a harder sell. Whether Robbins subscribed to McConnell's theory or not, his fiction after *Still Life* shows him leaving behind even the suggestion of tension between storyteller and story in favor of a less self-referential and more generally omniscient approach as author-narrator.

JITTERBUG PERFUME

In *Even Cowgirls Get the Blues,* the Chink warns Sissy against relying too heavily on Eastern philosophical and religious traditions as she struggles to find meaning in existence. Instead, he advises going back for spiritual inspiration to the religious traditions that preceded Christianity in the West, namely, to the pagan ceremonies and rituals associated with the Old God, the Horned One, the bawdy goat-man Pan. Robbins attempts to do just that in *Jitterbug Perfume,* using our pagan ancestry as the background for a story that emphasizes the need to participate fully and joyfully in *life* and thereby to break the stranglehold death has over our lives and imaginations.

After the chaotic arrangements of Robbins's first three novels, what strikes a reader most distinctly about *Jitterbug* is the orderly manner in which he lays out his plot. Parts 1, 2, and 3 all follow the same pattern of presenting the activities of present-day characters in separate chapters devoted to Seattle, New Orleans, and Paris, followed by a more extended narrative in which the primary tale of Alobar's journey into individual consciousness and his subsequent discovery, with his wife, Kudra, of the secret to immortality is recounted. That journey begins in Europe at the time of Christianity's rise to preeminence in Western culture and winds through the centuries until in part 4 Robbins brings the strands of his narrative together in contemporary America.

The Seattle portions of the novel focus on a waitress named Priscilla, who spends her off-duty hours experimenting with chemical combinations, hoping to hit upon the formula for a perfume that will rescue her from the dismal circumstances of her life. Priscilla has in her possession a mysterious bottle containing an elixir of aromatic genius, which she hopes to re-create through her after-hours efforts. The main characters in the New Orleans chapters, Madame Devalier and her assistant V'lu, are also interested in that bottle. Madame D. is the proprietor of the Parfumerie Devalier and is known as the "Queen of the Good Smells" in the French Quarter. She and V'lu spend their days seeking the scent that will restore her shop to past glory. Meanwhile in the Paris chapters Claude and Marcel LeFever, owners of a prestigious fragrance house, contemplate what scent will follow up the commercial success of their 1980s synthetic wonder New Wave. As the novel opens the characters in these three cities are the puzzled recipients of a gift from an anonymous donor. That gift? A beet. The real pleasure of Robbins's plot is its unveiling of how Alobar and Kudra's adventures through the centuries lead inexorably to the intertwined lives of the contemporary chapters and of exactly what role beets play in that process.

After discovering the secret to immortality (a regimen that involves incorporating the rhythms of air, water, earth, and fire into the regular practices of breathing, bathing, eating, and sex), Alobar and Kudra witness the transition from the nature-based ceremonies and rituals of paganism to the otherworld spirituality of Christian belief. They also make the acquaintance of the reigning deity of that disappearing pagan world, the half-goat, half-man Pan. As the years pass and Pan's influence wanes, his corporal existence fades as well, to the point that when Alobar and Kudra meet up with him in eighteenth-century Paris, during the Age of Reason, he has become invisible and announces his presence only by a pronounced odoriferous display. Pan's appearance, or disappearance, in *Jitterbug Perfume* enacts the evolution addressed in the debate between Tarzan and Jesus near the end of *Another Roadside Attraction.* Tarzan argues there that Pan's sensual union of nature and culture, flesh and spirit gave way to Christianity's separation of humans from nature, which meant "culture [would] dominate nature, the phallus [would] dominate the womb, perma-

nence [would] dominate change, and the fear of death [would] dominate everything."

When Kudra dematerializes attempting a new mode of travel to America, Pan and Alobar travel to the New World by boat, hoping to find a people more receptive to Pan's earthy and sensual influence. Their trip is aided by a bottle of K23, Alobar's new elixir with a secret beet pollen ingredient, created to mask Pan's overpowering odor while in transit. Eventually, though, Pan finds himself disoriented and confused by his lack of musky aroma and flings the bottle of K23 over the ship as it nears the Gulf Coast. Later retrieved from the Mississippi mud, the bottle makes its way to Madame Devalier's shop, where the lines of Robbins's story intersect. More than being united by a bottle of perfume, however, those story lines come together through the larger, evocative, unifying power of smell itself. As Marcel LeFever tells his brother:

> Fragrance is a conduit for our earliest memories, on the one hand; on the other, it may accompany us as we enter the next life. In between, it creates mood, stimulates fantasy, shapes thought, and modifies behavior. It is our strongest link to the past, our closest fellow traveler to the future. Prehistory, history, and the afterworld, all are its domain. Fragrance may well be the signature of eternity.

One character in the novel who certainly shares Marcel's belief is Wiggs Dannyboy, director of the Last Laugh Foundation in Seattle, who seeks to defeat death and believes the sense of smell's direct link to the neocortex might be the key to a newly evolving level of human consciousness. Wiggs serves as the Robbins persona in *Jitterbug,* the means by which the author delivers his philosophical bulletins. Wiggs also bears an uncanny resemblance to Robbins's friend and fellow shopper in the supermarket of human consciousness theories, Leary. The theory Wiggs expounds in *Jitterbug* concerns the evolution from reptilian to floral consciousness, through which humans will be able to suspend time and achieve immortality.

Wiggs makes the acquaintance of Alobar in a New Hampshire prison and learns only that the secret to K23 is connected somehow to beets. Sensing that Alobar's fragrance could be vital to his own research, Wiggs sets the plot in motion by secretly delivering beets to those he believes most capable of uncovering the magic of K23. This sends Priscilla, now Wiggs's lover, and Marcel, lover and employer of the industrial spy V'lu, to New Orleans for a rendezvous with Madame Devalier as they all seek to unlock the mystery of the next great scent. The bottle itself winds up smashed under a float in the Mardi Gras parade (with the assistance of the invisible Pan), and once Alobar reveals the secret of the beet pollen, the company of perfumers ultimately decides to make the creation of *Kudra* a joint venture. Largely through Alobar's influence, the ambitions and personal animosities of all those hoping to cash in on K23 are transformed into less-egotistical, more-cooperative motivations for seeing *Kudra* produced.

Over the course of centuries Alobar's immortality has taught him one primary thing—that "the spirit of one individual can supersede and dismiss the entire clockworks of history." He tells Pan:

> Our individuality is all, *all,* that we have. There are those who barter it for security, those who repress it for what they believe is the betterment of the whole society, but blessed in the twinkle of the morning star is the one who nurtures it and rides it, in grace and love and wit, from peculiar station to peculiar station along life's bittersweet route.

This as much as anything else seems the point of *Jitterbug Perfume,* to make the most of our individual spheres of existence.

When Kudra returns from the Other Side at the end of the book, she arrives in Paris and recounts to Claude LeFever the nature of her experience there. She has discovered that attendants within that nether realm weigh the hearts of persons who pass through, because "Should a person possess a heart that is as light as a feather, then that person is granted immortality." Kudra returns to the corporeal world by passing through a door marked "ERLE-ICHDA," which, roughly translated and in keeping with Alobar's lesson on the grace and love and wit of individual consciousness, means "Lighten up."

SKINNY LEGS AND ALL

About a third of the way through *Skinny Legs and All* (1990), a hungover Ellen Cherry Charles finds herself estranged from her husband, whom she loves; chronically horny, with no satisfaction imminent; and working as a waitress, although she came to New York to make a splash in the art world. Yet as she walks down a New York City street, she suddenly feels light and giddy. "Was she simply too shallow to suffer indefinitely," she wonders, "or was she too wise to become attached to her suffering, too feisty to permit it to rule her life? She voted for wise and feisty, and walked on, kicking leaves." Ellen's wise and feisty determination to walk on, kicking leaves, is a good way to characterize her creator's continuing pursuit of answers to some of life's more perplexing questions in his inimitably cheerful and linguistically lush manner.

Through the 1980s and 1990s Robbins faced critics who felt they had of necessity moved on from the crazy romanticism and spiritual idealism of the 1960s and 1970s, while Robbins unfortunately had not. Even in the area of his greatest attribute as a writer, his play with language, critics began to carp about his prose being overloaded or simply too much of a good thing. In a review shaped as a Dear John letter to Robbins, Zsuzsi Gartner, previously an admirer of Robbins's fiction, bemoans the wordplay in his novel *Fierce Invalids Home from Hot Climates* before asking, "Were you always like this and I just didn't notice?" She then finishes her reader's sayonara to Robbins with the words of a commiserating friend: "We loved him so much because we were so puerile and he was too. Then we grew up."

Despite this kind of revisionism, Robbins has blithely continued kicking leaves. His philosophy overall by the time of *Skinny Legs* had changed little from that espoused in *Roadside* and *Cowgirls*. In fact *Skinny Legs* seems a kind of summing up, with its self-conscious articulation of the seven veils of illusion. The language also appears to be vintage Robbins, although it has lost a bit of its metaphorical wildness and incongruity over the years. As to its freshness and energy overall, one has to wonder whether the change in some readers' reactions to Robbins's prose is due to a diminishment in the prose itself or simply due to a diminishment in readers' patience for such linguistic playfulness as they have grown older.

If Robbins has remained wise and feisty in his overall outlook and the stylistic expression of that outlook, however, he also has made some concessions to changing times in the nature of his plots and their arrangements in the later novels. They still maintain elements of his signature goofiness, but they are also more mainstream in the way they present manifestations of the illusions that interfere with individual happiness and freedom. And they retain some of *Jitterbug Perfume*'s orderliness as well. *Skinny Legs,* for instance, divides into seven sections according to the seven veils of Salome's climactic dance. At the end of each section Robbins includes a brief homily on the illusion about life or death represented by that veil, an illusion also illustrated through the episodes in his narrative.

The plot of *Skinny Legs* has all the markings of a Robbins farce as it opens with newlyweds Boomer Petway and Ellen Cherry Charles speeding across the United States in a trailer redesigned to resemble a roast turkey. Boomer used the wacky re-creation to help convince his waitress-artist girlfriend Ellen to marry him. They are now headed for New York from Seattle, where Ellen had fled to escape the provincialism and Christian fundamentalism of her Colonial Pines, Virginia, hometown. The first quarter of the book relates the couple's adventures, erotic and otherwise, on the road and fills in the backgrounds of their former lives back in Colonial Pines. It also introduces Ellen's uncle Buddy, a fundamentalist preacher with a nationally syndicated radio program who is partly responsible for Ellen's departure from Virginia. Buddy teamed with Ellen's father to accuse her of being a Jezebel because she sketched nude models in one of her art classes.

Robbins uses Ellen's curiosity about who Jezebel really was and why she gained such a reputation for sinfulness and betrayal as a pretext for exploring both the biblical story and its historical analogues, coming to the conclusion that Jezebel's real transgression was her devotion to the Great Goddess Mother Astarte at a time when patriarchy was asserting it hegemony over spiritual matters. This becomes the historical backdrop for the Dance of the Seven Veils at the book's end and once again establishes Robbins's view that civilization took a wrong turn when it abandoned the matriarchal ways of its distant past.

When Ellen and Boomer arrive in New York, Boomer and his roast turkey mobile become the toast of the fickle and faddish New York art world. The reversal in fortune for the newlyweds leads to discord and distance, especially after Boomer becomes involved with his new agent Ultima Sommervell. In despair over her own fizzled career, Ellen abandons art and takes up waitressing again, this time at Isaac and Ishmael's, jointly owned by an Arab and a Jew as a gesture of reconciliation for the warring factions in the Middle East. The conspiratorial presence of Ellen's uncle Buddy haunts the chapters about the difficulties and dangers of operating Isaac and Ishmael's, so visible and so symbolic a target for ideological anger. Buddy plots to hasten the arrival of Armageddon by blowing up the holy mosque, the Dome of the Rock, in Jerusalem.

All of this affords Robbins the opportunity to go into the political and religious history of Jerusalem's First and Second Temples, including the fading influence of the goddess cults and how the Dome of the Rock came to be built on the site of those former temples. It now stands in the way of the prophesied Third Temple. Often tagged as Robbins's most overtly political novel, *Skinny Legs and All* does explore the historical precedence for contemporary tensions in the Middle East. But it does so only to point out the futility of political solutions. The way to change the situation in the Middle East, according to Robbins, is for the people to change individually. Spike Cohen and Roland Abu Hadee's restaurant is an expression of the two men's attempt to accomplish just that. Thus it becomes the perfect setting for the modern-day Salome's Dance of the Seven Veils and the lifting of illusions that stand in the way of such individual transformation.

Perhaps the most intriguing of Robbins's seven veils is the second, which involves human beings recognizing they are not superior to other inhabitants of the physical world, like plants, animals, and even objects. This explains the subplot involving the conversations and locomotive antics of a stick, a shell, a spoon, a sock, and a can of beans, all of whom are bona fide characters in the novel. They set out on a pilgrimage to the Third Temple of Jerusalem but wind up in the basement of St. Patrick's Cathedral in New York City, awaiting passage across the ocean. Robbins treats incredulous readers to a refresher in contemporary physics:

The inertia of objects is deceptive. The inanimate world appears static, "dead," to humans only because of our neuromuscular chauvinism. We are so enamored of our own activity range that we blind ourselves to the fact that most of the action of the universe is unfolding outside our range, occurring at speeds so much slower or faster than our own that it is hidden from us as if by a . . . a veil.

This rallying cry for objecthood once again imparts Robbins's recognition of the relative nature of time and space. "In the immobile," he writes, "whirls the infinite." The Conch Shell itself asks, "How long can humankind continue to slight these integral pieces of the whole reality?"

Robbins aligns an awareness of the whole reality with the artistic temperament. As a child Ellen played what she called her eye game, "sliding her focus to muffle or distort the normal associative effects of object and space, stripping them of common meaning or symbolic function, forcing them to settle in the highly mysterious region that lies between the cornea and the brain." From the game grew her fascination with art. Her sojourn in the New York art world and her disappointment at Boomer's easy success have robbed her of the magic of her artistic impulses. But late in the novel, befuddled by her reunion with a spoon she left behind in a cave, where she and Boomer passed a carnal afternoon in North Dakota (that reunion a result of the spoon's leaping into Ellen's bag on the steps of St. Patrick's Cathedral), Ellen applies the long abandoned eye game to the utensil, with startling results:

For one giddy moment she felt that she had oriented herself at the interface of the visible and invisible worlds, that she was contemplating wholeness, an ultimate state in which all forms and motions were imminent but protected by physical or metaphysical law from the process of selection or favoritism that would compromise them.

Ellen's renewed appreciation for "the whole reality" makes her especially receptive to the revelatory aspects of Salome's dance at the end of the book, which in turn makes a reconciliation with Boomer possible. Throughout the novel Robbins makes periodic visits to the "room of the wolfmother wallpaper," his nomenclature for the state of wholeness Ellen achieved while staring at her magically recovered spoon and for the unified state of existence embodied in the goddess cults of our matriarchal past. When the veils are lifted and our illusions about sex, about nature, about politics, about religion, about money, about time are laid bare, then, Robbins suggests, one has the chance to establish a one-on-one relationship with reality, the message revealed by lifting the seventh veil.

HALF ASLEEP IN FROG PAJAMAS

In his first five novels Robbins ranged freely over time and space in sprawling narrative configurations. Even as he imposed more order on these narratives with *Jitterbug Perfume* and *Skinny Legs and All,* he still managed to traverse centuries and continents. In contrast, *Half Asleep in Frog Pajamas* (1994) is confined to just a few days over an Easter weekend in Seattle and focuses on the exploits of, for Robbins, relatively few interlinked characters. *Frog Pajamas* is noteworthy for a couple of other stylistic features as well—its reliance throughout on the second-person "you" and its delineation of chapters by specific references to time, with some of those chapters separated by a few hours, others by only a minute or two. The novel begins at 4:00 P.M. on the Thursday before Easter and ends at 5:55 A.M. the following Monday. "You," the reader, are never really allowed to forget what time it is.

Robbins makes clear in the text of course that the Christian celebration of Easter is an appropriation from an ancient pagan festival representing "Mother Nature in her fundamental, unexpurgated, paradoxical, bud-sprouting, blood-guzzling guise." But that doesn't prevent him from using its Christian resurrection symbolism for his own purposes, which have to do with a decidedly nontraditional form of personal rebirth. And his constant reminders of the ticking clock emphasize the way our lives are too often governed by the arbitrary measurement of minutes and hours, with predictably dismal results.

The matter of the second-person narrative is more of a problem. As a reader, "you" take on the character of Gwen Mati, an ethically challenged Seattle stockbroker and dedicated materialist. Given that Gwen is thoroughly dislikable in many parts of the novel, a reader might reasonably and determinedly resist that responsibility. Given also Gwen's all-consuming lust for monetary rewards, a reader might wonder what the finger-pointing implications for himself or herself are in Robbins's selection of the ubiquitous "you." And aside from the tricky dynamic between author, character, and reader, the second person seems to paint Robbins into some awkward prose corners. For the most part his renowned facility with words and sentences carries the day, despite the uncustomarily frequent presence of the funny-sounding pronoun. At times, however, the energy and ease of Robbins's delivery is jarred by statements like, "Don't make you laugh" or "Let you count the ways." Robbins often calls readers' attention to the artificial construct of words by which he creates his narrative, but in these instances the attention seems less salutary than is usually the case.

Gwen Mati's fateful Easter weekend begins with a crash in the stock market that may expose some of her less-than-ethical not to mention illegal practices. When the market closes for the long holiday weekend, her main ambition becomes to figure out a way to save herself from professional and financial collapse. Gwen's boyfriend Belford Dunn, who even Gwen believes suffers from "terminal dullness," is of little help since he is preoccupied with finding his reformed-jewel-thief, born-again-Christian monkey Andre, who has run away. Gwen's neighbor Q-Jo Huffington makes her living reading Tarot cards and sitting through the slide shows of vacation bores who cannot get anyone else to do so. Although a skeptic when it comes to the Tarot, Gwen is intrigued by Q-Jo's first reading of the cards for her, and the two women become friends despite the fact that Gwen is embarrassed to be seen in public with the three-hundred-pound woman.

Gwen's life becomes entwined with that of Larry Diamond, a disgraced but legendary former broker, when Q-Jo disappears after a scheduled appointment to view Diamond's slides from a trip to Timbuktu. Gwen follows Q-Jo's trail to Diamond, and the two ostensibly set out to find the missing Tarot reader. Along the way Gwen concocts a plan by which Larry, with his manipulative expertise, will help her make a futures play that would rescue her from professional demise before the market opens again on Monday. And Larry has plans of his own, as he makes painfully clear to Gwen at their second meeting—"What I'd really like to get into is your pants"—when they run into each other at Seattle's Science Center. Added to the context of their awkward partnership in finding Q-Jo are recurring references to a Dr. Yamaguchi's visit to Seattle after announcing his discovery of a potential cure for cancer, the details of which have not been revealed and understandably pique Diamond's interest since he suffers from cancer of the rectum.

Shortly before she disappeared, Q-Jo did a Tarot reading for Gwen in which the Fool emerged predominant, as it had a few times in the recent past. Q-Jo tells Gwen the Fool suggests she is ready to break from her past, from the "bogus melodrama" of pursuing wealth, to seek a more worthy and self-satisfying goal. "The only ones who'll ever reach that goal," Q-Jo emphasizes, "are the ones who have the courage to make fools of themselves along the way." That her words stir Gwen becomes

evident in a dream Gwen has about theatergoers presented the wrong libretto for a play but who never complain, blithely following the action with "a text for an entirely different drama than the one that was being staged." A voice in the dream notes that human beings do the same, observing reality while following with the wrong librettos. Gwen's chaotic search for Q-Jo over the Easter weekend also becomes the search for a suitable libretto from which to follow the action of her own life. No doubt Robbins intended for the second person pronoun "you" throughout the book to indicate the distance between Gwen's surface existence and her deeper yearnings as a human being.

Larry Diamond emerges as a quasi-instructor in that pursuit, because he underwent the same process of self-education after his own meltdown in the late 1980s. He refers to that process as "cognitive redecorating" or discovering that imagination creates reality rather than the other way around. He now wants Gwen to see the Lie of progress and unlimited economic expansion, that jobs are a mechanism through which the state exerts control over individuals, and that the yearning for "security" is actually a yearning after purgatory, while insecurity makes paradise possible. In keeping with Robbins's fascination with the mind-expanding properties of hallucinogens, Diamond reveals how mushrooms, those "microphones of the overmind," helped him realize that the world is different from what most people believe it to be and that they are too scared to find that out.

Diamond's discoveries are also linked with his visits to and study of the Bozo and Dogon tribes of western Africa, including the mysterious fact that they identified Sirius B even before astronomers did. This in turn gets mingled with theories of aliens and amphibians, in true Robbins fashion, where enough fact-based research is inserted to make the more speculative parts enticing. Diamond talks also of Timbuktu and his stay at the university there. And as much as he refers to it as a physical place, Timbuktu is also "a place in the brain" far removed from our normal understanding and expectations in regard to "reality," the place also where Q-Jo ultimately turns up and hopes Gwen will join her. The visiting faculty at this university are people like Timothy Leary, Carlos Castaneda, Terence McKenna, Fritjof Capra, and R. D. Laing, all influential in Robbins's own discovery of the appropriate libretto for perceiving the world.

Larry Diamond encourages Gwen to "move outside the realm of normal expectations," to "relocate outside the bounds of control and definition." He, like Q-Jo, wants her to join him "on the pad," ready for the next breakthrough in human evolution. This is the Easter resurrection Robbins celebrates in *Half Asleep in Frog Pajamas*. And Gwen, although reticent about believing much of what Diamond tells her in regard to Bozos and aliens and the intermediary role of frogs, is nonetheless tempted by the offer to accompany him to Timbuktu. The temptation stems in part from Gwen's awakening to the pleasures of sex. This too is familiar Robbins territory. When Larry introduces Gwen to the earth-moving sensations of oral sex, her renewed devotion to the transformative powers of the "carnal embrace" lead her to reconsider other dimensions of her life as well.

Diamond makes it clear to Gwen that what they share is a *collision,* not a relationship, because where a relationship might fulfill, a collision transforms. And the power in that process is passion itself. "Passion isn't a path through the woods," Diamond tells her. "Passion *is* the woods. It's the deepest, wildest part of the forest; the grove where the fairies still dance and obscene old vipers snooze in the boughs." Later in the novel, after Gwen has been temporarily reunited with Belford, Robbins as narrator offers an ode to lust that makes the liberating dimension of sex even more explicit:

Love makes the world go 'round, it's true, but lust stops the world in its tracks; love renders bearable the passage of time, lust causes time to stand still; lust kills time, which is not to say that it wastes it or whiles it away but rather that it annihilates it, cancels it, extirpates it from the continuum; preventing, while it lasts, any lapse into the tense and shabby woes of temporal society; lust is the thousand-pound odometer needle on the dashboard of the absolute.

Robbins acknowledges that the "plunge into the erotic" is often used simply as a means of escape, but it can also serve as a centering device, which is clearly the case for Gwen Mati.

Robbins's joyful and gung ho approach to sex has always been at the heart of his appeal to readers. But a seediness seeps into it through the character of Larry Diamond that can raise the hackles even among his fans. That seediness also adds an ambivalent flavor to some of Robbins's more direct narrative passages. Diamond makes no secret of his lust for Gwen from the moment he meets her, and once he establishes the terms of their "collision" about midway through the book, he takes to referring to her with pet names that always begin with "pussy." When he first refers to her as "pussy latte," it just seems a spontaneous if silly eruption. But as the terms pile up—pussy pudding, pussy sugar, pussy butter, pussy nougat, chops, pie, gravy, burger, gumbo, fondue, fricassee, frangipane, prosciutto, kimchi—something less liberating seems at work than Robbins's ode to lust might suggest.

Robbins has little patience for objections to such sex talk, seeing those objections as the overprotective whining of the politically correct. And his own objections to some liberal shibboleths appear elsewhere in *Frog Pajamas*. He attacks the tenets of multiculturalism that Belford Dunn and "his ilk" admire and makes a case for the homeless being responsible for their own bad choices in life rather than the victims of a heartless and unjust society. Gwen confronts Belford's social worker mentality near the end of the novel with arguments picked up from Diamond that carry a distinctively libertarian flavor: "The extent to which a society focuses on the needs of its lowest common denominator is the extent to which that society'll be mired in mediocrity."

Robbins's readers have grown accustomed to establishing friendly and philosophically compatible relationships with his narrators and primary characters over the years. In *Half Asleep in Frog Pajamas* things get a bit more prickly. Gwen Mati and Larry Diamond are frequently hard to like or admire, and the narrator sometimes ducks into philosophical alleys where readers might just as soon not venture. The fact that all of this comes through "you," as a stand-in for Gwen, makes it all the more discomforting and all the more provocative in its interplay of the light and dark forces that govern any human personality.

FIERCE INVALIDS HOME FROM HOT CLIMATES

After six novels built around the exploits of female protagonists, Robbins marks a departure with *Fierce Invalids Home from Hot Climates* (2000) in that its narrative focus stays squarely on Switters, a wheelchair-bound CIA operative with a philosophical outlook resembling that of his creator. Switters continues the more troublesome interplay between author, narrator, and characters begun in *Half Asleep in Frog Pajamas* as a cranky smugness seeps into many of his pronouncements. Of all Robbins's novels, *Fierce Invalids* seems most like *Still Life with Woodpecker* because of its tone of impatience for those who do not see things the same way as Switters.

Robbins's philosophizing is tinged with a nastiness in *Fierce Invalids* that is missing from earlier works, even *Still Life*. Switters and his aunt Maestra expound on a theory of "missing links," those individuals "north of the animal kingdom but south of humanity" because they lack the six essentials that separate human beings from the lower orders—humor, imagination, eroticism, spirituality, rebelliousness, and aesthetics. In his review of *Fierce Invalids* for the *Washington Post Book World,* Richard Grant refers to Switters's "contempt for the citizens and institutions of modern democracies." A reader of the novel might sympathize with that assessment as he or she wades through Switters's defense of the "virtues of true elitism" or his attack on the "inertia of the masses."

Switters's view also gets entangled with the narrator's (whom one easily comes to see as Robbins) when the narrator expands on a Switters remark:

> Presumably he was referring to the manner in which the powers that be, with the greedy compliance of the media and the eager assistance of the evangelicals, were busily bovinizing humanity, seeking to produce a vast herd of homogenized consumers, individually expendable, docile, and, beyond basic job skills, not too smart; two-legged cows that could easily be milked and, when necessary, guiltlessly slaughtered.

None of what Robbins writes here really alters the philosophy he has entertained readers with for three decades, but in the past his expression of that philosophy put him on the side of those who need to resist such bovinizing, offering encouragement, especially for young people. In *Fierce Invalids* it often appears simply to write them off.

If a dourness creeps into Robbins's moralizing, no slackening appears in the playful inventiveness he brings to his plot. While on assignment in Peru, Switters makes a side trip to the rain forest to fulfill an obligation for his wealthy Aunt Maestra in Seattle. His mission is to release her parrot back into the wild. While there he meets a British anthropologist named Potney Smythe. Smythe puts him onto the trail of a Kandakandero shaman deep in the jungle whose own name translates as End of Time or Today is Tomorrow but whose most distinguishing characteristic is a pyramid-shaped head. In exchange for the "knowledge of mysteries" that Switters seeks from him, Today is Tomorrow places a taboo on Switters, not allowing his feet to ever touch the ground or he will die. Inclined to respect the shaman's sanction anyway, Switters's willingness to do so is reinforced when Potney Smythe ignores a taboo placed on him earlier by the same shaman and drops dead right in front of Switters. For most of the rest of the novel, Switters keeps his feet at least two inches off the ground, relying on a wheelchair for mobility.

The knowledge he pays so dearly for concerns the secret to living beyond life's dualities. The Kandakandero people had always possessed a deeply imbedded spiritual sense that allowed them to confront life's mysteries, but they lacked an essential component that would consummate the "marriage of darkness and light." That component, Today is Tomorrow eventually discovered, was "Western man's comedic sense." Switters surmises that when scientists finally "split the most minute particle" and get down to the absolute most fundamental level of the universe, they will find "an energy field in which light and darkness intermingle." Today is Tomorrow's discovery suggests that such an intermingling can occur also "on the biomolecular plane, the social plane. That a people who could move in the primal realm of laughter could live free of all of life's dualities."

Switters extrapolates from Today is Tomorrow's epiphany a theory on joy itself being a form of wisdom: "If people are nimble enough to move freely between different perceptions of reality and if they maintain a relaxed, playful attitude well-seasoned with laughter, then they would live in harmony with the universe; they would connect with all matter, organic and inorganic, at its purest, most basic level." Robbins's penchant for mixing physics and metaphysics reaches a crescendo of sorts in

Fierce Invalids, tying together various loose ends of the philosophy he has explored throughout his novels with a justification for the very nature of his fiction.

Of course the turns of his plot extend beyond the encounter with Today is Tomorrow in the Peruvian jungle. These include Switters's lusting after his sixteen-year-old stepsister Suzy and his extended visit with an order of nuns in the Syrian desert. Switters's desire for Suzy leaves him in a quandary, as Robbins again explores the play of dualities in the human heart. Switters decries society's unnatural denial of the fact that adolescent girls are "horny as jackrabbits" and "highly charged sexual dynamos," but he also does not wish to deny Suzy the innocent process of trial and error by which most young girls attain information about sex. An obvious Nabokovian influence flavors this aspect of *Fierce Invalids,* with echoes also of Humbert Humbert's murderous prose style.

Switters's stay at the Order of St. Pachomius in the Syrian desert follows a freelance mission to supply gas masks to the Iraqi Kurds (he is relieved of his CIA duties once he confines himself to a wheelchair). While there he makes the acquaintance of Masked Beauty, the head abbess, whose past includes having posed for Henri Matisse's *Blue Nude 1942,* a painting Switters's Aunt Maestra just happens to own and Switters himself covets. The abbess has kept her face masked ever since praying for and being granted a release from her beauty, that release coming in the form of a gigantic and hideous wart. Switters also meets and falls in love with another of the convent's nuns, Domino Thiry, whom he engages in spirited debates, religious and otherwise. Those debates serve as a prelude to equally spirited demonstrations of the pair's physical attraction for each other, demonstrations that creatively but libidinously work around Domino's already miraculously restored virginity.

Estranged from the Vatican for their views on birth control, the nuns of St. Pachomius are eventually excommunicated, which precipitates negotiations over the order's prize possession, a document containing the three prophecies of Our Lady of Fatima. The third of those prophecies, a closely guarded Vatican secret, links a coming age of wisdom and joy with a pyramid, something the church fears will be interpreted as a prediction of Islam's succeeding Christianity as the world's dominant religion. Switters offers a different reading, associating the pyramid with the similarly shaped head of Today is Tomorrow and Switters's theory of darkness and light, spirituality and laughter, and joy as a form of wisdom. The deadlocked negotiations over possession of the Fatima document lead to a showdown at the Vatican, during which Switters is drawn from his chair to protect the threatened Domino. And he does not drop dead.

Robbins begins the unwinding of his complicated plot with four short, disconnected chapters that leapfrog from two different locations in Peru to Syria and to Vatican City. Their only unifying element is the presence of Switters. In the last of these opening chapters the narrator reflects on the disjointed nature of the novel so far, concluding,

> That's the way the mind works: the human brain is genetically disposed toward organization, yet if not tightly controlled, will link one imagerial fragment to another on the flimsiest of pretense and in the most freewheeling manner, as if it takes a kind of organic pleasure in creative association, without regard for logic or chronological sequence.

Still, the narrator continues, that is not the way "an effective narrative ought to unfold," and then the narrator indicates that henceforth the book will proceed in a more timely and orderly fashion.

Earlier in his writing career Robbins went to great lengths to make his novels reflect in some way the not-so-orderly and arbitrary nature of time and space. The structures of both *Another Roadside Attraction* and *Even Cowgirls Get the Blues* mimic the freewheeling manner and creative association of the mind at work, escaping the chronological, sequential demands of imposed conceptions of time. About halfway through *Fierce Invalids,* however, in the midst of a defense of disorder as a healthy complement to order, Switters tells Domino, "Besides, if properly employed, language can provide all of the order a person might ever need in life." In addition to suggesting a rationale for Robbins's shift to a more orderly arrangement of his fictional worlds, Switters's comment suggests something about the significance Robbins attaches to language itself as a vital means for establishing a healthy and joyful state of being.

Robbins also relays in the novel a story told by Tennessee Williams of people living their lives as though they were trapped in a house on fire, looking out an upstairs window while the house burns down around them. Robbins adds:

> What Tennessee failed to mention was that if we look out of that window with an itchy curiosity and a passionate eye; with a generous spirit and a capacity for delight; and, yes, the language with which to support and enrich the things we see, then it DOESN'T MATTER that the house is burning down around us. It doesn't matter. Let the motherfucker blaze!

Throughout *Fierce Invalids,* Robbins carries on a discussion through Switters about language, emphasizing its capacity to support and enrich, even as language itself evolves and "the electron rather than the word [becomes] the primary information link between the brain and the external word."

Switters is a language junkie. His Bible is James Joyce's *Finnegan's Wake* (1939). He reflects on the relationship between grammar and the actions of his daily life. He lectures on the importance of understanding that "unique" is not a synonym for "unusual." But he also offers lengthy discourses on how language in cyberculture is not contracting but expanding, beyond the body, out into the universe, usurping physical reality. He even recognizes that this could signal the "connectedness of electronic technology and primal mythology." Still, he remains devoted to the word and to the role that language can play in consciously creating individual realities. And in that respect, he embodies Tom Robbins's own attempt, through his fiction, to let the house burn.

While reviewing *Still Life with Woodpecker* in 1980, Barry Hannah described Tom Robbins as "abundant." It seems a particularly apt description for Robbins's literary output to date. In *Fierce Invalids* in fact Robbins writes that "human beings are by nature comprehensive," even as he worries about the effects of our contemporary mania for overspecialization. Robbins's seven novels certainly reflect that instinct for comprehensiveness in their exploration of matters large and small that bedevil and delight readers' journeys through life. They also show abundance in their love for language and the comic spirit. But most of all they demonstrate abundance in the principle that unites them all. Switters acknowledges that principle when Domino asks where the spiritual center of Catholicism would go if Rome itself were spiritually broken. "To the individual heart," he says. "The only church that ever was."

Selected Bibliography

WORKS BY TOM ROBBINS

NOVELS

Another Roadside Attraction. Garden City, N.Y.: Doubleday, 1971. Reprint, New York: Bantam, 1990.

Even Cowgirls Get the Blues. New York: Bantam, 1976. Reprint, 1990.

Still Life with Woodpecker. New York: Bantam, 1980. Reprint, 1990.

Jitterbug Perfume. New York: Bantam, 1984.

Skinny Legs and All. New York: Bantam, 1990.

Half Asleep in Frog Pajamas. New York: Bantam, 1994.

Fierce Invalids Home from Hot Climates. New York: Bantam, 2000.

ARTICLES

"Notes on Nukes, Nookie, and Neo-Romanticism." *Seattle Weekly,* June 21–27, 1978, pp. 11–15. (Letters and Robbins's response July 19–25, 1978, p. 5. Reprinted in many newspapers as "Feminismo" or "Move over Macho, Here Comes Feminismo.")

"The Purpose of the Moon." *Playboy,* January 1979, pp. 237, 330.

"Why I Live Where I Live." *Esquire,* October 1980, pp. 82–84.

"Ray Kroc Did It All for You." *Esquire,* December 1983, pp. 340–342, 344.

"The Hair of the Beast." *Esquire,* November 1984, pp. 236–238, 240, 242–244, 247.

"Writing and Politics." *fiction international* 15, no. 1:24 (1984).

"The Day the Earth Spit Wart Hogs." *Esquire,* October 1985, p. 124+.

"Wishing for Milton's Power and Tolstoy's Zaniness." *New York Times Book Review,* December 8, 1985, pp. 46–47.

"Treasured Places: Favorite Wilderness Areas of Eight American Writers." *Life,* July 1987, pp. 35–42+.

"The Real Valley of the Dolls." *Esquire,* December 1988, pp. 202–207.

"Nadia Salerno-Sonnenberg." *Esquire,* November 1989, pp. 172–173.

"The Kiss." *Playboy,* February 1990, pp. 92–93.

"Two in the Bush." *Esquire,* March 1990, pp. 50, 54.

"The Genius Waitress: An Ode to Women Who Serve." *Playboy,* December 1991, pp. 144–145.

"Confessions of a Reluctant Sex Goddess: Debra Winger as Encountered by Tom Robbins." *Esquire,* February 1993, pp. 71–76.

"You Gotta Have Soul." *Esquire,* October 1993, p. 164.

"Imagination." *Self,* May 1994, p. 230.

"Writing from the Inside Out: Style Is Not the Frosting; It's the Cake." Lecture delivered at Yale University, New Haven, Conn. October 6, 1994.

"Mini, a Natural High." *New York Times,* April 6, 1995, pp. C1, C6.

"Tom Robbins Considers the Man in the Tower." Liner notes for *Tower of Song: The Songs of Leonard Cohen.* By Leonard Cohen. A&M Records, 1995. Compact disk.

MEDIA

Even Cowgirls Get the Blues. Read by Michael Nouri. Dove Audio, 1993. Audiotape. (Unabridged, 9 cassettes, 13 hours.)

Even Cowgirls Get the Blues. Directed by Gus Van Sant. Narrative voice-over by Tom Robbins. Full Line Features, 1994. Film.

CRITICAL AND BIOGRAPHICAL STUDIES

Akers, Cynthia. *From Bubblegum to Personism: The Cycle of Choice in the Novels of Tom Robbins.* Emporia State Research Studies Vol. 38, no. 2, Emporia, Kans.: Emporia State University, 1992.

"*Another Roadside Attraction.*" *Playboy,* September 1971 pp. 22, 26.

Cameron, Ann. "A Nose Thumb at Normality." *Nation,* August 28, 1976, pp. 152–153.

Cantor, Jay. "Yet Another Roadside Attraction." *Washington Post Book World,* March 25, 1990, pp. 1, 9.

Capra, Fritjof. *The Tao of Physics: An Exploration of the Parallels between Modern Physics and Eastern Mysticism.* Berkeley, Calif.: Shambhala, 1975.

Cassill, R. V. "Whimsy with Moral." *New York Times Book Review,* September 28, 1980, p. 15.

Clark, Tom. "Through Salome's Veils to Ultimate Cognition." *Los Angeles Times Book Review,* April 15, 1990, pp. 1, 9.

Dutton, Thomas. "Behind the Best Sellers." *New York Times Book Review,* October 19, 1980, p. 58.

Egan, Timothy. "Perfect Sentences, Imperfect Universe." *New York Times,* December 30, 1993, pp. C1, C9.

"Five Ws for the Counterculture." *Horizon,* May 1977, p. 70.

Gartner, Zsuzsi. "Dear John . . . um, Tom." *Toronto Globe and Mail,* May 13, 2000, p. D7.

Geringer, Laura. "Romper Room." *Newsweek,* September 29, 1980, pp. 82–83.

Grant, Richard. "Jungle Fever." *Washington Post Book World,* May 28, 2000, p.7.

Gross, Beverly. "Misfits: Tom Robbins' *Even Cowgirls Get the Blues.*" *North Dakota Quarterly* 50, no. 3:36–51 (summer 1982).

Halpern, Sue M. "A Pox on Dullness." *Nation,* October 25, 1980, pp. 415–417.

Hannah, Barry. "Tom Robbins and Other Outrages." *Washington Post Book World,* September 28, 1980, p. 5.

Hettinga, Donald R. "Tom Robbins's *Still Life with Woodpecker.*" *Chicago Review* 32, no. 2:123–125 (autumn 1980).

House, John. "They Brake for Unicorns." *New York Times Book Review,* December 9, 1984, p. 11.

Hoyser, Catherine E., and Lorena Laura Stookey. *Tom Robbins: A Critical Companion.* Critical Companions to Popular Contemporary Writers. Westport, Conn.: Greenwood Press, 1997.

Jenks, Tom. "How Writers Live Today." *Esquire,* August 1985, pp. 123–127.

Karbo, Karen. "The Ocean's Zither." *New York Times Book Review,* October 30, 1994, p. 27.

Klinkowitz, Jerome. "Epilogue: Avant-garde and After." In his *The Practice of Fiction in America: Writers from Hawthorne to the Present.* Ames: Iowa State University Press, 1980. Pp. 114–128.

LeClair, Thomas. "*Even Cowgirls Get the Blues.*" *New York Times Book Review,* May 23, 1976, p. 5.

Lownsbrough, John. "A Shot of Tequila, a Dose of Whimsy." *Maclean's,* October 6, 1980, p. 82.

Mitchell, Greg. ". . . And Cowgirls Jumped over the Moon." *Crawdaddy,* August 1977, pp. 29–33.

McConnell, Frank. "Should We Trust a Cuddly Novelist?" *Commonweal,* March 13, 1981, pp. 153–155.

Nadeau, Robert L. "Physics and Cosmology in the Fiction of Tom Robbins." *Critique* 20, no. 1:63–74 (August 1978).

———. "Tom Robbins." In his *Readings from the New Book on Nature: Physics and Metaphysics in the Modern Novel.* Amherst: University of Massachusetts Press, 1981. Pp. 149–160.

Nelson, William. "The Comic Grotesque in Recent Fiction." *Thalia: Studies in Literary Humor* 5, no. 2:36–40 (fall/winter 1982–1983).

———. "Unlikely Heroes: The Central Figures in *The World According to Garp, Even Cowgirls Get the Blues,* and *A Confederacy of Dunces.*" In *The Hero in Transition.* Edited by Ray B. Browne and Marshall W. Fishwick. Bowling Green, Ohio: Bowling Green University Popular Press, 1983. Pp. 163–170.

Norman, Peter. "Being Kind to Objects." *Times Literary Supplement,* October 31, 1980, p. 1220.

Peters, Julie B. *"Still Life with Woodpecker."* *Saturday Review,* September 1980, pp. 71–72.

Poniewozik, James. "Sex, Drugs, and Subatomic Particles." *New York Times Book Review,* May 21, 2000, p. 12.

Queenan, Joe. "Then the Spoon Speaks Up." *New York Times Book Review,* April 15, 1990, p. 12.

Ross, Mitchell. "The Beet Goes On." *National Review,* June 28, 1985, pp. 44–45.

Rucker, Rudy. "In Search of the Ultimate Love Potion." *Washington Post Book World,* November 25, 1984, pp. 1, 9.

———. "The Transcendent Wisdom of Amphibians." *Washington Post Book World,* December 18, 1994, p.1.

Sharlin, Shifra. "Square and Groovy Gods Made Flesh." *Books & Religion,* fall 1990, pp. 5–6, 14.

Siegel, Mark. *Tom Robbins.* Western Writers Series no. 42. Boise, Idaho: Boise State University, 1980.

———. "The Meaning of Meaning in the Novels of Tom Robbins." *Mosaic* 14, no. 3:119–131 (summer 1981).

Skow, John. *"Skinny Legs and All."* *Time,* May 7, 1990, p. 112.

Strachan, Don. *"Another Roadside Attraction."* *Rolling Stone,* September 16, 1971, p. 52.

———. *"Jitterbug Perfume."* *Los Angeles Times Book Review,* December 16, 1984, pp. 6–7.

Sturgeon, Theodore. "Peaks and Beacons." *National Review,* January 19, 1973, pp. 103–104, 106.

Sutton, Roger. "'Grokking' the YA Cult Novels." *School Library Journal,* October 1983, pp. 131–132.

"Tom Robbins." In *Dictionary of Literary Biography Yearbook: 1980.* Detroit, Mich.: Gale, 1981. Pp. 301–303.

Treglown, Jeremy. "Such Style." *New Statesman,* August 12, 1977, p. 219.

Waugh, Auberon. "Butterfly Nut." *Spectator,* March 24, 1973, pp. 365–366.

Whittemore, Reed. "Rain Forest and Old Plantation." *New Republic,* June 26, 1971, pp. 29–30.

Wilson, Raymond J. "A Synthesis of Modernism." *Prairie Schooner* 51, no. 1:99–100 (spring 1977).

INTERVIEWS

Christy, George. "Interview: Tom Robbins." *Interview,* November 1993, pp. 126–131.

Cleary Miller, Patricia E. "An Interview with Tom Robbins." In her "Reconciling Science and Mysticism: Characterization in the Novels of Tom Robbins." Ph.D. dissertation. University of Kansas, Lawrence, 1979. Pp. 268–293.

Cott, Jonathan. "Drugstore Cowgirl." *Rolling Stone,* November 11, 1993, pp. 58–62.

Dougherty, Steve. "Cowgirls May Get the Blues, but Not Tom Robbins, Who Pours It on in *Jitterbug Perfume.*" *People,* April 1, 1985, pp. 123–124+.

Edlin, Mari. "PW Interviews: Tom Robbins." *Publishers Weekly,* May 25, 1990, pp. 41–42.

Lyons, Len. "Why Even Colleges Get Tom Robbins." *Book Views,* February 1978, p. 23.

Maxwell, Jessica. "Tom Robbins's Book of Bozo." *Esquire,* January 1995, p. 18.

McCaffery, Larry, and Sinda Gregory. "An Interview with Tom Robbins." In their *Alive and Writing: Interviews with American Authors of the 1980s.* Urbana: University of Illinois Press, 1987. Pp. 222–239.

Rogers, Michael. "Taking Tom Robbins Seriously." *Rolling Stone,* November 17, 1977, pp. 66–69.

Ross, Mitchell S. "The Prince of the Paperback Literati." *New York Times Magazine,* February 12, 1978, pp. 16–17, 66–69.

Strelow, Michael. "Dialogue with Tom Robbins." *Northwest Review* 20, no. 2–3:97–102 (1982).

Strickland, Bill. "Joy in Spite of Everything: An Interview with Tom Robbins, Part 1." *Writer's Digest,* February 1988, pp. 30–33, 69.

———. "Joy in Spite of Everything: An Interview with Tom Robbins, Part 2." *Writer's Digest,* March 1988, pp. 32–36.

Whitmer, Peter. "Cosmic Comedian." *Saturday Review,* January/February 1985, pp. 50–55.

Whitmer, Peter O., with Bruce VanWyngarden. "The Post-Modernist Outlaw Intellectual." In his *Aquarius Revisited: Seven Who Created the Sixties Counterculture That Changed America.* New York: Macmillan, 1987. Pp. 235–249.

—BRIAN KENT

Amy Tan

1952–

AMY TAN, THE American-born daughter of Chinese immigrants, published her first novel, the best-selling *The Joy Luck Club* (1989), when she was thirty-seven years old. At the time she was a highly successful business writer who had recently returned from her first trip to China with her mother, Daisy Tan. She would later say that she wrote *The Joy Luck Club* to gain a better understanding of the generational and cultural tensions between herself and her mother.

The Joy Luck Club was a commercial and critical success. It remained on the *New York Times* best-seller list for nearly a year and was a Book-of-the-Month Club selection. It was a finalist for a National Book Award as well as a National Book Critics Circle Award. Tan received the Bay Area Book Reviewers Award for fiction and the Commonwealth Club Gold Award. The book has been translated into seventeen languages, including Chinese.

The Joy Luck Club is made up of a masterful blend of voices that alternately tells the stories of four Chinese immigrant mothers and their Americanized daughters. With its bicultural themes, its human interest stories, and its evocative history of Chinese culture, the book immediately became popular in contemporary American literature courses.

In 1991 Tan published *The Kitchen God's Wife,* which was partially inspired by her mother's stories of life in China before the Communist Revolution. Tan continued to explore the complete range of Chinese American experience with her third novel, *The Hundred Secret Senses* (1995). She is also the author of short stories and two children's books, *The*

Moon Lady (1992) and *The Chinese Siamese Cat* (1994). With national and international acclaim for her writing, Tan is one of the best-known living American writers of Chinese ancestry.

EARLY YEARS

Tan was born on February 19, 1952, in Oakland, California. Her parents, Daisy and John Tan, were recent immigrants from China. Amy Tan's Chinese name, An-mei, means "blessing from America." Amy Tan is the second of three children. Her brother Peter was born in 1950 and her brother John in 1954.

Although her parents were Chinese, Tan grew up as an assimilated Asian American. She was aware at an early age of contradictions between her ethnicity and American culture. Her traditional Chinese parents expected her to become a neurosurgeon and a concert pianist. Tan felt uneasy balancing American lifestyles with more traditional Chinese customs. Her limited Chinese language skills and her parents' weak English added to the problem. Tan later expressed a painful awareness about her biculturalism. Speaking to Dorothy Wang of *Newsweek,* she recalled: "There was shame and self hate. There is this myth that America is a melting pot." She also felt uncomfortable with her physical appearance. As a child she slept for a week with a clothespin on her nose, hoping to alter her Asian features (noted in *Amy Tan: A Critical Companion*).

The family moved frequently in California and finally settled in Santa Clara. Tan showed an early gift for writing and won an essay contest in elementary school. When she was fifteen both her father and older brother Peter died of malignant brain tumors. Daisy Tan felt the loss deeply and renewed her ancient Chinese customs by invoking help from Chinese deities and soothsayers. Amy Tan was immersed into Chinese culture, an experience that would later infuse her novels. Also during that time Daisy Tan confessed to her daughter painful details from her life in China.

Daisy Tan was born into a wealthy Shanghai family. Her father, a scholar, died when she was young. Daisy spent part of her childhood in exile with her mother, Jing-mei, on an island off the coast of Shanghai. Jing-mei's one son was taken away from her and she eventually committed suicide. At nine years old, Daisy was left to grow up alone. She suffered through the trials of World War II and an extremely abusive marriage before fleeing to the United States. Daisy left behind three daughters. This amazing revelation inspired a major section of *The Joy Luck Club* in the narrative history of Suyuan Woo.

In 1968 Daisy Tan moved Amy and her brother John to Montreux, Switzerland, where Amy Tan went to school and enjoyed the novelty of being Asian American in Europe. Tan fell in with a wild crowd. Her boyfriend was a drug dealer and an escapee from a German mental hospital. Tan's mother was instrumental in breaking up this union, and soon after the Tan family returned to the United States.

Tan enrolled in San Jose State University and while there changed her major from pre-medical to a double major in English and linguistics, much to her mother's disappointment. She earned a bachelor of arts degree in English and linguistics in 1973 and a master of arts degree in linguistics in 1974, both at San Jose State. She married her Italian American boyfriend, Louis DeMattei, in 1974. Tan studied toward a

doctorate at the University of California at Santa Cruz and Berkeley before dropping out in 1976.

Tan then worked as a language development consultant to the Alameda County Association for Retarded Citizens. She branched out into business writing in the early 1980s. Using racially neutral pseudonyms like May Brown, Tan drafted speeches for salespersons and chief executives. Within a short time she had established her own business and attracted clients like IBM, for whom she wrote a twenty-six-chapter monograph entitled "Telecommunications and You." In a few years she had saved enough to buy her mother a house, but the long hours and stress took their toll.

In an effort to change her lifestyle, Tan took up jazz piano and began to write fiction. She read Eudora Welty, Flannery O'Connor, and Alice Munro. Louise Erdrich's novel, *Love Medicine* (1984), particularly influenced Tan with its voice and narrative structure, which consists of a collection of stories shared by individuals representing several generations of a Native American family.

Tan's first short story, "Endgame," about a precocious young chess champion who has a stormy relationship with her overprotective Chinese mother, was published in *FM* magazine and reprinted in *Seventeen*. Her second story, "Waiting between the Trees," was never published but did attract a literary agent. In the summer of 1987 Tan began working on a book of short stories, titled "Wind and Water," which later evolved into her first novel.

After Daisy was hospitalized for a heart condition, Tan decided to travel with her mother to China, where she met her three half sisters and learned firsthand about her mother's past. The trip was a turning point in Tan's quest to understand her heritage.

Upon her return from China, Tan was astounded by the news that her agent had negotiated a substantial contract for a book to be published by G. P. Putnam's Sons. Tan named her book *The Joy Luck Club* in reference to the mah-jongg–playing social and investment clubs formed by Chinese American mothers. *The Joy Luck Club* was published in March 1989 to great critical praise and popular success.

ASIAN AMERICAN LITERATURE

Chinese immigration to the United States was very high in the nineteenth century, particularly on the West Coast. Subsequently, the Chinese Exclusion Act of 1882 limited the flow of immigrants. At the same time, many Chinese in the United States were denied citizenship purely on racial grounds. The mainstream conception of Chinese culture was vastly distorted by the stereotypical portrayal of Chinese in popular media. Exaggerated character figures such as Charlie Chan, Fu Manchu, and Anna May Wong predominated in the public mind.

The earliest successful Chinese American authors were Edith and Winnifred Eaton, daughters of an English artist and his Chinese wife. Edith and Winnifred immigrated to the United States in the early twentieth century. Writing in the period between the world wars, the Eatons used pen names to mask their identities. Edith became Sui Sin Far and Winnifred became the Japanese writer Onoto Watanna.

Edith's writing was unusual for the period in that she presented original Chinese American characters without stereotypes based on race, gender, or class. She deftly portrayed the mixed heritage dilemma in which an individual does not belong to one culture or the other. Winnifred, on the other hand, wrote romance novels about delicate Japanese women in conflict with powerful men, often white. She later went on to a very successful career as a Hollywood scriptwriter.

Other early Asian American writers did little to alter accepted ideas of Chinese culture. Writers such as Lin Yutang in *My Country and My People* (1936) professed to explain Chinese culture, but the writer's popular appeal was based on his depiction of the Chinese as otherworldly and artistic. Pardee Lowe's *Father and Glorious Descendant* (1943) and Jade Snow Wong's *Fifth Chinese Daughter* (1950) were also based on formulaic romantic conceptions. The three sisters Adet, Anor, and Mei-mei Yutang wrote personalized accounts of World War II and its effects on China, as did Mai-mai Sze and Helena Kuo. Han Suyin was a prolific writer who focused on interracial relationships in exotic locales. Her books honestly portrayed the difficulties of mixed-blood marriages and families. *The House That Tai Maing Built* (1963), by Virginia Chin-lan Lee, is a semi-autobiographical account of the Chinese in America but lacks a cultural critique.

The Chinese Exclusion Act was repealed in 1943, allowing significant numbers of Chinese men and women to enter the United States. In 1945 the War Brides Act opened up immigration to Chinese women who had married U.S. servicemen during World War II. After the war a new honesty and realism about Asian American culture become more evident in the literary output of a number of writers. Louis Chu's *Eat a Bowl of Tea* (1961) introduced themes that anticipated the focus of Asian American women writers of the 1980s, in particular the debilitating effects of American racism and Chinese patriarchal culture on most Chinese American families. Set in 1947, the book discusses conflicts between elder immigrant Chinese and their American-born children. Hua Chuang's experimental novel, *Crossings* (1968), was another groundbreaking book that wove an interracial romance into a critique of the Korean War, which pitted China and the United States against each other. Her narrative experiments foreshadowed the work of Maxine Hong Kingston and Amy Tan.

Maxine Hong Kingston's *The Woman Warrior* (1976) was the first book by an Asian American to gain immense popular readership and acclaim. The novel is a semi-autobiographical treatment of conflicts and change within a Chinese American family. The struggle between mother and daughter over bicultural issues anticipates Amy Tan's work in the next decade. The book incorporates a combination of genres and styles that relies heavily on a Chinese oral tradition called *gong gu tsai* ("talk story"), in which women tell stories that combine folktale, poetry, and song into entertaining and instructive narratives. It also is a way of communicating wisdom through the use of parables, proverbs, and biographies of heroines and heroes. Kingston's second novel, *China Men* (1980), won the American Book Award.

Many valuable anthologies of Asian American writers were published in the 1970s. They include *Asian American Authors* (1972), edited by Kai-yu Hsu and Helen Palubinskas; *Aiiieeeee! An Anthology of Asian-American Writers* (1974), edited by The Combined Asian Resources Project; and *Asian American Heritage: An Anthology of Prose and Poetry* (1974), edited by David Hsin-fu Wand.

In the following decade Cathy Son won the Yale Series of Younger Poets competition for *Picture Bride* (1982). Garrett Hongo won the Lamont Poetry prize of the Academy of American Poets in 1987 for *Ring of Heaven: Poems* (1987), and the play *M Butterfly* won several Tony Awards in 1988, among them "best play" for David Henry Hwang. *Charlie Chan Is Dead: An Anthology of Contemporary Asian American Fiction*, edited by Jessica Hagedorn appeared in 1993.

LITERARY TECHNIQUE IN TAN'S WORK

Tan's writing breakthrough happened after she listened to her mother's story about her life in China. Daisy Tan's revelations of a former marriage and abandoned children opened up a world that Amy Tan had purposefully blocked out.

Her own Chinese cultural heritage now became the focus of her writing. The influence of Daisy Tan's stories can be seen in all of Amy Tan's novels, but particularly in *The Kitchen God's Wife*, which reads much like her mother's autobiography.

Tan uses writing techniques introduced by other Asian American writers, including Maxine Hong Kingston: she combines Western and Eastern storytelling methods, her novels explore Chinese and Chinese American life over many centuries in a nonlinear fashion, and her primary literary device comes from the honored and ancient Chinese tradition of communication called "talk story." Tan applies "talk story" to dual cultures and generations separated by language, time, and space. She combines stories from a variety of women speakers in her novels, most of them using their own voice. A frame story organizes these tales by tying different perspectives into a coherent and meaningful whole. A continuous, overlapping narrative, the frame story eventually becomes more than the sum of its parts.

Tan's novels incorporate nonfiction, poetry, biography, autobiography, and history to elucidate different time periods and national geographies. Realistic, allegorical, and fantastic styles of writing are all used to convey different states of mind. The narratives parallel and intersect each other as episode after episode accumulates.

Mothers and daughters struggle with troubled and ambiguous relationships in Tan's novels. The daughters are confused by their Chinese heritage. They have uneasy assimilated lives in the United States and their Chinese mothers' customs, clothes, and language often embarrass them. The mothers use traditional oral forms to transmit the remnants of Chinese culture that are fading from their own lives. They tell their histories while at the same time reconfiguring Chinese myths and parables. Their stories bridge the gap between the Old and New Worlds and provoke reflection on the part of their daughters.

Because *The Joy Luck Club* was first conceived as a collection of short stories, the episodic structure of the book reflects this early intent. It contains sixteen stories divided into four sections with four stories in each section. Each section presents a definitive moment in the lives of four Chinese women, including an important stage in their relationship with their daughters. A short parable prefaces each section. The theme of the parables foreshadows the main concerns that follow. As the separate stories of the characters are told, parallels between the episodes become apparent. Each narrator speaks with her own voice. Interestingly, none of the daughters directly addresses her mother.

In Tan's second novel, *The Kitchen God's Wife,* Winnie Louie reveals the secrets of her hidden past to her daughter Pearl. Her story provides a way for the daughter to strengthen her understanding of her mother and herself. At the center of the book is the revelation that Pearl is the child of a rape by Winnie Louie's brutal Chinese husband and that Winnie fled China under threat of death.

Winnie achieves wholeness by reshaping and understanding her life through the act of storytelling. She breaks out of silence imposed by her adopted culture and by her daughter, who represents that culture. Pearl also works toward wholeness by accompanying her mother back to China. Just as Winnie told her story to Pearl, Pearl will in turn pass the history to her children.

Tan's third work, *The Hundred Secret Senses,* features two narrators, Olivia and Kwan, half-sisters, one Chinese American and the other Chinese. The book employs the flashback technique to provide multiple versions and various perspectives on important events. The contemporary framing story involves Olivia, her husband, Simon, and her much older half sister Kwan. Olivia artfully traces her Chinese American upbringing in the San Francisco area. She tells of her first meeting with Kwan when she was a child and Kwan a young woman. Within the context of Olivia's story, Kwan speaks of her own life in China. She relates the tragic nineteenth-century Chinese tale of a servant named Nunumu, an American woman named Miss Banner, and Miss Banner's lover Yiban. The lives of these individuals parallel those of herself, Olivia, and Simon. Kwan's memory and mystical powers unite the two sets of characters. In *The Hundred Secret Senses* the past prefigures the present while the present revises the past.

As Olivia narrates her own story she reveals her unhappiness in her fully assimilated American lifestyle. Her older sister Kwan's voice, in contrast, is strong and firmly rooted in her memories of China and her love of Chinese culture. Kwan's voice embodies faith in the universe and in herself and has the rhythms of myth, legend, and folktale, leading Olivia to wonder, "So which part was her dream, which part was mine? Where did they intersect?" Although the novel is Olivia's story, Kwan gradually takes over with her distinctive "talk story" blend of legend, folktale, and history. Olivia ultimately realizes that the half sisters have a connection through their Chinese heritage that transcends division.

CHINESE AMERICAN BICULTURALISM

Tan's novels blend the contemporary concerns of uneasily assimilated Chinese Americans with stories about China by Chinese women. Tan's comprehensive perspective engages bicultural issues on a number of different levels, but the dislocations of living in two cultures lie at the heart of Tan's fiction.

The Chinese have retained a distinctive culture within United States in part because of marginalization by the mainstream society, but also as a consequence of the purposeful preservation of Chinese culture by Chinese immigrants. Tan's second-generation voice speaks to members of the Chinese community on both sides of the divide as it explores the web of bicultural forces that directs their lives.

In *The Joy Luck Club* the tensions between mothers and daughters and between U.S. and Chinese influences are constantly expressed in bicultural ways. The mothers are firmly rooted in their Chinese cultural heritage and are comfortable with being Chinese. The daughters are awkward with their own Chinese features, the Chinese language, and their repressed Chinese spirituality. The mothers identify with their ethnicity, but the daughters are ambivalent about who they are.

Biculturalism is manifest in the struggle for control between mothers and daughters. The generation that was born in China survived by immigrating to the United States. They have two lives. The first life in China cannot be erased by a geographical relocation. China lives within them. Their Chinese lifestyles are constant complements to their present lives in United States.

The daughters carve out independent lives and reject their mothers' ways but their successes in American society do not satisfy them. They seem ignorant of or oblivious to what their mothers endured. The mothers feel that their daughters' indifference is influenced by the dominant white culture. The mothers express bewilderment at their daughters' complaints about how difficult and unrewarding their lives are. As June in *The Joy Luck Club* notes, "My mother believed you could be anything you wanted to be in America. You could open a restaurant. You could work for the government and get good retirement. You could buy a house with almost no money down. You could become rich. You could become instantly famous." It is this dream that has brought the women of her mother's generation to America.

The schisms deepen and become very painful as the years pass. The problems of assimilation and acculturation create an imbalance of power

between older and younger generations in Chinese American families. The continued use of Chinese language and customs affects personal relationships, as young people eagerly adopt American influences despite the best efforts of their elders to maintain the traditional Chinese way of life.

In *The Joy Luck Club* the daughters are weighted down with guilt. They feel they disappointed their mothers by failing to live up to unreal expectations of fame and success. The mothers are seen as distant figures who make impossible demands. The mothers are aware of this gulf. Their daughters are strangers to them and have little respect for their values. They blame American culture for estranging their daughters from the old Chinese traditions. The mothers "see that joy and luck do not mean the same to their daughters, that to . . . American born minds 'joy luck' . . . does not exist."

Even so, an uneasy bridge is erected between mothers and daughters. The daughters' search for a usable and recognizable past comes to fruition through listening to their mothers' stories. They come to terms with the links between those stories and their own lives.

The Kitchen God's Wife, like Tan's first novel, addresses the complex relationship between a Chinese immigrant mother and her Americanized daughter. In this book the daughter, Pearl, is highly Americanized and determined to shed all vestiges of old-fashioned Chinese ways. Pearl rarely visits her mother, Winnie Louie, whose bossy criticisms and pervasive superstitions have created an emotional and cultural gulf between the two women. In turn, Pearl has concealed for seven years the fact that she is afflicted with multiple sclerosis.

When Pearl returns to San Francisco's Chinatown, Winnie Louie reveals to her daughter her own terrible secrets. As a refugee from China just before the Communist takeover in 1949, Winnie was desperately fleeing a brutal past. She tells Pearl that the man to whom she is married is not Pearl's father. Rather, Pearl's father is the nefarious Wen Fu, a cowardly pilot whom Winnie had wed at a young age in China. Wen Fu is so corrupt he assumes his brother's identity to advance his career, repeatedly rapes Winnie, and forces her at gunpoint to witness him rape and abuse his servants. Traveling across China during World War II, Winnie loses three daughters, one of whom is inadvertently killed because of Wen Fu's negligence. Winnie's narrative raises questions about the status of women in traditional Chinese culture and the consequences of war.

In Tan's third novel, *The Hundred Secret Senses,* she explores the relationships between two sisters, two cultures, and two centuries. At the heart of the novel is the complex and uneasy relationship between California-born Olivia and her much older, Chinese-born half sister Kwan. Kwan comes to America in 1962 when she is eighteen years old. Olivia is almost six years old when she is introduced to the adult half sister she never knew existed.

Kwan is the daughter of Jack Yee and his discarded first wife. She is markedly Chinese, while Olivia—whose mother is Jack Yee's second, American wife—is definitely American. Kwan is an adult when she emigrates and never truly assimilates into American culture. Olivia as a child is embarrassed by her unusual new sister, who has a decidedly mystical bent and is too Chinese to suit her.

Kwan has special talents and a "hundred secret senses" that connect her to a range of experiences unavailable to Olivia. Her aura disrupts electronic appliances, and she has regular conversations with the dead, whom she calls yin people. Kwan maintains a one-sided relationship with Olivia. For Olivia, Kwan represents ethnicity, a diaspora culture, and racial origins that threaten Olivia's uneasy relationship with American culture.

Olivia represents Western rationality while Kwan, who communes with spirits from the past, is more mystical and imbued with Eastern spirituality. When Olivia and her husband, Simon, a white American, initiate divorce proceedings, Kwan takes them to China. In Kwan's universe, Olivia and Simon are simply continuing a great romance that began during the Taiping Rebellion (1851–1864), when they were Miss Banner and Yiban Johnson.

When Olivia visits Kwan's native village for the first time, she is overwhelmed by the feeling that she has come home. Her kinship with Kwan strengthens and the past comes alive. Olivia comes to believe that she and Kwan have known each other in two lifetimes. They are empowered to correct the mistakes of an earlier time, rewrite their story together, and find an integrated self for Olivia and peace for Kwan.

CHINESE CULTURE

Chinese culture—both in United States and in China—plays an important role in all of Tan's novels. Tan explores Chinese culture as it survives in the United States. Furthermore, through the reconstruction of history she shows ancient Chinese culture in many different guises.

Tan uses repetitive symbols and motifs as well as folktales and songs to emphasize the Chinese cultural presence. Her fiction also employs dreams, ritual use of food, and descriptions of clothing to portray Chinese culture. Dreams connect characters in important ways and are used to foreshadow events to come. They help to emphasize associations with Chinese culture buried deep within the dreamer. Dreams also function as bridges between the modern world and older Chinese civilizations. Dreams reveal hidden selves and deeply repressed yearnings and fears. Food rituals help situate the novels in a specific historical or seasonal time. Festivals identify geographical locations and bring characters together. Gatherings around important Chinese holidays also introduce new characters to each other. Clothes can visually represent Chinese eras as well as the attitude and deportment of the individual. Tan uses clothing to show how people advertise their states of mind and their cultural bias. Clothes can also conceal and create manufactured identities. Characters who are unable to integrate their two cultures or who are experiencing some form of cultural dislocation show their duality through clothes.

Another important aspect of Chinese culture is the respect shown for ancestors and the elderly. The wise older woman embodies the history of the family or a people. She manifests ancient wisdom and the speech of her community. Paradoxically, she can represent growth and nurturance and at the same time domination and self-righteousness. Tan's mothers have enormous influence on their children. Through matrilineage they feel connected to their own mothers and their mothers' mothers. "Your mother is in your bones," says An-Mei Hsu to June in *The Joy Luck Club*.

In *The Joy Luck Club* four mothers meet in a group they call the Joy Luck Club to play mahjongg and converse about their families and business. As well as a social gathering, the club is an investment group that pools money for investment in the stock market. The group has met for over thirty years and the novel opens shortly after the death of the founding member, Suyuan Woo.

To correct an imbalance of players and to fill the empty east corner left by Suyuan, the three remaining members ask her daughter, June, to join them as her mother's replacement. The section that contains the story of June helps define the main theme of struggle for control between mothers and daughters.

The mothers in Tan's first novel are well versed in Chinese culture. Their tales are saturated with Chinese folk stories and parables. Their instinctual belief in Chinese gods and goddesses and their intimate presentation of Chinese historical events creates a broad panorama of cultural retention.

The Kitchen God's Wife continues this pattern of cultural revelations. The title refers to the wronged but eternally forgiving wife of the Chinese deity who doles out luck. During each New Year, the Kitchen God reports to the emperor the names of those who should be rewarded with good luck for their exemplary lives, as well as the names of those who deserve bad luck as punishment for having behaved badly.

The Chinese deities are alive and functioning in the worldview of the immigrant Chinese. The assimilated Chinese Americans have little respect for these holdover religious symbols. Even so, as Pearl listens and truly hears her mother's stories, she understands more of Winnie's complicated life. As the novel progresses it becomes apparent that Chinese culture and religion can provide lessons still relevant to the modern condition.

Three ritual events—an engagement party, a funeral, and a wedding—anchor the novel's plot and illustrate the importance of Chinese culture in the everyday life of Chinese Americans. These important family gatherings also define and introduce the novel's conflicts and resolution.

The Kitchen God's Wife also uses food and dreams as leitmotivs of Chinese cultural expression. Food creates the illusion of verisimilitude, evoking the China of Winnie's girlhood. It individualizes the characters through preference, represents continuity and family life, and highlights the difference between the immigrant generation and its American-born children.

In the final scene between mother and daughter, Winnie proudly presents a new goddess to Pearl. She replaces the traditional and patriarchal Kitchen God's Wife with Lady Sorrowfree, the divine protector of all women who must endure pain and loneliness. Winnie tells Pearl to unburden her soul to the goddess: "She will wash away everything sad with her tears. . . . See her name: Lady Sorrowfree, happiness winning over bitterness, no regrets in this world." Through her mother's example, Pearl finds the courage to share her own secrets.

In *The Hundred Secret Senses* there are collisions between present and past, the actual and the imaginary, this life and the afterlife, skepticism and mysticism. Kwan's voice dominates in this novel and through her stories the reader is introduced to fascinating fragments of actual Chinese history. The novel is liberally dotted with dreams that impart the patterns and symbols of myth as well as secrets.

The most unnerving of those secrets is Kwan's unshakable belief that she is gifted with yin eyes. She has frequent conversations with people who are already dead and inhabit an otherworldly existence called "the world of Yin." Kwan's stories about a previous life in nineteenth-century China form one of the main themes of the novel.

Another major symbol in the novel is food and its importance in the continuity of Chinese culture. It is also a symbol of the culture shock that Olivia and Simon experience when they travel to China and are initiated into the food rituals of the peasant Chinese. Eventually, their acceptance of Chinese culture becomes Olivia's salvation. She is shown the unbreakable connections between past and present through the ancient ritual of preserved and honored duck eggs.

SETTINGS

For many Chinese Americans, life in the United States is made up of a series of dualities: two identities, two voices, two cultures, and even two names. In Tan's books this duality is also represented by the settings of the various episodes. Settings give life to states of mind and cultural realities. They provide historical records of important periods of Chinese history and describe specific conditions, or ways of life. Tan renders the settings of her novels with evocative detail, and the reader is transported to different times and places.

Tan uses the particulars of place to enlarge upon themes important to biculturalism. Many of the generational conflicts are reflected in the clashes between the places the characters inhabit. Tan's American locations have boundaries in small sections of Oakland and San Francisco. These boundaries suggest a context of cultural struggle. The distance between Chinatown and a San Francisco suburb might be only a matter of miles, but each place represents two separate ways of life. San Francisco's Chinatown is a haven from discrimination and prejudice. It is a place at the heart of Chinese culture in United States. Chinatown's bustling neighborhoods contain the intricately textured world of the Chinese American community in United States.

The mothers in *The Joy Luck Club* and in *The Kitchen God's Wife* live and work in Chinatown, while the daughters inhabit other parts of the city. Psychologically they live on the border between two worlds, belonging to neither world completely. This bifurcation shows itself in the shattered condition of their lives. For example, Pearl in *The Kitchen God's Wife* grows up in the 1950s in a suburban neighborhood in California, a setting in which her ethnicity produces self-doubt and trauma. Because the dominant culture demands adaptation, Pearl represses her Chinese heritage. As she matures into an isolated life away from Chinatown she becomes more alienated from her mother, Winnie Louie, who opens her Ding Ho Flower Shop in the heart of Chinatown after her daughter has grown. Mother and daughter attempt to straddle the geography of mainstream America and Chinatown but they fail. With her American husband and her frantic lifestyle, Pearl becomes a foreigner to her mother, Winnie.

The plot of *The Hundred Secret Senses* follows two narrative threads: Olivia's search for an integrated self and Kwan's desire to undo the damage of a century-old mistake. Olivia's story is set in her dislocated modern life with its unhappiness and lack of fulfillment. She is about to be divorced and is dissatisfied with just about every aspect of her life.

Kwan seems to inhabit two places at once. She lives in Chinatown and is closely connected to the Chinese culture there but she also inhabits a world of the imagination, where she has an alternative life played out in nineteenth-century China. Kwan's supernatural bond with the past has important connections with her half sister Olivia, but Olivia has lost touch with her ability to visit the past. As a rational American woman of the 1990s, Olivia is inclined to doubt. "If I believe what she says, does that mean I now believe she has yin eyes?" When Olivia opens up her heart to a world that she has repressed since childhood, she steps into a reality that defies rational explanation.

Kwan's narratives of her past life as a girl named Nunumu are replete with naturalistic detail. As Nunumu, she worked as a servant in a household of English missionaries. Kwan's need to reconcile past and present and connect her former life with that of Olivia's serves as a catalyst for the novel's climax. As the story spins out across two centuries and two continents, it unravels the mysteriously interwoven stories of Olivia Bishop and her half sister Li Kwan, Nelly Banner, and her loyal friend Nunumu.

Tan covers tremendous geographical territory over the space of decades and sometimes centuries in all of her novels. The tensions between East and West are presented by contrasting geographical realities. Often Tan's settings reflect cultural dislocations by parallel presentation of different times and places. Through the recreation of the historical landscapes of China, Tan is able to demonstrate contrasting patterns of thought and changing cultural realities. She interrogates actual historical events and places and shows how class and gender differences in these places have affected the lives of her characters. This juxtaposition of past and present functions as a narrative device. What has been and what is parallel and mirror each other, serving as bridges between characters as well as between China and America.

In each novel the place of origin is China, and a trip to China brings out a rebirth in the characters. The country renews cyclical change and reconnects the characters to a circular infinity that lies outside of time. The characters' return to China acts symbolically as a journey into the unconscious in search of wholeness. Unification can be attained only when the second generation recognizes and understands the ancestral landscape of the first. With this unification the family's entire heritage becomes a creative force.

The Joy Luck Club explores post-feudal China, China during World War II, and China under Communist rule. Each section has its own period setting and each setting provides a different piece of the cultural puzzle. The completion of the puzzle often demands a journey to ancient places. For example, June, after discarding her American name in favor of her Chinese name, Jing-mei, travels to her ancestral homeland to unite with her Chinese half sisters. The reconciliations are healing bonds in which the Chinese culture is recognized as a connective reality.

In *The Kitchen God's Wife* China is a homeland that exists only in the memories and stories of the older generation. Winnie Louie's horrific tales of her attempt to survive her brutal husband and a war-torn landscape give a personal reality to China. It is only when China itself is revisited, however, that the full impact of Winnie's story enters the consciousness of her daughter.

The juxtaposition of American life with Winnie's memory highlights the emotional and physical distance of China from San Francisco. Winnie's narrative brings to life an exotic, alien China in all its feudal glory and beauty with a rich text of ancient festivals and celebrations. It also magnifies the brutal existence of demolished towns and cities as the Chinese are occupied by the Japanese during World War II.

In *The Hundred Secret Senses* a good portion of the action is set in China in the mid-nineteenth century during the Taiping Rebellion. That uprising was the most important peasant-led revolt in Chinese history, during which widespread changes were demanded, including equality for women, agricultural reform, and the abolition of private property. Kwan's perspective relives the history of Nunumu, who loses her entire family and is forced into a life of servitude. In an attempt to reunite the past and the present, Kwan takes Olivia and Simon Bishop to China and her home village of Changmian. Surprisingly, foreign China immediately feels familiar to Olivia. The environment allows for a total personal reassessment of her life. Olivia must come to terms with her relationship to her mother. Further, Olivia and Simon are forced to confront the hidden resentments and disguised angers that have destroyed their marriage.

Together, Olivia and Kwan embark on their shared journey toward wholeness. Kwan believes that the rightness of Olivia and Simon's union was determined by events in the distant past. As the novel progresses, Kwan's tales increase in intensity. The story of Yiban, the last days in the Ghost Merchant's house, and the encounter of the flight to the mountains clarifies connections between the characters. Olivia and Simon are Miss Banner and Yiban brought to Changmian to reunite.

Changmian, China, is an emotional and psychological homeland that fulfills dreams. Miss Banner's music box plays a significant role in the nineteenth-century Changmian years. The box, hidden in a cave in the mountains, is a safe hiding place for her diary and assorted keepsakes. A century later Kwan and Olivia find the box. At that moment Olivia experiences an epiphany, realizing that she and Kwan have had a shared history stretching back a century.

Events in the past significantly influence the lives of both Olivia and Kwan. Jack Yee's abandonment of a wife and child, and his discarding of an identity, is followed by a new life and new family in America. Yet that action does not obliterate a past that returns to haunt the characters.

Kwan bridges the chronological gap between her two lives. Olivia is shown that her connection with Kwan could have begun in an earlier century. The recovered music box and the discovered jars of duck eggs that Nunumu buried during the Taiping Rebellion are proof of a deep bond that has withstood the test of time.

At the end of the novel Kwan vanishes into the Changmian caves and is never found. Olivia believes that her daughter Samantha, born nine months later, is a gift from Kwan. In this new being the past and the present are fused. Olivia understands that "The world is not a place but the vastness of the soul. And the soul is nothing more than love, limitless, endless."

SUMMARY

Amy Tan's books are about self and identity and a search for family roots and connections. *The Joy Luck Club* is a recognized classic that illuminates an important aspect of the American experience. This story about the complicated relationships between Chinese mothers and Chinese American daughters hit a popular nerve when it was published in 1989 and it was quickly turned into a successful movie.

Tan's novels tell the story of families in crisis. The struggle to maintain family ties cross-culturally and between countries resonates deeply in the contemporary American consciousness. Also, the issues of acculturation and ethnicity in American society presented in Tan's books are shared by other minority groups.

Tan uses storytelling as a device that shapes the family histories and makes sense of the significant events in the lives of her characters. Through "talk story" they keep the past alive and build a bridge to the present. Their Chinese heritage is maintained and proves the salvation for contemporary Chinese American characters.

Tan's novels do a great service to women and the bonds between mothers and daughters and sisters. Her male characters, however, remain stock villains reminiscent of those in Asian romance fiction. Not until her third book did she present the male protagonist, Simon, with some rounding of personality.

In a short writing career, Amy Tan has achieved wide popular success. Tan speaks primarily to the community of Chinese Americans by expressing its traditions and cultural connections, but the universality of her themes also appeals to a wider, cross-cultural audience outside the Chinese American community.

Selected Bibliography

WORKS OF AMY TAN

NOVELS
The Joy Luck Club. New York: Putnam, 1989.
The Kitchen God's Wife. New York: Putnam, 1991.
The Hundred Secret Senses. New York: Putnam, 1995.

CHILDREN'S BOOKS
The Moon Lady. New York: Macmillan, 1992.
The Chinese Siamese Cat. New York: Macmillan, 1994.

ESSAYS
"The Language of Discretion." In *The State of the Language.* Edited by Christopher Ricks and Leonard Michaels. Berkeley, Calif.: University of California Press, 1990.
"Mother Tongue." *The Threepenny Review* 11:7–8 (fall 1990).

SHORT STORIES
"Two Kinds." *The Atlantic,* February 1989, pp. 53–57.
"Peanut's Fortune." *Grand Street* 10:10–22 (winter 1991).

CRITICAL AND BIOGRAPHICAL STUDIES

Asian Women United of California, ed. *Making Waves: An Anthology of Writings by and about Asian American Women.* Boston: Beacon, 1989.
Chen, Victoria. "Chinese American Women, Language, and Moving Subjectivity." *Women and Language* 18:3–7 (spring 1995).
Cheung, King-Kok. *Asian-American Literature: An Annotated Bibliography.* New York: Modern Language Association, 1988.
Chiu, Christina. *Notable Asian Americans: Literature and Education.* New York: Chelsea House, 1995.
Downing, Christine. *Psyche's Sisters: Re-Imagining the Meaning of Sisterhood.* San Francisco: Harper & Row, 1988.
Huntley, E. D. *Amy Tan: A Critical Companion.* Westport, Conn.: Greenwood Press, 1998.
Kim, Elaine H. *Asian American Literature: An Introduction to the Writings and Their Social Context.* Philadelphia: Temple University Press, 1982.
Wang, Dorothy. "A Game of Show Not Tell." *Newsweek,* April 17, 1989, pp. 68–69.
Wu, William F. *The Yellow Peril: Chinese Americans in American Fiction, 1850–1940.* Hamden, Conn.: Archon Books, 1982.

FILM BASED ON A WORK BY AMY TAN

The Joy Luck Club. Screenplay by Amy Tan and Ronald Bass. Hollywood Pictures, 1993.

—*STEPHEN SOITOS*

David Foster Wallace

1962–

BORN IN ITHACA, New York, on February 21, 1962, to a philosophy professor and an English teacher, David Foster Wallace has emerged as one of American fiction's most original and influential talents. In an interview, Wallace told Larry McCaffery that as a child he was "bookish and reading a lot, on the one hand, [and] watching grotesque amounts of TV, on the other." This combination of high and low culture formed his aesthetic, which encompasses "technical philosophy and continental European theory, and extreme avant-garde" writing as well as a willingness to sit in front of the television, "slack-jawed," for hours (Donahue). Wallace wants to write fiction "that has some of the richness and challenge and emotional and intellectual difficulty of avant-garde literary stuff, stuff that makes the reader confront things rather than ignore them, but to do that in such a way that it's also pleasurable to read." His primary subjects—communication, entertainment, addiction—establish a consistent focus within his body of formally innovative work.

In 1985 Wallace received his Bachelor of Arts in philosophy from Amherst College, where he also studied mathematical logic. In 1987 he received a Master of Fine Arts in creative writing from the University of Arizona in Tucson. His first novel, *The Broom of the System* (1987), appeared while Wallace was still a graduate student, and his first collection of short stories, *Girl with Curious Hair* (1989), appeared two years later. Briefly enrolled in the Ph.D. program in philosophy at Harvard University in the late 1980s, Wallace quit to pursue the life of a fiction writer. After several fallow years, he began *Infinite Jest* (1996), the novel that made him a

literary celebrity. Since early in his career Wallace has published short fiction in prestigious magazines, such as *Harper's* and the *Paris Review,* and in anthologies, such as *The Best American Short Stories*. He received a 1997 MacArthur Foundation "Genius" Grant, a 1996 Lannan Literary Award, a 1987 Whiting Writers Award, a fellowship from the National Endowment for the Arts, and the Paris Review Award. In 1993 he began teaching at Illinois State University in Bloomington, Illinois.

The typical critical reaction to Wallace's writing is to praise him for the ambition and complexity of his works and for his intellect, linguistic dexterity, and cultural incisiveness while admonishing him for being long-winded and self-indulgent. His verbal prowess is his strongest asset as well as his biggest weakness. Wallace's style is characterized by excess and by self-consciousness, self-reference, and self-consciousness about self-reference. Much of his work employs a hyper-irony that uses irony as a means toward greater honesty. The critic A. O. Scott claims that Wallace's

> gambit is to turn irony back on itself, to make his fiction relentlessly conscious of its own self-consciousness, and thus to produce work that will be at once unassailably sophisticated and doggedly down to earth. . . . He wants to be at once earnest and ironical, sensitive and cerebral, risible and scriptible, . . . straight man and clown.

Although Wallace has been called the heir to postmodernists such as Thomas Pynchon, William Gaddis, John Barth, and William Gass, he is not the most well-behaved of disciples. The critic Michiko Kakutani has asserted, "For all his narrative pyrotechnics, he has not wholly embraced the chilly, irony-suffused aesthetic of so many of his contemporaries, but has instead tried to meld his mythic, avant-garde ambitions with a more intimate sense of his characters' emotional and spiritual lives." According to Vince Passaro, Wallace's "work is bitingly funny and remarkably, even wildly, imaginative; at the same time he aims for very large psychological, emotional and social issues, issues of how we live or fail to live, love and fail to love, survive or destroy ourselves." And Scott believes that "Wallace is deeply suspicious of novelty, even as he scrambles to position himself on the cutting edge."

This "cutting edge" is Wallace's experimental style, which includes elaborate, sometimes page-long sentences; the use of numerous forms and genres within a single work; a fondness for footnotes; "a brilliant ear not only for the noise in his own head . . . but for the harsh polyphonies of contemporary American speech" (A. O. Scott); and the compound conjunction (for instance, "and but now"). But discussing Wallace's work primarily for its stylistic innovations and signatures risks overlooking its emotional elements. As Alex Abramovich points out:

> There's a geometry to his writing, a symmetry of levels and recursions, that makes it easy to admire his form and forget his purpose. . . . A thread running through all of Wallace's work is our need to understand one another, the substitutes we seek to ease the pain of failing to do so, and the ways in which those substitutes aggravate that failure.

The need for and failures of understanding and communication ultimately become the crux of Wallace's writing.

THE BROOM OF THE SYSTEM

Published when Wallace was twenty-five years old, his first novel, *The Broom of the System* (1987), immediately established him as a major talent in American fiction, an heir to innovators such as Gaddis, Pynchon, Gass, and Barth. The book's expansiveness and highly stylized writing distinguished it at a time when American fiction was dominated by the minimalist school. The stylistic elements that became Wallace's trademarks—versatility, a comic sensibility that enlivens the work's emotional and intellectual seriousness, an exceptional facility with dialogue and speech, complex syntax, and a penchant for minute yet compelling descriptions—are all on display in his debut.

Though criticized for its extravagance, *The Broom of the System* received an unusual amount of attention and praise for a first novel. Kakutani, writing for the *New York Times,* called the book "an unwieldy, uneven work—by turns, hilarious and stultifying, daring and derivative." Nevertheless, Kakutani believes "Wallace possesses a wealth of talents—a finely-tuned ear for contemporary idioms; an old-fashioned story-telling gift . . . ; a seemingly endless capacity for invention and an energetic refusal to compromise." Similarly Caryn James's review in the *New York Times Book Review* asserts that "the charms and flaws of David Foster Wallace's book are due to its exuberance—cartoonish characters, stories within stories, impossible coincidences, a hip but true fondness for pop culture and above all the spirit of playfulness that has slipped away from so much recent fiction." This vacillation between ecstatic praise and admonishment, sometimes in the same review, foretells critical responses to all of Wallace's subsequent books.

The most unusual element of *The Broom of the System* is the absence of a strong plot. The writer Rudy Rucker commented on the novel's "ramshackle, exfoliating, synchronistic plot," comparing it to those of Pynchon's novels. The plot of Wallace's book is almost negligible. Lenore Beadsman's ninety-two-year-old great-grandmother disappears from her nursing home in Cleveland, Ohio, along with twenty other residents, and Lenore is determined to find her. This determination takes Lenore to other members of her family—a despotic father, a psychologically wounded sister, and a brilliant yet perpetually intoxicated brother. These trips are always both humorous and sad, revealing Wallace's determination to locate hilarity in pathos. Yet they do not cohere, and the novel's many subplots overrun its main narrative.

Because the novel is so light on plot, its "heart," James says, "is its verbal extravagance and formal variations." Thus the novel's primary achievements are stylistic. In his interview with McCaffery, Wallace himself commented on the novel being "a coldly cerebral take on fiction." But what the novel lacks in plot it compensates for in sheer invention. Wallace's style encompasses first-person stream-of-consciousness narrative; third-person omniscient narrative; transcripts of business meetings, therapy sessions, and television programs; dialogue without any accompanying narrative; journal entries; the texts of short stories; and the re-creations of short stories.

The book begins in 1981, when Lenore Beadsman, a precocious fifteen-year-old, visits her "ravingly lovely" sister Clarice at Mount Holyoke College. In the space of a short chapter Wallace acutely and economically conveys the life of a first-year student at a women's college. This chapter also introduces Andy Lang, who, with his Amherst College roommate Bernard Diggerence, terrorizes the young women because they need their buttocks signed by five women as part of their initiation into a fraternity. The novel then shifts to 1990, the year in which the rest of the novel takes place. Because *The Broom of the System* was published in 1987, most of the events in the book occur in a near future, a technique Wallace also uses in his later works.

A graduate of Oberlin College, where she majored in philosophy, Lenore Beadsman now lives in East Corinth, Ohio, a town built by her grandfather and designed to resemble the full-body profile of Jayne Mansfield. Lenore works as a switchboard operator at Frequent and Vigorous, a publishing company in Cleveland that is "a corporate entity interested in failure for tax purposes . . . publishing things perhaps even slightly more laughable than nothing at all." Lenore, the youngest member of one of Cleveland's wealthiest and most powerful families, suffers from "disorientation and identity-confusion and lack of control." Though eighteen years his younger, Lenore is romantically involved with Rick Vigorous, a partner in Frequent and Vigorous and editor of the literary quarterly *Frequent Review*. Rick describes himself as "grossly and pathetically and fiercely and completely in love" with Lenore, and he is extraordinarily possessive and insecure. Wallace's prose style lends Vigorous's interior monologues a hilarious prolixity, as when he describes a kiss from Lenore:

> A kiss with Lenore is, if I may indulge a bit for a moment here, not so much a kiss as it is a dislocation, a removal and rude transportation of essence from self to lip, so that it is not so much two human bodies coming together and doing the usual things with their lips as it is two sets of lips spawned together and joined in kind from the beginning of post-Scarsdale time, achieving full ontological status only in subsequent union and trailing behind and below them, as they join and become whole, two now utterly superfluous fleshly bodies, drooping outward and downward from the kiss like the tired stems of overblossomed flora, trailing shoes on the ground, husks.

Rick's extreme love for Lenore, however, cannot be consummated because he has a "freakishly small penis" that forces him to "remain part of the world that is external to and other from Lenore Beadsman." This is "a source of profound grief" to Rick, who admits to Lenore: "I know I'm more than a little neurotic. I know I'm possessive. I know I'm fussy and vaguely effeminate. . . . And sexually intrinsically inadequate. . . . I cannot possibly satisfy you. We cannot unite. . . . I cannot be truly inside you."

Throughout the novel Wallace dramatizes Ludwig Wittgenstein's philosophical questioning of language, as when the elder Lenore (a former student of Wittgenstein's at Cambridge University) convinces her great-granddaughter that her life exists only in words, that the sum of her life is what can be said about it. This makes the younger Lenore wonder what differentiates her life from that of a character in a story and leads her to question her role in and ability to control her own life. She has come to see no difference between her life and "a telling" of her life. The elder Lenore is, according to Rick, "a hard woman, a cold woman, a querulous and thoroughly selfish woman, one with vast intellectual pretensions" who is "obsessed with words." But Rick himself tries to exercise the same control over Lenore through language, as when he tells her stories submitted to the *Frequent Review*. He attempts to possess her through these stories; if she exists only through language, then surrounding her with language will entrap her. Similarly her brother LaVache's statement "you're real insofar as you're told about, so that to the extent that you're real you're controlled" does not allay Lenore's anxiety about her existence.

As Lenore searches for her great-grandmother, various subplots emerge and intersect with the novel's primary narrative. One of the more humorous subplots involves Norman Bombardini, owner of the Bombardini Building, which houses Frequent and Vigorous. Bombardini is a "monstrously fat" man whose wife has just left him. Reversing the philosophy behind weight reduction, he intends to "grow and grow, and fill the absence that surrounds me with the horror of my own gelatinous presence." One night Rick and Lenore watch in horror as he orders nine steak dinners at a restaurant and declares to the waiter, "I am an obese, grotesque,

prodigal, greedy, gourmandizing, gluttonous pig. . . . I am more hog than human. . . . You see before you a swine. An eating fiend of unlimited capacity." His aim is to become an "autonomously full universe" and "to grow to infinite size." He becomes infatuated with Lenore and offers to save a space for her in the universe he is eating to fill.

Lenore goes to Amherst to visit her brother LaVache to try to determine if the elder Lenore had spoken with him before disappearing. Rick accompanies her, apparently to offer emotional support. In truth Rick has been secretly hired by Lenore's father to travel with her. When they arrive in Amherst, Rick, overcome by nostalgia, leaves Lenore to speak with LaVache while he walks the grounds of Amherst College for the first time in twenty years. By coincidence he meets Andy Lang at a bar that both frequented in college. After a conversation that reveals more coincidences—Lang and Rick were in the same fraternity at college and Lang met Lenore at Mount Holyoke College and married Clarice's roommate Mindy Metalman, who is also Rick's former next-door neighbor and the object of his infatuation—Rick, although jealous of the handsome, sociable, and wealthy Lang, hires him to work for Lenore's father on a special project.

Lang quickly falls in love with Lenore and pursues her despite her hatred of him: "How come I feel like the whole universe is playing pimp for me with you? . . . When I didn't ask for it at all? . . . When I didn't even *like* you? I didn't *want* you?" The question of free will, of existence outside of language, is never resolved for Lenore, who eventually leaves Rick for Lang, but not before Rick accompanies Lenore to the Great Ohio Desert (G.O.D.) under the pretense of searching for her great-grandmother there. In the G.O.D., which was created because the governor believed the people of Ohio needed "a point of savage reference," Rick tells Lenore an intricate story that clearly symbolizes his own position—particularly his inability to consummate his relationship with Lenore—while Lang watches them from a rowboat on the lake. When Rick realizes Lang is following them, he handcuffs himself to Lenore so they can be "joined" in "negation and discipline." Lang breaks the toy handcuffs and returns with Lenore to the Bombardini Building to remove her personal items from her work space. The lobby fills with various people—Rick and Lenore's psychologist, Lenore's father and several of his employees, a technician from the telephone company, and Rick, who tries to hide in the shadows—as Norman Bombardini, too large to fit through the revolving door, batters at a wall with his stomach, demanding "admission to Ms. Beadsman's space." It becomes apparent that the elder Lenore has inexplicably moved into the telephone tunnel below the Bombardini Building. Despite the numerous narrative threads in play at the end of the novel, Wallace does not inform the reader of the fates of any of these characters. *The Broom of the System* ends without resolution and, appropriately, in mid-sentence, and the omitted word most likely is "word."

THE SHORT FICTION

Wallace's first book of short stories, *Girl with Curious Hair* (1989), bolstered his reputation as an innovative fiction writer. The book presents an array of dysfunctional and unsympathetic characters within a formally varied collection. As with *The Broom of the System,* critical reaction to the book was largely enthusiastic. Reviewing the stories for the *New York Times Book Review,* the critic Jennifer Levin asserts:

> Mr. Wallace is such a bold writer that his failures can be almost as interesting as his successes. . . . Ever willing to experiment, he lays his artistic self on the line with his incendiary use of language, at times seeming to rip both the mundane and the unusual from their moorings, then setting them down anew, freshly described.

As a result, she continues, "he succeeds in restoring grandeur to modern fiction, reminding us of the ecstasy, terror, horror and beauty of which it is capable."

The novella and the nine short stories in *Girl with Curious Hair* present Wallace's fascination with television culture, alienation, and human relationships. "Little Expressionless Animals" explores the romance between Julie Smith and Faye Goddard against the backdrop of the *Jeopardy!* game show. Julie is a *Jeopardy!* champion whose 740-show winning streak is broken by her autistic yet eidetic brother, and Faye is a researcher for the show. Julie possesses the ability to make facts "transcend their internal factual limitations and become, in and of themselves, meaning, feeling." Although Julie's popularity on the show is a result of her magnetic presence and her overt hatred of its host, her success is attributed to her childhood, when she memorized an encyclopedia and read it to her brother because the two were frequently locked in a room while her mother entertained men. The show's executives eventually become disturbed by the relationship between Faye and Julie and the possible consequences it might have on the show, so they plot Julie's downfall by bringing her brother onto the show and including an unusually high number of animal questions. Julie cannot answer animal questions because of a mental block against animals, whose faces are incapable of expression.

Another twist on the love story, "Here and There," takes the form of alternating monologues narrated by a young man and a young woman who recently have separated. Their statements, though discrete, combine on the page to form a dialogue that does not occur in their lives. This dialogue is a metafictional technique that soon reveals itself as a contrivance of Bruce, the fore-grounded author-narrator of the story who is undergoing "fiction therapy" to accept the end of his relationship. Bruce describes himself as a hulking, pigeon-toed, blond, pale, red-lipped Midwestern boy, twenty-two, freshly graduated in electrical engineering from MIT, . . . freshly returned in putative triumph with my family to Bloomington, Indiana, there to be kicked roundly in the psychic groin by a certain cool, tight, wasteless, etcetera, Indiana University graduate student, the object of my theoretical passion, distant affection, and near-total loyalty for three years.

Bruce and his unnamed lover have separated because he has withdrawn into himself to the point of excluding all others. This withdrawal is a result of his intellectual pursuits, which center on an "epic poem about variable systems of information- and energy-transfer." An "aesthetician of the cold, the new, the right, the truly and spotlessly *here*," Bruce is extremely intelligent yet unable to love humanly. After the breakup he drives to Maine to visit his uncle and aunt and to get "very away" from everything. But Maine eventually "becomes another here instead of a there," and his mental health worsens until he breaks down while trying to fix an old electric stove. Despite being a brilliant student of electrical engineering, Bruce is unable to fix the stove, and at that moment, "behind the stove, with [his] aunt kneeling down to lay her hand on [his] shoulder," he realizes he is "afraid of absolutely everything there is." This statement closes the story and resonates with the alienation and fear that characterize most of the stories in *Girl with Curious Hair*.

Alienation makes up the center of the book's title story, which is narrated by Sick Puppy, a "corporate liability trouble shooter" who earns over $100,000 per year and spends his free time with "punk rockers" with names like Big, Gimlet, and Mr. Wonderful. His friends call him Sick Puppy because he enjoys burning people with cigarettes and lighters. Unaffected by drugs or any other stimuli that affect normal people, he always seems happy, and he explains his happiness as a natural result of his income, possessions, and sexual acts. Wallace attributes Sick Puppy's severe dysfunction to a childhood experience. His father, a highly ranked officer in the marines, burned the boy's penis when he tried to copulate with his ten-year-old sister. Sick Puppy, now impotent except when fellated, declares, "What would make me the happiest corporate liability trouble shooter in the history of the planet earth would be to kill my father and . . . bathe in his blood."

Despite his obvious problems, Sick Puppy is fond of describing himself in positive terms, as when he says:

I am fortunately an entirely handsome devil and appear even younger than twenty-nine. I look like a clean cut youth, a boy next door, and a good egg, and my mother stated at one time that I have the face of a heaven's angel. I have the eyes of an attractive marsupial, and I have baby-soft and white skin, and a fair complexion. I do not even have to shave, and I have finely styled hair without any of dandruff's unsightly itching or flaking. I keep my hair perfectly groomed, neat, and short at all times. I have exceptionally attractive ears.

Although he talks about himself constantly, he has a total lack of self-awareness and seems unable to realize that he is not a good person: "I am especially pleased and challenged in my career when it really happens that a manufacturer's product has a bug and has injured a consumer." His outwardly respectable appearance contradicts his despicable thoughts and actions, making him the most disturbing character in the collection.

One of the fundamental concerns in Wallace's writing—self-consciousness—becomes the primary theme of "My Appearance." The story's narrator, Edilyn, is a television actress scheduled to appear on *Late Night with David Letterman*. She has no misgivings about appearing on the show until her husband, Rudy, and their friend Ron insist on coaching her before her appearance. Their coaching escalates into an absurd workshop on irony and public image, as when Ron says, "If you know in advance that you're going to be made to look ridiculous, then you're one step ahead of the game, because then you can make *yourself* look ridiculous, instead of letting *him* do it for you." What ensues is a paranoia-inducing journey through the world of anti-television, and *Late Night with David Letterman* emerges as the ultimate anti-show. Edilyn maintains her composure and her belief in David Letterman's basic harmlessness, yet her naive optimism hints that she will be set up for humiliation during her appearance. However, with the help of the tranquilizer Xanax, her optimism prevails. She enjoys herself on the show and emerges unscathed and relieved. At the story's conclusion she asserts: "I have remembered and worked hard to show that, if nothing else at all, I am a woman who speaks her mind. It is the way I have to see myself, to live."

This veiled attack on irony leads to the outright assault in the novella "Westward the Course of Empire Takes Its Way," the last piece in *Girl with Curious Hair*. A metafictional novella about a student in a graduate creative writing program who distrusts metafiction, the piece is also a metafictional interpretation of John Barth's metafictional story "Lost in the Funhouse" (1968) and an antimetafictional analysis of metafiction. Convoluted and confusing, Wallace's novella attempts to expose the illusions of metafiction in a manner similar to how metafictionists attempt to expose the illusions of realism. In a 1993 interview with McCaffery, Wallace referred to the novella as "crude and naive and pretentious," but its concerns illuminate all of his work.

"Westward the Course of Empire Takes Its Way" presents an unlikable cast of characters, yet Wallace's intelligence and talent keep the piece from becoming thoroughly unlikable itself. The novella's title recalls Emanuel Leutze's 1860 painting *Westward the Course of Empire*, an image of manifest destiny during American expansion. Wallace's choice of titles extends manifest destiny into the realm of American fiction, implying that categorization is imperialistic in theory and practice. The putative villain of the novella is the metafictionist Professor C—— Ambrose, who is the author of "Lost in the Funhouse," an obvious stand-in for both Barth and the protagonist of Barth's story. Ambrose has entered into a business venture—a nightclub franchise called the Funhouse—with the advertising genius J. D. Steelritter, who has "built the second-largest advertising agency in American history from the fringe that is the country's center, from a piss-poor little accidental town." To launch the Funhouse franchise, Steelritter has invited everyone who has acted in a McDonald's commercial to Collision, Illinois, for a reunion. The reunion will be filmed and transformed into a commercial.

The novella's protagonist is Mark Nechtr, a trust fund beneficiary and a student in the East Chesapeake Tradeschool Writing Program (a thinly veiled Johns Hopkins University, where Barth taught for many years). Though lionized by his peers for his radiance and reticence, Mark has "professionally diagnosed emotional problems"; he suffers from the delusion that "he's the only person in the world who feels like the only person in the world." Mark has married Drew-Lynn Eberhardt (D. L.), a prolific yet unpopular member of Ambrose's class. "Conspicuously" weird, D. L. seems "greedy and self-serving," and she insists on "*calling* herself a post-modernist." After her work is received unenthusiastically by Ambrose, she quits the writing program but writes a limerick on the blackboard immediately before his class. The limerick, "graphed critically over Professor Ambrose's—and American metafiction's—most famous story," is a concise version of Wallace's novella:

For lovers, the Funhouse is fun.
For phonies, the Funhouse is love.
But *for whom,* the proles grouse,
Is the Funhouse a house?
Who lives there, when push comes to shove?

Shortly after the limerick incident, Mark and D. L. engage in sexual intercourse, and she pretends to be pregnant, hence their marriage.

The tension between Ambrose and Mark occurs primarily in Mark's head, since their relationship remains cordial throughout the novella. Mark "distrusts wordplay" and "regards metafiction the way a hemophiliac regards straight razors." He describes metafiction as "the act of a lonely solipsist's self-love" and "desires, some distant hard-earned day, to write something that stabs you in the heart. That pierces you, makes you think you're going to die." Mark is unsure of the type of writing to commit to: "Maybe it's called metalife. Or metafiction. Or realism. Or gfhrytytu." Mark's point is that the label does not matter to the art. In fact the term used to categorize art can prove harmful, since Mark believes:

> Dividing this fiction business into realistic and naturalistic and surrealistic and modern and postmodern and new-realistic and meta- is like dividing history into cosmic and tragic and prophetic and apocalyptic; is like dividing human beings into white and black and brown and yellow and orange. It atomizes, does not bind crowds, and, like everything timelessly dumb, leads to blind hatred, blind loyalty, blind supplication.

Whatever its terminology, Mark thinks, "the stuff would probably use metafiction as a bright smiling disguise."

As if fulfilling Mark's own desire, Wallace's novella consistently employs metafictional techniques. He includes some of Ambrose's theories of fiction writing as well as those of the author-narrator and Mark, and he allows various intrusions into the narrative. For example, the author-narrator writes, "OK true, that was all both too quick and too slow, for background—both intrusive and sketchy" and "the preceding generation of cripplingly self-conscious writers, obsessed with their own interpretation, would mention at this point, just as we're possibly getting somewhere, that the story isn't getting anywhere." The novella's narrative is also interspersed with unnumbered sections with titles such as "Background that Intrudes and Looms," "Why the Kids Are Late," and "A Really Blatant and Intrusive Interruption." The last begins,

> As mentioned before—and if this were a piece of metafiction, which it's NOT, the exact number of typeset lines between this reference and the pre-nominate referent would very probably be mentioned, which would be a princely pain in the ass, not to mention cocky, since it would assume that a straightforward and anti-embellished account of a slow and hot and sleep-deprived and basically clotted and frustrating day in the lives of three kids, none of whom are all that sympathetic, could actually get published, which these days good luck, but in metafiction it would, nay *needs* be mentioned, a required postmodern convention aimed at drawing the poor old reader's emotional attention to the fact that the narrative bought and paid for and now under time-consuming scrutiny is *not* in fact a barely-there window onto a different and truly diverting world, but rather in fact an "artifact," an object . . . —this self-conscious explicitness and deconstructed disclosure supposedly making said metafiction "realer" than a piece of pre-postmodern "Realism" that depends on certain antiquated techniques to create an "illusion" of a windowed access to a "reality" isomorphic with ours but possessed of and yielding up higher truths to which all authentically human persons stand in the relation of applicand.

The author/narrator's derogatory references to metafiction are themselves metafictional, and Wallace knowingly includes aspects of his own fiction in what he criticizes.

Wallace's other collection of short fiction, *Brief Interviews with Hideous Men* (1999), is his most disturbing and psychologically complex book to date. Throughout the collection Wallace presents an unnerving array of insincere and manipulative narrators who compulsively dissect their insincerity and manipulativeness. Critics met the book and its dark yet effective examinations of the human condition with a mixture of awe and contempt. Passaro, for example, believes that *Brief Interviews with Hideous Men*

> blends the languages of modern philosophy, sexual angst and suburban psychological breakdown in a way that manages both to be thoroughly new in literary terms, and yet still evoke in the reader that state of mind that all great literature evokes, that sense of encounter with phenomena long familiar and suddenly, perfectly identified.

As Abramovich notes, the collection "explores the bleakest regions of family, friendship, and desire" and shows Wallace working "toward sincere and hard-earned compassion."

The separate pieces in *Brief Interviews with Hideous Men* are unified by loneliness, as is evident from the collection's first piece, "A Radically Condensed History of Postindustrial Life," which begins on page zero:

> When they were introduced, he made a witticism, hoping to be liked. She laughed extremely hard, hoping to be liked. Then each drove home alone, staring straight ahead, with the very same twist to their faces.
>
> The man who'd introduced them didn't much like either of them, though he acted as if he did, anxious as he was to preserve good relations at all times. One never knows, after all, now did one now did one now did one.

The collection includes twenty-three pieces, three called "Yet Another Example of the Porousness of Certain Borders" (numbered six, eleven, and twenty-four from an apparent series), two called "The Devil Is a Busy Man," and four called "Brief Interviews with Hideous Men." As with most of Wallace's work, *Brief Interviews with Hideous Men* is structurally innovative. The futuristic "Datum Centurio" defines the word "date" according to "contemporary" usage: "the process of voluntarily submitting one's nucleotide configurations and other Procreativity Designators to an agency empow-

ered by law to identify an optimal female neurogenetic complement for the purposes of Procreative Genital Interface." "Octet," a series of pop quizzes, culminates with a metafictional quiz or a "metaQuiz": "These intranarrative acknowledgments have the . . . advantage of slightly diluting the pretentiousness of structuring the little pieces as so-called 'Quizzes,' but it also has the disadvantage of flirting with metafictional self-reference." And "Death Is Not the End" parodies the typical author's biographical note and ends with a footnote—"That is not wholly true"—that negates the story's conclusion.

Three of the four "Brief Interviews with Hideous Men" contain several interviews; the book includes a total of eighteen interviews. In the interviews the interrogator is most often silent, represented only by a "Q," whereas the "hideous men" questioned are quoted at length. Their dysfunctions are wide-ranging and often extreme. One has the unfortunate habit of shouting "Victory for the Forces of Democratic Freedom!" upon ejaculation; another has a compulsion to tie up women; another uses his deformed arm, which he calls "the Asset," to attract pity from women so he can seduce them. Other stories in the collection are equally distressing. "The Depressed Person" narrates the life of a woman depressed because depression is what her identity is based on: "The depressed person was in terrible and unceasing emotional pain, and the impossibility of sharing or articulating this pain was itself a component of the pain and a contributing factor in its essential horror." Compelled to describe her pain only through anecdote, she becomes so self-absorbed that she grows even more depressed, and the cycle of depression continues without end.

The psychological complexities and pathological behaviors of Wallace's characters fascinate as much as they repel, paying tribute to the power of fiction to capture the multifariousness of the human mind. Despite the desolate emotional landscape charted by *Brief Interviews with Hideous Men,* Passaro writes, "the hope of redemption . . . flickers through the text like a weak but still present flame." In "Think," for example, a man is about to commit adultery and, kneeling before the woman as if to undress her, begins instead to pray. In keeping with Wallace's resistance to pat resolutions, the reader does not learn if the man's prayers lead to his redemption, but small gestures like this cast light on a dark book.

INFINITE JEST

Wallace's second novel, *Infinite Jest: A Novel* (1996), extends the talents and intellectual prowess of his previous work and has become known as one of the most ambitious and complex novels published in the 1990s. At 1,079 pages and with 97 pages of footnotes, *Infinite Jest* is unusually long and intricate. The novel's scope and subject matter caused a sensation in the publishing industry and received largely enthusiastic reviews as well as a sizable readership. The book was reviewed in such unusual venues as *Entertainment Weekly* and *Spin* as well as in more conventional places, such as the *New York Times,* and Wallace became the subject of many articles and interviews.

Despite its length and scope, *Infinite Jest* is a fragmentary novel. Like *The Broom of the System* and much of Wallace's short fiction, it does not resolve itself. Yet the book is not entirely experimental in that many of Wallace's aims in the novel are rooted in traditional fiction. As the critic Alexander Star notes, Wallace "tries to write intimate, heartfelt fiction about a nation overrun with information and images." And Kakutani, writing for the *New York Times,* describes the Wallace of *Infinite Jest* as "a writer of virtuosic skills who can seemingly do anything, someone who can write funny, write

sad, write serious, write satiric . . . [a writer] who's also able to create flesh-and-blood characters and genuinely moving scenes." With *Infinite Jest,* Wallace attempts to reconcile difficulty and enjoyment by offering challenging ideas while remaining accessible.

The underlying themes of *Infinite Jest*—addiction and entertainment and how they intertwine—establish the pulse of the book, which emerges as a simultaneously sad and humorous dystopic novel. The novel explores the central irony of the American way of life: despite the country's freedom, many of its citizens are slaves to pleasure. Free will, Wallace implies, is virtually a myth. One of the central points of the novel is that anything—from sleep to sleep deprivation, shopping to shoplifting, sex to abstention, exercise to eating, friendship to solitude—can become an "emotional escape" and can be abused like a drug. Characters are obsessive-compulsive, sex addicts, drug addicts, alcoholics, slaves to entertainment.

The novel's setting—an imaginary Boston suburb in which the Enfield Tennis Academy shares land with the Ennet House Drug and Alcohol Recovery Center—creates a locus of dependency that eventually sees the students becoming addicted to drugs and, like the residents of Ennet House, receiving no pleasure from those drugs. The students at Enfield Academy lead rigidly structured lives, and they know at all times their rank in relation to other students. Their dedication to tennis emerges as a kind of addiction. The life of a serious athlete resembles that of a drug addict in that both are based on repetition, and when the sport or the drug is withdrawn from the addict, the withdrawal reveals an inner void, an existentialist horror. Talking with some younger Enfield Academy students, an older student claims: "We're each deeply alone here. It's what we all have in common, this aloneness." Bound together by their isolation, the students, like the other characters in *Infinite Jest,* want to avoid the void that they perceive at the center of themselves and will do this however they can, through entertainment, tennis, drugs, or political causes.

Infinite Jest occurs in an unspecified near future, in which years have been "sold" to companies and the United States, Mexico, and Canada have formed the Organization of North American Nations (O.N.A.N.). Because the novel does not proceed chronologically, Wallace provides a "Chronology of Organization of North American Nations' Revenue-Enhancing Subsidized Time™, by Year" as a guide:

1) Year of the Whopper
2) Year of the Tucks Medicated Pad
3) Year of the Trial-Size Dove Bar
4) Year of the Perdue Wonderchicken
5) Year of the Whisper-Quiet Maytag Dishmaster
6) Year of the Yushityu 2007 Mimetic-Resolution-Cartridge-View-Motherboard-Easy-To-Install-Upgrade For Infernatron/InterLace TP Systems For Home, Office, Or Mobile [sic]
7) Year of Dairy Products from the American Heartland
8) Year of the Depend Adult Undergarment
9) Year of Glad

Such inventiveness appears also in the book's structure, which consists of third-person narrative, interior monologues, the text of E-mail messages, school papers, a magazine article, film scripts, and expositions by the author on subjects such as the demise of the videophone. Wallace employs many dictions in the novel, ranging from theoretical scientific language to street talk, to the platitudinous language of self-help programs, to teenage argot, to pharmaceutical jargon. The novel's information overload—its massive accumulation of detail—is mimetic of the ways contemporary Americans receive information. According to the critic Sven Birkerts, *Infinite Jest* "mimes, in its movements as well as in its dense loads of referential data, the distributed systems that are the new paradigm in communications." Chronologically nonlinear in its progression—Birkerts notes the novel's

"radically cantilevered plot conception"—*Infinite Jest* is full of digressions and is composed of numerous subplots connected via juxtaposition and association. In an interview with Donahue, Wallace described the novel as "designed more like a piece of music than like a book, so a lot of it consists of leitmotifs and things that curve back."

Its formal innovations notwithstanding, *Infinite Jest* emerges as an extended commentary on American consumerism—its wastefulness, its privileging of wants over needs, its harmfulness—and therefore on late capitalism and its extreme levels of consumption. The culture, as Valerie Stivers notes, is now "ruled by mass entertainment that is consumed mostly in solitude." But as with any worthwhile novel, *Infinite Jest* is much more than commentary. The book presents a myriad of characters whose lives are so convincingly portrayed that Wallace succeeds in making a fictional world unforgettably realistic.

The novel opens in the Year of Glad (chronologically the last year in the book) with protagonist Hal Incandenza at a recruiting/admissions interview at the University of Arizona. Hal, ranked fourth in the United States and sixth in North America among tennis players under eighteen years old, seems a likely candidate for a tennis scholarship if not a professional tennis career. Hal has memorized the unabridged *Oxford English Dictionary* and "is now being encouraged to identify himself as a late-blooming prodigy and possible genius at tennis who is on the verge of making every authority-figure in his world and beyond very proud indeed." Yet Hal is miserable and extremely self-conscious. When asked to explain the discrepancies between his low standardized test scores, his excellent grades, and his arcane writing samples with titles such as "Montague Grammar and the Semantics of Physical Modality," Hal cannot make himself understood to the university administrators, who mistake his words for the "*sub*animalistic" sounds of a seizure and therefore restrain him and call for an ambulance. The cause of Hal's speech problem is never answered explicitly, yet it reflects the horrors of not being able to communicate.

This problem of communication also arises when Hal's father, James Incandenza, thinks his son never speaks to him. Either James hallucinates that Hal does not talk to him, or Hal hallucinates that he speaks to his father. Hal offers words, but he does not communicate; crippled by solipsism, he is encased in the shell that is himself. He frequently feels empty inside and tries to fill the void with recreational drugs, eventually becoming addicted to marijuana. His intellectual and athletic virtuosity have created high expectations for him, and the American obsession with excellence places enormous pressure on Hal to perform constantly. Late in the novel Hal realizes, "It had begun to occur to me . . . that if it came down to a choice between continuing to play competitive tennis and continuing to be able to get high, it would be a nearly impossible choice to make." In an attempt to conquer his marijuana addiction, Hal visits Ennet House for help.

The novel's other protagonist is Don Gately, a former burglar and oral narcotics addict trying to repair his life while hiding from Boston's assistant district attorney. Gately has personally insulted the assistant district attorney and contributed to his wife's mental decline. In addition Gately accidentally kills a person in one of his burglaries, even more reason to fear being found by the assistant district attorney. Much of Wallace's focus on Gately centers on his efforts to overcome his drug addiction with the help of Alcoholics Anonymous. He makes progress in his struggle toward sobriety, becomes a staff member at Ennet House, and is shot while protecting a resident of Ennet House from an attack. When hospitalized, he refuses painkillers because they would destroy the progress he has made in his recovery from addiction.

Although most of the novel is concerned with individuals' various stages of addictions and their various attempts to conquer those addictions, the primary action results from a terrorist group's attempts to obtain the film that gives the novel its name. *Infinite Jest* was created by James Incandenza, a talented optical physicist and tennis player, founder of the Enfield Tennis Academy, and alcoholic who has committed suicide by the time the novel begins. The film is rumored to be so addictively, perfectly entertaining that anyone who watches it wants nothing else in life but to watch the film. Those who view the film will forget everything else, even thirst and hunger, and eventually will die because of this addiction. If forcibly withdrawn from the film (no one voluntarily stops watching it), the viewer must be hospitalized for catatonia.

The terrorists, French Canadian separatists known as *Les Assassins des Fauteuils Rollents* (the Wheelchair Assassins), want to use the film to turn Americans' addiction to pleasure against them. The terrorists resent the formation of O.N.A.N. and Canada's alliance with consumption-crazed Americans, and they want Quebec to secede from O.N.A.N. by any means necessary. They also despise the United States because that country, after transforming most of northern New England into a landfill, forcefully ceded the region to Canada. The area, now known as the Concavity, receives other states' garbage and toxic waste via enormous catapults aimed toward the northeast. The Wheelchair Assassins compete with two agents from the U.S. Office of Unspecified Services to acquire the film. The terrorists want the film to destroy the United States; the U.S. government agents want it to save the country. The two groups' efforts to locate the film involve virtually every character in the novel.

While the plot of the film remains one of the novel's central mysteries, several allusions and incomplete descriptions of it provide enough detail for a general summary. A perfectly beautiful woman (played by Joelle van Dyne, who later checks into Ennet House for an addiction to freebase cocaine after attempting suicide) apologizes repeatedly to the viewer because, according to the cosmology of the film, she is both the viewer's mother and the viewer's murderer in his or her previous life. The film mimics the acts of birth and death simultaneously using special lenses and holography. Gately seems to be watching *Infinite Jest* in the hospital when he describes a dream in which a veil-less Joelle is "the figure of Death, Death incarnate" and:

> Death is explaining that Death happens over and over, you have many lives, and at the end of each one (meaning life) is a woman who kills you and releases you into the next life. . . . Death says that this certain woman that kills you is always your next life's mother.

By the end of his dream "it's as if he's seeing her through a kind of cloud of light, a milky filter that is the same as the wobbly blur through which a baby sees a parental face bending over its crib." Apparently unaffected by *Infinite Jest*, Gately has reached a point beyond temptation and addiction and emerges as the novel's hero.

A member of the Union of the Hideously and Improbably Deformed, Joelle joined the organization either because of her staggering beauty or because of the acid scars on her face (the reader is led to believe that Joelle's mother, jealous of Joelle's beauty and of Joelle's father's incestuous feelings toward her, throws acid in Joelle's face and then commits suicide, but the context of this information—an anecdote told by Joelle—casts the facts in doubt). Joelle herself says, "I used to go around saying the veil was to disguise lethal perfection, that I was too lethally beautiful for people to stand." Although her tone is ironic, her ability to fixate

viewers of *Infinite Jest* suggests that she is indeed "lethally beautiful."

Elsewhere Joelle explains the processes behind the film, which coincide markedly with Gately's dream, and tells the government agents questioning her that the film was buried with James Incandenza. Joelle's assertion reinforces Hal's own memory, relayed at the beginning of the novel, when Hal is in the hospital and thinking "of John N. R. Wayne, who would have won this year's Whataburger, standing watch in a mask as Donald Gately and I dig up my father's head." Hal's aside implies that Wayne, the tennis star at Enfield Academy, is an undercover Quebecois terrorist and has not entered the Whataburger tournament because he has left the academy. At the novel's opposite end Gately

> dreams he's with a very sad kid and they're in a graveyard digging some dead guy's head up and it's really important, like Continental-Emergency important . . . and the sad kid is trying to scream at Gately that the important thing was buried in the guy's head and to divert the Continental Emergency to start digging the guy's head up before it's too late. . . . The sad kid holds something terrible up by the hair and makes the face of somebody shouting in panic: *Too Late.*

Hal's and Gately's recollections of the grave-digging scene connect the novel's protagonists in a mysterious yet powerful way. Both are sympathetic characters, yet only Gately overcomes that which cripples him.

In one of Gately's other dreams, James Incandenza's ghost appears and explains that he made *Infinite Jest* to compel Hal to communicate with him. James wanted to

> make something so bloody compelling it would reverse thrust on a young self's fall into the womb of solipsism, anhedonia, death in life. A magically entertaining toy to dangle at the infant still somewhere alive in the boy, to make its eyes light and toothless mouth open unconsciously, to laugh. To bring him "out of himself," as they say.

Sadly Hal's solipsism only intensifies after his father's death, and the novel ends with Gately in the hospital and its numerous narrative strands unresolved. Nevertheless the novel's close resonates with the rest of the book, compelling the reader to revisit all that has occurred in *Infinite Jest* in an attempt to make all the fragments cohere.

THE NONFICTION

A self-acknowledged novice at nonfiction, Wallace nevertheless has redefined the nonfiction essay by creating meta-nonfiction, essays that express anxiety about writing essays and make that anxiety an integral part of the work. Originally commissioned by different magazines (*Harper's, Esquire, Premiere, Review of Contemporary Fiction, Harvard Book Review*), the seven essays collected in *A Supposedly Fun Thing I'll Never Do Again: Essays and Arguments* (1997) vary in subject and length. They reflect Wallace's primary obsessions—film, television, tennis, the pursuit of pleasure, literature, and literary theory—yet do not simply rehash ideas presented in his fiction. Because the book appeared one year after *Infinite Jest,* however, some critics, such as Kakutani, consider it "a sort of nonfiction addendum [to *Infinite Jest*], an echo of chamber musings, reportage and, of course, footnotes that recapitulate many of the author's favorite preoccupations."

As with all of Wallace's books, critics met *A Supposedly Fun Thing I'll Never Do Again* with both admiration and consternation. Kakutani believes it "boasts some marvelously demented set pieces that take the absurdities of contemporary American life and freeze them." But she believes that it also "is sorely in need of some editing: even its liveliest, most compelling pieces are larded with repetitions, self-indulgent digressions and a seeming need on Wallace's part to set down whatever random thoughts or afterthoughts that happen to trundle through his mind." Yet Wallace's primary achievement in his essays is his determination not to filter out "random thoughts or afterthoughts" or what many people would see as extraneous details. Because he is first and foremost a fiction writer, not a professional journalist or essayist, Wallace's approach to nonfiction is to write not an "essay" but "a directionless essay thing" that resembles his apparently disheveled novels. But circuitousness has a purpose here because it redefines the genre.

Wallace's nonfiction informs and illuminates his previous work, *Infinite Jest* in particular, while remaining worthwhile reading on its own. The essays on tennis and film are especially enlightening. A sixty-eight-page paean to the film director, "David Lynch Keeps His Head" attempts to explain David Lynch's accomplishments, examine his career and films, and speculate on the plot and meaning of Lynch's 1997 film *Lost Highway*. The essay is most interesting for what it reveals about the workings of Wallace's own mind, which, like Lynch's, seems drawn to the intersection of the mundane and the horrific.

In one of the collection's two essays on tennis, "Derivative Sport in Tornado Alley," Wallace claims he was "a near-great junior tennis player" between the ages of twelve and fifteen not because of his physical prowess but because of his "geometric thinking" and locale:

> My flirtation with tennis excellence had way more to do with the township where I learned and trained and with a weird proclivity for intuitive math than it did with athletic talent. I was, even by the standards of junior competition in which everyone's a bud of pure potential, a pretty untalented tennis player. . . . What I could do was "Play the Whole Court."

Wallace learned how to use a violent and capricious wind to his advantage.

In "Getting Away from Already Pretty Much Being Away from It All," Wallace visits the

1993 Illinois State Fair and is so concerned about missing any important details that he describes almost everything he sees and hears in exhaustive detail. This absence of selectivity becomes a signature of his nonfiction. He digresses on topics such as community, land ownership, sexual harassment, boxing, food consumption, and T-shirts with logos, and his prose oscillates between the lyrical and the deadpan, the expansive and the terse. These inconsistencies would be a deficiency in a journalist, but they are part of what makes Wallace's nonfiction prose distinctive and entertaining.

Throughout the essay, as Wallace levels his satirist's gaze on the spectacle that is the Illinois State Fair, he also takes aim at his own neuroses and hypocrisies. Wallace is not averse to exposing his own fears along with the hypocrisies and idiosyncrasies of others. His obsession with how he appears to others emerges most powerfully in the book's ninety-eight-page title essay, in which Wallace is the narrator-protagonist paid to go on a seven-night Caribbean cruise that promises to "pamper" him beyond his expectations. Rather than feeling relaxed or fortunate, Wallace "felt as bleak as I've felt since puberty." The ocean is for Wallace "one enormous engine of decay," and he considers the cruise more a test of his inner strength than a "respite from unpleasantness."

The cruise ship's business of carefully managed pleasure amplifies his feelings of self-consciousness and produces guilt, embarrassment, and paranoia. Nevertheless, most of the essay consists of humorous, sometimes absurd observations that skewer Wallace as much as the pleasure-seeking passengers. He loses a game of chess to a nine-year-old girl; he shows up at a formal dinner as the only person not wearing a tuxedo; and he fears his toilet, which

produces a brief but traumatizing sound, a kind of held high-B gargle, as of some gastric disturbance on a cosmic scale, [and is capable of] a concus-

sive suction so awesomely powerful that it's both scary and strangely comforting—your waste seems less removed than *hurled* from you, and hurled with a velocity that lets you feel as though the waste is going to end up someplace so far away from you that it will have become an abstraction.

In the book's most intellectual and influential essay, "E Unibus Pluram: Television and U.S. Fiction," Wallace argues that, while "irony and ridicule are entertaining and effective," they are "agents of a great despair and stasis in U.S. culture" and "pose especially terrible problems" for young fiction writers. The essay is an inspired and sophisticated analysis of self-consciousness, cynicism, irony, and television and their effects on late-twentieth-century American fiction. After diagnosing television as America's national addiction, Wallace proceeds to describe its effects on the country, its culture, and its literature.

In the beginning of the essay Wallace discusses television's stranglehold on American minds. Everything, he claims, is defined through television: "If we want to know what American normality is—i.e. what Americans want to regard as normal—we can trust television." Television, Wallace argues, contributes to solipsism and alienation because television viewing replaces human interaction for many people, offering an illusion of interaction that makes the viewer increasingly unlikely to seek out real interaction with other people. Television appeals to lonely people because it allows people to watch other people without being seen. This parallels the desire of most fiction writers to watch others but not to be the objects of attention themselves. However, television watchers are not voyeurs like fiction writers are; the people on television know they are being watched and are paid to pretend otherwise. Furthermore television offers a window onto an illusion of reality, whereas voyeurism is a window onto reality itself.

This dynamic becomes problematic for aspiring fiction writers, since "the nexus where television and fiction converse and consort is self-conscious irony." Early metafiction "was deeply informed by the emergence of television and the metastasis of self-conscious watching." "By offering young, overeducated fiction writers a comprehensive view of how hypocritically the U.S.A. saw itself circa 1960, early television helped legitimize absurdism and irony as not just literary devices but sensible responses to a ridiculous world." But Wallace believes that irony now "serves an almost exclusively negative function" in fiction because it levels without rebuilding. For Wallace:

> The most dangerous thing about television for U.S. fiction writers is that we don't take it seriously enough as both a disseminator and a definer of the cultural atmosphere we breathe and process. . . . So much of the pleasure my generation takes from television lies in making fun of it.

Television now caters to the lone viewer's desire to be both an individual and part of a group by courting irreverence, cynicism, and parody, often under the rubric of irony. The result has been even more alienation and indifference, which Wallace considers "the '90's version of frugality for U.S. young people: wooed several gorgeous hours a day for nothing but our attention, we regard that attention as our chief commodity, our social capital, and we are loath to fritter it." Because television "revolves off just the sorts of absurd contradictions irony's all about exposing, . . . avant-garde irony and rebellion have become dilute and malign . . . absorbed, emptied, and redeployed by the very televisual establishment they had originally set themselves athwart."

Thus Wallace bemoans the moral and ethical evasions American fiction writers have undertaken, and he feels that cultural disengagement does not excuse fiction writers from remaining engaged and passionate about moral issues. Although "a certain subgenre of pop-conscious postmodern fiction, written mostly by young Americans, has lately arisen and made a real at-tempt to transfigure a world of and for appearance, mass appeal, and television," this kind of fiction fails to enact change because "television has been ingeniously absorbing, homogenizing, and re-presenting the very same cynical post-modern aesthetic that was once the best alternative to the appeal of Low, over-easy, mass-marketed narrative." Wallace believes:

> the old postmodern insurgents risked the gasp and squeal: shock, disgust, outrage, censorship, ac-cusations of socialism, anarchism, nihilism. . . . [But] today's risks are different. The new rebels might be artists willing to risk the yawn, the rolled eyes, the cool smile, the nudged ribs, the parody of gifted ironists, the "Oh how *banal*." To risk ac-cusations of sentimentality, melodrama. Of over-credulity. Of softness.

Wallace's essay is ultimately a rallying cry for young fiction writers, and its central ques-tions—"how to rebel against TV's aesthetic of rebellion, how to snap readers awake to the fact that our televisual culture has become a cynical, narcissistic, essentially empty phenomenon, when television regularly *celebrates* just these features in itself and its viewers?"—have no easy answers. For such a gifted ironist, parodist, and satirist to call for old-fashioned and unfash-ionable values, such as sincerity and conviction, seems contradictory. Yet behind the stylized surfaces of his fiction is always a core of sincer-ity, a moral conviction doing its best to become visible.

Selected Bibliography

WORKS OF DAVID FOSTER WALLACE

NOVELS AND SHORT STORIES
The Broom of the System. New York: Viking Penguin, 1987.
Girl with Curious Hair. New York: Norton, 1989.
Infinite Jest: A Novel. Boston: Little, Brown, 1996.

Brief Interviews with Hideous Men. Boston: Little, Brown, 1999.

NONFICTION

Signifying Rappers: Rap and Race in the Urban Present, with Mark Costello. New York: Ecco Press, 1990.

A Supposedly Fun Thing I'll Never Do Again: Essays and Arguments. Boston: Little, Brown, 1997.

Up, Simba!: 7 Days on the Trail of an Anticandidate. New York: Time Warner, 2000. (Electronic book.)

CRITICAL AND BIOGRAPHICAL STUDIES

Abramovich, Alex. "Fear and Self-Loathing." (http://www.villagevoice.com/issues/9923/abramovich.shtml), June 9–15, 1999. (Review of *Brief Interviews with Hideous Men. Voice Literary Supplement.*)

Anderson, Jason. "Surely He Jests." *Eye* (http://www.eye.net/eye/issue/issue_04.03.97/plus/anderson.html), April 3, 1997.

Asahina, Robert. Review of *The Broom of the System. Los Angeles Times Book Review,* February 1, 1987, pp. 1, 9.

Bell, Madison Smartt. "At Play in the Funhouse of Fiction." *Washington Post Book World,* August 6, 1989, p. 4. (Review of *Girl with Curious Hair.*)

Birkerts, Sven. "The Alchemist's Retort: A Multi-Layered Postmodern Saga of Damnation and Salvation." *Atlantic Monthly* February 1996, pp. 106–108. (Review of *Infinite Jest.*)

Bruni, Frank. "The Grunge American Novel." *New York Times Magazine,* March 24, 1996, pp. 38–41.

Card, Orson Scott. Review of *The Broom of the System. Magazine of Fantasy and Science Fiction* 73, no. 2:41–42 (August 1987).

Caro, Mark. "The Next Big Thing." *Chicago Tribune,* February 23, 1996, pp. 1, 25.

Costello, Mark. "Fighting to Write: A Short Reminiscence of D. F. Wallace." *Review of Contemporary Fiction* 13, no. 2:235–236 (summer 1993).

Cryer, Dan. Review of *Infinite Jest. Newsday,* February 12, 1996, p. B02.

Gates, David. "Levity's Rainbow." *Newsweek,* February 12, 1996, pp. 80–81. (Review of *Infinite Jest.*)

Gessen, Keith. "The Null Set." *Feed Magazine* (http://www.feedmag.com/deepread/dr292_master.html), February 11, 1999.

James, Caryn. "Wittgenstein Is Dead and Living in Ohio." *New York Times Book Review,* March 1, 1987, p. 22. (Review of *The Broom of the System.*)

Kakutani, Michiko. Review of *The Broom of the System. New York Times,* December 27, 1986, p. 13.

———. Review of *Infinite Jest. New York Times,* February 13, 1996, p. C17.

———. "'A Supposedly Fun Thing': Musing on Life's Absurdities." *New York Times,* February 4, 1997, p. C15. (Review of *A Supposedly Fun Thing I'll Never Do Again.*)

Kipen, David. "Terminal Entertainment." *Los Angeles Times Book Review,* February 11, 1996, pp. 1, 9. (Review of *Infinite Jest.*)

LeClair, Tom. "The Prodigious Fiction of Richard Powers, William T. Vollmann, and David Foster Wallace." *Critique* 38, no. 1:12–37 (fall 1996).

Levin, Jennifer. "Love Is a Federal Highway." *New York Times Book Review,* November 5, 1989, p. 31. (Review of *Girl with Curious Hair.*)

McInerney, Jay. "The Year of the Whopper." *New York Times Book Review,* March 6, 1996, p. 8. (Review of *Infinite Jest.*)

Miller, Laura. "The Road to Babbittville." *New York Times,* March 16, 1997, p. 71. (Review of *A Supposedly Fun Thing I'll Never Do Again.*)

Moore, Steven. *Review of Contemporary Fiction* 16, no. 1:141–142 (spring 1996). (Review of *Infinite Jest.*)

Olsen, Lance. "Termite Art; or, Wallace's Wittgenstein." *Review of Contemporary Fiction* 13, no. 2:199–215 (1993).

Passaro, Vince. "A Baffling Man." *Salon* (http://www.salon.com/books/feature/1999/05/28/hideousmen/index.html), May 28, 1999. (Review of *Brief Interviews with Hideous Men.*)

Perlstein, Rick. Review of *Infinite Jest. Nation,* March 4, 1996, pp. 27–29.

Rother, James. "Reading and Riding the Post-Scientific Wave: The Shorter Fiction of David Foster Wallace." *Review of Contemporary Fiction* 13, no. 2:216–234 (summer 1993).

Rucker, Rudy. "From the Mixed-Up Future of Lenore Beadsman." *Washington Post Book World,*

January 11, 1987, pp. 1, 13. (Review of *The Broom of the System.*)

Scott, A. O. "The Panic of Influence." *New York Review of Books* February 10, 2000, pp. 39–43.

Shepard, R. Z. "Mad Maximalism." *Time,* February 19, 1996, pp. 70–71. (Review of *Infinite Jest.*)

———. "Sex, Lies, and Semiotics." *Time,* May 31, 1999, p. 97. (Review of *Brief Interviews with Hideous Men.*)

Star, Alexander. Review of *Infinite Jest* and *A Supposedly Fun Thing I'll Never Do Again. New Republic,* June 30, 1997, pp. 27–34.

Stern, Richard. "Verbal Pyrotechnics." *Chicago Tribune,* March 9, 1997, pp. 1, 11. (Review of *A Supposedly Fun Thing I'll Never Do Again.*)

INTERVIEWS

Donahue, Anne Marie. "Interview with David Foster Wallace." *Boston Phoenix,* March 21–28, 1996. (Available at http://www.bostonphoenix.com/alt1/archive/books/reviews/03-96/DAVID_FOSTER_WALLACE.html.)

McCaffery, Larry. "An Interview with David Foster Wallace." *Review of Contemporary Fiction,* no. 13:127–150 (1993).

Miller, Laura. "The *Salon* Interview: David Foster Wallace." *Salon* (http://www.salon.com/09/features/wallace1.html), March 8, 1996.

O'Connor, Chris, and Rob Elder. "Interview with David Foster Wallace." *Oregon Voice* (http://darkwing.uoregon.edu/~ovoice/DFW.html), March 1998.

Stivers, Valerie. "The Jester Holds Court: A Conversation with David Foster Wallace." *Stim* (http://www.stim.com/Stim-x/0596May/Verbal/dfwmain.html), May 1996.

Weissman, Benjamin. "A Sleek and Brilliant Monster: David Foster Wallace Comes Clean." *LA Weekly,* April 30–May 6, 1999, p. 45.

Wiley, David. Interview. *Minnesota Daily* (http://www.mndaily.com/ae/Print/1997/08/st/interv.html), February 27, 1997.

—BRIAN HENRY

John Edgar Wideman
1941–

JOHN EDGAR WIDEMAN opens *Damballah* (1981), the first novel of his Homewood trilogy, with the character Orion, who shares his namesake's keen affinity for the hunt with all of its attendant freedom and sense of adventure. Unlike his Greek counterpart, however, Wideman's Orion is not cut down in heraldic pursuit, but instead undergoes a spiritual killing, captured to endure life as a slave in the American South during the mid-nineteenth century. He wanders the plantation's cane rows and dirt paths, sure that the very air of this "strange land" is "wearing out his skin, rubbing it thinner and thinner," until one day he will be unable to "separate" what is inside "from everything outside." Clearly, Wideman's hero is haunted by the reality that his enslavement ultimately will usurp his African identity, trading all his indigenous qualities of masculinity for the humiliations that come with a life of forced servitude. Orion laments that he was once destined to hold a position of tribal leadership, replete with the responsibilities accorded the head of a prominent tribal household. He daydreams of using the "fishing magic," an uncanny power that enables men to talk their prey out of the water, until his fantasy is broken by his captive state.

Seeking to maintain a shred of dignity that was once his birthright, he vows never to speak "Merican" and submit to Christianity. Instead, Orion indulges in the strength provided by Damballah, "the good spirit of the sky," who remains unchanged by the present and, thus, simultaneously inhabits the ancient past and the future. Orion's belief in the African deity allows him to transcend bondage mentally and to become emboldened enough to knock the plantation overseer off his horse, an act that secures his own demise. Damballah, however, enables the ancient past to serve as a "solid, contemporary ground beneath one's feet." Thus, Orion's uncompromising invocation of the spirit signifies that only his current life, which had little to offer him, has been forsaken. His ensuing death moves him to a more self-realized existence. The ironic twisting of death to mean life has as much to do with African American existence as it does with African mythology. Common among slaves was their belief that the afterlife secured liberation from the master's chains. Figuring Orion's end conversely to represent a beginning bespeaks Wideman's merging of African American sensibilities with African lore.

Beyond such cultural integration, the quality of enduring strength offered by Orion's story is parabolic for many reasons. For one, this first chapter of *Damballah* serves as the ancestral start of the family that came to dominate much of Wideman's subsequent work, both fictional and nonfictional. After chronicling the life of Orion, the novel moves quickly to Homewood, an African American neighborhood in Pittsburgh, and begins an introduction, on a multigenerational level, to the household of John and Freeda French. Indeed, it is their marriage and house on Cassina Way that serve as the nexus for much of the action that unfolds in several of Wideman's texts. The tentative link between the Frenches and Orion is indicative of the vague genealogical history of many African Americans whose family ties were weakened, if not broken altogether, by the slave trade. Much of

Wideman's writing, however, works to solidify connections between family, despite threatening forces that materialize in many ways. In fact, competing elements of adversity and endurance provide the tension that belies much of his work.

Almost as a means to underscore the tenacious ability of African Americans to survive in the face of instability thrust upon their lives, Wideman seldom follows a linear narrative. For instance, in *Damballah,* as he charts John and Freeda's history, he moves back and forth to those who came before and after and even to those who surround the couple. The reader is made to move in and out of a particular scenario, following one character only to come upon another who supersedes the original. In one of his autobiographical works, *Fatheralong: A Meditation on Fathers and Sons, Race and Society* (1994), Wideman explains how his mother tells stories in the same manner. He writes:

> I'm jealous, astounded as always, at her skill in weaving these stories, making them real through just the right choice of detail, how precipitously and seamlessly she switches from some gossipy joke about somebody to a funeral or an unexpected teenage pregnancy then back to this or that . . . , mimicked exactly, telling nonstop but never in a hurry.

Although he does not formally cite his mother as an influence, he admires and also replicates in much of his work her ability to hold on to a single narrative through a series of plots.

By the end of *Damballah,* Freeda's Aunt May legitimizes the author's own seemingly haphazard style by explaining that "digressions within digressions" allow recovery of each part of the story. Nothing is lost. Again, such a piecemeal structure, to a certain degree, replicates African American history, where broken moments were more emblematic of life than continuous episodes building one upon the next. Wideman testified in his essay "The Language of Home" that "being black and poor reinforced the

wisdom of a tentative purchase on experience." He continues by explaining the staccato structure of his work through a litany of watchwords: "Don't get too close, doubt what you see. Need, commitment set you up for a fall, create the conditions for disaster." The very way in which Wideman constructs his stories is more in keeping with the reality of their unfolding. Besides, good storytelling, Aunt May stresses, is a process whereby the listener, in addition to the author, plays an active role in making connections between the various pieces.

Recognizing links among different texts, like those contained in a single volume, is crucial when reading Wideman. He seldom leaves a character or development entirely behind. For instance, one might expect to find threads from *Damballah* in later installments of the Homewood trilogy, *Hiding Place* (1981) and *Sent for You Yesterday* (1983). Yet *Brothers and Keepers* (1984) and *Fatheralong* also contain elements from the novel, even though both works are autobiographical and therefore represent an entirely different genre. Aspects from the trilogy also echo in the work that preceded it, such as *A Glance Away* (1967), *Hurray Home* (1970), and *The Lynchers* (1973), as well as in work that followed, such as *Reuben* (1987), *Fever: Twelve Stories* (1989), and *All Stories Are True* (1993). Moreover, the fruits from *Damballah* can be seen in the way the rich, regenerative terrain for storytelling coalesced in the novel and beyond it and also because its characters, plots, and themes initiated the substantial amount of recognition Wideman's work has received. In 1984, *Sent for You Yesterday* won the PEN/Faulkner Award, as did *Philadelphia Fire* (1990) in 1990. Both *Brothers and Keepers* and *Fatheralong* were finalists for the National Book Award in 1984 and 1995, respectively. In 1993 Wideman garnered a MacArthur "genius" fellowship. His work was the entire focus of the summer 1999 issue of *Callaloo,* which garnered an international reception and response. His piece "Weight" won the O. Henry Award for best story of 2000. The Wideman Society was instituted by academic scholars to provide a forum for regular discussion of research relative to his work.

PERSEVERANCE OF FAMILY

Central to Wideman's corpus is his illustration of the perseverance of the family. In fact, a "Begat Chart" and a "Family Tree," provided at the start of *Damballah,* visibly demonstrate that the community of Homewood, in all of its manifestations, has endured and even been prolific. Like Orion, nearly all the major characters inhabiting the neighborhood possess a spiritual ability to exist beyond what the author himself calls the confines of material poverty and racial stereotypes that often are considered emblematic of black life. His oeuvre, for that matter, predominantly concerns itself with the qualities endemic to human existence rather than the extraneous forces that seek to marginalize African Americans.

Although Wideman was born in Washington, D.C., on June 14, 1941, his family moved to Homewood when he was a year old. Many of the scenarios cast in his fiction reflect a subsistence existence where whites intrude as bosses, the police, doctors, bill collectors, and others in positions of authority. More important, however, and more to Wideman's interest, Homewood reflects a world where successive generations grow amid those who came before. In this way, there is an interconnectedness among families that engenders fierce loyalties to one another and among neighbors despite individual peccadilloes, ranging from vanity to stubbornness, and more serious transgressions, such as heroin addiction and murder. Often, when a character is on the brink of destruction, someone from the neighborhood, either a friend or a relation, intrudes or intercedes and, at the very least, provides a sustaining power. In *Sent for You Yesterday,* Wideman describes the house on Cassina Way, his grandparents' address, as an "ark" or an "island" that, to a certain degree, provides protection from the "arbitrary boundaries" established by those on the outside, explicitly the white world of Pittsburgh or, worse, the South. As a result, the neighborhood and, even more so, the family home, with all of the various personalities within, represent a kind of Genesis where something new is born.

It is not as if no one dies or lives in despair in Homewood. Quite the contrary is true. The narrator of *Sent for You Yesterday* explains that the houses on Cassina Way once were little more than rows of wooden shanties built quickly and cheaply to house the "floods of black migrants" moving North from the South for a better way of life after the Civil War. Likewise, Tommy, one of the main characters in *Hiding Place,* describes that it sometimes feels as if the winter wind could tear the shacks' walls apart. As Wideman established with Orion in *Damballah,* however, present-day life is often beleaguered, while the past offers a steadfast ability to move beyond daily adversity, ultimately infusing the future with hope. The Homewood community affords a touchstone to the liberating strength of what came before and beyond individual existence and vulnerabilities. In *Brothers and Keepers,* Wideman literally acknowledges the way the "living arrangements" of the neighborhood are connected to strengths of "ancient African patterns." He writes:

> The high wall of the family, the collective, communal reality of other souls, other huts like yours eliminated some of the dread, the isolation experienced when you turned inside and tried to make sense out of the chaos of your individual feelings. No matter how grown you thought you were or how far you believed you'd strayed, you knew you could cry *Mama* in the depths of the night and somebody would tend to you. Arms would wrap round you, a soft soothing voice lend its support. If not a flesh-and-blood mother then a

mother in the form of song or story or a surrogate, Aunt Geral, Aunt Martha, drawn from the network of family numbers.

Like the tribal villages of Africa, Homewood gives a broad sense of security in the way the community functions as a family, freeing one from the forces of alienation and isolation inflicted by the larger society.

In the concluding story of *Damballah,* titled "The Beginning of Homewood," Wideman makes the connection between the neighborhood and an understanding of freedom and security even more concrete as well as complex. Like the beginning of the novel, its end concerns an enslaved African American whose namesake was a figure in ancient Greece with a somewhat parallel life. The main character is a woman named Sybela Owens, whose mythic counterpart was Sybil, a figure with her own history of captivity. Eventually, Sybela's lover, Charlie Bell, who happens to be her master's son, takes her from the plantation to Pittsburgh, free from the threat of speculation but not racism. The couple is forced to reside on the outskirts of the city to avoid the condemnation imposed on an interracial marriage. In the ensuing years they have eighteen children, and their progeny become the foundation of Homewood. Thus, Sybela's role as the community's matriarch makes her life significant.

The narrator, however, is quick to point out that Sybela's story is even more remarkable, because it is born out of action once considered criminal. She was, after all, an escaped slave who consorted with a white man, even though Wideman makes clear that she had no choice. Although by today's standards such behavior is heroic, in her own time Sybela would have been condemned. As a result, Wideman reveals that right and wrong are unstable notions with definitions that can shift in relation to what society fancies is moral and ethical. For such reasons, Sybela's story, like Orion's, carries a certain dismissal of our present state of reality.

Strength, and ultimately freedom, is imparted to those who challenge what is often upheld as legitimate. Likewise, Homewood, which has long been an unvalued part of Pittsburgh, becomes the very core of existence when cast through the work of Wideman.

The lessons of *Damballah* would have been lost if it were not for an unnamed boy, figured at the start of the novel, who secretly watches Orion and eventually is introduced to the staying power of the African god he worships. When the slave is murdered, the child literally rescues Orion's soul from the master's profane burial in desecrated land. He returns Orion's decapitated head to the river, which is the entrance to the ancient world so revered by Damballah. The child's action, however, becomes more than that of caretaker of the dead, as Wideman charges him with preserving and passing on Orion's story, ultimately keeping him and all his beliefs alive. Such an intermediary role connects the powers of life existent before slavery to the African Americans who followed. In fact, nearly all the subsequent stories in the Homewood trilogy are set in the twentieth century, alluding to the certainty that Damballah's potency has survived. Such a link to a more fulfilled existence also serves as another indicator of the way *Damballah* allows understanding of the larger resonance found in many of Wideman's literary endeavors.

Indeed, the necessity to remember and, more important, to tell or relate one's memory is crucial not only to self-preservation but also to survival of the entire race and culture. In many of the stories that Wideman tells there are those, like the boy in Orion's life, who keep the narrative close to heart, ready for transmission. Moreover, characters also cherish certain signifiers of memory, such as photographs, letters, souvenirs, or keepsakes, as a means to validate the real-life importance of the story. For example, "The Beginning of Homewood," in its entirety, is a letter to an unnamed prisoner intended as a means of support and inspiration beyond a life of incarceration. At the end, the narrator admits that even though "the struggle doesn't ever end," the pieces of the story addressed to the inmate make life seem "better than the way it was before." In closing, the speaker tells the reader (presumably the person in jail) to "hold on," suggesting the sustaining power of the letter's contents.

In "Lizabeth: The Caterpillar Story," another chapter of *Damballah,* the main character also suggests the saving importance of the narrative. She realizes at a young age, before she can even speak, that she knows her family story so well that she can tell when it is related accurately or when "somebody got it wrong." When Lizabeth is an old woman, with grandchildren of her own, she contemplates the fact that her life can sometimes seem strange and empty until she recollects the voices of those closest to her, perhaps long dead. Invoking the past, even if she is the only one to listen, enables her to keep a vital sense of herself alive. In *Brothers and Keepers,* Wideman expands on the way the stories of Homewood are a life force for those inhabiting the neighborhood. He writes, "Face-to-face contact, shared language and values, a large fund of communal experience rendered individual lives extremely visible in Homewood. Both a person's self-identity ('You know who you are') and accountability ('Other people know who you are') were firmly established." The community, therefore, and all that transpired within it, imparts a sense of validation to its people that otherwise is not available.

Subsequent stories in *Damballah* explain that Wideman's fictional world and its concerns often call attention to or hark back to realities and meditations relative to his own life. Although such a characteristic is not unusual for any writer—and Wideman himself cautions that sometimes his casting of fact within fiction is unreliable—what makes his employment of such a trait unique is his earnest and skillful attempt to honor and lend understanding to a real community often disregarded, sometimes even by the author, for its poverty and crime rate. Like "Lizabeth," the chapter "The Chinaman" revolves around Freeda French, who on her deathbed must "dismantle" her voice, tell her stories, so she can revive the family that she bore. For in the story of her demise is the birth of her daughter, Lizabeth, who the reader subsequently learns is Wideman's own mother.

Moreover, Freeda's funeral was the spawning ground for many of the stories that make up the Homewood trilogy as well as so much of the work that followed. It is explained that after Freeda's burial (which is also remarkable for its resemblance to an Irish wake, replete with rain and whiskey), the family unites at Lizabeth's house and eventually encircles Aunt May, who tells the stories of Homewood. Freeda's life and death are tantamount to Wideman's literal and literary origins. Three months later, when Wideman and his wife and children experience car trouble near the shores of the Mississippi in Iowa, he yearns for his Aunt May's tales to replace the sound of steamers filled with cotton and slaves that haunts him in his hotel room and prevents a night of sleep. Wideman could be viewed as the unnamed boy of *Damballah,* who strives to save the story, an act of salvation from forces that limit his people's self-actualization. It is almost as if the power of Damballah intrudes into the author's own psyche and seeks to free him from the reality that entrapped his family, transporting him to experiences that fused their strength through communion with one another. Noting the importance of the story to his own sense of self, Wideman, in an essay for the *New York Times Book Review* titled "The Language of Home," says:

> The stance, the habit of looking long and hard, especially at those things—a face, a hand, a home—that matter, makes them matter more and

more. I examine minutely the place I come from, repeat its stories, sing its songs, preserve its language and values, because they make me what I am and because if I don't, who will?

Through such sentiments it is possible to witness just how close Wideman's characters are to his own sensibilities.

His dispensation to be a writer seems a natural inclination, given the many laurels Wideman has received throughout his life. Before graduating from the University of Pennsylvania with a bachelor's degree in English (1963), he was inducted into Phi Beta Kappa (1959–1963) and named a Rhodes Scholar (1963). While studying in England on the Rhodes scholarship, he was awarded a second bachelor's degree from Oxford University (1966). He began his teaching career at the University of Pennsylvania in 1966 and was awarded tenure in 1971. Subsequently, he taught at the University of Wyoming (1975) and the University of Massachusetts (1985). In addition to such successes, which certainly reflect Wideman's intellectual acumen, his literary accomplishments also gain magnitude when examined alongside the history of African Americans and higher education. When Wideman was attending the University of Pennsylvania as an undergraduate in the early 1960s, there was little awareness, never mind understanding or inclusion, of the black experience in the curriculum. Such was the case at universities across the country.

Given that Wideman's formal education was rooted so firmly in the establishment, which exhibited marginal cognizance of African American contributions, it is no wonder that he did not fully take into account his own cultural and historic background, endemic in his work. Indeed, when he initially cited the influences on his early fiction, novels such as *A Glance Away* and *Hurray Home,* Wideman credited such writers as the American-born English poet T. S. Eliot and, particularly, the British novelist Lau-

rence Sterne, whom he studied in depth while he was at Oxford. He also names his conventional academic background, which introduced him to Eliot as well as to the Irish novelist James Joyce, as crucial to his learning of "the language, how to write, . . . the technique" (*Conversations with John Edgar Wideman*). Furthermore, he has testified to his minimal exposure to black writers in both high school and college, including Langston Hughes, James Baldwin, and Ralph Ellison. Although all three of these writers may have been included in the particular anthologies that were used in classes, Wideman acknowledges that they were neglected in the actual course material.

With protests at many major American universities, demands for a reformed curriculum to include black studies were given promise. Moreover, such anthologies as LeRoi Jones and Larry Neal's *Black Fire* (1968), Houston A. Baker Jr.'s *Black Literature in America* (1971), and Ruth Miller's *Blackamerican Literature, 1760–Present* (1971) were published, giving more credence to claims that a substantive body of writing by African Americans existed and could not be ignored by college and university English departments. Wideman readily admits that such circumstances had an impact on him. The events of the 1960s made it necessary for him, and so many others, to examine his race and heritage in relation to self, even though he was reluctant to do so at first. Such hesitancy initially surfaced when he was approached by a group of students at the University of Pennsylvania, where he was a faculty member, and requested to teach a course in African American literature. In the beginning he made excuses that it was not his field of expertise and that he had his own work to complete, but ultimately he consented and, for the first time, began to read in earnest the work of other black writers. He subsequently was asked to organize and chair one of the first African American studies departments in the country.

Since Wideman's initial immersion in the African American literary endeavor, he has become one of its advocates in ways reaching beyond the classroom. Simultaneous to his development of a course focusing on the work of African American writers, he became an editor for W. W. Norton, the New York publishing house whose anthologies of literature of various periods and styles are used by many English departments at academic institutions. Wideman was one of the initial scholars involved in the compilation of *The Norton Anthology of African American Literature,* which took more than twenty years to produce, under the wing of several editors. He was also influential in the first attempts to "integrate" the work of black writers into the standard *Norton Anthology of American Literature.* Like his contemporaries Toni Morrison and Alice Walker, Wideman began publishing essays in established venues, among them, *Esquire,* the *Nation,* the *New York Times Book Review,* and even *Modern Maturity* "legitimizing" as he put it, "the language of my tribe." Such initiatives were part of a host of efforts by scholars and writers alike to incorporate black culture and history fully into the national psyche on both academic and popular levels.

BROTHERS AND KEEPERS

Wideman's self-schooling in the black literary canon, however, had its most profound impact on his own consciousness and, as a result, on his writing. His autobiographical work *Brothers and Keepers* is the first instance where he fully and openly recognizes the influence of African American culture and tradition in relation to his own perceptions, even if such an impact manifested itself slowly and, at times, painfully. The book was published about fifteen years after he developed the course in African American literature at the University of Pennsylvania. This span of time shows that the class may have been the impetus for his discovery of black writers as well as the significance of his own heritage, but it in no way functioned as his complete meditation on their importance to him professionally. Ironically, *Brothers and Keepers* does not focus exclusively on Wideman. The book charts the relationship between him and his brother Robby, who is serving a life sentence in Western State Penitentiary in Pennsylvania for armed robbery and murder. As the text evolves, however, it becomes apparent that the narrative cum biography has as much to do with Wideman's own sense of imprisonment—the result of feelings that he has been dislocated culturally because he is a successful black man—as it does with Robby's literal incarceration.

Brothers and Keepers begins in the midst of the national manhunt for Robby. Wideman, like the rest of his family, is beset with worry. He starts a letter to his fugitive brother that serves several purposes. Because Wideman was living at the time in Laramie, Wyoming, and teaching at the university, relating recent news as well as reliving fabled family experiences allowed the writer a sense of proximity during a time of crisis to those living in Pittsburgh, including Robby. Moreover, just as telling stories in previous texts often rescued various characters from conflicts they were confronting, Wideman's letter, even though it could not be delivered, carries with it a modicum of salvation. "Reach out and touch. That's what the old songs could do," Wideman writes. In time, Robby makes his way to Laramie, allowing Wideman to feed and shelter him for a night before his eventual capture across the border in Colorado. The letter that he begins writing at the time of Robby's trouble, however, has far-reaching implications, including an opportunity for Wideman to scrutinize and simultaneously to excoriate circumstances that led to his success but to his brother's delinquency.

As the text proceeds, Robby, unlike Wideman, becomes a figure fully immersed in the web of life that Homewood has to offer. Through a photograph taken the last time the family was together, Wideman describes his brother's hair as an exploding Afro and goes on to relate his propensity for the poolrooms, Saturday-night basement socials, and hangout corners of the neighborhood. Beyond indulgences in the communal world of Homewood, Robby also becomes fully engaged in aspects of life there that have a much more sinister quality. Because this brother is the youngest of the family, a full ten years separating he and Wideman, Wideman explains that the neighborhood of Robby's formative years was different from the one where he and his other siblings, and especially his mother, had grown up. Instead of a community that reinforces a sense of pride and security, Homewood became a place where the forces of "racial discrimination, economic exploitation, white hate and fear" began to encroach in ways that would "choke the life" out of it.

One particular example of the stultifying effect of prejudice relative to Robby is the illness of his friend Garth, which is misdiagnosed by the white doctors who serve the neighborhood and eventually result in the boy's death. Although tension always accompanies a white presence in Homewood, when Garth dies, the anxiety becomes more palpable and causes Robby to enlist his trust exclusively in aspects of life that were removed from the white power structure. By his own admission, Robby laments that his choices and actions are often ones that hurt him the most, as well as his family, even if they arise from a desire to shun the establishment that places the black community in a stranglehold. At the same time, he also acknowledges that because the level of racism against African Americans is so extreme, restricting success to a very small percentage of the population, there is a level of respect for those who operate outside the system, even if they are criminals and drug abusers. He states that

"we can't help but feel some satisfaction seeing a brother, a black man, get over on these people, on their system without playing their rules." His admiration for the derelict and his aspirations to be one among them, even if it causes his own downfall, is born out of a desire to free himself from the subjugation of a nation disinterested in the black community.

Even if only instinctually, Wideman himself identifies with Robby's rejection of the establishment on the day of his arraignment in Colorado. When he is brought into the courtroom handcuffed and in leg irons, Wideman greets his brother with the sign for black power. Although he does not condone Robby's crime, his salutation is a means to acknowledge that underpinning his brother's actions is a challenge, in some measure, to the power structure, represented by the courts, that persistently seeks to disenfranchise African Americans. Earlier, in the final chapter of *Damballah,* the motivations behind Robby's actions echo when the narrator considers whether the circumstances surrounding black existence have changed in the years between slavery and the present. Was Robby, like Sybela, forced to commit a crime because society provided few alternatives? The narrator asks, "Were there names other than 'outlaw' to call you, were there words other than 'crime' to define your choice?" In *Brothers and Keepers,* Wideman's raised, clenched fist is his only way to recognize Robby's humanity in the presence of those who deny it, whether or not he is a law-abiding citizen.

Likewise, Wideman charts the way in which his mother increasingly comes to realize during the course of Robby's incarceration that the establishment not only seeks to punish her son but also plays a large role in perpetrating the conditions that got him into trouble in the first place. Her recognition of the way African Americans have been systematically disenfranchised is all the more remarkable, Wideman explains, because before Robby's sentencing she dismissed, more often than not, the symptoms of racism that were destroying Homewood as "petty" and "not worth bothering about." While she witnesses the way the courts and then the prison ignore the role that society has played in the neighborhood's deterioration, however, she grows increasingly bitter and less willing to overlook particular discriminatory attitudes and actions. At the end of *Damballah,* the narrator states, "The Court could ask why you are where you are, and why the rest of us are here." Given that those in charge of the system acknowledge no such responsibility, Wideman writes that his mother now "understands they have a master plan that leaves little to accidents, that most of the ugliest things happening to black people are not accidental but the predictable results of the working plan." Robby's imprisonment, in many ways, raised Wideman's awareness, as well as that of his family, regarding the limitations imposed on their lives because of bigotry.

WOMEN AND ALIENATION

In the story "Solitary," a chapter in *Damballah* as well as in the novel *Hiding Place,* Wideman concentrates on the isolation experienced, particularly by women, in a society that shuns African American existence. The titles suggest that both texts focus on portraits of the convicted, but their real concern is a growing sense of alienation felt by those outside prison who must confront the hostility of those with legitimized power during the course of day-to-day existence. For instance, although the backdrop of "Solitary" is a black man's incarceration, the foreground addresses the way a prisoner's mother is dehumanized by the criminal justice system. First, long bus rides and uncomfortable waiting rooms in filthy conditions strip away the main character's dignity and sense of identity when she travels to visit her son. Then, after the trip, she must leave a further shard of her self behind when she sur-

renders her loved one back to prison life. The narrator affirms that "the hardships connected with the visits to her son were not accidental. Somebody had arranged it that way. An evil somebody who didn't miss a trick." Presumably, this individual is the same person or group of people that Wideman's mother had in mind in *Brothers and Keepers,* when she considers that Robby's imprisonment was an intended eventuality.

As "Solitary" progresses, the story becomes a meditation in which the mother recounts actions she took or did not take that may have caused her son's criminal behavior, how he has changed while in prison, how she will contend with neighbors inquiring after his health and well-being. She also recalls her family history in the neighborhood, which reaches back to a time when "bears and wildcats" roamed the streets of Homewood. In true Wideman fashion, the main character invokes her relatives as a means to gain their strength. As she stands on a railway overpass, with her arm in her brother's, she vows to stand up to the forces threatening her own and, ultimately, her family's existence.

Likewise, *Hiding Place* revolves around a female character who, at the end of the text, assumes a position of defiance to those seeking to incarcerate her grand-nephew. Bess, the elderly heroine of the novel, like the main character of "Solitary," becomes aware of the larger injustices facing the community when Tommy, her niece's son, uses her property to evade the Pittsburgh police after he has been involved in a murder. At first, Bess rejects Tommy's pleas for sanctuary, satisfied to provide him with only a brief moment of refuge before she demands that he find another place to hide. Before their acquaintance, she was content to live out her dying days on the top of Bruston Hill, site of the first black settlement in Homewood, a place where she could invoke memories of her childhood and adolescence. Yet through a series of conversations that she and Tommy share, Bess becomes reacquainted with the lives of her family and the forces of racism undermining the community. The novel ends with her poised to descend the hill, ready to argue Tommy's innocence and demand that they give him one more chance. Like the mother in "Solitary," Bess refuses to continue a life of indifference to those denying her grand-nephew's right to justice.

In *Brothers and Keepers,* Wideman continues to portray the consciousness-raising effect brought about by Robby's imprisonment, but its magnitude is all the more profound given that the account is nonfiction. The very way that Wideman constructed the text underscores how his brother's incarceration is imbedded in a system of discrimination. In large part the book uses elements of a slave narrative as a means to convey the story as well as its purpose. An obvious connection is the way in which Robby's autobiography, like its black counterparts of the nineteenth century, seeks to validate and impart to the larger society the methodical injustices confronting the African American community. Whereas slave narratives fueled the abolitionist movement's efforts to reform, so, too, does Robby's story bring understanding to the inequality brought to the fore by the Civil Rights movement of the twentieth century. Wideman is cautious, however, when he explains that *Brothers and Keepers* provides no great epiphany at the end, whereby the narrator moves from captivity to freedom. Indeed, Robby is not released from prison. Instead, the text explains how Wideman's brother incrementally learns to preserve a sense of himself, even though the day-to-day reality of his life as a convict seeks to destroy him. Freedom, as a result, is transformed from a physical to a mental state.

In producing Robby's account, Wideman does not simply replicate the techniques used by an earlier generation of black writers. Indeed, certain narrative strategies that were part of African American autobiography reveal levels of discrimination that black writers were made to confront even by those who sought to assist them through publication. For instance, the introductory pages of a slave narrative often carried an endorsement by a white person that was intended to authenticate the credibility of the writer. Although they were meant to have the opposite effect, such testimonies proved to be an implicit demonstration of belief that an African American, as articulate as he or she might be, did not possess the intellect required to write a convincing account of slavery's brutality. Given that Wideman had all of the legitimate credentials of a writer, his presence as the author within his brother's story could be interpreted as fulfilling the same mediating role played by whites in previous black narratives, which in the end belittled the storyteller's authority.

Wideman admits that his own history of disparagement toward Robby made it more than possible to view his motives as exploitative. Ironically, while teaching the African American literature course at the University of Pennsylvania, Wideman writes that he never considered that his brother could have a meaningful influence on his life, connecting him to his heritage. Instead, "the quiet of the classroom," reading Jones and Neal's *Black Fire,* replaced any identification that Robby was "living through the changes in black culture and consciousness." Preferring the safety afforded by academia, Wideman laments that he never even "spoke to Robby. Never knew until years later that he was the one who could have told me much of what I needed to hear."

Such regrets relate to earlier confessions in *Brothers and Keepers,* where Wideman chronicles his willful rejection of Homewood. He stresses that it was not as if he and his brother never had opportunities to indulge in each other's company. Rather, until Robby's incarceration, Wideman felt it necessary to deny where he came from, to run away "from black-ness" in order to accomplish his goals. "To suc-ceed in the man's world," he believed, "you must become like the man and the man sure didn't claim no bunch of nigger relatives in Pittsburgh." Therefore, Wideman came to view his good grades, his ability to speak and write standard English, and his scholarships, academic record, and appointments all as antithetical to his background. Robby's "words and gestures belonged to a language [he] was teaching [himself] to unlearn."

Even in *Hiding Place,* Wideman portrays a character named John, who returns from the university and provides a rare glimpse of impatience with Tommy, the fugitive in the text, who is similar to Robby:

> Sometimes I get close to hating him. Everything inside me gets cold and I don't care what happens to him. I think about all he's done, all the people he's hurt. . . . I know it's not all Tommy's fault. I know he's a victim in a way too. But on the other hand he's hurt people and done wrong and he can't expect to just walk away.

Only with his brother's sentencing and Wideman's subsequent visits to the prison, where he and Robby truly become acquainted, did Wideman come to realize that his own sense of himself, to a certain degree, was incomplete.

As central as his brother becomes to his identity, Wideman is also mindful that his own life history not supersede Robby's. He recog-nizes that *Brothers and Keepers* could easily turn into a book "about a writer who goes to a prison to interview his brother but comes away with his own story." Through such a scenario, Wideman would become like his brother's keep-ers, working to suppress any sense of dignity that could result from Robby's account of his life. Incumbent upon Wideman was the need to develop a narrative strategy that at once dimin-ished his own voice while at the same time upheld Robby's, thereby preserving the integrity

of black existence, a fundamental component of his brother's story. Because Wideman was trained as a writer, however, his ability to curb his own literary instincts often proved difficult. As he listened to Robby, his own interpretive ear often "swallowed" his brother until another voice would interrupt and say, "Stop. Stop and listen, listen to him."

As a result, the text is made up of a series of two narratives playing off each other. In one, Wideman reveals his own need to know Robby's story, functioning as a means to instill within him a sense of black character so absent from his formal education. In the other, Robby, in his own words, examines the forces that fueled his veneration of Homewood and, at the same time, proved to be his undoing. By setting the text up as a series of juxtaposed accounts, Wideman re-creates the feel of a dialogue between him and Robby that is void of self-consciousness and also avoids promoting himself to the detriment of his brother.

Robby actually boasts that he has achieved a modicum of recognition, in his own right, for his storytelling capabilities, beyond his col-laboration in the authoring of *Brothers and Keepers.* In high school his teachers would often call him to the front of the class to perform original sketches and monologues for his classmates. Likewise, other prisoners frequently ask him to recite his own poetry or read from a book. "Fellows like my poems," he says. "They say I write about the things they be thinking. Say it's like listening to their own self thinking. That's cause we all down there together." As with Wideman's own work, Robby's provides a sense of support for him and his fellow inmates, allowing them to transcend the confines of their reality.

Beyond the actual events that make up *Broth-ers and Keepers,* the fact that the text uses so much of Robby's speech patterns demonstrates on one more level Wideman's thwarting of publication demands often placed upon the black writer that, in reality, undercut their authenticity. Indeed, the inclusion of his brother's vernacular enhances the book's articulation and promotion of a genuine black experience. One of the more potent exhibitions of an urban, African American voice is evident when Robby testifies about his circle's political and social awareness despite their recklessness. He states:

> See. Ain't all of us out there in the street crazy. We know what's going down. We look round and what do we see? Homewood look like five miles of bad road. Ain't nothing happening. We see that. We know it. So what we supposed to do? Go to church like the old folks? Be O. J. or Dr. J? Shit. Ain't everybody in the street crazy. We see what's going down. We supposed to die. That ain't news to nobody. It's what's happening every day in Homewood. Them little checks and drugs. What else is out there? The streets out there. The hard-ass curb. That's why the highest thing you can say about a cat is he made his from the curb. That's a bad cat. That's a cat took nothing and made something. . . .
>
> I knew I was doing wrong. Knew I was hurting people. But then I'd look around and see Homewood and see what was going down. Shit. I ain't gon lay down and die. Shit. Ima punch that rock with my bare hand till it bleeds money.

In addition to the way the passage lends understanding to the motivating forces behind street life, the way in which Robby utters the account makes it all the more convincing. Wideman explains that within the "first language" that African Americans speak, such as the language used by his brother, lies the "primal authenticity of experience." Although formal education demands that conventional linguistic codes and literary practices be used when writing to an audience, Wideman argues that such customs remove the black author and, thus, what they write from their culture. In *Brothers and Keepers,* Wideman recounts how his first impulse in relation to Robby's story was to "clean him up," admitting that his intellectual training gave him little confidence in the way his brother could speak for himself. Conversely, when the text was drafted a second time, Wideman included not only what Robby said but also the way in which he spoke, pushing the book to represent one of the individual contributions made by African American authors. Moreover, by witnessing the evocative quality of the rhetoric, it is possible to realize the profound hole apparent in American literature when such voices are missing.

STRONG FAMILY RELATIONSHIPS

Since publishing *Brothers and Keepers,* Wideman has continued to explore the enduring quality of African American existence and the way family relationships strengthen the ability to survive. In so doing, however, he also investigates the often lopsided domestic realities of the black household, where women typically provide the holding power that allows for or provokes perseverance. Yet strong female characters are not portrayed in Wideman's work at the expense of a male presence. Instead, the author reveals the larger context surrounding African American men, which denies a sustained involvement in home life. The importance of Wideman's portraits of noncohesive familial relations would be underestimated if they were not examined in light of circumstances related to the feminist movement and the ensuing popular discourse between authors that initially pitted women and men against each other.

During the mid-1980s African American female authors were indicted for the perception that their work often rendered black men as wife-beaters, rapists, unfit fathers, and child molesters. Such accusations became particularly virulent when Alice Walker published *The Color Purple* (1982) and Mel Watkins, in a front-page *New York Times Book Review* essay (June 15, 1986), charged that work by black women was akin to melodramatic propaganda that was incomplete and less rewarding because of its sweeping condemnation of black men.

Rather than engage in such regressive exchanges, as did some black male writers, including Ishmael Reed, Wideman readily acknowledges in his work that women bear the brunt of uniting the family. He also depicts men in myriad situations that help explain the difficulty, if not the impossibility, of their making constructive contributions to the home, given the obstacles that presently accompany African American existence. Certainly, some men inhabiting Wideman's work live the life of the gangster, but most of his male characters are deeply dissatisfied with the limitations imposed upon their lives that prevent them from maintaining roles as loving husbands and responsible fathers. Moreover, the household sometimes becomes the site where men and women fight together to achieve a modicum of intimacy when drugs and crime are their only avenues for material gain.

For instance, "Rashad," a chapter in *Damballah,* tells the story of a man struggling to maintain relations with his wife, Shirley, and their daughter, Keesha. The memories of Rashad quickly reveal that he and Shirley have bickered constantly, especially when she has suffered his physical abuse. What makes matters worse is that Rashad's only access to income is dealing heroin, for which Shirley habitually makes excuses, enabling him to come and go without offering any sustained support. He arrives in Homewood intermittently, showering his family with presents and letting Shirley drive his "customized Regal" to church, only to leave again before he is shot or arrested. Although Rashad's mother-in-law seems to yearn for more from his life, the story ends with Keesha fully grown and Rashad absent. There is a lack of any real resolution with the text ending as it began, empty of a constructive male presence and with one woman who is unable to free

herself from a destructive relationship and another who prays for everyone's salvation.

In *Hiding Place,* Wideman continues to demonstrate, through the character of Tommy, the way in which black men are hindered from making constructive contributions to their own homes and to the larger community. Unlike Rashad, however, Tommy is more vocal about the causes of his disenfranchisement. After his great-aunt Bess lectures to him that life is hard but the end will bring reward, Tommy responds, "Like I got all the time in the world. Like I got to suffer a little more and wait a little longer and . . . and what . . . what's supposed to happen after I suffer some more and wait some more? Tired of that bullshit."

Realizing that his options to succeed are minimal, Tommy embarks on a plan to sell stolen televisions to Indovina, a white businessman in the community. The scheme is significant because it is reminiscent of the crime committed by Wideman's brother, Robby, in *Brothers and Keepers* and also because in *Hiding Place* it functions as a form of retribution for the years of exploitation inflicted upon blacks by whites in the neighborhood. Indeed, Indovina is emblematic of all white men and the way they have institutionally thwarted black progress. As Tommy says, "He's so greedy he can't stand for the nigger to have nothing. . . . They been robbing us so long they think that's the way things supposed to be." When the plan goes sour, however, and one of Indovina's men is killed, Tommy is forced to run, and he loses any hope of advancement. The crime, like Robby's, will be viewed only as an individual transgression rather than the outcome of conditions that society as a whole has promulgated.

In addition to Tommy's inability to attain legitimate gainful employment, the novel also focuses on his unhappiness over the way his relationship with his wife, Sarah, dissolves. Before he devises the plan to steal televisions, he begins selling heroin as a way to make a living. Eventually he ends up using it. Unlike

Rashad's situation in *Damballah,* it is almost as if Tommy is repulsed by the extent to which his addiction causes the neglect of Sarah and their baby until it is too late to make amends. While he is in hiding, he recalls having arrived at their apartment stoned on junk when Sarah went into labor with their son, Clyde. "Sometimes I knew I was fucking up and sometimes I didn't know," he thinks to himself. "Sometimes I cared about fucking up and sometimes I didn't give a damn." He longs to apologize but "his feet aren't moving" and "she can't hear what he's saying."

Tommy ultimately recognizes the way in which his actions harm himself as well as those around him. Sarah understandably refuses to make excuses for him or allow him back into her life and her son's. She leaves him, unwilling to reconcile their relationship. "You can't come back whenever you're in the mood and put us through changes," she tells him. "You had your chance for a son but you didn't want him. You wanted the street, whatever you loved so much in those gutter-rotten streets, and that's what you chose and that's what you got. It's too late now." Through the portrait of Tommy and Sarah, Wideman presents characters striving for connection, but sustaining a relationship proves too difficult when opportunities that would nurture their union are beyond their reach.

In *Brothers and Keepers,* Robby recounts the real-life ways in which his relationship with his wife, Tia, dissolves. His imprisonment, like Tommy's criminal behavior in *Hiding Place,* proves a barrier too great to sustain their marriage. As he narrates the way in which Tia stands by him through his court trials and appeals, Robby also explains that his wife's visits to the prison eventually become less frequent. She begins developing a life apart from the one the two of them established before his incarceration. "She changed jobs," he says. "Was into seeing new people I didn't know. What we had wasn't going nowhere. Wasn't nowhere for it to go with me locked up in here." Although Robby and Tia want to remain married, like Tommy and Sarah, their separate lives foster more estrangement than harmony, eventually resulting in divorce. Eventually, Robby is introduced to another woman—Leslie, the friend of a fellow inmate. As the relationship unfolds, the limitations imposed by his life sentence once again begin to surface and disrupt the couple's ability to plan for the future. What makes matters worse is Leslie's impression that Robby is due for release in a year or two at most. In turn, Robby cannot face telling her the truth and, like Tommy, in *Hiding Place,* confesses a sense of self-disgust at his incapacity to do better by those he loves.

The inability to promote and sustain intimate relationships is complicated further in Wideman's work by the general sense of deeply embedded anomie exhibited by many of the African American men he writes about in his fiction and nonfiction. For instance, Tommy, in *Hiding Place,* envisions Clyde's life as better without him. Although his mother entreats him to keep contact with his son, Tommy responds, "I ain't hitting on nothing. No money. No job. Nothing. What I'm gon do for him or his mama? No point talking bout it. Easier if I just don't see him no more." Because *Hiding Place* is fiction, Wideman is limited in the elucidation he can give to Tommy's sentiments without becoming didactic and heavy-handed. In *Fatheralong,* however, the nonfiction form permits him to reveal the larger circumstances propelling Tommy's self-inflicted alienation from Clyde. Wideman writes:

Arrayed against the possibility of conversation between fathers and sons is the country they inhabit, everywhere proclaiming the inadequacy of black fathers, their lack of manhood in almost every sense the term's understood here in America. The power to speak, father to son, is mediated or withheld; white men, and the reality they subscribe to, stand in the way. Whites own the country, run the country, and in this world where possessions count more than people, where law values property more than person, the material reality speaks plainly to anyone who's paying attention, especially black boys who own nothing, whose fathers, relegated to the margins, are empty-handed ghosts.

Although he does not mention Tommy specifically, Wideman's explanation of the absence of intimacy between black men and their sons correlates to the situation in *Hiding Place.* In short, Tommy's logic that it would be better for Clyde to grow up without any meaningful paternal contact with him is indicative of his own sense of inadequacy with regard to the material support he can offer his son.

In *Fatheralong,* Wideman sets out to account for the history of alienation experienced by African American men in relation to their families as well as to reverse the way such estrangement has surfaced between him and his own father. As he demonstrated in *Hiding Place,* black fathers often measure their relevance to the family by how much material support they can offer. Given their disenfranchisement from economic opportunity, however, their ability to satisfy their intentions often becomes impossible. In Wideman's case, such tensions surfaced early in his childhood when any outing he shared with his father, Edgar Lawson Wideman, had to be squeezed between the variety of jobs he held as a means to provide for his family. Because their time together was so minimal, Wideman often found himself breaking minor household rules, such as stealing food that was off limits in the refrigerator, as a way to garner his father's attention, even if it was anger.

Eventually the pressure of making a steady income and providing an emotional presence in the lives of his family members became too great for his father, and Wideman's parents separated. In the text, his father tries to reproduce his own reasoning at the time, stating, "For once in my life I wanted to be able to do the things I wanted to do. Not worry about every-

body and everything the way your mother does. Worry worry worry." The fact that Wideman, his siblings, and his mother were the embodiment of a reality that prevented his father from "enjoying a life of his own" has a near tangible resonance. Wideman also seems grateful, however, that his father has attempted for the first time to admit, explain, and apologize "for deserting his family." Moreover, the text reveals that because economic security was so difficult to come by, the anxiety faced by the senior Wideman to provide for his family proved an overwhelming responsibility.

With his father's move out of the house, it became even more difficult for the family to spend time together; matters became complicated by Wideman's mother's discomfort at being present when her ex-husband was around. When Wideman married, began a family of his own, and moved away from Pittsburgh, he often found himself seeing his father less and less. The two could manage to establish contact only during the course of a ride to the airport or in instances of "elaborately choreographed pop-in visits" (*Fatheralong*) that occurred only in the absence of his mother. Perhaps because his writing endeavors were also examining relations between African American men and their families, Wideman became extremely conscious of the sad "inadequacy" of the relationship between him and his father. In conversation with a friend whose father has died, Wideman envisions his own eventual regret over exchanges that will never take place because of his tenuous association with his father. His father's eventual passing without resolution to their fragile relations, Wideman feels, also would make regaining a relationship impossible.

Thirteen years before the publication of *Fatheralong,* Wideman expressed a similar kind of remorse in "Across the Wide Missouri," a chapter in *Damballah.* Like the real-life Edgar Wideman, the narrator's father works as a waiter in the dining room of Kaufman's Department

Store in Pittsburgh. One afternoon, as soon as his shift is over, he and his son make plans to spend a rare afternoon together seeing a movie. While the boy waits at a table vacated by patrons of the restaurant, he succumbs to a variety of emotions on which Wideman eventually elaborates in *Fatheralong*. For example, the narrator notices that the dining room embodies the country's racial divide, describing it as a "red-carpeted chaos of white people and black waiters."

Moreover, just as Wideman himself committed negligible transgressions to achieve his father's attention, so, too, does the narrator, stealing an eighty-cent tip left under a saucer. His feelings of guilt, however, are supplanted by delight regarding his and his father's plans. As they muse over which movie to take in, the boy thinks, "Words were unimportant because what mattered was his presence, talking or silent didn't matter. Point was he was with me and would stay with me the whole afternoon." While recounting that they finally settled on a western starring Clark Gable and entitled "Across the Wide Missouri," the narrator shifts to the present and his own relationship with his children, lamenting that they have grown up, like him, removed from knowing their grandfather. Although as an adult, the narrator realizes why he and his father could not spend more time together, he also acknowledges that such understanding makes their remoteness from each other no less difficult. He implies that society's condemnation of their race relegated his father to a certain station that prevented economic success and ultimately impinged upon his ability to establish long-lasting ties with his family. As true as such knowledge may be, the narrator surmises that simply knowing it offers little comfort.

In many ways *Fatheralong* works to repair the gulf between father and son that concludes "Across the Wide Missouri." Likewise, in his novel *Philadelphia Fire*, Wideman fictively explores the establishment of relations between a man and a boy when the main character, Cudjoe, sets out to find a missing child. *Fatheralong*, however, is provocative for the way Wideman examines his own contact with his father as well as the larger contextual circumstance that led to the chasm between them. Instead of leaving the relationship in a stalemate, Wideman takes the initiative to invite his father on a trip to South Carolina so the two can get to know each other and at the same time trace the genealogical origins of the Wideman clan. Between the episodes of the excursion, Wideman expounds on the social realities that came between him and his father, preventing them from forming a more enduring relationship beginning with his childhood. He asserts that existence in the United States hinges on a "corrupted version" of its basic institutions and values, which has produced a "paradigm of race" at the expense of its children. When a black child is born, Wideman explains, a father becomes a "burden," unable to give his offspring what every white father can provide: "full, unquestioned, unconditional citizenship. . . . You can't pretend 'race' doesn't exist, and 'race' defines you both as something other, something less than a white man."

Such realities become especially manifest when Wideman reveals that his father's people were considerably darker than his mother's family and, as a result, faced disaffection even within their families. When relatives from South Carolina visited Pittsburgh, Wideman, as an adult, realizes that they were rarely invited to the house. Although he wishes he could approach his father directly about it, he also knows that such frankness would cause more hurt. Instead, Wideman contemplates the way the "legacy" of racism, of "evil and unkindness," has an "inexhaustible capacity to mutate and proliferate into ugly new forms."

Although his plan to establish an enduring sense of intimacy in the face of such rejection could seem artificial and grandiose, Wideman stresses that he wants only to become acquainted with the ordinary man who is his father. He envisions the trip to South Carolina as a way to get to know the "actual life" of a person "excited" and "anxious to get the hell away from the everyday tedium of growing old, alone and poor." Once they arrive in Abbeville, the town of Wideman's forefathers, they spend time poring over local historical records and trying to establish the family lineage. Given that no immediate relations still live in the community, the graveyard and the abandoned homestead prove to be the remaining vestiges that establish that Widemans once resided in the locale. More important is their reacquaintance with James Harris, a cousin nicknamed Littleman. Over dinner in a bar, with a ballgame on the television, the three reminisce about their ancestors and about particular family legends. Wideman recognizes that within this gathering he has happened upon what he traveled to South Carolina with his father to find. He writes:

> Along with the silliness, something rich and good about being with men of my family. Another kind of spice, a mellow, simple contentment arising from this meal together, a ball game, this serendipitous reunion in South Carolina. Knowing we were connected, knowing what it cost in time and blood was like savoring a delicious secret. Somehow in spite of terrible odds our ancestors had managed to survive. Not only survive, but to cache in a cave on a mountaintop a treasure, our past, our history, the inheritance we held in common. And the treasure was bountiful, there was more than enough for each of us and generations to come. We could draw from it whenever we needed it. A family.

Like so much of Wideman's writing, *Fatheralong* proves to be a way to recover and record the exploits of his people as well as to demonstrate their relationship to the extended realm of African American existence. Granted that the repossession and chronicling are born out of a fracturing and are qualified by fragility, however, such characteristics are frequently apparent in Wideman's writing and prove his larger point regarding the capacity to survive in spite of a reality that continually threatens otherwise. Indeed, *Fatheralong* poignantly demonstrates the persistent frailty of life, if not continual tragedy of existence, in its conclusion. A series of the "Father Stories" make vague references to Wideman's son Jake, whom the text, in part, is dedicated to and who is serving a life sentence for murdering Eric Kane while the two were at summer camp in Flagstaff, Arizona. Given Wideman's brother's history, the pain caused by Jake's actions would seem insurmountable. In fact, at one point in the text Wideman beseeches God to take him instead of Jake. He writes, "Free my son from the terrible things happening to him. Take me in his place. Let them happen to me." Because it is impossible, however, for Wideman to supplant himself in the place of his son, he rationalizes in the monologue that begins this section with testimony that his role as a writer functions as its own life sentence, meaning he must tell the story to both preserve it and survive it.

Selected Bibliography

WORKS OF JOHN EDGAR WIDEMAN

BOOKS

A Glance Away. New York: Harcourt, Brace & World, 1967.

Hurray Home. New York: Harcourt Brace & World, 1970.

The Lynchers. New York: Harcourt Brace Jovanovich, 1973.

Damballah. New York: Avon, 1981.

Hiding Place. New York: Avon, 1981.

Sent for You Yesterday. New York: Avon, 1983.

Brothers and Keepers. New York: Holt, Rinehart and Winston, 1984.

Reuben. New York: Henry Holt, 1987.

Fever: Twelve Stories. New York: Henry Holt, 1989.

Philadelphia Fire. New York: Henry Holt, 1990.

All Stories Are True. New York: Random House, 1993.

Fatheralong: A Meditation on Fathers and Sons, Race and Society. New York: Pantheon, 1994.

The Cattle Killing. Boston: Houghton Mifflin, 1996.

Two Cities. Boston: Houghton Mifflin, 1998.

UNCOLLECTED ESSAYS

"Frame and Dialect: The Evolution of the Black Voice in American Literature." *American Poetry Review* 5, no. 5:34–47 (September–October 1976).

"Defining the Black Voice in Fiction." *Black American Literature Forum* 11, no. 3:79–82 (fall 1977).

"*Stomping the Blues*: Ritual in Black Music and Speech." *American Poetry Review* 7, no. 4:42–45 (July–August 1978).

"The Language of Home." *New York Times Book Review,* January 13, 1985, pp. 1, 35–36.

"The Black Writer and the Magic of the Word." *New York Times Book Review,* January 24, 1988, pp. 1, 28–29.

"The Color of Fiction." *Mother Jones* 15, no. 7:59–60 (November–December 1990).

"Dead Black Men and Other Fallout from the American Dream." *Esquire,* September 1992, pp. 149–156.

"Father Stories." *The New Yorker,* August 1, 1994, p. 36.

"Doing Time, Marking Race." *Nation* 261, no. 14:503–505 (October 30, 1995).

"Playing Dennis Rodman." *The New Yorker,* April 29, 1996, p. 94.

"My Daughter the Hoopster." *Essence,* November 1996, pp. 79–80.

"What Is a Brother?" *Esquire,* June 1998, p. 96.

CRITICAL AND BIOGRAPHICAL STUDIES

Abu-Jamal, Mumia. "The Fictive Realism of John Edgar Wideman." *Black Scholar* 28, no. 1:75–79 (spring 1998).

Bennion, John. "The Shape of Memory in John Edgar Wideman's *Sent for You Yesterday.*" *Black American Literature Forum* 20:143–150 (spring/summer 1986).

Berben, Jacqueline. "Beyond Discourse: The Unspoken Versus Words in the Fiction of John Edgar Wideman." *Callaloo* 8:525–534 (fall 1985).

Byerman, Keith Eldon. *John Edgar Wideman: A Study of the Short Fiction.* Madison, Wis.: Twayne, 1998.

Coleman, James W. *Blackness and Modernism: The Literary Career of John Edgar Wideman.* Jackson: University Press of Mississippi, 1989.

Hoem, S. I. "Shifting Spirits: Ancestral Constructs in the Postmodern Writing of John Edgar Wideman." *African American Review* 34, no. 2:249–262 (2000).

Julien, Claude, ed. "John Edgar Wideman: The European Response." *Callaloo* (Special Issue) 22, no. 3 (summer 1999).

Mbalia, Doreatha Drummond. *John Edgar Wideman: Reclaiming the African Personality.* Selinsgrove, Penn.: Susquehanna University Press, 1995.

TuSmith, Bonnie, ed. *Conversations with John Edgar Wideman.* Jackson: University Press of Mississippi, 1998.

—PATRICIA FERREIRA

Index

Index

Arabic numbers printed in bold-face type refer to extended treatment of a subject.

A Complete Listing of Authors in
American Writers

Adams, Henry   Volume I
Addams, Jane   Supplement I
Agee, James   Volume I
Aiken, Conrad   Volume I
Albee, Edward   Volume I
Alcott, Louisa May   Supplement I
Algren, Nelson   Supplement IX
Alvarez, Julia   Supplement VII
Ammons, A. R.   Supplement VII
Anderson, Sherwood   Volume I
Angelou, Maya   Supplement IV
Ashbery, John   Supplement III
Auchincloss, Louis   Supplement IV
Auden, W. H.   Supplement II
Baldwin, James   Supplement I
Banks, Russell   Supplement V
Baraka, Amiri   Supplement II
Barlow, Joel   Supplement II
Barnes, Djuna   Supplement III
Barth, John   Volume I
Barthelme, Donald   Supplement IV
Bausch, Richard   Supplement VII
Beattie, Ann   Supplement V
Bell, Madison Smartt   Supplement X
Bellow, Saul   Volume I
Berry, Wendell   Supplement X
Berryman, John   Volume I
Bierce, Ambrose   Volume I
Bishop, Elizabeth   Supplement I
Blackmur, R. P.   Supplement II
Bly, Robert   Supplement IV
Bogan, Louise   Supplement III
Bourne, Randolph   Volume I
Bowles, Paul   Supplement IV
Boyle, T. C.   Supplement VIII
Bradbury, Ray   Supplement IV

Bradstreet, Anne   Supplement I
Brodsky, Joseph   Supplement VIII
Brooks, Gwendolyn   Supplement III
Brooks, Van Wyck   Volume I
Brown, Charles Brockden   Supplement I
Bryant, William Cullen   Supplement I
Buck, Pearl S.   Supplement II
Burke, Kenneth   Volume I
Burroughs, William S.   Supplement III
Caldwell, Erskine   Volume I
Capote, Truman   Supplement III
Carson, Rachel   Supplement IX
Carver, Raymond   Supplement III
Cather, Willa   Volume I
Cather, Willa   Retrospective Supplement I
Chandler, Raymond   Supplement IV
Cheever, John   Supplement I
Chopin, Kate   Supplement I
Cisneros, Sandra   Supplement VII
Clampitt, Amy   Supplement IX
Cooper, James Fenimore   Volume I
Coover, Robert   Supplement V
Cowley, Malcolm   Supplement II
Cozzens, James Gould   Volume I
Crane, Hart   Volume I
Crane, Stephen   Volume I
Creeley, Robert   Supplement IV
Crèvecoeur, Michel-Guillaume Jean de   Supplement I
Cullen, Countee   Supplement IV
Cummings, E. E.   Volume I
DeLillo, Don   Supplement VI
Dickey, James   Supplement IV
Dickinson, Emily   Volume 1
Dickinson, Emily   Retrospective Supplement I
Didion, Joan   Supplement IV

Jong, Erica   Supplement V
Justice, Donald   Supplement VII
Kazin, Alfred   Supplement VIII
Kennedy, William   Supplement VII
Kenyon, Jane   Supplement VII
Kerouac, Jack   Supplement III
Kincaid, Jamaica   Supplement VII
King, Stephen   Supplement V
Kingsolver, Barbara   Supplement VII
Kingston, Maxine Hong   Supplement V
Kinnell, Galway   Supplement III
Kosinski, Jerzy   Supplement VII
Kumin, Maxine   Supplement IV
Kunitz, Stanley   Supplement III
Kushner, Tony   Supplement IX
LaBastille, Anne   Supplement X
Lanier, Sidney   Supplement I
Lardner, Ring   Volume 2
Lee, Harper   Supplement VIII
Levertov, Denise   Supplement III
Levine, Philip   Supplement V
Lewis, Sinclair   Volume 2
Lindsay, Vachel   Supplement I
London, Jack   Volume 2
Longfellow, Henry Wadsworth   Volume 2
Lowell, Amy   Volume 2
Lowell, James Russell   Supplement I
Lowell, Robert   Volume 2
McCarthy, Cormac   Supplement VIII
McCarthy, Mary   Volume 2
McCullers, Carson   Volume 2
Macdonald, Ross   Supplement IV
McGrath, Thomas   Supplement X
McKay, Claude   Supplement X
MacLeish, Archibald   Volume 3
McMurty, Larry   Supplement V
McPhee, John   Supplement III
Mailer, Norman   Volume 3
Malamud, Bernard   Supplement I
Marquand, John P.   Volume 3
Mason, Bobbie Ann   Supplement VIII
Masters, Edgar Lee   Supplement I
Mather, Cotton   Supplement II
Matthews, William   Supplement IX

Matthiessen, Peter   Supplement V
Maxwell, William   Supplement VIII
Melville, Herman   Volume 3
Melville, Herman   Retrospective Supplement I
Mencken, H. L.   Volume 3
Merrill, James   Supplement III
Merton, Thomas   Supplement VIII
Merwin, W. S.   Supplement III
Millay, Edna St. Vincent   Volume 3
Miller, Arthur   Volume 3
Miller, Henry   Volume 3
Minot, Susan   Supplement VI
Momaday, N. Scott   Supplement IV
Monette, Paul   Supplement X
Moore, Lorrie   Supplement X
Moore, Marianne   Volume 3
Morison, Samuel Eliot   Supplement I
Morris, Wright   Volume 3
Morrison, Toni   Supplement III
Muir, John   Supplement IX
Mumford, Lewis   Supplement III
Nabokov, Vladimir   Volume 3
Nabokov, Vladimir   Retrospective Supplement I
Naylor, Gloria   Supplement VIII
Nemerov, Howard   Volume 3
Niebuhr, Reinhold   Volume 3
Nin, Anaïs   Supplement X
Norris, Frank   Volume 3
Oates, Joyce Carol   Supplement II
O'Brien, Tim   Supplement V
O'Connor, Flannery   Volume 3
Odets, Clifford   Supplement II
O'Hara, John   Volume 3
Olds, Sharon   Supplement X
Oliver, Mary   Supplement VII
Olson, Charles   Supplement II
O'Neill, Eugene   Volume 3
Ortiz, Simon J.   Supplement IV
Ozick, Cynthia   Supplement V
Paine, Thomas   Supplement I
Paley, Grace   Supplement VI
Parker, Dorothy   Supplement IX

ADX – 9208

12|5.

5.0

PS
129
ASS

supp. 10

124.